The
HUMAN
RECORD

Volume I

The

HUMAN
RECORD

SOURCES OF GLOBAL HISTORY

▼▼▼

THIRD EDITION / Volume I: To 1700

Alfred J. Andrea
University of Vermont

James H. Overfield
University of Vermont

HOUGHTON MIFFLIN COMPANY   BOSTON   NEW YORK

Sponsoring Editor: Andrea Shaw
Assistant Editor: Keith Mahoney
Project Editor: Anne Holm
Senior Production/Design Coordinator: Jill Haber
Manufacturing Manager: Florence Cadran
Marketing Manager: Sandra McGuire

Cover design: Sarah Melhado and Sam Shaw
Cover image: Bibliotheque Nationale, Paris

Source credits appear on pages 481–485.

Library of Congress Catalog Card Number: 97-72433

ISBN: 0-395-87087-9

123456789-DH-02 01 00 99 98

As always, our love and thanks to
Juanita B. Andrea and Susan L. Overfield

Contents

GEOGRAPHIC CONTENTS   xiii

TOPICAL CONTENTS   xvii

PREFACE   xxvii

*Prologue: Primary Sources and
How We Read Them*   *P-1*

WHAT IS HISTORY?   P-1

PRIMARY SOURCES: THEIR VALUE
AND LIMITATIONS   P-2

EXAMINING THE SOURCES   P-4

YOU AND THE SOURCES   P-6

  "With the Royal Standard Unfurled"
    Christopher Columbus,
    A Letter Concerning
    Recently Discovered Islands   P-8

INTERPRETING COLUMBUS'S LETTER   P-15

UNWRITTEN SOURCES   P-19

    An Anonymous Woodcut of 1511   P-19

INTERPRETING THE WOODCUT   P-21

Part One ▼ The Ancient World   I

Chapter 1: The First Civilizations   5

MESOPOTAMIA: THE LAND OF TWO RIVERS   6

  The Search for Eternal Life in Mesopotamia
    1. The Epic of Gilgamesh   7
  Bringing Order to an Uncertain World
    2. The Judgments of Hammurabi   12
EGYPT: THE LAND OF TWO LANDS   17

  The Search for Eternal Life in Egypt
    3. Three Funerary Documents   18
  Making a Living in Ancient Egypt
    4. A Scribal Exercise Book   22
CHINA: THE LAND OF THE YELLOW RIVER   25

  The Mandate of Heaven
    5. The Classic of History   26
  Courtship and Marriage in Ancient China
    6. The Classic of Odes   29
MUTE TESTIMONY   31

  Bringing in the Sheaves
    7. A Tassili Rock Painting   31
  Cultural Impressions
    8. Indus, Mesopotamian, and
    Cretan Seals   33
  Sacred Kingship along the Nile
    9. Two Temple Reliefs   36
  The Were-Jaguar
    10. Four Olmec Statuettes   38

Chapter 2: New Peoples   41

THE INDO-EUROPEANS   42

  Life, Death, and the Gods in Aryan India
    11. The Rig Veda   43
  A Journey to the Underworld
    12. Homer, The Odyssey   47
THE HEBREWS AND THEIR NEIGHBORS   52

  Establishing a Covenant with Humanity
    13. The Book of Genesis   53
  Establishing a Covenant with
  the Chosen People
    14. The Book of Deuteronomy   57
  Keeping and Breaking the Covenant
    15. The Book of Judges   60

*Chapter 3: Transcendental Reality:
Developing the Spiritual Traditions
of India and Southwest Asia:
800–200 B.C.E.*   63

THE EMERGENCE OF BRAHMINICAL HINDUISM   65

  The Hindu Search for Divine Reality
    16. The Upanishads   66

Dharma: The Imperative of Caste Law
    17. The Bhagavad Gita   68
CHALLENGERS OF CASTE:
THE MAHAVIRA AND THE BUDDHA   71

    A Call to the Heroic Life
        18. The Book of Good Conduct   72
    The Path to Enlightenment
        19. The Buddha, Two Lessons   74
    Admitting Women to the Mendicant Life
        20. The Discipline Basket   79
PERSIANS, ISRAELITES, AND THEIR GODS   83

    The Fight between Good and Evil
        21. Zarathustra, Gathas   83
    A New Covenant for All Peoples
        22. The Book of Isaiah   86

**Chapter 4: The Secular Made Sacred:
Developing the Humanistic Traditions
of China and Hellas: 600–200 B.C.E.   90**

CHINA: THREE WAYS OF THOUGHT   91

    Daoism: The Way That Is and Is Not
        *23. Laozi, The Classic of
        the Way and Virtue   93*
    Confucianism: The Way of the Superior Man
        24. Confucius, The Analects   96
    Legalism: The Way of the State
        *25. Han Fei, The Writings of
        Master Han Fei   100*
    The Legalist Policies of Qin
        *26. Sima Qian, The Records of
        the Grand Historian   101*
HELLENIC CIVILIZATION: A RATIONAL
INQUIRY INTO LIFE   104

    The Science of Medicine
        *27. Hippocrates, On the
        Sacred Disease   106*
    The Athenian as Citizen
        *28. Thucydides, The History of
        the Peloponnesian War   108*
    An Inquiry into the Horrors of War
        29. Euripides, The Women of Troy   114
    Socrates and the Laws of Athens
        30. Plato, Crito   119

**Chapter 5: Regional Empires and
Afro-Eurasian Interchange:
300 B.C.E.–500 C.E.   124**

THE GRECO-ROMAN WORLD   126

    Images of the Hellenistic World
        31. Four Hellenistic Statues   127
    The World According to Strabo
        32. Strabo, Geography   131
    The Blessings of the Roman Peace
        *33. Aelius Aristides,
        The Roman Oration   134*
    Isis: The Goddess Who Saves
        *34. Lucius Apuleius,
        Metamorphoses   137*
HAN CHINA   140

    Establishing an Imperial
    Confucian Academy
        *35. Sima Qian, The Records of
        the Grand Historian   141*
    The Views of a Female Confucian
        36. Ban Zhao, Lessons for Women   145
INDIA IN THE AGE OF EMPIRES   149

    The Softening Effects of Dharma
        37. Asoka, Rock and Pillar Edicts   150
    Sacred Law in Classical India
        38. The Laws of Manu   154
    Gupta India as Viewed by
    a Chinese Monk
        *39. Faxian, Travels in
        India and Ceylon   159*
TRAVEL ALONG THE SILK ROAD   162

    Zhang Qian's Western Expedition
        *40. Sima Qian, The Records of
        the Grand Historian   163*
    The Transit of Images along
    the Silk Road
        41. Four Robed Statues   167
TRAVEL ACROSS THE INDIAN OCEAN   171

    The Transit of the Buddha Image to Funan
        42. A Buddha from Funan   171
    Faxian's Homeward Voyage
        *43. Faxian, Travels in
        India and Ceylon   173*

**Part Two ▼ Faith, Devotion, and Salvation:
Great World Religions to 1500 C.E.**   175

*Chapter 6: New Developments in
Three Ancient Religions*   177

HINDUISM: THE WAY OF DEVOTION   178

  Vishnu, Destroyer of Sin
    44. The Vishnu Purana   179
  Shiva, Auspicious Destroyer
    45. Shiva Nataraja   180

MAHAYANA BUDDHISM: A RELIGION OF
INFINITE COMPASSION   183

  Perceiver of the World's Sounds:
  A Universal Bodhisattva
    46. The Lotus Sutra   184
  The Bodhisattva Image
    47. Three Bodhisattvas   187

RABBINICAL JUDAISM   190

  A Defense of the Law
    *48. Flavius Josephus,
    Against Apion*   191
  A Commentary on the Law
    49. The Babylonian Talmud   195

*Chapter 7: Christianity:
Conquering the World for Christ*   198

THE FOUNDATIONS OF CHRISTIANITY   199

  Becoming Spiritually Perfect
    50. The Gospel of St. Matthew   200
  The Path to Righteousness:
  The Law or Faith?
    *51. St. Paul, The Epistle to
    the Romans*   202

CHRISTIANITY AND THE ROMAN WORLD   205

  Persecution and Deliverance
    *52. Eusebius of Caesarea,
    Ecclesiastical History*   206
  The Imperial Religion
    53. Christ the Redeemer   211
  The Origins of Christian Monasticism

    *54. St. Ephraem of Edessa,
    The Life of St. Mary the Harlot*   213

RELIGIOUS EXCHANGE AND INTERCHANGE   216

  Gnostic Christianity:
  The Secret Knowledge of Jesus
    55. The Gospel of Thomas   216
  Manichaeism: Enlightening the World
    *56. The Parable about
    the World-Ocean*   219

*Chapter 8: Islam:
Universal Submission to God*   223

THE FOUNDATIONS OF ISLAMIC LIFE   225

  The Word of God
    57. The Qur'an   225
  The Tales of Tradition
    *58. Imam Nawawi, Gardens of
    the Righteous*   229

VARIETY AND UNITY IN ISLAM   233

  God's Martyrs: The Party of Ali
    *59. Ibn Babawayh al-Saduq,
    Creed Concerning the Imams*   234
  God's Vice-Regent on Earth
    *60. Abu'l Hasan Ali al-Mawardi, Book
    of the Principles of Government*   237
  Sufi Mysticism
    *61. Abu Hamid Muhammad al-Ghazali,
    The Alchemy of Happiness*   240
  An African Pilgrim to Mecca
    *62. Mahmud Kati,
    The Chronicle of the Seeker*   242

ISLAM AND UNBELIEVERS   245

  The *Dhimma*: A Contract with the
  People of the Book
    63. The Pact of Umar   245
  The Jewish Community of
  Twelfth-Century Baghdad
    *64. Benjamin of Tudela,
    Book of Travels*   247
  Fourteenth-Century Hindu *Dhimmis*
    *65. The Deeds of Sultan
    Firuz Shah*   250

**Part Three ▼ Continuity, Change, and
Interchange: 500–1500**   **253**

**Chapter 9: Asia: Change in
the Context of Tradition**   **255**

JAPAN: CREATING A DISTINCTIVE CIVILIZATION   256

The Constitution of Prince Shotoku
    66. Chronicles of Japan   257
An Aristocratic Woman in
Eleventh-Century Japan
    67. Murasaki Shikibu, Diary   260
The Ideal Samurai
    *68. Chronicle of the
    Grand Pacification   264*
CHINA: THE AGES OF TANG AND SONG   269

Open to the World: Christianity in
Tang China
    *69. Bishop Adam,
    The Christian Monument   271*
Troubles in Late Tang
    70. Du Fu, Poems   275
The Dao of Agriculture in Song China
    *71. Chen Pu,
    The Craft of Farming   277*
Thirteenth-Century Hangzhou
    *72. A Record of Musings on
    the Eastern Capital   280*
BUDDHISM IN EAST ASIA: ACCEPTANCE, REJECTION,
AND ACCOMMODATION   284

A Conflict of Values: Foreign Religions in
Late Tang China
    *73. Han Yu, Memorial on Buddhism, and
    Emperor Tang Wuzong,
    Proclamation Ordering the Destruction of
    the Buddhist Monasteries   285*
Zen Buddhism in Japan
    74. Dogen, On Life and Death   289
SOUTHWEST ASIA: CROSSROADS OF
THE AFRO-EURASIAN WORLD   291

The Arrival of the Turks
    *75. Al-Jahiz, The Merits of the Turks
    and of the Imperial Army as
    a Whole   292*
The Arrival of the Franks

    *76. Usamah ibn Munqidh,
    The Book of Reflections   296*
Sinbad's First Voyage
    *77. A Thousand and One
    Arabian Nights   300*
INDIA: CONTINUITY AND CHANGE   305

Islam and Hindu Civilization: Cultures in
Conflict
    *78. Abu'l Raihan al-Biruni, Description
    of India   306*
The Perfect Wife
    *79. Dandin, Tales of the Ten
    Princes   310*
A Sati's Sacrifice
    80. Vikrama's Adventures   312

**Chapter 10: Two Christian
Civilizations: Byzantium and
Western Europe**   **315**

BYZANTIUM AND ITS NEIGHBORS   317

Two Imperial Portraits:
Justinian and Theodora
    81. The Mosaics of San Vitale   318
Emperor Basil II and the Apogee
of Byzantine Power
    *82. Michael Psellus,
    The Chronographia   322*
Economic Regulation
    83. The Book of the Eparch   325
Bringing Christianity to the Rus'
    *84. The Russian
    Primary Chronicle   327*
WESTERN EUROPE: THE EMERGENCE OF
A NEW CIVILIZATION   331

Charlemagne: Europe's First Emperor
    *85. Einhard,
    The Life of Charles the Great   332*
A Papal Portrait: Leo III and
Charles the Great
    86. A Lateran Palace Mosaic   337
The Feudal Perspective
    87. The Song of Roland   338
Bringing Christianity to the Magyars
    *88. Pope Sylvester II,
    Letter to St. Stephen of Hungary   342*

A Conflict of Authorities
89. *Four Documents from the*
Investiture Controversy   *345*
The Merchants of Southampton
90. *Ordinances of the Merchant Guild*
of Southampton   *351*
BYZANTIUM AND THE WEST:
THE DIVIDING OF CHRISTENDOM   355

The West and the First Crusade from
a Byzantine Perspective
91. *Anna Comnena, The Alexiad*   *356*
Byzantium and the Fourth Crusade from
a Western Perspective
92. *Gunther of Pairis,*
A Constantinopolitan History   *359*

Chapter 11: Africa and
the Americas   *363*

AFRICA   365

The Land of Zanj: Tenth-Century East Africa
93. *Abu'l-Hasan Ali al-Mas'udi,*
Meadows of Gold   *366*
The Land of Ghana:
Eleventh-Century Western Sudan
94. *Abu Ubaydallah al-Bakri,*
The Book of Routes and Realms   *370*
The Land of Seyon:
Fourteenth-Century Ethiopia
95. *The Glorious Victories of*
'Amda Seyon   *374*
A Yoruba Woman of Authority?
96. *Seated Female Figure*   *378*
THE AMERICAS   380

The God Who Descended from
the Mountains
97. *A Moche Ceramic*   *381*
Taino Culture
98. *Ramón Pane, A Report Concerning the*
Antiquities of the Indians   *383*
Quiché Mayan Gods and Monarchs
99. *The Book of the Community*   *389*
Governing the Inca Empire
100. *Pedro de Cieza de León,*
Chronicles   *392*

Part Four ▼ Travel, Encounter, and
Exchange: 1000–1700   397

Chapter 12: Adventurers, Merchants,
Diplomats, Pilgrims, and Missionaries:
A Half Millennium of Travel and
Encounter: 1000–1500   *399*

PILGRIMS AND MERCHANTS BEFORE
THE MONGOL AGE   401

The Pilgrimage to Rome
101. *Benedict of St. Peter,*
The Marvels of the City of Rome   *402*
A Jewish Merchant Writes Home
102. *A Letter from the*
Cairo Geniza   *407*
TRAVEL IN THE AGE OF
THE *PAX MONGOLICA*   410

Mongol Culture
103. *William of Rubruck,*
Journey to the Land of the Tartars   *410*
Another View of Mongol Society
104. *Marco Polo,*
Description of the World   *415*
A European Missionary in China
105. *John of Monte Corvino,*
Letter to the West   *418*
Khmer Society in Chinese Eyes
106. *Zhou Daguan, Recollections of*
the Customs of Cambodia   *423*
Advice for Merchants Traveling to Cathay
107. *Francesco Pegolotti, The Book*
of Descriptions of Countries   *426*
TRAVEL BEYOND THE MONGOL ECUMENE   428

A Moroccan Visitor in Sub-Saharan Africa
108. *Ibn Battuta, A Donation to*
Those Interested in Curiosities   *429*
A European View of the World
109. *John Mandeville, Travels*   *433*
Zheng He's Western Voyages
110. *Ma Huan, The Overall Survey of*
the Ocean's Shores   *438*
The Origins of Portugal's Overseas Empire
111. *Gomes Eannes de Azurara,*
Chronicle of Guinea   *442*

Chapter 13: Transoceanic Encounters:
1500–1700   *445*

EUROPEANS IN THE AMERICAS   446

The Battle for Tenochtitlán:
An Aztec Perspective
   112. *Bernardino de Sahagún, General*
   History of the Things of New Spain   447
The Mountain of Silver and the Mita System
   113. *Antonio Vazquez de Espinosa,*
   Compendium and Description of
   the West Indies   453

AFRICAN REACTIONS TO THE
EUROPEAN PRESENCE   458

An African Voice of Protest
   114. *Nzinga Mbemba (Afonso I),*
   Letters to the King of Portugal   459
Images of the Portuguese in the Art of Benin
   115. *A Benin-Portuguese Saltcellar and*
   A Benin Wall Plaque   462

The Economics of the West African
Slave Trade
   116. *James Barbot,*
   A Voyage to New Calabar River in
   the Year 1699   465

CHINESE AND JAPANESE REACTIONS TO
THE WEST   467

The Jesuits in China
   117. *Matteo Ricci, Journals*   468
The Seclusion of Japan
   118. *Tokugawa Iemitsu, Closed Country*
   Edict of 1635 and Exclusion of
   the Portuguese, 1639   472

THE GREAT MUGHALS AND THE WEST   475

Dealing with the Faringis
   119. *Abul Fazl, Akbarnama*   476
Seventeenth-Century Commerce in India
   120. *Jean-Baptiste Tavernier,*
   Travels in India   478

SOURCES   481

Geographic Contents

Africa

Three Funerary Documents	18
A Scribal Exercise Book	22
A Tassili Rock Painting	31
Two Temple Reliefs	36
Strabo	131
Lucius Apuleius	137
The Gospel of Thomas	216
Mahmud Kati	242
Al-Mas'udi	366
Al-Bakri	370
The Glorious Victories of 'Amda Seyon	374
Seated Female Figure	378
A Letter from the Cairo Geniza	407
Ibn Battuta	429
Azurara	442
Nzinga Mbemba	459
A Benin-Portuguese Saltcellar	462
A Benin Wall Plaque	462
Barbot	465

The Americas

Columbus	P-8
Woodcut of 1511	P-19
Four Olmec Sculptures	38
A Moche Ceramic	381
Pane	383
The Book of the Community	389
Cieza de León	392
Sahagun	447
Espinosa	453

The Ancient Mediterranean

Three Funerary Documents	18
A Scribal Exercise Book	22
A Tassili Rock Painting	31
Cretan Seal	33
Two Temple Reliefs	36

Homer	47
Genesis	53
Deuteronomy	57
Judges	60
Isaiah	86
Hippocrates	106
Thucydides	108
Euripides	114
Plato	119
Four Hellenistic Statues	127
Strabo	131
Aelius Aristides	134
Lucius Apuleius	137
Caesar Augustus as Pontifex Maximus	167
Josephus	191
The Gospel of Matthew	200
St. Paul	202
Eusebius of Caesarea	206
Christ the Redeemer	211
St. Ephraem of Edessa	213
The Gospel of Thomas	216

Byzantium

Eusebius of Caesarea	206
Christ the Redeemer	211
St. Ephraem of Edessa	213
The Mosaics of San Vitale	318
Psellus	322
The Book of the Eparch	325
The Russian Primary Chronicle	327
Anna Comnena	356
Gunther of Pairis	359

Central Asia

Sima Qian	163
Four Robed Statues	167
The Lotus Sutra	184
The Parable about the World-Ocean	219

Bishop Adam   271
Du Fu   275
Al-Jahiz   292
William of Rubruck   410
Polo   415
Pegolotti   426
Mandeville   433

China

The Classic of History   26
The Classic of Odes   29
Laozi   93
Confucius   96
Han Fei   100
Sima Qian   101, 141, 163
Ban Zhao   145
Northern Wei Buddha   167
Faxian   173
The Lotus Sutra   184
Guanyin   187
Bishop Adam   271
Du Fu   275
Chen Pu   277
Musings on the Eastern Capital   280
Han Yu   285
Tang Wuzong   285
Al-Mas'udi   366
John of Monte Corvino   418
Ma Huan   438
Ricci   468

Europe

The Russian Primary Chronicle   327
Einhard   332
A Lateran Palace Mosaic   337
The Song of Roland   338
Sylvester II   342
The Investiture Controversy   345
The Guild of Southampton   351
Anna Comnena   356
Benedict of St. Peter   402
Mandeville   433
Azurara   442

India

Indus Seals   33
The Rig Veda   43
The Upanishads   66
The Bhagavad Gita   68
The Book of Good Conduct   72
The Buddha   74
The Discipline Basket   79
Asoka   150
The Laws of Manu   154
Faxian   159
Sima Qian   163
Gandharan Buddha   167
The Vishnu Purana   179
Shiva Nataraja   180
The Lotus Sutra   184
Firuz Shah   250
Al-Biruni   306
Dandin   310
Vikrama's Adventures   312
Al-Mas'udi   366
A Letter from the Cairo Geniza   407
Ma Huan   438
Abul Fazl   476
Tavernier   478

The Indian Ocean

Strabo   131
A Buddha from Funan   171
Faxian   173
Hevajra   187
A Thousand and One Arabian Nights   300
Al-Mas'udi   366
A Letter from the Cairo Geniza   407
Zhou Daguan   423
Ma Huan   438
Abul Fazl   476
Tavernier   478

Japan

Chronicles of Japan   257
Murasaki Shikibu   260
Chronicle of the Grand Pacification 264

Dogen	289
Tokugawa Iemitsu	472

Southeast Asia

A Buddha from Funan	171
Faxian	173
Hevajra	187
Arapacana	187
Zhou Daguan	423
Ma Huan	438

Southwest Asia

The Epic of Gilgamesh	7
The Judgments of Hammurabi	12
Mesopotamian Seals	33
Genesis	53
Deuteronomy	57
Judges	60

Zarathustra	83
Isaiah	86
Sima Qian	163
Parthian Noblewoman	167
Josephus	191
The Babylonian Talmud	195
The Gospel of Matthew	200
The Parable about the World-Ocean	219
The Qur'an	225
Imam Nawawi	229
Al-Saduq	234
Al-Mawardi	237
Al-Ghazali	240
The Pact of Umar	245
Benjamin of Tudela	247
Al-Jahiz	292
Ibn Munqidh	296
A Thousand and One Arabian Nights	300
A Letter from the Cairo Geniza	407
Ma Huan	438

Topical Contents

Cultural Encounter, Exchange, and Conflict

Columbus	P-8
Woodcut of 1511	P-19
Indus, Mesopotamian, and Cretan Seals	33
Two Temple Reliefs	36
Judges	60
Isaiah	86
Four Hellenistic Statues	127
Strabo	131
Aelius Aristides	134
Lucius Apuleius	137
Faxian	159
Sima Qian	163
Four Robed Statues	167
A Buddha from Funan	171
The Lotus Sutra	184
Three Bodhisattvas	187
Josephus	191
St. Paul	202
Eusebius of Caesarea	206
Christ the Redeemer	211
The Parable about the World-Ocean	219
The Pact of Umar	245
Benjamin of Tudela	247
Firuz Shah	250
Chronicles of Japan	257
Bishop Adam	271
Han Yu	285
Tang Wuzong	285
Al-Jahiz	292
Ibn Munqidh	296
Al-Biruni	306
The Russian Primary Chronicle	327
Sylvester II	342
Anna Comnena	356
Gunther of Pairis	359
Al-Mas'udi	366
Al-Bakri	370
Cieza de León	392

John of Monte Corvino	418
Zhou Daguan	423
Ibn Battuta	429
Ma Huan	438
Azurara	442
Sahagun	447
Nzinga Mbemba	459
A Benin-Portuguese Saltcellar	462
A Benin Wall Plaque	462
Barbot	465
Ricci	468
Tokugawa Iemitsu	472
Abul Fazl	476
Tavernier	478

Death and the Beyond

The Epic of Gilgamesh	7
Three Funerary Documents	18
The Rig Veda	43
Homer	47
The Upanishads	66
The Bhagavad Gita	68
The Buddha	74
Lucius Apuleius	137
The Vishnu Purana	179
Shiva Nataraja	180
The Lotus Sutra	184
Three Bodhisattvas	187
St. Paul	202
Christ the Redeemer	211
The Gospel of Thomas	216
The Qur'an	225
Imam Nawawi	229
Firuz Shah	250
Dogen	289
Vikrama's Adventures	312
The Song of Roland	338
Pane	383

Disease and Healing

Hippocrates	106
Thucydides	108
The Laws of Manu	154
Faxian	159
Guanyin	187
St. Ephraem of Edessa	213
Firuz Shah	250
Pane	383
Sahagun	447
Nzinga Mbemba	459

Economic Activity

Artisans

The Judgments of Hammurabi	12
A Scribal Exercise Book	22
Abul Fazl	476

Commerce

The Judgments of Hammurabi	12
Strabo	131
Aelius Aristides	134
Faxian	159, 173
Sima Qian	163
Musings on the Eastern Capital	280
A Thousand and One Arabian Nights	300
The Book of the Eparch	325
The Guild of Southampton	351
Al-Mas'udi	366
A Letter from the Cairo Geniza	407
Polo	415
Zhou Daguan	423
Pegolotti	426
Ibn Battuta	429
Mandeville	433
Ma Huan	438
Azurara	442
Nzinga Mbemba	459
A Benin Wall Plaque	462
Barbot	465
Tokugawa Iemitsu	472
Abul Fazl	476
Tavernier	478

Governmental Intervention and Supervision

The Judgments of Hammurabi	12
Sima Qian	101
Al-Mas'udi	366
Cieza de León	392
Pegolotti	426
Ibn Battuta	429
Ma Huan	438
Azurara	442
Tokugawa Iemitsu	472

Occupations

A Scribal Exercise Book	22
The Book of Good Conduct	72
The Buddha	74
The Discipline Basket	79
The Laws of Manu	154
Faxian	159
St. Ephraem of Edessa	213
Musings on the Eastern Capital	280
The Book of the Eparch	325
William of Rubruck	410
Polo	415
Abul Fazl	476
Tavernier	478

(*See also* Economic Activity: Commerce; Farming, Fertility, and Mining)

Farming, Fertility, and Mining

Columbus	P-8
A Scribal Exercise Book	22
A Tassili Rock Painting	31
The Rig Veda	43
Sima Qian	101
Strabo	131
Chronicles of Japan	257
Chen Pu	277
Al-Mas'udi	366
Al-Bakri	370
A Moche Ceramic	381
Cieza de León	392
Espinosa	453

Government

Authority: Its Source and Exercise

The Epic of Gilgamesh	7
The Judgments of Hammurabi	12
A Scribal Exercise Book	22
The Classic of History	26
Indus, Mesopotamian, and Cretan Seals	33
Two Temple Reliefs	36
Deuteronomy	57
Judges	60
Isaiah	86
Han Fei	100
Sima Qian	101, 141
King Euthydemos I of Bactria	127
Aelius Aristides	134
Asoka	150
Faxian	159
Caesar Augustus as Pontifex Maximus	167
Al-Mawardi	237
Firuz Shah	250
Chronicles of Japan	257
The Mosaics of San Vitale	318
Psellus	322
Einhard	332
A Lateran Palace Mosaic	337
Sylvester II	342
The Investiture Controversy	345
Anna Comnena	356
Al-Bakri	370
The Glorious Victories of 'Amda Seyon	374
Seated Female Figure	378
The Book of the Community	389
Cieza de León	392
Zhou Daguan	423
Ibn Battuta	429
A Benin Wall Plaque	462

Empires and Empire Building

Columbus	P-8
A Scribal Exercise Book	22
Sima Qian	101, 163
Strabo	131
Aelius Aristides	134
Al-Mawardi	237
Du Fu	275

Psellus	322
The Russian Primary Chronicle	327
Einhard	332
The Glorious Victories of 'Amda Seyon	374
Cieza de León	392
Nzinga Mbemba	459
A Benin-Portuguese Saltcellar	462
Tokugawa Iemitsu	472
Abul Fazl	476

Ideal Government

The Judgments of Hammurabi	12
The Classic of History	26
Laozi	93
Confucius	96
Han Fei	100
Sima Qian	101, 141
Thucydides	108
Asoka	150
Al-Mawardi	237
Chronicles of Japan	257
The Mosaics of San Vitale	318
Einhard	332
A Lateran Palace Mosaic	337
The Investiture Controversy	345
The Book of the Community	389
Cieza de León	392
Mandeville	433

Law, Trial, and Punishment

The Judgments of Hammurabi	12
A Scribal Exercise Book	22
Han Fei	100
Sima Qian	101
Plato	119
Asoka	150
The Laws of Manu	154
Faxian	159
Al-Mawardi	237
The Pact of Umar	245
Firuz Shah	250
Ibn Munqidh	296
The Book of the Eparch	325
The Guild of Southampton	351
The Glorious Victories of 'Amda Seyon	374
Seated Female Figure	378

Cieza de León   392
Ricci   468
Tokugawa Iemitsu   472

Taxes and Tribute
A Scribal Exercise Book   22
The Qur'an   225
Al-Mawardi   237
Benjamin of Tudela   247
Firuz Shah   250
Du Fu   275
Tang Wuzong   285
The Guild of Southampton   351
Al-Bakri   370
Cieza de León   392
Zhou Daguan   423
Ma Huan   438
Espinosa   453
Barbot   465
Tavernier   478
(*See also* Economic Activity: Governmental
Intervention and Supervision;
Religion: Pilgrimage)

Nature and Humanity

The Epic of Gilgamesh   7
The Classic of History   26
Indus, Mesopotamian, and Cretan Seals   33
Four Olmec Sculptures   38
The Rig Veda   43
Genesis   53
Laozi   93
Hippocrates   106
Murasaki Shikibu   260
Chen Pu   277
A Moche Ceramic   381
Pane   383
Zhou Daguan   423
(*See also* Religion: Animism, Shamanism,
and Folk Religion)

Philosophy

Confucianism
The Classic of History   26

The Classic of Odes   29
Confucius   96
Sima Qian   101, 141
Ban Zhao   145
Chronicles of Japan   257
Murasaki Shikibu   260
Du Fu   275
Chen Pu   277
Han Yu   285
Ricci   468

**Secular Ethics and the
Well-Lived Life**
The Epic of Gilgamesh   7
The Classic of History   26
Laozi   93
Confucius   96
Thucydides   108
Euripides   114
Plato   119
Ban Zhao   145
Chronicles of Japan   257
Murasaki Shikibu   260
Du Fu   275
Dogen   289
Dandin   310

Religion

Animism, Shamanism, and Folk Religion
Indus, Mesopotamian, and Cretan Seals   33
Four Olmec Statues   38
The Rig Veda   43
Al-Mas'udi   366
Al-Bakri   370
A Moche Ceramic   381
Pane   383
The Book of the Community   389
William of Rubruck   410
Polo   415
Sahagun   447

Buddhism
The Buddha   74
The Discipline Basket   79
Asoka   150
Faxian   159, 173

Gandharan Buddha	167
Northern Wei Buddha	167
Buddha from Funan	171
The Lotus Sutra	184
Three Bodhisattvas	187
Chronicles of Japan	257
Han Yu	285
Tang Wuzong	285
Dogen	289

Christianity

Columbus	P-8
The Gospel of Matthew	200
St. Paul	202
Eusebius of Caesarea	206
Christ the Redeemer	211
St. Ephraem of Edessa	213
The Gospel of Thomas	216
Bishop Adam	271
Ibn Munqidh	296
The Mosaics of San Vitale	318
The Russian Primary Chronicle	327
Einhard	332
A Lateran Palace Mosaic	337
The Song of Roland	338
Sylvester II	342
The Investiture Controversy	345
Anna Comnena	356
Gunther of Pairis	359
The Glorious Victories of 'Amda Seyon	374
Benedict of St. Peter	402
John of Monte Corvino	418
Mandeville	433
Azurara	442
A Benin-Portuguese Saltcellar	462
Ricci	468

Divinity

The Epic of Gilgamesh	7
Three Funerary Documents	18
Indus, Mesopotamian, and Cretan Seals	33
Two Temple Reliefs	36
Four Olmec Statues	38
The Rig Veda	43
Homer	47
Genesis	53
Deuteronomy	57

Judges	60
The Upanishads	66
The Bhagavad Gita	68
Zarathustra	83
Isaiah	86
Lucius Apuleius	137
Four Robed Statues	167
Buddha from Funan	171
The Vishnu Purana	179
Shiva Nataraja	180
The Lotus Sutra	184
Three Bodhisattvas	187
The Gospel of Matthew	200
St. Paul	202
Christ the Redeemer	211
The Gospel of Thomas	216
The Qur'an	225
Al-Ghazali	240
A Moche Ceramic	381
Pane	383
The Book of the Community	389

Hinduism

Indus Seals	33
The Rig Veda	43
The Upanishads	66
The Bhagavad Gita	68
The Book of Good Conduct	72
The Laws of Manu	154
Faxian	159
The Vishnu Purana	179
Shiva Nataraja	180
Al-Biruni	306
Vikrama's Adventures	312

Islam

The Qur'an	225
Imam Nawawi	229
Al-Saduq	234
Al-Mawardi	237
Al-Ghazali	240
Mahmud Kati	242
The Pact of Umar	245
Firuz Shah	250
Al-Mas'udi	366
Al-Bakri	370
The Glorious Victories of 'Amda Seyon	374

Ibn Battuta 429

Abul Fazl 476

Judaism

Genesis 53

Deuteronomy 57

Judges 60

Isaiah 86

Josephus 191

The Babylonian Talmud 195

The Gospel of Matthew 200

St. Paul 202

The Qur'an 225

Benjamin of Tudela 247

The Russian Primary Chronicle 327

The Glorious Victories of 'Amda Seyon 374

A Letter from the Cairo Geniza 407

Pilgrimage

Lucius Apuleius 137

Faxian 159, 173

Mahmud Kati 242

Benjamin of Tudela 247

Ibn Munqidh 296

Anna Comnena 356

Gunther of Pairis 359

Benedict of St. Peter 402

Religious Codes of Conduct

The Negative Confession 18

Genesis 53

Deuteronomy 57

Judges 60

The Bhagavad Gita 68

The Book of Good Conduct 72

The Buddha 74

The Discipline Basket 79

Lucius Apuleius 137

Asoka 150

The Laws of Manu 154

Josephus 191

The Babylonian Talmud 195

The Gospel of Matthew 200

St. Paul 202

St. Ephraem of Edessa 213

The Gospel of Thomas 216

The Qur'an 225

Imam Nawawi 229

Al-Saduq 234

Ritual

The Epic of Gilgamesh 7

Three Funerary Documents 18

Indus, Mesopotamian, and Cretan Seals 33

Two Temple Reliefs 36

Four Olmec Sculptures 38

Homer 47

Genesis 53

Deuteronomy 57

The Old Woman 127

Asoka 150

The Laws of Manu 154

Faxian 159

Four Robed Statues 167

The Vishnu Purana 179

The Lotus Sutra 184

The Gospel of Matthew 200

St. Paul 202

The Pact of Umar 245

Han Yu 285

Ibn Munqidh 296

The Mosaics of San Vitale 318

The Russian Primary Chronicle 327

A Lateran Palace Mosaic 337

Pane 383

The Book of the Community 389

Benedict of St. Peter 402

William of Rubruck 410

John of Monte Corvino 418

Mandeville 433

Sahagun 447

Toleration and Persecution,
Amity and Hostility

Deuteronomy 57

Judges 60

Asoka 150

Faxian 159, 173

Josephus 191

Eusebius of Caesarea 206

Christ the Redeemer 211

The Qur'an 225

Imam Nawawi 229

Al-Saduq — 234
Al-Mawardi — 237
The Pact of Umar — 245
Benjamin of Tudela — 247
Firuz Shah — 250
Bishop Adam — 271
Han Yu — 285
Tang Wuzong — 285
Ibn Munqidh — 296
Al-Biruni — 306
The Song of Roland — 338
Anna Comnena — 356
Gunther of Pairis — 359
Al-Bakri — 370
The Glorious Victories of 'Amda Seyon — 374
Mandeville — 433
Ricci — 468
Tokugawa Iemitsu — 472
Abul Fazl — 476

Society and Social Groups

Court Life and Ceremony

Two Temple Reliefs — 36
Benjamin of Tudela — 247
Murasaki Shikibu — 260
The Mosaics of San Vitale — 318
Einhard — 332
Al-Bakri — 370
Seated Female Figure — 378
Cieza de León — 392
Zhou Daguan — 423
Ibn Battuta — 429
A Benin Wall Plaque — 462
Abul Fazl — 476

Fringe Peoples and the Exotic Other

Columbus — P-8
Woodcut of 1511 — P-19
The Gaul and Wife — 127
Strabo — 131
Asoka — 150
Sima Qian — 163
Han Yu — 285
Tang Wuzong — 285
Al-Jahiz — 292

Ibn Munqidh — 296
A Thousand and One Arabian Nights — 300
Al-Biruni — 306
The Russian Primary Chronicle — 327
Anna Comnena — 356
Al-Mas'udi — 366
Al-Bakri — 370
Pane — 383
Cieza de León — 392
Rubruck — 410
Polo — 415
Monte Corvino — 418
Zhou Daguan — 423
Ibn Battuta — 429
Mandeville — 433
Ma Huan — 438
Azurara — 442
Sahagun — 447
A Benin Wall Plaque — 462
Barbot — 465
Ricci — 468
Tokugawa Iemitsu — 472
Abul Fazl — 476

Marriage and the Family

Columbus — P-8
Woodcut of 1511 — P-19
Hammurabi — 12
The Classic of Odes — 29
Homer — 47
Deuteronomy — 57
Judges — 60
Confucius — 96
Euripides — 114
The Gaul and Wife — 127
Ban Zhao — 145
The Laws of Manu — 154
The Babylonian Talmud — 195
Imam Nawawi — 229
Du Fu — 275
Dandin — 310
Vikrama's Adventures — 312
Einhard — 332
A Letter from the Cairo Geniza — 407
Rubruck — 410
Polo — 415

Ibn Battuta   429
(*See also* Women: Cultural and
Occupational Roles)

Slaves and Forced Laborers
Columbus   P-8
The Judgments of Hammurabi   12
A Scribal Exercise Book   22
The Rig Veda   43
Deuteronomy   57
Euripides   114
The Laws of Manu   154
Asoka   150
Mahmud Kati   242
The Pact of Umar   245
Tang Wuzong   285
Cieza de León   392
Zhou Daguan   423
Ibn Battuta   429
Azurara   442
Espinosa   453
Nzinga Mbemba   459
Barbot   465

Urban Life
The Judgments of Hammurabi   12
Thucydides   108
Aelius Aristides   134
Faxian   159
Benjamin of Tudela   247
Musings on the Eastern Capital   280
The Book of the Eparch   325
The Guild of Southampton   351
Al-Bakri   370
Cieza de León   392
Benedict of St. Peter   402
Zhou Daguan   423
(*See also* Economic Activity: Artisans;
Economic Activity: Commerce;
Economic Activity: Occupations)

Travel and Exploration
Columbus   P-8
The Epic of Gilgamesh   7
Homer   47
Strabo   131

Faxian   159, 173
Sima Qian   163
Mahmud Kati   242
Benjamin of Tudela   247
A Thousand and One Arabian Nights   300
Al-Mas'udi   366
A Letter from the Cairo Geniza   407
Rubruck   410
Polo   415
Monte Corvino   418
Zhou Daguan   423
Pegolotti   426
Ibn Battuta   429
Mandeville   433
Ma Huan   438
Azurara   442
A Benin-Portuguese Saltcellar   462
Barbot   465
Tokugawa Iemitsu   472
Tavernier   478
(*See also* Religion: Pilgrimage)

Violence, War, and Warriors

The Effects of War
A Scribal Exercise Book   22
Euripides   114
Asoka   150
Du Fu   275
Al-Biruni   306
Anna Comnena   356
Sahagun   447

Heroes and Warrior Cultures
The Epic of Gilgamesh   7
Indus, Mesopotamian, and Cretan Seals   33
The Rig Veda   43
Homer   47
Deuteronomy   57
Judges   60
The Bhagavad Gita   68
Thucydides   108
Euripides   114
The Gaul and Wife   127
Christ the Redeemer   211

Chronicle of the Grand Pacification   264
Al-Jahiz   292
Psellus   322
Einhard   332
The Song of Roland   338
The Glorious Victories of 'Amda Seyon   374
Polo   415
Sahagun   447
A Benin Wall Plaque   462

Holy War
Deuteronomy   57
Judges   60
The Bhagavad Gita   68
Isaiah   86
Eusebius of Caesarea   206
Christ the Redeemer   211
The Qur'an   225
Imam Nawawi   229
Al-Mawardi   237
Einhard   332
A Lateran Palace Mosaic   337
The Song of Roland   338
Anna Comnena   356
Gunther of Pairis   359
The Glorious Victories of 'Amda Seyon   374
Mandeville   433
Sahagun   447

Nonviolence
The Book of Good Conduct   72
The Buddha   74
Laozi   93
Confucius   96
Asoka   150
Faxian   159
The Gospel of Matthew   200
The Parable about the World Ocean   219
Du Fu   275
Dogen   289
(*See also* Violence, War, and Warriors:
Peace and Peace Making)

Peace and Peace Making
Isaiah   86
Sima Qian   101, 163
Aelius Aristides   134

Asoka   150
Faxian   159
The Gospel of Matthew   200
Eusebius of Caesarea   206
The Qur'an   225
Imam Nawawi   229
The Pact of Umar   245
The Russian Primary Chronicle   327
The Glorious Victories of 'Amda Seyon   374
Cieza de León   392

Women

Cultural and Occupational Roles
Hammurabi   12
The Classic of Odes   29
A Tassili Rock Painting   31
The Discipline Basket   79
Euripides   114
The Old Woman   127
Ban Zhao   145
The Laws of Manu   154
St. Ephraem of Edessa   213
Imam Nawawi   229
Murasaki Shikibu   260
Du Fu   275
Musings on the Eastern Capital   280
Dandin   310
Vikrama's Adventures   312
The Mosaic of Empress Theodora   318
Seated Female Figure   378
Rubruck   410
Polo   415
Zhou Daguan   423
Pegolotti   426
Ibn Battuta   429
Mandeville   433
(See also Society and Social Groups:
Marriage and the Family)

Goddesses
The Epic of Gilgamesh   7
"The Negative Confession"   18
Two Temple Reliefs   36
Deuteronomy   57
Judges   60

Lucius Apuleius 137
Faxian 173
Guanyin 187
Chronicle of the Grand Pacification 264

Legal Status
Hammurabi 12
The Discipline Basket 79
The Laws of Manu 154

Property Owners
Hammurabi 12
The Laws of Manu 154

Providers
Hammurabi 12
A Tassili Rock Painting 31
Dandin 310
Rubruck 410
Polo 415
Zhou Daguan 423

Women as Models and Types
The Classic of Odes 29
The Discipline Basket 79

Euripides 114
The Gaul and Wife 127
The Old Woman 127
Ban Zhao 145
Asoka 150
St. Paul 202
Eusebius of Caesarea 206
St. Ephraem of Edessa 213
Imam Nawawi 229
Dandin 310
Vikrama 312
Seated Female Figure 378
Polo 415

Women of Authority
The Parthian Noblewoman 167
St. Paul 202
Eusebius of Caesarea 206
St. Ephraem of Edessa 213
Murasaki Shikibu 260
The Mosaic of Empress Theodora 318
The Russian Primary Chronicle 327
The Glorious Victories of 'Amda Seyon 374
Seated Female Figure 378

Preface

Many goals and principles have guided our work on the third edition of *The Human Record.* Foremost is our commitment to the proposition that all students of history must meet the challenge of analyzing primary sources, thereby becoming active inquirers into the past, rather than passive recipients of historical facts. Involvement with primary-source evidence enables students to see that historical scholarship is principally the intellectual process of drawing inferences and discovering patterns from clues yielded by the past, not of memorizing someone else's conclusions. Moreover, such analysis motivates students to learn by stimulating curiosity and imagination, and it helps them develop into critical thinkers who are comfortable with complex challenges.

Not only does primary-source evidence enable the student of history to discover what people in the past thought and did, it also allows the researcher to detect significant changes, as well as lines of continuity, in the institutions and ideas of a culture or cluster of cultures. This in turn allows the historian to divide the past into meaningful periods that highlight the turning points, as well as the constancies, that constitute the human story. In short, primary-source analysis is the essence of the historian's craft and the basis of all historical understanding.

Themes and Structure

We have compiled a source collection that traces the long and intricate course of human history. Volume I follows the evolution of the cultures that most significantly influenced the history of the world from around 3500 B.C.E. to 1700 C.E., with emphasis on the development of the major religious, social, intellectual, and political traditions of that supercontinent of interconnected societies known as the *Afro-Eurasian Ecumene.* Although our primary focus in Volume I is on the eastern hemisphere, we do not neglect the Americas. This first volume concurrently develops the theme of the growing links and increasingly important exchanges among the world's cultures down to the early modern era. Volume II picks up this theme of growing human interconnectedness by tracing the gradual establishment of Western global hegemony; the simultaneous historical developments in other civilizations and societies around the world; the anti-Western, anticolonial movements of the twentieth century; and the emergence of today's still often bitterly divided but integrated *one world.*

To address these themes in depth, we have chosen and arranged selections that present an overview of global history in mosaic form, in which each source contributes to a single large composition. We have been careful to avoid isolated sources that provide a taste of some culture or age but, by their dissociation, shed no light on patterns of cultural creation, continuity, change, and interchange — the essential components of world history.

In selecting and placing the various pieces of our mosaic, we have sought to create a balanced picture of human history and to craft a book that reveals the contributions of the world's major societies. We also have attempted to give our readers a collection of sources representing a wide variety of perspectives and experiences. Believing that the study of history properly concerns every aspect of past human activity and thought, we have sought sources that mirror the practices and concerns of a wide variety of representative persons and groups.

Our pursuit of historical balance has also led us into the arena of unwritten evidence. Although most historians center their research on documents, the discipline requires us to consider all of the clues surrendered by the past, and these include artifacts. Moreover, we have discovered that students enjoy analyzing artifacts and seem to remember vividly the conclusions they draw from them. For these reasons, we have included a number of illustrations of works of art and other artifacts that users of this book can analyze as historical sources.

Learning Aids

Source analysis can be a daunting exercise for students. Therefore, to make these selections as accessible as possible, we have provided our readers with a variety of aids. First there is the *Prologue,* in which we explain — initially in a theoretical manner and then through concrete examples — how a student of history interprets written and artifactual sources. Next we offer *part, chapter, section, and individual source introductions,* all to help the reader place each selection into a meaningful context and understand its historical significance. Because we consider *The Human Record* an interpretive overview of global history and therefore a survey of the major patterns of global history that stands on its own as a text, our introductions are significantly fuller than those normally encountered in a book of sources.

Suggested *Questions for Analysis* precede each source; their purpose is to help the student make sense of each piece of evidence and wrest from it as much insight as possible. The questions are presented in a three-tiered format designed to resemble the historian's approach to source analysis and to help students make historical comparisons on a global scale. The first several questions are usually quite specific and ask the reader to pick out important pieces of information. These initial questions require the student to address the issues What does this document or artifact say? and What meaningful facts can I garner from it? Addressing concrete questions of this sort prepares the student researcher for the next, more significant level of critical thinking and analysis: drawing inferences. Questions that demand inferential conclusions follow the fact-oriented questions. Finally, whenever possible, we offer a third tier of questions that challenge the student to compare the individual or society that produced a particular source with another individual, group, or culture encountered earlier in the volume. We believe such comparisons help students fix more firmly in their minds the distinguishing cultural characteristics of the various societies they encounter in their survey of world history. Beyond that, we believe that global history is, by its very nature, comparative history.

Another form of help we offer is to *gloss the sources,* explaining fully words and allusions that college students cannot reasonably be expected to know. To facilitate reading and to encourage reference, the notes appear at the bottoms of the pages on which they are cited. Some documents also contain *interlinear notes* that serve as transitions or provide needed information.

Some instructors might use *The Human Record* as their sole textbook. Most, however, will probably use it as a supplement to a standard narrative textbook, and many of these professors might decide not to require their students to analyze every entry. To assist instructors (and students) in selecting sources that best suit their interests and needs, we have prepared *two analytical tables of contents* for each volume. The first lists readings and artifacts by geographic and cultural area, and the second, by topic. These two tables of contents suggest to professors and students alike the rich variety of material available within these pages, particularly for essays in comparative history.

New to This Edition

A major goal in crafting *The Human Record* has been to do our best to prepare the student-reader for success — *success* being defined as comfort with historical analysis, proficiency in critical thinking, an understanding of how to view history on a global scale, and a deepened awareness of the rich cultural varieties, as well as shared characteristics, of the human family. To continue to meet these objectives, we have made a number of changes in this third edition. Moreover, because the study of history is an ongoing dialogue between the present and the past, recent developments — the eruption of bitter ethnic rivalries in many parts of the world, the growing appeal of militant religious fundamentalism, and the continuing rapid economic growth of China, Hong Kong, Singapore, Taiwan, and Korea — have made revision of some portions of our book desirable. In addition, recent scholarly discoveries, such as the excavation of a human site at Monte Verde, Chile, that has been dated to at least 10,500 B.C.E., have made revision not just desirable but necessary.

Users of the second edition will discover that about one-third of the documents and artifacts are new to the third edition. Volume I has a whole new chapter (Chapter 10) devoted to the parallel and often mutually hostile cultures of two medieval Christian civilizations: Western Europe and Byzantium. New sections have also been added within several chapters of Volume I, all of which focus on various aspects of cross-cultural exchange. These sections include "Travel along the Silk Road" and "Travel across the Indian Ocean" in Chapter 5; "Christianity and the Roman World" and "Religious Exchange and Interchange" in Chapter 7; "Buddhism in East Asia: Acceptance, Rejection, and Accommodation" and "Southwest Asia: Crossroads of the Afro-Eurasian

World" in Chapter 9; and "Pilgrims and Merchants before the Mongol Age" in Chapter 12.

Likewise, Volume II has received a top-to-bottom overhauling, with expanded coverage in some areas and the addition of a number of new areas and topics. For example, religious fundamentalism is the focus of several new sources, including selections from the writings of the late-eighteenth-century African political and religious leader Usman den Fodio (Chapter 6); a summary of the principles of the Muslim Brotherhood, the twentieth-century movement dedicated to Islamic revival (Chapter 12); and a statement of Hindu nationalism by the Indian journalist Girilal Jain (Chapter 13). Economic and political problems of former colonies in Africa and Asia provide the topic for a new section in Chapter 13, which, in addition to Jain's editorials, includes selections from the speeches and writings of C. Odumwegwu Ojukwu, a leader of the Biafran independence movement in the 1970s, and a new set of statistics on world economic development. Finally, excerpts from Deng Xiaoping's speeches and writings shed light on China's ongoing economic transformation.

Other new sources reflect our ongoing commitment to social-cultural history. In this vein we added a number of documentary and artifactual sources that reflect everyday life (and death) and gender issues — topics emphasized in the first two editions but important enough to justify expanded coverage in this new edition. Additionally, some of the new sources appearing in Volume I — such as the Buddha statue from Funan, the Gnostic *Gospel of Thomas,* the Manichaean *Parable about the World-Ocean,* the Nestorian-Chinese *Christian Monument,* Pope Sylvester II's *Letter to St. Stephen of Hungary,* and al-Mas'udi's *Meadows of Gold* — were chosen because they reveal stages in the important process of cultural *syncretism,* in which elements from two or more cultures merge to form a new cultural complex. This essential aspect of global history is a major theme throughout both volumes of *The Human Record.*

Because of the long expanse of time covered by Volume I, several new sources were added to illustrate the way in which some cultures and their institutions evolved over extended periods of time. Thus in Chapter 1, the three documents that comprise source 3, "Three Funerary Documents," allow the student to see how Egyptian notions of a blissful afterlife took shape over a period of more than a thousand years. Likewise, the addition of the vedic hymn "Who Is Indra?" helps clarify essential shifts in the Indo-Aryan cosmology over the period of roughly a millennium.

Always on the lookout for new artifacts that can stimulate student inquiry and aid understanding, we are happy to report that both volumes have received an infusion of new visual sources.

In addition, some new items are actually new translations of documents that appeared in previous editions, and a number of these are our own translations. Our goal is to provide selections that are written in clear and idiomatic modern English. Other new sources have been added simply because we believe they will provide effective material for classroom use.

To reflect up-to-date scholarship, as well as our rethinking and restructuring of a number of source selections, we have revised many of the book's introductions and explanatory notes, occasionally expanding them in order to provide even greater help to the student-reader.

Using The Human Record: Suggestions from the Editors

Specific suggestions for assignments and classroom activities appear in the manual entitled *Using The Human Record: Suggestions from the Editors.* In this manual, prepared by the editor-authors, we explain why we have chosen the sources that appear in this book and what insights we believe students should be capable of drawing from them. We also describe classroom tactics for encouraging thought and discussion on the various sources. The advice we present is the fruit of our own use of these sources in the classroom.

Acknowledgments

We are in debt to the many professionals who offered their expert advice and assistance during preparation of this edition. Scholars and friends at the University of Vermont who generously shared their expertise with us include Doris Bergen, Robert V. Daniels, Carolyn Elliott, Shirley Gedeon, Eric Gilbert, William Haviland, Kristin M. Peterson-Ishaq, Abubaker Saad, Wolfe W. Schmokel, Peter Seybolt, John W. Seyller, Marshall True, Diane Villemaire, and Denise Youngblood. We wish to thank especially Peter D. Andrea, who drew the prototype for the map of "Strabo's world" that appears in Volume I.

We also wish to acknowledge the following instructors, who read and commented on portions of this edition in its earliest stages of revision: Robert Babcock, Hastings College; Blake Beattie, University of Louisville; Norman Bennett, Boston University; Joel Berlatsky, Wilkes University; Jack Betterly, Emma Willard School; Orazio Ciccarelli, The University of Southern Mississippi; Steve Davidson, Southwestern University; David Fahey, Miami University; Frederick Gifun, University of Massachusetts-Dartmouth; Bernice Guillaume, St. Louis University; Howard Holter, California State University-Dominguez Hills; Paul Madden, Hardin-Simmons University; Patrick Manning, Northeastern University; Delores McBroome, Humboldt State University; Pamela McVay, Ursuline College; Richard Negron, Central Washington University; James B. M. Schick, Pittsburg State University; Marvin G. Slind, Washington State University; and Charlotte Staelin, Wesley College.

Finally, our debt to our spouses is beyond payment, but our dedication to them of each edition of this book reflects in some small way how deeply we appreciate their constant support and good-humored tolerance.

A. J. A.
J. H. O.

The HUMAN RECORD

Volume I

Prologue

———— ▾▾▾ ————

Primary Sources and How We Read Them

What Is History?

Many students believe that the study of history involves simply memorizing dates, names, battles, treaties, and endless numbers of similar, usually uninteresting facts with seemingly no relevance to their lives and concerns. After all, so they think, the past is over and done with. Historians know what has happened, and all that is left for students is to absorb this body of knowledge, for reasons known only to educators.

But these notions are wrong — totally wrong. History involves discovery and interpretation, and its content is vitally relevant to our lives. Our understanding of history is constantly changing and deepening, as historians learn more about the past and shed new light on its meaning. Just as significant, each person who studies the past brings to it a unique perspective and raises questions that are meaningful to him or her. Although there is certainly an objective past, which we all should endeavor to discover and understand as fully as possible, each of us also must explore a past that has personal meaning in order to find in it insights and truths relevant to our own concerns. The drive to understand what has gone before us is innately human and springs from our need to know who we are. History serves this function of self-discovery in a special way because of its universality. Contrary to the opinion of many people, the study of history does not focus exclusively or even primarily on politics. It deals with all aspects of past human activity and belief, for there is no subject or concern that lacks a history. Therefore, each of us can and should explore the origins and historical evolution of whatever is most important to us.

Regardless of our individual interests or questions, the study and interpretation of our historical heritage involves coming to grips with the dynamics of the historical process. It means exploring the ways in which human societies reacted to the environments in which they found themselves and the ways in which they sought to reshape those environments to meet their needs. It means exploring the complex interplay of geography, technology, religion, social structures, and a myriad of other historical factors. It means exploring the ways in which societies change in response to stimuli and the ways in which they resist change, as well. It means exploring the traditions that have imprinted themselves upon various cultures and the ways those traditions have provided continuity over long periods of time. It means exploring the roles of individuals in shaping the course of history and the ways in which individuals have been shaped by historical circumstances. Indeed, the questions we ask of the past are limited only by our imaginations; the answers we arrive at are limited only by the evidence at hand and our ability to use that evidence thoroughly and creatively. Our answers, no matter how partial or tentative, certainly reveal the inner dynamics of whatever historical culture we are investigating. More than that, those insights help us better understand the challenges we face in our own day by enlarging our field of vision. When applied to the global community, historical perspective enables us to appreciate the richness of human experience and expression and the factors underlying the striking similarities and differences that exist among the world's peoples.

This collection of sources will help you discover some of the major lines of global historical development and understand many of the major cultural traditions and forces that have shaped history around the world. As editors we will not hand you answers; you will have to work for them because hard work lies at the heart of historical study. The word *history,* which is Greek in origin, means "learning through inquiry," and that is precisely what historians do. They discover and interpret the past by asking questions and conducting research. Their inquiry revolves around an examination of evidence left by the past. For lack of a better term, historians call that evidence *primary source material.*

Primary Sources: Their Value and Limitations

Primary sources are records that for the most part have been passed on in written form, thereby preserving memories of past events. These written sources include, but are not limited to, official records, law codes, private correspondence, literature, religious texts, merchants' account books, memoirs, and the list goes on and on. No source by itself contains unadulterated truth or the whole picture. Each gives us only a glimpse of reality, and it is the historian's task to fit these fragments of the past into a coherent picture.

Imagine for a moment that some historian in the mid twenty-first century decides to write a history of your college class. Think about the primary sources this researcher would seek out: the school catalogue, the registrar's class lists, academic transcripts, and similar official documents; class lecture notes, course syllabi, examinations, term papers, and possibly even textbooks; diaries and private letters; school newspapers, yearbooks, and sports programs; handbills, posters, and even photographs of graffiti; and recollections written down or otherwise recorded by some of your classmates long after they graduated. With a bit of thought you could add other items to the list, among them some nonwritten sources, such as recordings of popular music and photographs and videotapes of student life and activity. But let us confine ourselves for the moment to written records. What do all these documentary sources have in common?

Even this imposing list of sources does not and cannot present the past in its entirety. Where do we see the evidence that never made it into any official record, including long telephone calls home, all-night study groups, afternoons spent at the student union, or complaints shared among classmates about professors and courses? Someone possibly recorded memories of some of these events and opinions, but how complete and trustworthy is that evidence? Also consider that all the documents available to this twenty-first-century historian will be fortunate survivors. They will represent only a small percentage of the vast bulk of written material generated during your college career. Thanks to the wastebasket, the "delete" key, the disintegration of materials, and the inevitable loss of life's memorabilia as years slip by, the evidence available to the future historian will be fragmentary. This is always the case with historical evidence. We cannot preserve the records of the past in their totality. Clearly, the more remote the past, the more fragmentary our documentary evidence. Imagine the feeble chance any particular document from the twelfth century had of surviving the wars, worms, and wastebaskets of the past eight hundred years.

Now let us consider the many individual pieces of documentary evidence relating to your class's history that have survived. As we review the list, we see that no single primary source gives us a pure, unvarnished, and complete picture. Each has its perspective, value, and limitations. Imagine that the personal essays submitted by applicants for admission were your only sources of information about the student body. Given this, would you not conclude that the school attracted only the most gifted and interesting people imaginable? Also consider that these essays by aspiring students are not the only potential sources available to you that are, at least in part, exercises in creative advertising. You certainly are aware of how every college catalogue presents an idealized picture of campus life.

Despite their flaws, however, essays composed by applicants for admission and the school's official catalogue are still important pieces of historical evidence — when used judiciously. The essays certainly reflect the would-be students' perceptions of the school's cultural values and the types of people it hopes to attract, and usually the applicants are right on the mark because they have read the school's catalogue. That catalogue, of course, reflects the values of the faculty and administrators who composed it. It also provides quite a bit of useful information concerning rules and regulations, courses, instructors, school organizations, and similar items. That factual information, however, is the raw material of history, not history itself, and certainly it does not reflect the full historical reality of your class.

What is true of the catalogue is equally true of the student newspaper and every other piece of evidence generated by or pertinent to your class. Each primary source is part of a larger whole, but as we have already seen, we do not have all the pieces. Think of historical evidence in terms of a jigsaw puzzle. Even though many of the pieces are missing, it is possible to put most, though probably not all, of the remaining pieces together in a reasonable fashion to form a fairly accurate and coherent picture. The picture that emerges might not be complete (it never is), but it is useful and valid. The keys to fitting these pieces together are hard work and imagination. Each is absolutely necessary.

Examining the Sources

Hard work speaks for itself, but students are often unaware that a historian also needs an imagination to reconstruct the past. After all, many students ask, doesn't history consist of strictly defined and irrefutable dates, names, and facts? Where does imagination enter into the process of learning these facts?

Again let us consider your class's history and its documentary sources. Many of those documents provide factual data — dates, names, grades, statistics. And while these data are important, individually and collectively they have no historical meaning until they have been interpreted. Your college class is not a collection of statistics and facts. It is a group of individuals who, despite their differences, share and help mold a collective experience. It is a community evolving within a particular time and place. Influenced by its environment, it is in turn an influence on that world. Any valid or useful history must reach beyond a mere list of dates, names, and facts and interpret the historical characteristics and role of your class: What were its values? How did it change and why? What impact did it have? These are some of the important questions a historian asks of the evidence. The answers the historian arrives at help us gain insight into ourselves, our society, and our human nature.

In order to arrive at answers, the historian must examine each and every piece of relevant evidence in its full context and wring from that evidence as many *inferences* as possible. Facts are the foundation stones of history, but inferences are its edifices. An inference is a logical conclusion drawn from evidence, and it is the heart and soul of historical inquiry.

Every American schoolchild learns that "In fourteen hundred and ninety-two, Columbus sailed the ocean blue." That fact is worthless, however, unless the individual understands the motives, causes, and significance of this late-fifteenth-century voyage. Certainly a historian must know when Columbus sailed west. After all, time is history's framework. Yet the questions historians ask go far beyond simple chronology: Why did Columbus sail west? What factors made possible Spain's engagement in such enterprises at this time? Why were Europeans willing and able to exploit, as they did, the so-called New World? What were the short- and long-term consequences of the European presence in the Americas? These are some of the significant questions to which historians seek inferential answers, and those answers can only be found in the evidence.

One noted historian, Robin Winks, has written a book entitled *The Historian as Detective,* and the image is appropriate although inexact. Like the detective, the historian examines clues in order to reconstruct events. However the detective is essentially interested in discovering what happened, who did it, and why, whereas the historian goes one step beyond and asks what it all means. In addressing the question of meaning, the historian transforms simple curiosity about past events into a humanistic discipline.

As a humanist, the historian seeks wisdom and insight into the human condition, but that wisdom cannot be based on theories spun out of fantasy, wishful thinking, or preconceived notions. It must be based on a methodical and probing investigation of the evidence. Like a detective interrogating witnesses, the historian must also carefully examine the testimony of sources, and both investigators must ask similar questions. First and foremost the historian must evaluate the *validity* of the source. Is it what it purports to be? Artful forgeries have misled many historians. Even if the source is authentic (and most are), it still can mislead the historian. The possibility always exists that the source's author lied or otherwise deliberately misrepresented reality. Even if this is not the case, the historian can easily be led astray by not fully understanding the *perspective* reflected in the document. As any detective who has examined a number of eyewitnesses to an event knows, what each individual reports he or she saw often differs radically due to a number of factors. The police detective has the opportunity to re-examine witnesses and offer them the opportunity to change their testimony in the light of new evidence and deeper reflection. The historical researcher is usually not so fortunate. Even when the historian compares a piece of documentary evidence with other evidence in order to uncover its flaws, there is no way to cross-examine it in detail. What is written is written. Given this fact, it is absolutely necessary for the historian to understand as fully as possible the source's perspective. Thus the historian must ask several key questions: *What* kind of document is this? *Who* wrote it? For *whom* and *why*? *Where* was it composed and *when*?

The *what* is important because understanding the nature of a particular source can save the historian a great deal of frustration. Many historical sources simply do not address the questions a historian would like to ask of them. That twenty-first-century historian would be foolish to try to learn much about the academic quality of your school's courses from a study of the registrar's class lists and grade sheets. Student and faculty class notes, copies of old syllabi, examinations, papers, and textbooks would be far more fruitful sources.

Who, for whom, and *why* are equally important questions. The official school catalogue undoubtedly addresses some issues pertaining to student social life. But should this document — designed to attract potential students and place the school in the best possible light — be read and accepted uncritically? Obviously not. It must be tested against student testimony and discovered in such sources as private letters, memoirs, posters, student newspapers, and yearbooks.

Where and *when* are also important questions to ask of any primary source. As a general rule, distance in space and time from an event colors perceptions and can adversely affect the validity of a source's testimony. The recollections of a person celebrating a twenty-fifth class reunion could be quite insightful and valuable. Conceivably this graduate now has a perspective and information that were absent one-quarter century earlier. Just as conceivably, that person's memory might be playing tricks. A source can be so close to or distant from the event it documents that its view is distorted or totally erroneous. Even so the source is not necessarily worthless. Often the blind spots and misinformation within a source reveal to the researcher important insights into the author's attitudes and sources of information.

The historical detective's task is difficult. In addition to constantly questioning the validity and particular perspectives of available sources, the historical researcher must often use whatever evidence is available in imaginative ways. The researcher must interpret these fragmentary and flawed glimpses of the past and piece together the resultant inferences and insights as well as possible. While recognizing that a complete picture of the past is impossible, the historian assumes the responsibility of recreating a past that is valid and has meaning for the present.

You and the Sources

This book will actively involve you in the work of historical inquiry by asking you to draw inferences based on your careful analysis of primary source evidence. This is not an easy task, especially at first, but it is well within your capability. Moreover, along with your professor, we will be helping you all along the way.

You realize by now that historians do not base their conclusions on analyses of single, isolated sources. Historical research consists of laborious sifting through mountains of documents. We have already done much of this work for you by selecting, paring down, and annotating important sources that individually allow you to gain some significant insight into a particular issue or moment in the long and complex history of our global community. In doing this for you, we do not relieve you of the responsibility of recognizing that no single source, no matter how rich it might appear, offers a complete picture of the individual or culture that produced it. Each source that appears in this book is a piece of valuable evidence, but it is only partial evidence. You should never forget this.

You will analyze two types of evidence: documents and artifacts. Each source will be authentic, so you do not have to worry about validating it. We will also supply you with the information necessary to place each piece of evidence into its proper context and will suggest questions you legitimately can and should ask of each source. If you carefully read the introductions and notes, the suggested Questions for Analysis, and, most important of all, the sources themselves — and think about what you are doing — solid inferences will follow.

To illustrate how you should go about this task and what is expected of you, we will take you through a sample exercise, step by step. The exercise consists of our analyzing two sources: a document from the pen of Christopher Columbus and a reproduction of an early sixteenth-century woodcut. By the end of this exercise, if you have worked closely with us, you should be ready to begin interpreting sources on your own.

Before we begin we want to offer a cautionary note. Please understand that we will wring from this sample document many more inferences than we or your professor should expect from you. After all, we bring to this task quite a bit of background that you do not yet have. We have read books on Christopher Columbus that you might never have the opportunity to view, and that reading inevitably has had an influence on how we interpret this particular document. Nevertheless, we believe that leading you through this exercise has value, insofar as it will demonstrate the general way to go about drawing historical inferences and the rich possibilities for insight that lie within a piece of documentary evidence. So please do not be intimidated by what follows. Take from it whatever of value you find in it.

That noted, let us now look at the document. We present it just as it would appear in any chapter of this book: first an introduction, then suggested Questions for Analysis, and finally the source itself, with explanatory footnotes. Because we want to give you a full introduction to the art of documentary source analysis, the excerpt in our example is a bit longer than the average document in this book. The notes that comment on the text are probably also fuller than necessary, but we prefer to err on the side of providing too much information and help, rather than too little. Again do not let the length of the document or its many notes intimidate you. Once you get into the source, you should find it fairly easy going.

Your first step in analyzing any source in this book is to read the introduction and the Questions for Analysis. The former is intended to place the source into context; the latter should provide direction when it comes time to analyze the source. One important point to keep in mind is that every historian approaches a source with at least one question in mind, even though it might be vaguely formulated. Very much like the detective, the historian wants to discover some particular truth or shed light on a given issue. This requires asking specific questions of the witnesses or, in the historian's case, of the evidence. These questions of course should not be prejudgments. One of the worst errors a historian can make is setting out to prove a point or to defend an ideological position. Questions are simply starting points, nothing else, but they are essential. Therefore, as you approach a source, have your question or questions fixed in your mind, and as you work your way through a source, constantly remind yourself what issue or issues you are investigating. We have provided you with a number of suggested questions for each source. Perhaps you or your professor will want to ask other questions. Whatever the case, keep focused on these questions and issues, and take notes as you read each source. Never rely on unaided memory; it will almost inevitably lead you astray.

Needless to say, you must be honest and thorough as you study a source. Read each explanatory footnote carefully, lest you misunderstand a word or allusion. Try to understand exactly what the source is saying and what its author's perspective is. Be careful not to wrench items, words, or ideas out of context, thereby distorting them. Above all, read the entire source so that you understand as fully as possible what it says and, just as important, what it does not say.

This is not as difficult as it sounds. It just takes concentration and a bit of work. To illustrate the point, let us read and analyze Christopher Columbus's letter and in the process try to answer this core question: What evidence is there in this document that allows us to judge Columbus's reliability as an objective reporter? By addressing this issue, we will actually answer questions 3–6 and 8.

"With the Royal Standard Unfurled"
▼▼▼

▼ *Christopher Columbus,*
A LETTER CONCERNING
RECENTLY DISCOVERED ISLANDS

Sixteenth-century Spain's emergence as the dominant power in the Americas is forever associated with the name of a single mariner: Christopher Columbus (1451–1506). Sponsored by King Ferdinand V of Aragon and Queen Isabella I of Castile, this Genoese sea captain sailed westward into the Atlantic seeking a new route to the empires of East Asia described by John Mandeville (Volume I, Chapter 12, source 109), Marco Polo (Volume I, Chapter 12, source 104), and others whose books of travels Columbus had avidly read and digested. On October 12, 1492, his fleet of three ships dropped anchor at a small Bahamian island, which Columbus claimed for Spain, naming it San Salvador. The fleet then sailed to two larger islands, which he named Juana and Española (today known as Cuba and Hispaniola).

After exploring these two islands and establishing on Española the fort of Navidad del Señor, Columbus departed for Spain in January 1493. On his way home, the admiral prepared a preliminary account of his expedition to the "Indies" for Luis de Santángel, a counselor to King Ferdinand and one of Columbus's enthusiastic supporters. In composing the letter, Columbus borrowed heavily from his official ship's log, often lifting passages verbatim. When he landed in Lisbon, Portugal, in early March, Columbus dispatched the letter overland, expecting it to precede him to the Spanish royal court in faraway Barcelona, where Santángel would communicate its contents to the two monarchs. The admiral was not disappointed. His triumphal reception at the court in April was proof that the letter had served its purpose.

As you analyze the document, be aware of several facts. The admiral was returning with only two of his vessels. He had lost his flagship, the *Santa Maria,* when it was wrecked on a reef off present-day Haiti on Christmas Day. Also many of Columbus's facts and figures reflect more his enthusiasm than dispassionate analysis. His estimates of the dimensions of the two main islands he explored grossly exaggerate their sizes, and his optimistic report of the wide availability of such riches as gold, spices, cotton, and mastic was not borne out by subsequent exploration and colonization. Although he obtained items of gold and received plenty of reports of nearby gold mines, the metal was rare in the islands. Moreover, the only indigenous spice proved to be the fiery chili pepper; the wild cotton was excellent but not plentiful; and mastic, an eastern Mediterranean aromatic gum, was not native to the Caribbean.

QUESTIONS FOR ANALYSIS

1. How does Columbus indicate that these lands are worth the careful attention of the Spanish monarchs?
2. What does Columbus's description of the physical attributes of the islands suggest about some of the motives for his voyage?
3. Often the eyes only see what the mind prepares them to see. What evidence is there that Columbus saw what he wanted to see and discovered what he expected to discover? In other words, how had his environment prepared Columbus to see and interpret what he encountered in the Caribbean?
4. What evidence suggests that Columbus's letter was a carefully crafted piece of self-promotion by a person determined to prove he had reached the Indies?
5. Notwithstanding the obvious self-promotion, is there any evidence that Columbus also attempted to present an objective and fairly accurate account of what he had seen and experienced? In other words, to what extent, if at all, can we trust his account?
6. What do the admiral's admitted actions regarding the natives and the ways in which he describes these people allow us to conclude about his attitudes toward these "Indians" and his plans for them?
7. What does this letter tell us about the culture of the Tainos on the eve of European expansion into their world? Does Columbus tell us anything about these people that doesn't seem to ring totally true? What do you infer from your answer to that latter question?
8. How does this letter illustrate the fact that single historical sources read in isolation can mislead the researcher?

Sir, as I know that you will be pleased at the great victory with which Our Lord has crowned my voyage, I write this to you, from which you will learn how in thirty-three days, I passed from the Canary Islands to the Indies[1] with the fleet which the most illustrious king and queen, our sovereigns, gave to me. And there I found very many islands filled with people[2] innumerable, and of them all I have taken possession for their highnesses, by proclamation made and with the royal standard unfurled, and no opposition was offered to me. To the first island which I found, I gave the name *San Salvador,*[3] in remembrance of the Divine Majesty, Who has marvelously be-

---

[1]An inexact term that referred not just to India but the entire area of the Indian Ocean and East Asia.
[2]The Tainos, a tribal branch of the Arawak language family. Arawak speakers inhabited an area from the Amazon River to the Caribbean.

[3]The "Holy Savior," Jesus Christ.

stowed all this; the Indians call it "Guanahani." To the second, I gave the name *Isla de Santa Maria de Concepción;*[4] to the third, *Fernandina;* to the fourth, *Isabella;* to the fifth, *Isla Juana,*[5] and so to each one I gave a new name.

When I reached Juana, I followed its coast to the westward, and I found it to be so extensive that I thought that it must be the mainland, the province of Catayo.[6] And since there were neither towns nor villages on the seashore, but only small hamlets, with the people of which I could not have speech, because they all fled immediately, I went forward on the same course, thinking that I should not fail to find great cities and towns. And, at the end of many leagues,[7] seeing that there was no change and that the coast was bearing me northwards, which I wished to avoid, since winter was already beginning and I proposed to make from it to the south, and as moreover the wind was carrying me forward, I determined not to wait for a change in the weather and retraced my path as far as a certain harbor known to me. And from that point, I sent two men inland to learn if there were a king or great cities. They traveled three days' journey and found an infinity of small hamlets and people without number, but nothing of importance. For this reason, they returned.

I understood sufficiently from other Indians, whom I had already taken,[8] that this land was nothing but an island. And therefore I followed its coast eastwards for one hundred and seven leagues to the point where it ended. And from that cape, I saw another island, distant eighteen leagues from the former, to the east, to which I at once gave the name "Española." And I went

there and followed its northern coast, as I had in the case of Juana, to the eastward for one hundred and eighty-eight great leagues in a straight line. This island and all the others are very fertile to a limitless degree, and this island is extremely so. In it there are many harbors on the coast of the sea, beyond comparison with others which I know in Christendom, and many rivers, good and large, which is marvelous. Its lands are high, and there are in it very many sierras and very lofty mountains, beyond comparison with the island of Teneriffe.[9] All are most beautiful, of a thousand shapes, and all are accessible and filled with trees of a thousand kinds and tall, and they seem to touch the sky. And I am told that they never lose their foliage, as I can understand, for I saw them as green and as lovely as they are in Spain in May, and some of them were flowering, some bearing fruit, and some in another stage, according to their nature. And the nightingale was singing and other birds of a thousand kinds in the month of November there where I went. There are six or eight kinds of palm, which are a wonder to behold on account of their beautiful variety, but so are the other trees and fruits and plants. In it are marvelous pine groves, and there are very large tracts of cultivatable lands, and there is honey, and there are birds of many kinds and fruits in great diversity. In the interior are mines of metals, and the population is without number. Española is a marvel.

The sierras and mountains, the plains and arable lands and pastures, are so lovely and rich for planting and sowing, for breeding cattle of every kind, for building towns and villages. The harbors of the sea here are such as cannot be be-

---

[4]"Holy Mary of the Immaculate Conception," the Virgin Mary, Mother of Jesus, who Catholics believe was absolutely sinless, to the point of being conceived without the stain of Original Sin (the sin of Adam and Eve) on her soul.
[5]Named for Prince Juan, heir apparent of Castile.
[6]The Spanish term for *Cathay.* Technically Cathay was that area along China's northern frontier ruled from 907 to 1125 by the Khitans, a proto-Mongol people. Columbus understood Cathay to be the entire Chinese Empire of the Great Khan, not realizing that the Chinese had expelled the Mongol khans in the mid fourteenth century. (See Volume I, Chapter 12, sources 103–107 for more on the Mongols.)

[7]A league is three miles.
[8]Columbus took seven Tainos on board at San Salvador to instruct them in Spanish and use them as guides and interpreters.
[9]One of the Canary Islands.

lieved to exist unless they have been seen, and so with the rivers, many and great, and good waters, the majority of which contain gold. In the trees and fruits and plants, there is a great difference from those of Juana. In this island, there are many spices and great mines of gold and of other metals.

The people of this island, and of all the other islands which I have found and of which I have information, all go naked, men and women, as their mothers bore them,[10] although some women cover a single place with the leaf of a plant or with a net of cotton which they make for the purpose. They have no iron or steel or weapons, nor are they fitted to use them, not because they are not well built men and of handsome stature, but because they are very marvelously timorous. They have no other arms than weapons made of canes, cut in seeding time, to the ends of which they fix a small sharpened stick. And they do not dare to make use of these, for many times it has happened that I have sent ashore two or three men to some town to have speech, and countless people have come out to them, and as soon as they have seen my men approaching they have fled, even a father not waiting for his son. And this, not because ill has been done to anyone; on the contrary, at every point where I have been and have been able to have speech, I have given to them of all that I had, such as cloth and many other things, without receiving anything for it; but so they are, incurably timid. It is true that, after they have been reassured and have lost their fear, they are so guileless and so generous with all they possess, that no one would believe it who has not seen it. They never refuse anything which they possess, if it be asked of them; on the contrary, they invite anyone to share it, and display as much love as if they would give their hearts, and whether the thing be of value or whether it be of small price, at once with whatever trifle of whatever kind it may be that is given to them, with that they are content.[11] I forbade that they should be given things so worthless as fragments of broken crockery and scraps of broken glass, and ends of straps, although when they were able to get them, they fancied that they possessed the best jewel in the world. So it was found that a sailor for a strap received gold to the weight of two and a half *castellanos,*[12] and others much more for other things which were worth much less. As for new *blancas,*[13] for them they would give everything which they had, although it might be two or three *castellanos'* weight of gold or an *arroba*[14] or two of spun cotton. . . . They took even the pieces of the broken hoops of the wine barrels and, like savages, gave what they had, so that it seemed to me to be wrong and I forbade it. And I gave a thousand handsome good things, which I had brought, in order that they might conceive affection, and more than that, might become Christians and be inclined to the love and service of their highnesses and of the whole Castilian nation, and strive to aid us and to give us of the things which they have in abundance and which are necessary to us. And they do not know any creed and are not idolaters;[15] only they

---

[10]Marco Polo described a number of islanders in South Asia who went naked. Compare also Columbus's description of this nudity with John Mandeville's account of the people of Sumatra (see Volume I, Chapter 12, source 109).

[11]Compare this with Mandeville's description of the people of Sumatra's attitude toward possessions (see Volume I, Chapter 12, source 109).

[12]A gold coin of considerable value that bore the seal of Castile.

[13]The smallest and least valuable Spanish coin, worth about one-sixtieth of a castellano. Composed of billon, a mixture of copper and silver, it had a whitish hue; hence the name *blanca,* or "white."

[14]The equivalent of about sixteen skeins, or balls, of spun textile.

[15]Normally the term *idolater* means anyone who worships idols, or sacred statues, but it is uncertain exactly what Columbus means here. The Tainos worshipped a variety of deities and spirits known as *cemis,* whom they represented in stone statues and other handcrafted images, also known as cemis. (For further information on Taino cemis, see Volume I, Chapter 11, source 98.) It is hard to imagine Columbus's not having seen carved cemis, which filled the Tainos' villages. To compound the problem of what Columbus meant by their not being idolaters, consider the next-to-last paragraph of this letter, in which the admiral refers to idolaters who will be enslaved.

all believe that power and good are in the heavens, and they are very firmly convinced that I, with these ships and men, came from the heavens, and in this belief they everywhere received me, after they had overcome their fear. And this does not come because they are ignorant; on the contrary, they are of a very acute intelligence and are men who navigate all those seas, so that it is amazing how good an account they give of everything, but it is because they have never seen people clothed or ships of such a kind.

And as soon as I arrived in the Indies, in the first island which I found, I took by force some of them, in order that they might learn and give me information of that which there is in those parts, and so it was that they soon understood us, and we them, either by speech or signs, and they have been very serviceable. I still take them with me, and they are always assured that I come from Heaven, for all the intercourse which they have had with me; and they were the first to announce this wherever I went, and the others went running from house to house and to the neighboring towns, with loud cries of, "Come! Come to see the people from Heaven!" So all, men and women alike, when their minds were set at rest concerning us, came, so that not one, great or small, remained behind, and all brought something to eat and drink, which they gave with extraordinary affection. In all the island, they have very many canoes, like rowing *fustas,*[16] some larger, some smaller, and some are larger than a *fusta* of eighteen benches. They are not so broad, because they are made of a single log of wood, but a *fusta* would not keep up with them in rowing, since their speed is a thing incredible. And in these they navigate among all those islands, which are innumerable, and carry their goods. One of these canoes I have seen with seventy and eighty men in her, and each one with his oar.

In all these islands, I saw no great diversity in the appearance of the people or in their manners and language. On the contrary, they all understand one another,[17] which is a very curious thing, on account of which I hope that their highnesses will determine upon their conversion to our holy faith, towards which they are very inclined.

I have already said how I have gone one hundred and seven leagues in a straight line from west to east along the seashore of the island Juana, and as a result of that voyage, I can say that this island is larger than England and Scotland together, for, beyond these one hundred and seven leagues, there remain to the westward two provinces to which I have not gone. One of these provinces they call "Avan,"[18] and there the people are born with tails;[19] and these provinces cannot have a length of less than fifty or sixty leagues, as I could understand from those Indians whom I have and who know all the islands.

The other, Española, has a circumference greater than all Spain, from Colibre, by the seacoast, to Fuenterabia in Vizcaya, since I voyaged along one side one hundred and eighty-eight great leagues in a straight line from west to east. It is a land to be desired and, seen, it is never to be left. And . . . I have taken possession for their highnesses . . . in this Española, in [a] situation most convenient and in the best position for the mines of gold and for all intercourse as well with the mainland . . . belonging to the Grand Khan,[20] where will be great trade and gain. I have taken possession of a large town, to which I gave the name *Villa de Navidad,*[21] and in it I have made

---

[16]A small, oared boat, often having one or two masts.

[17]This is not totally accurate. Columbus's Taino interpreters knew only a little of the language of the Ciguayos, whom the admiral encountered on Española in January 1493 (note 27).

[18]Which the Spaniards transformed into La Habana, or Havana.

[19]Marco Polo reported the existence of tailed humans (possibly orangutans) in the islands of Southeast Asia. John Mandeville also listed hairy persons who walked on all fours and climbed trees in his description of the various fantastic people who supposedly inhabited the islands of Southeast Asia.

[20]The Mongol emperor of Cathay.

fortifications and a fort, which now will by this time be entirely finished, and I have left in it sufficient men for such a purpose with arms and artillery and provisions for more than a year, and a *fusta,* and one, a master of all seacraft, to build others, and great friendship with the king of that land, so much so, that he was proud to call me, and to treat me as, a brother. And even if he were to change his attitude to one of hostility towards these men, he and his do not know what arms are and they go naked, as I have already said, and are the most timorous people that there are in the world, so that the men whom I have left there alone would suffice to destroy all that land, and the island is without danger for their persons, if they know how to govern themselves.[22]

In all these islands, it seems to me that all men are content with one woman, and to their chief or king they give as many as twenty.[23] It appears to me that the women work more than the men. And I have not been able to learn if they hold private property; what seemed to me to appear was that, in that which one had, all took a share, especially of eatable things.[24]

In these islands I have so far found no human monstrosities, as many expected,[25] but on the contrary the whole population is very well-formed, nor are they negroes as in Guinea,[26] but their hair is flowing, and they are not born where there is intense force in the rays of the sun; it is true that the sun has there great power, although it is distant from the equinoctial line twenty-six degrees. In these islands, where there are high mountains, the cold was severe this winter, but they endure it, being used to it and with the help of meats which they eat with many and extremely hot spices. As I have found no monsters, so I have had no report of any, except in an island "Quaris," the second at the coming into the Indies, which is inhabited by a people who are regarded in all the islands as very fierce and who eat human flesh. They have many canoes with which they range through all the islands of India and pillage and take as much as they can.[27] They are no more malformed than the others, except that they have the custom of wearing their hair long like women, and they use bows and arrows of the same cane stems, with a small piece of wood at the end, owing to lack of iron which they do not possess. They are ferocious among these other people who are cowardly to an excessive degree, but I make no more account of them than of the rest. These are those who have intercourse with the women of "Matinino," which is the first island met on the way from Spain to the Indies, in which there is not a man. The women engage in no feminine occupation, but use bows and arrows of cane, like those al-

---

[21]The "Village of the Nativity" (of the Lord). The destruction of the *Santa Maria* off the coast of Española on Christmas Day (Navidad del Señor) forced Columbus to leave behind thirty-nine sailors at the garrison, which he named after the day of the incident.

[22]When Columbus returned in November 1493, he discovered the entire garrison had been killed by the native inhabitants in reaction to abuses. Some of Columbus's actions prior to departing for Europe, such as his staging a mock battle, suggest that he was uneasy about leaving these men behind and wanted to impress the Tainos with a display of Spanish firepower and fighting skills.

[23]Generally only chiefs could afford large numbers of wives because of the substantial bride prices that were paid in goods or services to women's families. Notwithstanding, many commoners could and did have two or three wives.

[24]See note 11.

[25]Europeans were prepared to find various races of monster humans and semihumans in the Indies. Accepted accounts of the wonders of the East, such as the travelogue of John Mandeville, told of dog-headed people and a species of individuals who, lacking heads, had eyes on their shoulders. Such stories had been inherited from ancient Greek, Roman, and Arabic ethnographies.

[26]Sub-Saharan West Africa (see Volume I, Chapter 12, source 111).

[27]The Caribs, who shortly before the arrival of Columbus began to displace the Arawak peoples of the Lesser Antilles, the archipelago to the east and south of Hispaniola. Sixteenth-century Spanish writers unanimously agreed that the Caribs were fierce warriors and cannibalistic. On January 13, 1453, Columbus and his men had a short skirmish on Española with some previously unknown natives, whom the admiral incorrectly assumed were Caribs. They were actually Ciguayos, who were less peaceful than the Tainos.

ready mentioned, and they arm and protect themselves with plates of copper, of which they have much.[28]

In another island, which they assure me is larger than Española, the people have no hair.[29] In it, there is gold incalculable, and from it and from the other islands, I bring with me Indians as evidence.[30]

In conclusion, to speak only of that which has been accomplished on this voyage, which was so hasty, their highnesses can see that I will give them as much gold as they may need, if their highnesses will render me very slight assistance; moreover, spice and cotton, as much as their highnesses shall command; and mastic,[31] as much as they shall order to be shipped and which, up to now, has been found only in Greece, in the island of Chios,[32] and the Seignory[33] sells it for what it pleases; and aloe wood, as much as they shall order to be shipped, and slaves, as many as they shall order to be shipped and who will be from the idolaters.[34] And I believe that I have found rhubarb and cinamon,[35] and I shall find a thousand other things of value, which the people

whom I have left there will have discovered, for I have not delayed at any point, so far as the wind allowed me to sail, except in the town of Navidad, in order to leave it secured and well established, and in truth, I should have done much more, if the ships had served me, as reason demanded.

This is enough . . . and the eternal God, our Lord, Who gives to all those who walk in His way triumph over things which appear to be impossible, and this was notably one; for, although men have talked or have written of these lands, all was conjectural, without suggestion of ocular evidence, but amounted only to this, that those who heard for the most part listened and judged it to be rather a fable than as having any vestige of truth. So that, since Our Redeemer[36] has given this victory to our most illustrious king and queen, and to their renowned kingdoms, in so great a matter, for this all Christendom ought to feel delight and make great feasts and give solemn thanks to the Holy Trinity[37] with many solemn prayers for the great exaltation which they shall have, in the turning of so many people to our holy faith, and afterwards for temporal

---

[28]This same account appears in Columbus's log. Father Ramón Pane, who composed an ethnographic study of Taino culture during Columbus's second voyage of 1493–1494 (see Volume I, Chapter 11, source 98), also related in great detail the legend of the island of Matinino, where only women resided. As reported by Pane, however, the story contains no hint that these were warlike women. Apparently Columbus took this Taino legend and combined it with the Greco-Roman myth of the warrior Amazons. Mandeville wrote of the land of Amazonia, populated totally by warrior women, and Marco Polo described two Asian islands, one inhabited solely by women and another exclusively by men. There is no evidence that the female society reported by Columbus and Pane ever existed in the Caribbean. The Tainos, however, who were essentially a stone-age people, did import from South America an alloy of copper and gold, which they used for ornaments.
[29]John Mandeville described people with little body hair, and Marco Polo told of Buddhist monks whose heads and faces were shaved.
[30]Columbus brought seven Tainos back to Spain, where they were baptized, with King Ferdinand and Prince Juan acting as godparents. One remained at the Spanish court, where he died, and the others returned with Columbus on his second voyage of 1493.

[31]Columbus and his men mistook a native gumbo-limbo tree, which does contain an aromatic resin, for the rare mastic tree, whose costly resin was a profitable trade item for Genoa (note 33).
[32]An island in the eastern Mediterranean.
[33]The ruling body of Genoa, an Italian city-state. Chios was a possession of Genoa, whose merchants controlled the mastic trade.
[34]Church law forbade the enslavement of Christians, except in the most exceptional circumstances.
[35]Actually when members of the crew showed Columbus what they thought were aloe, mastic, and cinnamon, the admiral accepted the aloe and mastic as genuine but rejected the supposed cinnamon. One of his lieutenants reported seeing rhubarb while on a scouting expedition.
[36]Jesus Christ.
[37]The Christian belief of three divine persons — Father, Son, and Holy Spirit — contained in a single divine essence.

benefits, for not only Spain but all Christians will have hence refreshment and gain.

This in accordance with that which has been accomplished, thus briefly.

Done in the caravel,[38] off the Canary Islands, on the fifteenth of February, in the year one thousand four hundred and ninety-three.

At your orders.   El Almirante.[39]

---

[38]A Spanish ocean-going ship.

[39]The Admiral.

Interpreting Columbus's Letter

Columbus's letter contains a number of interesting and potentially important facts. For example, the natives Columbus initially encountered were largely homogeneous and communicated with one another through interisland travel. Yet as fascinating and important as these facts are, knowing them does not necessarily make you (or anyone else) a historian. Similarly, garnering such isolated items from a source does not constitute full historical analysis. True historical analysis consists of drawing as much inferential insight as possible from a source and trying to answer, at least in part, the central question of historical study: What does it all mean? This document allows us to do just that.

Historians use no secret method or magic formula to draw historical insights from documentary evidence. All they need are attention to detail, thoroughness, common sense, and a willingness to enter imaginatively into the mind of the document's author as fully and honestly as possible, while trying to set aside personal values and perspectives. Anyone who is willing to work at it can profitably interpret written primary sources.

The researcher always has to evaluate the worth of each source, which means understanding its point of view and reliability. In this letter several things are obvious. Columbus believed he had reached Asian islands. John Mandeville's *Travels* and other accounts of Asia provided a number of reference points by which to recognize the Orient, and Columbus believed he had found many of them. Equally obvious is the fact that Columbus tried to present his discoveries in the best light possible. He sent this letter ahead to the court of Ferdinand and Isabella to ensure that when he arrived he would be received with due honor.

Certainly there is exaggeration, self-puffery, error, and possibly even deliberate distortion in this account. As the introduction to the letter informs us, Columbus overestimated the size of several islands, and except for chilies, the spices he claimed to have discovered proved to be mirages. The admiral also failed to mention that the *Santa Maria* had been lost. There is no way he could escape informing his royal patrons of this unhappy incident, but presumably Columbus wanted to wait until he was at the court, where he could put his own spin on the facts surrounding the incident. Also not mentioned is a skirmish that he and his men had on January 13, 1493, with some hostile strangers, whom he incorrectly assumed were Caribs. Perhaps that incident, if reported without explanation, would have weakened the admiral's claim that Spain could easily subjugate these timid Indians. Generally, however, despite Columbus's enthusiasm and understandable tendency to exaggerate, to conveniently neglect to mention anything negative, and to see what he wanted to see, the admiral *seems* to have wanted to present an essentially factual account — at least that is how it appears to us.

Columbus's reading of popular travel accounts had prepared him to encounter every sort of human monstrosity, and undoubtedly he would have enjoyed reporting such contacts. But he honestly reported that all the natives he encountered were quite unmonstrous in appearance and temperament. Of course the admiral reported stories of people with tails, cannibals, and war-like women who lived apart from men, but it is unlikely that he was deliberately misleading anyone on this issue. The Carib cannibals were real enough. Rumors of tailed people and latter-day Amazons conceivably were nothing more than the natives' trying to please Columbus or simply the result of poor communication. It is not difficult to imagine that the admiral inquired after the locations of those various human curiosities whom Mandeville, Polo, and others had placed in the islands of the Indian Ocean and that the Tainos, not knowing what he was asking, agreeably pointed across the waters to other islands.

In fact this raises one issue that has long vexed us and that goes straight to the heart of the question of this source's overall reliability: *How well was Columbus able to communicate with these people?* Columbus insisted that through gestures and learned words the Spaniards and Tainos were able to communicate with one another, and he certainly learned enough of the Tainos' language to report that they called the island on which he initially landed *Guanahani.* Nevertheless, we suspect that only the most primitive forms of communication were possible between Europeans and Native Americans in 1492–1493. Therefore we should have a healthy skepticism about anything that Columbus reports about the Tainos' beliefs and cosmological perspectives.

Still, all things considered, it seems reasonable to conclude that Columbus's letter can be accepted as a generally honest if not totally accurate account of his discoveries and experiences. That basic honesty, compromised to an extent by an understandable enthusiasm and desire to present his accomplishments positively, comes through in his attempt to describe the islands' physical qualities as well as the people he encountered there. The picture that emerges tells us a lot about the complex motives that underlay his great adventure.

We notice that Columbus had matter of factly taken possession of the lands in the names of the monarchs of Spain and even renamed the islands without once giving thought to the claims of anyone else. He also thought nothing of seizing some natives as soon as he arrived and of carrying several Indians back to Spain. Moreover, he noted toward the end of his letter that the monarchs of Spain could obtain as many *slaves* as they desired from among the islands' "idolaters." At the same time (and this might strike the modern student as curious), Columbus claimed that he had always acted kindly toward the native people, and his letter conveys a tone of admiration and even affection for the people whom he had encountered. Indeed the admiral expressed a deep interest in protecting and winning over the native people of the Indies in an avowed hope that they might become Christians and loyal subjects of Ferdinand and Isabella. According to Columbus, the Indians' intelligence, timidity, naiveté, ignorance, sense of wonder at the Europeans, and ability to communicate freely among themselves made them prime candidates for conversion. It also made them ripe for subjugation, however.

The tone of this letter suggests that Columbus was concerned with these people as humans and genuinely interested in helping them achieve salvation through conversion. It is equally clear, however, that Columbus believed it to be his and Catholic Spain's right and duty to subjugate and exploit these same people. Here we see a tension that continued throughout the Spanish colonial experience in the Americas.

Subjugation of the Indians and their lands involved more than just a sense of divine mission and Christian altruism — as real as those motives were. Columbus, his royal patrons, and most others who joined overseas adventures expected to gain in earthly wealth, as well. Even a superficial reading of his letter reveals the admiral's preoccupation with the riches of the islands — riches that it seems he knowingly exaggerated. (See note 35 regarding the supposed discovery of cinnamon.) Gold, spices, cotton, aromatic mastic, and, of course, slaves were the material rewards that awaited Christian Europeans. Columbus was fully interested in these rewards and wanted Ferdinand and Isabella to underwrite future trips so that he could discover them in abundance. So while exaggeration can be found in this account, it seems to be exaggeration based on conviction.

Was Columbus being cynical, hypocritical, or deliberately ironic when in his closing words he claimed that Jesus Christ had provided this great victory to the Spanish monarchs (and indeed to all Christendom) and from that would flow the dual benefits of the conversion of so many people and worldly riches? Cynicism, hypocrisy, and conscious irony are not likely explanations. It seems more likely that these closing remarks reveal the mind of a man who saw no contradiction between spreading the faith and benefiting materially from that action, even if doing so meant exploiting the converts.

Please note that in presenting this insight we have tried to avoid intruding any moral judgments. This does not mean that, as far as our own standards of right and wrong are concerned, we accept slavery as justifiable or believe it is proper to dispossess people of their lands and cultures. What it does mean is that we are trying to understand Columbus and his world view, not sit in judgment of a society whose values were in some respects radically different from those of our own. Passing moral judgment on a distant society's actions might be emotionally satisfying, but it will not change what has happened. Doing so also could conceivably blind the judge to the historical context in which those actions took place. As suggested earlier, we study the past in order to gain insight and wisdom regarding the human condition. If that insight is to have any validity, it must be based on as dispassionate a study of the evidence as possible.

Another point merits mention here. Perhaps you disagree with our conclusion that Columbus's letter is basically an honest and valuable source, despite its shortcomings. If you do, you are in excellent company. Two eminent historians — William D. Phillips, Jr., and Carla Rahn Phillips, in their book *The Worlds of Christopher Columbus* — characterize this letter as "a tissue of exaggerations, misconceptions, and outright lies." We obviously disagree with these authors in our interpretation of the degree, nature, and extent of the letter's misstatements. Well, no historian is infallible, and certainly we do not claim that distinction. Moreover, no source is so clear in all respects that it presents no areas of potential disagreement for historians. That, in fact, is one of the exciting aspects of historical research. Despite all the facts and conclusions that historians generally agree on, there are numerous areas in which they carry on spirited debate. The very nature of history's fragmentary, flawed evidence makes debate inevitable.

What is more, no historian can possibly see everything there is to be seen in every source. What this means, so far as you are concerned, is that there is plenty of latitude in the sources that appear in this book for you to arrive at insights that are unique to you. In so doing, however, you must at all times attempt to divorce yourself of present mindedness and to enter imaginatively into the world of the author whose work you are analyzing. You will note that, as is the case with this letter from Columbus, we have endeavored to help you do this through suggested Questions for Analysis that often are quite leading — perhaps too leading. Do not be constrained by these questions. If you find a question misleading or wrong headed in its presumed assumptions, feel free to follow your own mind. Just be ready to defend the questions you have chosen to ask along with the conclusions you have reached in answering them.

We could ask many other questions of Columbus's letter and garner other insights from it. Certainly it tells us a lot about Taino culture. Despite his cultural blinders, his naiveté, his tendency to see what he wanted to see, and his probably exaggerated belief in his ability to communicate with these people, Columbus seems to be a reasonably accurate and perceptive observer. Thus anyone interested in what the cultures of the Caribbean peoples were like before the Europeans had much of a chance to influence them must necessarily look to this and similar accounts of first contacts. In fact it would be good practice for you, right now, to try to answer question 7, which we have deliberately left unanswered. You will be surprised at how much you can learn about the Tainos from this brief description. As you do this exercise, however, do not forget to ask yourself constantly: How reliable does Columbus appear to be on this specific point, and why do I conclude this?

After you have tested your own powers of historical analysis in this little exercise, it would be wise to put the letter aside for the present. We trust that by now you have a good idea of how to examine and mine a documentary source. Now let us consider artifacts.

Unwritten Sources

Historians distinguish between the prehistorical and historical past, with the chief defining feature of any historical culture being that it provides written records from which we can reconstruct its past. Without a large volume and variety of documentary sources, it is impossible to write any society's history in detail. This is not to say that the unwritten relics of the past are worthless. Archeology proves their value, and even historians use such sources. As a rule, however, no matter how extensive a culture's physical remains might be, if it has not left us records we can read, its history largely remains a closed book. The ancient civilizations of Harappan India and Minoan Crete, for example, knew and practiced the art of writing, but until we learn how to decipher their texts, we can draw only vague pictures of their respective histories.

Given the central role documents play in our reconstruction of the past, it should surprise no one to learn that most historians concentrate their research almost exclusively on written sources. Yet historians would be foolish to overlook *any* piece of evidence from the past. As we suggested earlier, photographs could be a rich source for anyone researching the history of your class. Our future historian might also want to study all of the extant souvenirs and supplies sold in your school's bookstore. Examined properly they could help fill in some gaps in the story of your class's cultural history.

Artifacts can be illuminating, particularly when used in conjunction with written records. Coins can tell us a lot about a society's ideals or its leaders' programs. Art in its many forms can reveal the interests, attitudes, and modes of perception of various segments of society, from the elites to the masses. More down-to-earth items, such as domestic utensils and tools, allow us to infer quite a bit about the lives of common individuals. In this book we concentrate largely on written sources, for reasons already outlined. It would be wrong, however, if we totally overlooked artifacts. So scattered throughout these chapters you will find important pieces of nonwritten evidence. Let us look at an example and proceed to "read" it.

▼ AN ANONYMOUS WOODCUT OF 1511

Columbus arrived in Barcelona in April 1493 to learn not only had his letter arrived, but it had already been published and publicly circulated. Within months the letter was translated into several languages; the Latin translation alone went through nine editions, several of which were lavishly illustrated, before the end of 1494. Printers discovered that educated Europeans had an almost insatiable desire to learn about the peoples and lands Columbus and other explorers were discovering, and they catered to that interest. Their clientele wanted not only to

read about the fascinating peoples, plants, and animals of these lands — they wanted also to see them. Consequently, as books on the new explorations proliferated, so did the number of printed illustrations. Many are quite fanciful and tell us more about the Europeans who created them than the peoples and regions they supposedly portrayed. The woodcut print we have chosen appeared in a popular English pamphlet of 1511.

QUESTIONS FOR ANALYSIS

1. What scene has the artist set? What has the artist placed to the immediate right of the standing man, and what function does it have in this scene?

2. What do each person's actions, dress, and demeanor tell us about her or him?
3. What does this illustration tell us about popular European notions concerning the natives of the New World?

Interpreting the Woodcut

What a charming, even idyllic domestic scene. An attractive mother nurses an infant at her breast while amusing an older child with a feather. A well-muscled, equally attractive, and proud father stands nearby, holding the tools of his trade while next to him the family's dinner is slowly cooking. Dinner, of course, may strike us as macabre, as these are cannibals, and it looks like roast European is on the menu. The tools of the father's trade are weapons. Both children are naked, and the parents are virtually nude, save for what appear to be leaves that cover their loins, decorative necklaces, armbands and anklets of some indeterminate material, and feathers in their hair.

What is the message? What we have is a reprise of the image provided by Columbus in his letter of 1493: the *noble savage.* These are fully human beings with human bonds and affections. Yet they are still savages, as their clothing (or lack of it), decorations, weapons, and choice of food would have suggested to most sixteenth-century Europeans. Here, as Columbus and many of those who followed agreed, were a people who could become Christians but who also, by virtue of their backwardness, were to be subjugated. There is something appealing about their innocent savagery, but what of that poor fellow whose severed leg and head are slowly roasting?

Have we read too much into the woodcut? It is arguable that we may have. The historian always faces this problem when trying to analyze an isolated piece of evidence, particularly a nonverbal source. Yet this artifact is not completely isolated, for we brought to its analysis insight gained from documentary evidence — Columbus's letter. That is how we generally read the artifacts of historical cultures. We attempt to place them in the context of what we have already learned or inferred from documentary sources. Documents illuminate artifacts, and artifacts make more vivid and tangible the often shadowy world of words.

As you attempt to interpret the unwritten sources in this book, keep in mind what you have learned from the documents you have already read, your textbook, and class lectures. Remember that we have chosen these artifacts to illustrate broad themes and general trends. You should not find their messages overly subtle. As with the documents, always try to place each piece of nonverbal evidence into its proper context, and in that regard, read the introductions and Questions for Analysis very carefully. We will do our best to provide you with all the information and clues you need.

Good luck and have fun!

Part One

▼▼▼

The Ancient World

The term *the ancient world* presents a problem to the student of global history because it is a creation exclusively of Western historical thought. Historians in the West originally used the term to refer only to the early history of one small region of the world — the area that stretches from the northwest corner of the Indian subcontinent to Western Europe. Understood within this narrow context, ancient history involves the period from the rise of civilization in Southwest Asia (known today as the *Middle East*) to the collapse of the Roman Empire, approximately 3500 Before the Common Era (B.C.E.) to 500 in the Common Era (C.E.). Within this Western scheme of history, antiquity passed away about fifteen hundred years ago but not before it had laid the roots of Western civilization. Having spent itself, the ancient world was followed by the so-called *Middle Ages* (500–1500), and this era, in turn, was followed by the early modern (1500–1789), modern (1789–1914), and contemporary eras.

Such neat divisions of the past, which might reflect the Western historical experience (and there is debate over their accuracy, even in regard to the history of the West), make little sense when history is studied globally. Nevertheless, the category *the ancient world* is useful for the global historian, if it is redefined in two ways: by expanding the term to include all of the world's primary, or earliest, civilizations and by distinguishing between the Afro-Eurasian and American worlds of antiquity.

Ancient civilizations arose independently on two grand *world islands:* the Afro-Eurasian landmass and the Americas. The first to witness this phenomenon was the Afro-Eurasian supercontinent, where primary civilizations appeared in the river valleys of Mesopotamia, Egypt, northwest India, and northern China between approximately 3500 and 2000 B.C.E. Although distinct and largely indigenous, these four early centers of civilization influenced one another in varying degrees. Mesopotamia, the world's first known civilization, had early contact with the nascent civilizations of Egypt and India, and by the middle of the second millennium (the 1000s) B.C.E. wheat, barley, and chariots had made their way from Southwest Asia to northern China.

Across the Atlantic and Pacific Oceans, unknown to and uninfluenced by the civilizations of Eurasia and Africa, civilizations appeared along the gulf coast of Mexico around 1200 B.C.E. and, about the same time or shortly thereafter, along the Pacific coast and Andean highlands of Peru. As was the case in the Afro-Eurasian world island, the civilizations of the Americas cross-fertilized one another through their trade networks but were essentially isolated from the rest of the world. As was also the case in the Afro-Eurasian hemisphere of the globe, the original centers of civilization in the Americas served as the American hemisphere's dominant matrices of civilized culture for thousands of years and well beyond the period Europeans characterize as *antiquity.*

The original centers of the Afro-Eurasian network of separate but connected civilizations were four fairly self-contained river valleys. Over the course of several thousand years, however, these first civilizations spread outward, each encompassing a large region on which it imprinted a distinctive culture. By 300 B.C.E. the four major Afro-Eurasian cultural regions, or pools, were Southwest Asia, the Mediterranean, India, and China. Of these, China's relative isolation at the eastern end of the Eurasian landmass dictated that its culture would be the most singular and least stimulated by foreign influences. Conversely, the culture of Southwest Asia — the crossroads of the Afro-Eurasian world — was the most variegated and eclectic.

During the last few centuries B.C.E. and for the first several centuries C.E., the cultures at both ends of the great Eurasian expanse of land — China and the Greco-Roman world — achieved political unity and consequently expanded at the expense of their less organized neighbors, such as Koreans and Southeast Asians in the East and various Celtic peoples in the West. The result was two massive empires linked by Central Asiatic, Indian, Southwest Asian, and East African intermediaries. Consequently, goods, ideas, and diseases were exchanged throughout Eurasia and portions of Africa more freely and quickly than ever before.

Between approximately 200 and 550 C.E. internal and external pressures, including diseases that had traveled along the trade routes, precipitated the collapse of empires in China, India, Southwest Asia, and the Roman Mediterranean. With those disasters, which were neither totally contemporaneous nor equally severe, the first grand epoch of Afro-Eurasian history — the ancient world — was essentially at an end. The era that followed rested on the foundations of antiquity but also differed substantially from the ancient world, in part because of three world religions — Mahayana Buddhism, Christianity, and Islam — which played transforming roles throughout Eurasia and Africa between roughly 600 and 1500 C.E.

Across the oceans, the civilizations of Mexico and Central and South America continued their development in isolation from the cares and trends of the eastern hemisphere. Cities and empires rose and fell, and societies continued to develop along cultural lines set down by the Americas' first civilizations. To be sure, changes took place. One important new trend between roughly 600 and 1200 C.E. was the rise of North American civilizations in what are today the deserts of the southwest United States and the lands washed by the Mississippi and Ohio Rivers. Despite these new centers of civilization, the Amerindian world was only wrenched out of its ancient patterns when European invaders and colonists began arriving in significant numbers in the early sixteenth century.

Because of a relative lack of documentary evidence relating to preconquest Amerindian cultures and civilizations, the sources in Part One deal almost exclusively with ancient Afro-Eurasian history. We will more fully consider the story of antiquity in the western hemisphere in Part Three, Chapter 11.

Chapter 1

▼▼▼

The First Civilizations

The word *civilization* is derived from the Latin adjective *civilis,* which means "political" or "civic." No matter how else we define civilization, an organized civic entity, known as a *state,* stands at the center of every society we call civilized. A state is a sovereign public power that binds large numbers of people together at a level that transcends the ties of family, clan, tribe, and local community and organizes them for projects far beyond the capabilities of single families or even villages and towns.

Modern states tend to be *secular,* or of this world, and most rulers today claim no particular spiritual or religious authority. Indeed, many modern states are based on the principle that legitimate power comes solely from the people. The world's first states were different, inasmuch as they were all sacred states and their rulers claimed to govern by divine mandate. Such rulers either governed in the name of some divine authority or were themselves perceived as gods. Religious beliefs, as well as political and social institutions, varied greatly among the world's ancient civilizations, but ancient civilized peoples shared a common perception that authority is indivisible because it is divine. In other words, they saw no distinction between the state's sacred and secular functions.

Rulers and those who carried out their wills — priests, bureaucrats, and soldiers — were a small minority and maintained power by exploiting the many. This was a fact of early civilized life largely because, until recent times, states could produce only severely limited surpluses of resources, due to the narrow agrarian base of their economies. That surplus of goods, which is so necessary for the creation of a state, could only be channeled into state-building activities if rulers kept the majority of their subjects at a fairly low level of subsistence by exacting from them a major portion of the surplus through taxes, labor services, and military conscription. Consequently, the more agreeable benefits of civilization, such as literature and the other arts, were largely the exclusive property and tools of the few.

Most of the world's first civilizations evolved systems of writing, and in each case the art of writing served, at least initially, to strengthen the authority of rulers. Whether writing was used to record temple possessions or tax obligations, to give permanence to laws, or to provide priests with a coherent body of sacred texts, writing set apart the powerful from the powerless.

Not all of the records left behind by the first civilizations are open to us. Some ancient systems of writing still defy decipherment. Happily this is not the case with the written languages of Mesopotamia, Egypt, and China. The documentary sources left behind by these three civilizations reveal societies that were strikingly different in perspective and structure, even as they shared characteristics common to all early civilizations.

▼▼▼

Mesopotamia: The Land of Two Rivers

According to the eminent historian Samuel N. Kramer, "History begins at Sumer," and there is a good deal of truth to this judgment. It is in *Sumer,* which lay just to the north of the Persian Gulf in an area encompassed by the southern regions of modern Iraq, that we find the first evidence of human civilization. By 3500 B.C.E. a number of *Sumerian* city-states had emerged, and humanity was embarked on the adventure of civilization.

Generally, we call the Sumerians, and the other peoples who succeeded them in this region of Southwest Asia, *Mesopotamians.* The term, which means "those who dwell between the rivers," acknowledges the origin of the world's first known civilization in the valley created by the Tigris and Euphrates Rivers.

By approximately 1800 B.C.E., the Sumerians had been absorbed by waves of infiltrators and invaders and ceased to exist as an identifiable people. Moreover, the cultural center within Mesopotamia had shifted northward to the region of middle Mesopotamia, centering on the city of Babylon.

Despite their disappearance as a people, the Sumerians had set the framework for what proved to be a dynamic Mesopotamian civilization that exercised profound cultural influence throughout West Asia and beyond for about three thousand years. Between roughly 3500 and 500 B.C.E. Mesopotamia was where much of the action was, so far as the history of West Asian civilization was concerned.

That action was both constructive and destructive. The Mesopotamians have been credited with such firsts as the world's first governments, schools, codes of law, ethical systems, and epic literature. Just as prominent in Mesopotamian life were disasters, both natural and human generated.

The geography of Mesopotamia provided its people with the challenge of harnessing the waters of its two great rivers, and from that necessary cooperative effort civilization arose. Yet those rivers also threatened to destroy the fragile fabric of civilized society because they were unpredictable and could easily turn into uncontrollable torrents. Moreover, most of southern Mesopotamia was covered by either arid wasteland or marsh. Consequently, Sumerian civilization was built upon heroic labor in the midst of a hostile environment.

Another significant geographical aspect of Mesopotamian life, which also proved to be an important factor throughout its history, is the land's openness to incursions. To the north and east lie the hills and mountains of Iran and Armenia, from which wave after wave of invaders descended into the inviting valley of cities. To the south and west lies the desert of Arabia, out of which came countless nomads century after century. In many instances these invaders toppled a preexisting state and then settled down to become, in turn, Mesopotamians.

Whether they came from the desert fringes, as did the *Amorites,* who established the first Babylonian empire around 1800 B.C.E., or were mountain folk, such as the chariot-driving *Kassites,* who conquered Babylon soon after 1700, they all eventually became part of a Mesopotamian cultural complex, with modes of life and thought the Sumerians had set in place at the dawn of human civilization.

The Search for Eternal Life in Mesopotamia
▼▼▼

1 ▼ THE EPIC OF GILGAMESH

Humans share many basic concerns, and among them two are of primary importance: finding meaning in life and confronting the reality of death. In Mesopotamia, where life and human fortune were so precarious, people deeply probed these issues and made them the subjects of numerous *myths*. The word *myth* derives from the ancient Greek word for "a poetic story." As understood by modern scholars, however, myths are not just any poetic stories, and they certainly are not deliberate pieces of fiction or stories told primarily to entertain, even though myths do have entertainment value. First and foremost, myths are vehicles through which prescientific societies explain the workings of the universe and humanity's place within it. Whereas the scientist objectifies nature, seeing the world as an *it,* the myth-maker lives in a world where everything has a soul, a personality, and its own story. For instance, a raging river is not a body of water responding to physical laws but an angry or capricious god. In the same manner, the fortunes of human society are not the consequences of chance, history, or any patterns discoverable by social scientists. Rather, the gods and other supernatural spirits intervene directly into human affairs, punishing and rewarding as they wish, and divine interventions become the subjects of mythic stories. The stories in turn provide insight into the ways of the gods, thereby largely satisfying the emotional and intellectual needs of the myth-maker's audience.

So far as the issues of the meaning of life and death were concerned, ancient Mesopotamia eventually evolved its classic mythic answer in the form of its greatest work of literature, *The Epic of Gilgamesh*. An *epic* is a long narrative poem that celebrates the feats of some legendary hero who is involved in a journey or similar severe test. In the process of his trials the hero gains wisdom and, because of that wisdom, greater heroic stature.

The most complete extant version of *The Epic of Gilgamesh* was discovered on twelve clay tablets in the ruins of an Assyrian library that dated to the late seventh century B.C.E. Other earlier versions of the epic show, however, that the story, at least in its basic outline, is Sumerian in origin and goes back to the third millennium B.C.E. (2000s).

The hero, Gilgamesh, was a historical figure who ruled the city-state of Uruk sometime between 2700 and 2500 B.C.E. and was remembered as a great warrior, as well as the builder of Uruk's massive walls and temple. His exploits were so impressive that he became the focal point of a series of oral sagas that recounted his legendary heroic deeds. Around 2000 B.C.E. an unknown Babylonian poet reworked some of these tales, along with other stories — such as the adventure of Utnapishtim that appears in our selection — into an epic masterpiece that became widely popular and influential throughout Southwest Asia and beyond.

The epic contains a profound theme: the conflict between humanity's talents and aspirations and its mortal limitations. Gilgamesh, "two-thirds a god and one-third human," as the poem describes him, is a man of heroic proportions and appetites who still must face the inevitability of death.

As the epic opens, an arrogant Gilgamesh, not yet aware of his human limitations and his duties as king, is exhausting the people of Uruk with his manic energy. The people cry to Heaven for relief from his abuse of power, and the gods respond by creating Enkidu, a wild man who lives among the animals. Enkidu enters Uruk, where he challenges Gilgamesh to a contest of strength and fighting skill. When Gilgamesh triumphs, Enkidu embraces him as a brother, and the two heroes set out on a series of spectacular exploits.

In the course of their heroic adventures they insult Ishtar, goddess of love and fertility, and for this a life is owed. The one chosen by the gods to die is Enkidu. As our selection opens, Enkidu, after having cursed his heroic past, which has brought him to this fate, tells Gilgamesh of a vision he has had of the place Mesopotamians knew as "the land of no return."

QUESTIONS FOR ANALYSIS

1. What was the Mesopotamian view of the afterlife?
2. What is the message of Siduri's advice to Gilgamesh?
3. Consider Utnapishtim's initial response to Gilgamesh's request for the secret of eternal life. How does his message complement what Siduri has said? What do these two messages suggest about the Mesopotamian view of life?

4. Consider the story of Utnapishtim. What do the various actions of the gods and goddesses allow us to infer about how the Mesopotamians viewed their deities?

5. According to the epic, what are the respective roles of the gods and humans? What do the Mesopotamian deities require of humans? What do humans expect of their gods?

6. What wisdom has Gilgamesh gained from his epic struggles? How has he changed as a result of his quest?

7. Despite the apparent failure of his quest for eternal life, has Gilgamesh earned a type of immortality? If so, what is it?

8. Reconsider your answers to questions 2 and 3 in light of the epilogue, where the poet lays out for us the moral of the story. Basing your answer on the entire story, and especially the epilogue, what would you say was the Mesopotamian vision of the meaning of life?

As Enkidů slept alone in his sickness, in bitterness of spirit he poured out his heart to his friend. "It was I who cut down the cedar, I who leveled the forest, I who slew Humbaba[1] and now see what has become of me. Listen, my friend, this is the dream I dreamed last night. The heavens roared, and earth rumbled back an answer; between them stood I before an awful being, the sombre-faced manbird; he had directed on me his purpose. His was a vampire face, his foot was a lion's foot, his hand was an eagle's talon. He fell on me and his claws were in my hair, he held me fast and I smothered; then he transformed me so that my arms became wings covered with feathers. He turned his stare towards me, and he led me away to the palace of Irkalla, the Queen of Darkness,[2] to the house from which none who enters ever returns, down the road from which there is no coming back.

"There is the house whose people sit in darkness; dust is their food and clay their meat. They are clothed like birds with wings for covering, they see no light, they sit in darkness.

I entered the house of dust and I saw the kings of the earth, their crowns put away forever; rulers and princes, all those who once wore kingly crowns and ruled the world in the days of old. They who had stood in the place of the gods like Anu and Enlil,[3] stood now like servants to fetch baked meats in the house of dust, to carry cooked meat and cold water from the waterskin. In the house of dust which I entered were high priests and acolytes, priests of the incantation and of ecstasy; there were servers of the temple, and there was Etana, that king of Kish whom the eagle carried to heaven in the days of old.[4] There was Ereshkigal[5] the Queen of the Underworld; and Belit-Sheri squatted in front of her, she who is recorder of the gods and keeps the book of death. She held a tablet from which she read. She raised her head, she saw me and spoke: 'Who has brought this one here?' Then I awoke like a man drained of blood who wanders alone in a waste of rushes; like one whom the bailiff has seized and his heart pounds with terror."

---

[1]The giant who guarded the cedar forest and was slain by Enkidu and Gilgamesh.
[2]Goddess of the Underworld.
[3]Dead earthly kings. Anu was the supreme king of the gods and the source of all order and government; Enlil was the storm god, who supported royal authority.

[4]A legendary king of the Sumerian city of Kish.
[5]Another name for Irkalla, goddess of the Underworld.

▷ Enkidu dies, and Gilgamesh now realizes that heroic fame is no substitute for life. Facing the reality of his own death, he begins a desperate search for immortality. In the course of his search he meets Siduri, a goddess of wine, who advises him:

"Gilgamesh, where are you hurrying to? You will never find that life for which you are looking. When the gods created man they allotted to him death, but life they retained in their own keeping. As for you, Gilgamesh, fill your belly with good things; day and night, night and day, dance and be merry, feast and rejoice. Let your clothes be fresh, bathe yourself in water, cherish the little child that holds your hand, and make your wife happy in your embrace; for this too is the lot of man."

▷ Gilgamesh, however, refuses to be deflected from his quest. After a series of harrowing experiences, he finally reaches Utnapishtim, a former mortal whom the gods had placed in an eternal paradise, and addresses him.

"Oh, father Utnapishtim, you who have entered the assembly of the gods, I wish to question you concerning the living and the dead, how shall I find the life for which I am searching?"

Utnapishtim said, "There is no permanence. Do we build a house to stand forever, do we seal a contract to hold for all time? Do brothers divide an inheritance to keep forever, does the flood-time of rivers endure? It is only the nymph of the dragon-fly who sheds her larva and sees the sun in his glory. From the days of old there is no permanence. The sleeping and the dead, how alike they are, they are like a painted death. What is there between the master and the servant when both have fulfilled their doom? When the Anunnaki,[6] the judges, come together, and Mam-

metun[7] the mother of destinies, together they decree the fates of men. Life and death they allot but the day of death they do not disclose."

Then Gilgamesh said to Utnapishtim the Faraway, "I look at you now, Utnapishtim, and your appearance is no different from mine; there is nothing strange in your features. I thought I should find you like a hero prepared for battle, but you lie here taking your ease on your back. Tell me truly, how was it that you came to enter the company of the gods and to possess everlasting life?" Utnapishtim said to Gilgamesh, "I will reveal to you a mystery, I will tell you a secret of the gods."

"You know the city Shurrupak, it stands on the banks of Euphrates? That city grew old and the gods that were in it were old. There was Anu, lord of the firmament, their father, and warrior Enlil their counselor, Ninurta[8] the helper, and Ennugi[9] watcher over canals; and with them also was Ea.[10] In those days the world teemed, the people multiplied, the world bellowed like a wild bull, and the great god was aroused by the clamor. Enlil heard the clamor and he said to the gods in council, 'The uproar of mankind is intolerable and sleep is no longer possible by reason of the babel.' So the gods agreed to exterminate mankind. Enlil did this, but Ea because of his oath[11] warned me in a dream. He whispered their words to my house of reeds, 'Reed-house, reed-house! Wall, O wall, hearken reed-house, wall reflect; O man of Shurrupak, son of Ubara-Tutu; tear down your house and build a boat, abandon possessions and look for life, despise worldly goods and save your soul alive. Tear down your house, I say, and build a boat. . . . Then take up into the boat the seed of all living creatures.'

"When I had understood I said to my lord, 'Behold, what you have commanded I will honor and perform, but how shall I answer the people, the city, the elders?' Then Ea opened his mouth and said to me, his servant, 'Tell them this: I

---

[6]Gods of the Underworld who judge the dead.
[7]Goddess of fate.
[8]God of war.
[9]God of irrigation.

[10]God of wisdom and providence.
[11]Apparently an oath to protect humanity, because Ea was the god of life-giving water and good fortune.

have learnt that Enlil is wrathful against me, I dare no longer walk in his land nor live in his city; I will go down to the Gulf to dwell with Ea my lord. But on you he will rain down abundance, rare fish and shy wildfowl, a rich harvest-tide. In the evening the rider of the storm will bring you wheat in torrents.' . . .

"On the seventh day the boat was complete. . . .

"I loaded into her all that I had of gold and of living things, my family, my kin, the beast of the field both wild and tame, and all the craftsmen. I sent them on board. . . . The time was fulfilled, the evening came, the rider of the storm sent down the rain. I looked out at the weather and it was terrible, so I too boarded the boat and battened her down. . . .

"For six days and six nights the winds blew, torrent and tempest and flood overwhelmed the world, tempest and flood raged together like warring hosts. When the seventh day dawned the storm from the south subsided, the sea grew calm, the flood was stilled; I looked at the face of the world and there was silence, all mankind was turned to clay. The surface of the sea stretched as flat as a roof-top; I opened a hatch and the light fell on my face. Then I bowed low, I sat down and I wept, the tears streamed down my face, for on every side was the waste of water. I looked for land in vain, but fourteen leagues distant there appeared a mountain, and there the boat grounded; on the mountain of Nisir the boat held fast, she held fast and did not budge. . . . When the seventh day dawned I loosed a dove and let her go. She flew away, but finding no resting-place she returned. Then I loosed a swallow, and she flew away but finding no resting-place she returned. I loosed a raven, she saw that the waters had retreated, she ate, she flew around, she cawed, and she did not come back. Then I threw everything open to the four winds, I made

a sacrifice and poured out a libation[12] on the mountain top. Seven and again seven cauldrons I set up on their stands, I heaped up wood and cane and cedar and myrtle. When the gods smelled the sweet savor, they gathered like flies over the sacrifice.[13] Then, at last, Ishtar also came, she lifted her necklace with the jewels of heaven that once Anu had made to please her. 'O you gods here present, by the lapis lazuli round my neck I shall remember these days as I remember the jewels of my throat; these last days I shall not forget.[14] Let all the gods gather round the sacrifice, except Enlil. He shall not approach this offering, for without reflection he brought the flood; he consigned my people to destruction.'

"When Enlil had come, when he saw the boat, he was wrath and swelled with anger at the gods, the host of heaven, 'Has any of these mortals escaped? Not one was to have survived the destruction.' Then the god of the wells and canals Ninurta opened his mouth and said to the warrior Enlil, 'Who is there of the gods that can devise without Ea? It is Ea alone who knows all things.' Then Ea opened his mouth and spoke to warrior Enlil, 'Wisest of gods, hero Enlil, how could you so senselessly bring down the flood?' . . . It was not that I revealed the secret of the gods; the wise man learned it in a dream. Now take your counsel what shall be done with him.

"Then Enlil went up into the boat, he took me by the hand and my wife and made us enter the boat and kneel down on either side, he standing between us. He touched our foreheads to bless us saying, 'In time past Utnapishtim was a mortal man; henceforth he and his wife shall live in the distance at the mouth of the rivers.' Thus it was that the gods took me and placed me here to live in the distance, at the mouth of the rivers."

Utnapishtim said, "As for you, Gilgamesh, who will assemble the gods for your sake, so that

---

[12]Poured out wine or some other beverage as an offering to the gods.
[13]Many myth-making people believe that the gods gain nourishment from the greasy smoke of burnt sacrifices.

[14]The necklace is a rainbow.

you may find that life for which you are searching?"

___

▷ After telling his story, Utnapishtim challenges Gilgamesh to resist sleep for six days and seven nights. When Gilgamesh fails the test, Utnapishtim points out how preposterous it is to search for immortality when one cannot even resist sleep. Out of kindness, Utnapishtim does tell Gilgamesh where he can find a submarine plant that will at least rejuvenate him. Consequently, the hero dives to the bottom of the sea and plucks it. However, humanity is to be denied even the blessing of forestalling old age and decrepitude, because the plant is stolen from Gilgamesh by a serpent. His mission a failure, Gilgamesh returns to Uruk.

___

The destiny was fulfilled which the father of the gods, Enlil of the mountain, had decreed for Gilgamesh: "In nether-earth the darkness will show him a light: of mankind, all that are known, none will leave a monument for generations to come to compare with his. The heroes, the wise men, like the new moon have their waxing and waning. Men will say, 'Who has ever ruled with might and with power like him?' As in the dark month, the month of shadows, so without him there is no light. O Gilgamesh, this was the meaning of your dream. You were given the kingship, such was your destiny, everlasting life was not your destiny. Because of this do not be sad at heart, do not be grieved or oppressed; he has given you power to bind and to loose, to be the darkness and the light of mankind. He has given unexampled supremacy over the people, victory in battle from which no fugitive returns, in forays and assaults from which there is no going back. But do not abuse this power, deal justly with your servants in the palace, deal justly before the face of the Sun." . . .

Gilgamesh, the son of Ninsun, lies in the tomb. At the place of offerings he weighed the bread-offering, at the place of libation he poured out the wine. In those days the lord Gilgamesh departed, the son of Ninsun, the king, peerless, without an equal among men, who did not neglect Enlil his master. O Gilgamesh, lord of Kullab,[15] great is thy praise.

___

[15]Part of Uruk.

Bringing Order to an Uncertain World
▼▼▼
2 ▼ *THE JUDGMENTS OF HAMMURABI*

Mesopotamia's characteristic sense of insecurity resulted in its producing not only great philosophical literature but also detailed legal codes. The so-called *Code of Hammurabi* is the most famous but certainly not the earliest of the many collections of law produced throughout the first three thousand years of Mesopotamian civilization. Discovered in 1901, this Babylonian document from the eighteenth-century B.C.E. is inscribed on a stone pillar that measures over seven feet in height and more than six feet in circumference.

Whether Mesopotamia's numerous compilations of law were Sumerian, Babylonian, Assyrian, or Chaldean, a number of common elements united them. Chief among these elements was the expressed purpose, as the prologue to Hammurabi's collection declares, "to promote the welfare of the people, . . . to cause justice to prevail in the land, to destroy the wicked and the evil, that the strong might not oppress the weak." There is good reason to believe that even conquerors such as Hammurabi (reigned ca. 1792–1750 B.C.E.), who briefly united

Mesopotamia and transformed Babylon into the capital of an empire, sought to promote justice through law.

Hammurabi's code is actually a collection of decisions or *misharum* (equity rulings) that the king made in response to specific cases and perceived injustices. Although this is a compilation of judgments rather than a systematic code, the collection covers a wide variety of crimes and circumstances, thereby allowing extensive insight into the structure and values of eighteenth-century Babylonian society.

QUESTIONS FOR ANALYSIS

1. What specific actions did Hammurabi take in his attempt to provide for the good order of society and the basic welfare of his subjects?
2. What evidence is there of class distinctions in Babylon?
3. What was the status of women in this society? Did they enjoy any protection or liberties?
4. What about children? What was their status? Did they enjoy any protection or liberties?
5. Mesopotamian society has been characterized as a *patriarchal* society (dominated by male heads of households). Does the evidence in this collection of decisions tend to support or refute that judgment?
6. The principle of "An eye for an eye and a tooth for a tooth" usually means in modern idiom a philosophy of retribution that is noted for its severity and lack of compassion. Does such a characterization do justice to the spirit behind Hammurabi's code?
7. What principles and assumptions seem to underlay these judgments? In other words, what does this collection reveal about the world view, basic values, and ideals of Hammurabi's Babylon?

PROLOGUE

When Marduk[1] had instituted me governor of men, to conduct and to direct, Right and Justice I established in the land, for the good of the people.

THE ADMINISTRATION OF JUSTICE

3. If in a lawsuit a man gives damning evidence, and his word that he has spoken is not justified, then, if the suit be a capital one,[2] that man shall be slain. . . .

5. If a judge has heard a case, and given a decision, and delivered a written verdict, and if afterward his case is disproved, and that judge is convicted as the cause of the misjudgment, then he shall pay twelve times the penalty awarded in that case. In public assembly he shall be thrown from the seat of judgment; he shall not return; and he shall not sit with the judges upon a case. . . .

---

[1] The chief god of Babylon.

[2] A case in which death is the penalty.

FELONS AND VICTIMS

22. If a man has perpetrated brigandage, and has been caught, that man shall be slain.
23. If the brigand has not been taken, the man plundered shall claim before god[3] what he has lost; and the city and governor in whose land and boundary the theft has taken place shall restore to him all that he has lost.
24. If a life, the city and governor shall pay one mina[4] of silver to his people.[5] . . .

PROPERTY

29. If his son is under age, and unable to administer his [deceased] father's affairs, then a third part of the field and garden shall be given to his mother, and his mother shall bring him up. . . .
38. A captain, soldier, or official may not give his field, or garden, or house to his wife or his daughter; neither can they be given as payment for debt.[6]
39. He may bequeath in writing to his wife or daughter a field, a garden, or a house that he may have bought, and may give it as payment for debt. . . .

WINESELLERS AND TAVERNS

109. If rebels meet in the house of a wineseller and she[7] does not seize them and take them to the palace, that wine-seller shall be slain.
110. If a priestess who has not remained in the temple,[8] shall open a wine-shop, or enter a wine-shop for drink, that woman shall be burned. . . .

DEBT SLAVERY

117. If a man has contracted a debt, and has given his wife, his son, his daughter for silver or for labor, three years they shall serve in the house of their purchaser or bondsmaster; in the fourth year they shall regain their original condition. . . .

MARRIAGE AND THE FAMILY

129. If the wife of a man is found lying with another male, they shall be bound and thrown into the water. If the husband lets his wife live, then the king shall let his servant live. . . .
134. If a man has been taken prisoner, and there is no food in his house, and his wife enters the house of another, then that woman bears no blame.
135. If a man has been taken prisoner, and there is no food before her, and his wife has entered the house of another, and bears children, and afterward her husband returns and regains his city, then that woman shall return to her spouse. The children shall follow their father.
136. If a man has abandoned his city, and absconded, and after that his wife has entered the house of another, if that man comes back and claims his wife, because he had fled and deserted his city, the wife of the deserter shall not return to her husband.
138. If a man has decided to divorce . . . a wife who has presented him with children, then he shall give back to that woman her dowry,[9] and he shall give her the use of field, garden, and property, and she shall

---

[3]The god of the city. Each city had its special protector deity.
[4]About five hundred grams of silver. A mina was divided into sixty shekels.
[5]The family of the slain person.
[6]The monarch retained ultimate ownership of the property handed out to soldiers and bureaucrats who received land as payment for their services.

[7]Women traditionally filled this role in ancient Mesopotamia, perhaps because the wine deity was the goddess Siduri (see *The Epic of Gilgamesh,* source 1).
[8]Thereby breaking her vow to devote her life to serving the temple deity.
[9]The required money or goods she brought to the marriage.

bring up her children. After she has brought up her children, she shall take a son's portion of all that is given to her children, and she may marry the husband of her heart.

138. If a man divorces his spouse who has not borne him children, he shall give to her all the silver of the bride-price,[10] and restore to her the dowry which she brought from the house of her father; and so he shall divorce her.

139. If there was no bride-price, he shall give her one mina of silver for the divorce.

140. If he is a peasant, he shall give her one-third of a mina of silver.

141. If a man's wife, dwelling in his house, has decided to leave, has been guilty of dissipation, has wasted her house, and has neglected her husband, then she shall be prosecuted. If her husband says she is divorced, he shall let her go her way; he shall give her nothing for divorce. If her husband says she is not divorced, her husband may marry another woman, and that [first] woman shall remain a slave in the house of her husband.

142. If a woman hates her husband, and says "You shall not possess me," the reason for her dislike shall be inquired into. If she is careful, and has no fault, but her husband takes himself away and neglects her, then that woman is not to blame. She shall take her dowry and go back to her father's house. . . .

148. If a man has married a wife, and sickness has seized her, and he has decided to marry another, he may marry; but his wife whom the sickness has seized he shall not divorce. She shall dwell in the house he has built, and he shall support her while she lives. . . .

168. If a man has decided to disinherit his son, and has said to the judge, "I disown my son," then the judge shall look into his reasons. If the son has not been guilty of a serious offense which would justify his being disinherited, then the father shall not disown him.

169. If the son has committed a serious offense against his father which justifies his being disinherited, still the judge shall overlook this first offense. If the son commits a grave offense a second time, his father may disown him. . . .

PERSONAL INJURY

195. If a son has struck his father, his hands shall be cut off.

196   If a man has destroyed the eye of another free man, his own eye shall be destroyed.

197. If he has broken the bone of a free man, his bone shall be broken.

198. If he has destroyed the eye of a peasant, or broken a bone of a peasant, he shall pay one mina of silver.

199. If he has destroyed the eye of a man's slave, or broken a bone of a man's slave, he shall pay half his value.

200. If a man has knocked out the teeth of a man of the same rank, his own teeth shall be knocked out.

201. If he has knocked out the teeth of a peasant, he shall pay one-third of a mina of silver.

202. If a man strikes the body of a man who is superior in status, he shall publicly receive sixty lashes with a cowhide whip. . . .

206. If a man has struck another man in a dispute and wounded him, that man shall swear, "I did not strike him knowingly"; and he shall pay for the physician.

207. If he dies of his blows, he shall swear likewise; and if it is the son of a free man, he shall pay half a mina of silver.

208. If he is the son of a peasant, he shall pay a third of a mina of silver.

---

[10]The price he paid her family in order to marry her.

209. If a man strikes the daughter of a free man, and causes her fetus to abort, he shall pay ten shekels of silver for her fetus.
210. If that woman dies, his daughter shall be slain.
211. If he has caused the daughter of a peasant to let her fetus abort through blows, he shall pay five shekels of silver.
212. If that woman dies, he shall pay half a mina of silver. . . .

CONSUMER PROTECTION

215. If a physician has treated a man with a metal knife for a severe wound, and has cured the man, or has opened a man's tumor with a metal knife, and cured a man's eye, then he shall receive ten shekels of silver.
216. If the son of a peasant, he shall receive five shekels of silver. . . .
218. If a physician has treated a man with a metal knife for a severe wound, and has caused the man to die, or has opened a man's tumor with a metal knife, and destroyed the man's eye, his hands shall be cut off. . . .
229. If a builder has built a house for a man, and his work is not strong, and if the house he has built falls in and kills the householder, that builder shall be slain.
230. If the child of the householder is killed, the child of that builder shall be slain.
231. If the slave of the householder is killed, he shall give slave for slave to the householder.
232. If goods have been destroyed, he shall replace all that has been destroyed; and because the house that he built was not made strong, and it has fallen in, he shall restore the fallen house out of his own personal property.

233. If a builder has built a house for a man, and his work is not done properly, and a wall shifts, then that builder shall make that wall good with his own silver. . . .

EPILOGUE

The oppressed, who has a lawsuit, shall come before my image as king of justice. He shall read the writing on my pillar, he shall perceive my precious words. The word of my pillar shall explain to him his cause, and he shall find his right. His heart shall be glad [and he shall say,] "The Lord Hammurabi has risen up as a true father to his people; the will of Marduk, his god, he has made to be feared; he has achieved victory for Marduk above and below. He has rejoiced the heart of Marduk, his lord, and gladdened the flesh of his people for ever. And the land he has placed in order." . . .

In after days and for all time, the king who is in the land shall observe the words of justice which are written upon my pillar. He shall not alter the law of the land which I have formulated, or the statutes of the country that I have enacted. . . . If that man has wisdom, and desires to keep his land in order, he will heed the words which are written upon my pillar. . . . The . . . people he shall govern; their laws he shall pronounce, their statutes he shall decide. He shall root out of the land the perverse and the wicked; and the flesh of his people he shall delight.

Hammurabi, the king of justice, am I, to whom Shamash[11] has granted rectitude. My words are well weighed: my deeds have no equal, leveling the exalted, humbling the proud, expelling the haughty. If that man heeds my words that I have engraved upon my pillar, departs not from the laws, alters not my words, changes not my sculptures, then may Shamash make the scepter of that man to endure as long as I, the king of justice, and to lead his people with justice.

---

[11]The sun god, god of justice and vindicator of the oppressed. During the eighteenth century B.C.E. he rose in prominence among the deities of Babylon. Apparently his new status indicates a new emphasis on justice and equity.

▼▼▼

Egypt: The Land of Two Lands

Civilization seems to have arisen in Egypt shortly after it first appeared in Sumer. Although there is evidence of early Sumerian contact with the Egyptians, Egypt's civilization was largely self-generated, and its history and cultural patterns differed substantially from those of Mesopotamia. Egyptians, however, shared the same myth-making way of perceiving reality.

An integral element of Egyptian myth was the belief that Egypt was the land of divine harmony ruled by a living god-king, or *pharaoh,* who balanced all conflicting cosmic forces. Around 3100 B.C.E. the land of the Nile was unified into a single state, although culturally it remained two distinctive lands: the rich delta region of the north, known as *Lower Egypt* (because the Nile flows northward), and the long but narrow strip of green land that borders the Nile to the south, known as *Upper Egypt.* Before their unification, Lower and Upper Egypt had been separate kingdoms. As far as Egyptians were concerned, they forever remained two antithetical yet complementary lands that were brought into harmony by a unifying king who was a god on earth. As the embodiment of the union of Upper and Lower Egypt, the king was likewise the personification on earth of the goddess *Maat,* whose name in a general sense meant "what is right." In other words, the god-king of Egypt *was* truth, law, and justice.

The state that resulted from the union of Egypt's two lands enjoyed about three thousand years of unparalleled prosperity and stability. Between approximately 3100 and 343 B.C.E. Egypt experienced only a handful of relatively short-lived periods of either major internal turmoil and the consequent breakdown of central authority or domination by foreign powers. This long history of centralized monarchy and native rule was due in large part to the blessings of geography. Egypt was fairly secure behind its barriers of sea and desert, and the Nile's annual flooding was predictable and beneficial.

The sense of security that followed from these geographical and historical circumstances was reflected in the life-affirming spirit that was evident in much of Egyptian religion and philosophy. This spirit also left its imprint on Egypt's arts. Whether painting charming scenes of everyday activities or composing tender love poems, Egyptian artists celebrated the joys of life. At the same time, codes of law, which figure so prominently in the historical records of Mesopotamia, are not to be found in the literature of ancient Egypt. Though the Egyptians were equally concerned with maintaining a well-ordered society, their avenue to this goal differed greatly from that of the Mesopotamians.

The Search for Eternal Life in Egypt

▼▼▼

3 ▼ *THREE FUNERARY DOCUMENTS*

Historians have traditionally divided the first two thousand years of Egyptian civilization into six ages: the Early Dynastic Period (ca. 3100–2600 B.C.E.); the Old Kingdom (ca. 2600–2125); the First Intermediate Period (ca. 2125–2025); the Middle Kingdom (ca. 2060–1700); the Second Intermediate Period, or Age of the Hyksos (ca. 1700–1550); and the New Kingdom, or Empire (ca. 1550–1069).

The Early Dynastic Period was Egypt's era of initial unification and state building under the guidance of its first three royal dynasties. The Old Kingdom that followed centered on Egypt's god-kings, whose mummified remains were reverently entombed in pyramids, in preparation for the journey to eternal life in the *Land of the West.* During this age, Egyptians believed (or at least the priests taught) that immortality was the exclusive preserve of the divine pharaoh, members of the royal family, the priests, and a handful of favored royal servants. They further believed that in order to ensure the king's safe journey to the afterlife, all that was needed was proper attention to the many details of the royal funeral ceremony. Beginning with the entombment of King Unas, who died around 2345 B.C.E., Egyptians carved magical incantations on the walls of royal burial chambers as a means of assuring the king's safe journey into eternal life. Modern scholars have discovered and catalogued over seven hundred fifty distinct incantations, which they term collectively the *Pyramid Texts.* We do not know what the Egyptians called them, but regardless, they provide a privileged view of funeral practices and beliefs regarding immortality during the Old Kingdom. Our first selection comes from the tomb of King Teti, who followed Unas to the throne.

Egyptians continued to bury their dead with great ceremony for thousands of years to come, but it was essentially only during the Old Kingdom that they constructed the great burial pyramids, which for over four and one-half thousand years have served as tokens of the power wielded by early Egypt's god-kings. The reign of Pepi II (ca. 2275–2185 B.C.E.) marked the end of the Old Kingdom. Shortly after Pepi's death, pharaonic power collapsed, plunging Egypt into an era of internal turmoil known as the First Intermediate Period. A century later this age of local rule and social upheaval gave way to the Middle Kingdom, an era of revived central authority and a deepening awareness of social justice and personal moral responsibility. Befitting the new spirit, many Egyptians came to view eternal life as available to all Egyptians who met certain criteria.

A new body of funerary inscriptions now appeared, which scholars today refer to as the *Coffin Texts.* The texts, usually inscribed within the wooden coffins of people who could afford elaborate funerals, were ritual resurrection spells. Some were modeled upon the earlier *Pyramid Texts,* but most were quite new and displayed an obsession with the dangers of earth and the terrors of death that was lacking in the pyramid inscriptions. Despite the essential life-affirming nature of their culture, the Egyptians were not immune to the miseries and fears, especially fears of disaster and death, that beset all humans.

Our second selection is a much used coffin spell that takes the form of a two-part speech. In the first part the sun god Re speaks, reminding humanity of his four good deeds at the time of creation. In the second part the deceased speaks, laying his claim on eternal life.

The process of widening access to the afterlife evolved to another level with the creation of *The Book of the Dead*. This is actually the modern name for a collection of papyrus texts that the Egyptians knew as *The Chapters for Coming Forth by Day*. Although it did not reach its final form until around the sixth century B.C.E., this collection of chapters was largely a creation of the New Kingdom. Like the pyramid and coffin inscriptions from which it evolved, it was a body of magical incantations for use in burial ceremonies, but unlike the pyramid and coffin inscriptions, it had a fairly standardized text. It was also available to a larger but still necessarily prosperous clientele. Divided into more than one hundred fifty chapters, which were gathered together into papyrus scrolls, the book had a certain mass-produced quality. One could purchase a scroll, fill in the name of the deceased, and bury it with the person's body. Resurrection had become a cut-rate enterprise.

Of all the chapters, the most famous is Chapter 125, the lengthy "Judgment of the Dead," from which we have extracted the "Negative Confession." The scene is the Hall of the Two Truths, or the Double Maat, where Osiris, king of the Underworld, presides over an assembly of forty-two minor deities. It is these forty-two who will judge the deceased's suitability to become an eternally blessed spirit. Upon entering the hall, the deceased (*N,* or fill in the name) proclaims his or her purity.

QUESTIONS FOR ANALYSIS

1. What were King Teti's expectations regarding the afterlife?
2. What allows us to infer that the Egyptians believed that King Teti had become a resurrected god?
3. It has been said that our second selection, the coffin text, contains a strong egalitarian message. Where are those presumed egalitarian statements, and what do you make of them?
4. Consider the speech of Re. Does it contain a moral element? If so, how is that message connected, if at all, with the dead person's spell?
5. According to the coffin text, how does a person guarantee eternal life? What do you conclude from your answer?
6. One scholar has written of the coffin texts, "Because the individuals who were seeking an afterlife as divine beings stood outside the royal circle, their coffin inscriptions reflected both paranoid fear and delusions of grandeur." Do you agree or disagree?
7. What does "The Negative Confession" allow us to infer about Egyptian values in the New Kingdom?
8. Each of the three texts provides a path to eternal life. What do their similarities and differences suggest about continuities and changes within Egyptian society over this millennium?
9. Compare these three texts with *The Epic of Gilgamesh* (source 1). What are their different messages? What do those messages suggest about the differences between the two civilizations?

A PYRAMID TEXT

Oho! Oho! Rise up, O Teti!
Take your head,
Collect your bones,
Gather your limbs,
Shake the earth from your flesh!
Take your bread that rots not,
Your beer that sours not,
Stand at the gates that bar the
  common people!
The gatekeeper comes out to you,
He grasps your hand,
Takes you into heaven, to your father Geb.[1]
He rejoices at your coming,
Gives you his hands,
Kisses you, caresses you,
Sets you before the spirits, the
  imperishable stars.
The hidden ones worship you,
The great ones surround you,
The watchers wait on you.
Barley is threshed for you,
Emmen is reaped for you,
Your monthly feasts are made with it,
Your half-month feasts are made with it,
As ordered done for you by Geb, your father,
Rise up, O Teti, you shall not die!

A COFFIN TEXT

Words spoken by Him-whose-names-are-hidden, the All-Lord, as he speaks before those who silence the storm, in the sailing of the court:[2]

Hail in peace! I repeat to you the good deeds which my own heart did for me from within the serpent-coil,[3] in order to silence strife. I did four good deeds within the portal of lightland:

I made the four winds, that every man might breathe in his time. This is one of the deeds.

I made the great inundation,[4] that the humble might benefit by it like the great. This is one of the deeds.

I made every man like his fellow; and I did not command that they do wrong. It is their hearts that disobey what I have said. This is one of the deeds.

I made that their hearts are not disposed to forget the West,[5] in order that sacred offerings be made to the gods of the nomes.[6] This is one of the deeds.

I have created the gods from my sweat, and the people from the tears of my eye.

The dead speaks

I[7] shall shine and be seen every day as a dignitary of the All-Lord, having given satisfaction to the Weary-hearted.[8]

I shall sail rightly in my bark,[9] I am lord of eternity in the crossing of the sky.

I am not afraid in my limbs, for Hu and Hike[10] overthrow for me that evil being.

I shall see lightland, I shall dwell in it. I shall judge the poor and the wealthy.

I shall do the same for the evil-doers; for mine is life, I am its lord, and the scepter will not be taken from me.

I have spent a million years with the Weary-hearted, the son of Geb, dwelling with him in one place; while hills became towns and towns hills, for dwelling destroys dwelling.

I am lord of the flame who lives on truth; lord of eternity maker of joy, against whom that worm shall not rebel.

I am he who is in his shrine, master of action who destroys the storm; who drives off the ser-

---

[1]The god of the earth and father of Osiris, the god of resurrection and king of the dead.
[2]The deities who accompany Re as he sails daily across the sky (note 9).
[3]The serpent-dragon Apophis, a mythic symbol of the lurking dangers in the world.
[4]The annual flooding of the Nile.
[5]The Land of the Resurrected Dead.
[6]The forty-two religious and administrative districts into which Egypt was divided.

[7]The dead person now becomes the speaker, assuming the identity of Re.
[8]One of Osiris's titles. One must first satisfy Osiris before joining Re.
[9]Re sails across the sky in a bark, or boat.
[10]Personifications of effective speech and magic; they are probably a reference to this magical spell, which has been uttered at entombment and carved in the coffin.

pents of many names when he goes from his shrine.

Lord of the winds who announces the north-wind, rich in names in the mouth of the Ennead.[11]

Lord of lightland, maker of light, who lights the sky with his beauty.

I am he in his name! Make way for me, that I may see Nun[12] and Amun![13] For I am that equipped spirit who passes by the guards.[14] They do not speak for fear of Him-whose-name-is-hidden, who is in my body. I know him, I do not ignore him! I am equipped and effective in opening his portal!

As for any person who knows this spell, he will be like Re in the eastern sky, like Osiris in the netherworld. He will go down to the circle of fire, without the flame touching him ever!

THE NEGATIVE CONFESSION

(1) To be said on reaching the Hall of the Two Truths[15] so as to purge N of any sins committed and to see the face of every god:

Hail to you, Great God, Lord of the
    Two Truths!
I have come to you, my Lord,
I was brought to see your beauty.
I know you, I know the names of the forty-
    two gods,
Who are with you in the Hall of the
    Two Truths.
Who live by warding off evildoers,
Who drink of their blood,

On that day of judging characters
    before Wennofer.[16]
Lo, your name is "He-of-Two-Daughters,"
(And) "He-of-Maat's-Two-Eyes."
Lo, I come before you,
Bringing Maat to you,
Having repelled evil for you.

I have not done crimes against people,
I have not mistreated cattle,
I have not sinned in the Place of Truth.[17]
I have not known what should not
    be known,[18]
I have not done any harm.
I did not begin a day by exacting more than
    my due,
My name did not reach the bark of the
    mighty ruler.[19]
I have not blasphemed a god,
I have not robbed the poor.
I have not done what the god abhors,
I have not maligned a servant to his master.
I have not caused pain,
I have not caused tears.
I have not killed,
I have not ordered to kill,
I have not made anyone suffer.
I have not damaged the offerings in
    the temples,
I have not depleted the loaves of the gods,
I have not stolen the cakes of the dead.[20]
I have not copulated nor defiled myself.
I have not increased nor reduced
    the measure, . . .

---

[11]The company of Egypt's nine chief deities.

[12]The watery void outside the temporal and spatial boundaries of creation from which the creator emerged; Nun was personified as the god of the Abyss.

[13]A primeval god who existed as a force before creation; he became the chief god of Thebes. He rose to preeminence in Egypt when the princes of Thebes reunited Egypt after the Second Intermediate Period (see source 4, note 1).

[14]The guards to the Land of the West.

[15]Maat takes a dual form here in Isis, goddess of Right, and Nephthys, goddess of Truth. Isis was the sister and wife of Osiris. It was she who brought the dead and dismembered Osiris back to life, thereby assuring his status as god of resurrection and king of the Underworld. Nephthys, also Osiris's sister, had assisted in his resurrection.

[16]One of Osiris's names.

[17]He has not sinned in any holy place.

[18]Secrets of the gods.

[19]As he sails across the sky in his bark, Re has not heard of any misdeeds by the deceased.

[20]Food to accompany the dead on their journey.

I have not cheated in the fields.
I have not added to the weight of
    the balance,
I have not falsified the plummet of
    the scales.
I have not taken milk from the mouth
    of children,
I have not deprived cattle of their pasture.
I have not snared birds in the reeds of
    the gods,
I have not caught fish in their ponds.
I have not held back water in its season,
I have not dammed a flowing stream,

I have not quenched a needed fire.
I have not neglected the days of
    meat offerings,
I have not detained cattle belonging to
    the god,
I have not stopped a god in his procession.

I am pure, I am pure,
I am pure, I am pure! . . .
No evil shall befall me in this land,
In this Hall of the Two Truths;
For I know the names of the gods in it,
The followers of the great God!

Making a Living in Ancient Egypt
▼▼▼
4 ▼ A SCRIBAL EXERCISE BOOK

We would be greatly mistaken if we viewed the ancient Egyptians as so preoccupied with death and the afterlife that they had little concern with the affairs of this world. The literature and art of Egypt provide many glimpses into everyday life, and one of the best in this regard is a large body of exercise pieces for student scribes that compare the scribe's profession to other ways of making a living. Needless to say, scribes believed that all crafts were inferior to their own. Despite its blatant prejudice in favor of the scribe's way of life, this description of the wretchedness of nonscribal activities gives a good overview of the types of employment in which Egyptians were engaged. Examples of this genre go back at least to the Middle Kingdom; our selection dates from the twelfth century B.C.E. in the age of the late New Kingdom.

QUESTIONS FOR ANALYSIS

1. According to the teacher, what attributes do all nonscribal trades share?
2. Most of Egypt's peasants were free. Taking the obvious exaggeration into account, what does this text suggest about the lives of these peasants?
3. The New Kingdom was an era of empire and foreign military adventure. What does this text tell us about the soldiers who bore the brunt of Egypt's imperial ambitions?
4. What are the presumed advantages of the scribe's profession?
5. Does this seem to be a fair picture of the dichotomy that existed in ancient society between the literate and the illiterate?
6. How would you characterize the economy of Egypt as revealed in this text?

The idle scribe is worthless

The royal scribe and chief overseer of the cattle of Amun-Re,[1] King of Gods, Nebmare-nakht, speaks to the scribe Wenemdiamun, as follows. You are busy coming and going, and don't think of writing. You resist listening to me; you neglect my teachings.

You are worse than the goose of the shore, that is busy with mischief. It spends the summer destroying the dates, the winter destroying the seed-grain. It spends the balance of the year in pursuit of the cultivators. It does not let seed be cast to the ground without snatching it in its fall. One cannot catch it by snaring. One does not offer it in the temple. The evil, sharpeyed bird that does no work!

You are worse than the desert antelope that lives by running. It spends no day in plowing. Never at all does it tread on the threshing-floor. It lives on the oxen's labor, without entering among them. But though I spend the day telling you "Write," it seems like a plague to you. Writing is very pleasant!

*All occupations are bad
except that of the scribe*

See for yourself with your own eye. The occupations lie before you.

The washerman's day is going up, going down. All his limbs are weak, [from] whitening his neighbors' clothes every day, from washing their linen.

The maker of pots is smeared with soil, like one whose relations have died. His hands, his feet are full of clay; he is like one who lives in the bog.

The cobbler mingles with vats.[2] His odor is penetrating. His hands are red with madder,[3] like one who is smeared with blood. . . .

The watchman[4] prepares garlands and polishes vase-stands. He spends a night of toil just as one on whom the sun shines.

The merchant travels downstream and upstream. They are as busy as can be, carrying goods from one town to another. They supply him who has wants. But the tax collectors carry off the gold, that most precious of metals.

The ships' crews from every house [of commerce], they receive their loads. They depart from Egypt for Syria, and each man's god is with him. [But] not one of them says: "We shall see Egypt again!"

The carpenter who is in the shipyard carries the timber and stacks it. If he gives today the output of yesterday, woe to his limbs! The shipwright stands behind him to tell him evil things.

His outworker who is in the fields, his is the toughest of all the jobs. He spends the day loaded with his tools, tied to his tool-box. When he returns home at night, he is loaded with the toolbox and the timbers, his drinking mug, and his whetstones.

The scribe, he alone, records the output of all of them. Take note of it!

The misfortunes of the peasant

Let me also expound to you the situation of the peasant, that other tough occupation. [Comes] the inundation and soaks him – – –,[5] he attends to his equipment. By day he cuts his farming tools; by night he twists rope. Even his midday hour he spends on farm labor. He equips himself to go to the field as if he were a warrior. The dried field lies before him; he goes out to get his team. When he has been after the herdsman for many days, he gets his team and comes back with it. He makes for it a place in the field. Comes dawn, he goes to make a start and does not find it in its place. He spends three days

---

[1]The composite chief deity of the New Kingdom, Amun-Re was a result of the joining of Amun, chief god of Thebes (source 3, note 13), with Re, the chief deity of the Old and Middle Kingdoms.
[2]For tanning leather.

[3]A red plant dye.
[4]The watchman-custodian of a temple, who prepares for the next day's rituals.
[5]There is a gap in the document here.

searching for it; he finds it in the bog. He finds no hides on them; the jackals have chewed them. He comes out, his garments in his hand, to beg for himself a team.

When he reaches his field he finds [it] broken up. He spends time cultivating, and the snake is after him. It finishes off the seed as it is cast to the ground. He does not see a green blade. He does three plowings with borrowed grain. His wife has gone down to the merchants and found nothing for barter. Now the scribe lands on the shore. He surveys the harvest. Attendants are behind him with staffs, Nubians[6] with clubs. One says [to him]: "Give grain." "There is none." He is beaten savagely. He is bound, thrown in the well, submerged head down. His wife is bound in his presence. His children are in fetters. His neighbors abandon them and flee. When it's over, there's no grain.

If you have any sense, be a scribe. If you have learned about the peasant, you will not be able to be one. Take note of it!

Be a scribe

The scribe of the army and commander[7] of the cattle of the house of Amun, Nebmare-nakht, speaks to the scribe Wenemdiamun, as follows. Be a scribe! Your body will be sleek; your hand will be soft. You will not flicker like a flame, like one whose body is feeble. For there is not the bone of a man in you. You are tall and thin. If you lifted a load to carry it, you would stagger, your legs would tremble. You are lacking in strength; you are weak in all your limbs; you are poor in body.

Set your sight on being a scribe; a fine profession that suits you. You call for one; a thousand answer you. You stride freely on the road. You will not be like a hired ox. You are in front of others.

I spend the day instructing you. You do not listen! Your heart is like an [empty] room. My

teachings are not in it. Take their [meaning] to yourself!

The marsh thicket is before you each day, as a nestling is after its mother. You follow the path of pleasure; you make friends with revellers. You have made your home in the brewery, as one who thirsts for beer. You sit in the parlor with an idler. You hold the writings in contempt. You visit the whore. Do not do these things! What are they for? They are of no use. Take note of it!

The scribe does not suffer like the soldier

Furthermore. Look, I instruct you to make you sound; to make you hold the palette freely. To make you become one whom the king trusts; to make you gain entrance to treasury and granary. To make you receive the ship-load at the gate of the granary. To make you issue the offerings on feast days. You are dressed in fine clothes; you own horses. Your boat is on the river; you are supplied with attendants. You stride about inspecting. A mansion is built in your town. You have a powerful office, given you by the king. Male and female slaves are about you. Those who are in the fields grasp your hand, on plots that you have made. Look, I make you into a staff of life! Put the writings in your heart, and you will be protected from all kinds of toil. You will become a worthy official.

Do you not recall the [fate of] the unskilled man? His name is not known. He is ever burdened [like an ass carrying] in front of the scribe who knows what he is about.

Come, [let me tell] you the woes of the soldier, and how many are his superiors: the general, the troop-commander, the officer who leads, the standard-bearer, the lieutenant, the scribe, the commander of fifty, and the garrison-captain. They go in and out in the halls of the palace, saying: "Get laborers!" He is awakened at any hour. One is after him as [after] a donkey. He toils until the Aten[8] sets in his darkness of night.

---

[6]Mercenaries from the land south of Egypt (source 9).
[7]A joke whereby the scribe Nebmare-nakht, who holds the post of overseer of the cattle of the god Amun-Re, now takes the military title of *commander*.

[8]The divine sun disk.

He is hungry, his belly hurts; he is dead while yet alive. When he receives the grain-ration, having been released from duty, it is not good for grinding.

He is called up for Syria. He may not rest. There are no clothes, no sandals. The weapons of war are assembled at the fortress of Sile. His march is uphill through mountains. He drinks water every third day; it is smelly and tastes of salt. His body is ravaged by illness. The enemy comes, surrounds him with missiles, and life recedes from him. He is told: "Quick, forward, valiant soldier! Win for yourself a good name!" He does not know what he is about. His body is weak, his legs fail him. When victory is won, the captives are handed over to his majesty, to be taken to Egypt. The foreign woman faints on the march; she hangs herself [on] the soldier's neck. His knapsack drops, another grabs it while he is burdened with the woman. His wife and children are in their village; he dies and does not reach it. If he comes out alive, he is worn out from marching. Be he at large, be he detained, the soldier suffers. If he leaps and joins the deserters, all his people are imprisoned. He dies on the edge of the desert, and there is none to perpetuate his name. He suffers in death as in life. A big sack is brought for him; he does not know his resting place.

Be a scribe, and be spared from soldiering! You call and one says: "Here I am." You are safe from torments. Every man seeks to raise himself up. Take note of it!

▼▼▼

China: The Land of the Yellow River

The study of history has been one of China's most revered and continuous traditions for well over two thousand years. Already by the second century B.C.E., the Chinese confidently claimed a detailed history that reached back into the early third millennium. According to this vision of their past, Chinese civilization was sparked not by the actions of gods but by extraordinary men, beginning with the Yellow Emperor, who established an organized state around 2700 B.C.E. Four other monarchs succeeded in turn, each of whom ascended the throne by virtue of merit and genius rather than by birth. Following these five predynastic *Sage Emperors,* who laid down all of the basic elements of Chinese culture, the *Xia* family established China's first royal dynasty and ruled from 2205 to 1766 B.C.E. After Xia's collapse, the *Shang* Dynasty held power, until it gave way to the *Zhou* Dynasty.

Until the late 1920s we had no irrefutable evidence that either the Xia or Shang Dynasties ever existed, and Western historians generally dismissed them as romantic legends. The work of archeologists over the past sixty years, however, has proved beyond any shadow of a doubt that Shang royal rule was a historical reality. Dating it precisely, however, has proved to be a problem, due to the ambiguity of the archeological record. Some scholars date its origins to the eighteenth century B.C.E.; other historians place it no earlier than around 1600 B.C.E. Locating Xia's time and place has proved to be even more difficult, but recent excavations strongly suggest that the Xia Dynasty also existed, possibly as early as 2200 or 2100 B.C.E. (or later — the evidence is also quite ambiguous). The picture of earliest Chinese civilization remains cloudy and controversial at best, but recent archeological evidence *seems* to indicate that Xia, Shang, and Zhou were originally three coexisting centers of civilization in North China, and the Shang and Zhou successions were largely the shifting of dominance through warfare from one state and family of royal warlords to another. The state of our present knowledge of earliest Chinese civilization is that northern China most likely had civilized centers of government as early as the late third millennium B.C.E. (or soon after 2000 B.C.E.), but the details still largely elude us. Most of the stories related by Sima Qian and other classical Chinese historians about the predynastic Sage Emperors and China's first royal dynasties still seem to most modern historians to be more the stuff of legend than historical fact. But who knows what tomorrow's archeological discovery will bring?

Our knowledge of the Xia state and its age of predominance is sketchy at best. We know much more about the Shang, thanks to the work of modern archeologists, who have unearthed magnificent bronze ceremonial vessels, two huge capital cities, and a primitive form of Chinese ideographic writing on what are known as *oracle bones*. Although scholars can read them, the oracle bones provide little detail about the social and political history of the Shang because they served only one purpose: magical divination of the future.

China's earliest extant literary and political documents date from the age of Zhou rule, and thus we know much more about the Zhou Dynasty than about the Xia and Shang. Even so, Zhou's date of origin remains a subject for debate. (All Chinese dates before 800 B.C.E. are quite imprecise.) The era of Zhou rule *seems* to have begun around 1100, when the Zhou conquered the Shang and established a royal dynasty that lasted eight hundred years or more. The Zhou Era is divided into two periods: Western and Eastern. The age of Western Zhou witnessed a fairly strong *feudal* monarchy that presided over fifty or more *vassal,* or subordinate, states. What this means is that the Zhou kings delegated authority to the rulers of these states in elaborate ceremonies that emphasized the king's primacy. As time went on, however, power tended to slip away from the Western Zhou kings into the hands of the vassal lords. In 771 B.C.E. a group of rebellious northern nobles killed King Yu and overran the capital city, Xi'an, and the royal heir fled eastward to Loyang. Here the Zhou continued to reside as kings until 256 B.C.E. The kings of Eastern Zhou, however, never enjoyed the power of their western forbearers. For five hundred years they reigned over but did not rule a kingdom where all real power resided in the hands of local lords.

The Mandate of Heaven
▼▼▼
5 ▼ *THE CLASSIC OF HISTORY*

The *Shu Jing,* or *The Classic of History,* is the oldest complete work among what are known as the five Confucian classics. (The introduction to source 24 in Chapter 4 contains a biography of Confucius, and note 6 of source 35 in Chapter 5 describes the classics.) The five classics were canonized as the basic elements of the Confucian educational system during the second century B.C.E., when the books were reconstructed by order of several emperors of the Han Dynasty (202 B.C.E.–220 C.E.). Although Han scholars probably refashioned elements of the *Shu Jing,* the work was already ancient in Confucius's day, and the book, as we have received it, is probably essentially the same text that Confucius (551–479 B.C.E.) knew, studied, and accepted as an authentic record of Chinese civilization.

Despite its title, *The Classic of History* is not a work of historical interpretation or narration. Rather, it is a collection of documents spanning some seventeen hundred years of Chinese history and legend, from 2357 to 631 B.C.E. Many of the documents, however, are the spurious creations of much later periods and therefore reflect the attitudes of those subsequent eras.

The document that appears here was composed in the age of Zhou but purports to be the advice given by the faithful Yi Yin to King Tai Jia, second of the Shang kings. According to the story behind the document, when the first Shang king, Cheng Tang, died around 1753, his chief minister, Yi Yin, took it upon himself to instruct the new, young king in the ways and duties of kingship and the workings of the Mandate of Heaven.

The Mandate of Heaven was a political-social philosophy that served as the basic Chinese explanation for the success and failure of monarchs and states down to the end of the empire in 1912 C.E. Whenever a dynasty fell, the reason invariably offered by China's sages was that it had lost the moral right to rule, which is given by Heaven alone. In this context, Heaven did not mean a personal god but a cosmic, all-pervading power. The theory of the Mandate of Heaven was probably created by the Zhou and used to justify their overthrow of the Shang. The king, after all, was the father of his people, and paternal authority was the basic cement of Chinese society from earliest times. Rebellion against a father, therefore, needed extraordinary justification.

QUESTIONS FOR ANALYSIS

1. How does a monarch lose the Mandate of Heaven, and what are the consequences of this loss?
2. What evidence can you find here of the Chinese cult of reverence for the ancestors?
3. What evidence can you find to support the conclusion that Chinese political philosophers perceived the state as an extended family?
4. What sort of harmony does the monarch maintain?
5. Would Yi Yin accept the notion that one must distinguish between a ruler's private morality and public policies?
6. What does the theory of the Mandate of Heaven suggest about the nature of Chinese society?
7. American politicians often promise innovative answers to the challenges of tomorrow. What would Yi Yin think about such an approach to statecraft? What would Yi Yin think about modern politicians who attempt to appear youthful? What would he think of popular opinion polls?

8. Compare the Chinese vision of its ideal monarch with Egyptian and Mesopotamian views of kingship. Despite all their obvious cultural differences, did each of these societies expect its king to perform essentially the same task? If so, what was that task?

In the twelfth month of the first year . . . Yi Yin sacrificed to the former king, and presented the heir-king reverently before the shrine of his grandfather. All the princes from the domain of the nobles and the royal domain were present; all the officers also, each continuing to discharge his particular duties, were there to receive the orders of the chief minister. Yi Yin then clearly described the complete virtue of the Meritorious Ancestor[1] for the instruction of the young king.

He said, "Oh! of old the former kings of Xia cultivated earnestly their virtue, and then there were no calamities from Heaven. The spirits of the hills and rivers likewise were all in tranquility; and the birds and beasts, the fishes and tortoises, all enjoyed their existence according to their nature. But their descendant did not follow their example, and great Heaven sent down calamities, employing the agency of our ruler[2] who was in possession of its favoring appointment. The attack on Xia may be traced to the orgies in Ming Tiao.[3] . . . Our king of Shang brilliantly displayed his sagely prowess; for oppression he substituted his generous gentleness; and the millions of the people gave him their hearts. Now your Majesty is entering on the inheritance of his virtue; — all depends on how you commence your reign. To set up love, it is for you to love your relations; to set up respect, it is for you to respect your elders. The commencement is in the family and the state. . . .

"Oh! the former king began with careful attention to the bonds that hold men together. He listened to expostulation, and did not seek to resist it; he conformed to the wisdom of the ancients; occupying the highest position, he dis-

played intelligence; occupying an inferior position, he displayed his loyalty; he allowed the good qualities of the men whom he employed and did not seek that they should have every talent. . . .

"He extensively sought out wise men, who should be helpful to you, his descendant and heir. He laid down the punishments for officers, and warned those who were in authority, saying, 'If you dare to have constant dancing in your palaces, and drunken singing in your chambers, — that is called the fashion of sorcerers; if you dare to set your hearts on wealth and women, and abandon yourselves to wandering about or to the chase, — that is called the fashion of extravagance; if you dare to despise sage words, to resist the loyal and upright, to put far from you the aged and virtuous, and to seek the company of . . . youths, — that is called the fashion of disorder. Now if a high noble or officer be addicted to one of these three fashions with their ten evil ways, his family will surely come to ruin; if the prince of a country be so addicted, his state will surely come to ruin. The minister who does not try to correct such vices in the sovereign shall be punished with branding.' . . .

"Oh! do you, who now succeed to the throne, revere these warnings in your person. Think of them! — sacred counsels of vast importance, admirable words forcibly set forth! The ways of Heaven are not invariable: — on the good-doer it sends down all blessings, and on the evil-doer it sends down all miseries. Do you but be virtuous, be it in small things or in large, and the myriad regions will have cause for rejoicing. If you not be virtuous, be it in large things or in small, it will bring the ruin of your ancestral temple."

---

[1]Cheng Tang, founder of the Shang Dynasty.
[2]Cheng Tang (see note 1).

[3]According to legend, Jie, the last Xia king, held notorious orgies at Ming Tiao.

Courtship and Marriage in Ancient China
▼▼▼
6 ▼ THE CLASSIC OF ODES

The *Shih Jing,* or *The Classic of Odes,* is another of the five Confucian classics that served as the basic texts of an educational system that molded China's leaders for more than two thousand years. The work consists of 305 poetic songs, covering a variety of topics from love to war; their dates of composition largely fall into the period of about 900 to 600 B.C.E. The book ultimately became Confucian because Confucius and his many generations of disciples used the songs as texts for moral instruction. No good reason exists to believe that Confucius had a hand in crafting any of the poems or even in assembling the collection.

The following ballads reveal several important customs, attitudes, and realities relating to love, courtship, and marriage in early China. Traditional Chinese society revolved around the family to the point that all larger social and political units were viewed as its extensions. In any society in which family ties are the primary bond, courtship and marriage assume great significance, and as far back as the record goes, the Chinese have consistently exhibited a preoccupation with the proper rites of courtship and stable marriages.

The first ode concerns a woman who resists the attempt of a man to marry her and argues her case before a court of law; the second poem is analogous, insofar as it is a widow's protest against being urged to remarry. The third ballad recounts the affection a husband feels for his bride. The fourth song reveals a woman's change of mood upon her husband's return. In the fifth ode a man compares his middle-aged spouse with some young women whom he encounters.

QUESTIONS FOR ANALYSIS

1. On what apparent grounds has the woman in poem 1 refused to marry her suitor? Does she believe she has a good case? What do you infer from this?

2. From what you can infer from poem 1, how seriously were betrothal vows normally taken?

3. Why does the widow in poem 2 refuse to remarry? What does her refusal suggest about the power and status of widows in Zhou society?

4. What does poem 3 tell us about the traditional Chinese formula for a successful marriage? Normally, first marriages in traditional China were arranged between the families of the bride and groom. Notwithstanding this, was it possible for the prospective partners to have some control over whom they would marry?

5. Women of high class tended to have more power and freedom in the ages of Shang and Zhou than did Chinese women a thousand years later. What evidence is there in these poems of female power?

6. Did the Chinese believe that love was possible within an arranged marriage? What is the evidence for your answer?

1. I WILL NOT MARRY YOU

The dew thick on the wet paths lay;
Thither at early dawn my way
I might have taken; but I said, "Nay.
The dew is thick, at home I'll stay." . . .

You say this trial is a proof
That I exchanged betrothal vows.
But though you've made me here appear
    in court,
Yet at betrothal what you did fell short. . . .

You say this trial proves my vows
Of plighted troth were perfect all.
But though to court you've forced me here
    to come,
My will is firm; — I'll not with you go home.

2. NO SECOND MARRIAGE FOR ME

In the mid river that cypress boat floats free,
While friends a second marriage press on me,
I see my husband's youthful forehead there,
And on it the twin tufts of falling hair.
Rather than wed again I'll die, I swear!
O mother dear, O Heaven supreme,
    why should
You not allow my vow, and aid my
    purpose good?

Near to the bank that cypress boat floats free,
While friends a second marriage press on me.
He was my only one, with forehead fair,
And on it the twin tufts of falling hair.
Till death to shun the evil thing I swear!
O mother dear, O Heaven supreme,
    why should
You not allow my vow, and aid my
    purpose good?

3. YOUNG LOVE

With axle creaking, all on fire I went,
To fetch my young and lovely bride.
No thirst or hunger pangs my bosom rent,

I only longed to have *her* by my side.
I feast with her, whose virtue fame had told,
Nor need we friends our rapture to behold.

The long-tailed pheasants surest cover find,
Amid the forest on the plain.
Here from my virtuous bride, of noble mind,
And person tall, I wisdom gain.
I praise her while we feast, and to her say,
"The love I bear you ne'er will know decay.

"Poor we may be; spirits and foods fine
My humble means will not afford.
But what we have, we'll taste and not repine;[1]
From us will come no grumbling word.
And though to you no virtue I can add,
Yet we will sing and dance, in spirit glad.

"I oft ascend that lofty ridge with toil,
And hew large branches from the oaks;
Then of their leafy glory them I spoil,
And fagots form with vigorous strokes.
Returning tired, your matchless grace I see,
And my whole soul dissolves in ecstasy.

"To the high hills I looked, and urged
    each steed;
The great road next was smooth and plain.
Up hill, o'er dale, I never slackened speed;
Like lutestring sounded every rein.
I knew, my journey ended, I should come
To you, sweet bride, the comfort of my home."

4. MY BELOVED RETURNS

Cold is the wind, fast falls the rain,
The cock aye shrilly crows.
But I have seen my lord again; —
Now must my heart repose.

Whistles the wind, patters the rain,
The cock's crow far resounds.
But I have seen my lord again,
And healed are my heart's wounds.

All's dark amid the wind and rain,
Ceaseless the cock's clear voice!

---

[1]Complain.

But I have seen my lord again; —
Should not my heart rejoice?

Dressed in a thin white silk, with coiffure gray,
Is she, my wife, my joy in life's low way.

5. MATURE LOVE

My path forth from the east gate lay,
Where cloudlike moved the girls at play.
Numerous are they, as clouds so bright,
But not on them my heart's thoughts light.

Forth by the covering wall's high tower,
I went, and saw, like rush in flower,
Each flaunting girl. Brilliant are they,
But not with them my heart's thoughts stay.
In thin white silk, with headdress
    madder-dyed,
Is she, my sole delight, 'foretime my bride.

▼▼▼

Mute Testimony

Some of the world's earliest civilizations have left written records that we cannot yet decipher and might never be able to read. These include India's Harappan civilization, which was centered in the Indus valley from before 2500 to some time after 1700 B.C.E.; the Minoan civilization of the Aegean island of Crete, which flourished from roughly 2500 to about 1400 B.C.E.; and the African civilization of Kush, located directly south of Egypt, which reached its age of greatness after 800 B.C.E. but with much earlier origins as a state. For many other early civilizations and cultures we have as yet uncovered no written records. This is the case of the mysterious peoples who, between approximately 6000 B.C.E. and the first century C.E., painted and carved thousands of pieces of art on the rocks of Tassili n' Ajjer in what is today the central Saharan Desert. It is also true of the Olmec civilization of Mexico, which appeared around 1200 B.C.E.

The following pieces of artifactual evidence provide glimpses into these often forgotten cultures. As is always the case when dealing with unwritten sources, however, the historian discovers that such clues from the past raise more questions than they answer.

Bringing in the Sheaves
▼▼▼

7 ▼ *A TASSILI ROCK PAINTING*

Tassili n' Ajjer is today a desiccated, largely uninhabited plateau deep in the heart of southern Algeria's Sahara Desert. Its name, however, which translates as "plateau of the rivers," suggests a past quite different from its present condition. Before the Sahara crept into the region about two thousand years ago, Tassili n' Ajjer was a lush area that supported a wide variety of animal species and human cultures. The latter left behind a rich artistic record of over six thousand years of habitation on the plateau.

In 1956 an expedition of French scholars studied and copied more than four thousand rock paintings at Tassili along with an equally impressive number of rock carvings. This art reflects four major cultural stages of the peoples who lived there. The earliest examples of rock paintings reach back to before 6000 B.C.E. and were the products of a preagricultural, gatherer-hunter society. The rock art produced between about 5000 and 1200 B.C.E. was the work of a pastoral people whose cattle figure prominently in their paintings. Around 1200 B.C.E. the horse and chariot appear in Tassili's rock art, evidence of a significant new equine technology due to influences from the Mediterranean. Finally, as the desert was expanding, the domesticated single-humped Arabian camel appears on the faces of these rocks, signifying yet another and now final stage of cultural development for the terminally endangered people of this area.

The painting that appears here is generally interpreted as portraying a group of people harvesting wild grains. It might date anywhere from 4000 to 1500 B.C.E.

QUESTIONS FOR ANALYSIS

1. What appears to be the sex of the harvesters?
2. What does your answer suggest about gender roles in this society?
3. If these are wild grains that are being gathered, what would be the next cultural step?
4. Based on your answer to question 3, what do you think was likelihood that agriculture developed indigenously at Tassili?

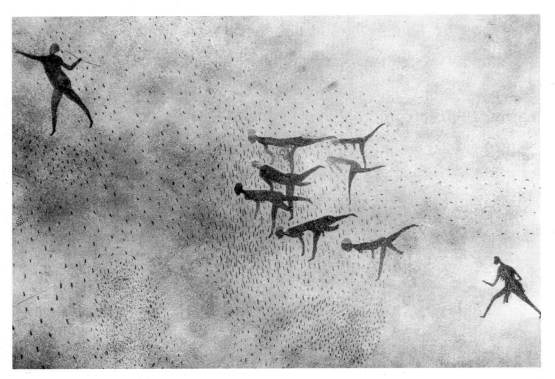

Tassili Rock Painting: Grain Harvesters

Cultural Impressions

▼▼▼

8 ▼ *INDUS, MESOPOTAMIAN, AND CRETAN SEALS*

The stamps and seals that grace the many documents certifying who we are and what we have attained have their origins in the carved magic amulets of prehistory. As official signatures and tokens of authority, seals and stamps have been used by individuals and states since the dawn of civilization. In Mesopotamia carved stone cylinder seals that were rolled into soft clay were used at Uruk and other Sumerian cities as early as 3500 B.C.E. and continued to be produced in large numbers throughout Southwest Asia for the next three thousand years. When papyrus and parchment replaced clay as preferred writing surfaces, stamps and stamp seals replaced cylinder seals in popularity.

Ancient Southwest Asians did not have a monopoly on the use of such marks of ownership, authenticity, and official approval. More than two thousand stamp seals and seal impressions have been discovered at Harappan sites in the Indus valley of what is today the nation of Pakistan. Collectively, the seals contain some four hundred different characters of what appears to be a pictographic form of writing. However, scholars have as yet been unable to crack the code represented by these signs. Happily, the seals contain more than undecipherable words; they contain carved images that allow us to infer something about this largely mysterious civilization.

Our first grouping contains six modern drawings of Indus seal impressions from the period 2100–1750 B.C.E., the age of Harappan cultural maturity. Seal 1 depicts a hairy person holding two tigers by the throat. Seal 2 portrays a horned, tailed, and cloven-foot individual grappling with a horned tiger under a tree. Seal 3 depicts two unicorn (single-horned) animal heads twisted around what appears to be a stylized *pipal,* or fig, tree, the sacred tree of India. Seal 4 shows four human figures somersaulting forward and backward over the raised horns of a bull. Seal 5 shows a humped bull, often called a Brahman bull. Seal 6 presents a male individual with a deeply furrowed or painted face who is wearing a water buffalo-horn headdress, numerous bangles, bracelets, and a V-shaped collar or necklace. The individual is sitting with his knees angled to either side and the soles of his feet pressed together in front of him. His arms extend away from his body and his hands rest on his knees, with fingers pointed downward. Surrounding him are wild animals: a rhinoceros and water buffalo to his left; an elephant and tiger to his right; underneath him are two antelopelike creatures (one is largely broken off; only its horns remain). A stick-figure human also stands or walks to his right.

For reasons of comparison, consider the second group of three seal impressions. Items 7 and 8 are rolled-out impressions from Mesopotamian cylinder seals. Number 7, which is from Sumer and dates to somewhere between 2600 and 2350 B.C.E., depicts two heroes struggling with animals. On the left is a nude, muscular, hairy man fighting two bulls. This is probably Gilgamesh (source 1). On the right is a creature who is half bull and half human grasping two lions. This is probably Gilgamesh's companion Enkidu. Seal 8 was crafted in Akkad in central Mesopotamia in the period 2340–2180 B.C.E. and shows a bull-man on the left and a hairy hero on the right (probably Enkidu and Gilgamesh). Each holds a rampant bull by the mane and tale. The forelegs of each bull touch the top of a stylized mountain and what might be a sacred tree on the mountain.

The final impression (9) is of a seal from the island civilization of Crete. The seal dates to circa 1550–1500 B.C.E. and depicts two bulls and two acrobats. One athlete has just vaulted over a bull, while the second bull leaper stands ready to vault.

(See "Questions for Analysis" on page 36.)

1

4

2

5

3

6

Indus Seals

Mesopotamian Seals

Cretan Seal

QUESTIONS FOR ANALYSIS

1. Seals 2 through 9 contain horned figures. What do you suppose the horn symbolized to these societies? Why, of all horned creatures, do you think the bull figures so prominently in these seals? Based on your answers, what can you infer about the religious and social values of these societies?
2. Consider the hairy males in seals 1, 7, and 8. What does hairiness seem to symbolize in each instance? Again, what do you infer about these societies' religious and social values, based on this evidence?
3. Consider the central figure in seal 6. How do you interpret his posture, and what does your answer suggest about the individual and his function? Consider his dress and the figures that surround him. Do they suggest humanity or divinity? If a human, what is his class? If a god, what sort of god?
4. What can you infer from these seals about possible lines of cultural contact and influence? Who *seems* to have influenced whom and how? On a map, trace the possible routes of cultural exchange.

Sacred Kingship along the Nile
▼▼▼

9 ▼ TWO TEMPLE RELIEFS

It is unclear whether several of the Indus seals we have studied portray humans or deities, but the two temple reliefs (raised carvings on flat backgrounds) that follow clearly depict gods. The piece on the top is Egyptian and dates from the thirteenth century B.C.E. Located at the temple of King Seti I at Abydos in Upper Egypt, it portrays, from right to left, Horus the falcon god, King Seti, and the goddess Isis (see source 3). We will use it solely for comparison with the relief below it. This piece of religious art is Kushite and dates from after 300 B.C.E. It is a small fragment (6½ inches) of a temple tablet from Meroë, a Nubian city considerably distant from Abydos. It portrays a Nubian king of Kush and the lion god Apedemak.

The Nubians, who were black Africans inhabiting the region directly south of Egypt, were drawn into the orbit of their powerful neighbor to the north at an early date. Yet while they borrowed from the Egyptians, the Nubians managed to retain their indigenous culture. Around 800 B.C.E. the Nubians created the independent kingdom of Kush and around 730 B.C.E. were strong enough to conquer Egypt, which Kushite pharaohs ruled for nearly a century. After being driven out of Egypt by the Assyrians, the Kushites eventually established a new capital for their kingdom at Meroë on the Middle Nile. Between about 350 B.C.E. and the early fourth century C.E., Kush was a major economic power in Northeast Africa, largely because of Meroë's rich iron deposits.

In the relief on the right, one of those mighty monarchs of Kush stands face to face with the Nubians' most powerful deity. Unfortunately, we cannot decipher the writing above each figure, so we can only guess at the meaning of this scene. Perhaps the relief of Seti I provides a vital clue. There, Horus, the divine son of

Temple Relief: Seti I and Horus

Temple Relief: Kushite King and Apedemak

Isis, is handing the scepter of power to Seti, who as long as he lives on earth will be identified with Horus, upon whose throne he sits. Note that the Meroitic tablet also portrays both god and king with what appear to be scepters.

QUESTIONS FOR ANALYSIS

1. What do these two sculptures allow us to infer about the nature of royal power in Kush?
2. What do they suggest about the balance that the Kushites struck between accepting Egyptian influences and retaining traditional Nubian ways?

The Were-Jaguar
▼▼▼

10 ▼ FOUR OLMEC STATUETTES

Olmec civilization, which emerged in the gulf region of southeastern Mexico around 1200 B.C.E. and spread out from there, apparently laid the cultural basis for all subsequent pre-Columbian civilizations in Mexico and Central America. Evidence strongly suggests that later societies — such as the Maya, the Toltec, and the Aztec — continued to develop ways of thought and behavior articulated by the Olmec centuries and even millennia earlier.

As far as we know, the Olmec created no written language. We do not even know what they called themselves. The term *Olmec,* which means "People of the Rubber Country," is Aztec in origin and refers to the fact that the Olmec inhabited a tropical, coastal region noted for its rubber trees. Although they left behind no written records, the Olmec bequeathed to posterity a rich artistic heritage, especially stone carvings. Carved in a variety of sizes and motifs, ranging from monumental basalt heads of several tons to delicate jade masks and ornaments, these sculptures allow us to glimpse the world as seen by the Olmec.

One recurring figure in Olmec art is a creature who is part human and part jaguar. Known technically as a *were-jaguar,* this individual appears to have been central to Olmec religion. The following four statuettes, which date from the period circa 900–300 B.C.E., suggest the Olmec fascination with the jaguar, a mostly nocturnal predator.

QUESTIONS FOR ANALYSIS

1. Consider the statuettes in sequence, from 1 through 4. What is happening here?
2. What do you think this sequence of events means? (Hint: Within many Amerindian cultures, *shamans,* who served as intermediaries between the visible and spirit worlds, underwent rituals that they believed enabled them to be transformed into nonhuman {or superhuman] creatures.)
3. Why do you think the were-jaguar was such an important shamanic being?
4. What might these statuettes suggest about the Olmec view of humanity's place in regard to nature?

2

1

4

3

Chapter 2

v̌v̌v̌

New Peoples

The oldest town yet excavated by archeologists is Jericho, which has been inhabited, almost continuously, for the past eleven thousand years. Around 8000 B.C.E. this site, immediately west of the River Jordan, covered more than eight acres and supported a population of over three thousand. Most impressive of all are the town's massive watchtower, walls, and encircling ditch, which serve as silent evidence of the residents' fear of outsiders.

That fear was well based. Archeological evidence shows that Jericho suffered destruction on several occasions, and it is easy to imagine that some of those catastrophes were the handiwork of invading nomads, attracted by the city's wealth.

The tension between wandering pastoral peoples, tending herds of domesticated animals, and settled farmers, who became the backbone of civilization, is as old as agriculture itself, and it continued to be a major factor in global history into the seventeenth century C.E. To be sure, there were many mutually beneficial relationships between civilized communities and the pastoralists who wandered their borders. However, fringe peoples who served as mercenary soldiers, traders, and carriers of new ideas could also be formidable foes, threatening the very existence of some civilizations.

Afro-Eurasian civilizations were subjected to two periods of especially intense pressure from nomadic outsiders prior to 1000 B.C.E. Around 1800 B.C.E. nomads living on the Iranian plateau perfected the two-wheeled chariot. Within the relatively short span of several centuries, groups of pastoralists used this new master weapon to establish a number of warrior kingdoms as far west as Greece and at least as far east as northern India. These peoples included the Greeks of Mycenae, the Hittites of Anatolia, the Kassites and Mitanni of Mesopotamia, the Hyksos of Egypt, and the Aryans of India.

The second age of major nomadic disturbance took place around 1200 B.C.E., as an expanding knowledge of iron metallurgy enabled new fringe groups to challenge many of the now old and tired chariot kingdoms. With plentiful and therefore cheap weapons available to both their external and internal enemies, a number of these civilized societies found themselves fighting for their very survival, and several succumbed. Mycenaean Greece slipped back into a precivilized state after it was overwhelmed by waves of ruder Greek cousins; the mighty Hittite Empire was wiped out and soon became a faded memory. Other regions rode out these invasions with greater resilience. Egypt successfully fought off the invaders but only at great cost. The land of Syria-Palestine experienced invasion and settlement by Philistines, Hebrews, and others, but in the end it managed to absorb all without losing the essential elements of civilization.

Geographic isolation protected China from these Iron Age migrations. Iron would not be produced in China until the sixth century B.C.E. Around 1200 B.C.E., however, the chariot made its appearance in China and was used to great effect by the Zhou in their toppling of the Shang.

Around 1000 B.C.E. the general level of nomadic violence subsided for awhile across Eurasia and North Africa, but the previous eight centuries had seen successive waves of nomads challenge, at times overwhelm, and in a few isolated instances eradicate centers of civilization.

▼▼▼

The Indo-Europeans

Sometime around 2000 B.C.E. and following, pastoral people living on the steppes of western Asia — roughly in the area that lies north of the Caucasus Mountains, between the Black and Caspian Seas — began to migrate out of their traditional grazing lands and, in successive waves, wandered into Europe, Asia Minor, Mesopotamia, Iran, and India. These bronze-armed nomads spoke a variety of related languages that shared a common origin in a prehistoric tongue scholars call *proto-Indo-European.* Through their migrations, these people eventually spread their family of languages from Central Asia to the British Isles. The fact that *Aryan, Eire* (the Gaelic name for the Republic of Ireland), and *Iran* derive from the common archaic root word *aryo,* which means "lord," eloquently attests to the extent of the ancient Indo-European wanderings and settlements.

Among the many significant waves of Indo-European newcomers were the *Aryans,* who spoke Sanskrit, and the *Achaeans,* who spoke an early form of Greek. The Sanskrit speakers moved eastward across the Hindu Kush mountain range and into the fertile Indus valley, where they encountered Harappan civilization. The Greek speakers moved westward into the Balkans, absorbing or displacing the native agricultural people they encountered.

Life, Death, and the Gods in Aryan India
▼▼▼

11 ▼ *THE RIG VEDA*

It is unclear whether the Aryans conquered and destroyed a vigorous Harappan civilization or, what seems more likely, took over a society already in eclipse. Whatever the case, by 1500 B.C.E. the Aryans were ruling northwest India as an illiterate warrior aristocracy, and the Harappan arts of writing and statecraft had disappeared. India would not reemerge into the light of recorded history until around 600 B.C.E.

Because the early Aryans were a preliterate people, what little we know about them we derive from their oral tradition, which survives chiefly in four great collections of priestly hymns, chants, incantations, and ritual formulas known as the *Vedas. Veda* means "wisdom" or "knowledge," and the Aryans accepted these collections of sacred poetry as the eternal word of the gods.

The most celebrated and earliest of the four is the *Rig Veda,* a collection of 1,028 songs, which probably was compiled for the most part between 1200 and 900 B.C.E., although it contains many elements that stretch back to a time long before the Aryans arrived in India. This Sanskrit masterpiece remains, even today, one of the sacred books of Hinduism. It is also the earliest extant major work of literature in an Indo-European tongue, predating by several centuries the Homeric Greek epics.

As is common in preliterate societies, Aryan priests, known as *Brahmins,* were trained to perform prodigious feats of memory. Generation after generation, they sang these songs and passed them on to those who followed. As a result, although the Vedas would not be written down until long after 1000 B.C.E., many of the songs reflect the religious, social, and political realities of Aryan life around 1500 B.C.E. or earlier. Conversely, other vedic hymns were the products of much later centuries and mirror the more sophisticated culture of an emerging Indo-Aryan civilization.

The following three poems illustrate the evolution of Indo-Aryan religious thought. The first celebrates the victory over *Vritra,* the dragon of drought, by *Indra,* the *Rig Veda*'s chief deity. A lusty god of war, Indra was noted for imbibing large amounts of *Soma,* a sacred hallucinogenic drink reserved for the gods and their priests, and his military victories over the *Dasas* (the slaves), the indigenous people of northern India whom the Aryans were subduing. In this particular hymn, however, Indra conquers another foe, Vritra, known as the *Encompasser,* and liberates the universe, which Vritra has swallowed. In his conquest Indra releases life-giving monsoon rains, irrigating waters that were vital to the Aryans, who were now settling down and farming the land. As the Aryans were absorbed into the rich cultural fabric of India, their forms of religious expression also changed. Indra, whose worship was the central reality of early vedic religious life, largely fell out of favor as a major deity in post-Vedic India, becoming simply the god of weather. Our second hymn hints at the change in religious perception that was taking place in later Indo-Aryan society as some Aryans even dared to doubt the very existence of this ancient god of battle. As this second hymn also indicates, the Aryans had originally envisioned Indra as the creator god. Our third hymn, which is clearly one of the last vedic songs to be crafted, presents another vision of creation. In this poem the gods create the universe (and themselves) by sacrificing *Purusha,* the Primeval Man, to himself. The paradoxical view of reality presented in this hymn would become a hallmark of classic Hindu thought, as we shall see in Chapter 3.

QUESTIONS FOR ANALYSIS

1. The hymn regarding the victory over Vritra is the earliest of the three poems. What sort of god is the Indra who appears in poem 1? What does your answer suggest about the society that worshipped him as its chief deity?
2. Compare the Indra of hymn 1 with the Indra whom we see in the second hymn. In what ways has he remained the same? Are there any important attributes ascribed to him in this second hymn that are lacking in the first hymn? If so, what are they? What inferences do you draw from them?
3. What inferences do you draw from the fact that the second hymn seems to have been composed to refute doubts about Indra's very existence? What does this suggest about Indo-Aryan society at that time?
4. What are the clues in the hymn to Purusha that point to its late composition?
5. What evidence is there in hymn 3 for the emergence of what would become the Hindu *caste* system (Chapter 3, source 17), and how is that system explained and justified?
6. Can you find in the hymn to Purusha evidence of the basic Hindu concept of the unity of all life? How is it articulated?
7. If Purusha brings forth all life by self-sacrifice, what does this suggest about the Indo-Aryan view of life and death? Is death a negation of life? Are they mutually exclusive states?
8. Compare Indra and Purusha as deities. In what ways do they represent significant historical changes that took place within Indo-Aryan society?

VICTORY OVER VRITRA

I will declare the manly deeds of Indra, the first that he achieved, the thunder-wielder.

He slew the dragon, then disclosed the waters, and cleft the channels of the mountain torrents.

He slew the dragon lying on the mountain: his heavenly bolt of thunder Twashtar[1] fashioned.

Like lowing cows in rapid flow descending, the waters glided downward to the ocean.

Impetuous as a bull, he chose the Soma, and quaffed in threefold sacrifice the juices.

Maghavan[2] grasped the thunder for his weapon, and smote to death this firstborn of the dragons.

---

[1] The divine artisan.

[2] Lord Bountiful — another name for Indra.

When, Indra, you had slain the dragon's first-born, and overcome the charms of the enchanters.

Then, giving life to sun and dawn and heaven, you found not one foe to stand against you.

Indra with his own great and deadly thunder smote into pieces Vritra worst of Vritras.[3]

As trunks of trees, what time the axe has felled them, low on the earth so lies the prostrate dragon.

He, like a mad weak warrior, challenged Indra, the great impetuous many-slaying hero.

He, brooking not the clashing of the weapons, crushed — Indra's foe — the shattered forts in falling,[4]

Footless and handless still[5] he challenged Indra, who smote him with his bolt between the shoulders.

Emasculated yet claiming manly vigor, thus Vritra lay with scattered limbs dissevered. . . .

Nothing availed him. Lightning, nothing, nor thunder, hailstorm or mist which he had spread around him.[6]

When Indra and the dragon strove in battle, Maghavan gained the victory for ever. . . .

Indra is king of all that moves and moves not, of creatures tame and horned, the thunder-wielder.

Over all living men he rules as sovereign, containing all as spokes within a rim.

WHO IS INDRA?

The god who had insight the moment he was born, the first who protected the gods with his power of thought, before whose hot breath the two world-halves[7] tremble at the greatness of his manly powers — he, my people, is Indra.

He who made fast the tottering earth, who made still the quaking mountains, who measured out and extended the expanse of the air, who propped up the sky — he, my people, is Indra.

He who killed the serpent and loosed the seven rivers, who drove out the cows that had been pent up by Vala,[8] who gave birth to fire between two stones,[9] the winner of booty in combats — he, my people, is Indra.

He by whom all these changes were rung, who drove the race of Dasas down into obscurity, who took away the flourishing wealth of the enemy as a winning gambler takes the stake — he, my people, is Indra.

He about whom they ask, 'Where is he?,' or they say of him, the terrible one, 'He does not exist,' he who diminishes the flourishing wealth of the enemy as a gambler does — believe in him! He, my people, is Indra.

He who encourages the weary and the sick, and the poor priest who is in need, who helps the man who harnesses the stones to press Soma, he who has lips fine for drinking — he, my people, is Indra.

He under whose command are horses and cows and villages and all chariots, who gave birth to the sun and the dawn and led out the waters, he, my people, is Indra.

He who is invoked by both of two armies, enemies locked in combat, on this side and that side, he who is even invoked separately by each of two men standing on the very same chariot,[10] he, my people, is Indra.

---

[3]"Dragon, worst of dragons."
[4]The clouds are pictured as forts imprisoning moisture.
[5]Vritra is serpentlike, lacking feet and hands.
[6]Vritra used magic to surround himself with storms and mist, but they failed him.
[7]Heaven and earth.
[8]A demon who penned up Indra's cows, cows being tokens of wealth among the early Aryans.

[9]Indra is the bringer of fire, which is kindled by striking two flints. He is also the creator of lightning (the fire between [the stones of] heaven and earth) and Soma, which is made by being crushed between stones. He also created the sun, another fire between heaven and earth.
[10]Two persons rode in a war chariot, the priest-charioteer and the warrior-noble (see Chapter 3, source 17).

He without whom people do not conquer, he whom they call on for help when they are fighting, who became the image of everything, who shakes the unshakeable — he, my people, is Indra.

He who killed with his weapon all those who had committed a great sin, even when they did not know it, he who does not pardon the arrogant man for his arrogance, who is the slayer of the Dasyus,[11] he, my people, is Indra.

He who in the fortieth autumn discovered Sambara living in the mountains,[12] who killed the violent serpent, the Danu,[13] as he lay there, he, my people, is Indra.

He, the mighty bull who with his seven reins let loose the seven rivers to flow, who with his thunderbolt in his hand hurled down Rauhina[14] as he was climbing up to the sky, he, my people, is Indra.

Even the sky and the earth bow low before him, and the mountains are terrified of his hot breath; he who is known as the Soma-drinker, with his thunderbolt in his hand, with the thunderbolt in his palm, he, my people, is Indra.

He who helps with his favor the one who presses and the one who cooks,[15] the praiser and the preparer, he for whom prayer is nourishment, for whom Soma is the special gift, he, my people, is Indra.

You[16] who furiously grasp the prize for the one who presses and the one who cooks, you are truly real. Let us be dear to you, Indra, all our days, and let us speak as men of power in the sacrificial gathering.

TO PURUSHA

A thousand heads had Purusha,[17] a thousand eyes, a thousand feet.

He covered earth on every side, and spread ten fingers' breadth beyond.

This Purusha is all that yet has been and all that is to be;

The lord of immortality which waxes greater still by food.

So mighty is his greatness; yea, greater than this is Purusha.

All creatures are one-fourth of him, three-fourths eternal life in heaven.[18]

With three-fourths Purusha went up: one-fourth of him again was here.

Thence he strode out to every side over what eats not and what eats.

From him Viraj[19] was born; again Purusha from Viraj was born.

As soon as he was born he spread eastward and westward o'er the earth.

When gods prepared the sacrifice with Purusha as their offering,

Its oil was spring, the holy gift was autumn; summer was the wood.

They balmed as victim on the grass[20] Purusha born in earliest time.

With him the deities and all Sadhyas[21] and Rishis[22] sacrificed.

---

[11]The Dasas, or slaves.
[12]A demon who kept Soma from Indra in mountain fortresses.
[13]Vritra.
[14]An obscure enemy about whom nothing else is known.
[15]Those who press and those who cook Soma.
[16]Indra.
[17]Purusha, the all-pervading universal spirit and source of all life, is conceived as a god with countless eyes, hands, and feet. Purusha is both limitless and able to be enclosed in the smallest of spaces. In an act celebrated by this poem, Purusha is simultaneously the sacrifice and the sacrificer.
[18]One-quarter of Purusha is found in all mortal creation; three-fourths of Purusha is divine and eternal.
[19]The female creative germ.
[20]Special grasses laid out during vedic sacrifices for the gods to sit upon.
[21]A class of demigods.
[22]Sages.

From that great general sacrifice the dripping fat was gathered up.

He formed the creatures of the air, and animals both wild and tame.

From that great general sacrifice Richas and Samahymns[23] were born:

Therefrom the meters were produced,[24] the Yajus[25] had its birth from it.

From it were horses born, from it all creatures with two rows of teeth:

From it were generated cows, from it the goats and sheep were born.

When they divided Purusha how many portions did they make?

What do they call his mouth, his arms? What do they call his thighs and feet?

The Brahmin[26] was his mouth, of both his arms was the Rajanya[27] made.

His thighs became the Vaisya,[28] from his feet the Sudra[29] was produced.

The Moon was gendered from his mind, and from his eye the Sun had birth;

Indra and Agni[30] from his mouth were born, and Vayu[31] from his breath.

Forth from his navel came mid-air; the sky was fashioned from his head;

Earth from his feet, and from his ear the regions. Thus they formed the worlds.

Seven fencing-logs had he, thrice seven layers of fuel were prepared,[32]

When the gods, offering sacrifice, bound, as their victim, Purusha.

Gods, sacrificing, sacrificed the victim: these were the earliest holy ordinances.

The mighty ones attained the height of heaven, there where the Sadhyas, gods of old, are dwelling.

---

[23]The constituent elements of the *Rig Veda*.
[24]The verses of the *Sama Veda*. The *Sama Veda* is largely a collection of elements from the *Rig Veda* arranged for religious ceremonial use.
[25]The ritual formulas of the *Yajur Veda*. It was compiled a century or two after the *Rig Veda* and served as a collection of sacrificial chants.
[26]An Aryan priest.
[27]The *Rajanyas*, or *Kshatriyas*, comprised the ruling or warrior class.

[28]This class initially encompassed free herders and farmers; later it included traders and artisans.
[29]The slave and servant class. The term was originally applied to the Dasas, the native people whom the Aryans conquered and subjugated when they entered India.
[30]The god of fire and sacrifice. This Sanskrit word is cognate with *ignis,* the Latin word for "fire" (hence, *ignite* in English).
[31]The wind.
[32]For a sacrificial fire.

A Journey to the Underworld
▼▼▼

12 ▼ *Homer, THE ODYSSEY*

By 1600 B.C.E. history's first identifiable Greeks, a people who called themselves the *Achaeans,* had created in the Balkan Peninsula a decentralized, warrior civilization, which we term *Mycenaean.* The name derives from *Mycenae,* a city that exercised a loose leadership over the petty principalities of southern and central Greece. Around 1450 B.C.E. the Achaeans were masters of the island civilization of Crete and, as accomplished pirates and maritime merchants, a major force in the eastern Mediterranean. It is against this background that we must place the Achaean expedition against Troy, a city in Anatolia (modern Asiatic Turkey), which took place around 1260.

The sack of rival Troy was the high-water mark for the Achaeans. Within a century Mycenaean civilization was collapsing, at least in part, it appears, because of internecine wars among the various Achaean principalities. What other factors were involved remain a mystery. By 1100 B.C.E. the arts and crafts, including literacy, that had characterized Bronze Age Greece at its height had disappeared or were severely reduced in quality and quantity. Greece had entered a period we call the *Greek Dark Age* (ca. 1100–ca. 800), a term that, more than anything else, implies our overall ignorance of what was happening in the Greek world during these centuries. About all we can say with any degree of certainty is that the Greeks lost the art of writing, their political and economic structures seem to have been drastically reduced in size, and a relatively weak and impoverished Greek world ceased, for awhile, to be a major power in the eastern Mediterranean. At the same time, however, recent archeological finds have tended to underscore the continuities between late Mycenaean society and the classical Hellenic world that arose after 750 B.C.E.

When Greek literacy and high civilization reemerged around the middle of the eighth century B.C.E., it was centered along the western shores of Anatolia in a region known as *Ionia,* where Greek colonists had settled during the so-called Dark Age. Here, across the Aegean Sea, Greek settlers, benefiting from their contact with the far older civilizations of Southwest Asia (and to a lesser extent Egypt), produced the first Greek literature known to us (as opposed to the bureaucratic lists left behind by Mycenaean civilization). Of all of this early literature, the most significant are two epic poems, the *Iliad* and the *Odyssey,* both ascribed to a bard called *Homer*.

The ancients had no doubt there was a historical Homer who created both works. Modern scholars are less certain, and most would probably agree that we will never know the truth regarding Homer's identity. Arguments from internal evidence (the words, phrases, and allusions within each poem) have led many scholars to posit the theory that Homer was at least two different persons. According to this view, two eighth-century Asiatic Greeks, living a generation or more apart, orally composed the epics. Each poet crafted a single, coherent work of art. The first genius created the *Iliad;* the later genius created the *Odyssey*. Neither epic poet, however, worked in a vacuum or produced a totally new work of art. Rather, in their acts of creation, both drew heavily from a long tradition of oral poetic stories preserved in the memories of wandering professional bards. A century or more later — that is, after 650 and possibly closer to 550 B.C.E. — the two epics were finally written down in basically the forms we know them today. Other modern scholars dismiss this scenario and favor seeing both poems as products of a long, gradual, and unchartable process of compilation by numerous anonymous singers of heroic tales.

Whatever the process of their creation, when used judiciously, the two epics tell us a good deal about life in the thirteenth century B.C.E. — the age of the

Trojan War. At the same time, the poems also reveal a lot of the values and modes of perception of Late Dark Age society, especially that of the ninth and eighth centuries. The problem facing the historian is to separate one from the other.

On one level both poems celebrate such warrior virtues as personal honor, bravery, and loyalty to one's comrades, and on a deeper level they probe the hidden recesses of human motivation and emotion. On a third level the poems address the issue of the meaning of human suffering: Why do humans experience pain and sorrow? Are they captive to the whims of the gods? Are they and the gods subject to an overarching destiny that neither can avoid?

More to human scale than the *Iliad,* the *Odyssey* tells two intertwined stories. One traces the ten-year-long homeward voyage of the Achaean hero *Odysseus.* This clever adventurer has to battle, with cunning and skill, the enmity of Poseidon, god of the sea, and a variety of superhuman opponents before finally arriving home to his island kingdom of Ithaca. The second story details the attempts of Odysseus's wife and son, Penelope and Telemarchus, who with equal cunning and skill attempt to stall indefinitely the advances of a group of suitors who seek to marry the presumed widow. As the suitors impatiently wait to see whom she will marry, they despoil Odysseus and Penelope's home and waste Telemarchus's patrimony. The two story lines merge when Odysseus returns and, with the aid of his son and several loyal servants, wreaks vengeance on the suitors by killing them all. Unlike most epics, the story ends happily, with Penelope and Odysseus reunited and Telemarchus assured of his inheritance.

The following selection describes one of Odysseus's most daring adventures on his troubled homeward journey: a visit to the House of Hades, or the Land of the Dead. Here he consults Teiresias, the blind Theban seer, and also meets the shades of many famous women and men, including his old comrade-in-arms Achilles, the Achaeans' greatest warrior and the central character of the *Iliad,* who was killed prior to the fall of Troy.

QUESTIONS FOR ANALYSIS

1. What values did Odysseus's society hold in highest esteem?
2. How does Homer address the issue of human responsibility for ill fortune?
3. Is there a destiny humans cannot escape?
4. What role do the gods play in this destiny?
5. It is often stated that the Greeks focused on human beings and human concerns. Does this selection seem to support or contradict that judgment?
6. Compare Achilles's sentiment toward the land of the dead with Enkidu's vision in *The Epic of Gilgamesh* (Chapter 1, source 1). What do you conclude from your analysis?
7. Compare Greek society with that of the Aryans. Which strike you as more significant, the similarities or the differences? What do you conclude from your answer?

Now the spirit of Teiresias of Thebes came forward, bearing a golden staff in his hand. Knowing who I am, he addressed me: "Son of Laertes, sprung from Zeus,[1] Odysseus, known for your many wiles, why, unhappy man, have you left the sunlight to behold the dead in this cheerless region? Step back from the trench and put aside your sharp sword so that I might drink the blood[2] and thereby prophesy the truth to you." Thus he spoke. I, stepping backward, drove my silver-studded sword into its scabbard. When he had drunk the black blood, this noble prophet addressed me with these words.

"Lord Odysseus, you seek a honey-sweet homeward journey, but a god will make your travels difficult. I do not think you can escape the notice of the Earth-shaker,[3] who has set his mind in enmity against you, enraged because you blinded his beloved son.[4] Even so, you still might be able to reach home, although in sorry circumstances, if you are willing to restrain your desires, and those of your comrades, beginning when your seaworthy ship leaves the deep blue waters and approaches the island of Thrinacie,[5] where you will see the grazing cattle and fat sheep of Helios,[6] who sees and hears everything. If you leave the animals untouched and concentrate solely on getting home, it is possible that all of you might reach Ithaca, although in sorry circumstances. If you injure these animals, however, I foresee destruction for your ship and its crew, and even if you yourself manage to escape, you will return home late, in a sorry state, in an alien ship, having lost all your companions.[7] And even there at home you will find troubles. Overbearing men will be consuming your wealth, wooing your goddesslike wife, and offering her bridal gifts. Certainly, following your arrival, you will gain revenge on these suitors for their evil deeds. When you have slain the suitors in your halls, whether by stratagem or in an open fight with sharp bronze weapons, you must again set out on a journey. You must take a well-fashioned oar and travel until you reach a people who are ignorant of the sea and never eat food mixed with salt, and who know nothing about our purple-ribbed ships and the well-fashioned oars that serve as ships wings. And I say you will receive a sign, a very clear one that you cannot miss. When another traveler upon meeting you remarks that you are carrying a winnowing-fan across your broad back,[8] plant your well-fashioned oar in the earth and offer Lord Poseidon the sacrifice of a ram, a bull,[9] and a boar, the mate of the wild she-swine. Then return home and there make sacred offerings to all the immortal gods who inhabit wide heaven, and do so to each in order of rank. As for death, it will come to you at last gently out of the sea in a comfortable old age when you are surrounded by a prosperous people. This I tell you truly." . . .

Next came the spirits of Achilles, son of Peleus, of Patroclus,[10] of noble Antilochus,[11] and of Aias,[12] who surpassed all the Danaans[13] in beauty of physique and manly bearing, except for the flawless son of Peleus.[14] The spirit of swift-footed Achilles of the house of Aeacus[15] recognized me, and mournfully spoke in winged words: "Son of

---

[1]The greatest of the Greek gods. The title implies Odysseus's godlike heroic qualities.
[2]The spirits of the dead can communicate with Odysseus only after drinking blood from animals he has sacrificed.
[3]Poseidon, god of the sea and of earthquakes.
[4]The Cyclops, a son of Poseidon, was a one-eyed, cannibal giant whom Odysseus had blinded in self-defense.
[5]Identified by ancient Greeks as the island of Sicily.
[6]The sun god.
[7]The crew will kill and eat the sun god's flocks, and all, except Odysseus, will die as a result.
[8]Odysseus is in a region where no one knows what an oar's function is.

[9]The bull was sacred to Poseidon. (See Chapter 1, source 8 for examples of the popularity of the bull as a sacred animal.)
[10]Achilles's best friend, who also died at Troy.
[11]An Achaean hero who fell at Troy while defending his father, King Nestor of Pylos (note 20).
[12]The Achaeans' second-greatest warrior; he committed suicide at Troy.
[13]Another name for the Achaeans.
[14]Achilles.
[15]The ancestor from whom Peleus and his son Achilles were descended. Homer's heroes always identified themselves by reference to their fathers and other notable ancestors.

Laertes, sprung from Zeus, Odysseus, known for your many wiles! Rash man, what greater deed than this remains for you to devise in your heart? How did you dare to descend to Hades'[16] realm, where the dead dwell as witless images of worn-out mortals?"

Thus he spoke, and I answered in return. "Achilles, son of Peleus, by far the mightiest of the Achaeans, I came to consult with Teiresias in the hope of his giving me a plan whereby I might reach rocky Ithaca. For I have not yet come near the land of Achaea,[17] nor yet set foot on my own island, but have been constantly beset by misfortunes. How different from your situation, Achilles, you who are more fortunate than any man whoever was or will be. For in the old days, when you were alive, we Argives[18] honored you as though you were a god, and now that you are here, you rule nobly among the dead. Therefore, grieve not, Achilles, that you are dead."

So I spoke, and he immediately answered, saying: "Do not endeavor to speak soothingly to me of death, Lord Odysseus. I would rather live on earth as the hired help of some landless man whose own livelihood was meager, than be lord over all the dead who have perished. Enough of that. Tell me about my son, that lordly young man. Did he follow me to war and play a leading role in it? And tell me about noble Peleus. . . . I am not there in the sunlight to aid Peleus with that great strength that was once mine on the broad plains of Troy, where I slew the best of the enemy's army in defense of the Argives. If, but for an hour, I could return to my father's house with such strength as I once had, I would give those who do him violence and dishonor him cause to rue my might and my invincible hands."

So he spoke, and I answered: "I have heard nothing about noble Peleus, but I will give you all the news you desire of your dear son, Neoptolemus. It was I who brought him from Scyros[19] in my well-fashioned, hollow ship to join the ranks of the well-armed Achaeans. Whenever we held a council meeting during the siege of Troy, he was always the first to speak, and his words never missed the mark. God-like Nestor[20] and I alone surpassed him. As often as we fought with bronze weapons on the Trojan plain, he never lagged behind in the ranks or crowd, but would always run far out in front, yielding first place to no one, and he slew many men in mortal combat. I could not name all whom he killed in defense of the Argives. . . . Again, when we, the best of the Argives, were about to enter into the horse that Epeus made,[21] and responsibility lay solely with me to either open or keep closed the door of our stout-built ambush, the other Danaan leaders and chieftains were wiping away tears from their eyes and each man's limbs shook beneath him. But never did my eyes see his fair face grow pale, nor did I see him wiping away tears from his cheeks. Rather, he earnestly begged me to allow him to sally forth from the horse, and he kept handling his sword-hilt and his heavy bronze spear in his eagerness to inflict harm on the Trojans. Following our sack of the lofty city of Priam,[22] he boarded his ship with a full share of the spoils and his special prize.[23] And he was unscathed, never cut by a sharp sword or wounded in close combat, as often happens in war, since Ares[24] rages in a confused fashion."

So I spoke, and the spirit of the son of Aeacus departed with long strides across the field of asphodel,[25] rejoicing that his son was preeminent among men.

---

[16]The god of the dead.
[17]The land of the Achaeans.
[18]Another name for the Achaeans.
[19]The Aegean island where Achilles's son had been raised.
[20]The aged king of Pylos noted for his wisdom and sage advice.
[21]The so-called Trojan horse, through which the Achaeans finally were able to capture Troy.

[22]The last king of Troy.
[23]At the division of the Trojan survivors, Neoptolemus was awarded Andromache, widow of Hector, Troy's greatest hero, whom Achilles had killed in single combat (see Chapter 4, source 29).
[24]The god of war.
[25]A flower that carpeted the Elysian Fields, where the spirits of dead heroes, such as Achilles, resided.

▼▼▼

The Hebrews and Their Neighbors

Recent excavations at the site of the long-forgotten city of Ebla in the modern nation of Syria reveal that the land of Syria-Palestine, which serves as a land bridge between Egypt and Mesopotamia, has known civilization since about 3000 B.C.E. As is the fate of most small lands that lie next to more powerful neighbors, the region has historically been prey to invaders. Its earliest known conqueror was Sargon the Great of Akkad in Mesopotamia, who sacked Ebla sometime before 2300 B.C.E.

Around 1200 B.C.E., in the midst of the great nomadic upheavals that were testing all the civilizations of the Middle East, several different invaders penetrated the lands of Syria-Palestine and established themselves at the expense of the indigenous Canaanite population. One of these was a mixed group of invaders from the Mediterranean, who settled down in cities along the coast of what is today the state of Israel. These people, who included a large percentage of uprooted Greeks and Cretans, became known as the *Philistines. A* second major wave was comprised of another hybrid mass of people who spoke a language that belongs to a family of tongues we term *Semitic.* These people, known as the *Hebrews,* infiltrated the region from the southern and eastern deserts and settled the inland high ground overlooking the Philistine cities.

Prior to the waves of nomadic invaders of around 1200, the Hittite and Egyptian Empires had fought one another for mastery over Syria-Palestine. With the destruction of Hittite civilization and the concurrent severe weakening of the Egyptian Empire, a momentary power vacuum occurred along the eastern rim of the Mediterranean. In the absence of any outside imperial power, the various cultural groups of Syria-Palestine had several centuries of relative freedom in which to struggle with one another and to amalgamate.

For the Hebrews, amalgamation was both seductively easy and potentially disastrous. The vast majority of the various peoples who already inhabited this land known as *Canaan* were, like the Hebrews, Semites. Hebrews and Canaanites spoke related languages that had a common place of origin (probably the Arabian Peninsula before 3000 B.C.E.), and they shared many other cultural similarities. As the Hebrews coalesced as a people, however, they evolved the idea that they enjoyed the special protection of a god they called *YHWH* (probably pronounced "Yahveh"). In return for that protection, this deity demanded their sole devotion. A corollary of that belief was the conviction that if the Hebrews were to prosper in Canaan, which YHWH had promised them, they had to maintain religious (and therefore cultural) distance from all other people.

Establishing a Covenant with Humanity
▼▼▼
13 ▼ *THE BOOK OF GENESIS*

The major documentary source for both the process of cultural fusion and the fierce struggles that took place among the various groups of Iron Age settlers in Syria-Palestine is a collection of sacred Hebrew writings known as the *Bible* (from the Greek word *biblos,* which means "book"). The exclusively Hebrew, or Jewish, portion of the Bible, known to Jews as the *Tanakh* but called by Christians the *Old Testament,* consists of many different types of literature. These were mainly composed, edited, and reedited from roughly 1000 B.C.E. to possibly as late as the second century B.C.E., although Jewish religious authorities did not fix the *Tanakh*'s final canon, or official body of accepted texts, until 100 C.E. This means that biblical accounts of early Hebrew history are, in many cases, centuries removed from the events they narrate. It is nevertheless clear that these later authors often used early written and oral sources that are now lost to us. Moreover, although these authors primarily wrote history from a theological perspective and consequently clothed their stories in myth, independent archeological evidence has often confirmed the basic historical outline of many but not all of the biblical stories concerning the fortunes of the Hebrews in Canaan, the Promised Land.

The first book of the Bible is known as *Genesis* (the beginning) and recounts the story of humanity's relationship with YHWH from Creation through the settlement of the Hebrew people, known as the *Children of Israel,* in Egypt. Tradition ascribes its authorship to Moses, who lived during the thirteenth century B.C.E., but within the context of the culture of ancient Israel this did not necessarily mean that Moses actually wrote or dictated the book. Rather, he was the one who provided the initial and pervading spirit behind the work. In all likelihood, a number of different authors composed and reworked Genesis over the period from before 900 to after 721 B.C.E.

The following selection recounts a popular Southwest Asian theme that we saw in Chapter 1: the Flood. As you read it, be aware not only of the striking similarities between it and the story told by Utnapishtim but of the even more significant differences. Remember that the author is making a religious statement.

QUESTIONS FOR ANALYSIS

1. Can you find any inconsistencies in this text in regard to the numbers of animals brought into the ark? What does this suggest about the story's creation process?
2. Why does YHWH destroy all humanity except Noah and his family? How does YHWH's reasoning compare with the Mesopotamian gods' reason for wanting to destroy humans and Ea's decision to warn Utnapishtim (Chapter 1, source 1)?

3. Compare YHWH's treatment of Noah and his descendants after the Flood with the Mesopotamian gods' treatment of Utnapishtim after the waters had receded.

4. What do the Mesopotamian gods demand of humans? What does Noah's God demand?

5. From these several comparisons, what picture emerges of the God of the Hebrews? In what ways is their deity similar to the gods of Mesopotamia? In what ways does their god differ?

6. YHWH establishes a covenant, or agreement, with all humanity, and indeed with all living creation, through Noah. What is that covenant?

7. Consider the story of Noah's curse on Canaan. What has Ham done to deserve such anger, and why is it that his son suffers as a consequence? Do your answers tell us anything about Hebrew social values and practices at this time? How is the story of the curse relevant to the Hebrews' settlement in the land of Canaan? What does this suggest about the story's date of composition? How does this illustrate the Hebrews' use of myth to explain and justify historical events?

8. How might we explain the fact that both the Mesopotamians and the Hebrews had flood stories as part of their mythology? Does the Hebrews' belief that Abraham, father of all Hebrews, was born in the Sumerian city of Ur provide a clue?

The Lord saw that the wickedness of man was great in the earth, and that every imagination of the thoughts of his heart was only evil continually. And the Lord was sorry that he had made man on the earth, and it grieved him to his heart. So the Lord said, "I will blot out man whom I have created from the face of the ground, man and beast and creeping things and birds of the air, for I am sorry that I have made them." But Noah found favor in the eyes of the Lord. . . .

Noah was a righteous man, blameless in his generation; Noah walked with God. And Noah had three sons, Shem,[1] Ham, and Japheth.

Now the earth was corrupt in God's sight, and the earth was filled with violence. And God saw the earth, and behold, it was corrupt; for all flesh had corrupted their way upon the earth. And God said to Noah, "I have determined to make an end of all flesh; for the earth is filled with vio-

lence through them; behold, I will destroy them with the earth. Make yourself an ark of gopher wood; make rooms in the ark, and cover it inside and out with pitch. . . . For behold, I will bring a flood of waters upon the earth, to destroy all flesh in which is the breath of life from under heaven; everything that is on the earth shall die. But I will establish my covenant with you; and you shall come into the ark, you, your sons, your wife, and your sons' wives with you. And of every living thing of all flesh, you shall bring two of every sort into the ark, to keep them alive with you; they shall be male and female. Of the birds according to their kinds, and of the animals according to their kinds, of every creeping thing of the ground according to its kind, two of every sort shall come in to you, to keep them alive. Also take with you every sort of food that is eaten, and store it up; and it shall serve as food

[1]Shem was the eldest of Noah's sons and the one from whom the Hebrews claimed direct descent. The term *Semite* (one who speaks any Semitic language, such as Akkadian, Assyrian, Hebrew, and Arabic) is derived from the name.

for you and for them." Noah did this; he did all that God commanded him.

Then the Lord said to Noah, "Go into the ark, you and all your household, for I have seen that you are righteous before me in this generation. Take with you seven pairs of all clean animals,[2] the male and his mate; and a pair of the animals that are not clean, the male and his mate; and seven pairs of the birds of the air also, male and female, to keep their kind alive upon the face of all the earth. For in seven days I will send rain upon the earth forty days and forty nights; and every living thing that I have made will blot out from the face of the ground." And Noah did all that the Lord had commanded him.

Noah was six hundred years old when the flood of waters came upon the earth. And Noah and his sons and his wife and his sons' wives with him went into the ark, to escape the waters of the flood. Of clean animals, and of animals that are not clean, and of birds, and of everything that creeps on the ground, two and two, male and female, went into the ark with Noah, as God had commanded Noah. And after seven days the waters of the flood came upon the earth.

In the six hundredth year of Noah's life, in the second month, on the seventeenth day of the month, on that day all the fountains of the great deep burst forth, and the windows of the heavens were opened.[3] And rain fell upon the earth forty days and forty nights. . . .

And the waters prevailed so mightily upon the earth that all the high mountains under the whole heaven were covered. . . . He blotted out every living thing that was upon the face of the ground, man and animals and creeping things and birds of the air; they were blotted out from the earth. Only Noah was left, and those that were with him in the ark. And the waters prevailed upon the earth a hundred and fifty days.

But God remembered Noah and all the beasts and all the cattle that were with him in the ark. And God made a wind blow over the earth, and the waters subsided; the fountains of the deep and the windows of the heavens were closed, the rain from the heavens was restrained, and the waters receded from the earth continually. At the end of a hundred and fifty days the waters had abated; and in the seventh month, on the seventeenth day of the month, the ark came to rest upon the mountains of Ararat. And the waters continued to abate until the tenth month; in the tenth month, on the first day of the month, the tops of the mountains were seen.

At the end of forty days Noah opened the window of the ark which he had made, and sent forth a raven; and it went to and fro until the waters were dried up from the earth. Then he sent forth a dove from him, to see if the waters had subsided from the face of the ground; but the dove found no place to set her foot, and she returned to him to the ark, for the waters were still on the face of the whole earth. So he put forth his hand and took her and brought her into the ark with him. He waited another seven days, and again he sent forth the dove out of the ark; and the dove came back to him in the evening, and lo, in her mouth a freshly plucked olive leaf; so Noah knew that the waters had subsided from the earth. Then he waited another seven days, and sent forth the dove; and she did not return to him any more.

In the six hundred and first year,[4] in the first month, the first day of the month, the waters were dried from off the earth; and Noah removed the covering of the ark, and looked, and behold, the face of the ground was dry. . . . Then God said to Noah, "Go forth from the ark, you and your wife, and your sons and your sons' wives with you. Bring forth with you every living thing

---

[2]A ritually clean animal, such as a sheep, was one worthy of sacrifice to YHWH. An unclean animal, such as a predator or a scavenger, would never be offered in sacrifice.

[3]The view of the world shared by the peoples of Southwest Asia at this time was that the world's firmament, or land,

was totally surrounded, above and below, by water. The water above was normally kept in place by a translucent crystalline sphere. Rain was the seepage of water through that sphere.

[4]Of Noah's life.

that is with you of all flesh — birds and animals and every creeping thing that creeps on the earth — that they may breed abundantly on the earth, and be fruitful and multiply upon the earth." So Noah went forth, and his sons and his wife and his sons' wives with him. And every beast, every creeping thing, and every bird, everything that moves upon the earth, went forth by families out of the ark.

Then Noah built an altar to the Lord, and took of every clean animal and of every clean bird, and offered burnt offerings on the altar. And when the Lord smelled the pleasing odor, the Lord said in his heart, "I will never again curse the ground because of man, for the imagination of man's heart is evil from his youth; neither will I ever again destroy every living creature as I have done. While the earth remains, seedtime and harvest, cold and heat, summer and winter, day and night, shall not cease."

And God blessed Noah and his sons, and said to them, "Be fruitful and multiply, and fill the earth. The fear of you and the dread of you shall be upon every beast of the earth, and upon every bird of the air, upon everything that creeps on the ground and all the fish of the sea; into your hand they are delivered. Every moving thing that lives shall be food for you; and as I gave you the green plants, I give you everything. Only you shall not eat flesh with its life, that is, its blood.[5] For your lifeblood I will surely require a reckoning; of every beast I will require it and of man; of every man's brother I will require the life of man. Whoever sheds the blood of man, by man shall his blood be shed; for God made man in his own image. And you, be fruitful and multiply, bring forth abundantly on the earth and multiply in it."

Then God said to Noah and to his sons with him, "Behold, I establish my covenant with you and your descendants after you, and with every living creature that is with you, the birds, the cattle, and every beast of the earth with you, as many as came out of the ark. I establish my covenant with you, that never again shall all flesh be cut off by the waters of a flood, and never again shall there be a flood to destroy the earth." And God said, "This is the sign of the covenant which I make between me and you and every living creature that is with you, for all future generations: I set my bow[6] in the cloud, and it shall be a sign of the covenant between me and the earth. When I brink clouds over the earth and the bow is seen in the clouds, I will remember my covenant which is between me and you and every living creature of all flesh; and the waters shall never again become a flood to destroy all flesh. When the bow is in the clouds, I will look upon it and remember the everlasting covenant between God and every living creature of all flesh that is upon the earth." God said to Noah, "This is the sign of the covenant which I have established between me and all flesh that is upon the earth."

The sons of Noah who went forth from the ark were Shem, Ham, and Japheth. Ham was the father of Canaan. These three were the sons of Noah; and from these the whole earth was peopled.

Noah was the first tiller of the soil. He planted a vineyard; and he drank of the wine, and became drunk, and lay uncovered in his tent. And Ham, the father of Canaan, saw the nakedness of his father, and told his two brothers outside. Then Shem and Japheth took a garment, laid it upon both their shoulders, and walked backward and covered the nakedness of their father; their faces were turned away, and they did not see their father's nakedness. When Noah awoke from his wine and knew what his youngest son had done to him, he said

"Cursed be Canaan;
a slave of slaves shall he be to
his brothers."[7]

---

[5]Raw meat or meat dripping with blood could not be consumed.

[6]A rainbow. Compare this with Ishtar's rainbow (Chapter 1, source 1).

[7]According to Hebrew legend, Ham and his son Canaan were the direct ancestors of the Canaanites, the people whom the Hebrews were dispossessing of their lands.

He also said,

"Blessed by the Lord my God be Shem;
and let Canaan be his slave.
God enlarge Japheth,
and let him dwell in the tents of Shem;[8]
and let Canaan be his slave."

---

[8]Japheth, according to Hebrew tradition, was the ancestor of the Indo-European peoples of northern Syria and beyond, such as the Hittites and Hurrians. From the Hebrew perspective, the Hebrews and the northern Indo-Europeans were dividing up the land of Syria-Palestine between them.

After the flood Noah lived three hundred and fifty years. All the days of Noah were nine hundred and fifty years; and he died.

Establishing a Covenant with the Chosen People
▼▼▼
14 ▼ *THE BOOK OF DEUTERONOMY*

The story of Noah tells of YHWH's post-Deluge covenant with all living creatures; the story of the Hebrews' *Exodus* (flight) from Egypt tells of their special Covenant with this god and their becoming a Chosen People with a new identity. The Hebrews had probably entered Egypt in the time of the Hyksos' conquest of that land. With the overthrow of the Hyksos and the reestablishment of native Egyptian rule around 1570 B.C.E., significant numbers of Hebrews were enslaved. Probably during the reign of Ramesses the Great (r. 1279–1213 B.C.E.), a charismatic leader known as *Moses* led a band of these Hebrews out of Egypt into Canaan. In the process of this migration, he molded them into a people and wedded them to his god YHWH. No longer a loose band of nomads, they were now the *Israelites* — descendants of the patriarchs Abraham, Isaac, and Jacob (also called *Israel*).

The story of this thirteenth-century transformation is told in several books of the Bible. This selection comes from Deuteronomy, which, in its present form, dates from the reign of King Josiah of Jerusalem (r. 640–609 B.C.E.). It was composed or, more likely, recast at a time of religious reformation, when Josiah was attempting to abolish all forms of pagan worship in his kingdom, especially the practices of the Assyrians. Although Deuteronomy, as we know it, is essentially a seventh-century creation, it is doubtlessly based on sources that date from the time of Moses.

The setting of our excerpt is the frontier of Canaan, which, according to the story of the Exodus, the Israelites reached after forty years of wandering in the desert. Moses, realizing he will die before his people cross the Jordan River into the Promised Land, delivers a final message to them.

QUESTIONS FOR ANALYSIS

1. What is the Covenant between YHWH and the people of Israel? What does God promise and demand in return? What does YHWH threaten for those who break the Covenant?
2. Consider YHWH's promises again. What does YHWH have to say about rewards after death? What do you infer from your answer?
3. Compare this Covenant with that given after the Flood. How, if at all, do they differ, and what do those differences suggest?
4. Which elements of Moses' message would the religious reformers of seventh-century Jerusalem wish to emphasize?
5. Compare the Ten Commandments with the *Judgments of Hammurabi* (Chapter 1, source 2). Which strike you as more significant, the similarities or the differences? What do you conclude from your answer?
6. Compare these Ten Commandments with the Egyptian "Negative Confession" (Chapter 1, source 3). Which strike you as more significant, the similarities or the differences? What do you conclude from your answer?

And Moses summoned all Israel,[1] and said to them, "Hear, O Israel, the statutes and the ordinances which I speak in your hearing this day, and you shall learn them and be careful to do them. The Lord our God made a covenant with us in Horeb.[2] Not with our fathers did the Lord make this covenant, but with us, who are all of us here alive this day. The Lord spoke with you face to face at the mountain, out of the midst of the fire, while I stood between the Lord and you at that time, to declare to you the word of the Lord; for you were afraid because of the fire, and you did not go up into the mountain. He said:

"'I am the Lord your God, who brought you out of the land of Egypt, out of the house of bondage.

"'You shall have no other gods before me.

"'You shall not make for yourself a graven image, or any likeness of anything that is in heaven above, or that is on the earth beneath, or that is in the water under the earth; you shall not bow down to them or serve them; for I the Lord your God am a jealous God, visiting the iniquity of the fathers upon the children to the third and fourth generation of those who hate me, but showing steadfast love to thousands of those who love me and keep my commandments.

"'You shall not take the name of the Lord your God in vain: for the Lord will not hold him guiltless who takes his name in vain.

"'Observe the sabbath day, to keep it holy, as the Lord your God commanded you. Six days you shall labor, and do all your work; but the seventh day is a sabbath to the Lord your God; in it you shall not do any work, you, or your son, or your daughter, or your manservant, or your maidservant, or your ox, or your ass, or any of your cattle, or the sojourner who is within your gates, that your manservant and your maidservant may rest as well as you. You shall remember that you were a servant in the land of Egypt, and the Lord your God brought you out thence with a mighty

---

[1]The Hebrews referred to themselves as *Israel* and also as the *Children of Israel* and the *Israelites* because they traced their lineage to Jacob, whose name God had changed to *Israel* (God rules). Jacob, the grandson of Abraham and the son of Isaac, had twelve sons, each of whom became the patriarch of one of the twelve tribes of the Children of Israel.

[2]Also known as *Mount Sinai.* Here Moses had received the Law from YHWH, during the period of desert wandering.

hand and an outstretched arm; therefore the Lord your God commanded you to keep the sabbath day.

"'Honor your father and your mother, as the Lord your God commanded you; that your days may be prolonged, and that it may go well with you, in the land which the Lord your God gives you.

"'You shall not kill.

"'Neither shall you commit adultery.

"'Neither shall you steal.

"'Neither shall you bear false witness against your neighbor.

"'Neither shall you covet your neighbor's wife; and you shall not desire your neighbor's house, his field, or his manservant, or his maidservant, his ox, or his ass, or anything that is your neighbor's.'

"These words the Lord spoke to all your assembly at the mountain out of the midst of the fire, the cloud, and the thick darkness, with a loud voice; and he added no more. And he wrote them upon two tables of stone, and gave them to me. . . .

"Now this is the commandment, the statutes and the ordinances which the Lord your God commanded me to teach you, that you may do them in the land to which you are going over, to possess it; that you may fear the Lord your God, you and your son and your son's son, by keeping all his statutes and his commandments, which I command you, all the days of your life; and that your days may be prolonged. Hear therefore, O Israel, and be careful to do them; that it may go well with you, and that you may multiply greatly, as the Lord, the God of your fathers, has promised you, in a land flowing with milk and honey.

"Hear, O Israel: The Lord our God is one Lord; and you shall love the Lord your God with all your heart, and with all your soul, and with all your might. And these words which I command you this day shall be upon your heart; and you shall teach them diligently to your children, and shall talk of them when you sit in your house, and when you walk by the way, and when you lie down, and when you rise. And you shall bind them as a sign upon your hand, and they shall be as frontlets between your eyes. And you shall write them on the doorposts of your house and on your gates.

"And when the Lord your God brings you into the land which he swore to your fathers, to Abraham, to Isaac, and to Jacob, to give you, with great and goodly cities, which you did not build, and houses full of all good things, which you did not fill, and cisterns hewn out, which you did not hew, and vineyards and olive trees, which you did not plant, and when you eat and are full, then take heed lest you forget the Lord, who brought you out of the land of Egypt, out of the house of bondage. You shall fear the Lord your God; you shall serve him, and swear by his name. You shall not go after other gods, of the gods of the peoples who are round about you; for the Lord your God in the midst of you is a jealous God; lest the anger of the Lord your God be kindled against you, and he destroy you from off the face of the earth. . . .

"When the Lord your God brings you into the land which you are entering to take possession of it, and clears away many nations before you . . . seven nations greater and mightier than yourselves, and when the Lord your God gives them over to you, and you defeat them; then you must utterly destroy them; you shall make no covenant with them, and show no mercy to them. You shall not make marriages with them, giving your daughters to their sons or taking their daughters for your sons. For they would turn away your sons from following me, to serve other gods; then the anger of the Lord would be kindled against you, and he would destroy you quickly. But thus shall you deal with them: you shall break down their altars, and dash in pieces their pillars, and hew down their Asherim,[3] and burn their graven images with fire.

---

[3]Sacred poles raised to Astarte (or Asherah), the Canaanite counterpart of Ishtar, the Mesopotamian goddess of fertility and love.

"For you are a people holy to the Lord your God; the Lord your God has chosen you to be a people for his own possession, out of all the peoples that are on the face of the earth. It was not because you were more in number than any other people that the Lord set his love upon you and chose you, for you were the fewest of all peoples; but it is because the Lord loves you, and is keeping the oath which he swore to your fathers, that the Lord has brought you out with a mighty hand, and redeemed you from the house of bondage, from the hand of Pharaoh king of Egypt. Know therefore that the Lord your God is God, the faithful God who keeps covenant and steadfast love with those who love him and keep his commandments, to a thousand generations, and repays those who hate him, by destroying them; he will not be slack with him who hates him. . . . You shall therefore be careful to do the commandments, and the statutes, and the ordinances, which I command you this day.

"And because you hearken to these ordinances, and keep and do them, the Lord your God will keep with you the covenant and the steadfast love which he swore to your fathers to keep; he will love you, bless you, and multiply you; he will also bless the fruit of your body and the fruit of your ground, your grain and your wine and your oil, the increase of your cattle and the young of your flock, in the land which he swore to your fathers to give you. You shall be blessed above all peoples; there shall not be male or female barren among you, or among your cattle. And the Lord will take away from you all sickness; and none of the evil diseases of Egypt, which you knew, will he inflict upon you, but he will lay them upon all who hate you. And you shall destroy all the peoples that the Lord your God will give over to you, your eye shall not pity them; neither shall you serve their gods, for that would be a snare to you."

Keeping and Breaking the Covenant
▼▼▼

15 ▼ THE BOOK OF JUDGES

Following Moses' death, Joshua led the Israelites into Canaan. Unable to wipe out or displace all the indigenous peoples, the Israelites settled in the hills and became one of several major cultural groups in the region. Between Joshua's death, which took place around 1150 B.C.E., and the rise of the kingdom of Israel around 1050 B.C.E., various leaders, known as *judges,* arose to lead the Israelites in times of crisis. These were not judges in a narrow juridical or institutional sense but men and women who were defenders of YHWH's law and justice.

The following story from The Book of Judges tells why the first of the major judges, Othniel, was called to lead Israel. The book, which is based on a cycle of written epics that date to around 1000 B.C.E., was probably put into its final form by the same group of seventh-century reformers in Jerusalem who were recasting Deuteronomy.

QUESTIONS FOR ANALYSIS

1. In what ways did the Israelites break the Covenant, and what were the consequences?
2. What was the message or lesson to be learned from this experience?

3. What does this source suggest about the historical realities of the Hebrew experience in the Promised Land?
4. What do you think happened after Othniel died?
5. Compare the troubles of the Israelites with the fall of the Xia and Shang Dynasties in China as recorded in *The Classic of History* (Chapter 1, source 5). In what ways do these two explanations of history, the Mandate of Heaven and the Covenant, parallel one another? In what ways do they differ? Which are more significant, the similarities or the differences? What do you conclude from your answer?

When Joshua dismissed the people, the people of Israel went each to his inheritance to take possession of the land. And the people served the Lord all the days of Joshua, and all the days of the elders who outlived Joshua, who had seen all the great work which the Lord had done for Israel. And Joshua the son of Nun, the servant of the Lord, died. . . . And all that generation also were gathered to their fathers; and there arose another generation after them, who did not know the Lord or the work which he had done for Israel.

And the people of Israel did what was evil in the sight of the Lord and served the Baals;[1] and they forsook the Lord, the God of their fathers, who had brought them out of the land of Egypt; they went after other gods, from among the gods of the peoples who were round about them, and bowed down to them; and they provoked the Lord to anger. They forsook the Lord, and served the Baals and the Ashtaroth.[2] So the anger of the Lord was kindled against Israel, and he gave them over to plunderers, who plundered them; and he sold them into the power of their enemies round about, so that they could no longer withstand their enemies. Whenever they marched out, the hand of the Lord was against them for evil, as the Lord had warned, and as the Lord had sworn to them; and they were in sore straits.

Then the Lord raised up judges, who saved them out of the power of those who plundered them. And yet they did not listen to their judges;

for they played the harlot after other gods and bowed down to them; they soon turned aside from the way in which their fathers had walked, who had obeyed the commandments of the Lord, and they did not do so. Whenever the Lord raised up judges for them, the Lord was with the judge, and he saved them from the hand of their enemies all the days of the judge; for the Lord was moved to pity by their groaning because of those who afflicted and oppressed them. But whenever the judge died, they turned back and behaved worse than their fathers, going after other gods, serving them and bowing down to them; they did not drop any of their practices or their stubborn ways. So the anger of the Lord was kindled against Israel; and he said, "Because this people have transgressed my covenant which I commanded their fathers, and have not obeyed my voice, I will not henceforth drive out before them any of the nations that Joshua left when he died, that by them I may test Israel, whether they will take care to walk in the way of the Lord as their fathers did, or not." So the Lord left those nations, not driving them out at once, and he did not give them into the power of Joshua.

Now these are the nations which the Lord left, to test Israel by them, that is, all in Israel who had no experience of any war in Canaan; it was only that the generations of the people of Israel might know war, that he might teach war to such at least as had not known it before. These are the nations: the five lords of the Philistines, and all

---

[1] Baal was the chief Canaanite god. Here, however, the term means "all the gods of the native peoples of the region."

[2] See source 14, note 3. In this context, the phrase means all the native gods, not just Baal and Astarte.

the Canaanites, and the Sidonians, and the Hivites. . . . They were for the testing of Israel, to know whether Israel would obey the commandments of the Lord, which he commanded their fathers by Moses. So the people of Israel dwelt among the Canaanites, the Hittites, the Amorites, the Perizzites, the Hivites, and the Jebusites; and they took their daughters to themselves for wives, and their own daughters they gave to their sons; and they served their gods.

And the people of Israel did what was evil in the sight of the Lord, forgetting the Lord their God, and serving the Baals and the Asheroth. Therefore the anger of the Lord was kindled against Israel, and he sold them into the hand of Cushanrishathaim[3] king of Mesopotamia and the people of Israel served Cushanrishathaim eight years. But when the people of Israel cried to the Lord, the Lord raised up a deliverer for the people of Israel, who delivered them, Othniel the son of Kenaz, Caleb's younger brother. The Spirit of the Lord came upon him, and he judged Israel; he went out to war, and the Lord gave Cushanrishathaim king of Mesopotamia into his hand; and his hand prevailed over Cushanrishathaim. So the land had rest forty years. Then Othniel the son of Kenaz died.

---

[3]A king who held major portions of Syria.

Chapter 3

▼▼▼

Transcendental Reality

Developing the Spiritual Traditions
of India and Southwest Asia:
800–200 B.C.E.

Between about 800 and 200 B.C.E. profound changes in
thought, belief, social organization, and government took
place in China, India, Southwest Asia, and *Hellas* (the land of
the Greeks). During these six centuries the Chinese, Indians,
Southwest Asians, and *Hellenes* (the name by which the
Greeks of classical antiquity identified themselves) formulated distinctive traditions and institutions that became essential features of their civilizations. In essence, their classical
cultures took shape.

These developments became especially pronounced during the sixth century B.C.E. and following. It is no coincidence
that Confucius, the Buddha, the Mahavira, several of the late
authors of the Upanishads, Zarathustra, Second Isaiah, and
the earliest Greek scientists and philosophers all lived during or around the sixth century. Moreover, the Hindu caste
system was in place and the Persian Empire and the Hellenic
city-states were thriving by the end of this century.

What accounts for these parallel developments? The Age
of Iron, which began after about 1000 B.C.E., witnessed the
development of considerably larger, more complex, and more
competitive political and economic entities that challenged
older social systems and values. This disruption of life was
unsettling and led to the search for answers to some fundamental questions: What is the meaning and goal of life? How
does one relate to the spiritual world? To the natural world?
To other humans? What is the ideal government?

The historical frameworks of the various civilizations pos-
ing such questions often differed radically. Their respective
answers consequently varied significantly. In one way, however, they displayed a striking similarity: Each emerging tra-

dition challenged the myth-making notion that humankind is held hostage by a capricious, god-infested nature.

Indian thinkers did this by denying the ultimate reality and importance of the world of observable nature. China witnessed several other approaches. One school of thought sought mystical union with nature, and two other schools sought to control nature by imposing human discipline upon it. One of these latter schools of philosophy saw the solution in a moral order of virtuous behavior; the other, in the order of strict and dispassionately applied human law. In Southwest Asia freedom from myth-laden nature was partially achieved through worship of and obedience to a totally spiritual yet personal God of the universe, who stood completely outside nature yet imposed moral and historical order upon it. In Hellas the attempt to master nature took the form of rational philosophy and science. Here certain thinkers sought to control nature by studying it objectively, thereby discovering laws that would enable humans to define more surely their place in the universe. In this manner four major world traditions emerged: Indian transcendental spirituality; China's distinctive blend of practical worldliness with a mystical appreciation of nature; Southwest Asia's preoccupation with monotheism; and Greek rationalism, with its special focus on the human condition.

In this chapter we shall explore the spiritual and religious traditions that took shape in India and Southwest Asia. Religion has played a central role in human history, especially in the region of southern Asia that stretches from Syria-Palestine in the west to the Bay of Bengal in the east. This vast area, which encompasses all of Southwest Asia and the whole Indian subcontinent, has been the birthplace of most of the world's major religions. Time and again we shall return to this region of the world to marvel at its spiritual fertility. For the present we concentrate on the emergence of two major spiritual traditions. The first was a world- and self-denying transcendentalism that took shape in India. Its most classic expressions were Brahminical Hinduism, Jainism, and Buddhism. All three religious traditions sprang out of a common Indian notion that true peace and bliss do not lie in the momentary pleasures that come from satisfying the illusory desires of this world. Rather, lasting tranquility comes only with the discovery of Immutable Reality through a radical transformation of one's self. The second major religious tradition of southern Asia was the concept of a single, sole God of the universe. This god is totally transcendental, existing outside of time, space, and matter, all of which are this deity's creations. But this Universal God is also a personal, caring deity who directs human history and uses humans as historical agents. Moreover, this god demands a high degree of moral behavior from those called to divine service because by directing human history, God has sanctified it. This notion, which we term *ethical monotheism,* found expression in Persia's Zoroastrian faith and in Judaism.

▼▼▼

The Emergence of Brahminical Hinduism

The *Rig Veda*'s hymn to Purusha, which appears in Chapter 2, illustrates the emergence of what eventually became one of Hinduism's major beliefs: the unity of all being. During the period spanning the tenth through fourth centuries B.C.E., most of the other elements of classical Hindu thought and practice took shape.

It is wrong to think of Hinduism, either modern or ancient, as a single set of beliefs and practices. To the contrary, it is a fluid mass of religious and social expressions, which collectively encompass the living faiths of all the diverse peoples of India who call themselves *Hindu.* Hinduism comfortably includes folk rituals and beliefs, which have changed little over many millennia, and the most abstract and speculative thought on the nature of God. It is polytheistic and monotheistic; it is simultaneously earthy and metaphysical. Indeed, Hindus can choose from a variety of beliefs and modes of worship dizzying to the outside observer, because ultimately the basic religious insight of Hinduism is that there are an infinite number of paths to and manifestations of the One. Thus Hindus, unlike Christians or Muslims, for example, do not believe that the fullness of religious truth can be summed up in a neat package of doctrinal statements, nor do they believe that religion consists of a clear-cut struggle of truth versus error. The notion that something either is or is not, but cannot be both, has no place in the Hindu world, where countless apparent contradictions exist comfortably alongside one another.

Hinduism is also more than just a family of often seemingly contradictory beliefs and religious rituals. It involves all the ways in which Hindus live and relate to one another. Therefore, as we study Hinduism's historical evolution, it is necessary to put aside the modern Western notion of a meaningful dichotomy between religion and social organization. Hinduism is a total way of life, and this is best seen in the *caste* system.

Not all Hindus are members of castes, but most are, which suggests that beneath the variety of beliefs and rituals we term Hindu, there are some fairly common elements. These include the notion of the oneness of the universe; a belief in the ultimate reality of the spiritual and the nonreality of the corporeal world; the caste system; and *dharma* (caste law), *samsara* (the cycle of birth, suffering, death, and rebirth), and *karma* (the fruits of action performed in a previous life).

The Hindu Search for Divine Reality

▼▼▼

16 ▼ *THE UPANISHADS*

Between about 800 and 500 B.C.E. Indo-Aryan religious teachers brought the Vedic Age to a spectacular close. Taking certain concepts that were implied in the later vedic hymns, these teachers developed a vision of an all-inclusive Being, or Ultimate Reality, called *Brahman* and enunciated that theological breakthrough in a number of speculative treatises known as *Upanishads.*

Upanishad means "additional sitting near a teacher," and these texts often take the form of a dialogue between a teacher and a pupil who seek to go beyond the Vedas in their search for ultimate wisdom. As we might expect, there are many contradictions among the numerous upanishadic texts, yet a fundamental message binds them: Not only is there a Universal Soul, or Brahman, but the innermost essence of a person, the *atman,* or spiritual self, is one with Brahman, the Self. Humans, therefore, are not outside Divine Reality; they are part of it.

The first selection, which comes from the early and especially revered *Chandogya Upanishad,* presents two analogies to explain this theological message. The second excerpt, taken from the later but equally important *Brihadaranyaka Upanishad,* deals with the issue of how that spark of Brahman, the Self, which is contained within each mortal body, finally achieves release and rejoins the One. Here we see an early enunciation of what will become two essential elements of Hindu religious thought: reincarnation and the law of karma. The third selection, also from the *Brihadaranyaka,* describes the state of consciousness of a person who is on the verge of attaining release from the cycle of rebirth and union with Brahman.

QUESTIONS FOR ANALYSIS

1. What sort of truth does Uddalaka offer his son when he instructs him in "that . . . by which we know what cannot be known"?
2. What does the father mean when he states, "You, Svetaketu, are it"?
3. What is the law of karma?
4. Why are souls reincarnated?
5. How does one end the cycle of rebirth?
6. How important or real is this world to the soul returning to Brahman?
7. Why do good and evil cease to have any meaning to the soul that has found Brahman?
8. How is the upanishadic view of Brahman a logical development from the message of the hymn to Purusha (Chapter 2, source 11)?

There lived once Svetaketu. . . . To him his father Uddalaka . . . said: "Svetaketu, go to school; for no one belonging to our race, dear son, who, not having studied, is, as it were, a Brahmin[1] by birth only."

Having begun his apprenticeship when he was twelve years of age, Svetaketu returned to his father, when he was twenty-four, having then studied all the Vedas, — conceited, considering himself well-read, and stern.

His father said to him: "Svetaketu, as you are so conceited, considering yourself so well-read, and so stern, my dear, have you ever asked for that instruction by which we hear what cannot be heard, by which we perceive what cannot be perceived, by which we know what cannot be known?"

"What is that instruction, Sir?" he asked. . . .

"Fetch me . . . a fruit of the Nyagrodha tree."

"Here is one, Sir."

"Break it."

"It is broken, Sir."

"What do you see there?"

"These seeds, almost infinitesimal."

"Break one of them."

"It is broken, Sir."

"What do you see there?"

"Not anything, Sir."

The father said: "My son, that subtle essence which you do not perceive there, of that very essence this great Nyagrodha tree exists.

"Believe it, my son. That which is the subtle essence, in it all that exists has its self. It is the True. It is the Self, and you, . . . Svetaketu, are it."

"Please, Sir, inform me still more," said the son.

"Be it so, my child," the father replied.

"Place this salt in water, and then wait on me in the morning."

The son did as he was commanded.

The father said to him: "Bring me the salt, which you placed in the water last night."

The son having looked for it, found it not, for, of course, it was melted.

The father said: "Taste it from the surface of the water. How is it?"

The son replied: "It is salt."

"Taste it from the middle. How is it?"

The son replied: "It is salt."

"Taste it from the bottom. How is it?"

The son replied: "It is salt."

The father said: "Throw it away and then wait on me."

He did so; but the salt exists forever.[2]

Then the father said: "Here also, in this body,[3] . . . you do not perceive the True, my son; but there indeed it is.

"That which is the subtle essence,[4] in it all that exists has its self. It is the True. It is the Self, and you, Svetaketu, are it."

▼ ▼ ▼

"And when the body grows weak through old age, or becomes weak through illness, at that time that person, after separating himself from his members, as a mango, or fig, or Pippala-fruit is separated from the stalk,[5] hastens back again as he came, to the place from which he started, to new life. . . .

"Then both his knowledge and his work take hold of him[6] and his acquaintance with former things.[7]

"And as a caterpillar, after having reached the end of a blade of grass, and after having made another approach to another blade, draws itself together towards it, thus does this Self, after having thrown off this body and dispelled all ignorance, and after making another approach to another body, draw himself together towards it.

---

[1]A member of the priestly caste (see Chapter 2, source 11). *Brahmin* is a male gender variation of the neuter noun *Brahman*.

[2]The salt, although invisible, remains forever in the water.

[3]The human body.

[4]The soul, or atman.

[5]The image is of a fruit that carries the seed of new life, even as it decays.

[6]The law of karma, which is defined more fully later in this source.

[7]One's acquaintance with things in a former life explains the peculiar talents and deficiencies evident in a child.

"And as a goldsmith, taking a piece of gold, turns it into another, newer and more beautiful shape, so does this Self, after having thrown off this body and dispelled all ignorance, make unto himself another, newer and more beautiful shape. . . .

"Now as a man is like this or like that, according as he acts and according as he behaves, so will he be: — a man of good acts will become good, a man of bad acts, bad. He becomes pure by pure deeds, bad by bad deeds.

"And here they say that a person consists of desires. And as is his desire, so is his will; and as is his will, so is his deed; and whatever deed he does, that he will reap.

"And here there is this verse: 'To whatever object a man's own mind is attached, to that he goes strenuously together with his deed; and having obtained the consequences of whatever deed he does here on earth, he returns again from that world . . . to this world of action.'[8]

"So much for the man who desires. But as to the man who does not desire, who, not desiring, freed from desires, is satisfied in his desires, or desires the Self only, his vital spirits do not de-part elsewhere, — being Brahman, he goes to Brahman.[9]

"On this there is this verse: 'When all desires which once entered his heart are undone, then does the mortal become immortal, then he obtains Brahman.'"

▼ ▼ ▼

"Now as a man, when embraced by a beloved wife, knows nothing that is without, nothing that is within, thus this person, when embraced by the intelligent Self, knows nothing that is without, nothing that is within. This indeed is his true form, in which his wishes are fulfilled, in which the Self only is his wish, in which no wish is left, — free from any sorrow.

"Then a father is not a father, a mother not a mother, the worlds not worlds, the gods not gods, the Vedas not Vedas. Then a thief is not a thief, a murderer not a murderer, a Kandala not a Kandala,[10] a Sramana not a Sramana,[11] a Tapasa not a Tapasa.[12] He is not followed by good, not followed by evil, for he has then overcome all the sorrows of the heart."

---

[8]This is the law of karma.
[9]Thereby ending the painful cycle of samsara.
[10]*Kandalas* were the lowest and most "unclean" of all caste-less persons. (See Chapter 5, sources 38 and 39, for additional sources and notes that deal with the Kandalas.)

[11]A holy beggar.
[12]A person performing penance.

Dharma: The Imperative of Caste Law
▼▼▼
17 ▼ *THE BHAGAVAD GITA*

The *Bhagavad Gita* (*Song of the Blessed Lord*) is Hinduism's most beloved sacred text. The poem appears in its present form as an episode in the *Mahabharata* (*The Great Deeds of the Bharata Clan*), the world's longest epic, which was composed over a period from perhaps 500 B.C.E. to possibly 400 C.E. but which certainly drew from much earlier Aryan oral traditions. Like the Homeric Greek epics, the *Mahabharata* deals on one level with the clash of armies and the combat of individual heroes, and simultaneously on a higher plane it expounds theological and philosophical insights. Of all its spiritual interjections, the *Bhagavad Gita* is the most profound.

The *Gita*'s date of final composition is uncertain; scholars fix it anywhere from 300 B.C.E. to 300 C.E.. What is certain is that Hindu commentators have consistently considered the song to be the last and greatest of the upanishadic texts, for they see it as the crystallization of all that was expressed and implied in the upanishadic tradition.

The core question addressed in the *Bhagavad Gita* is how a person can become one with Brahman while still functioning in this world. The answer comes from Lord Krishna, the incarnation of Vishnu, the Divine Preserver. In this particular corporeal form, or *avatara,* Krishna/Vishnu serves as charioteer to the warrior hero Arjuna. Arjuna, a brave soldier, shrinks from entering battle when he realizes that he must fight close relatives. The hero god Krishna then proceeds to resolve Arjuna's quandary by explaining to him the moral imperative of caste-duty, or dharma.

QUESTIONS FOR ANALYSIS

1. Why should Arjuna not grieve for those whom he might kill?
2. According to Krishna, how real is the corporeal world?
3. Why should one perform one's caste duty in a totally disinterested fashion?
4. Why is it better to perform one's caste duty poorly than to perform the duties of another caste well?
5. According to Krishna, what constitutes sin? What is evil?
6. What hope, if any, does Krishna's theological message hold for the lowest elements of Hindu society?
7. The Hindu caste system is based on several elemental religious beliefs. What are they?
8. In what ways is Krishna's message the same as that of the Upanishads?

The deity said, you have grieved for those who deserve no grief. . . . Learned men grieve not for the living nor the dead. Never did I not exist, nor you, nor these rulers of men; nor will any one of us ever hereafter cease to be. As in this body, infancy and youth and old age come to the embodied self, so does the acquisition of another body; a sensible man is not deceived about that. The contacts of the senses, O son of Kunti! which produce cold and heat, pleasure and pain, are not permanent, they are ever coming and going. Bear them, O descendant of Bharata! For, O chief of men! that sensible man whom they (pain and pleasure being alike to him) afflict not, he merits immortality. There is no existence for that which is unreal; there is no non-existence for that which is real. And the correct conclusion about both is perceived by those who perceive the truth. Know that to be indestructible which pervades all this. . . . He who thinks it[1] to be the killer and he who thinks it to be killed, both know nothing. It kills not, is not killed. It is not born, nor does it ever die, nor, having existed, does it exist no more. Unborn, everlasting, unchangeable, and primeval, it is not killed when the body is killed. O son of Pritha! how can that man who

---

[1]The atman, or individual soul, and Brahman, which are one and the same.

knows it thus to be indestructible, everlasting, unborn, and inexhaustible, how and whom can he kill, whom can he cause to be killed? As a man, casting off old clothes, puts on others and new ones, so the embodied self casting off old bodies, goes to others and new ones. . . . It is everlasting, all-pervading, stable, firm, and eternal. It is said to be unperceived, to be unthinkable, to be unchangeable. Therefore knowing it to be such, you ought not to grieve. But even if you think that it is constantly born, and constantly dies, still, O you of mighty arms! you ought not to grieve thus. For to one that is born, death is certain; and to one that dies, birth is certain. . . . This embodied self, O descendant of Bharata! within every one's body is ever indestructible. Therefore you ought not to grieve for any being. Having regard to your own duty also, you ought not to falter, for there is nothing better for a Kshatriya[2] than a righteous battle. Happy those Kshatriyas, O son of Pritha! who can find such a battle . . . an open door to heaven! But if you will not fight this righteous battle, then you will have abandoned your own duty and your fame, and you will incur sin. . . . Your business is with action alone; not by any means with fruit. Let not the fruit of action be your motive to action. Let not your attachment be fixed on inaction. Having recourse to devotion . . . perform actions, casting off all attachment, and being equable in success or ill-success; such equability is called devotion. . . . The wise who have obtained devotion cast off the fruit of action,[3] and released from the shackles of repeated births, repair to that seat where there is no unhappiness. . . . The man who, casting off all desires, lives free from attachments, who is free from egoism, and from the feeling that this or that is

mine, obtains tranquility. This, O son of Pritha! is the Brahmic state; attaining to this, one is never deluded; and remaining in it in one's last moments, one attains the Brahmic bliss.[4] . . .

I have passed through many births, O Arjuna! and you also. I know them all, but you, O terror of your foes! do not know them. Even though I am unborn and inexhaustible in my essence, even though I am lord of all beings, still I am born by means of my delusive power. Whensoever, O descendant of Bharata! piety languishes, and impiety is in the ascendant, I create myself. I am born age after age, for the protection of the good, for the destruction of evil-doers, and the establishment of piety. . . . The fourfold division of castes was created by me according to the appointment of qualities and duties. . . . The duties of Brahmins, Kshatriyas, and Vaisyas, and of Sudras, too, O terror of your foes! are distinguished according to the qualities born of nature.[5] Tranquility, restraint of the senses, penance, purity, forgiveness, straightforwardness, also knowledge, experience, and belief in a future world, this is the natural duty of Brahmins. Valor, glory, courage, dexterity, not slinking away from battle, gifts, exercise of lordly power, this is the natural duty of Kshatriyas. Agriculture, tending cattle, trade, this is the natural duty of Vaisyas. And the natural duty of Sudras, too, consists in service. Every man intent on his own respective duties obtains perfection. Listen, now, how one intent on one's own duty obtains perfection. Worshiping, by the performance of his own duty, him from whom all things proceed, and by whom all this is permeated, a man obtains perfection. One's duty, though defective, is better than another's duty well performed. Performing the duty prescribed by nature, one does

---

[2]A member of the ruling warrior caste.

[3]They do not concern themselves with the earthly consequences of their actions and develop no attachments to the rewards of this world (fame, wealth, family) that might result from those actions.

[4]Brahma-nirvana, or merging with Brahman and release (*moksha*) from the cycle of rebirth. It is a state of simultaneous being and nonbeing.

[5]Each caste consists of persons born to that station by virtue of their nature. Each person's karma has made his or her nature suitable for a particular caste and only that caste. Brahmins teach and offer sacrifices; Kshatriyas rule and fight; Vaisyas work; and Sudras serve. (See Chapter 2, source 11, and *The Laws of Manu*, Chapter 5, source 38.)

not incur sin. O son of Kunti! one should not abandon a natural duty though tainted with evil; for all actions are enveloped by evil, as fire by smoke. One who is self-restrained, whose understanding is unattached everywhere, from whom affections have departed, obtains the supreme perfection of freedom from action by renunciation. Learn from me, only in brief, O son of Kunti! how one who has obtained perfection attains the Brahman, which is the highest culmination of knowledge. A man possessed of a pure understanding, controlling his self by courage, discarding sound and other objects of sense, casting off affection and aversion; who frequents clean places, who eats little, whose speech, body, and mind are restrained, who is always intent on meditation and mental abstraction, and has recourse to unconcern, who abandoning egoism, stubbornness, arrogance, desire, anger, and all belongings, has no thought that this or that is mine, and who is tranquil, becomes fit for assimilation with the Brahman.

▼▼▼

Challengers of Caste: The Mahavira and the Buddha

By 600 B.C.E. the central spiritual question in Indian society was how one finds liberation from karma and the cycle of rebirth. As we have seen, the upanishadic teachers offered their answers. The eventual result by about 300 B.C.E. was establishment of the caste system throughout most of Indian society and fairly general acceptance of the notion that dharma (the law) meant caste-duty. This was not, however, the only answer.

Even as the Brahmin, or priestly, class was in the process of turning itself into the dominant Hindu caste and defining what would become mainstream Hinduism, several teachers emerged from the Kshatriya, or warrior, class to offer alternatives to the caste system. One of these was Nataputta Vardhamana (ca. 599–527 B.C.E.), known to history as the *Mahavira* (the Great Hero). The other was Siddhartha Gautama (ca. 563–483 B.C.E.), better known as the *Buddha* (the Enlightened One).

Each teacher and his doctrine is understandable only within the context of an Indo-Aryan cosmology. Although both formulated philosophies that denied certain concepts basic to what was emerging as classical, Brahminical Hinduism, the questions each asked and the answers each offered were predicated upon the world-denying assumptions underlying all Indian religious thought.

Ironically, although both doctrines began as philosophies in which divinities played no role, they became in time theistic (god-centered) religions. *Jainism,* which developed out of the Mahavira's teachings, would win adherents only in India, but it has survived to the present. Half a millennium after the Buddha's release from the bonds of matter, his teachings had been transformed into a family of related religions, many of which worshiped the Buddha himself as a divine being. For well over two thousand years *Buddhism* in its various forms has profoundly shaped the lives of countless devotees throughout South and East Asia and remains a vital force today.

A Call to the Heroic Life
▼▼▼
18 ▼ *THE BOOK OF GOOD CONDUCT*

Our picture of the Mahavira and his teachings is hazy, in part because the earliest written sources for the Great Hero's life and doctrine date no earlier than two centuries after his death. One of these sources is the *Acaranga Sutra* (*The Book of Good Conduct*), which Jains revere as the first of their eleven major sacred texts.

Here we encounter reincarnation, karma, and dharma, but with a Jain twist, and we discover Jain *ahimsa,* or absolute nonviolence toward all life. The first excerpt defines dharma, the second tells how the Mahavira conquered karma, and the third outlines the five great Jain vows.

QUESTIONS FOR ANALYSIS

1. What is *dharma,* according to Jainism?
2. What is the Jain definition of *karma?*
3. What sort of heroic life does the Great Hero challenge his followers to lead?
4. The Mahavira was acknowledged as the *Jina,* or Conqueror. Consequently, his followers are Jains. What do Jains seek to conquer?
5. Compare Jain notions of dharma and karma with those of conventional Hinduism. Compare Jain notions of sin and evil with those articulated in the *Bhagavad Gita.* Which strike you as more significant, the differences or the similarities? What do you conclude from this?
6. Both Lord Krishna in the *Bhagavad Gita* and the Mahavira teach a doctrine of nonattachment to this world. How do their teachings parallel one another? Where do they diverge? Which are more pronounced, the differences or the similarities? What do you conclude from this?
7. Compare the five Jain vows with the Hebrew Ten Commandments (Chapter 2, source 14). Which are more pronounced, the differences or the similarities? What do you conclude from this?

The Arhats[1] . . . of the past, present, and future, all say thus, speak thus, declare thus, explain thus: all breathing, existing, living, sentient creatures[2] should not be slain, nor treated with violence, nor abused, nor tormented, nor driven away.

This is the pure, unchangeable, eternal law [dharma], which the clever ones, who understand the world, have declared: among the zealous and the not zealous, among the faithful and the not faithful, among the not cruel and the cruel, among those who have worldly weakness and

---

[1]Perfect souls, or saints.

[2]Not only the higher forms of sentient life, such as humans and animals, but also insects, plants, seeds, lichens, and even beings known as *earth bodies, wind bodies, water bodies,* and *fire bodies.*

those who have not, among those who like social bonds and those who do not: "that is the truth, that is so, that is proclaimed in this."

Having adopted the law, one should not hide it, nor forsake it. Correctly understanding the law, one should arrive at indifference for the impressions of the senses, and "not act on the motives of the world." "He who is not of this mind, how should he come to the other?"[3]

▼ ▼ ▼

Beings which are born in all states become individually sinners by their actions.[4]

The Venerable One[5] understands thus: he who is under the conditions of existence, that fool suffers pain. Thoroughly knowing karma, the Venerable One avoids sin.

The sage, perceiving the double karma,[6] proclaims the incomparable activity,[7] he, the knowing one; knowing the current of worldliness, the current of sinfulness, and the impulse.

Practicing the sinless abstinence from killing, he[8] did no acts, neither himself nor with the assistance of others; he to whom women were known as the causes of all sinful acts, he saw the true state of the world. . . .

He well saw that bondage comes through action. Whatever is sinful, the Venerable One left that undone: he consumed clean food.[9]

Knowing measure in eating and drinking, he was not desirous of delicious food, nor had he a longing for it. . . .

The Venerable One, exerting himself, did not seek sleep for the sake of pleasure; he waked up himself, and slept only a little, free from desires. . . .

Always well guarded, he bore the pains caused by grass, cold, fire, flies, and gnats; manifold pains.

He traveled in the pathless country of the Ladhas.[10] . . .

In Ladha natives attacked him; the dogs bit him, ran at him.

Few people kept off the attacking, biting dogs. . . .

Such were the inhabitants. Many other mendicants,[11] eating rough food . . . and carrying about a strong pole [to keep off the dogs], . . . lived there.

Even thus armed they were bitten by the dogs, torn by the dogs. It is difficult to travel in Ladha.

Ceasing to use the stick against living beings, abandoning the care of the body, the houseless, the Venerable One endures the thorns of the villages being perfectly enlightened.

As an elephant at the head of the battle, so was Mahavira there victorious. . . .

The Venerable One was able to abstain from indulgence of the flesh. . . .

Purgatives and emetics, anointing of the body and bathing, shampooing and cleansing of the teeth do not behoove him, after he learned [that the body is something unclean]. . . .

In summer he exposes himself to the heat, he sits squatting in the sun; he lives on rough food: rice, pounded jujube, and beans. . . .

Sometimes the Venerable One did not drink for half a month or even for a month.

Or he did not drink for more than two months, or even six months, day and night, without desire for drink. Sometimes he ate stale food. . . .

Having wisdom, Mahavira committed no sin himself, nor did he induce others to do so, nor did he consent to the sins of others.

Having entered a village or a town, he begged for food which had been prepared for somebody else. Having got clean food, he used it, restraining the impulses. . . . The Venerable One slowly

---

[3]How is it possible for a person to sin ("come to the other") who does not "act on the motives of the world"?
[4]The law of karma, as understood by Jains.
[5]The Mahavira.
[6]The present and the future.
[7]The life of the true Jain.

[8]The Mahavira.
[9]Food that does the absolute minimum violence to sentient life in all its forms.
[10]Possibly western Bengal.
[11]Wandering holy people who beg for their food (see source 20).

wandered about, and, killing no creatures, he begged for his food.

Moist or dry or cold food, old beans, old pap, or bad grain, whether he did or did not get such food he was rich. . . .

Himself understanding the truth and restraining the impulses for the purification of the soul, finally liberated, and free from delusion, the Venerable One was well guarded during his whole life.

The Venerable Ascetic[12] Mahavira endowed with the highest knowledge and intuition taught the five great vows.

▼ ▼ ▼

The first great vow, Sir, runs thus:

I renounce all killing of living beings, whether subtle or gross, whether movable or immovable. Nor shall I myself kill living beings, nor cause others to do it, nor consent to it. As long as I live, I confess and blame, repent and exempt myself of these sins, in the thrice threefold way,[13] in mind, speech, and body. . . .

The second great vow runs thus:

I renounce all vices of lying speech arising from anger or greed or fear or mirth. I shall neither myself speak lies, nor cause others to speak lies, nor consent to the speaking of lies by others. . . .

The third great vow runs thus:

I renounce all taking of anything not given,[14] either in a village or a town or a wood, either of little or much, of small or great, of living or lifeless things. I shall neither take myself what is not given, nor cause others to take it, nor consent to their taking it.

The fourth great vow runs thus:

I renounce all sexual pleasures, either with gods or men or animals. I shall not give way to sensuality. . . .

The fifth great vow runs thus:

I renounce all attachments, whether little or much, small or great, living or lifeless; neither shall I myself form such attachments, nor cause others to do so, nor consent to their doing so.

---

[12]A person who leads a life of rigorous self-denial for religious reasons.
[13]Acting, commanding, or consenting in mind, speech, or body in the past, present, or future.

[14]The Jain must live as a beggar.

The Path to Enlightenment
▼▼▼
19 ▼ *The Buddha, TWO LESSONS*

Many parallels exist between the legendary lives of the Mahavira and the Buddha, and several of their teachings are strikingly similar. Each rejected the special sanctity of vedic literature, and each denied the meaningfulness of caste distinctions and duties. Yet a close investigation of their doctrines reveals substantial differences.

Like the Mahavira, young Prince Siddhartha Gautama, shrinking in horror at the many manifestations of misery in this world, fled his comfortable life and eventually became an ascetic. Unlike the Mahavira, who found victory over karma in severe self-denial and total nonviolence, Prince Gautama found only severe disquiet. The ascetic life offered him no enlightenment as to how one might escape the sorrows of mortal existence. After abandoning extreme asceticism,

Gautama achieved Enlightenment in a flash while meditating under a sacred pipal tree (see Chapter 1, source 9, seal 3). He was now the Buddha, the Enlightened One.

Legend tells us he then proceeded to share the way to Enlightenment, which he termed the *Middle Path,* by preaching a sermon in a deer park at Benares in northeastern India to five ascetics, who became his first disciples. Buddhists refer to that initial sermon as "Setting in Motion the Wheel of the Law," which means that the Buddha had embarked on a journey (turning the wheel) on behalf of the Law of Righteousness (dharma).

Our first text is a reconstruction of that sermon. The second document is a dialogue between the Buddha and one of his disciples. Known as "The Lesson on Questions That Tend Not to Edification," it deals with issues on which the Buddha refused to speculate.

Both sources are preserved in a body of Buddhist literature known as the *Pali Canon,* which contains the most authentic texts relating to the Buddha and his doctrine known to exist today. Assembled as an authoritative collection, or *canon,* of orally transmitted remembrances during the period between the Buddha's death and the late third century B.C.E., the texts were probably not written down in the form in which we have them until the late first century B.C.E. Composed in Pali, a language that is close to classical Sanskrit, they first appeared in the island of Ceylon (modern Sri Lanka) and traveled from there to Burma and Thailand, where they became the core canonical books of the branch of Buddhism known as *Theravada* (see Chapter 6). Each text is located in one of three groupings, or "baskets"; hence the entire collection is known as the *Tipitaka,* or *Three Baskets.* Our first document comes from *The Discipline Basket,* which consists of a number of books that concern the discipline, or regimented life, of Buddhist monks and nuns. The second source comes from *The Basket of Discourses,* which contains a series of books that supposedly contain all of the Buddha's sermons and lessons.

QUESTIONS FOR ANALYSIS

1. What is the *Middle Path?* Why is it, according to the Buddha, the proper path to Enlightenment?
2. What are the *Four Noble Truths,* and how does one's total comprehension and acceptance of them lead to *Nirvana,* or escape from the cycle of suffering?
3. Buddhists call the law taught by the Buddha *dharma.* How does Buddhist dharma differ from that of Brahminical Hinduism?
4. What issues or questions did the Buddha refuse to consider? Why? What does his refusal to speculate on these issues suggest about his doctrine?
5. In what ways have the Mahavira and the Buddha rejected the caste system? Why might Jainism and Buddhism appeal to non-Brahmins?
6. Both the Mahavira and the Buddha came from the warrior caste. Do their respective doctrines hint at this fact?

7. It has been said that Brahminical Hinduism, Jainism, and Buddhism all emphasize *selflessness,* but each defines it differently. Do you agree or disagree? Why?

8. What elements do these three Indian religious traditions share? Where do they differ? Which are more significant, the similarities or the differences? What conclusions follow from your answer?

SETTING IN MOTION THE WHEEL OF THE LAW

And the Blessed One thus addressed the five Bhikkhus.[1] "There are two extremes, O Bhikkhus, which he who has given up the world ought to avoid. What are these two extremes? A life given to pleasures, devoted to pleasures and lusts: this is degrading, sensual, vulgar, ignoble, and profitless; and a life given to mortifications: this is painful, ignoble, and profitless. By avoiding these two extremes, O Bhikkhus, the Tathagata[2] has gained the knowledge of the Middle Path which leads to insight, which leads to wisdom, which conduces to calm, to knowledge, to the Sambodhi,[3] to Nirvana.[4]

"Which, O Bhikkhus, is this Middle Path the knowledge of which the Tathagata has gained, which leads to insight, which leads to wisdom, which conduces to calm, to knowledge, to the Sambodhi, to Nirvana? It is the Holy Eightfold Path, namely, Right Belief,[5] Right Aspiration,[6] Right Speech,[7] Right Conduct,[8] Right Means of Livelihood,[9] Right Endeavor,[10] Right Memory,[11] Right Meditation.[12] This, O Bhikkhus, is the

Middle Path the knowledge of which the Tathagata has gained, which leads to insight, which leads to wisdom, which conduces to calm, to knowledge, to the Sambodhi, to Nirvana.

"This, O Bhikkhus, is the Noble Truth of Suffering: Birth is suffering; decay is suffering; illness is suffering; death is suffering. Presence of objects we hate, is suffering; Separation from objects we love, is suffering; not to obtain what we desire, is suffering. Briefly, . . . clinging to existence is suffering.

"This, O Bhikkhus, is the Noble Truth of the Cause of suffering: Thirst, that leads to rebirth, accompanied by pleasure and lust, finding its delight here and there. This thirst is threefold, namely, thirst for pleasure, thirst for existence, thirst for prosperity.

"This, O Bhikkhus, is the Noble Truth of the Cessation of suffering: it ceases with the complete cessation of this thirst, — a cessation which consists in the absence of every passion — with the abandoning of this thirst, with the doing

---

[1]Ascetics. The term later was used to refer to Buddhism's mendicant monks (see source 20).

[2]One of the Buddha's titles; its derivation is not totally clear. It seems to mean "He who has arrived at the Truth."

[3]Total enlightenment.

[4]The state of release from the limitations of existence and rebirth. The word means literally "extinction," in the sense that one has extinguished all worldly desires. In essence, it is Buddhahood. Like the Hindu Brahma-nirvana, Buddhist Nirvana is a state of absolute being and nonbeing.

[5]Understanding the truth about the universality of suffering, knowing the path leading to its extinction, and realizing it is attainable.

[6]Preparing for the journey to Enlightenment by freeing one's mind of ill will, sensuous desire, and cruelty.

[7]Abstaining from lying, harsh language, and gossip.

[8]Acting honestly by avoiding killing, stealing, and unlawful sexual intercourse.

[9]Avoiding any occupation that harms any living being directly or indirectly.

[10]Going beyond simply acting morally; a person now avoids all distractions and temptations of the flesh.

[11]Now that a person has put aside distractions, he or she focuses the entire mind fully on important issues, such as life, suffering, and death.

[12]Total discipline of the mind, body, and spirit leading to a state of absolute awareness that transcends consciousness.

away with it, with the deliverance from it, with the destruction of desire.

"This, O Bhikkhus, is the Noble Truth of the Path which leads to the cessation of suffering: that Holy Eightfold Path, that is to say, Right Belief, Right Aspiration, Right Speech, Right Conduct, Right Means of Livelihood, Right Endeavor, Right Memory, Right Meditation. . . .

"As long, O Bhikkhus, as I did not possess with perfect purity this true knowledge and insight into these four Noble Truths . . . so long, O Bhikkhus, I knew that I had not yet obtained the highest, absolute Sambodhi in the world of men and gods. . . .

"But since I possessed, O Bhikkhus, with perfect purity this true knowledge and insight into these four Noble Truths . . . then I knew, O Bhikkhus, that I had obtained the highest, universal Sambodhi. . . .

"And this knowledge and insight arose in my mind: The emancipation of my mind cannot be lost; this is my last birth; hence I shall not be born again!"

QUESTIONS THAT TEND NOT TO EDIFICATION

Thus I have heard.

On certain occasion the Blessed One[13] was dwelling at Savatthi in Jetavana monastery in Anathapindika's Park. Now it happened to the venerable Malunkyaputta,[14] being in seclusion and plunged in meditation, that a consideration presented itself to his mind as follows:

"These theories that the Blessed One has left unexplained, has set aside and rejected — that the world is eternal, that the world is not eternal, that the world is finite, that the world is infinite, that the soul and the body are identical, that the soul is one thing and the body another, that the saint[15] exists after death, that the saint does not exist after death, that the saint both

exists and does not exist after death, that the saint neither exists nor does not exist after death — these the Blessed One does not explain to me. And the fact that the Blessed One does not explain them to me does not please me nor suit me. Therefore I will draw near to the Blessed One and inquire of him concerning this matter. If the Blessed One will explain them to me, . . . I will lead the religious life under the Blessed One. If the Blessed One will not explain them to me, . . . I will abandon religious training and return to the lower life of a layman."

Then the venerable Malunkyaputta arose in the evening from his seclusion, and drew near to where the Blessed One was; and having drawn near and greeted the Blessed One, he sat down respectfully at one side. And seated respectfully at one side, the venerable Malunkyaputta spoke to the Blessed One as follows:

"Reverend Sir, it happened to me, as I was just now in seclusion and plunged in meditation, that a consideration presented itself to my mind, as follows: 'These theories that the Blessed One has left unexplained, has set aside and rejected — that the world is eternal, that the world is not eternal . . . that the saint neither exists nor does not exist after death — these the Blessed One does not explain to me. And the fact that the Blessed One does not explain them to me does not please me nor suit me. I will draw near to the Blessed One and inquire of him concerning this matter. If the Blessed One will explain to me, either that the world is eternal, or that the world is not eternal . . . or that the saint neither exists nor does not exist after death, in that case I will lead the religious life under the Blessed One. If the Blessed One will not explain to me, either that the world is eternal, or that the world is not eternal . . . or that the saint neither exists nor does not exist after death, in that case I will abandon religious training and return to the lower life of a layman.'

---

[13]The Buddha.
[14]One of the Buddha's disciples.

[15]An *arahat,* or "worthy person," who has achieved Enlightenment and thereby Nirvana.

"If the Blessed One knows that the world is eternal, let the Blessed One explain to me that the world is eternal; if the Blessed One knows that the world is not eternal, let the Blessed One explain to me that the world is not eternal. If the Blessed One does not know either that the world is eternal or that the world is not eternal, the only upright thing for one who does not know, or who has not that insight, is to say, 'I do not know; I have not that insight.'"

"Pray Malunkyaputta, did I ever say to you, 'Come, Malunkyaputta, lead the religious life under me, and I will explain to you either that the world is eternal, or that the world is not eternal . . . or that the saint neither exists nor does not exist after death'?"

"No, indeed, Reverend Sir."

"Or did you ever say to me, 'Reverend Sir, I will lead the religious life under the Blessed One, on condition that the Blessed One explain to me either that the world is eternal, or that the world is not eternal . . . or that the saint neither exists nor does not exist after death'?"

"No, indeed, Reverend Sir." . . .

"That being the case, vain man, whom are you so angrily denouncing?

"Malunkyaputta, any one who should say, 'I will not lead the religious life under the Blessed One until the Blessed One shall explain to me either that the world is eternal. Or that the world is not eternal . . . or that the saint neither exists nor does not exist after death'; — that person would die, Malunkyaputta, before the Tathagata had ever explained this to him.

"It is as if, Malunkyaputta, a man had been wounded by an arrow thickly smeared with poison, and his friends and companions, his relatives and kinsfolk, were to procure for him a physician or surgeon; and the sick man were to say, 'I will not have this arrow taken out until I have learned whether the man who wounded me belonged to the warrior caste, or to the Brahmin caste, or to the agricultural caste, or to the menial caste.'

"Or again he were to say, 'I will not have this arrow taken out until I have learned the name of the man who wounded me, and to what clan he belongs.'

"Or again he were to say, 'I will not have this arrow taken out until I have learned whether the man who wounded me was tall, or short, or of the middle height.'

"Or again he were to say, 'I will not have this arrow taken out until I have learned whether the man who wounded me was black, or dusky, or of a yellow skin.'

"Or again he were to say, 'I will not have this arrow taken out until I have learned whether the man who wounded me was from this or that village, or town, or city.' . . .

▷   Many similar possibilities are mentioned.

"That man would die, Malunkyaputta, without ever having learned this.

"In exactly the same way, Malunkyaputta, any one who should say, 'I will not lead the religious life under the Blessed One until the Blessed One shall explain to me either that the world is eternal, or that the world is not eternal . . . or that the saint neither exists nor does not exist after death'; — that person would die, Malunkyaputta, before the Tathagata had ever explained this to him.

"The religious life, Malunkyaputta, does not depend on the dogma that the world is eternal; nor does the religious life, Malunkyaputta, depend on the dogma that the world is not eternal. Whether the dogma obtain, Malunkyaputta, that the world is eternal, or that the world is not eternal, there still remain birth, old age, death, sorrow, lamentation, misery, grief, and despair, for the extinction of which in the present life I am prescribing. . . .

"Accordingly, Malunkyaputta, bear always in mind what it is that I have not explained, and what it is that I have explained. And what, Malunkyaputta, have I not explained? I have not explained, Malunkyaputta, that the world is eternal; I have not explained that the world is not eternal; I have not explained that the world is finite; I have not explained that the world is infinite; I have not explained that the soul and the body are identical; I have not explained that the soul is one thing and the body another; I have not explained that the saint exists after death; I have not explained that the saint does not exist after death; I have not explained that the saint both exists and does not exist after death; I have not explained that the saint neither exists nor does not exist after death. And why, Malunkyaputta, have I not explained this? Because, Malunkyaputta, this profits not, nor has to do with the fundamentals of religion, nor tends to aversion, absence of passion, cessation, quiescence, the supernatural faculties, supreme wisdom, and Nirvana; therefore I have not explained it.

"And what, Malunkyaputta, have I explained? Misery, Malunkyaputta, have I explained; the origin of misery have I explained; the cessation of misery have I explained; and the path leading to the cessation of misery have I explained. And why, Malunkyaputta, have I explained this? Because, Malunkyaputta, this does profit, has to do with the fundamentals of religion, and tends to aversion, absence of passion, cessation, quiescence, knowledge, supreme wisdom, and Nirvana; therefore have I explained it. Accordingly, Malunkyaputta, bear always in mind what it is that I have not explained, and what it is that I have explained."

Thus the Blessed One spoke and, delighted, the venerable Malunkyaputta applauded the speech of the Blessed One.

Admitting Women to the Mendicant Life
▼▼▼
20 ▼ THE DISCIPLINE BASKET

Although the Buddha originally preached his message of enlightenment to a group of five male ascetics, his teachings soon attracted large numbers of people who desired to follow the Middle Path, in the hope of achieving release from the shackles of existence. These aspirants to Buddhahood fell into two categories. Some enthusiastic disciples, like Malunkyaputta in our previous source, became *mendicant,* or begging, monks and attempted to live the Holy Eightfold Path to its fullest. They were known collectively as the *Sangha,* or Order (of monks). Most people attracted to the Buddha's message, however, remained enmeshed in the affairs of the world and constituted a class of faithful laity who supported the Sangha's holy beggars and attempted in individual ways to translate the Buddhist Middle Path into a code of conduct that enabled them to balance their attachments to this world with their desire to find a means of escaping the bonds of suffering.

This group of lay followers from the start contained women, as well as men, whereas the Sangha appears to have originally been composed only of men. Soon, however, the question arose: What to do about women who wish to become monastic beggars? According to a venerable tradition, the first woman to challenge the Buddha on this issue was his maternal aunt and foster mother, Queen Maha-Prajapati, who had recently been widowed.

The following story of Maha-Prajapati's attempt to become a mendicant is preserved in *The Discipline Basket,* a collection of texts that is explained in the introduction to source 19. As we saw, although these texts were written down in their present form many centuries after the Buddha's death, they are based on strong oral traditions. As such, they probably contain more than just a few germs of historical truth.

QUESTIONS FOR ANALYSIS

1. Why does the Buddha finally relent and allow his aunt and other women to embrace the mendicant life?
2. Even after giving his permission, what does he think about the wisdom of allowing women to enter the monastic life?
3. Consider the eight special rules for Buddhist nuns. What is their combined effect?
4. Do you think you can legitimately infer anything from this document concerning the general status of women in north India in the age of the Buddha?
5. Regardless of your answer to question 4, what can you infer from this document about the status of women in Theravada Buddhist society around the late first century B.C.E.?
6. Notwithstanding the special rules laid upon them, as well as the profession's natural rigor, why would some women find the mendicant monastic life attractive?

Now the Blessed Buddha was staying among the Sakyas[1] in Kapilavatthu. . . . And Maha-Prajapati the Gotami[2] went to the place where the Blessed One was, and on arriving there, bowed down before the Blessed One, and remained standing on one side. And so standing she spoke thus to the Blessed One:

"It would be well, lord, if women should be allowed to renounce their homes and enter the homeless state under the doctrine and discipline proclaimed by the Tathagata."[3]

"Enough, Gotami. Let it not please you that women should be allowed to do so."

[And a second and a third time Maha-Prajapati the Gotami made the same request in the same words, and received the same reply.]

Then Maha-Prajapati the Gotami, sad and sorrowful that the Blessed One would not permit women to enter the homeless state, bowed down before the Blessed One, and keeping him on her right hand as she passed him, departed . . . weeping and in tears.

Now when the Blessed One had remained at Kapilavatthu as long as he thought fit, he set out on his journey toward Vesali; and traveling straight on he in due course arrived there. And there at Vesali the Blessed One stayed. . . .

And Maha-Prajapati the Gotami cut off her hair, and put on orange-colored robes,[4] and set out, with a number of women of the Sakya clan, toward Vesali; and in due course she arrived at Vesali. . . . And Maha-Prajapati the Gotami, with

---

[1]The Buddha's clan.
[2]Her family name; before renouncing his patrimony, the Buddha had been surnamed *Gautama*.

[3]One of the Buddha's titles. (See note 2 in the previous document.)
[4]Orange robes are the distinguishing costume of Buddhist monks.

swollen feet and covered with dust, sad and sorrowful, weeping and in tears, took her stand outside under the entrance porch.

And the venerable Ananda[5] saw her so standing there, and on seeing her so he said to
Maha-Prajapati: "Why are you standing there,
outside the porch, with swollen feet and covered
with dust, sad and sorrowful, weeping and in
tears?"

"Because Ananda, the lord, the Blessed One,
does not permit women to renounce their homes
and enter the homeless state under the doctrine
and discipline proclaimed by the Tathagata."

Then the venerable Ananda went up to the
place where the Blessed One was, and bowed
down before the Blessed One, and took his seat
on one side. And, so sitting, the venerable
Ananda said to the Blessed One:

"Behold, lord, Maha-Prajapati the Gotami is
standing outside under the entrance porch, with
swollen feet and covered with dust, sad and sorrowful, weeping and in tears, because the Blessed
One does not permit women to renounce their
homes and enter the homeless state under the
doctrine and discipline proclaimed by the Blessed
One.

"It would be well, lord, if women were to have
permission granted to them to do as she desires."

"Enough, Ananda. Let it not please you that
women should be allowed to do so." . . .

[And a second and a third time Ananda made
the same request, in the same words, and received
the same reply.]

Then the venerable Ananda thought: "The
Blessed One does not give his permission, let
me now ask the Blessed One on another ground."
And the venerable Ananda said to the Blessed
One:

"Are women, lord, capable when they have
gone forth from the household life and entered
the homeless state, under the doctrine and discipline proclaimed by the Blessed One — are they
capable of realizing the fruit of conversion, or of
the second path, or of the third path,[6] or of
Arahantship?"[7]

"They are capable, Ananda."

"If then, lord, they are so capable, since
Maha-Prajapati the Gotami has proved herself
of great service to the Blessed One, when as aunt
and nurse she nourished him and gave him milk,
and on the death of his mother suckled the
Blessed One at her own breast, it would be well,
lord, that women should have permission to go
forth from the household life and enter the homeless state under the doctrine and discipline proclaimed by the Tathagata."

"If then, Ananda, Maha-Prajapati the Gotami
takes upon herself the eight chief rules, let
that be reckoned as her ordination.[8] They are
these:

1. "A nun, even if of a hundred years standing,
   shall make salutation to, shall rise up in the
   presence of, shall bow down before, and shall
   perform all proper duties toward a monk,
   even a newly initiated monk. This is a rule
   to be revered and reverenced, honored and
   observed, and her life long never to be transgressed.
2. "A nun is not to spend the rainy season[9] in a
   district in which there is no monk. This is a
   rule . . . never to be transgressed.
3. "Every half month a nun is to await from the
   order of Bhikkhus[10] two things, . . . the date
   of the uposatha ceremony,[11] and the time
   when the monk will come to give the exhor-

---

[5] The Buddha's beloved disciple and personal attendant.
[6] The three states that anticipate Enlightenment ("crossing
the stream") once one has received and accepted the message of the Four Noble Truths: the fruit of entering the
stream; the fruit of the once returner; the fruit of the
nonreturner.

[7] Enlightenment (see source 19, note 15).
[8] By accepting these eight special rules, she is ordained to
the monastic life.
[9] The time of spiritual retreat.
[10] Male monks.
[11] The twice-monthly monastic meeting.

tation. This is a rule . . . never to be transgressed.

4. "After keeping the rainy season the nun is to hold Pavarana,[12] to inquire whether any fault can be laid to her charge, before both orders — monks as well as nuns — with respect to three matters, namely, what has been seen, and what has been heard, and what has been suspected. This is a rule . . . never to be transgressed.

5. "A nun who has been guilty of a serious offense is to undergo suitable discipline toward both orders, monks and nuns. This is a rule . . . never to be transgressed.

6. "When a nun, as novice, has been trained for two years in the . . . rules, she is to ask leave for . . . ordination from both orders, monks as well as nuns. This is a rule . . . never to be transgressed.

7. "A nun is on no pretext to revile or abuse a monk. This is a rule . . . never to be transgressed.

8. "From henceforth official admonition by nuns of monks is forbidden, whereas the official admonition of nuns by monks is not forbidden. This is a rule . . . never to be transgressed.

"If, Ananda, Maha-Prajapati the Gotami take upon herself these eight chief rules, let that be reckoned . . . as her ordination."

Then the venerable Ananda, when he had learned from the Blessed One these eight chief rules, went to Maha-Prajapati the Gotami and told her all that the Blessed One had said, to which she replied: . . .

"I, Ananda, take upon me these eight chief rules never to be transgressed my life long."

Then the venerable Ananda returned to the Blessed One, and bowed down before him, and took his seat on one side. And, so sitting, the venerable Ananda said to the Blessed One: "Maha-Prajapati the Gotami, lord, has taken upon herself the eight chief rules, the aunt of the Blessed One has received . . . ordination."

"If, Ananda, women had not received permission to go out from the household life and enter the homeless state, under the doctrine and discipline proclaimed by the Tathagata, then would the pure religion, Ananda, have lasted long, the good law would have stood fast for a thousand years. But since, Ananda, women now have received that permission, the pure religion, Ananda, will not now last so long, the good law will now stand fast for only five hundred years. Just, Ananda, as houses in which there are many women and but few men, are easily violated by robbers, by burglars; just so, Ananda, under whatever doctrine and discipline women are allowed to go out from the household life into the homeless state, that religion will not last long.

"And just, Ananda, as when disease, called mildew, falls upon a field of rice in fine condition, that field of rice does not continue long; just so, Ananda, under whatsoever doctrine and discipline women are allowed to go forth from the household life into the homeless state, that religion will not last long. And just, Ananda, as when disease, called blight, falls upon a field of sugar-cane in good condition, that field of sugar-cane does not continue long; just so, Ananda, under whatsoever doctrine and discipline women are allowed to go forth from the household life into the homeless state, that religion does not last long. And just, Ananda, as a man would in anticipation build an embankment to a great reservoir, beyond which the water should not overpass; just even so, Ananda, have I in anticipation laid down these eight chief rules for the nuns, their life long not to be overpassed."

---

[12]The final ceremony of the religious retreat, in which one seeks to discover his or her faults.

Persians, Israelites, and Their Gods

By the sixth century B.C.E. two peoples of Southwest Asia, the Hebrews and the Persians, had evolved separate visions of a single God of the universe who demanded wholehearted devotion and imposed an uncompromising code of moral behavior upon all believers. Both the Persian Ahura Mazda (Wise Lord) and the Hebrew YHWH (I Am Who I Am) were originally perceived as male sky gods, existing among a multiplicity of other gods of nature; by the sixth century, however, their respective devotees worshiped each as the sole creator of the entire universe and envisioned each as transcending all material creation. This totally spiritual nature did not prevent either from also being a god of history. That is, each God used humans as agents to serve the Divine Will and thereby to assist in the realization of the Divine Plan for humanity. For both the Persians and Hebrews, human history had a purpose and a goal. By serving as agents in the unfolding of God's plan for creation, humans thus assumed a spiritual dignity and importance that they could otherwise never have hoped to attain.

The Fight between Good and Evil

▼▼▼

21 ▼ *Zarathustra, GATHAS*

Some time after 1400 B.C.E. a group of Indo-Europeans settled the Iranian highlands. The religion and general culture of these people initially resembled that of the vedic Aryans. For example, they celebrated the slaying of Verethra, the drought, by their war god Indara. The parallel with Indra's striking down Vritra, the dragon of drought, is obvious (see Chapter 2, source 11). In time, however, these settlers, of what is today largely Iran, developed a civilization that differed radically from that of the Indo-Aryans. We call that ancient civilization *Persian.*

By the late sixth century B.C.E. the Persians possessed the largest empire the world had yet seen. For nearly two centuries they united Southwest Asia and portions of Central Asia, Northeast Africa, and the Balkan region of Europe into a politically centralized yet culturally diverse entity. During the reign of Darius the Great (r. 522–486 B.C.E.), who rightly styled himself King of Kings, the royal house of Persia officially adopted as its religion the teachings of a native son, Zarathustra. The highly ethical message of this Persian religious visionary appears to have been one of the major factors contributing to the empire's general policy of good government.

We know little about the life of Zarathustra. Apparently, he flourished in eastern Iran around 660 B.C.E. and taught his disciples to uphold, through ritual and moral conduct, the cause of *Ahura Mazda,* the sole deity of the universe. It is clear that Zarathustra claimed to be a *prophet* (a person speaking by divine inspiration, thereby revealing the will of God). It is equally clear that Zarathustra transmitted to his followers the message that Ahura Mazda required all humans to join in the cosmic struggle against Angra Mainyu (Enemy Spirit). Although in no way the equal of Ahura Mazda, Angra Mainyu (known also as the *Liar*) afflicted human souls with evil and led them away from the path of righteousness.

Zarathustra's teachings took hold in Persia, evolving into a complex religion we call *Zoroastrianism* (after Zoroaster, the Greek version of Zarathustra). In the process, however, Zarathustra's strict monotheism was lost. From 224 to 651 C.E. Zoroastrianism was the official state religion of a revived Persian Empire under the Sassanian house, but Zoroastrianism had by then lapsed into polytheism. Moreover, Angra Mainyu was now seen as coeternal and coequal with Ahura Mazda. One deity was the creator of all goodness; the other was the origin of all evil.

The *Avesta,* the Zoroastrian collection of holy scripture, was compiled only in the early Sassanian Era and strongly reflects this later dualism. It also contains, however, a few short devotional hymns, known as *Gathas,* which date from the age of Zarathustra and probably owe their composition to him or an early disciple. Essentially our only reliable sources for the teachings of the Persian prophet, they illustrate his vision and message.

QUESTIONS FOR ANALYSIS

1. Where and how does Zarathustra refer to Ahura Mazda's use of humanity and history to realize certain sacred purposes? How does each person's life become a microcosm of the battle between Ahura Mazda and the Liar?
2. What is promised to those who serve Ahura Mazda faithfully? Compare those promises with what YHWH promised the Children of Israel for their faithful service (Chapter 2, source 14). What do you conclude from this comparison?
3. What does Zarathustra think of those persons who do not accept and serve Ahura Mazda?
4. How do we know that Zarathustra believed Ahura Mazda would ultimately triumph over evil?
5. What evidence indicates that Zarathustra saw Ahura Mazda as the sole creator of the universe?
6. Does Zarathustra see his faith as only one of many paths to the truth, or is it the Truth?
7. Compare the message proclaimed by Zarathustra with the messages of the Mahavira and the Buddha. Which strike you as more significant, their similarities or differences, and what do you conclude from your answer?

Then shall I recognize you as strong and holy, Mazda,[1] when by the hand in which you yourself hold the destinies that you will assign to the Liar and the Righteous . . . the might of Good Thought[2] shall come to me.

As the holy one I recognized you, Mazda Ahura,[3] when I saw you in the beginning at the birth of Life, when you made actions and words to have their reward — evil for the evil, a good Destiny for the good — through your wisdom when creation shall reach its goal.

At which goal you will come with your holy Spirit, O Mazda, with Dominion, at the same with Good Thought, by whose action the settlements[4] will prosper through Right. . . .

As the holy one I recognized you, Mazda Ahura, when Good Thought came to me and asked me, "Who are you? to whom do you belong? By what sign will you appoint the days for questioning about your possessions and yourself?"

Then I said to him: "To the first question, I am Zarathustra, a true foe to the Liar, to the utmost of my power, but a powerful support would I be to the Righteous, that I may attain the future things of the infinite Dominion, as I praise and proclaim you, Mazda." . . .

As the holy one I recognized you, Mazda Ahura, when Good Thought came to me, when the still mind taught me to declare what is best: "Let not a man seek again and again to please the Liars, for they make all the righteous enemies."

And thus Zarathustra himself, O Ahura, chooses that spirit of thine that is holiest, Mazda. May Right be embodied, full of life and strength! May Piety abide in the Dominion where the sun shines! May Good Thought give destiny to men according to their works!

▾ ▾ ▾

This I ask you, tell me truly, Ahura. Who is by generation the Father of Right, at the first? Who determined the path of sun and stars? Who is it by whom the moon waxes and wanes again? This, O Mazda, and yet more, I want to know.

This I ask you, tell me truly, Ahura. Who upheld the earth beneath and the firmament from falling? Who the waters and the plants? Who yoked swiftness to winds and clouds? Who is, O Mazda, creator of Good Thought?

This I ask you, tell me truly, Ahura. What artist made light and darkness? What artist made sleep and waking? Who made morning, noon, and night, that call the understanding man to his duty? . . .

This I ask you, tell me truly, Ahura. Who created together with Dominion the precious Piety? Who made by wisdom the son obedient to his father? I strive to recognize by these things you, O Mazda, creator of all things through the holy spirit. . . .

This I ask you, tell me truly, Ahura. The Religion which is the best for all that are, which in union with Right should make prosperous all that is mine, will they duly observe it, the religion of my creed, with the words and action of Piety, in desire for your future good things, O Mazda?

This I ask you, tell me truly, Ahura — whether Piety will extend to those to whom your Religion shall be proclaimed? I was ordained at the first by you: all others I look upon with hatred of spirit.

This I ask you, tell me truly, Ahura. Who among those with whom I would speak is a righteous man, and who a liar? On which side is the enemy? . . .

This I ask you, tell me truly, Ahura — whether we shall drive the Lie away from us to those who being full of disobedience will not strive after

---

[1]*Mazda* means "wise" or "wisdom."
[2]Zarathustra appears to have conceived of Good Thought, Piety, Right, and other such entities as angelic spirits and not simply abstract virtues.

[3]*Ahura* means "lord."
[4]Settled or civilized people.

fellowship with Right, nor trouble themselves with counsel of Good Thought. . . .

This I ask you, tell me truly, Ahura — whether through you I shall attain my goal . . . and that my voice may be effectual, that Welfare and Immortality may be ready to unite according to that promise with him who joins himself with Right.

This I ask you, tell me truly, Ahura — whether I shall indeed, O Right, earn that reward, even ten mares with a stallion and a camel,[5] which was promised to me, O Mazda, as well as through you the future gift of Welfare and Immortality.

▾ ▾ ▾

I will speak of that which Mazda Ahura, the all-knowing, revealed to me first in this earthly life. Those of you that put not in practice this word as I think and utter it, to them shall be woe at the end of life. . . .

I will speak of that which the Holiest declared to me as the word that is best for mortals to obey: he, Mazda Ahura said, "They who at my bidding render him[6] obedience, shall all attain Welfare and Immortality by the actions of the Good Spirit." . . .

In immortality shall the soul of the righteous be joyful, in perpetuity shall be the torments of the Liars. All this does Mazda Ahura appoint by his Dominion.

---

[5]Symbols of good fortune and earthly prosperity.

[6]Zarathustra.

A New Covenant for All Peoples
▾▾▾
22 ▾ *THE BOOK OF ISAIAH*

As we saw in Chapter 2, around 1200 B.C.E. the Israelites moved into the land of Canaan. Once settled there, they waged a continuing battle to retain their independence, cultural identity, and exclusive devotion to YHWH. In the late eleventh century B.C.E., largely in response to Philistine pressure, the Israelites created a kingdom. Around 1020 B.C.E. their second king, David, captured Jerusalem and converted it into the religious and political capital of the Israelites.

The political stability of this kingdom was precarious at best. In 922 it was split into two independent entities: the larger kingdom of Israel in the north and the kingdom of Judah, centering on Jerusalem, in the south. In 722 the Assyrians obliterated Israel. The more compact and remote kingdom of Judah survived until 586 B.C.E., when finally a Semitic people from Mesopotamia known as the *Chaldeans* captured and destroyed Jerusalem and carried off most of Judah's upper classes into exile in Babylon, an episode known forever after as the *Babylonian Captivity.*

Cultural and religious stability was equally precarious. The cult of YHWH was in many ways more suitable to the life of the desert herder than to that of the settled farmer. As the Hebrews settled down, they adopted many of the religious practices of their Canaanite neighbors. This action occasioned angry protests from a group of religious reformers known as the *prophets.* The prophets, who claimed inspiration from YHWH, now increasingly referred to simply as *the Lord,* protested vehemently against debasement of the Mosaic religion, but in the process of their protest they broadened considerably the moral and theological scope of the worship of the Lord.

One of the greatest and last of these prophets was a person we know only as *Second Isaiah.* He served as the voice of a new faith that was born out of the anguish of the Babylonian Captivity. We call that faith *Judaism.*

The original Prophet Isaiah had towered over the religious scene of Jerusalem from the middle to late eighth century B.C.E. and left behind a rich legacy of teaching on the Lord's role as the God who controls the destinies of all people. Second Isaiah, who lived in the mid and late sixth century B.C.E., carried on this tradition. Consequently, the prophecies of this otherwise unknown person were appended to the writings of the earlier Isaiah and appear as chapters 40 through 55 in the Bible's Book of Isaiah.

The following passages were composed around 538 B.C.E., when Cyrus the Great, king of Persia and conqueror of the Chaldean (Neo-Babylonian) Empire, released the Israelites from captivity. Here Second Isaiah metaphorically describes the people of Israel as YHWH's *Suffering Servant* and delineates the historical role that the Lord has decreed for this servant.

QUESTIONS FOR ANALYSIS

1. Consider the opening lines of this selection. In what manner has YHWH's special relationship with the people of Israel remained unchanged since the days of Moses?
2. Consider the Lord's relationship with King Cyrus and the Persians. Even though Cyrus does not know or honor Him, the Lord has chosen Cyrus as a servant. Why? In what ways does this represent a departure from the Israelites' traditional view of their neighbors (Chapter 2, source 15)?
3. What does Second Isaiah mean by the prophecy that the Lord will present Israel "as a light to the nations"? How will the Children of Israel's redemption from exile in Babylon serve a universal purpose?
4. What are the essential elements of Second Isaiah's vision of the Lord and this deity's Chosen People?
5. In what way has the Lord's Covenant with Israel been given a new meaning? How does this new interpretation of the Covenant relate to the covenant Yahweh entered into with Noah (Chapter 2, source 13)?
6. In what ways are Ahura Mazda and the Lord both universal gods of righteousness? How do their attitudes toward good and evil differ from that expressed by Lord Krishna in the *Bhagavad Gita* (source 17)? What do you conclude from this?
7. "For the Hebrews and Persians religion became the means of transforming the world, not negating it." What does the author of this statement mean? Do you agree or disagree? Why?
8. How do Ahura Mazda and the Lord differ from Brahman?

"But now hear, O Jacob[1] my servant,
Israel whom I have chosen!
Thus says the Lord who made you, who formed
    you from the womb and will help you:
Fear not, O Jacob my servant,
Jeshurun[2] whom I have chosen.
For I will pour water on the thirsty land,
and streams on the dry ground;
I will pour my Spirit upon your descendants,
and my blessing on your offspring.
They shall spring up like grass amid waters,
like willows by flowing streams;
This one will say, 'I am the Lord's,
another will call himself by the name of Jacob,
and another will write on his hand,
    'The Lord's,'[3]
and surname himself by the name of Israel.
Thus says the Lord, the King of Israel[4]
and his Redeemer, the Lord of hosts:
"I am the first and I am the last;
besides me there is no God. . . .
Remember these things, O Jacob,
and Israel, for you are my servant;
I formed you, you are my servant;
O Israel, you will not be forgotten by me.
I have swept away your transgressions like
    a cloud,
and your sins like mist;
return to me, for I have redeemed you. . . .
I am the Lord, who made all things,
who stretched out the heavens alone,
who spread out the earth —
    Who was with me? —
who frustrates the omens of liars,
and makes fools of diviners;
who turns wise men back,
and makes their knowledge foolish;
who confirms the word of his servant,
and performs the counsel of his messengers;

who says of Jerusalem, 'She shall be inhabited,'
and of the cities of Judah, 'They shall be built,
and I will raise up their ruins,' . . .
who says of Cyrus, 'He is my shepherd.
and he shall fulfill all my purpose';
saying of Jerusalem, 'She shall be built,'
and of the temple, 'Your foundation shall
    be laid.'"
Thus says the Lord to his anointed, to Cyrus,
whose right hand I have grasped,
to subdue nations before him
and ungird the loins of kings,
to open doors before him
that gates may not be closed:
"I will go before you
and level the mountains,
I will break in pieces the doors of bronze
and cut asunder the bars of iron,[5]
I will give you the treasures of darkness
and the hoards in secret places,
that you may know that it is I, the Lord,
the God of Israel, who call you by your name.
For the sake of my servant Jacob,
and Israel my chosen,
I call you by your name,
I surname you,[6] though you do not know me.
I am the Lord, and there is no other,
besides me there is no God;
I gird you, though you do not know me,
that men may know, from the rising of the sun
and from the west, that there is none
    besides me;
I am the Lord, and there is no other. . . .
I made the earth,
and created man upon it;
it was my hands that stretched out
    the heavens,
and I commanded all their host.
I have aroused him[7] in righteousness,

[1]Here *Jacob* means all of Jacob's descendants — the Children of Israel.
[2]"Upright one" — a term of endearment.
[3]Compare this with Moses' command that the Israelites tie the Law to their arms and wear it on their foreheads (Chapter 2, source 14).

[4]This refers to all of the Israelites and should not be confused with the kingdom of Israel, which the Assyrians destroyed in 722 B.C.E.
[5]A reference to the great walls of Babylon.
[6]The Lord bestows on Cyrus the title *the Great.*
[7]Cyrus.

and I will make straight all his ways;
he shall build my city[8]
and set my exiles free,
not for price or reward,"
says the Lord of hosts. . . .
"I the Lord speak the truth,
I declare what is right.
"Assemble yourselves and come,
draw near together,
you survivors of the nations![9]
They have no knowledge
who carry about their wooden idols,
and keep on praying to a god
that cannot save.
Declare and present your case;
let them take counsel together!
Who told this long ago?
Who declared it of old?
Was it not I, the Lord?
And there is no other god besides me,
  a righteous God and a Savior;
there is none besides me.
"Turn to me and be saved,
all the ends of the earth!
For I am God, and there is no other.
By myself I have sworn,
from my mouth has gone forth
  in righteousness
a word that shall not return:
'To me every knee shall bow,
every tongue shall swear.'
"Only in the Lord, it shall be said of me,
are righteousness and strength;
to him shall come and be ashamed,
all who were incensed against him.

In the Lord all the offspring of Israel
shall triumph and glory." . . .
Listen to me, O coastlands,
and hearken, you peoples from afar.
The Lord called me[10] from the womb,
from the body of my mother he named
  my name.
He made my mouth like a sharp sword,
in the shadow of his hand he hid me;
he made me a polished arrow,
in his quiver he hid me away.
And he said to me, "You are my servant,
Israel, in whom I will be glorified."
But I said, "I have labored in vain,
I have spent my strength for nothing
  and vanity;
yet surely my right is with the Lord,
and my recompense with my God."
And now the Lord says, . . .
"It is too light a thing that you should be
  my servant
to raise up the tribes of Jacob
and to restore the preserved of Israel;
I will give you as a light to the nations,
that my salvation may reach to the end of
  the earth."
Thus says the Lord,
the Redeemer of Israel and his Holy One,
to one deeply despised, abhorred by
  the nations,
the servant of rulers:
"Kings shall see and arise;
princes, and they shall prostrate themselves;
because of the Lord, who is faithful,
the Holy One of Israel, who has chosen you."

---

[8] Jerusalem will be rebuilt.
[9] All peoples who survive the collapse of the Chaldean, or Neo-Babylonian, Empire.

[10] The Children of Israel.

Chapter 4

▾▾▾

The Secular
Made Sacred

Developing the Humanistic Traditions of China and Hellas: 600–200 B.C.E.

The Chinese and the Greeks, who inhabited the eastern and western extremes of civilized Eurasia in the sixth century B.C.E., had deities and spirits for every imaginable function and a wide range of religious taboos and rituals. But religion in its narrowest sense — reverence for a supernatural being — offered them little in the way of either intellectual stimulation or emotional outlet. While contemporaries in India and Southwest Asia were raising religious speculation to high levels of abstract thought, religion for the Chinese and Greeks remained, for the most part, a practical affair. One sacrificed to the gods and spirits in order to assure their benevolence. Religion was a form of magical insurance and not a relationship with Ultimate Reality.

At the same time, the social and psychic crises of the Age of Iron were just as real in China and Greece as elsewhere. In fashioning responses to the questions occasioned by the dislocation of traditional ways of life, both the Chinese and Greeks looked more toward this world than the Beyond and created cultures that were essentially *humanistic* and *secular* (of this world) in the sense that they focused on humanity's position within an observable universe of finite space and time. Social philosophy rather than theology engaged the intellectual energies of the Chinese and the Greeks as they endeavored to meet the challenges of the Iron Age.

In China various philosophers offered insights into how humans should behave in regard to their families, the state, and nature. These philosophers also struggled with the issue of personal excellence. They first inquired whether such a goal was achievable or even desirable, and many ultimately concluded that the cult of individuality that was inherent in such a quest for personal perfection threatened the harmony of the family, the state, and even the natural order. For those who accepted, however tentatively and reluctantly, even a modified search for personal excellence, several questions remained: How is it achieved, and what purposes does it serve? Does one's cultivation of virtue have only personal value, or is it subordinate to a higher social purpose?

Many of the same human-centered concerns preoccupied Greek rationalists. Two issues particularly dominated Greek social thought: (1) How does the individual achieve excellence, a quality the Greeks assumed was the natural goal of all human striving and which they termed *arete*? (2) How does the individual function as an effective citizen within the city-state? Most Greek social philosophers, at least during the fifth and fourth centuries B.C.E., assumed that cultivation of one's personal talents and good citizenship were complementary and not antithetical pursuits. Additionally, a small but highly influential group of Greek rationalists turned their attention to an objective study of the physical environment, thereby becoming the West's first natural scientists. Like its social philosophers, Greece's scientists attempted to explain the workings of the physical universe in response to human needs, the most basic of which was to provide information that would allow people to control their lives and environment.

The Chinese and the Greeks did not look to divine forces for direction and meaning in life. Rather they fashioned cultures in which humanity and the natural world were the measure of all that was important to them. However, concentration on the human-sized matters of this world did not mean that the Chinese and the Greeks lacked a sense of a sacred mystery. Nothing could be farther from the truth. In essence, they made the secular sacred.

▼▼▼

China: Three Ways of Thought

Ages of political and social unrest often prove to be periods of significant intellectual ferment, and this was certainly true of the era of Eastern Zhou (770–256 B.C.E.). The collapse of the Western Zhou monarchy in 771 signaled the end of royal power in China and ushered in a five hundred–year period when regional states held center stage. Zhou kings continued to perform their traditional religious roles and received tokens of nominal obedience from the great feudal lords. True power, however, lay in the hands of the regional lords, who developed bureaucratic governments and strong standing armies. With each local prince essentially a sovereign, military and diplomatic maneuvering among their states became a constant fact of life. As disruptive as this was at times, it also proved to be a stimulus to intellectual activity. Both the demands of statecraft at the regional level and the occasional social dislocation that resulted from the conflicts among these states encouraged the development of political theory and social philosophy.

This was especially true from the fifth century B.C.E. onward, as wars became more frequent and bitter. Chinese historians traditionally catalogue the period from 403 to 221 B.C.E. as the Age of Warring States. Innovations such as cavalry, iron weapons, and the crossbow broke the battlefield superiority of the chariot-driving aristocracy. Armies of conscripted foot and horse soldiers became larger and more deadly. Concomitantly, intellectuals sought to keep pace with this changing world.

Between 260 and 221 B.C.E., Qin, the most aggressive and best organized of the warring states, conquered all rival powers in China and established a new royal family, the short-lived but pivotal Qin Dynasty (221–206 B.C.E.). The triumph of the lord of Qin, the self-styled Qin Shi Huangdi (the First Emperor of Qin, r. 221–210 B.C.E.) not only inaugurated China's first empire, it brought with it the momentary victory of a political philosophy known as *Legalism.* In conforming to the principles of Legalism, the Qin regime was ruthless and brutal in its drive for complete centralization of authority. Undone by the harshness of its laws and policies, the Qin Dynasty collapsed in early 206 in the midst of rebellion and civil war. Within four years, however, a commoner general, Liu Bang, reformulated the empire by establishing the successful and long-lived Han Dynasty (202 B.C.E.–220 C.E.).

Although the extreme measures of the Qin regime discredited Legalism as a philosophy, Legalist-inspired organizational structures and administrative procedures served as the framework of the highly centralized Han Empire. By the late second century B.C.E., however, the Han Dynasty adopted as its official ideology the gentler and more humane philosophy of *Confucianism,* which had also taken shape in the disturbing period of Eastern Zhou.

Han imperial policies and institutions were, therefore, the products of a Confucian-Legalist synthesis, but these were not the only modes of thought to play a prominent role both then and ever after in China. *Daoism,* an antirational, quite antipolitical, and somewhat antisocial philosophy, also emerged as an articulated school of thought in the confusion of Eastern Zhou and survived the hostility of Qin censors.

These three schools of Chinese thought, each of which claimed to offer the only correct Way, or path, to social harmony, were not the only important intellectual currents in China in the age of Han. They were, however, destined to become three major foundational blocks of Chinese civilization. Although they offered different answers to the social ills of their day and presented some striking differences of perspective, they were not mutually exclusive; indeed, they have served for more than two thousand years as intertwined and complementary elements of Chinese thought and action.

Daoism: The Way That Is and Is Not
▼▼▼

23 ▼ *Laozi,*
THE CLASSIC OF THE WAY AND VIRTUE

Few if any philosophies are as enigmatic as *Daoism* — the teachings of the Way (Dao). The opening lines of this school's greatest masterpiece, *The Classic of the Way and Virtue* (*Dao De Jing*), which is ascribed to the legendary *Laozi,* immediately confront the reader with Daoism's essential paradox: "The Way that can be trodden is not the enduring and unchanging Way. The name that can be named is not the enduring and unchanging name." Here is a philosophy that purports to teach *the* Way (of truth) but simultaneously claims that the True Way transcends human understanding. Encapsulated within a little book of some five thousand words is a philosophy that defies definition, spurns reason, and rejects words as inadequate.

The Dao is limitless and its origins are infinite; somewhat like the Way that it purports to teach and not teach, Daoism has many manifestations and numerous origins. No one knows when or where it originated, but its roots probably lie in the animistic religions of prehistorical China. Daoism's earliest sages are equally shadowy. According to tradition, the author of Daoism's greatest classic was Laozi, who supposedly was born around 604 B.C.E. and died about 517, making him an older contemporary of Confucius (source 24). According to one popular story, when Confucius visited him, Laozi instructed the younger man to rid himself of his arrogant airs and then bade him farewell. As another story has it, the aged Laozi decided to leave the state in which he lived because he foresaw its imminent decay. At the frontier he was delayed by a border official, who implored him not to depart without first leaving behind his wisdom. In response Laozi dashed off the *Dao De Jing* and left, never to be heard from again (although according to one story that sprang up in Daoist circles in the fourth century C.E., Laozi went to India where he became the Buddha). The fact that *Laozi* means "Old Master" suggests to many that this sage was more a composite figure of legend and imagination than a historic individual of flesh and blood. Indeed, many scholars conclude that the bulk of the language, ideas, and allusions contained within this classic indicate an intellectual environment closer to 300 than to 500 B.C.E.

Whatever its date and circumstances of composition, the *Dao De Jing* is one of the most profound and beautiful works ever written in Chinese. This little book has exercised an incalculable influence on Chinese life and art over the centuries. There is a good deal of truth to the cliché that traditional Chinese upper-class men were Confucians in public and Daoists in private.

As you study the following selections, pay particular attention to the Daoist notion of *Actionless Activity.* Known in Chinese as *wuwei* and also translated as

"Effortlessness," "Nonaction," and "Nonstriving," this idea pervades all Daoist thought and comes closest to being Daoism's universal principle and driving force, if such is possible.

QUESTIONS FOR ANALYSIS

1. How does one define the Way? How permanent is it? How limited is it? Is there anything it does not encompass?
2. Does the Way acknowledge absolute right and wrong?
3. How does a sage ruler who is in harmony with the Way govern?
4. How does *wuwei* function? Why is it the greatest form of action?
5. What are Daoism's major criticisms of Confucianism and Legalism?
6. Why would Daoism appeal to some individuals in the Age of Warring States?
7. Compare *wuwei* with the teachings of the Mahavira and the Buddha (Chapter 3, sources 18 and 19). Do you see any similarities? What are more significant, the similarities or the differences?
8. Compare the Way with the Supreme Beings of India and Southwest Asia (Chapter 3, sources 16, 17, 21, and 22). Does it share any common characteristics with Brahman, Ahura Mazda, or YHWH? Which are more significant, the similarities or the differences?

THE WAY

The Dao that can be trodden is not the enduring and unchanging Dao. The name that can be named is not the enduring and unchanging name.

Conceived of as having no name, it is the Originator of heaven and earth; conceived of as having a name, it is the Mother of all things.

▼ ▼ ▼

The Dao produces all things and nourishes them; it produces them and does not claim them as its own; it does all, and yet does not boast of it; it presides over all, and yet does not control them. This is what is called "The mysterious quality" of the Dao.

▼ ▼ ▼

When the Great Dao ceased to be observed, benevolence and righteousness came into vogue. Then appeared wisdom and shrewdness, and there ensued great hypocrisy.[1]

▼ ▼ ▼

Man takes his law from the Earth; the Earth takes its law from Heaven; Heaven takes its law from the Dao. The law of the Dao is its being what it is.

▼ ▼ ▼

All-pervading is the Great Dao! It may be found on the left hand and on the right.

All things depend on it for their production, which it gives to them, not one refusing obedience to it. When its work is accomplished, it

---

[1]This is a criticism of the supposed hypocrisy of Confucians who claim to know and practice virtue (see source 24).

does not claim the name of having done it. It clothes all things as with a garment, and makes no assumption of being their lord; — it may be named in the smallest things; . . . it may be named in the greatest things.

▼ ▼ ▼

He who has in himself abundantly the attributes of the Dao is like an infant.

▼ ▼ ▼

The Dao in its regular course does nothing, for the sake of doing it, and so there is nothing which it does not do.

THE WISE PERSON

When we renounce learning we have no troubles.[2]

▼ ▼ ▼

If we could renounce our sageness and discard our wisdom, it would be better for the people a hundredfold. If we could renounce our benevolence and discard our righteousness, the people would again become filial and kindly.[3] If we could renounce our artful contrivances and discard our scheming for gain, there would be no thieves nor robbers.

▼ ▼ ▼

The sage manages affairs without doing anything, and conveys his instructions without the use of speech.

▼ ▼ ▼

Therefore the sage holds in his embrace the one thing of humility, and manifests it to all the world. He is free from self-display, and therefore he shines; from self-assertion, and therefore he is distinguished; from self-boasting, and therefore his merit is acknowledged; from self-complacency, and therefore he acquires superiority. It is because he is thus free from striving that therefore no one in the world is able to strive with him.

▼ ▼ ▼

When gold and jade fill the hall, their possessor cannot keep them safe. When wealth and honors lead to arrogance, this brings its evil on itself. When the work is done, and one's name is becoming distinguished, to withdraw into obscurity is the way of Heaven.

THE IDEAL GOVERNMENT

A state may be ruled by measures of correction;[4] weapons of war may be used with crafty dexterity; but the kingdom is made one's own only by freedom from action and purpose.

How do I know that it is so? By these facts: — In the kingdom the multiplication of prohibitive enactments increases the poverty of the people; the more implements to add to their profit that the people have, the greater disorder is there in the state and clan; the more acts of crafty dexterity that men possess, the more do strange contrivances appear; the more display there is of legislation, the more thieves and robbers there are.

Therefore a sage has said, "I will do nothing, and the people will be transformed of themselves; I will be fond of keeping still, and the people will of themselves become correct. I will take no trouble about it, and the people will of them-

---

[2]According to the Confucians, careful study and emulation of the virtues of the past is the primary avenue to harmony.
[3]These first two sentences reject the Confucian values of wisdom (saintliness), knowledge, human-heartedness, and righteousness, all of which, according to the Confucians, will result in *filial piety* (proper devotion to one's parents and ancestors).

[4]This aphorism rejects the principles and methods of Legalism (see sources 25 and 26).

selves become rich; I will manifest no ambition, and the people will of themselves attain to the primitive simplicity."

▾ ▾ ▾

Not to value and employ men of superior ability is the way to keep the people from rivalry among themselves; not to prize articles which are difficult to procure is the way to keep them from becoming thieves; not to show them what is likely to excite their desires is the way to keep their minds from disorder.

Therefore the sage, in the exercise of his government, empties their minds, fills their bellies, weakens their wills, and strengthens their bones.

He constantly tries to keep them without knowledge and without desire, and where there are those who have knowledge, to keep them from presuming to act on it. When there is this abstinence from action, good order is universal.

Confucianism: The Way of the Superior Man
▾▾▾
24 ▾ *Confucius, THE ANALECTS*

The Chinese refer to the period of Eastern Zhou as the age of *The Hundred Schools.* Of the many schools of thought that flourished then, none has had more impact on Chinese culture than Confucianism.

Unlike the case of Laozi, we are certain there was a historical Confucius. According to tradition, he was born in 551 B.C.E. into the impoverished, lower-aristocratic Kong family. He became a high-ranking civil servant in his native state of Lu but was forced into exile as a result of political intrigue. There followed ten years of wandering from state to state as he attempted without success to convince the princes of the states he visited to employ his theory of how to achieve a harmonious and just society. Disappointed at his inability to win over the lords of his day, Master Kong turned to teaching, seeking out students who showed promise of rising to eminent posts in the various states of feudal China. In this way he hoped his philosophy of life and government — his moral Way — would essentially transform Chinese society to the point that it returned to the values and practices of the age of the duke of Zhou, a twelfth-century B.C.E. legislator and consolidator of the Zhou Dynasty, whom Confucius deeply admired. For his educational efforts, posterity accorded him the elegant title *Kong Fuzi* (Kong the Philosopher), which Western scholars have Latinized into *Confucius.* Tradition records that he died in 479, a decade before the birth of his great Greek counterpart, Socrates (source 30).

Somewhat like Socrates, who claimed that if he was wise it was because he recognized his own ignorance, Confucius claimed to possess no special genius or knowledge. He simply saw himself as someone who revered the old ways and followed them zealously. There is no question that much of what Confucius taught was already part of Chinese culture. However, he took such traditional values as *filial piety* (respect for one's parents and ancestors) and *propriety* (regard for proper decorum) and turned them into moral principles. He insisted that human beings are moral creatures with social obligations and are, by that fact, obliged to comport themselves humanely and with integrity. He also believed that humans, or at least men, are capable of perfecting themselves as upright individuals. His ideal moral agent was the superior man (*zhunzi*) who cultivated virtue through study and imitation of the moral Way of the past. By knowing the good, this person would choose the good. What is more, he would act as an example to others, who would irresistibly follow the path he set along the Way of Goodness.

Confucius had few pupils; we know the names of only about twenty. Although Master Kong appears to have been a widely respected sage, he was only one of many itinerant teachers of his age and probably not the most popular. There is reason to conclude he died believing himself a failure. Such failure should happen to us all. In time Confucianism became virtually synonymous with Chinese culture and played an almost equally important role in shaping Korean, Japanese, and Vietnamese thought.

As is true of so many great teachers whose words and example have placed a permanent stamp on a civilization, Confucius was not a productive writer. As far as we know, nothing he wrote or edited survives. Early Confucian disciples, however, managed to transmit to posterity a number of sayings ascribed to Confucius and his immediate pupils. In time these were gathered into a book known as *The Analects (Lun Yu)*. We do not know which of these maxims Confucius actually uttered, but collectively they provide us with the best available view of Kong Fuzi's teachings as remembered by those who knew and followed him.

As you study the following selections, note the role that propriety (*li*) plays in Confucius's system. For him propriety meant much more than good manners or proper etiquette. It was the primary interior quality that set the superior man apart from all other humans.

QUESTIONS FOR ANALYSIS

1. How does Confucius define *filial piety?*
2. What does Confucius mean by the term *propriety,* and how does it serve as the keystone of his philosophical system?
3. What is Confucius's concept of the ideal state?
4. What is the superior man? Is he born or made? If the latter, how?
5. According to Confucius, what was the most practical form of education, and what was its purpose? What do your answers suggest about Confucius's social views?
6. Consider the four topics Confucius did not discuss. Why do you suppose this was the case? What does this suggest about the man and his philosophy?
7. Compare the topics that Confucius refused to discuss with the questions that the Buddha refused to answer (Chapter 3, source 19). Which strike you as more significant, the similarities or the differences? What conclusions do you draw from your answer?
8. Confucius, like Laozi, speaks of the Way and claims to teach it. How does his Way differ from that of Daoism? What do you think his attitude was toward those who preached either the way of Nonstriving or the idea that there are no absolute standards of behavior?

FILIAL PIETY

Zi, you asked what filial piety was. The Master said, "The filial piety of now-a-days means the support of one's parents. But dogs and horses likewise are able to do something in the way of support; — without reverence, what is there to distinguish the one support given from the other?"

▼ ▼ ▼

The Master said, "In serving his parents, a son may remonstrate with them, but gently; when he sees that they do not incline to follow his advice, he shows an increased degree of reverence, but does not abandon his purpose; and should they punish him, he does not allow himself to murmur."

▼ ▼ ▼

Mang I asked what filial piety was. The Master said, "It is not being disobedient."

Soon after, as Fan Chih was driving him, the Master told him, saying, "Mang Sun asked me what filial piety was, and I answered him, 'not being disobedient.'"

Fan Chih said, "What did you mean?" The Master replied, "That parents, when alive, should be served according to propriety; that, when dead, they should be buried according to propriety; and that they should be sacrificed to according to propriety."

PROPRIETY

The Master said, "Respectfulness, without the rules of propriety, becomes laborious bustle; carefulness, without the rules of propriety, becomes timidity; boldness, without the rules of propriety, becomes insubordination; straightforwardness, without the rules of propriety, becomes rudeness."

IDEAL GOVERNMENT

The Master said, "When rulers love to observe the rules of propriety, the people respond readily to the calls on them for service."

▼ ▼ ▼

The Master said, "If the people be led by laws, and uniformity sought to be given them by punishments,[1] they will try to avoid the punishment, but have no sense of shame.

"If they be led by virtue, and uniformity sought to be given them by the rules of propriety, they will have the sense of shame, and moreover will become good."

▼ ▼ ▼

The Master said, "He who exercises government by means of his virtue may be compared to the north polar star, which keeps its place and all the stars turn towards it."

▼ ▼ ▼

The duke Ai[2] asked, saying, "What should be done in order to secure the submission of the people?" Confucius replied, "Advance the upright and set aside the crooked, then the people will submit. Advance the crooked and set aside the upright, then the people will not submit."

Ji Kang asked how to cause the people to reverence their ruler, to be faithful to him, and to go on to nerve themselves to virtue. The Master said, "Let him preside over them with gravity; — then they will reverence him. Let him be filial and kind to all; — then they will be faithful to him. Let him advance the good and teach the incompetent; — then they will eagerly seek to be virtuous."

▼ ▼ ▼

Ji Kang asked Confucius about government. Confucius replied, "To govern means to rectify.

---

[1]This was the Way of the Legalists (sources 25 and 26).

[2]The lord of the state of Lu (r. 494–468 B.C.E.), whom several of Confucius's disciples served.

If you lead on the people with correctness, who will dare not to be correct?"

▼ ▼ ▼

The Master said, "If a minister make his own conduct correct, what difficulty will he have in assisting in government? If he cannot rectify himself, what has he to do with rectifying others?"

▼ ▼ ▼

The Master said, "'If good men were to govern a country in succession for a hundred years, they would be able to transform the violently bad, and dispense with capital punishments.' True indeed is this saying!"

THE SUPERIOR MAN

Confucius said, "There are three things of which the superior man stands in awe. He stands in awe of the ordinances of Heaven. He stands in awe of great men. He stands in awe of the words of sages.

"The mean man does not know the ordinances of Heaven, and consequently does not stand in awe of them. He is disrespectful to great men. He makes sport of the words of sages."

▼ ▼ ▼

Zi Gong asked what constituted the superior man. The Master said, "He acts before he speaks, and afterward speaks according to his actions."

▼ ▼ ▼

The Master said, "The mind of the superior man is conversant with righteousness; the mind of the mean man is conversant with gain."

▼ ▼ ▼

The Master said, "If the will be set on virtue,

there will be no practice of wickedness."

The Master said, "Riches and honors are what men desire. If it cannot be obtained in the proper way, they should not be held. Poverty and meanness are what men dislike. If it cannot be obtained in the proper way, they should not be avoided.

"If a superior man abandon virtue, how can he fulfill the requirements of that name?

"The superior man does not, even for the space of a single meal, act contrary to virtue. In moments of haste, he cleaves to it. In seasons of danger, he cleaves to it."

▼ ▼ ▼

The Master said, "By nature, men are nearly alike; by practice, they get to be wide apart."

▼ ▼ ▼

The Master said, "By extensively studying all learning, and keeping himself under the restraint of the rules of propriety, one may thus likewise not err from what is right."

▼ ▼ ▼

The Master said, "The accomplished scholar is not a utensil."[3]

SPIRITS

The subjects on which the Master did not talk, were extraordinary things,[4] feats of strength,[5] disorder, and spiritual beings.[6]

▼ ▼ ▼

Ji Lu asked about serving the spirits of the dead. The Master said, "While you are not able to serve men, how can you serve their spirits?" Ji Lu added, "I venture to ask about death?" He was answered, "While you do not know life, how can you know about death?"

---

[3]A specialist, or technician.
[4]Extraordinary phenomena that cause delight and wonder among the ignorant.

[5]Confucius and his disciples had only contempt for soldiers and all other persons who exercised power by virtue of physical strength. The Confucians believed in the exclusive exercise of moral and intellectual power.
[6]The spirits of the ancestors.

Legalism: The Way of the State
▼▼▼

25 ▼ Han Fei,
THE WRITINGS OF MASTER HAN FEI

Daoism offered no active political program, whereas Confucius and his disciples preached a doctrine of benevolent reform based on virtuous imitation of the past. A third school of thought that emerged in the chaos of the late Zhou Era was *Legalism,* which rejected both the Way of nature, as embraced by the Daoists, and Confucianism's emphasis on the primacy of the moral Way of antiquity. Legalist writers, to the contrary, emphasized law as government's formulative force and advocated a radical restructuring of society in ways that were totally rational and up to date.

Legalism reached its apogee in the late third century B.C.E. in the writings of Han Feizi (Master Han Fei) and the policies of Emperor Qin Shi Huangdi. Han Fei was a prince of the state of Han who defected to its chief rival, the state of Qin, but eventually he ran afoul of Qin's chief minister, Li Si (d. 208 B.C.E.), and was forced to commit suicide in 233 B.C.E. Before he died, he composed a number of essays on how to construct a stable and peaceful state. The following selections present Han Fei's major principles of political philosophy.

QUESTIONS FOR ANALYSIS

1. In Han Fei's ideal state what is the supreme governing authority, the will of the ruler or the law?
2. What are the "two handles," and how important are they to a Legalist state? Why must the sovereign never surrender control over the two handles?
3. What roles do individuality and private initiative play in Han Fei's ideal state?
4. Why do you think Legalism appealed to some people?
5. Imagine a series of conversations among a Daoist, a Confucian, and a Legalist. How would each respond to the following issues: What is the purpose of good government? What role does morality play in formulating law? What are the qualities of a superior ruler? What is the validity of the proposition "Might makes right"?

HAVING REGULATIONS

No country is permanently strong. Nor is any country permanently weak. If conformers to law are strong, the country is strong; if conformers to law are weak, the country is weak. . . .

Any ruler able to expel private crookedness and uphold public law, finds the people safe and the state in order; and any ruler able to expunge private action and act on public law, finds his army strong and his enemy weak. So, find out men following the discipline of laws and regulations, and place them above the body of officials. Then the sovereign cannot be deceived by anybody with fraud and falsehood. . . .

Therefore, the intelligent sovereign makes the law select men and makes no arbitrary promotion himself. He makes the law measure merits and makes no arbitrary regulation himself. In consequence, able men cannot be obscured, bad characters cannot be disguised; falsely praised fellows cannot be advanced, wrongly defamed people cannot be degraded. . . .

To govern the state by law is to praise the right and blame the wrong.

The law does not fawn on the noble. . . . Whatever the law applies to, the wise cannot reject nor can the brave defy. Punishment for fault never skips ministers, reward for good never misses commoners. Therefore, to correct the faults of the high, to rebuke the vices of the low, to suppress disorders, to decide against mistakes, to subdue the arrogant, to straighten the crooked, and to unify the folkways of the masses, nothing could match the law. To warn the officials and overawe the people, to rebuke obscenity and danger, and to forbid falsehood and deceit, nothing could match penalty. If penalty is severe, the noble cannot discriminate against the humble. If law is definite, the superiors are esteemed and not violated. If the superiors are not violated, the sovereign will become strong and able to maintain the proper course of government. Such was the reason why the early kings esteemed Legalism and handed it down to posterity. Should

the lord of men discard law and practice selfishness, high and low would have no distinction.

THE TWO HANDLES

The means whereby the intelligent ruler controls his ministers are two handles only. The two handles are chastisement and commendation. What are meant by chastisement and commendation? To inflict death or torture upon culprits, is called chastisement; to bestow encouragements or rewards on men of merit, is called commendation.

Ministers are afraid of censure and punishment but fond of encouragement and reward. Therefore, if the lord of men uses the handles of chastisement and commendation, all ministers will dread his severity and turn to his liberality. The villainous ministers of the age are different. To men they hate they would by securing the handle of chastisement from the sovereign ascribe crimes; on men they love they would by securing the handle of commendation from the sovereign bestow rewards. Now supposing the lord of men placed the authority of punishment and the profit of reward not in his hands but let the ministers administer the affairs of reward and punishment instead, then everybody in the country would fear the ministers and slight the ruler, and turn to the ministers and away from the ruler. This is the calamity of the ruler's loss of the handles of chastisement and commendation.

The Legalist Policies of Qin
▼▼▼

26 ▼ *Sima Qian,*
THE RECORDS OF THE GRAND HISTORIAN

Born around 145 B.C.E., Sima Qian was educated in the Confucian classics, served his emperor on a variety of missions, and in 107 succeeded his father as Grand Historian of the Han court. Even before rising to this position, Sima Qian had avidly collected historical records during his travels on imperial service. Upon his appointment as Grand Historian, he embarked on an initial project of collecting additional sources, especially from the imperial library, and verifying his facts. Only in 104 was he ready to begin the process of composition, a labor that lasted until 91 B.C.E. The result was a history monumental in scope. In 130 chapters he traced the story of China from the age of the legendary Five Sage Emperors, who preceded the Xia and Shang Dynasties, to his own day. In later years he made small additions and changes and probably continued to revise his masterpiece in minor ways until his death at an unknown date.

The result was well worth the effort. The Chinese rightly consider *The Records of the Grand Historian* to be traditional China's greatest piece of historical writing. Sima Qian aimed at telling the whole truth, insofar as he could discover it, and in pursuit of that truth he scoured all available archives. As he composed his work, he included verbatim many of the records he had found, thereby providing modern historians with a wealth of documentary evidence that would otherwise have been lost, for many of the sources Sima Qian quoted, paraphrased, and cited exist today only in his history. In the first excerpt the Grand Historian quotes a memorial that the First Emperor, Qin Shi Huangdi (r. 221–210 B.C.E.), built to proclaim his accomplishments. The second selection tells of an edict of 213 that banned almost all non-Legalist literature.

QUESTIONS FOR ANALYSIS

1. Of what accomplishments does the emperor boast?
2. In what ways does this memorial emphasize the government's standardization of society?
3. What general principles and policies underlie this memorial?
4. Does the inscription contain any claims that Confucius would have applauded? What claims would Confucius have found troubling?
5. What would a Daoist think of the emperor's policies?
6. How and for what reason did Li Si reject all non-Legalist schools of thought and especially Confucian principles? What does his rejection of the "hundred schools" and Confucianism in particular suggest about the way in which Legalists viewed the world and themselves?
7. Why do you think books on medicine, divination, and agriculture were exempted from the general prohibition of 213 B.C.E.? What does your answer suggest about Legalist policies?
8. Consider the Legalist view of the proper subject matter and purpose of education. How does it differ from the educational philosophy of the Confucians? How does it differ from the Daoist view of education?
9. Have you been able to find any elements that are common to the three schools? If so, what are they?
10. How do you think it is possible for the Chinese to reconcile these three schools?

The emperor had a tower built on Mount Langya and a stone inscription set up to praise the power of Qin and make clear his will. The inscription read:

A new age is inaugurated by the Emperor;
Rules and measures are rectified,
The myriad things set in order,
Human affairs are made clear
And there is harmony between fathers
    and sons.
The Emperor in his sagacity, benevolence
    and justice
Has made all laws and principles manifest.
He set forth to pacify the east,
To inspect officers and men;
This great task accomplished
He visited the coast.
Great are the Emperor's achievements,
Men attend diligently to basic tasks,
Farming is encouraged, secondary
    pursuits discouraged,
All the common people prosper;
All men under the sky
Toil with a single purpose;
Tools and measures are made uniform,
The written script is standardized;
Wherever the sun and moon shine,
Wherever one can go by boat or by carriage,
Men carry out their orders
And satisfy their desires;
For our Emperor in accordance with the time
Has regulated local customs,
Made waterways and divided up the land.
Caring for the common people,
He works day and night without rest;
He defines the laws, leaving nothing in doubt,
Making known what is forbidden.
The local officials have their duties,
Administration is smoothly carried out,
All is done correctly, all according to plan.
The Emperor in his wisdom
Inspects all four quarters of his realm;

High and low, noble and humble,
None dare overshoot the mark;
No evil or impropriety is allowed,
All strive to be good men and true,
And exert themselves in tasks great and small;
None dares to idle or ignore his duties,
But in far-off, remote places
Serious and decorous administrators
Work steadily, just and loyal.
Great is the virtue of our Emperor
Who pacifies all four corners of the earth,
Who punishes traitors, roots out evil men,
And with profitable measures
    brings prosperity.
Tasks are done at the proper season,
All things flourish and grow;
The common people know peace
And have laid aside weapons and armor;
Kinsmen care for each other,
There are no robbers or thieves;
Men delight in his rule,
All understanding the law and discipline.
The universe entire
Is our Emperor's realm,
Extending west to the Desert,
South to where the houses face north,
East to the East Ocean,
North to beyond Daxia;
Wherever human life is found,
All acknowledge his suzerainty,
His achievements surpass those of the
    Five Emperors,[1]
His kindness reaches even the beasts of
    the field;
All creatures benefit from his virtue,
All live in peace at home.

▾ ▾ ▾

Chunyu Yueh, a scholar of Chi . . . said, "I have yet to hear of anything able to endure that was not based on ancient precedents. . . .

The emperor ordered his ministers to debate this question.

---

[1] The mythical Five Sage Emperors of predynastic China.

The prime minister Li Si said, "The Five Emperors did not emulate each other nor did the Three Dynasties[2] adopt each other's ways, yet all had good government. This is no paradox, because times had changed. Now Your Majesty has built up this great empire to endure for generations without end. Naturally this passes the comprehension of a foolish pedant. Chunyu Yueh spoke about the Three Dynasties, but they are hardly worth taking as examples. In times gone by different barons fought among themselves and gathered wandering scholars. Today, however, the empire is at peace, all laws and order come from one single source, the common people support themselves by farming and handicrafts, while students study the laws and prohibitions.

"Now these scholars learn only from the old, not from the new, and use their learning to oppose our rule and confuse the black-headed people.[3] As prime minister I must speak out on pain of death. In former times when the world, torn by chaos and disorder, could not be united, different states arose and argued from the past to condemn the present, using empty rhetoric to cover up and confuse the real issues, and employing their learning to oppose what was established by authority. Now Your Majesty has conquered the whole world, distinguished between black and white, set unified standards. Yet these opinionated scholars get together to slander the laws and judge each new decree according to their own school of thought, opposing it secretly in their hearts while discussing it openly in the streets. They brag to the sovereign to win fame, put forward strange arguments to gain distinction, and incite the mob to spread rumors. If this is not prohibited, the sovereign's prestige will suffer and factions will be formed among his subjects. Far better put a stop to it!

"I humbly propose that all historical records but those of Qin be burned. If anyone who is not a court scholar dares to keep the ancient songs, historical records or writings of the hundred schools, these should be confiscated and burned by the provincial governor and army commander. Those who in conversation dare to quote the old songs and records[4] should be publicly executed; those who use old precedents to oppose the new order should have their families wiped out; and officers who know of such cases but fail to report them should be punished in the same way.

"If thirty days after the issuing of this order the owners of these books have still not had them destroyed, they should have their faces tattooed and be condemned to hard labor at the Great Wall.[5] The only books which need not be destroyed are those dealing with medicine, divination, and agriculture. Those who want to study the law can learn it from the officers." The emperor sanctioned this proposal.

---

[2]Xia, Shang, and Zhou.
[3]The common people.
[4]A reference to *The Classic of Odes* (Chapter 1, source 6) and *The Classic of History* (source 5).

[5]The First Emperor began the process of linking frontier fortresses together to form the Great Wall. Labor on the Great Wall, which was tantamount to a death sentence, was a common penalty under Qin.

▼▼▼

Hellenic Civilization: A Rational Inquiry into Life

Early in the sixth century B.C.E., a small group of Greek intellectuals, beginning, according to tradition, with a semilegendary figure known as *Thales of Miletus* (ca. 640–562 B.C.E.), started to challenge age-old mythic ways of explaining the workings of the universe by looking at the world as an objective phenomenon that could be studied in a rational, systematic manner. These thinkers, who sought to discover the physical underpinnings of the universe, are acknowledged as ancient Hellas's first philosophers and scientists and the people who established the Greek intellectual tradition of rational inquiry into all aspects of the physical and moral world.

As important as reason was in the formation of Greek thought, it never threatened to totally displace myth, mysticism, and religion. We would very much misunderstand Greek civilization by concluding that rational inquiry dominated every element of Greek life from the sixth century onward. Indeed, the nonrational permeated Greek society. This fact should not be surprising, nor should it cause us to undervalue the achievements of Greek rationalists, whose modes of analysis became a hallmark of Greek civilization.

As we survey the developments of Greek rationalism, it would be helpful to keep in mind the broad division of Greek history favored by historians. The period from about 750 B.C.E. down to the death of Alexander the Great in 323 B.C.E. is known as the *Hellenic Age* because, as we have seen, the people we call *Greeks* referred to themselves as *Hellenes* and their land as *Hellas*. (It was the Romans who began the tradition of calling all Hellenes *Greeks*.) The period from 323 to 30 B.C.E. is known as the *Hellenistic Age*. In this case, *Hellenist* means a non-Hellene who adopted the Greek language and culture.

During the Hellenic Age the Greek world was a frontier society along the western periphery of the ancient civilized world. As a result, the Greeks were able to draw from the experiences of their more deeply rooted neighbors while enjoying a certain amount of freedom to experiment culturally, especially in the areas of politics and thought. This age was characterized by general Greek independence from foreign domination, political decentralization, intense rivalry among Hellas's many city-states, and a deep-seated ethnocentrism and even contempt for the non-Hellenic World. The Hellenes coined the term *barbarian* to refer to all non-Greek speakers, even the most civilized, because their alien languages sounded to Greek ears like so much babble, or *bar-bar*. The two characteristic and dominating events of this period were the Persian Wars (499–450 B.C.E.) and the Peloponnesian War (431–404 B.C.E.). In the first, Greeks, under the leadership of Athens and Sparta, successfully withstood the threat of Persian domination. In the latter, again under Athenian and Spartan leadership, the whole Greek world was embroiled in a bitter family bloodletting.

Under the leadership of King Philip and his son Alexander (r. 336–323 B.C.E.) the Macedonians finally forced internal peace and unity on the Greeks. Alexander the Great's conquest of the Persian Empire and his penetration even into northwest India ushered in a new age for western Eurasia. Whereas the Hellenic World had been parochial, the Hellenistic World was cosmopolitan and culturally *syncretic* (characterized by combining different cultural traditions to create new hybrid cultures). The armies of Alexander and the state builders who followed helped create a cultural amalgamation of Southwest Asian, North African, and even some Indian elements, over which lay a deep layer of Greek language, thought, and artistic expression. What emerged was, to use a Greek word, a cultural *ecumene* (a unity of diverse civilized peoples). This ecumenical culture stretched from Afghanistan and northwest India in the east to the regions of the central Mediterranean in the west, and much of it was Greek in form and inspiration. Greek science and philosophy matured during the Hellenistic Age. Although the Roman Empire later expanded the boundaries of this rich cultural ecumene into northwest Africa and portions of western Europe, it is convenient to date the end of the Hellenistic Age as 30 B.C.E., when Egypt, the last independent and arguably most brilliant of the Hellenistic kingdoms, passed into Roman hands.

The Science of Medicine
▼▼▼

27 ▼ *Hippocrates, ON THE SACRED DISEASE*

No matter how much they differed among themselves, early Greek scientists shared two basic assumptions: The world is a physical entity governed by regular, natural laws and not by mysterious supernatural forces or divine whims; and the human mind, unaided by magic or divine revelation, can understand how those laws function.

One area of Hellenic science that proved especially fruitful was medicine, especially as pioneered by the physicians of the island of Cos. Of all the healers of Cos, the most famous in history and legend was *Hippocrates.* For all of his fame and reputed dominance in his field, we know very little about Hippocrates' life. Born on Cos around 460, he served as a member of that community's Guild of Aesculapius, a group of physicians who traced their origin to the priesthood of the god of healing. Hippocrates' abilities as a practitioner and teacher of medicine eventually earned him a pan-Hellenic reputation, and he found himself traveling from city to city teaching his art and science — a science that stressed careful clinical observation of the nature and course of diseases. A late tradition holds that the Master Physician died in Thessaly in northern Greece around 377 B.C.E.

Succeeding generations of physicians looked to Hippocrates as the preeminent figure in their profession, and consequently his legend and stature grew beyond simple human proportions as the years passed. By 300 B.C.E. some seventy-two books were ascribed to him, but this Hippocratic body of medical knowledge clearly shows the hands of many different authors. It is impossible to say precisely which, if any, of these books Hippocrates composed, but it is safe to assume that they represent the medical tradition that he and generations of his students practiced and taught.

Our document comes from one of the earliest treatises within this body of Hippocratic texts, *On the Sacred Disease,* in which the author, putatively Hippocrates, deals with the issue of epilepsy.

QUESTIONS FOR ANALYSIS

1. Why does Hippocrates reject the notion that epilepsy comes from the gods?
2. In his rejection of the idea that this is a sacred disease, does he show any atheistic tendencies?
3. How does he propose to cure this ailment?

4. **Do you consider Hippocrates' explanation of the origins and treatment of epilepsy scientific? Why or why not?**

In regard to the disease called "sacred," it seems to me to be no more divine or sacred than other diseases but has a natural cause from which it originates, like other afflictions. People regard its nature and cause as divine out of ignorance and credulity, because it is unlike other diseases. This notion of its divinity persists by virtue of people's inability to comprehend it and the simplicity of the means by which it is "cured," for those afflicted are supposedly freed from it by purifications and incantations. If people reckon it divine because it incites awe, then instead of one sacred disease there would be many. As I will show, other diseases are no less awe-inspiring and strange, yet no one considers them sacred. . . . For example, one can see people grow mad and demented for no apparent reason and doing many strange things. I have known many persons to groan and cry out in their sleep, . . . some jumping up and rushing out of doors, all deprived of their reason until they wake up. Afterward they are as healthy and rational as before, although pale and weak. And this will occur not once but frequently. There are many similar phenomena that it would be tedious to enumerate.

In my view, they who first associated this disease with the gods were people just like our present-day magicians, purifiers, charlatans, and quacks, who claim great piety and superior knowledge. Such persons, using superstition as camouflage for their own inability to offer any help, proclaimed the disease "sacred" . . . and instituted a method of treatment which protected them, namely purifications, incantations, and enforced abstinence from bathing and from many types of food. . . . Their course of treatment forbids the patient to have a black robe, because black is symbolic of death, or to sleep on a goatskin, or to wear one, or to put one foot on another, or one hand on another. All these things are reputed to be impediments to healing. . . . If

the patient recovers they reap the honor and credit; if the patient dies, they have a perfect defense: the gods, not they, are to blame, seeing as they had administered nothing to eat or drink in the way of medicine, and they had not overheated the patient with baths. . . . To my way of thinking, if this course of treatment were correct, no Libyan living in the interior of Africa would be free of the disease, since they all sleep on goatskins and live on goat meat. . . . Then again, if such things, when administered as food, aggravate the disease, and if it is cured by abstinence from them, then the disease cannot be divine in origin, and the rites of purification provide no benefit. It is the food which is either beneficial or harmful. . . . Therefore, they who attempt to cure this disease in such a manner appear to me to be incapable of believing the disease is sacred or divine. . . .

Neither do I believe it to be a worthy opinion to maintain that a human body is polluted by the divine: the most impure substance being polluted by the most pure. . . . For it is the godhead that purifies, makes holy, and cleanses us from the greatest and most wicked of our offenses. . . . When we enter temples and the groves of gods we are sprinkled with holy water, not as a pollution but as a means of cleansing whatever pollution we had. And this principle seems to me to be the same in regard to purifications offered by charlatan healers.

Consequently, this disease seems to me to be no more divine than others. It has the same nature and cause as other diseases. It is also no less curable than other diseases. . . . The key to its origin, as is the case with other diseases, lies in heredity. . . . There is nothing to prevent it from happening that where one or the other parent suffers from this malady, some of their children likewise suffer from it. . . . Another strong proof that this disease is no more divine in origin than any other is that it afflicts those who are by nature phlegmatic,[1] but it does not attack the bilious.[2] If this disease were more divine than other diseases, it should afflict all groups equally, making no distinction between the bilious and the phlegmatic. . . .

Since the brain, as the primary center of sensation and of the spirits, perceives whatever occurs in the body, if any unusual change takes place in the air, due to the seasons, the brain is changed by the state of the air. . . . And the disease called "sacred" arises from . . . those things that enter and leave the body, such as cold, the sun, and winds, which are constantly changing and never at rest. . . . Therefore the physician should understand and distinguish each individual situation, so that at one time he might add nourishment, at another time withhold it. In this disease, as in all others, he must endeavor not to feed the disease, but he must attempt to wear it out by administering whatever is most contrary to each disease and not that which favors and is allied to it. For it grows vigorous and increases through that which is allied to it, but it wears out and disappears under the administration of whatever is opposed to it.[3] Whoever is knowledgeable enough to render a person humid or dry, hot or cold by regimen can also cure this disease, if the physician recognizes the proper season for administering remedies. The physician can do so without attention to purifications, spells, and all other forms of "hocus-pocus."

---

[1] A calm temperament that can reach sluggishness (see note 3).

[2] A peevish, sour-tempered disposition (see note 3).

[3] The physicians of Cos believed the body contains four basic fluids, or *humors:* blood, phlegm, black bile, and yellow bile. They further believed that an excess of any humor — by reason of hereditary factors, environment, or accident — causes physical and psychic imbalance. Depending on the humor that has thrown the body out of balance, the patient becomes sanguine, phlegmatic, melancholy, or bilious. Of course, no one is ever in perfect harmony; some humor always is dominant, which explains why there are different personality types. When, however, the imbalance becomes so great as to cause clinical illness, the physician must intervene. The Greek physician's art and science consisted of helping the body reestablish its natural harmony by administering or withholding foods and medicines that either reduced or increased one or more of the humors.

The Athenian as Citizen

▼▼▼

28 ▼ *Thucydides,* *THE HISTORY OF THE PELOPONNESIAN WAR*

During the eighth century B.C.E. Homer, the putative author of the *Iliad* and the *Odyssey* (Chapter 2, source 12), interpreted the past through the medium of poetic myth. By the mid fifth century certain Hellenic researchers were recapturing and interpreting the past through the more prosaic but accurate medium of history. The word *historia* is Greek and means "knowledge achieved through inquiry." As we have seen, the Hebrews and Persians had already evolved a sense of divinely directed history (Chapter 2, sources 13 to 15, and Chapter 3, sources 21 and 22). However, it was the Greeks who became western Eurasia's first students of secular history. That means researchers who systematically studied worldly affairs divorced from any consideration of divine intervention or control. The particular genius of Greek *historiography* (the writing of history) was that certain thinkers, largely beginning with Herodotus (ca. 484–424 B.C.E.), believed that human events could be reconstructed and made comprehensible through careful research into the human record.

One such student of the human past was Thucydides (ca. 460–400 B.C.E.), widely regarded as classical Hellas's greatest historian. Thucydides was a citizen of Athens in an age when Hellenic civilization was dominated by rivalry among its many different city-states, or *poleis* (the plural of *polis*). During Thucydides' youth and young manhood, Athens was led by Pericles, who from 461 to 429 B.C.E. helped shape the last stages in the evolution of Athenian democracy. In 431 Pericles led democratic Athens into the Peloponnesian War against the *oligarchic* (ruled by a few) polis of Sparta and its allies. The war dragged on for a generation, ending in 404 with a Spartan victory. In the early stages of the conflict it had seemed as though Athens could not lose the war. In the winter of 431/430 a confident Athens paused to honor those citizens who had fallen in battle during the first year of fighting and called upon Pericles, its unofficial First Citizen, to deliver the eulogy. Pericles used the occasion to praise the polis for which those citizens had lived and died.

Thucydides undoubtedly attended that funeral and perhaps dreamed of his own glorious service to Athens. Six years later Thucydides commanded a small naval squadron that failed to relieve a besieged Athenian infantry force, and for that failure he was forced into exile. An avid student of human affairs, especially politics, Thucydides used his enforced retirement to study the war and write its history. As he noted in the opening lines of his *History,* he had begun writing about the war from its outbreak because he believed it would prove to be the most memorable conflict in all of Hellenic history, outstripping even the Trojan and Persian Wars in magnitude. His purpose was simple: to provide all Hellenes with "an everlasting possession," whose careful study would enable them to avoid similar errors in the future.

In his attempt to create an aura of dramatic verisimilitude, thereby assuring his work's being read and preserved, Thucydides used the convention of including large numbers of speeches in his *History.* As he admitted, the speeches were not verbatim accounts, but he claimed to preserve the sense of either what was said or what he judged should have been said on a particular occasion. Because Pericles' Funeral Oration was such a public and memorable speech, there is good reason to believe Thucydides preserved the essence of Pericles' message. That message tells us a good deal about Hellenic culture in the fifth century B.C.E.

Just as telling is Thucydides' description of the plague that ravaged Athens in the summer of 430. Plato (source 30) implies that Hippocrates (source 27) visited and taught medicine in Athens. Although it is not possible to verify this, it is clear that Hippocratic medical principles were part of Athens's intellectual atmosphere by the end of the fifth century B.C.E. It is equally clear that Thucydides had enjoyed all of the educational benefits available to a wealthy Athenian citizen.

QUESTIONS FOR ANALYSIS

1. How does Pericles define Athenian democracy? According to him, what sort of citizens does this democracy breed, and how does Athens help its citizens achieve their full potential?

2. According to Pericles, what role should public affairs play in a citizen's life? Why?
3. In his idealized portrait of Athens, Pericles contrasts Athens's spirit with that of Sparta. According to him, how do the Spartans live? As Pericles sees it, what is wrong with the Spartan way of life?
4. Why is Athens, in Pericles' words, "the school of Hellas"?
5. How does Pericles' speech provide evidence of Hellenic preoccupation with the human individual, the life of the polis, and rational analysis?
6. In what ways, if at all, does Thucydides' description of the plague conform to the principles of Hippocratic medicine?
7. How, if at all, does Thucydides' description of the consequences of the plague serve as a commentary on Pericles' speech? Please be specific.
8. Compose a commentary on this entire excerpt, the speech and the plague sequence, by either Confucius or Qin Shi Huangdi.

During the . . . winter, . . . the funeral of those who first fell in this war was celebrated by the Athenians at the public charge. . . . Over those who were the first buried Pericles was chosen to speak. At the fitting moment he advanced from the sepulcher to a lofty stage, which had been erected in order that he might be heard as far as possible by the multitude, and spoke as follows: . . .

"I will speak first of our ancestors, for it is right and becoming that now, when we are lamenting the dead, a tribute should be paid to their memory. There has never been a time when they did not inhabit this land, which by their valor they have handed down from generation to generation, and we have received from them a free state. But if they were worthy of praise, still more were our fathers, who added to their inheritance, and after many a struggle transmitted to us their sons this great empire. And we ourselves assembled here today, who are still most of us in the vigor of life, have chiefly done the work of improvement, and have richly endowed our city with all things, so that she is sufficient for herself both in peace and war. Of the military exploits by which our various possessions were acquired, or of the energy with which we or our fathers drove back the tide of war, Hellenic or Barbarian, I will not speak; for the tale would be long and is familiar to you. But before I praise

the dead, I should like to point out by what principles of action we rose to power, and under what institutions and through what manner of life our empire became great. For I conceive that such thoughts are not unsuited to the occasion, and that this numerous assembly of citizens and strangers may profitably listen to them.

"Our form of government does not enter into rivalry with the institutions of others. We do not copy our neighbors, but are an example to them. It is true that we are called a democracy, for the administration is in the hands of the many and not of the few. But while the law secures equal justice to all alike in their private disputes, the claim of excellence is also recognized; and when a citizen is in any way distinguished, he is preferred to the public service, not as a matter of privilege, but as the reward of merit. Neither is poverty a bar, but a man may benefit his country whatever be the obscurity of his condition. There is no exclusiveness in our public life, and in our private intercourse we are not suspicious of one another, nor angry with our neighbor if he does what he likes; we do not put on sour looks at him which, though harmless, are not pleasant. While we are thus unconstrained in our private intercourse, a spirit of reverence pervades our public acts; we are prevented from doing wrong by respect for authority and for the laws, having a special regard to those which are ordained for the protection of the injured as well as to those unwritten laws which bring upon the transgressor of them the reprobation of the general sentiment.

"And we have not forgotten to provide for our weary spirits many relaxations from toil; we have regular games and sacrifices throughout the year; at home the style of our life is refined; and the delight which we daily feel in all these things helps to banish melancholy. Because of the greatness of our city the fruits of the whole earth flow in upon us; so that we enjoy the goods of other countries as freely as of our own.

"Then, again, our military training is in many respects superior to that of our adversaries. Our city is thrown open to the world, and we never expel a foreigner or prevent him from seeing or learning anything of which the secret if revealed to an enemy might profit him. We rely not upon management or trickery, but upon our own hearts and hands. And in the matter of education, whereas they from early youth are always undergoing laborious exercises which are to make them brave, we live at ease, and yet are equally ready to face the perils which they face. . . .

"If then we prefer to meet danger with a light heart but without laborious training, and with a courage which is gained by habit and not enforced by law, are we not greatly the gainers? Since we do not anticipate the pain, although, when the hour comes, we can be as brave as those who never allow themselves to rest; and thus too our city is equally admirable in peace and in war. For we are lovers of the beautiful, yet simple in our tastes, and we cultivate the mind without loss of manliness. Wealth we employ, not for talk and ostentation, but when there is a real use for it. To avow poverty with us is no disgrace; the true disgrace is in doing nothing to avoid it. An Athenian citizen does not neglect the state because he takes care of his own household; and even those of us who are engaged in business have a very fair idea of politics. We alone regard a man who takes no interest in public affairs, not as a harmless, but as a useless character; and if few of us are originators, we are all sound judges

of a policy. The great impediment to action is, in our opinion, not discussion, but the want of that knowledge which is gained by discussion preparatory to action. For we have a peculiar power of thinking before we act and of acting too, whereas other men are courageous from ignorance but hesitate upon reflection. And they are surely to be esteemed the bravest spirits who, having the clearest sense both of the pains and pleasures of life, do not on that account shrink from danger. . . . To sum up: I say that Athens is the school of Hellas, and that the individual Athenian in his own person seems to have the power of adapting himself to the most varied forms of action with the utmost versatility and grace. This is no passing and idle word, but truth and fact; and the assertion is verified by the position to which these qualities have raised the state. For in the hour of trial Athens alone among her contemporaries is superior to the report of her. No enemy who comes against her is indignant at the reverses which he sustains at the hands of such a city; no subject complains that his masters are unworthy of him. And we shall assuredly not be without witnesses; there are mighty monuments of our power which will make us the wonder of this and of succeeding ages; we shall not need the praises of Homer or of any other panegyrist whose poetry may please for the moment, although his representation of the facts will not bear the light of day. For we have compelled every land and every sea to open a path for our valor, and have everywhere planted eternal memorials of our friendship and of our enmity. Such is the city for whose sake these men nobly fought and died; they could not bear the thought that she might be taken from them; and every one of us who survives should gladly toil on her behalf.

"I have dwelt upon the greatness of Athens because I want to show you that we are contending for a higher prize than those who enjoy none of these privileges, and to establish by manifest proof the merit of these men whom I am now commemorating. Their loftiest praise has been already spoken. For in magnifying the city I have magnified them, and men like them whose virtues made her glorious. . . ."

Such was the order of the funeral celebrated in this winter, with the end of which ended the first year of the Peloponnesian War. As soon as summer returned, the Peloponnesian army[1] . . . invaded Attica,[2] where they established themselves and ravaged the country. They had not been there many days when the plague broke out at Athens for the first time. A similar disorder is said to have previously smitten many places, particularly Lemnos,[3] but there is no record of such a pestilence occurring elsewhere, or of so great a destruction of human life. For a while physicians, in ignorance of the nature of the disease, sought to apply remedies; but it was in vain, and they themselves were among the first victims, because they most often came into contact with it. No human art was of any avail, and as to supplications in temples, inquiries of oracles,[4] and the like, they were utterly useless, and at last men were overpowered by the calamity and gave them all up.

The disease is said to have begun south of Egypt in Ethiopia; thence it descended[5] into Egypt and Libya,[6] and after spreading over the greater part of the Persian empire, suddenly fell upon Athens. It first attacked the inhabitants of the Piraeus,[7] and it was supposed that the Peloponnesians had poisoned the cisterns, no conduits having as yet been made there. It afterwards reached the upper city, and then the mortality became far greater. As to its probable origin or the causes which might or could have produced such a disturbance of nature, every man, whether a physician or not, will give his own opinion. But I shall describe its actual course, and the symptoms by which any one who knows them beforehand may recognize the disorder should it ever reappear. For I was myself attacked and witnessed the sufferings of others.

The season was admitted to have been remarkably free from ordinary sickness and if anybody was already ill of any other disease, it was absorbed in this. Many who were in perfect health, all in a moment, and without any apparent reason, were seized with violent heats in the head and with redness and inflammation of the eyes. Internally the throat and the tongue were quickly suffused with blood, and the breath became unnatural and fetid. There followed sneezing and hoarseness; in a short time the disorder, accompanied by a violent cough, reached the chest; then fastening lower down, it would move the stomach and bring on all the vomits of bile to which physicians have ever given names; and they were very distressing. An ineffectual retching producing violent convulsions attacked most of the sufferers; some as soon as the previous symptoms had abated, others not until long afterwards. The body externally was not so very hot to the touch, nor yet pale; it was of a livid color inclining to red, and breaking out in pustules and ulcers. But the internal fever was intense; the sufferers could not bear to have on them even the finest linen garment; they insisted on being naked, and there was nothing which they longed for more eagerly than to throw themselves into cold water. And many of those who had no one to look after them actually plunged into the cisterns, for they were tormented by unceasing thirst, which was not in the least assuaged whether they drank little or much. They could not sleep; a restlessness which was intolerable never left them. While the disease was at its height the body, instead of wasting away, held out amid these sufferings in a marvelous manner, and either they died on the seventh or ninth day, not of weakness, for their strength was not exhausted, but of internal fever, which was the end of most; or, if they survived, then the disease descended into the bowels and there produced violent ulceration; severe

---

[1] The Spartans and their allies. Sparta was located in the Peloponnesus, the southern peninsula of the Greek mainland.
[2] The peninsula on which Athens was located.
[3] An Aegean island.

[4] Priestesses of Apollo who looked into the future.
[5] The Nile flows northward; therefore, one descends the river while traveling from south to north.
[6] The region of North Africa immediately west of Egypt.
[7] Athens's port.

diarrhoea at the same time set in, and at a later stage caused exhaustion, which finally with few exceptions carried them off. For the disorder which had originally settled in the head passed gradually through the whole body, and, if a person got over the worst, would often seize the extremities and leave its mark, attacking the privy parts and the fingers and the toes, and some escaped with the loss of these, some with the loss of their eyes. Some again had no sooner recovered than they were seized with a forgetfulness of all things and knew neither themselves nor their friends.

The malady took a form not to be described, and the fury with which it fastened upon each sufferer was too much for human nature to endure. There was one circumstance in particular which distinguished it from ordinary diseases. The birds and animals which feed on human flesh, although so many bodies were lying unburied, either never came near them, or died if they touched them. This was proved by a remarkable disappearance of the birds of prey, who were not to be seen either about the bodies or anywhere else; while in the case of the dogs the fact was even more obvious, because they live with man.

Such was the general nature of the disease: I omit many strange peculiarities which characterized individual cases. None of the ordinary sicknesses attacked any one while it lasted, or, if they did, they ended in the plague. Some of the sufferers died from want of care, others equally who were receiving the greatest attention. No single remedy could be deemed a specific; for that which did good to one did harm to another. No constitution was of itself strong enough to resist or weak enough to escape the attacks; the disease carried off all alike and defied every mode of treatment. Most appalling was the despondency which seized upon any one who felt himself sickening, for he instantly abandoned his mind to despair and, instead of holding out, absolutely threw away his chance of life. Appalling too was the rapidity with which men caught the infection; dying like sheep if they attended

on one another; and this was the principal cause of mortality. When they were afraid to visit one another, the sufferers died in their solitude, so that many houses were empty because there had been no one left to take care of the sick; or if they ventured they perished, especially those who aspired to heroism. For they went to see their friends without thought of themselves and were ashamed to leave them, even at a time when the very relations of the dying were at last growing weary and ceased to make lamentations, overwhelmed by the vastness of the calamity. But whatever instances there may have been of such devotion, more often the sick and the dying were tended by the pitying care of those who had recovered, because they knew the course of the disease and were themselves free from apprehension. For no one was ever attacked a second time, or not with a fatal result. All men congratulated them, and they themselves, in the excess of their joy at the moment, had an innocent fancy that they could not die of any other sickness.

The crowding of the people out of the country into the city aggravated the misery; and the newly-arrived suffered most. For, having no houses of their own, but inhabiting in the height of summer stifling huts, the mortality among them was dreadful, and they perished in wild disorder. The dead lay as they had died, one upon another, while others hardly alive wallowed in the streets and crawled about every fountain craving for water. The temples in which they lodged were full of the corpses of those who died in them; for the violence of the calamity was such that men, not knowing where to turn, grew reckless of all law, human and divine. The customs which had hitherto been observed at funerals were universally violated, and they buried their dead each one as best he could. Many, having no proper appliances, because the deaths in their household had been so frequent, made no scruple of using the burial-place of others. When one man had raised a funeral pile, others would come, and throwing on their dead first, set fire to it; or when some other corpse was already burning, before they could be stopped would throw their own dead upon it and depart.

There were other and worse forms of lawlessness which the plague introduced at Athens. Men who had hitherto concealed their indulgence in pleasure now grew bolder. For, seeing the sudden change, — how the rich died in a moment, and those who had nothing immediately inherited their property, — they reflected that life and riches were alike transitory, and they resolved to enjoy themselves while they could, and to think only of pleasure. Who would be willing to sacrifice himself to the law of honor when he knew not whether he would ever live to be held in honor? The pleasure of the moment and any sort of thing which conduced to it took the place both of honor and of expediency. No fear of god or law of man deterred a criminal. Those who saw all perishing alike, thought that the worship or neglect of the gods made no difference. For offences against human law no punishment was to be feared; no one would live long enough to be called to account. Already a far heavier sentence had been passed and was hanging over a man's head; before that fell, why should he not take a little pleasure?

An Inquiry into the Horrors of War
▼▼▼
29 ▾ *Euripides, THE WOMEN OF TROY*

Notwithstanding Pericles' claims to the contrary, each of classical Hellas's poleis, including Athens, was a brotherhood of warriors organized for the primary purpose of waging war — usually against other Hellenes. The most destructive of all the Hellenic wars fought during the fifth and fourth centuries B.C.E. was the Peloponnesian War (431–404), which grew ever more bitter as the fighting dragged on. Both sides were guilty of atrocities, but one of the most infamous was Athens's doing. During a brief truce in the autumn of 416, Athens tried to compel the neutral island of Melos to join its confederacy. When the Melians declined, an Athenian fleet captured the island, killed all of Melos's adult male citizens, and enslaved all its women and children. It is against the background of the capture of Melos and the spirited public debate early the following year over whether Athens should launch a massive naval expedition against the Greek city of Syracuse in Sicily that we should place *The Women of Troy*. Written and produced by Euripides (ca. 480–406 B.C.E.) in the spring of 415, the play was performed while the expeditionary force against Syracuse was assembling in Athens's harbor. As Euripides seems to have feared, that expedition proved disastrous for Athens and became the tragic turning point in the war for the city. After the debacle at Syracuse, Athens never fully recovered, and the defeat that came in 404 was almost a foregone conclusion.

Euripides' audience was well acquainted with the legends of the troubles and disasters that beset the victorious Greeks after they sailed away from Troy (Chapter 2, source 12), and it could not fail to miss the playwright's implied warning about the Syracusan adventure. It was an article of Hellenic social-ethical philosophy that acts of *hubris* (unrestrained arrogance) inevitably invite the punishment of *nemesis* (retributive justice). How prophetic the playwright turned out to be.

Whereas Hippocrates studied the clinical course of physical disease, Euripides specialized in diagnosing emotional disorders and mental breakdowns, especially those brought about by social ills. Deep compassion underlay his dissections of tortured human psyches. Although his extant plays show him to be a person who sought more to understand than to judge, he was an outspoken critic of the indignities visited upon those whom society exploited. In *The Women of Troy* his sympathies went out to the victims of war, especially its female victims, but he also reserved some sympathy for otherwise honorable soldiers who were coarsened and often destroyed by war.

Significantly, toward the very end of his life Euripides voluntarily left Athens, choosing to live in the wilds of faraway Thessaly. Athens had become a much less pleasant place in which to live as a result of the ongoing war that was turning out so badly for the city. Its chief architect of the war, Pericles, had strongly implied in his funeral oration that Athens could not fail to win the war, given its presumed moral superiority over Sparta, its chief enemy. How wrong he was — on several levels.

As is true of most Greek tragedies, the setting is in the legendary past. The scene is Troy, following its capture by the Achaeans. All the men of Troy are dead or have fled the city. Amid the ruins we meet four characters: Hecuba, widowed queen of Troy; her daughter-in-law, Andromache, the widow of Troy's greatest hero, Hector; Talthybius, the official messenger of the Greek army; and Astyanax, the child of Andromache and Hector. Looming behind the scenes but never appearing on stage is Odysseus, whom we saw in the *Odyssey* (Chapter 2, source 12), but this Odysseus is quite different from the hero of Homeric epic song. As our excerpt begins, Hecuba is about to learn the fate of her daughter Polyxena.

QUESTIONS FOR ANALYSIS

1. What picture emerges from this scene of the fate of war captives in the Hellenic World?
2. What does Andromache's initial speech allow us to infer about the role and place of women in Euripides' society?
3. Assuming Euripides intended this play to be a commentary on the Melian massacre and the projected expedition against Syracuse, what was his message?
4. The *Iliad* and the *Odyssey* served as Hellas's core cultural texts, and Achilles, Odysseus, and their comrades were regarded as great ethnic heroes. What does Euripides' characterization of the Achaeans at Troy suggest about his art and message?
5. Were he alive, what do you think would be Pericles' reaction to this play? Be specific in your answer.
6. This is a strange tragic play. The protagonists are passive; there is no plot to speak of and little action, and nothing is resolved. Horror simply follows upon horror. What, if anything, is so humanistic about this nondramatic drama?

7. **Compare the social criticism of Thucydides with that of Euripides. What do they share, and what do those common elements suggest about Hellenic rationalism?**

ANDROMACHE
Polyxena lies dead upon Achilles' tomb,
a gift to a corpse, to a lifeless thing.

HECUBA
My sorrow! That is what Talthybius meant —
I could not read his riddle.[1] Oh, too plain.

ANDROMACHE
I saw her there and left the chariot
and covered her dead body with my cloak,
and beat my breast.

HECUBA
Murdered — my child. Oh, wickedly!
Again I cry to you. Oh, cruelly slain!

ANDROMACHE
She has died her death, and happier by far
dying than I alive.

HECUBA
Life cannot be what death is, child.
Death is empty — life has hope.

ANDROMACHE
Mother, O Mother, hear a truer word.
Now let me bring joy to your heart.
I say to die is only not to be,
and rather death than life with bitter grief.
They have no pain, they do not feel
    their wrongs.
But the happy person who has come
    to wretchedness,
his soul is a lost wanderer,
the old joys that were once, left far behind.
She is dead, your daughter — to her the same
as if she never had been born.
She does not know the wickedness that
    killed her.
While I — I aimed my shaft at good repute.

I gained full measure — then
    missed happiness.
For all that is called virtuous in a woman
I strove for and I won in Hector's house.
Always because we women, whether right
    or wrong,
are spoken ill of
unless we stay within our homes, my longing
I set aside and kept the house.
Light talk, glib women's words,
could never gain an entrance there.
My own thoughts were enough for me,
best of all teachers to me in my home.
Silence, a tranquil eye, I brought my husband,
knew well in what I should rule him,
and when to give him obedience.
And this report of me came to the Greeks
for my destruction. When they captured me
Achilles' son[2] would have me.
I shall be a slave to those who murdered —
O Hector, my beloved — shall I thrust
    him aside,
open my heart to the man that comes to me,
and be a traitor to the dead?
And yet to shrink in loathing from him
and make my masters hate me —
One night, men say, one night in a man's bed
will make a woman tame —
Oh, shame! A woman throw her husband off
and in a new bed love another —
Why, a young colt will not run in the yoke
with any but her mate — not a dumb beast
that has not reason, of a lower nature.
O Hector, my beloved, you were all to me,
wise, noble, mighty, in wealth, in
    manhood, both.
No man had touched me when you took me,
took me from out my father's home

---

[1]Unable to tell Hecuba the truth, he had said that Polyxena was watching Achilles' tomb and was free from trouble.

[2]Neoptolemus (see Chapter 2, source 12).

and yoked a girl fast to you.
And you are dead, and I, with other plunder,
am sent by sea to Greece. A slave's yoke there.
Your dead Polyxena you weep for,
what does she know of pain like mine?
The living must have hope. Not I,
    not anymore.
I will not lie to my own heart. No good will
    ever come.
But oh, to think it would be sweet.

A Woman[3]
We stand at the same point of pain. You
    mourn your ruin,
and in your words I hear my own calamity.

Hecuba
Those ships — I never have set foot on one,
but I have heard of them, seen pictures
    of them.
I know that when a storm comes which
    they think
they can ride out, the sailors do their best,
one by the sail, another at the helm,
and others bailing.
But if great ocean's raging overwhelms them,
they yield to fate.
They give themselves up to the racing waves.
So in my many sorrows I am dumb.
I yield, I cannot speak.
The great wave from God has conquered me.
But, O dear child, let Hector be,
and let be what has come to him.
Your tears will never call him back.
Give honor now to him who is your master.
Your sweet ways — use them to allure him.
So doing you will give cheer to your friends.
Perhaps this child, my own child's son,
you may rear to manhood and great aid
    for Troy,
and if ever you should have more children,
they might build her again. Troy once more be
    a city!
Oh — one thought leads another on.

But why again that servant of the Greeks?
I see him coming. Some new plan is here.

(*Enter Talthybius with soldiers. He is troubled
and advances hesitatingly.*)

Talthybius
Wife of the noblest man that was in Troy,
O wife of Hector, do not hate me.
Against my will I come to tell you.
The people and the kings have all resolved —

Andromache
What is it? Evil follows words like those.

Talthybius
This child they order — Oh, how can I
    say it —

Andromache
Now that he does not go with me to the
    same master —

Talthybius
No man in Greece shall ever be his master.

Andromache
But — leave him here — all that is left
    of Troy?

Talthybius
I don't know how to tell you. What is bad,
words can't make better —

Andromache
I feel you kind. But you have not good news.

Talthybius
Your child must die. There, now you know
the whole, bad as it is.

Andromache
Oh, I have heard an evil worse
than a slave in her master's bed.

Talthybius
It was Odysseus had his way. He spoke
to all the Greeks.

---

[3]One of the women of Troy, who comprise the chorus.

ANDROMACHE
O God. There is no measure to my pain.

TALTHYBIUS
He said a hero's son must not grow up —

ANDROMACHE
God, on his own sons may that counsel fall.

TALTHYBIUS
— but from the towering wall of Troy
    be thrown.
Now, now — let it be done — that's wiser.
Don't cling so to him. Bear your pain
the way a brave woman suffers.
You have no strength — don't look to
    any help.
There's no help for you anywhere.
    Think — think.
The city gone — your husband too. And you
a captive and alone, one woman — how
can you do battle with us? For your own good
I would not have you try, and draw
hatred down on you and be shamed.
Oh, hush — never a curse upon the Greeks.
If you say words that make the army angry
the child will have no burial,[4] and
    without pity —
Silence now. Bear your fate as best you can.
So then you need not leave him dead without
    a grave,
and you will find the Greeks more kind.

ANDROMACHE
Go die, my best beloved, my own, my treasure,
in cruel hands, leaving your
    mother comfortless.
Your father was too noble. That is why
they kill you. He could save others,
he could not save you for his nobleness.
My bed, my bridal — all for misery —
when long ago I came to Hector's halls
to bear my son — oh, not for Greeks to slay,
but for a ruler over a teeming Asia.
Weeping, my little one? There, there.

You cannot know what waits for you.
Why hold me with your hands so fast, cling so
    fast to me?
You little bird, flying to hide beneath
    my wings.
And Hector will not come — he will
    not come,
up from the tomb, great spear in hand, to
    save you.
Not one of all his kin, of all the Trojan might.
How will it be? Falling down — down —
    oh, horrible.
And his neck — his breath — all broken.
And none to pity. You little thing,
curled in my arms, you dearest to your mother,
how sweet the fragrance of you.
All nothing then — this breast from where
your baby mouth drew milk, my travail too,
my cares, when I grew wasted watching you.
Kiss me — Never again. Come, closer, closer.
Your mother who bore you — put your arms
    around my neck.
Now kiss me, lips to lips.
O Greeks, you have found out ways to torture
that are not Greek.
A little child, all innocence of wrong —
you wish to kill him. . . .
Quick! Take him — seize him — cast
    him down —
if so you will. Feast on his flesh.
God has destroyed me, and I cannot —
I cannot save my child from death.
Oh hide my head for shame and fling me
into the ship.

(She falls, then struggles to her knees.)

My fair bridal — I am coming —
Oh, I have lost a child, my own.

A WOMAN
O wretched Troy, tens of thousands lost
for a woman's sake,[5] a hateful marriage bed.

---

[4]And his shade will have no peace as a consequence.
[5]Helen. By running off to Troy with King Priam's son, Paris,
she had brought down on Troy the wrath of her husband
(Menelaus of Sparta), his brother (Agamemnon of Mycenae),
and their Achaean allies.

TALTHYBIUS (*drawing the child away*)
Come, boy, let go. Unclasp those loving hands,
poor mother.
Come now, up, up, to the very height,
where the towers of your fathers crown
 the wall,
and where it is decreed that you must die.

(*To the soldiers*)

Take him away.
A herald who must bring such orders
should be a man who feels no pity,
and no shame either — not like me.

Socrates and the Laws of Athens
▼▼▼

30 ▼ *Plato, CRITO*

In his "Funeral Oration," Pericles claims that Athenians respect authority and
the laws. The question is, how far does civic obedience extend when legal authorities have apparently perverted or misapplied the law? The question was
more than academic for the philosopher and social critic Socrates of Athens (ca.
469–399 B.C.E.). Socrates' uncompromising search for truth and goodness of soul
led him to expose humbuggery and hypocrisy wherever he found them, and he
earned the enmity of many who had been stung by his and his students' ability to
tie into logical knots people who were guilty of fuzzy thinking or moral obtuse-
ness. For most of his seventy years, Athens tolerated this self-proclaimed "gad-
fly," but in the mood of bitter recrimination that followed Athens's defeat in the
Peloponnesian War — a defeat that had been precipitated by the ill-considered
policies of one of Socrates' former students — the philosopher found himself
defending not only his teachings but his very life. In 399 a young conservative
politician charged the old man with impiety against the gods and corruption of
Athens's youth. Found guilty in a public trial, Socrates chose the sentence of
death rather than exile.

Much of what we know, or think we know, about Socrates comes from the
Dialogues of Plato (427–348 B.C.E.), one of Socrates' students and arguably the
most original philosopher produced by classical Hellas. The *Dialogues* consist of
a series of conversations that Socrates allegedly had with a number of contemporaries regarding ethical, social, and political issues. How much of what we read
in them is truly Socratic and how much is Platonic remains a subject of vigorous
debate among scholars.

The dialogue from which the present source is excerpted is known as the *Crito*.
The setting is prison, where Socrates awaits imminent execution. Crito, his friend
of many years, visits and informs the philosopher that escape is possible. A number of people stand ready to bribe some willing officials to let Socrates slip away
into exile. Socrates refuses and in doing so delivers what is known as "The Speech
of the Laws of Athens," in which he addresses the obligations of citizenship.

QUESTIONS FOR ANALYSIS

1. What are the Laws' essential arguments, and why does Socrates find them compelling?
2. Socrates speaks of following the will of God, but are his arguments regarding right and wrong based on a god-centered religious vision or on something else? What conclusions follow from your answer?
3. Compare Socrates' view of citizenship and its rights and responsibilities with those of Pericles (source 28). Do they agree? Based on your study of both sources, what inferences have you reached regarding the phenomenon of citizenship in Athens?
4. What would a Chinese Legalist, such as we saw in sources 25 and 26, think of this speech?

SOCRATES: In leaving the prison against the will of the Athenians, do I wrong any? or rather do I not wrong those whom I ought least to wrong? Do I not desert the principles which were acknowledged by us to be just — what do you say?

CRITO: I cannot tell Socrates; for I do not know.

SOCRATES: Then consider the matter in this way: — Imagine that I am about to play truant (you may call the proceeding by any name which you like), and the laws and the government come and interrogate me: "Tell us Socrates," they say, "what are you about? Are you not going by an act of yours to overturn us — the laws, and the whole state, as far as in you lies? Do you imagine that a state can subsist and not be overthrown, in which the decisions of law have no power, but are set aside and trampled upon by individuals?" What will be our answer, Crito, to these and the like words? Any one, and especially a rhetorician, will have a good deal to say on behalf of the law which requires a sentence to be carried out. He will argue that this law should not be set aside; and shall we reply, "Yes, but the state has injured us and gives an unjust sentence." Suppose I say that?

CRITO: Very good, Socrates.

SOCRATES: "And was that our agreement with you?" the law would answer, "or were you to abide by the sentence of the state?" And if I were to express my astonishment at their words, the law would probably add: "Answer, Socrates, instead of opening your eyes — you are in the habit of asking and answering questions. Tell us, — What complaint have you to make against us which justifies you in attempting to destroy us and the state? In the first place did we not bring you into existence? Your father married your mother by our aid and begat you. Say whether you have any objection to urge against those of us who regulate marriage?" None, I should reply. "Or against those of us who after birth regulate the nurture and education of children, in which you also were trained? Were not the laws which have the charge of education, right in commanding your father to train you in music and gymnastic?" Right, I should reply. "Well then, since you were brought into the world and nurtured and educated by us, can you deny in the first place that you are our child and slave, as your fathers were before you? And if this is true you are not on equal terms with us; nor can you think that you have a right to do to us what we are doing to you. Would you have any right to strike or revile or do any other evil to your father or your master, if you had one, because you have been struck or reviled by him, or received some other evil at his hands? — you would not say this? And because we think right to destroy you, do you think that you have any right to destroy us in return, and your country as far as in you lies? Will you, O professor of true virtue, pretend that you are justified in this? Has a philosopher like you failed to discover that our country is more to be valued and higher and holier far than mother or father or any ancestor, and more to be regarded in the eyes of the gods and of men of understanding? also to be soothed, and gently and reverently entreated when angry, even more than a father, and either to be persuaded, or if not persuaded, to be obeyed? And when we are punished by her, whether with imprisonment or stripes, the punishment is to be endured in silence; and if she lead us to wounds or death in battle, thither we follow as is right; neither may any one yield or retreat or leave his rank, but whether in battle or in a court of law, or in any other place, he must do what his city and his country order him; or he must change their view of what is just: and if he may do no violence to his father or mother, much less may he do violence to his country." What answer shall we make to this, Crito? Do the laws speak truly, or do they not?

CRITO: I think they do.

SOCRATES: Then the laws will say: "Consider, Socrates, if we are speaking truly that in your present attempt you are going to do us an injury. For, having brought you into the world, and nurtured and educated you, and given you and every other citizen a share in every good which we had to give, we further proclaim to any Athenian by the liberty that we allow him, that if he does not like us when he has become of age and has seen the ways of the city, and made our acquaintance, he may go where he pleases and take his goods with him. None of us laws will forbid him or interfere with him. Any one who does not like us and the city, and who wants to emigrate to a colony or to any other city, may go where he likes, retaining his property. But he who has experience of the manner in which we order justice and administer the state, and still remains, has entered into an implied contract that he will do as we command him. And he who

disobeys us is, as we maintain, thrice wrong; first, because in disobeying us he is disobeying his parents; secondly, because we are the authors of his education; thirdly, because he has made an agreement with us that he will duly obey our commands; and he neither obeys them nor convinces us that our commands are unjust; and we do not rudely impose them, but give him the alternative of obeying or convincing us; — that is what we offer, and he does neither.

"These are the sort of accusations to which as we were saying, you, Socrates, will be exposed if you accomplish your intentions; you, above all other Athenians." Suppose now I ask, why I rather than anybody else? They will justly retort upon me that I above all other men have acknowledged the agreement. "There is clear proof," they will say, "Socrates, that we and the city were not displeasing to you. Of all Athenians you have been the most constant resident in the city, which, as you never leave, you may be supposed to love. For you never went out of the city either to see the games,[1] except once when you went to Isthmus,[2] or to any other place unless when you were on military service; nor did you travel as other men do. Nor had you any curiosity to know other states or their laws. Your affections did not go beyond us and our state; we were your special favorites, and you acquiesced in our government of you; and here in this city you begat your children, which is proof of your satisfaction. Moreover, you might in the course of the trial, if you had liked, have fixed the penalty at banishment; the state which refuses to let you go now would have let you go then. But you pretended that you preferred death to exile and that you were not unwilling to die. And now you have forgotten these fine sentiments, and pay no respect to us the laws, of whom you are the destroyer; and are doing what only a miserable slave would do, running away and turning your back upon the compacts and agreements which you made as a

---

[1]Various religious festivals at which athletic games were held. The most famous were the pan-Hellenic Olympic Games.

[2]The Isthmian Games in honor of Poseidon and held by the city of Corinth, which commanded the isthmus that connects central Greece with the Peloponnesian Peninsula.

citizen. And first of all answer this very question: Are we right in saying that you agreed to be governed according to us in deed, and not in word only? Is that true or not?" How shall we answer, Crito? Must we not assent?

CRITO: We cannot help it, Socrates.

SOCRATES: Then will they not say: "You, Socrates, are breaking the covenants and agreements which you made with us at your leisure, not in any haste or under any compulsion or deception, but after you have had seventy years to think of them, during which time you were at liberty to leave the city, if we were not to your mind, or if our covenants appeared to you to be unfair. You had your choice, and might have gone either to Lacedaemon[3] or Crete, both which states are often praised by you for their good government, or to some other Hellenic or foreign state. Whereas you, above all other Athenians, seemed to be so fond of the state, or, in other words, of us her laws (and who would care about a state which has no laws?), that you never stirred out of her; the halt, the blind, the maimed were not more stationary in her than you were. And now you run away and forsake your agreements. Not so, Socrates, if you will take our advice; do not make yourself ridiculous by escaping out of the city.

"For just consider, if you transgress and err in this sort of way, what good will you do either to yourself or to your friends? That your friends will be driven into exile and deprived of citizenship, or will lose their property, is tolerably certain; and you yourself, if you fly to one of the neighboring cities, as, for example, Thebes or Megara, both of which are well governed, will come to them as an enemy, Socrates, and their government will be against you, and all patriotic citizens will cast an evil eye upon you as a subverter of the laws, and you will confirm in the minds of the judges the justice of their own condemnation of you. For he who is a corrupter of the laws

is more than likely to be a corrupter of the young and foolish portion of mankind. Will you then flee from well-ordered cities and virtuous men? And is existence worth having on these terms? Or will you go to them without shame, and talk to them, Socrates? And what will you say to them? What you say here about virtue and justice and institutions and laws being the best things among men? Would that be decent of you? Surely not. But if you go away from well-governed states to Crito's friends in Thessaly,[4] where there is great disorder and license, they will be charmed to hear the tale of your escape from prison, set off with ludicrous particulars of the manner in which you were wrapped in a goatskin or some other disguise, and metamorphosed as the manner is of runaways; but will there be no one to remind you that in your old age you were not ashamed to violate the most sacred laws from a miserable desire of a little more life? Perhaps not, if you keep them in good temper; but if they are out of temper you will hear many degrading things; you will live, but how? — as the flatterer of all men, and the servant of all men; and doing what? — eating and drinking in Thessaly, having gone abroad in order that you may get a dinner. And where will be your fine sentiments about justice and virtue? Say that you wish to live for the sake of your children — you want to bring them up and educate them — will you take them into Thessaly and deprive them of Athenian citizenship? Is this the benefit which you will confer upon them? Or are you under the impression that they will be better cared for and educated here if you are still alive, although absent from them; for your friends will take care of them? Do you fancy that if you are an inhabitant of Thessaly they will take care of them, and if you are an inhabitant of the other world that they will not take care of them? Nay; but if they who call themselves friends are good for anything, they will — to be sure they will.

---

[3] Sparta.

[4] A wild area of northern Greece. In 408 the playwright Euripides (source 29) left Athens for Thessaly, apparently disappointed at his lack of popular acclaim in his native city.

"Listen then, Socrates, to us who have brought you up. Think not of life and children first, and of justice afterwards, but of justice first, that you may be justified before the princes of the world below. For neither will you nor any that belong to you be happier or holier or juster in this life, or happier in another, if you do as Crito bids. Now you depart in innocence, a sufferer and not a doer of evil; a victim, not of the laws but of men. But if you go forth, returning evil for evil, and injury for injury, breaking the covenants and agreements which you have made with us, and wronging those whom you ought least of all to wrong, that is to say, yourself, your friends, your country, and us, we shall be angry with you while you live, and our brethren, the laws in the world below, will receive you as an enemy; for they will know that you have done your best to destroy us. Listen, then, to us and not to Crito."

This, dear Crito, is the voice which I seem to hear murmuring in my ears, like the sound of the flute in the ears of the mystic; that voice, I say, is humming in my ears, and prevents me from hearing any other. And I know that anything more which you may say will be vain. Yet speak, if you have anything to say.

CRITO: I have nothing to say, Socrates.

SOCRATES: Leave me then, Crito, to fulfill the will of God, and to follow whither he leads.

Chapter 5

▼▼▼

Regional Empires and Afro-Eurasian Interchange

300 B.C.E.–500 C.E.

By 300 B.C.E. the cultural traditions of China, India, Southwest Asia, and Hellas were solidly in place and ready to expand beyond their original boundaries. Expand they did, but expansion followed no single pattern. Imperial aggrandizement, largely by means of military conquest, played a major role in spreading Chinese, Southwest Asian, and Hellenic cultural influences, but it was not a factor in the creation in Southeast Asia of a *Greater India* (as many historians term it).

As early as the first century C.E. people of the coastal areas of Southeast Asia accepted elements of Indian culture, including Hindu and Buddhist traditions, from merchants traveling across the Bay of Bengal. Colonists, including Indian priests and scholars, soon followed. Traffic was not all one way, however, as youths from various Hindu and Buddhist kingdoms throughout Southeast Asia traveled to India for advanced religious instruction.

Chinese cultural influences traveled south, northeast, and west as a consequence of both military adventure — the imperialistic expansionism of the Qin and Han Dynasties — and more peaceful exchanges, especially the travels of merchants and the slow, steady southward migration of China's expanding peasant population. The armies of Han conquered Manchuria and northern Korea and established hegemony over non-Chinese peoples to the south in northern Vietnam and along the Himalayan foothills. To the west the armies of Han China penetrated deeply into Central Asia. Wherever its soldiers went, its merchants were not too far behind. The roads that China opened to the West also served as conduits for the influx of new ideas into the Middle Kingdom, particularly Buddhism, which flowed into China along its overland trade routes.

From the late sixth to the late fourth century B.C.E. the Persian Empire, centered in Southwest Asia, encompassed an area from the Nile to the Indus, from the Mediterranean to the Persian Gulf, and from the Black Sea to the Red Sea. Although the Persians were respectful of local traditions, their massive empire was a fertile medium for the blending and transmission of many different cultures. Then in the late fourth century Persia and Greece were merged into a single empire for one brief but significant moment. The conquest of the Persian Empire by Alexander the Great (r. 336–323 B.C.E.) and his penetration as far east as the Indus Valley ushered in a new era for western Eurasia: the *Hellenistic Age.* Whereas the Hellenic World had been parochial, the Hellenistic World was cosmopolitan and culturally eclectic. The armies of Alexander and the state builders who followed helped create a cultural amalgamation of Southwest Asian, North African, and even some Indian elements, over which was laid a layer of Greek language, thought, and artistic expression. What emerged was, to use a Greek word, a cultural *ecumene* (a unity of diverse civilized peoples). This world culture stretched from western Central Asia and northwest India in the east to the regions of the central Mediterranean in the West, and much of it was Greek in form and inspiration.

Alexander's empire did not survive him, but the amalgamation of peoples and cultures that he forged laid the basis for Hellenistic successor states in Egypt, Southwest Asia, and the Mediterranean. Of these, the most impressive was the Roman Empire. To be sure, the Romans spoke Latin and not Greek, and their civilization was as deeply influenced by the Etruscans of north central Italy as it was by Greeks and other Hellenistic cultures. Moreover, their empire was centered on the Mediterranean Sea — far away from the heartland of the original Hellenistic Ecumene. Notwithstanding all of these realities, it is still reasonable to see the Roman Empire as the last and greatest of the Hellenistic states and as the carrier of Hellenistic culture into such faraway western regions as Gaul, Germany, and Britain.

Rome was certainly not Eurasia's only great empire. By the end of the first century B.C.E. four great regional empires linked China, India, Southwest Asia, and the Greco-Roman Mediterranean in a chain of civilization from the Pacific to the Atlantic. Han China dominated East Asia and reached deeply into Central Asia. India, which was not politically united, was joined to Central Asia by the *Kushana Empire* in its northern regions. The *Parthian Empire,* which had arisen in the wake of the collapse of the most eastern Hellenistic state, controlled the Southwest Asian lands of Iran and Mesopotamia and aggressively butted up against the Roman Empire.

Sea and land routes, most notably the fabled *Silk Road,* now joined these civilized regions, creating the first age of Afro-Eurasian linkage. As is the case with most chains, the ends rarely came into direct contact with one another. Very few Mediterraneans traveled all the way to China, and fewer Chinese ventured even to the borders of the Roman Empire. Instead, a series of merchant intermediaries speeded along the silk, cotton, spices, plants and animals, manufactured goods, gold, ideas, and even killing diseases that traveled from one end of this great network to the other, with the Parthian Empire serving as a major site of exchange and interchange.

Although most of the major trade routes traversed the waters and lands of Eurasia, Africa also shared in this unification to the extent that its northern regions were an integral part of the Roman Empire and portions of its eastern coast were linked by regular trade with Arabia, India, and Southeast Asia.

This age of grand-scale linkage began to break down around 200 C.E., when both China and the Roman Empire entered periods of severe crisis. Despite political and economic disasters, however, trade along the Silk Road never totally ceased in the centuries that followed, even though it experienced periods of severe recession.

▼▼▼

The Greco-Roman World

Alexander the Great died in Babylon in 323 B.C.E. Tradition claims that when questioned as to whom he bequeathed his empire, he replied, "To the strongest." No single would-be successor proved strong enough to seize the entire empire. Rather, rival generals divided the Hellenistic World into a number of successor states. The two mightiest and most brilliant were the kingdom of the Seleucids, centered on Anatolia, Mesopotamia, and Syria, and the kingdom of Egypt, which fell to the family of Ptolemy, one of Alexander's Macedonian generals.

Ptolemy and his successors lavished money on their capital, Alexandria, transforming this new city, located in Egypt's northern delta region, into the most impressive cosmopolitan setting in the Hellenistic World. The city's twin crowning glories, at least in the opinion of scholars and scientists, were the Museum, which functioned as a center of advanced research, and the Library, which represented an attempt to gather under one roof the entire Hellenistic World's store of written knowledge and contained perhaps as many as a half million separate scrolls.

Both institutions enjoyed the continuous generous patronage of the Macedonian god-kings of Egypt and served as focal points for scientific and literary studies that were Greek in form and substance but cosmopolitan in scope and clientele. Educated Persians, Jews, Mesopotamians, Syrians, Italians, and members of many other ethnic groups flocked to Alexandria, where they formed an ecumenical community of scholars and artists whose common tongue and intellectual perspective were as Greek as that of their Ptolemaic hosts.

In 30 B.C.E. Cleopatra VII, the last Ptolemaic ruler of Egypt, died in Alexandria by her own hand, and Egypt passed under the direct control of the rising imperial power of Rome. By this time Rome had already seized control of Italy, Greece, major portions of Anatolia (which it termed *Asia Minor*), Syria, most of North Africa, all of the major Mediterranean islands, Spain, and the area north of the Alps and Pyrenees known as *Gaul*. The Mediterranean had truly become Rome's *Mare Nostrum* (Our Sea), and the Roman Empire now controlled a large portion of the Hellenistic World. As inheritor by conquest of eastern Mediterranean lands and culture, Rome would disseminate a Greco-Roman form of Hellenistic culture throughout the western Mediterranean, as well as among various barbarian peoples living in European lands well beyond the Mediterranean coastline. Well before the end of the first century C.E., Roman legions would be erecting Greek-style temples to the Persian god Mithras along the Rhine and in Britain, and Greek literature would be studied in schools throughout lands recently wrested from Gallic tribes.

Images of the Hellenistic World
▼▼▼
31 ▼ FOUR HELLENISTIC STATUES

The Hellenistic Ecumene was exceedingly cosmopolitan, but cosmopolitanism often carries a price. In more parochial societies — such as fifth-century Hellas, which centered on small, fairly homogenous poleis — people can often feel secure in the sense of living in a friendly and understandable environment. Conversely, living in societies that are open to the world and filled with a bewildering array of different and often contradictory cultural stimuli can be frightening and alienating. Such alienation and confusion can have profound effects on artistic expression. But even when people are comfortable with cultural differences and at home in a "universal city" (which is the literal meaning of *cosmopolitan*), they tend to view the world and themselves differently from people whose horizons are more limited. This comfort with a wider world also finds expression in the arts.

Hellenic sculptors of the fifth century B.C.E. had idealized the human body and placed the human being securely in the center of an ordered world — a world that they saw reflected in the poleis in which they were citizens (Chapter 4, source 28). As the following four pieces suggest, later Hellenistic sculptors had different visions.

Our first item is a marble bust of King Euthydemos I of *Bactria* (r. ca. 235–200 B.C.E.), which dates from around 200 B.C.E. The Greek-speaking kings of Bactria had carved out a realm on the far horizon of the Hellenistic World, a wild, mountainous region in western Central Asia shared by the modern nations of Turkmenistan, Tajikistan, Uzbekistan, and Afghanistan. A native of Anatolia, Euthydemos had risen to power by overthrowing his predecessor. Our second piece is a Roman marble copy of a bronze original that had been created around 230–220 B.C.E. Known as *The Gaul and Wife,* the original had served as one of a number of statues gracing a victory monument of King Attalos I of *Pergamon* (r. 241–197 B.C.E.) that celebrated his victories over invading Gallic, or Celtic, tribes. The kings of Pergamon, a city located near the northwestern coast of Anatolia, lavished money on their city's beautification, using art to trumpet their policies and achievements. Our third sculpture is *The Old Woman,* also known as *The Old Market Woman,* an original work in marble that dates from the late second or early first century B.C.E. One interpretation of the sculpture is that the woman is depicted in the act of calling out to potential customers, hoping that they purchase the chicken and basket of vegetables and fruits that she holds in her left hand. Another interpretation, which we favor, is that the laurel wreath on her head suggests she is offering the goods as part of a religious festival, possibly one in honor of Dionysus, the god of wine. Our fourth sculpture is a bronze boxer by the Athenian sculptor Apollonius. Created around 60 B.C.E. in Italy, possibly for some rich fan of the Greek sport of pugilism, the work shows us a veteran boxer, whose broken nose, battered face and ears, muscular body, and leather gloves with bands of lead at the knuckles clearly indicate his profession.

QUESTIONS FOR ANALYSIS

1. Consider the bust of King Euthydemos. How does the sculptor present the king? What reaction do you think the sculptor desired to evoke from the viewer?

2. Hellenistic people viewed the Gauls as barbarians; that is, they were a non-Hellenized people. How does the sculptor portray the Gallic warrior and his wife? What is the sculptor's message, and what emotions does the sculptor wish to evoke? What conclusions follow from your answers?

3. Consider the old woman and the boxer. How have their sculptors dealt with them? Have they been given any dignity, or are they devoid of it? Do their sculptors display contempt or compassion for the lowborn, the elderly, and those who suffer life's misfortunes? Perhaps the sculptors felt neither sympathy nor disdain but simply wanted to take a cold, hard look at reality. How do you answer these questions, and what conclusions follow from your answers?

(*"Questions for Analysis" continue on page 131.*)

The Gaul and Wife

King Euthydemos I of Bactria

The Boxer

The Old Woman

130

4. "Hellenistic art often exhibited an attitude toward life that was cynical and totally devoid of idealism." Based on your study of these four pieces, do you agree or disagree with this anonymous judgment? Why have you reached that conclusion?

5. Some commentators have characterized Hellenistic art as an attempt to create psychological portraits. Do any or all of these four works seem to meet that characterization? If so, what was there about the Hellenistic World that might have led some artists to emphasize the individual human psyche?

6. If art is a window on the society that produces it, what do these four sculptures allow you to infer about the Hellenistic World?

The World According to Strabo

▼▼▼

32 ▼ Strabo, GEOGRAPHY

The life and work of the late Hellenistic historian and geographer Strabo (ca. 64 B.C.E.–25 C.E.) reflect the hybrid nature and wide horizons of Hellenistic civilization. By descent Strabo was part Asian and part Greek. He was born in Amaseia in northeastern Anatolia but studied and worked at length in Rome and Alexandria. He admired the Romans and their empire but composed his historical and geographical works in Greek, the common language of educated Hellenistic people.

His only surviving work is the *Geography*. Its seventeen books are largely a compilation of information and misinformation garnered from accounts and studies by earlier Hellenistic travelers and geographers of the known lands of Europe, Asia (up to and including India), and Africa. Because most of Strabo's sources were lost forever when the Library of Alexandria was destroyed in late Roman times, his *Geography* is our main source of information on the Hellenistic World's geographical knowledge and lore. In this selection Strabo discusses the state of his society's knowledge of the world.

QUESTIONS FOR ANALYSIS

1. What kind of evidence did Strabo rely on?
2. Why does he prefer the accounts of contemporary writers and travelers to those of earlier ones, and what does this suggest about travel in his own day?
3. Using the map, trace that portion of the inhabited world Strabo knew from firsthand experience.
4. What level of contact did Strabo's society have with India? How did it compare with earlier exchanges in the age of the Ptolemies?

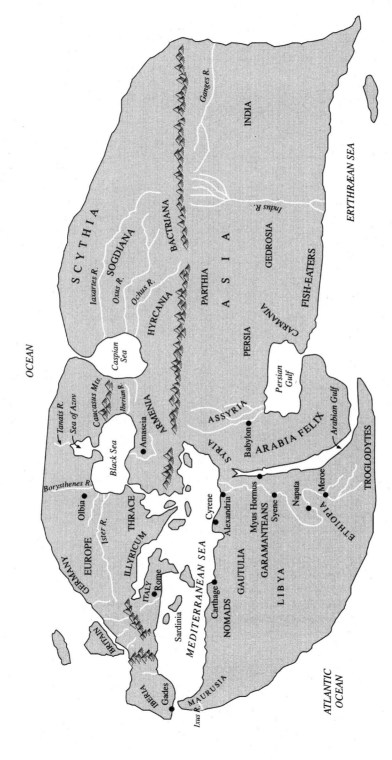

The World According to Strabo

5. Consider the map and Strabo's account of Asia. What does he know about lands east of India, and what does this suggest about direct Greco-Roman knowledge of China?
6. What does Strabo tell us about the physical and human geography of North Africa? What evidence does Strabo present to allow us to conclude that North Africa was more fertile and less desiccated in his day than in our own? What does he know about Africa's interior? From what he tells us and does not tell us, what do you infer about Greco-Roman knowledge of Africa?

Now I shall tell what part of the land and sea I have myself visited and concerning what part I have trusted to accounts given by others by word of mouth or in writing. I have traveled westward from Armenia as far as the regions of Tyrrhenia[1] opposite Sardinia, and southward from the Euxine Sea[2] as far as the frontiers of Ethiopia.[3] And you could not find another person among the writers on geography who has traveled over much more of the distances just mentioned than I; indeed, those who have traveled more than I in the western regions have not covered as much ground in the east, and those who have traveled more in the eastern countries are behind me in the western; and the same holds true in regard to the regions towards the south and north. However, the greater part of our material both they and I receive by hearsay and then form our ideas. . . . And men who are eager to learn proceed in just that way: they trust as organs of sense those who have seen or wandered over any region, no matter what, some in this and some in that part of the earth, and they form in one diagram their mental image of the whole inhabited world. . . . And he who claims that only those have knowledge who have actually seen abolishes the criterion of the sense of hearing, though this sense is much more important than sight for the purposes of science.

In particular the writers of the present time can give a better account of the Britons, the Germans, the peoples both north and south of the Ister, the Getans, the Tyregetans, the Bastarnians,[4] and, furthermore, the peoples in the regions of the Caucasus, such as the Albanians and the Iberians.[5] Information has been given us also concerning Hyrcania and Bactriana by the writers of Parthian histories (Apollodorus of Artemita[6] and his school), in which they marked off those countries more definitely than many other writers. Again, since the Romans have recently invaded Arabia Felix with an army, of which Aelius Gallus,[7] my friend and companion, was the commander, and since the merchants of Alexandria are already sailing with fleets by way of the Nile and of the Arabian Gulf as far as India, these regions also have become far better known to us of to-day than to our predecessors. At any rate, when Gallus was prefect of Egypt, I accompanied him and ascended[8] the Nile as far as Syene and the frontiers of Ethiopia, and I learned that as many as one hundred and twenty vessels were sailing from Myos Hormos[9] to India, whereas formerly, under the Ptolemies, only

---

[1]North central Italy.
[2]The Black Sea.
[3]In this context *Ethiopia* meant all the land of Southeast Africa (see the map of Strabo's world).
[4]Tribes wandering through the Balkans, especially in Thrace.
[5]These are the *eastern* Iberians, who resided in the region between the Black and Caspian Seas. The western Iberians inhabited the land that is today Spain and Portugal.

[6]A second-century B.C.E. geographer of Alexandria and Athens.
[7]A Roman prefect of Egypt who led a disastrous two-year expedition into southern Arabia in 25–24 B.C.E.
[8]Sailed south. Because the Nile flows north, upstream lies to the south.
[9]An African port on the Red Sea.

a very few ventured to undertake the voyage and to carry on traffic in Indian merchandise. . . .

And Libya,[10] is — as the others show, and indeed as Cnaeus Piso,[11] who was once the prefect of that country, told me — like a leopard's skin; for it is spotted with inhabited places that are surrounded by waterless and desert land. The Egyptians call such inhabited places "oases." But though Libya is thus peculiar, it has some other peculiarities, which give it a threefold division. In the first place, most of its coastline that lies opposite to us[12] is extremely fertile, and especially Cyrenaea and the country about Carthage up to Maurusia and to the Pillars of Heracles,[13] secondly, even its coastline on the ocean[14] affords only moderate sustenance; and thirdly, its interior region, which produces silphium,[15] affords only a wretched sustenance, being, for the most part, a rocky and sandy desert; and the same is also true of the straight prolongation of this region through Ethiopia, the Troglodyte Country,[16] Arabia, and Gedrosia where the Fish-Eaters live. The most of the peoples of Libya are unknown to us; for not much of it is visited by armies, nor yet by men of outside tribes; and not only do very few of the natives from far inland ever visit us, but what they tell is not trustworthy or complete either. But still the following is based on what they say. They call the most southerly peoples Ethiopians; those who live next north of the Ethiopians they call, in the main, Garamantians, Pharusians, and Nigritans; those who live still north of these latter, Gaetulans; those who live near the sea, or even on the seacoast, next to Egypt and as far as Cyrenaea, Marmaridans; while they call those beyond Cyrenaea and the Syrtes, Psyllians, Nasamonians, and certain of the Gaetulans, and then Asbystians and Byzacians, whose territory reaches to that of Carthage. The territory of Carthage is large, and beyond it comes that of the Nomads,[17] the best known of these are called, some of them, Masylians, and others Masaesylians. And last of all come the Maurusians. The whole country from Carthage to the Pillars is fertile, though full of wild beasts, as is also the whole of the interior of Libya. So it is not unlikely that some of these peoples were also called Nomads for the reason that in early times they were not able to cultivate the soil on account of the multitude of wild animals. But the Nomads of today not only excel in the skill of hunting (and the Romans take a hand in this with them because of their fondness for fights with wild animals), but they have mastered farming as well as the chase. This, then, is what I have to say about the continents.

---

[10]*Libya* here means all of Africa.
[11]Proconsul (governor) of the North African province of Africa in the early years following the birth of Jesus.
[12]The coast of North Africa.
[13]The Strait of Gibraltar.
[14]It is not clear which ocean he means here, the Indian or the Atlantic. Strabo know and wrote about each. Quite possibly he refers to both ocean coastlines.

[15]An aromatic plant grown for export in Cyrene, on Africa's northeast coast; its resin was a popular medicine.
[16]A stone-age people of sub-Saharan Africa.
[17]The Berber inhabitants of the North African Roman province of Numidia.

The Blessings of the Roman Peace

▼▼▼

33 ▼ *Aelius Aristides, THE ROMAN ORATION*

Following its victory over Carthage in the Second Punic War (218–201 B.C.E.), the Roman Republic was the major power in the Mediterranean and an empire in fact, if not in name. Rome's acquisition of an empire had major repercussions at home, and the resultant strains triggered more than a century of class discord and civil war. The civil wars ended in 30 B.C.E., when Octavian, the great nephew and adopted son of Julius Caesar (ca. 100–44 B.C.E.), defeated Mark Antony and became sole master of the Roman World. In 27 B.C.E. the Senate accorded him the title *Augustus* (Revered One), implying he possessed divine authority. Posterity remembers him as *Caesar Augustus* (63 B.C.E.–14 C.E.), Rome's first emperor and the man who created and presided over the first generation of the *Pax Romana* (the Roman Peace).

Despite a number of weaknesses within the Roman imperial system, the Roman Peace held up rather well for two centuries. During that two-hundred-year period the empire expanded its borders significantly, reaching the apex of its expansion and prosperity in the age of the Antonines, the so-called *Five Good Emperors.* Each of these emperors, beginning with Nerva (r. 96–98 C.E.) and ending with Marcus Aurelius (r. 161–180), displayed a sensitivity to law and good government. Each labored to maintain internal stability and prosperity, and their combined extensive public works projects in both Italy and the provinces beautified the empire and significantly improved its infrastructure. Of the five emperors, the most widely admired was Antoninus Pius (r. 138–161), whose long and peaceful reign, simple life, and even temper won him many friends and few enemies.

In the year 155, Publius Aelius Aristides (117 or 118–ca. 180), a wealthy landowner from Anatolia whose family had received Roman citizenship in 123, visited the imperial court in Rome, where, in the presence of Emperor Antoninus, he delivered a *panegyric*, or formal public speech of praise, on the glories of the Pax Romana. Although this Greek-speaking philosopher and rhetorician presented a highly stylized address that was filled with the clichéd phrases and hyperbolic flourishes of the Hellenistic oratorical tradition, he managed nonetheless to capture the spirit of prosperity, cosmopolitanism, and universal mission that characterized the attitude of so many of the Roman Empire's ruling elite during the second century C.E.

QUESTIONS FOR ANALYSIS

1. According to Aristides, what were the unique attributes and blessings of the Roman Empire?
2. According to Aristides, how did the Romans manage to offer all of their various subject peoples good government?
3. What does he mean when he claims that Rome created a "world democracy" under the rule of a single man?
4. Which of his claims strike you as obvious exaggerations and blatant pufferies? Which strike you as totally false? Why?
5. Granted the hyperbole, do any of Aristides' claims strike you as plausible? Which ones? Please explain.
6. What does this oration allow us to infer about the second-century Roman self-image?

It is an age-old tradition that travelers who journey forth on land or water offer a prayer whereby they pledge to fulfill some vow — something they have on their mind — on reaching their destination safely. . . . The vow I took as I journeyed here was not the usual stupid and irrelevant sort, nor was it one unrelated to the art I profess. I simply vowed that, if I arrived safely, I would salute your city with a public address. . . .

Some writer referring to Asia asserted that one man ruled as much territory as the sun passed over, but his statement was false, because he placed all of Africa and Europe outside of the area where the sun rises in the east and sets in the west.[1] Now, however, it has become fact. The land you possess equals what the sun can pass over, and the sun does encompass your land. . . . You do not reign within fixed boundaries, and another state does not dictate the limits of the land you control; rather, the sea[2] extends like a belt, situated in the middle of the civilized world and in the middle of the land over which you rule. Around that sea lie the great continents[3] massively sloping down to it, forever offering you in full measure what they possess. . . . Whatever each culture grows and manufactures cannot fail to be here at all times and in great profusion. Here merchant vessels arrive carrying these many commodities from every region in every season and even at every equinox,[4] so that the city takes on the appearance of a sort of common market for the world. One can see cargoes from India and even, if you will, from southern Arabia in such numbers that one must conclude that the trees in those lands have been stripped bare,[5] and if the inhabitants of those lands need anything, they must come here to beg for a share of what

they have produced. . . . Your farmlands are Egypt, Sicily, and all of cultivated Africa.[6] Seaborne arrivals and departures are ceaseless, to the point that the wonder is, not so much that the harbor has insufficient space for all these merchant vessels, but that the sea has enough space (if it really does). Just as . . . there is a common channel where all waters of the Ocean[7] have a single source and destination, so there is a common channel to Rome and all meet here: trade, shipping, agriculture, metallurgy — all the arts and crafts that are or ever were and all things that are produced or spring from the earth. What one does not see here does not exist. So it is not easy to decide which is the greater: the superiority of this city relative to cities that presently exist, or the superiority of this empire relative to all empires that ever existed. . . .

As vast and comprehensive as its size is, your empire is much greater for its perfection than for the area its borders encircle. . . . The entire civilized world prays with one voice that this empire endure forever. . . . For of all who have ever gained an empire, you alone rule over free men. . . . You, who conduct public business throughout the whole civilized world exactly as if it were one city-state, appoint governors, as if it were by election, to protect and care for the governed, not to act as slave masters over them. . . . One could say that the people of today are ruled by the governors sent out to them only to the degree that they wish to be ruled. . . .

You have divided into two parts all men throughout your empire . . . everywhere giving citizenship to all those who are more accomplished, noble, and powerful, even as they retain their native-born identities,[8] while the rest you

---

[1]This had been written of the King of Kings of Persia. The clear implication is that the Roman Empire is vaster than that of ancient Persia.

[2]The Mediterranean Sea.

[3]Africa, Asia, and Europe. (See the map of Strabo's world accompanying source 32.)

[4]In other words, without any break whatsoever, despite the time of year.

[5]Of aromatics from southern Arabia and various spices from India and points east.

[6]North Africa, which was much more fertile in Roman times than it is today (source 32), was a major producer of grain and other agricultural products.

[7]Ancient Greek and Roman geographers believed that the three continents were surrounded by a single great ocean. (See the map accompanying source 32.)

[8]Aristides, for example, retained his citizenship in the Anatolian city of Smyrna while simultaneously possessing Roman citizenship.

have made subjects and the governed. Neither the sea nor the great expanse of intervening land keeps one from being a citizen, and there is no distinction between Europe and Asia. . . . No one is a foreigner who deserves to hold an office or is worthy of trust. Rather, there is here a common "world democracy" under the rule of one man, the best ruler and director. . . . You have divided humanity into Romans and non-Romans, . . . and because you have divided people in this manner, in every city throughout the empire there are many who share citizenship with you, no less than they share citizenship with their fellow natives. And some of these Roman citizens have not even seen this city![9] There is no need for troops to garrison the strategic high points of these cities, because the most important and powerful people in each region guard their native lands for you. . . . Yet there is not a residue of resentment among those excluded.[10] Because your government is both universal and like that of a single city-state, its governors rightly rule not as foreigners but, as it were, their own people. . . . Additionally, all of the masses of subjects under this government have protection against the more powerful of their native countrymen, by virtue of your anger and vengeance, which would fall upon the more powerful without delay should they dare to break the law. Thus, the

present government serves rich and poor alike, and your constitution has developed a single, harmonious, all-embracing union. What in former days seemed impossible has in your time come to pass: You control a vast empire with a rule that is firm but not unkind. . . .

As on a holiday, the entire civilized world lays down the weapons that were its ancient burden and has turned to adornment and all glad thoughts, with the power to realize them. . . . Cities glisten with radiance and charm, and the entire earth has been made beautiful like a garden. . . . Like a perpetual sacred flame, the celebration is unending. . . . You, better than anyone else, have proved the truth of the proverb: The earth is everyone's mother and our common fatherland. It is now possible for Hellene and non-Hellene,[11] with or without property, to travel with ease wherever he wishes, as though passing from homeland to homeland. . . . As far as security is concerned, it suffices to be a Roman citizen, or rather one of those people united under your rule. . . .

Let us pray that all the gods and their children grant that this empire and this city flourish forever and never cease until stones float on water and trees cease to put forth shoots in spring, and that the Great Governor[12] and his sons be preserved and obtain blessings for all.

---

[9]Rome.

[10]From Roman citizenship and a share in the governance of the provinces.

[11]By this time the term *Hellene* did not refer simply to an ethnic Greek. It meant anyone who was a Roman citizen and who shared in the Greco-Roman high culture of the

empire. Thus, Aristides, a native of Asia Minor, was a Hellene. A non-Hellene, or barbarian, was either someone from outside the empire or one of the empire's uneducated masses.

[12]The emperor.

Isis: The Goddess Who Saves
▼▼▼

34 ▾ *Lucius Apuleius, METAMORPHOSES*

Much like practices and beliefs in China, early Roman religion centered on each family's *paterfamilias,* or male head of the household, who embodied that family's *genius,* or unique living spirit, and, as its chief priest, communicated with the spirits of the family's ancestors. These ceremonies, it was believed, assured familial harmony and prosperity. As was true also in China, religion that had begun as family ancestor worship was raised to a civic level in order to assure the state's harmony and prosperity. Such religion stressed public ceremony over private belief and was centered on worldly concerns. Rome's civic cults, which were presided over by the emperor who served as *pontifex maximus,* or "chief priest" (source 41), were designed to learn the will of the gods and to curry their favor. The rationale was that if the rituals were performed properly, Rome would prosper.

Such practical approaches to religion failed to satisfy individuals who desired religious experiences that offered personal comfort in an often hostile world and private relief from the ills and sorrows that attend all humans. Just as Mahayana Buddhism, a foreign import, provided solace to many millions of Chinese who sought a deeper and more personal spiritual experience than was provided by traditional household and state religious rituals (Chapter 6, sources 46 and 47), so also the so-called *mystery religions* of the eastern Mediterranean and Southwest Asia helped many Romans and non-Romans alike to cope with the stresses of life. The attraction of these religions from the East became pronounced in the first century C.E., when the Greco-Roman World became increasingly vast and complex, thereby contributing to a high level of anxiety and alienation. As the empire began to undergo frightening challenges from the late second century onward, conversions to the empire's many mystery religions multiplied many times over.

Members of the various mystery religions believed that through a process of conversion and ritual initiation, a devotee was transformed into a new person. By virtue of that transformation, or rebirth, the new member was admitted to the religion's mysteries, or secret knowledge that led to everlasting tranquility. Membership in this select body of initiates provided a believer with the immediate support of a cohesive community of like-minded individuals and the promise of personal salvation. The various savior deities who offered such aid to their worshipers included *Mithras,* an Iranian sun god whose cult was open only to men, and *Cybele,* or the Great Mother, a fertility goddess from Asia Minor. Most popular of all was the ancient Egyptian goddess *Isis* (Chapter 1, sources 3 and 9), the loving mother of humanity, whose temples could be found throughout the empire. Save for the fact that Isis's followers were not prevented from worshiping other deities, the cult of this goddess might almost be termed monotheistic, so all powerful was she believed to be.

The *Metamorphoses,* also known as *The Golden Ass,* is a multilayered, allegorical novel by Lucius Apuleius (ca. 123–185 C.E.), a native of the city of Madauros in North Africa (modern Algeria), who, through a sophisticated blending of bawdy comedy and moral instruction, traced his personal spiritual journey to Isis. In the following selection, the goddess miraculously appears to the novel's hero, Lucius, and promises him relief from his miseries.

QUESTIONS FOR ANALYSIS

1. What forms of service does Isis demand of her devotees?
2. What does Isis promise her devotees? By implication, what happens to those not devoted to her?

3. *Syncretism* is the combination or reconciliation of differing cultural values, traditions, and modes of belief or opinion. What evidence is there of this phenomenon in the present document? What does the evidence of syncretism in this source suggest about the Greco-Roman ecumene of the second century C.E.?

4. There was a tendency in the Greco-Roman World of late antiquity for many pious individuals to search for a common, unifying Divine Reality behind all of the different religious beliefs and practices of their day. Can you find evidence of this phenomenon here? Why do you think there was this tendency?

5. Compare the view of the afterlife presented in this work with that of the *Odyssey* (Chapter 2, source 12). What has changed, and what has remained the same? Which seem more significant, the continuities or the changes? What factors do you think might have influenced the changes?

"Behold, Lucius, here I am, moved by your prayers. I am the Mother of all Nature, the Mistress of all the elements, the First-Born of the ages, the Supreme Deity, Queen of the dead, the foremost heavenly being, the unchanging manifestation of all the gods and goddesses. By my will, I govern the lofty stars of heaven, the health-giving breezes of the sea, and the bitter silence of those in the Underworld. My single godhead is worshiped worldwide in various forms, in different rites, and under a variety of names. Thus the Phrygians,[1] the earliest race of people, call me Pessinuntia, Mother of the gods; the aboriginal natives of Attica[2] call me Cecropian Minerva;[3] the people of Cyprus, who travel the sea, call me Paphian Venus;[4] the archer Cretans call me Diana of Mount Dictys;[5] the trilingual[6] inhabitants of Sicily call me Ortygian Proserpina;[7] the Eleusinians know me as the ancient goddess Ceres;[8] some know me as Juno,[9] others as Bellona.[10] . . . Those, however, who are illuminated by the first rays of the rising sun god, the Ethiopians, the Africans, and those who excel in ancient lore, the Egyptians,[11] all these do me honor with my distinctive rites and call me by my true name, Queen Isis.

Here I am, taking pity on your miseries; here I am, benevolent and protective. Put aside your tears. Cease your lamentations. Stop grieving. Through my providence, a day of salvation is now dawning for you. . . . But above all remember and understand deep in the recesses of your heart that the remaining course of your life, right to the limit of your last breath, is pledged to me. It is not wrong that you render to her, through whose favor you shall return to human company,[12] the remainder of your life. You shall live as one of the blessed. You will live in full glory under

---

[1]A people of Asia Minor (modern Turkey).

[2]The peninsula in Greece on which Athens is located.

[3]Cecrops was the legendary founder and first king of Athens, who devoted the city to the goddess of wisdom, Athena (*Minerva* in Latin).

[4]Paphos, a seaside town on Cyprus, was the reputed birthplace and center of the cult of Aphrodite (*Venus* in Latin), goddess of love.

[5]Artemis (*Diana* in Latin) was the Greco-Roman goddess of light, the moon, and hunting.

[6]Greek, Latin, and their native language.

[7]Proserpina (*Persephone* in Greek) was queen of the Underworld; Ortygia was an island off of the Sicilian city of Syracuse.

[8]Eleusis was a town on the Attic peninsula dedicated to Demeter (*Ceres* in Latin), goddess of agriculture and mother of Persephone/Proserpina.

[9]Juno (*Hera* in Greek) was sister, consort, and female counterpart to Jupiter (*Zeus* in Greek), king of the gods. Hence, she was queen of Heaven.

[10]Roman goddess of war.

[11]Apuleius distinguishes among the black-skinned peoples of the south (the Ethiopians), the Mediterranean peoples of North Africa (the Africans), and the Egyptians.

[12]In this allegory, Lucius had been magically metamorphosed into an ass, the symbol of sexual debauchery and an unspiritual life. Now, through Isis's intervention, he is being returned to human form.

my protection, and when you have completed the span of time allotted to you, you will pass down to the Underworld. There also, in that subterranean hemisphere, you shall often worship me, whom you now see as the one who favors you, shining amid dark gloom of Acheron[13] and reigning in the Stygian[14] depths, while you dwell amidst the Elysian Fields.[15] If by diligent obedience, pious service, and steadfast purity[16] you prove worthy of Our godhead, know that I alone have the power to prolong your life even beyond the span prescribed by your destiny.

[13]Several rivers that were believed to be connected in the lower world.
[14]The Styx was the river that encircled the nether regions seven times.

[15]The area of the Underworld reserved for heroes and others beloved by the gods (Chapter 2, source 12, note 25).
[16]Keep in mind that Isis is saving the suppliant Lucius from a life of meaningless carnal pleasures (note 12).

▼▼▼

Han China

In 2 C.E. an imperial census counted 12,233,062 families, or approximately sixty million people, residing in China. A Roman imperial census of 14 C.E. recorded 4,937,000 citizens of the empire. Assuming that full-fledged citizens of Rome constituted less than ten percent of the empire's total population at that time, it is reasonable to conclude that the Roman Empire contained fifty to sixty million people in the early decades of the first century C.E. Therefore, as we survey Eurasia around the turn of the millennium, we see two massive empires of about equal size and population at the ends of this great land mass. For the next two centuries Han China and Rome dominated their respective regions, and although each experienced periods of crisis, each also offered its subjects fairly stable government and a degree of prosperity.

A measure of Rome's and China's greatness can be seen in their powerful mythic influences on those who followed. Well into the modern period, European emperors and kings claimed to be legitimate heirs of Roman authority. As late as the early twentieth century, German and Russian monarchs styled themselves *Kaiser* and *Tsar,* variations on the title *Caesar.* In China today, all ethnic Chinese — ninety-seven percent of the population of the People's Republic — proudly call themselves *Han.*

The Han Dynasty reigned during one of China's golden ages, creating a political and social order based on a synthesis of Legalist and Confucian principles. It expanded China's influence into Korea, Vietnam, and across the reaches of Central Asia, presided over a general economic upswing, and witnessed a period of rich cultural productivity. Han China flourished for nearly four centuries, but in the end, like the Roman Empire, the dynasty and its empire collapsed due to internal instabilities and invasions.

The age of Han was not one period but two. From 202 B.C.E. to 9 C.E. the Former Han ruled China, and its most powerful and important emperor was Han Wudi, the Martial Emperor of Han, who reigned from 141 to 87 B.C.E. His domestic and foreign policies provided his successors for the next two thousand years with *the* model of aggressive imperial greatness. Following an interlude in which Wang

Mang (9–23 C.E.) wrested the imperial throne temporarily from the Han family, the dynasty returned to power as the Later, or Eastern, Han (25–220 C.E.). After the first century, however, domestic and frontier conditions deteriorated. From 88 C.E. onward a series of ineffective rulers plagued the family.

By 220, when the Han Dynasty formally came to an end, local lords and invaders from the steppes ruled China. The stability of the earlier Han was only a memory as China plunged into a social, economic, and political chaos that would last for almost four centuries. This period has often been compared with the so-called Dark Ages that ensued after the disintegration of Roman imperial unity in the West, although the differences between the two are more significant than any superficial parallels.

Establishing an Imperial Confucian Academy
▼▼▼

35 ▼ *Sima Qian,* THE RECORDS OF THE GRAND HISTORIAN

During its short existence the Qin Dynasty had experimented with various procedures for recruiting competent and loyal officials. The early emperors of Former Han and their chief ministers continued the search for rational ways of discovering persons of ability. In 124 B.C.E. Emperor Han Wudi established an important precedent when he decreed that proven knowledge of one of the Confucian classics would be a basis for promotion into the imperial civil service and created a rudimentary imperial academy for educating aspiring scholar-officials in the various fields of Confucian learning. By this act he set in motion a process whereby centuries later Confucianism became the empire's ideological framework.

What began modestly as an academy designed to educate fifty young men became an institution that numbered upward of thirty thousand students in the last days of Later Han. Relatively few of these scholars, however, were called to the emperor's service, and the examinations Han Wudi initiated were irregularly held under his Han successors. Government office was still largely the privilege of the landed aristocracy right to the end of the Later Han Era. Only in the age of the *Tang* Dynasty (618–907) did a regular system of civil service examinations emerge as a consequence of the imperial court's successful attempt to break the power of the traditional landed aristocracy by creating a new class of salaried imperial officials. By the early tenth century education in all the Confucian classics was virtually the only route to civil office. China had not only established the world's first-known civil service examination system, it had also, for the most part, developed a system that conferred civil authority on a class of people who shared a common education and philosophy. This class of Confucian *literarchs* (literary rulers) would, more often than not, control China into the early twentieth century.

In the following selection, Sima Qian, one of Former Han's greatest Confucian scholars (whom we already saw in Chapter 4, source 26), traces the vicissitudes of

Confucianism as a practiced political doctrine from the days of Master Kong down to the time of the contemporary emperor, Han Wudi.

QUESTIONS FOR ANALYSIS

1. What vicissitudes did the school of Confucius experience in the four centuries following his death?
2. How were students selected for admission to the emperor's academy, and what sort of person was to be admitted? What do these standards for admission tell us of the values and purposes of Confucian education in the era of Han Wudi?
3. By approving this proposal, how has Han Wudi joined Confucianism with Legalism?
4. Consider what Confucius says in *The Analects* about government and the superior man (Chapter 4, source 24). How do you think he would respond to this academy, its students, curriculum, and purpose for existence? What would Confucius have thought about the tone of the imperial edict?

After the death of Confucius, his band of seventy disciples broke up and scattered among the feudal lords, the more important ones becoming tutors and high ministers to the rulers, the lesser ones acting as friends and teachers to the lower officials, while some went into retirement and were never seen again. . . . Among the feudal lords, however, only Marquis Wen of Wei had any fondness for literature. Conditions continued to deteriorate until the time of the First Emperor of the Qin; the empire was divided among a number of states, all warring with each other, and no one had any use for the arts of the Confucians. Only in Qi and Lu[1] did scholars appear to carry on the teachings and save them from oblivion. During the reigns of Kings Wei and Xuan of Qi (378–323 B.C.), Mencius[2] and Xun Qing[3] and their respective groups both honored the doctrines of the Master and worked to expand and enrich them, winning prominence among the men of the time by their learning.

Then followed the twilight[4] days of the Qin emperor, who burned the *Odes* and *Documents* and buried the scholars alive,[5] and from this time on the texts of the Six Classics[6] of the Confucians were damaged and incomplete. . . .

---

[1]Two of the Warring States.

[2]Mencius (the Latinized form of *Mengzi,* or Master Meng), lived from around 372 to about 289 B.C.E. and, except for Confucius, was the single most important thinker in the history of Confucian philosophy. His basic doctrines were that humans are innately good and that each person has the potential to become a sage. From these two principles he evolved a political philosophy of benevolent government.

[3]Master Xun Qing (ca. 300–235 B.C.E.) was the last great philosopher in the formative age of Confucian classical thought. Unlike Confucius and Mencius, he set his ideas down systematically in a detailed book. Although he might have been the most original and systematic of the three great Confucian sages, the Chinese valued his teachings far less than those of Confucius and Mencius because he was too much of a free thinker, rejecting the existence of spirits and doubting that humans are innately good.

[4]"Twilight" because, in Han Confucian eyes, this brief and evil reign was more the last stage of Zhou than a full-fledged dynasty itself. It had not followed the classic pattern, established in the first three dynasties, of vigorous growth, maturity, and decay (see Chapter 1, source 5).

[5]Chapter 4, source 26.

[6]*The Classic of History, The Classic of Odes* (Chapter 1, sources 5 and 6), *The Analects* (Chapter 4, source 24), *The Classic of Changes, The Classic of Rites,* and *The Spring and Autumn Annals. The Classic of Changes,* or *Yi Jing,* is a work of divination that enjoys popularity today among Western readers; *The Classic of Rites* is a compilation of proper rituals. See note 18 for a description of *The Spring and Autumn Annals.* Although *The Analects* always remained a revered book of Confucian wisdom, the other five classics assumed greater importance during the age of Later Han and collectively emerged as the *Wu Jing* — the core of the Confucian canon.

Later, when Gaozu[7] had defeated Xiang Yu,[8] he marched north and surrounded the state of Lu with his troops, but the Confucian scholars of Lu went on as always, reciting and discussing their books, practicing rites and music, and never allowing the sound of strings and voices to die out.[9] . . . And when the Han came to power, these scholars were at last allowed to study and teach their Classics freely and to demonstrate the proper rituals. . . .

Shusun Tong[10] drew up the ceremonial for the Han court and was rewarded with the post of master of ritual, while all the other scholars who assisted him were likewise given preferential treatment in the government. The emperor sighed over the neglected state of learning and would have done more to encourage its revival, but at the time there was still considerable turmoil within the empire and the region within the four seas had not yet been set at peace. Likewise, during the reigns of Emperor Zu[11] and Empress Lü[12] there was still no leisure to attend to the matter of government schools. Moreover, the high officials at this time were all military men who had won their distinction in battle.

With the accession of Emperor Wen,[13] Confucian scholars began little by little to be summoned and employed in the government, although Emperor Wen himself rather favored the Legalist teachings on personnel organization and control. Emperor Jing[14] made no effort to employ Confucian scholars, and his mother, Empress Dowager Dou,[15] was an advocate of the teachings of the Yellow Emperor[16] and Laozi. Thus various scholars were appointed to fill the posts of court councilor and to answer questions, but they had no prospects of advancement.

When the present emperor came to the throne there were a number of enlightened Confucian scholars . . . at court. The emperor was much attracted by their ideas and accordingly sent out a summons for scholars of moral worth and literary ability to take service in the government.

After Empress Dowager Dou passed away, the marquis of Wuan, Tianfan,[17] became chancellor. He rejected the doctrines of the Daoists, the Legalists, and the other philosophical schools, and invited several hundred Confucian scholars and literary men to take service in the government. Among them was Gongsun Hong who, because of his knowledge of the *Spring and Autumn Annals,*[18] advanced from the rank of commoner to that of one of the three highest ministers in the government and was installed as marquis of Pingjin. Scholars throughout the empire saw which way the wind was blowing and did all they could to follow his example.

As a scholar official, Gongsun Hong, who held the post of imperial secretary, was disturbed that the teachings of Confucius were being neglected and not put into greater practice and he therefore submitted the following memorial:

---

[7]*Gaozu* means "high ancestor" and was the throne name of Liu Bang, the first Han emperor (r. 202–195 B.C.E.).

[8]The brilliant but erratic noble whom the commoner Liu Bang defeated in a contest for the empire after the fall of Qin.

[9]Confucians emphasize music for several reasons: This art from the revered past creates harmony out of dissonance, soothes the hearer's troubled spirit, and raises the mind to a higher plane.

[10]A Confucian scholar who served both the Qin and early Han rulers.

[11]Known as the *Filial Emperor,* he reigned from 195 to 188 B.C.E. However, his mother, the Empress Dowager Lü, held all real power (see note 12).

[12]The widow of Han Gaozu (note 7); she ruled China as the power behind the throne between 195 and 180 B.C.E.

[13]Wen the Filial (r. 180–157 B.C.E.), the fourth son of Han Gaozu and the first strong emperor since his father's death fifteen years earlier.

[14]Wen's successor, who ruled from 157 to 141 B.C.E.

[15]This powerful woman, who died in 135 B.C.E., sponsored the study of Daoist teachings at the courts of her husband and son.

[16]Huang Di (the Yellow Emperor), one of the legendary predynastic Sage Emperors, supposedly reigned during the mid third millennium B.C.E. He was believed to be, along with Laozi, the founder of Daoism (Chapter 4, source 23).

[17]Maternal uncle of Han Wudi.

[18]A terse chronicle of events covering the period 722 to 481 B.C.E. and written from the perspective of Confucius's home state of Lu. This Confucian classic was also believed to be authored by the Great Master. There is no reason to believe he had a hand in composing it, but apparently he studied and admired the work.

The chancellor and the imperial secretary wish to make this statement. Your Majesty has issued an edict which reads:

"I have heard that the people are to be guided by rites and led to the practice of virtue through music, and that the institution of marriage is the basis of the family. Yet at the present time rites have fallen into disuse and music has declined, a fact which grieves me deeply. Therefore I have invited men of outstanding moral worth and wide learning from all over the empire to come and take service at court. Let the officials in charge of ritual encourage learning, hold discussions, and gather all the information they can to encourage the revival of rites in order to act as leaders of the empire. Let the master of ritual consult with the erudites[19] and their students on how to promote the spread of virtue in the countryside and open the way for men of outstanding talent."

In accordance with this edict we have respectfully discussed the matter with the master of ritual Kong Zang, the erudit Ping, and others, and they have told us that, according to their information, it was the custom under the Three Dynasties of antiquity to set up schools for instruction in the villages. In the Xia dynasty these were called *xiao,* in the Shang dynasty *xu,* and in the Zhou dynasty *xiang.* These schools encouraged goodness by making it known to the court and censured evil by applying punishments. Thus it was the officials of the capital who took the initiative in instructing and educating the people, and virtue spread from the court outwards to the provinces.

Now Your Majesty, manifesting supreme virtue and displaying a profound intelligence worthy to rank with that of heaven and earth, has sought to rectify human relations, encourage learning, revive the former rites, promote instruc-

tion in goodness, and open the way for men of worth so that the people of the four directions[20] may be swayed to virtue. This is indeed the way to lay the foundations for an era of great peace.

In earlier times, however, the instruction provided by the government was incomplete and the rites were not fully carried out. We therefore beg that the previous official system be utilized to increase the spread of instruction. In order to fill the offices of erudit we suggest that fifty additional students be selected and declared exempt from the usual labor services. The master of ritual shall be charged with the selection of these students from among men of the people who are eighteen years of age or older and who are of good character and upright behavior. In order to supply candidates for the selection, the governors, prime ministers, heads, and magistrates of the various provinces, kingdoms, districts, marches,[21] and feudal cities shall recommend to the two thousand picul officials[22] in their respective regions any men who are fond of learning, show respect for their superiors, adhere to the teachings of the government, and honor the customs of their village, and whose actions in no way reflect discredit upon their reputations. The two thousand picul officials shall in turn make a careful examination of the men recommended; those found worthy shall then be sent in company with the local accounting officials when the latter come to the capital to make their reports, and shall there be presented to the master of ritual. They shall then receive instruction in the same manner as the regular students of the erudits.

At the end of a year, all of them shall be examined. Those who have mastered one or more of the Classics shall be assigned to fill vacancies among the scholar officials in the provinces or among the officers . . . who serve under the mas-

---

[19]Erudites (*boshi*) were scholar-advisors to the imperial court by virtue of the fact that each was a specialist in one of the Confucian classics.
[20]That is, throughout all China.
[21]Frontier regions.

[22]A *picul* was 133.33 pounds of grain. Every office was graded according to its annual salary, and most salaries ranged between two thousand and one hundred piculs a year, although the emperor's chief counselor received ten thousand piculs. Salaries were paid partly in grain and partly in silk and cash equivalents.

ter of ritual. If there are any outstanding students who qualify for the post of palace attendant, the master of ritual shall present their names to the throne. In this way men of exceptional talent and ability will be brought at once to the attention of the ruler. If, on the contrary, there are any who have not applied themselves to their studies, whose ability is inferior, or who have failed to master even one Classic, they shall be summarily dismissed. In addition, if there are any among the recommending officials who have failed to carry out their duties properly, we suggest that they be punished. . . .

The emperor signified his approval of this proposal, and from this time on the number of literary men who held positions as ministers and high officials in the government increased remarkably.

The Views of a Female Confucian

▼▼▼

36 ▼ Ban Zhao, LESSONS FOR WOMEN

Education in the Confucian classics increasingly became one of several avenues to a position of social and political power in Han China. Confucian doctrine, however, did not accord women a status equal to that of men, and women generally were regarded as unworthy or incapable of a literary education. The Confucian classics themselves say little about women, which shows how little they mattered in the scheme of Confucian values. Most Confucians accepted women's subservience to men as natural and proper. In their view, failure to maintain a proper relationship between two such obviously unequal persons as husband and wife or brother and sister would result in social disharmony and a breakdown of all the rules of propriety.

Yet this was only part of the traditional Chinese view of women. Both Confucian doctrine and Chinese society at large accorded women, as both mothers and mothers-in-law, a good deal of honor, and with that honor came power within the family structure. In every age, moreover, a handful of extraordinary women managed to acquire literary educations or otherwise achieved positions of far-ranging influence and authority despite social constraints. The foremost female Confucian of the age of Han was Ban Zhao (ca. 45–116 C.E.), younger sister of the court historian Ban Gu (32–92 C.E.). Upon Gu's death, Zhao served as imperial historian under Emperor Han Hedi (r. 88–105) and completed her brother's *Han Annals,* a history of the Former Han Dynasty, which is generally regarded as second only to the historical work of Sima Qian (sources 26, 35, and 40). Ban Zhao also served as an advisor on state matters to Empress Deng, who assumed power as regent for her infant son in 106.

Madame Ban was the daughter of the widely respected writer and administrator Ban Biao (3–54 C.E.) and received her elementary education from her literate mother while still a child in her father's house. Otherwise, her early life appears to have been quite conventional. She married at the age of fourteen, thereby becoming the lowest-ranking member of her husband's family, and bore children. Although her husband died young, Ban Zhao never remarried, devoting herself instead to literary pursuits and acquiring a reputation for scholarship and stylistic grace that eventually brought her to the imperial court.

Among her many literary works, Ban Zhao composed a commentary on the popular *Lives of Admirable Women* by Liu Xiang (77–6 B.C.E.) and later in life produced her most famous work, the *Nü Jie,* or *Lessons for Women,* which purports to be an instructional manual on feminine behavior and virtue for her daughters. In fact, she intended it for a much wider audience. Realizing that Confucian texts contained little in the way of specific and practical guidelines for a woman's everyday life, Ban Zhao sought to fill that void with a coherent set of rules for women, especially young women.

QUESTIONS FOR ANALYSIS

1. What does Ban Zhao tell us about the status of daughters-in-law? How has she escaped from the fears of such servitude?
2. According to Ban Zhao, what rules of propriety should govern a marriage?
3. What does Ban Zhao consider the principal duty of a husband? Of a wife? How and why are they complementary parts of the natural order of the universe?
4. What sort of education does she advocate for women, and what is its purpose?
5. In what way and why does Ban Zhao advocate a departure from tradition?
6. What does her claim to lack of intelligence suggest? Do you think she was sincere in this claim?
7. What was there about Ban Zhao's essay that caused it to be so highly regarded by Confucian scholars over the following centuries?

I, the unworthy writer, am unsophisticated, unenlightened, and by nature unintelligent, but I am fortunate both to have received not a little favor from my scholarly father, and to have had a cultured mother and instructresses upon whom to rely for a literary education as well as for training in good manners. More than forty years have passed since at the age of fourteen I took up the dustpan and the broom in the Cao family.[1] During this time with trembling heart I feared constantly that I might disgrace my parents, and that I might multiply difficulties for both the women and the men of my husband's family. Day and night I was distressed in heart, but I labored without confessing weariness. Now and hereafter, however, I know how to escape from such fears.

Being careless, and by nature stupid, I taught and trained my children without system. Consequently I fear that my son Gu may bring disgrace upon the Imperial Dynasty by whose Holy Grace he has unprecedentedly received the extraordinary privilege of wearing the Gold and the Purple, a privilege for the attainment of which by my son, I a humble subject never even hoped. Nevertheless, now that he is a man and able to plan his own life, I need not again have concern for him. But I do grieve that you, my daughters, just now at the age for marriage, have not at this time had gradual training and advice; that you still have not learned the proper customs for married women. I fear that by failure in good manners in other families you will humiliate both your ancestors and your clan. I

---

[1]The family into which she married.

am now seriously ill, life is uncertain. As I have thought of you all in so untrained a state, I have been uneasy many a time for you. At hours of leisure I have composed . . . these instructions under the title, "Lessons for Women." In order that you may have something wherewith to benefit your persons, I wish every one of you, my daughters, each to write out a copy for yourself.

From this time on every one of you strive to practice these lessons.

HUMILITY

On the third day after the birth of a girl the ancients observed three customs: first to place the baby below the bed; second to give her a potsherd[2] with which to play; and third to announce her birth to her ancestors by an offering. Now to lay the baby below the bed plainly indicated that she is lowly and weak, and should regard it as her primary duty to humble herself before others. To give her potsherds with which to play indubitably signified that she should practice labor and consider it her primary duty to be industrious. To announce her birth before her ancestors clearly meant that she ought to esteem as her primary duty the continuation of the observance of worship in the home.

These three ancient customs epitomize a woman's ordinary way of life and the teachings of the traditional ceremonial rites and regulations. Let a woman modestly yield to others; let her respect others; let her put others first, herself last. Should she do something good, let her not mention it; should she do something bad, let her not deny it. Let her bear disgrace; let her even endure when others speak or do evil to her. Always let her seem to tremble and to fear. When

a woman follows such maxims as these, then she may be said to humble herself before others.

Let a woman retire late to bed, but rise early to duties; let her not dread tasks by day or by night. Let her not refuse to perform domestic duties whether easy or difficult. That which must be done, let her finish completely, tidily, and systematically. When a woman follows such rules as these, then she may be said to be industrious.

Let a woman be correct in manner and upright in character in order to serve her husband. Let her live in purity and quietness of spirit, and attend to her own affairs. Let her love not gossip and silly laughter. Let her cleanse and purify and arrange in order the wine and the food for the offerings to the ancestors. When a woman observes such principles as these, then she may be said to continue ancestral worship.

No woman who observes these three fundamentals of life has ever had a bad reputation or has fallen into disgrace. If a woman fails to observe them, how can her name be honored; how can she but bring disgrace upon herself?

HUSBAND AND WIFE

The Way of husband and wife is intimately connected with *Yin* and *Yang*,[3] and relates the individual to gods and ancestors. Truly it is the great principle of Heaven and Earth, and the great basis of human relationships. Therefore the "Rites"[4] honor union of man and woman; and in the "Book of Poetry"[5] the "First Ode" manifests the principle of marriage. For these reasons the relationships cannot but be an important one.

If a husband be unworthy, then he possesses nothing by which to control his wife. If a wife be unworthy, then she possesses nothing with

---

[2]A piece of broken pottery.
[3]According to Chinese cosmology, these were the two basic elements of the universe: *Yin,* the soft, yielding, feminine element; and *Yang,* the hard, aggressive, male element. Every substance contains both elements in varying proportions. As one element increases within a substance or being, the other decreases, but neither is ever eliminated.

[4]*The Classic of Rites* (see source 35, note 6).
[5]*The Classic of Odes* (Chapter 1, source 6).

which to serve her husband. If a husband does not control his wife, then the rules of conduct manifesting his authority are abandoned and broken. If a wife does not serve her husband, then the proper relationship between men and women and the natural order of things are neglected and destroyed. As a matter of fact the purpose of these two [the controlling of women by men, and the serving of men by women] is the same.

Now examine the gentlemen of the present age. They only know that wives must be controlled, and that the husband's rules of conduct manifesting his authority must be established. They therefore teach their boys to read books and study histories. But they do not in the least understand that husbands and masters must also be served, and that the proper relationship and the rites should be maintained.

Yet only to teach men and not to teach women — is that not ignoring the essential relation between them? According to the "Rites," it is the rule to begin to teach children to read at the age of eight years, and by the age of fifteen years they ought then to be ready for cultural training. Only why should it not be that girls' education as well as boys' be according to this principle?

RESPECT AND CAUTION

As *Yin* and *Yang* are not of the same nature, so man and woman have different characteristics. The distinctive quality of the *Yang* is rigidity; the function of the *Yin* is yielding. Man is honored for strength; a woman is beautiful on account of her gentleness. Hence there arose the common saying: "A man though born like a wolf may, it is feared, become a weak monstrosity; a woman though born like a mouse may, it is feared, become a tiger."

Now for self-culture nothing equals respect for others. To counteract firmness nothing equals compliance. Consequently it can be said that the Way of respect and acquiescence is woman's most important principle of conduct. So respect may be defined as nothing other than holding on to that which is permanent; and acquiescence nothing other than being liberal and generous. Those who are steadfast in devotion know that they should stay in their proper places; those who are liberal and generous esteem others, and honor and serve them.

If husband and wife have the habit of staying together, never leaving one another, and following each other around within the limited space of their own rooms, then they will lust after and take liberties with one another. From such action improper language will arise between the two. This kind of discussion may lead to licentiousness. Out of licentiousness will be born a heart of disrespect to the husband. Such a result comes from not knowing that one should stay in one's proper place.

Furthermore, affairs may be either crooked or straight; words may be either right or wrong. Straightforwardness cannot but lead to quarreling; crookedness cannot but lead to accusation. If there are really accusations and quarrels, then undoubtedly there will be angry affairs. Such a result comes from not esteeming others, and not honoring and serving them.

If wives suppress not contempt for husbands, then it follows that such wives rebuke and scold their husbands. If husbands stop not short of anger, then they are certain to beat their wives. The correct relationship between husband and wife is based upon harmony and intimacy, and conjugal love is grounded in proper union. Should actual blows be dealt, how could matrimonial relationship be preserved? Should sharp words be spoken, how could conjugal love exist? If love and proper relationship both be destroyed, then husband and wife are divided.

WOMANLY QUALIFICATIONS

A woman ought to have four qualifications: (1) womanly virtue; (2) womanly words; (3) womanly bearing; and (4) womanly work. Now what is called womanly virtue need not be brilliant ability, exceptionally different from others.

Womanly words need be neither clever in debate nor keen in conversation. Womanly appearance requires neither a pretty nor a perfect face and form. Womanly work need not be work done more skillfully than that of others.

To guard carefully her chastity; to control circumspectly her behavior; in every motion to exhibit modesty; and to model each act on the best usage, this is womanly virtue.

To choose her words with care; to avoid vulgar language; to speak at appropriate times; and not to weary others with much conversation, may be called the characteristics of womanly words.

To wash and scrub filth away; to keep clothes and ornaments fresh and clean; to wash the head and bathe the body regularly; and to keep the person free from disgraceful filth, may be called the characteristics of womanly bearing.

With whole-hearted devotion to sew and to weave; to love not gossip and silly laughter; in cleanliness and order to prepare the wine and food for serving guests, may be called the characteristics of womanly work.

These four qualifications characterize the greatest virtue of a woman. No woman can afford to be without them. In fact they are very easy to possess if a woman only treasure them in her heart. The ancients had a saying: "Is Love afar off? If I desire love, then love is at hand!" So can it be said of these qualifications. . . .

IMPLICIT OBEDIENCE

Whenever the mother-in-law says, "Do not do that," and if what she says is right, unquestionably the daughter-in-law obeys. Whenever the mother-in-law says, "Do that," even if what she says is wrong, still the daughter-in-law submits unfailingly to the command.

Let a woman not act contrary to the wishes and the opinions of parents-in-law about right and wrong; let her not dispute with them what is straight and what is crooked. Such docility may be called obedience which sacrifices personal opinion. Therefore the ancient book, "A Pattern for Women," says: "If a daughter-in-law who follows the wishes of her parents-in-law is like an echo and a shadow, how could she not be praised?"

▼▼▼

India in the Age of Empires

In its long history, India has been politically fragmented more often than not. Between the third century B.C.E. and the sixth century C.E., however, India witnessed the rise and flowering of two great native empires, each of which participated in the general interchange of goods, ideas, and peoples that characterized this age of Afro-Eurasian interchange.

First there was the mighty *Mauryan Empire* (ca. 315–183 B.C.E.), which controlled all but the most southern portions of the subcontinent. Centuries later the *Gupta Empire* (320–ca. 550 C.E.) arose, centered on the Ganges River in the northeast but exercising authority over most of northern and central India. Although neither equaled the Han and Roman Empires in size, military power, or longevity, both Indian empires provided peace and a general prosperity based in part on energetic administration and benign social intervention. At the height of the Gupta Empire under Chandragupta II (r. ca. 376–415 C.E.), India possibly was the most prosperous and peaceful society in all of Eurasia. China was then immersed in an interdynastic time of troubles; Greco-Roman civilization was undergoing severe stresses at every level; and the powerful *Sassanian Empire* of Persia was embroiled in internal religious turmoil and wars on its frontiers.

Between these two homebred imperial periods, India underwent a series of invasions from the northwest that resulted in portions of northern India falling under the domination of alien rulers and being joined to important Central Asian kingdoms and empires. The first of these invaders were Greeks from Bactria (source 31), who came in the early second century B.C.E. and established a number of competing kingdoms in northern India. The Greco-Bactrians did not remain in India long. They soon gave way to various nomadic invaders from East Asia, whose lives had been disrupted by the emergence of Chinese imperialism in the late third and second centuries B.C.E. and also by intertribal conflicts.

The most significant of the new invaders were the *Yuezhi,* who created the *Kushana Empire* toward the end of the first century B.C.E. The Kushana, whose imperial focus was always Central Asia, lasted into the third century C.E. and during their centuries of empire provided India with connections to Southwest Asia and China. Much of that interaction was the peaceful exchange of goods and ideas, but Chinese annals also tell how General Ban Chao, brother of the historians Ban Gu and Ban Zhao (source 36), destroyed a Yuezhi army in 90 C.E. when the Kushana emperor launched a retaliatory strike against the Chinese after he was refused the hand of a Han princess.

All of these important political developments should not blind us to the fact that the most significant developments taking place in India during the period 300 B.C.E. to 500 C.E. were cultural. The Gupta Era is especially important in this regard and is rightly acknowledged as one of traditional India's golden ages.

The Softening Effects of Dharma
▼▼▼

37 ▼ *Asoka, ROCK AND PILLAR EDICTS*

As Alexander the Great and his Macedonian generals pulled back from northwest India, a local lord, Chandragupta Maurya (r. ca. 315–281 B.C.E.), began the process of carving out what would become the greatest of India's ancient empires. Under the founder and his son, Bindusara, the empire expanded and functioned with brutal efficiency. Around 269 B.C.E. Bindusara's son *Asoka* (r. ca. 269–232) inherited the throne and initially continued his family's tradition of imperial aggression.

In the eighth year of his reign, however, he underwent a spiritual conversion when he beheld the bloodshed and misery that resulted from his conquest of the land of Kalinga, along India's southeastern flank. As a consequence, Asoka embraced the teachings of the Buddha and embarked on a new policy of government. Probably inspired by the public monuments of the kings of Persia, Asoka publicized his change of heart and new imperial policies in a series of engraved rock and pillar inscriptions scattered throughout his lands.

QUESTIONS FOR ANALYSIS

1. What evidence is there in these edicts of India's contacts with the outside world?
2. What evidence is there that Asoka attempted to export Buddhist teachings to his western neighbors?
3. Following his conversion, what did Asoka consider to be the purpose of good government? What structures and policies did he institute in order to achieve his vision?
4. What was Asoka's attitude and policy toward all non-Buddhist religions and ceremonies?
5. How did Asoka define *dharma?* Can you find any Hindu or Jain influences on his understanding of dharma?
6. Asoka saw himself as a follower of the Buddha's Law of Righteousness (dharma). Review source 19 in Chapter 3. Based on your reading of these two lessons by the Buddha, respond to the following questions: Where would the Buddha agree with Asoka's policies and beliefs? Where would he disagree? What would be the Buddha's overall evaluation of Asoka's understanding of Buddhist teachings?
7. Imagine that three Chinese travelers — a Confucian, a Legalist, and a Daoist — read these inscriptions. What would be their reactions?

ROCK EDICT XIII

The Kalinga country was conquered by King Priyadarsi,[1] Beloved of the Gods, in the eighth year of his reign. One hundred and fifty thousand persons were carried away captive, one hundred thousand were slain, and many times that number died.

Immediately after the Kalingas had been conquered, King Priyadarsi became intensely devoted to the study of Dharma,[2] to the love of Dharma, and to the inculcation of Dharma.

The Beloved of the Gods, conqueror of the Kalingas, is moved to remorse now. For he has felt profound sorrow and regret because the conquest of a people previously unconquered involves slaughter, death, and deportation.

But there is a more important reason for the King's remorse. The Brahmanas[3] and Sramanas[4] as well as the followers of other religions and householders — who all practiced obedience to superiors, parents, and teachers, and proper courtesy and firm devotion to friends, acquaintances, companions, relatives, slaves, and servants — all suffer from the injury, slaughter, and deportation inflicted on their loved ones. Even those who escaped calamity themselves are deeply afflicted by the misfortunes suffered by those friends, acquaintances, companions, and relatives for whom they feel an undiminished affection. Thus all men share in the misfortune, and this weighs on King Priyadarsi's mind. . . .

---

[1]Asoka's throne name; it means "one who sees to the good of others."

[2]Sources 17, 18, and 19 of Chapter 3 provide three different definitions of *dharma.*

[3]Hindu ascetics who were members of the Brahmin, or priestly, caste. They were divided into many sects.

[4]Another group of ascetics. In the context of this edict, *Brahmanas and Sramanas* means all Hindu and Buddhist holy people.

Therefore, even if the number of people who were killed or who died or who were carried away in the Kalinga war had been only one one-hundredth or one one-thousandth of what it actually was, this would still have weighed on the King's mind.

King Priyadarsi now thinks that even a person who wrongs him must be forgiven for wrongs that can be forgiven.

King Priyadarsi seeks to induce even the forest peoples who have come under his dominion[5] to adopt this way of life and this ideal. He reminds them, however, that he exercises the power to punish, despite his repentance, in order to induce them to desist from their crimes and escape execution.

For King Priyadarsi desires security, self-control, impartiality, and cheerfulness for all living creatures.

King Priyadarsi considers moral conquest the most important conquest. He has achieved this moral conquest repeatedly both here and among the peoples living beyond the borders of his kingdom, even as far away as six hundred *yojanas*,[6] where the Yona [Greek] king Antiyoka[7] rules, and even beyond Antiyoka in the realms of the four kings named Turamaya, Antikini, Maka, and Alikasudara,[8] and to the south among the Cholas and Pandyas[9] as far as Ceylon.[10]

Here in the King's dominion also, . . . everywhere people heed his instructions in Dharma.

Even in countries which King Priyadarsi's envoys have not reached, people have heard about Dharma and about his Majesty's ordinances and instructions in Dharma, and they themselves conform to Dharma and will continue to do so.

Wherever conquest is achieved by Dharma, it produces satisfaction. Satisfaction is firmly established by conquest by Dharma. Even satisfaction, however, is of little importance. King Priyadarsi attaches value ultimately only to consequences of action in the other world.

This edict on Dharma has been inscribed so that my sons and great-grandsons who may come after me should not think new conquests worth achieving. If they do conquer, let them take pleasure in moderation and mild punishments. Let them consider moral conquest the only true conquest.

This is good, here and hereafter. Let their pleasure be pleasure in morality. For this alone is good, here and hereafter.

PILLAR EDICT VII

King Priyadarsi, the Beloved of the Gods, speaks as follows: . . .

How can the people be induced to follow Dharma strictly? How can progress in morality be increased sufficiently? How can I raise them up by the promotion of Dharma? . . . This occurred to me. I shall issue proclamations on Dharma, and I shall order instruction in Dharma to be given to the people. Hearing these proclamations and instructions, the people will conform to Dharma; they will raise themselves up and will make progress by the promotion of Dharma. To this end I have issued proclamations on Dharma, and I have instituted various kinds of moral and religious instruction.

My highest officials, who have authority over large numbers of people, will expound and spread the precepts of Dharma. I have instructed the provincial governors, too, who are in charge of many hundred thousand people, concerning how to guide people devoted to Dharma. . . .

---

[5]The primitive, largely uncivilized folk of the southern jungle.
[6]About three thousand miles.
[7]Antiochus II Theos (r. 261–246 B.C.E.), a member of the Macedonian family of Seleucus and king of Syria.
[8]Ptolemy II Philadelphus of Egypt (r. 285–247 B.C.E.); Antigonos Gonatas of Macedonia (r. 278–239 B.C.E.); Magos of Cyrene in North Africa (r. 300–258 B.C.E.); and Alexander of Epirus in northwest Greece (r. ca. 272–258 B.C.E.).

[9]People of the southern tip of India.
[10]The major island off the southeast coast of India; today it is the nation of Sri Lanka.

My officers charged with the spread of Dharma are occupied with various kinds of services beneficial to ascetics and householders, and they are empowered to concern themselves with all sects. I have ordered some of them to look after the affairs of the Sangha,[11] some to take care of the brahmin . . . ascetics, some to work among the Nirgranthas,[12] and some among the various other religious sects. Different officials are thus assigned specifically to the affairs of different religions, but my officers for spreading Dharma are occupied with all sects. . . .

These and many other high officials take care of the distribution of gifts from myself as well as from the queens. They report in various ways . . . worthy recipients of charity. . . . I also ordered some of them to supervise the distribution of gifts from my sons and the sons of other queens, in order to promote noble deeds of Dharma and conformity to the precepts of Dharma. These noble deeds and this conformity consist in promoting compassion, liberality, truthfulness, purity, gentleness, and goodness. . . .

Whatever good deeds I have done the people have imitated, and they have followed them as a model. In doing so, they have progressed and will progress in obedience to parents and teachers, in respect for elders, in courtesy to priests and ascetics, to the poor and distressed, and even to slaves and servants. . . .

The people can be induced to advance in Dharma by only two means, by moral prescriptions and by meditation. Of the two, moral prescriptions are of little consequence, but meditation is of great importance. The moral prescriptions I have promulgated include rules making certain animals inviolable, and many others. But even in the case of abstention from injuring and from killing living creatures, it is by meditation that people have progressed in Dharma most.

This edict on Dharma has been inscribed in order that it may endure and be followed as long as my sons and great-grandsons shall reign and as long as the sun and moon shall shine. For one who adheres to it will attain happiness in this world and hereafter. . . .

This edict on morality should be engraved wherever stone pillars or stone slabs are available, in order that it may endure forever.

PILLAR EDICT II

King Priyadarsi says:

Dharma is good. But what does Dharma consist of? It consists of few sins and many good deeds, of kindness, liberality, truthfulness, and purity.

I have bestowed even the gift of spiritual insight on men in various ways. I have decreed many kindnesses, including even the grant of life, to living creatures, two-footed and four-footed as well as birds and aquatic animals. I have also performed many other good deeds.

I have ordered this edict on Dharma to be inscribed in order that people may act according to it and that it may endure for a long time. And he who follows it completely will do good deeds.

ROCK EDICT IX

King Priyadarsi, the Beloved of the Gods, says:

People perform various ceremonies. Among the occasions on which ceremonies are performed are sicknesses, marriages of sons or daughters, children's births, and departures on journeys. Women in particular have recourse to many diverse, trivial, and meaningless ceremonies.

It is right that ceremonies be performed. But this kind bears little fruit. The ceremony of Dharma,[13] on the contrary, is very fruitful. It consists in proper treatment of slaves and ser-

---

[11]Buddhist monastic groups (see Chapter 3, source 20).
[12]Jain ascetics (see Chapter 3, source 18).

[13]*Ceremony* should be understood in a metaphorical sense — the good works of dharma as encapsulated in the Holy Eightfold Path (Chapter 3, source 19).

vants, reverence to teachers, restraint of violence toward living creatures, and liberality to priests and ascetics. These and like actions are called the ceremonies of Dharma.

Therefore, a father, son, brother, master, friend, acquaintance, or even neighbor ought to say about such actions, "These are good; they should be performed until their purpose is achieved. I shall observe them."

Other ceremonies are of doubtful value. They may achieve their purpose, or they may not. Moreover the purposes for which they are performed are limited to this world.

The ceremony of Dharma, on the other hand, is not limited to time. Even if it does not achieve its object in this world, it produces unlimited merit in the next world. But if it produces its object in this world, it achieves both effects: the purpose desired in this world and unlimited merit in the next.

It has also been said that liberality is commendable. But there is no greater liberality than the gift of Dharma or the benefit of Dharma. Therefore, a friend, well-wisher, relative, or companion should urge one when the occasion arises, saying, "You should do this; this is commendable. By doing this you may attain heaven." And what is more worth doing than attaining heaven?

ROCK EDICT VII

King Priyadarsi wishes members of all faiths to live everywhere in his kingdom.

For they will seek mastery of the senses and purity of mind. Men are different in their inclinations and passions, however, and they may perform the whole of their duties or only part.

Even if one is not able to make lavish gifts, mastery of the senses, purity of mind, gratitude, and steadfast devotion are commendable and essential.

PILLAR EDICT IV

Impartiality is desirable in legal procedures and in punishments. I have therefore decreed that henceforth prisoners who have been convicted and sentenced to death shall be granted a respite of three days. During this period their relatives may appeal to the officials for the prisoners' lives; or, if no one makes an appeal, the prisoners may prepare for the other world by distributing gifts or by fasting.

For I desire that, when the period of respite has expired, they may attain happiness in the next world, and that various ways of practicing Dharma by self-control and the distribution of gifts may be increased among the people.

Sacred Law in Classical India
▼▼▼
38 ▾ *THE LAWS OF MANU*

Despite Asoka's promotion of the Buddhist principle of dharma, or the Law of Righteousness, the majority of classical India's population seems to have remained true to traditional Hindu ways and beliefs, which included acceptance of the caste system and the concept that dharma defined one's caste duties. Hindus, like Buddhists, believed that dharma was the moral law of the universe and the highest good upon which all reality was founded. Yet, for Hindus dharma was not an abstract, impersonal code of righteousness; it was Sacred Law and, as such, governed all of a person's social and religious activities. For most Hindus dharma became concrete in the innumerable rituals that Asoka found so useless and in Indian civilization's numerous forms of mandated social behavior. Faith, worship, and social duty all sprang from dharma.

The earliest extant codification of the Sacred Law of dharma is *The Laws of Manu,* which was compiled between the first century B.C.E. and the second or third century C.E. In Hindu mythology Manu was the primeval human being, the father of humanity, and its first king. In the Vedas he appears as the founder of all human social order and the original teacher of dharma, having been instructed in the Sacred Law by Brahman. Tradition also regarded him as an Indian Utnapishtim or Noah, the sole survivor of a catastrophic flood, after which he created a woman, through whom he generated the human species. The anonymous compilers of *The Laws of Manu* claimed that the rules and regulations contained in this code were universal and timeless. Each law was believed to be a manifestation of dharma, passed down uncorrupted from Brahman through Manu. In reality, this collection mirrors twenty-five hundred years of Indian social history and consequently contains what seem to an outside viewer to be numerous contradictions. These apparent discrepancies, however, are readily integrated in a cultural complex predicated on the idea that truth has infinite manifestations.

The selections here illustrate the two major determinants of classical Indian society: caste and gender. As far as we can ascertain, gender and class distinctions of one sort or another were common to all ancient civilizations, but the caste system was unique to India. The English word *caste* is derived from the Portuguese *casta.* Hindus use two different Sanskrit words for caste: *varna* (color) and *jati* (birth). Varna refers only to the four major social-religious divisions that "The Hymn to Purusha" (Chapter 2, source 11) enumerates: Brahmins (priests), Kshatriyas (warriors), Vaisyas (farmers, artisans, and merchants), and Sudras (workers). These classifications of Indian society apparently resulted from the Aryans' attempt to separate themselves from the darker-skinned natives they had conquered. The jati system, which today includes more than three thousand identifiable groupings, was not fully developed until around the Gupta period, long after the Aryans had disappeared into India's general population. Jatis are hereditary occupations, each with its own dharma. Hindus generally classify jatis as subdivisions of the varna system and steps in the ladder of reincarnation.

QUESTIONS FOR ANALYSIS

1. The lowest-ranking jatis are composed of people known as *untouchables.* Why are they called that, and what manner of life do they lead? What is there about their occupations that other Hindus find so offensive?
2. Under what circumstances might a person engage in work appropriate to a lower varna? How far may one go in this regard, and what are the consequences? May one legitimately assume the duties of a higher varna? Is intermarriage among the castes considered acceptable?
3. Each varna and jati has its own dharma. Is there, additionally, a universal dharma common to all Hindus?
4. How might the caste system make political and social unification difficult, if not impossible?
5. Why are women denied access to ceremonies where the vedic texts are recited? Notwithstanding this prohibition, do women perform any

necessary religious functions? If so, what are they, and what do the functions suggest about the status of women?

6. What constraints are placed on women, and why? What freedoms, if any, does a woman enjoy? How and why, if at all, are women protected and honored? What are the duties of their fathers and husbands?

7. Compare the status of Hindu women with that of women in Han China (source 36). How do their respective situations reflect the different cultures in which they live? Notwithstanding cultural differences, are their positions comparable, or does one group seem to enjoy greater freedom and power? Is one better protected than the other?

VARNA

The Brahmin, the Kshatriya, and the Vaisya castes are the twice-born ones,[1] but the fourth, the Sudra, has one birth only; there is no fifth caste. . . .

To Brahmins he[2] assigned teaching and studying the Vedas, sacrificing for their own benefit and for others, giving and accepting of alms.

The Kshatriya he commanded to protect the people, to bestow gifts, to offer sacrifices, to study the Vedas, and to abstain from attaching himself to sensual pleasures;

The Vaisya to tend cattle, to bestow gifts, to offer sacrifices, to study the Vedas, to trade, to lend money, and to cultivate land.

One occupation only the lord prescribed to the Sudra, to serve meekly . . . these other three castes.

JATIS

From a male Sudra are born an Ayogava, a Kshattri, and a Kandala, the lowest of men, by Vaisya, Kshatriya, and Brahmin females respectively, sons who owe their origin to a confusion of the castes.[3] . . .

Killing fish to Nishadas; carpenters' work to the Ayogava; to Medas, Andhras, Kunkus, and Madgus, the slaughter of wild animals. . . .

But the dwellings of Kandalas . . . shall be outside the village. . . .

Their dress shall be the garments of the dead, they shall eat their food from broken dishes, black iron shall be their ornaments, and they must always wander from place to place.

A man who fulfills a religious duty, shall not seek intercourse with them; their [Kandala] transactions shall be among themselves, and their marriages with their equals. . . .

At night they shall not walk about in villages and in towns.

By day they may go about for the purpose of their work, distinguished by marks at the king's command, and they shall carry out the corpses of persons who have no relatives; that is a settled rule.

By the king's order they shall always execute the criminals, in accordance with the law, and they shall take for themselves the clothes, the beds, and the ornaments of such criminals.

DHARMA

A king who knows the sacred law must inquire into the laws of castes [jatis], of districts, of guilds, and of families, and settle the peculiar law of each. . . .

---

[1]One's second birth was initiation into the recitation of the Vedas. Only men could be *twice born*.
[2]Brahman.
[3]This is a mythic explanation for the existence of certain low-born, or "unclean," jatis; they originated in mythic time as the result of illicit unions between people of different castes. The greatest profanation of all was when a male Sudra defiled (had sexual intercourse with) a female Brahmin, and the consequence was the origin of the Kandala jati — the basest of all jatis.

Among the several occupations the most commendable are, teaching the Veda for a Brahmin, protecting the people for a Kshatriya, and trade for a Vaisya.

But a Brahmin, unable to subsist by his peculiar occupations just mentioned, may live according to the law applicable to Kshatriyas; for the latter is next to him in rank. . . .

A man of low caste [varna] who through covetousness lives by the occupations of a higher one, the king shall deprive of his property and banish.

It is better to discharge one's own duty incompletely than to perform completely that of another; for he who lives according to the law of another caste is instantly excluded from his own.

A Vaisya who is unable to subsist by his own duties, may even maintain himself by a Sudra's mode of life, avoiding however acts forbidden to him, and he should give it up, when he is able to do so. . . .

Abstention from injuring creatures, veracity, abstention from unlawfully appropriating the goods of others, purity, and control of the organs,[4] Manu has declared to be the summary of the law for the four castes.

THE NATURE OF WOMEN

It is the nature of women to seduce men in this world; for that reason the wise are never unguarded in the company of females. . . .

For women no rite is performed with sacred texts, thus the law is settled; women who are destitute of strength and destitute of the knowledge of Vedic texts are as impure as falsehood itself; that is a fixed rule.

HONORING WOMEN

Where women are honored, there the gods are pleased; but where they are not honored, no sacred rite yields rewards.

Where the female relations live in grief, the family soon wholly perishes; but that family where they are not unhappy ever prospers.

FEMALE PROPERTY RIGHTS

A wife, a son, and a slave, these three are declared to have no property; the wealth which they earn is acquired for him to whom they belong. . . .

What was given before the nuptial fire, what was given on the bridal procession, what was given in token of love, and what was received from her brother, mother, or father, that is called the six-fold property of a woman.

Such property, as well as a gift subsequent and what was given to her by her affectionate husband, shall go to her offspring, even if she dies in the lifetime of her husband. . . .

But when the mother has died, all the uterine[5] brothers and the uterine sisters shall equally divide the mother's estate.

A WOMAN'S DEPENDENCE

In childhood a female must be subject to her father, in youth to her husband, when her lord is dead to her sons; a woman must never be independent.

She must not seek to separate herself from her father, husband, or sons; by leaving them she would make both her own and her husband's families contemptible. . . .

Him to whom her father may give her, or her brother with the father's permission, she shall obey as long as he lives, and when he is dead, she must not insult his memory.

BETROTHAL

No father who knows the law must take even the smallest gratuity for his daughter; for a man

---

[4]Control of all the senses and especially one's sexual drives.

[5]All natural siblings (born from her uterus).

who, through avarice, takes a gratuity, is a seller of his offspring. . . .

Three years let a damsel wait,[6] though she be marriageable,[7] but after that time let her choose for herself a bridegroom of equal caste and rank.

If, being not given in marriage, she herself seeks a husband, she incurs no guilt, nor does he whom she weds.

MARRIAGE AND ITS DUTIES

To be mothers were women created, and to be fathers men; religious rites, therefore, are ordained in the Veda to be performed by the husband together with the wife. . . .

No sacrifice, no vow, no fast must be performed by women apart from their husbands; if a wife obeys her husband, she will for that reason alone be exalted in heaven.[8] . . .

By violating her duty towards her husband, a wife is disgraced in this world, after death she enters the womb of a jackal, and is tormented by diseases as punishment for her sin. . . .

Let the husband employ his wife in the collection and expenditure of his wealth, in keeping everything clean, in the fulfilment of religious duties, in the preparation of his food, and in looking after the household utensils. . . .

Drinking spirituous liquor, associating with wicked people, separation from the husband, rambling abroad, sleeping at unseasonable hours, and dwelling in other men's houses, are the six causes of the ruin of women. . . .

Offspring, religious rites, faithful service, highest conjugal happiness and heavenly bliss for the ancestors and oneself, depend on one's wife alone. . . .

"Let mutual fidelity continue until death," . . . may be considered as the summary of the highest law for husband and wife.

Let man and woman, united in marriage, constantly exert themselves, that they may not be disunited and may not violate their mutual fidelity.

DIVORCE

For one year let a husband bear with a wife who hates him; but after a year let him deprive her of her property and cease to cohabit with her. . . .

But she who shows aversion towards a mad or outcaste[9] husband, a eunuch,[10] one destitute of manly strength, or one afflicted with such diseases as punish crimes,[11] shall neither be cast off nor be deprived of her property. . . .

A barren[12] wife may be superseded[13] in the eighth year, she whose children all die in the tenth, she who bears only daughters in the eleventh, but she who is quarrelsome without delay.

But a sick wife who is kind to her husband and virtuous in her conduct, may be superseded only with her own consent and must never be disgraced.

---

[6]To be offered in marriage by her father or brother.
[7]Twelve was a common age of marriage for women; men tended to wait until their twenties.
[8]While waiting for the next incarnation on the karmic journey to release from the bonds of matter, a soul can be assigned to one of an infinite number of heavens or hells. Thus, depending on how well or poorly a person followed dharma, there is a double reward or punishment: a heaven or a hell followed by incarnation into a higher or lower caste or even a lower life form.

[9]One who has so egregiously violated the dharma of his or her caste (varna) that the person has been made an *outcaste* — for example, a Brahmin who knowingly receives food or a gift from a Kandala or other unclean person.
[10]Sexually impotent.
[11]A disease incurred by reason of a sin in a previous incarnation (the law of karma). Hindu society evolved complex and lengthy lists of diseases and their corresponding sins.
[12]Childless.
[13]Replaced as primary wife by a second wife.

Gupta India as Viewed by a Chinese Monk
▼▼▼

39 ▼ *Faxian, TRAVELS IN INDIA AND CEYLON*

During the age of the Later, or Eastern, Han Dynasty (25–220 C.E.), Buddhist missionaries traveled to China along the overland routes of Central Asia and the oceanic trade routes of Southeast Asia. As China underwent increasing stresses during the last stages of the Han Empire, a form of salvationist Buddhism known as the *Mahayana doctrine* became quite popular (Chapter 6, sources 46 and 47). In the post-Han period of disunity it provided many Chinese with a comforting refuge from the evils of the world.

As Buddhism expanded in China, devotees of the new religion, particularly monks, avidly sought to add to the available body of Buddhist literature, which meant tracing down various Buddhist holy books, or *sutras,* in India and translating them into Chinese. The search for a complete and authentic library of Buddhist scripture, together with the desire to make pilgrimages to sites made sacred by the Buddha and his early disciples, resulted in a steady but small stream of Chinese travelers to India during the age of the Gupta Empire and thereafter.

The earliest known Chinese pilgrim to travel to India and return with sacred books was the monk Faxian. In 399 he set out from North China, traveling by a difficult overland route to India, where he visited sacred shrines, learned Sanskrit, and immersed himself in the legends and lore of Buddhism. From India he sailed to the island of Ceylon (modern Sri Lanka), which, according to one tradition, had received Buddhism through the efforts of Asoka and his missionary son, Mahendra. From there Faxian traveled to Java and in 414 reached home, where he spent the rest of his days translating the texts he had obtained in India.

In addition to these translations, Faxian left behind a record of his travels, in which he described Indian society in the reign of Chandragupta II. Although this pious Chinese monk was much more concerned with pilgrimage sites and holy books than with providing detailed descriptions of Indian culture, his travelogue is important, because it provides an outsider's view of India at the height of Gupta prosperity. One thing that Faxian failed to note (but which the reader should be aware of), is that Hinduism in all its forms enjoyed a resurgence of vitality during the Gupta Era to the point that it was absorbing and displacing Indian Buddhism (see Chapter 6, sources 44 and 45).

QUESTIONS FOR ANALYSIS

1. According to Faxian, how strong was Buddhism in northern India in his day?
2. How well or poorly did the Hindu and Buddhist communities interact? What conclusion follows from your answer?
3. Consider the Buddha's original teaching, which refused to deal with such questions as the existence of spirits, the soul, an afterlife, and gods (Chapter

3, source 19) and rejected all ritual. How had it by Faxian's day merged with folk beliefs and customs?

4. To what extent does Faxian's account of the life led by members of the Kandala jati agree with the evidence from *The Laws of Manu* (source 38)?

5. How did Buddhist principles influence the various social practices and values of Gupta India?

6. How prosperous and well governed do the land and its people appear to have been? Do they appear to have been intensively governed and restricted?

7. Play a bit of historical fantasy and compose Asoka's commentary on Gupta India.

From this place they[1] traveled southeast, passing by a succession of very many monasteries, with a multitude of monks, who might be counted by myriads. After passing all these places, they came to a . . . river on the banks of which, left and right, there were twenty monasteries, which might contain three thousand monks; and here the Law of Buddha was still more flourishing. Everywhere, from the Sandy Desert, in all the countries of India, the kings had been firm believers in that Law. When they make their offerings to a community of monks, they take off their royal caps, and along with their relatives and ministers, supply them with food with their own hands. That done, the king has a carpet spread for himself on the ground, and sits down on it in front of the leader of the monastery; — they dare not presume to sit on couches in front of the community. The laws and ways, according to which the kings presented their offerings when Buddha was in the world, have been handed down to the present day.

All south from this is named the Middle Kingdom. In it the cold and heat are finely tempered, and there is neither hoarfrost nor snow. The people are numerous and happy; they have not to register their households, or attend to any magistrates and their rules; only those who cul-

tivate the royal land have to pay a portion of the gain from it. If they want to go, they go; if they want to stay on, they stay. The king governs without decapitation or other corporal punishments. Criminals are simply fined, lightly or heavily, according to the circumstances of each case. Even in cases of repeated attempts at wicked rebellion, they only have their right hands cut off. The king's bodyguards and attendants all have salaries. Throughout the whole country the people do not kill any living creature, nor drink intoxicating liquor, nor eat onions or garlic. The only exception is that of the Kandalas.[2] That is the name for those who are held to be wicked men, and live apart from others. When they enter the gate of a city or a market-place, they strike a piece of wood to make themselves known, so that men know and avoid them, and do not come into contact with them. In that country they do not keep pigs and fowls, and do not sell live cattle; in the markets there are no butchers' shops and no dealers in intoxicating drink. . . . Only the Kandalas are fishermen and hunters, and sell flesh meat.

After Buddha attained to pari-nirvana[3] the kings of the various countries and the heads of the Vaisyas[4] built viharas[5] for the monks,[6] and endowed them with fields, houses, gardens, and

---

[1]Faxian and his fellow pilgrims.
[2]The lowest group of untouchables. See *The Laws of Manu* (source 38) for a fuller description of the Kandalas.
[3]The Buddha's release from the bonds of matter — his final death.

[4]The caste of merchants and prosperous farmers (see *The Laws of Manu*, source 38).
[5]A hermitage for a recluse or a little house built for a holy person.
[6]Chapter 3, source 20.

orchards, along with the resident populations and their cattle, the grants being engraved on plates of metal, so that afterwards they were handed down from king to king, without any one daring to annul them, and they remain even to the present time.

The regular business of the monks is to perform acts of meritorious virtue, and to recite their Sutras[7] and sit wrapt in meditation. When stranger monks arrive at any monastery, the old residents meet and receive them, carry for them their clothes and alms-bowl, give them water to wash their feet, oil with which to anoint them, and the liquid food permitted out of the regular hours.[8] When the stranger has enjoyed a very brief rest, they further ask the number of years that he has been a monk, after which he receives a sleeping apartment with its appurtenances, according to his regular order, and everything is done for him which the rules prescribe.

Where a community of monks resides, they erect stupas[9] to Sariputtra, to Mahamaudgalyayana, and to Ananda,[10] and also stupas in honor of the Abhidharma, the Vinaya, and the Sutras.[11] A month after the annual season of rest, the families which are looking out for blessing stimulate one another to make offerings to the monks, and send round to them the liquid food which may be taken out of the ordinary hours. All the monks come together in a great assembly, and preach the Law; after which offerings are presented at the stupa of Sariputtra, with all kinds of flowers and incense. All through the night lamps are kept burning, and skillful musicians are employed to perform. . . .

Having crossed the river, and descended south . . . the travelers came to the town of Pataliputtra,[12] in the kingdom of Magadha, the city where king Asoka ruled. . . .

By the side of the stupa of Asoka, there has been made a mahayana monastery, very grand and beautiful; there is also a hinayana[13] one; the two together containing six hundred or seven hundred monks. The rules of demeanor and the scholastic arrangements in them are worthy of observation.

Shamans[14] of the highest virtue from all quarters, and students, inquirers wishing to find out truth and the grounds of it, all resort to these monasteries. There also resides in this monastery a Brahmin teacher, whose name also is Manjusri, whom the shamans of greatest virtue in the kingdom, and the mahayana bhikshus[15] honor and look up to.

The cities and towns of this country are the greatest of all in the Middle Kingdom. The inhabitants are rich and prosperous, and vie with one another in the practice of benevolence and righteousness. Every year on the eighth day of the second month they celebrate a procession of images. They make a four-wheeled car, and on it erect a structure of five stories by means of bamboos tied together. This is supported by a king-post, with poles and lances slanting from it, and is rather more than twenty cubits high, having the shape of a stupa. White and silk-like cloth of hair is wrapped all round it, which is then painted in various colors. They make figures of devas[16] with gold, silver, and lapis lazuli grandly blended and having silken streamers and

---

[7]Sacred texts.

[8]Solid food was prohibited between sunrise and noon.

[9]A *stupa* was a large, domed structure built to house some relic of the Buddha or one of his early disciples. Asoka had commissioned the construction of a large number of these holy sites throughout his empire, and they continued to be built and refined architecturally long after the collapse of the Mauryan Empire.

[10]Three of the Buddha's principal disciples. Ananda appears in source 20 of Chapter 3.

[11]The *Tipitaka*, or "Three Baskets" — the three major collections of Buddhist sacred literature. (See the introduction to source 19 of Chapter 3.)

[12]Modern Patna.

[13]The *Hinayana* (Small Vehicle), or, more correctly, *Theravada*, school was the second of Buddhism's two major sects at this time. Both it and the *Mahayana* (Great Vehicle) school are treated in Chapter 6.

[14]He probably means Hindu *yogis* (practioners of the art of disciplining body and mind through the practice of *yoga*) and other holy persons. (Chapter 1, source 10, deals with shamanism.)

[15]Buddhist monks.

[16]Gods and goddesses.

canopies hung out over them. On the four sides are niches, with a Buddha seated in each, and a Bodhisattva[17] standing in attendance on him. There may be twenty cars, all grand and imposing, but each one different from the others. On the day mentioned, the monks and laity within the borders all come together; they have singers and skillful musicians; they pay their devotions with flowers and incense. The Brahmins come and invite the Buddhas to enter the city. These do so in order, and remain two nights in it. All through the night they keep lamps burning, have skillful music, and present offerings. This is the practice in all the other kingdoms as well. The heads of the Vaisya families in them establish in the cities houses for dispensing charity and medicines. All the poor and destitute in the country, orphans, widowers, and childless men, maimed people and cripples, and all who are diseased, go to those houses, and are provided with every kind of help, and doctors examine their diseases. They get the food and medicines which their cases require, and are made to feel at ease; and when they are better, they go away of themselves.

---

[17] A saint who voluntarily postpones Nirvana, or escape from this world, in order to work for the salvation of others. (See Chapter 6, sources 46 and 47.)

▼▼▼

Travel along the Silk Road

By the turn of the millennium two general routes connected the Greco-Roman Mediterranean with India and China. A sea route went down the Red Sea and across the Arabian Gulf to India, where Western merchants exchanged gold for pepper and other spices, jewels, and muslin cloth, as well as for Chinese manufactured commodities, such as lacquered boxes, iron ware, and silk. As we saw in source 32, the geographer Strabo claimed that in his day one hundred twenty vessels made the annual voyage from Egypt to India. There is even record of a group of supposedly Roman merchants (probably Syrians or Egyptians) who sailed from India to south China in the mid second century c.e., but such adventures were rare. For most merchant mariners from the Roman World, India was the main terminus and marketplace where East met West. The other more heavily traveled route connecting China to the Roman Empire was the romantically named *Silk Road,* a series of linked camel caravan routes that ran for five thousand miles from China to the eastern shores of the Mediterranean. As the name implies, Chinese silk was the major commodity that stimulated trade along these roads. Most Western merchants did their trading on the Silk Road in Parthia, which was centered in Mesopotamia and Iran. The Parthian Empire carefully protected its strategic position and role by policing the roads that ran through its territories and also by discouraging all direct commercial traffic through its regions. Western overland merchants who wanted silk and other Chinese items had to deal with Parthian intermediaries and generally traveled no farther east. Merchants from Central and East Asia likewise went no farther west.

Although Mediterranean merchants traded some Western manufactured goods, such as colored glass vessels and bronze statues, for silk and other Eastern luxury items, their main form of payment was gold and silver, which meant that the

Roman World suffered from a trade imbalance with the East
tury C.E. this trade imbalance contributed to the empire's ov
nomic miseries.

Rome's Asiatic trade introduced other even more dama'
From the mid second through the sixth centuries a series
appear to have traveled along the Silk Road from the ea
terranean. Each new disease, appearing as it did amon
tion, resulted in massive die offs. The impact of the suaa.
millions of Mediterraneans during these four and a half centuries
contributed to the eventual transformation of the Greco-Roman World.

Regardless of these tragic consequences, trade along the Silk Road continued,
at times somewhat tenuously, after the empires of Rome and Han China had
passed away. During the fifth and sixth centuries C.E. trade slowed to a trickle,
but it revived dramatically during the age of China's Tang Dynasty (618–907).
The riches that were available to the merchants willing to brave the hazards of
this caravan network that linked eastern and western Eurasia were just too attractive to ignore.

Our first source chronicles the efforts of a Chinese diplomat whose travels
westward in the late second century B.C.E. helped open up the Silk Road. Our
second source, a collection of four artifacts, suggests that more than just gold and
goods traveled in the caravans of the Silk Road.

Zhang Qian's Western Expedition
▼▼▼

40 ▼ Sima Qian,
THE RECORDS OF THE GRAND HISTORIAN

One of the most impressive achievements of Emperor Han Wudi (source 35) was
his extension of imperial power far beyond China's traditional borders. Under
his leadership, China entered into an age of confident military expansion, pushing vigorously against its neighbors to the north, west, and south. The emperor's
aggressive foreign policy brought China into conflict with the *Xiongnu,* a nomadic Turkish people of the steppes, whose mounted archers were formidable
foes. Searching for allies against the Xiongnu, the emperor dispatched one of his
courtiers, Zhang Qian, in 138 B.C.E. to the court of the *Yuezhi,* another Turkish
steppe people. After a series of harrowing adventures, the indomitable Zhang
Qian caught up with the Yuezhi in *Daxia,* which the West knew as *Bactria* (source
31), but was unable to convince them to ally with China against their common
foe, the Xiongnu. Although his mission ended in apparent failure, Zhang Qian
returned to the Chinese imperial court in 126 with exciting information about
West and South Asia, areas with which China had not had much direct contact
previously. Zhang Qian's travels ushered in a fruitful period of interchange between China and West Asia, and he is rightly remembered as one of the pioneers
who blazed the trail of what became the Silk Road.

n this selection the court historian Sima Qian (whom we saw in Chapter 4, ource 26) writes about events that took place during his own youth and young manhood. Remember, the Chinese place family names first, so these two Qians shared given names but were not related.

QUESTIONS FOR ANALYSIS

1. What evidence is there that at least some of the western barbarians desired closer contacts with China?
2. What evidence is there in this account for the existence of at least indirect trade between China and West Asia before Zhang Qian's travels? Which Chinese goods made their way west, and how did they get there?
3. How safe was it to travel from China to West Asia in the late second century B.C.E.?
4. What about Zhang Qian's report particularly caught the interest of Han Wudi?
5. How did Zhang Qian propose to establish contact between China and Daxia? What was the result of the emperor's following his proposal?
6. After studying this account, what do you conclude China first had to do before it was possible for there to be a Silk Road between East and West Asia?

Zhang Qian was the first person to bring back a clear account of Dayuan.[1] . . . At this time [139 B.C.E.] the emperor questioned various Xiongnu[2] who had surrendered to the Han, and they all reported that the Xiongnu had defeated the king of the Yuezhi people and had made his skull into a drinking vessel. As a result the Yuezhi had fled and bore a constant grudge against the Xiongnu, though as yet they had been unable to find anyone to join them in an attack on their enemy.

The Han at this time were engaged in a concerted effort to destroy the Xiongnu, and therefore, when the emperor heard this, he decided to try to send an envoy to establish relations with the Yuezhi. To reach them, however, an envoy would inevitably have to pass through Xiongnu territory. The emperor accordingly sent out a summons for men capable of undertaking such a mission. Zhang Qian, who was a palace attendant at the time, answered the summons and was appointed as envoy.

He set out, . . . accompanied by Kanfu, a Xiongnu slave. . . . They traveled west through the territory of the Xiongnu and were captured by the Xiongnu and taken before the Shanyu.[3] The Shanyu detained them and refused to let them proceed. "The Yuezhi people live north of me," he said. "What does the Han mean by trying to send an envoy to them! Do you suppose . . . the Han would let my men pass though China?"

The Xiongnu detained Zhang Qian for over ten years and gave him a wife from their own people, by whom he had a son. Zhang Qian never once relinquished the imperial credentials that marked him as an envoy of the Han, and after he

---

[1] A Central Asian steppe kingdom to China's northwest located in a region that today encompasses portions of Kyrgystan and Uzbekistan.

[2] The Xiongnu were possibly the ancestors of the Huns who devastated the Roman Empire in the fifth century C.E.
[3] The Xiongnu king.

had lived in Xiongnu territory for some time and was less closely watched than at first, he and his party finally managed to escape and resume their journey toward the Yuezhi.

After hastening west for twenty or thirty days, they reached the kingdom of Dayuan.[4] The king of Dayuan had heard of the wealth of the Han empire and wished to establish communication with it, though as yet he had been unable to do so. When he met Zhang Qian he was overjoyed and asked where Zhang Qian wished to go.

"I was dispatched as envoy of the Han to the Yuezhi, but the Xiongnu blocked my way and I have only just now managed to escape," he replied. "I beg Your Highness to give me some guides to show me the way. If I can reach my destination and return to the Han to make my report, the Han will reward you with countless gifts!"

The king of Dayuan trusted his words and sent him on his way, giving him guides and interpreters to take him to the state of Kangju.[5] From there he was able to make his way to the land of the Great Yuezhi.

Since the king of the Great Yuezhi had been killed by the Xiongnu, his son had succeeded him as ruler and had forced the kingdom of Daxia [Bactria] to recognize his sovereignty.[6] The region he ruled was rich and fertile and seldom troubled by invaders, and the king thought only of his own enjoyment. He considered the Han too far away to bother with and had no particular intention of avenging his father's death by attacking the Xiongnu. . . .

After spending a year or so in the area, Zhang Qian began to journey back, . . . but he was once

more captured by the Xiongnu and detained over a year. Just at this time the Shanyu died and the . . . King of the Left[7] attacked the Shanyu's heir and set himself up as the new Shanyu [126 B.C.E.]. As a result of this the whole Xiongnu nation was in turmoil and Zhang Qian, along with his Xiongnu wife and the former slave Kanfu, was able to escape and return to China.

The emperor honored Zhang Qian with the post of palace counselor and awarded Kanfu the title of "Lord Who Carries Out His Mission." . . . When Zhang Qian first set out on his mission, he was accompanied by over one hundred men, but after thirteen years abroad, only he and Kanfu managed to make their way back to China. Zhang Qian in person visited the lands of Dayuan, the Great Yuezhi, Daxia, and Kangju, and in addition he gathered reports on five or six other large states in the neighborhood. All of this information he related to the emperor on his return.

▷ Zhang Qian's report contained the following types of information. In the selection that appears below he describes Parthian Persia (Anxi), Mesopotamia (Tiaozhi), and India (Shendu), none of which he had personally visited:

Anxi [Parthian Persia] is situated several thousand *li*[8] west of the region of the Great Yuezhi. The people are settled on the land, cultivating the fields and growing rice and wheat. They also make wine out of grapes.[9] They have walled cities, . . . the region containing several hundred cities of various sizes. The kingdom . . . is very large, measuring several thousand square li. Some

---

[4]See note 1.
[5]A steppe kingdom located southeast of the Aral Sea and directly north of Bactria (note 6). Today the region forms part of Kazakhstan.
[6]Around 139 B.C.E. the Yuezhi conquered Bactria (Daxia). As we saw in source 31, Bactria was a west Central Asian remnant of the Hellenistic ecumene forged by Alexander the Great and his generals and, until its conquest by the Yuezhi, was governed by Greek-speaking rulers. The Yuezhi later used Bactria as the launching area from which it carved out the Kushana Empire during the late first century B.C.E.
[7]A formerly subordinate Xiongnu prince.

[8]A *li* is a bit more than one-third of a mile.
[9]Grape wine was up to this point apparently unknown in China. Tradition credits Zhang Qian with introducing the grapevine into China. Later Chinese envoys to the West apparently brought back for Chinese cultivation the chive, coriander, cucumbers, figs, sesame, safflower, and walnuts. In return, China sent westward knowledge of how to grow pears, peaches, oranges, roses, peonies, azaleas, camellias, and chrysanthemums. By the mid sixth century C.E. even the secret of silk manufacture had made its way to the eastern Mediterranean.

of the inhabitants are merchants who travel by carts or boats to neighboring countries, sometimes journeying several thousand li. The coins of the country are made of silver and bear the face of the king. When the king dies, the currency is immediately changed and new coins issued with the face of his successor. . . . To the west lies Tiaozhi [Mesopotamia]. . . .

Tiaozhi is situated several thousand li west of Anxi and borders the Western Sea [Persian Gulf?]. It is hot and damp, and the people live by cultivating the fields and planting rice. . . . The people are very numerous and are ruled by many petty chiefs. The ruler of Anxi[10] gives orders to these chiefs and regards them as his vassals. . . .

Southeast of Daxia is the kingdom of Shendu [India]. "When I was in Daxia," Zhang Qian reported, "I saw bamboo canes from Qiong[11] and cloth made in the province of Shu.[12] When I asked the people how they had gotten such articles, they replied, 'Our merchants go to buy them in the markets of Shendu.' Shendu, they told me, lies several thousand li southeast of Daxia. The people cultivate the land and live much like the people of Daxia. The region is said to be hot and damp. The inhabitants ride elephants when they go into battle. The kingdom is situated on a great river.[13]

"We know that Daxia is located twelve thousand li southwest of China. Now if the kingdom of Shendu is situated several thousand li southeast of Daxia and obtains goods that are produced in Shu, it seems to me that it must not be very far from Shu. At present, if we try to send envoys to Daxia by way of the mountain trails that lead through the territory of the Qiang people,[14] they will be molested by the Qiang, while if we send them a little farther north, they will be captured by the Xiongnu. It would seem that the most direct route, as well as the safest, would be that out of Shu."[15]

Thus the emperor learned of Dayuan, Daxia, Anxi, and the others, all great states rich in unusual products whose people cultivated the land and made their living in much the same way as the Chinese. All these states, he was told, were militarily weak and prized Han goods and wealth. He also learned that to the north of them live the Yuexi and Kangju[16] people who were strong in arms but who could be persuaded by gifts and the prospect of gain to acknowledge allegiance to the Han court. If it were only possible to win over these states by peaceful means, the emperor thought, he could then extend his domain ten thousand li, attract to his court men of strange customs who would come translating and retranslating their languages,[17] and his might would become known to all the lands within the four seas.

The emperor was therefore delighted, and approved Zhang Qian's suggestion. He ordered Zhang Qian to start out from . . . Shu on a secret mission to search for Daxia. The party broke into four groups. . . . All the groups managed to advance one or two thousand li, but were blocked on the north by the Di and Tso tribes and on the south by the Sui and Kunming tribes. The Kunming tribes have no rulers but devote themselves to plunder and robbery, and as soon as they seized any of the Han envoys they immediately murdered them. Thus none of the parties was ever able to get through to its destination. They did learn, however, that some one thousand or more li to the west there was a state called Tianyue[18] whose people rode elephants and that

---

[10]The Parthian monarchs Phraates II (r. 138–127 B.C.E.) and Artabanus I (r. 127–124).
[11]Qiongzhou in Szechwan province in southwest China.
[12]China's Szechwan province.
[13]Probably a reference to the Indus River.
[14]A Tibetan mountain people.
[15]In other words, in order to avoid the Xiongnu and the Qiang, Zhang Qian proposes traveling to Daxia by way of India.

[16]Another nomadic people (see note 5).
[17]Having no knowledge of Chinese, they would need to communicate through a series of intermediary languages.
[18]Probably Burma (modern Myanmar), which today borders China's Yunnan province; in the late second century B.C.E. Yunnan was not yet fully part of China and would not be for centuries to come. Burma, therefore, was a distant and mysterious land.

the merchants from Shu sometimes went there with their goods on unofficial trading missions.[19] In this way the Han, while searching for a route to Daxia, first came into contact with the kingdom of Tian.

Earlier the Han had tried to establish relations with the barbarians of the southwest, but the expense proved too great and no road could be found through the region and so the project was abandoned. After Zhang Qian reported that it was possible to reach Daxia by traveling through the region of the southwestern barbarians, the Han once more began efforts to establish relations with the tribes in the area.

---

[19]Smuggling.

The Transit of Images along the Silk Road
▼▼▼
41 ▼ FOUR ROBED STATUES

The most visible manifestation of this first age of Afro-Eurasian interchange was the manner in which artistic motifs and styles traveled across the four major cultural pools, especially from west to east. As these ideas and forms moved from one region to another, they were reshaped and blended with native elements to produce striking examples of syncretic art. The four sculptures that appear here illustrate the way in which a Greco-Roman artistic style traveled from the Mediterranean to China between the late first century B.C.E. and the fifth century C.E.

As is evident in *The Gaul and Wife* and *The Old Woman* in source 31, Hellenistic sculptors were masters at carving draped clothing that defined the human body concealed beneath. The creator of our first statue, *Caesar Augustus as Pontifex Maximus,* uses the emperor's draped robes as a means of evoking a mood of drama and mystery while simultaneously proclaiming Augustus's vitality and stolidity. This sculpture, crafted by an unknown eastern Mediterranean artist around 20 B.C.E., portrays Emperor Caesar Augustus in the fullness of his civil and religious power. As head of the Roman state, Augustus held the office of *Pontifex Maximus* (Chief Priest) and was responsible for presiding over Rome's major religious ceremonies. No member of the empire could gaze on this sculpture and not realize that the emperor embodied all of the Roman state's sacred authority.

Our second sculpture comes from Parthia. In 171 B.C.E. the Parthians, an Iranian steppe people, replaced the Macedonian Seleucids as masters of Persia and Mesopotamia and established an empire that lasted to 226 C.E. Although creative in military and administrative matters, the Parthians seem to have been content to be inheritors rather than innovators in the fine arts. As a consequence, their rise did not result in any immediate repudiation of the Hellenistic forms of artistic expression that had been a part of the fabric of Persian civilization since the late fourth century B.C.E. The Parthian Empire, however, bordered Central Asia, which meant that Parthian culture was a rich combination of many elements, of which Mediterranean Hellenism was only one.

The sculpture represented here of a woman in Iranian dress dates from the late second or early third century C.E. and illustrates a typical Parthian blend of Greco-Roman and Iranian components. It is one of over one hundred similar votive statues discovered at the many shrines of the city of Hatra in northern Mesopotamia. The unknown noblewoman it portrays offered it in devotion to an equally unknown deity. The statue, which is more than six feet high, affirms the importance of the donor, who stands with her hand raised in reverence.

Our third statue portrays the Buddha. Early Buddhists believed it was wrong to depict the Buddha artistically in human form, because he had broken the chains of matter and had achieved Nirvana. For over five hundred years Buddhist artists used such symbols as a wheel, a pipal tree (Chapter 1, source 8), a throne, a footprint, or a stupa (source 39, note 9) to symbolize his last earthly body. Toward the end of the first century C.E. artists in the Kushana province of *Gandhara,* which today comprises Afghanistan and northwest Pakistan, began representing the Buddha as a human. The sculpture of the standing Buddha that appears here is typical of the many carvings that have survived from this period and place. The setting is the Buddha's first sermon on the Law of Righteousness (Chapter 3, source 19). Many of the features are distinctively Buddhist. The knot on the top of the Buddha's head is known as the *ushnisha* and represents his cosmic consciousness; his pierced, distended earlobes symbolize his former royal life; the garment he wears is the *sanghati,* or monk's robe; the *halo,* or solar disk, that frames his head is typical of all Gandharan statues of the Buddha and represents his sanctity. His missing right hand probably was raised palm outward in the gesture of blessing. The lotuses, or water lilies, carved into the base of the statue are a Buddhist symbol of purity and peace, therefore Nirvana. But those lotuses are also an example of the syncretic nature of Buddhist art. The lotus first appeared in ancient Egyptian art as a symbol of rebirth, and it made its way to Gandhara and India through Mesopotamia and Iran. Therefore, it should not surprise us that many scholars claim that the style and majesty of the Roman imperial sculpture that emanated from the workshops of the eastern Mediterranean deeply influenced the creators of the early Gandharan statues of the Buddha.

Our fourth sculpture depicts the Buddha standing on a lotus flower. Composed of gilded bronze, it was crafted in 477 C.E. in the region of China ruled by the Northern Wei Dynasty (386–535). The Northern Wei, Turkic invaders who had conquered and unified northern China during China's long period of political disunity following the collapse of the Han Empire, had adopted the trappings of Chinese aristocratic culture but added a new element. They were deeply devoted to Mahayana Buddhism and patronized its rapid spread throughout northern China. The statue, missing only its original attached halo, deals largely with the same theme and setting as the Gandharan Buddha, but artistically it is somewhat different. An excellent example of an emerging Chinese style of Buddhist art, the statue's face and spiralling hairstyle, as well as its formality, are distinctly Chinese. However, the sensuousness of the statue, in which a well-formed body is revealed beneath diaphanous robes, is quite new to Chinese art and probably an import from India.

Caesar Augustus as Pontifex Maximus

Parthian Noblewoman

QUESTIONS FOR ANALYSIS

1. Consider Caesar Augustus's expression, posture, and dress. How has the artist evoked a sense of sacred authority?
2. Consider the Parthian woman's expression, posture, and dress. How has the sculptor evoked a sense of her authority?

Gandharan Buddha

Northern Wei Buddha

3. Compare the Gandharan and Chinese Buddhas. In what ways are they similar? How do they differ?
4. Consider the expressions, postures, and dress of the two Buddhas. What responses do their respective sculptors hope to evoke from viewers?
5. Compare all four sculptures. Do they share any common elements? Do any significant differences divide them?
6. What conclusions follow from your answers to questions 1–5?

Travel across the Indian Ocean

During the last centuries B.C.E. Indian merchants, especially from India's southern kingdoms, began sailing across the Bay of Bengal into the lands of Southeast Asia, which were rich in natural resources. These included gold, spices, and the aromatic woods and resins of the rain forests. Offsetting the considerable dangers of venturing into this vast region were the considerable profits that a successful entrepreneur could gain. The result was the creation, during the first several centuries C.E., of a network of routes and overseas trading stations tieing India and the island of Ceylon to the peoples of coastal Southeast Asia. Traffic flowed in both directions, as Southeast Asians made their way to India for trade and study, and Malay sailors even ventured as far as the east coast of Africa.

One significant consequence of this contact was the exportation of Indian culture, especially Hindu and Buddhist religious beliefs and practices, into a number of Southeast Asian lands during the first five centuries C.E. India was not, however, the only neighbor to leave a permanent imprint on Southeast Asia. China imparted many of its cultural ways to the northern regions of mainland Southeast Asia, especially northern Vietnam, through both overland and seaborne contacts. Indeed, the ports of Southeast Asia, especially those that commanded the narrow Strait of Malacca separating the Malay Peninsula from the island of Sumatra, became prosperous way stations on an oceanic trade route that joined India with southern China.

The Transit of the Buddha Image to Funan

▼▼▼

42 ▾ *A BUDDHA FROM FUNAN*

During the third century C.E. the kingdom of Funan, established by emigrant Hindus in an area that encompassed portions of modern Vietnam and Cambodia, was already deeply Indianized — at least as far as the culture of its rulers was concerned. The power and wealth of this kingdom attracted not only Indians and Chinese (the latter gave the region its name) but even sailors from the Sassanid Empire of Persia, which had replaced the Parthian Empire early in the third century. By the sixth century, however, due to successful competition from more southerly port areas, Funan's economic and political power was rapidly contracting.

Our source is a Buddha statue of Gandharan style that was excavated in the remains of Funan's harbor of Oc Eo. Of uncertain date, the statue suggests some of the Indian influences on Funan.

QUESTIONS FOR ANALYSIS

1. Compare this statue with the Gandharan Buddha in source 41. Do you see why scholars generally conclude that this was probably a local copy of a Gandharan original?
2. What inferences follow from your study of this statue?

Funan Buddha

Faxian's Homeward Voyage

▼▼▼

43 ▼ *Faxian,* TRAVELS IN INDIA AND CEYLON

After spending two years on the island of Ceylon, off the southern tip of India, where he obtained additional Buddhist sutras, Faxian (whom we met in source 39) prepared to travel by ship back to China. His plan was to reach the southern Chinese port of Guangzhou (Canton). However, when he finally set foot on Chinese soil in 414 he found himself far up the northeast coast in Shandong Province, which lies across the Yellow Sea from Korea. His adventures and misadventures on his homeward voyage shed light on the interesting nature of early fifth-century oceanic travel between India and China. In fact, his is the earliest extant account of this sea route.

QUESTIONS FOR ANALYSIS

1. What does Faxian tell us about the voyage to Java-dvipa and the ship in which he sailed?
2. Why do you think he waited five months in Java-dvipa before resuming his trip home?
3. What does he tell us about the last leg of his journey from Java-dvipa to China and the ship in which he sailed?
4. Based on your answers to questions 1–3, describe the state of travel between India and China in the early fifth century C.E.
5. What does this account allow us to infer about cultural interchanges in this region?

Faxian abode in this country[1] two years. . . . Having obtained these Sanskrit works,[2] he took passage in a large merchantman, on board of which there were more than 200 men, and to which was attached by a rope a smaller vessel, as a provision against damage or injury to the large one from the perils of the navigation. With a favorable wind, they proceeded eastwards for three days, and then they encountered a great wind. The vessel sprang a leak and the water came in. The merchants wished to go to the smaller vessel; but the men on board it, fearing that too many would come, cut the connecting rope. The merchants were greatly alarmed, feeling their risk of instant death. Afraid that the vessel would fill, they took their bulky goods and threw them into the water. Faxian also took his pitcher and washing-basin, with some other articles, and cast them into the sea; but fearing that the merchants would cast overboard his books and images, he could only think with all his heart of Guanshiyin,[3] and commit his life to [the protection of] the Buddhist congregation of the land of Han,[4] [saying in effect], "I have travelled far in search of our Law. Let me, by your dread and supernatural [power], return from my wanderings, and reach my resting place!"

---

[1]Ceylon (modern Sri Lanka).
[2]Four sutras to add to those he had collected in India.
[3]Literally, "Perceiver of the World's Sounds," or "One Who Hears the Cries of the World," this Bodhisattva is better known as *Guanyin.* (Consult Chapter 6, sources 46 and 47,

for fuller treatment of this Mahayana Buddhist intermediary.)
[4]The Han Dynasty had collapsed in 220 C.E., but the Chinese still referred to China as the "land of Han."

In this way the tempest continued day and night, till on the thirteenth day the ship was carried to the side of an island, where, on the ebbing of the tide, the place of the leak was discovered, and it was stopped, on which the voyage was resumed. On the sea [hereabouts] there are many pirates, to meet with whom is speedy death. The great ocean spreads out, a boundless expanse. There is no knowing east or west; only by observing the sun, moon, and stars was it possible to go forward. If the weather were dark and rainy, [the ship] went as she was carried by the wind, without any definite course. In the darkness of the night, only the great waves were to be seen, breaking on one another, and emitting a brightness like that of fire, with huge turtles and other monsters of the deep [all about]. The merchants were full of terror, not knowing where they were going. The sea was deep and bottomless, and there was no place where they could drop anchor and stop. But when the sky became clear, they could tell east and west, and [the ship] again went forward in the right direction. If she had come on any hidden rock, there would have been no way of escape.

After proceeding in this way for rather more than ninety days, they arrived at a country called Java-dvipa,[5] where various forms of error and Brahminism are flourishing, while Buddhism in it is not worth speaking of. After staying there for five months, [Faxian] again embarked in another large merchantman, which also had on board more than 200 men. They carried provisions for fifty days, and commenced the voyage on the sixteenth day of the fourth month.

Faxian kept his retreat on board the ship. They took a course to the north-east, intending to reach Guangzhou. After more than a month, when the night-drum sounded the second watch, they encountered a black wind and tempestuous rain, which threw the merchants and passengers into consternation. Faxian again with all his heart directed his thoughts to Guanshiyin and the monkish communities of the land of Han; and, through their awesome and mysterious protection, was preserved to day-break. After day-break, the Brahmins[6] deliberated together and said, "It is having this Sramana[7] on board that has occasioned our misfortune and brought us this great and bitter suffering. Let us land the bhikshu[8] and place him on some island-shore. We must not for the sake of one man allow ourselves to be exposed to such imminent peril." A patron of Faxian, however, said to them, "If you land the bhikshu, you must at the same time land me; and if you do not, then you must kill me. If you land this Sramana, when I get to the land of Han, I will go to the emperor, and inform against you. The emperor also reveres and believes the Law of Buddha, and honors the bhikshus." The merchants hereupon were perplexed, and did not dare immediately to land Faxian.

At this time the sky continued very dark and gloomy, and the sailing-masters looked at one another and made mistakes. More than seventy days passed [from their leaving Java], and the provisions and water were nearly exhausted. They used the salt-water of the sea for cooking, and carefully divided the [fresh] water, each man getting two pints. Soon the whole was nearly gone, and the merchants took counsel and said, "At the ordinary rate of sailing we ought to have reached Guangzhou, and now the time is passed by many days; — must we not have held a wrong course?" Immediately they directed the ship to the north-west, looking out for land; and after sailing day and night for twelve days, they reached the shore on the south of mount Lao,[9] . . . and immediately got good water and vegetables. They had passed through many perils and hardships, and had been in a state of anxious apprehension for many days together; and now suddenly arriving at this shore, . . . they knew indeed that it was the land of Han.

---

[5]Probably the western part of the island of Java, which lies just east of Sumatra.
[6]Here he possibly means all Hindus on board, not just members of the Brahmin caste.

[7]A Buddhist monk.
[8]Another term for a Buddhist monk.
[9]On the Shandong Peninsula.

Part Two

▼▼▼

Faith, Devotion, and Salvation: Great World Religions to 1500 C.E.

By about 200 B.C.E. two overarching religious traditions had taken shape in Eurasia: Indian civilization produced Buddhism and Hinduism, both of which denied the reality of this world and sought release from it. And in Southwest Asia two monotheistic faiths emerged — Judaism and Zoroastrianism — whose believers saw themselves as agents in the transformation of this world according to precepts decreed by their God.

During the next fifteen hundred years these four religions underwent significant change. Zoroastrianism essentially disappeared after the ninth century C.E., except for remnant communities in Iran, India, Central Asia, and China. Before it passed away as a major religion, however, Zoroastrianism had a profound impact on the teachings of several new salvation faiths: Christianity, *Manichaeism,* and *Islam.* Judaism, which also exhibited some Zoroastrian influences, survived, continued its historical evolution, and served as a major source for two of the new religions of salvation: Christianity and Islam. Meanwhile one school of Buddhist thought, the *Mahayana* sect, evolved into a faith that also offered its believers personal salvation. To the contrary, mainstream Brahminical Hinduism never developed a clearly articulated doctrine of heavenly salvation, but it did evolve a form of worship centered on an intensely personal and deeply emotional devotion to a single, select deity.

Four faiths — Buddhism (largely in its Mahayana form), Christianity, Manichaeism, and Islam — became universal religions. That is, they found homes in a wide variety of cultural settings and claimed to offer salvation to all humanity. Of the four, Buddhism was the most regional, confined largely to the vast, heavily populated lands of South and East Asia. Islam became the most global, at least until around 1500. Muslim communities dominated the east coast of Africa and the trading empires of interior West Africa. Islam stretched across the entire breadth of North Africa, Southwest Asia, and the northern and central portions of India. It spread through much of Central Asia and the island and coastal regions of Southeast Asia, and it also touched many parts of China. It even penetrated Europe. Islamic rulers controlled much of the Iberian Peninsula from the early eighth to the early thirteenth centuries, and it was not until 1492 that Christian powers were able to conquer the final Islamic state in Spain. Meanwhile, during the fourteenth century, Islam arrived in Europe's Balkan region, where it has remained a vital force down to today. Christianity in its various forms found homes in Ethiopia, in the lands that bordered the eastern rim of the Mediterranean, among the Slavs of Eastern and Central Europe, and throughout Western Europe. In addition, small groups of Christians inhabited portions of Central Asia, northern and western China, and the western shores of India. With the new age of European transoceanic explorations, which got underway in the fifteenth century, Westerners transplanted Christianity throughout the Americas, along the Atlantic and Indian Ocean coasts of Africa, and, in a very limited way, in various parts of East and South Asia. Manichaeism, which had its origins in third-century Babylonia, penetrated both the Roman and Chinese Empires but was never more than a minority movement in either area. Persecutions led to its ultimate disappearance in Southwest Asia and the Roman World, but it remained a vital force in Central Asia for a millennium more.

Meanwhile, Judaism and Hinduism also expanded beyond the confines of their ethnic and geographic origins. In addition to the *Diaspora,* or "Great Dispersion," of Jewish communities throughout much of Eurasia and northern Africa, Jews also welcomed *gentile* converts into their midst. The most notable example of conversion to Judaism was when the ruling families of the *Khazars,* a Turkic people inhabiting the Upper Volga region between the Black and Caspian Seas, embraced Judaism toward the middle of the eighth century, possibly under the influence of Jewish refugees from Persia. Yet conversions of this sort were rare in Jewish history, and generally Jews did not attempt to spread their religion beyond their ethnic boundaries. Indian merchants and Brahmin teachers were more active disseminators of culture and religion than their Jewish counterparts. As we saw in Chapter 5, Indians traveled in significant numbers across the waters of the Bay of Bengal, bringing Hindu culture, particularly that of southern India, to the coastal regions of Southeast Asia. The cults of *Shiva* and *Vishnu* found especially fertile soil in these lands across the sea. Despite this expansion, however, both Judaism and Hinduism remained far less universal in scope or appeal than Buddhism, Christianity, and Islam, and maybe even Manichaeism.

Chapter 6

▼▼▼

New Developments in Three Ancient Religions

During the first age of Afro-Eurasian interchange (Chapter 5), Hinduism, Judaism, and Buddhism all experienced profound changes. Within Hinduism a new movement known as *bhakti,* or the Way of Devotion, challenged the caste system without rejecting it. At the same time, it was this new form of Hindu religion, not the caste system, that Indian merchants transplanted among the emerging civilizations of Southeast Asia in the early centuries C.E. Without the Way of Devotion, Hinduism probably would not have spread significantly beyond the Indian subcontinent.

Hinduism and Judaism have historically been family religions, in the sense that each has been largely confined to the heirs of a single civilization. Normally their adherents are born into these religious-social complexes and are not converts. Even so, both religions have occasionally reached out beyond their cultural matrices. This was particularly so in the case of Judaism because of the Diaspora, or Great Dispersion, which scattered Jewish communities all over the Afro-Eurasian World. While Jews remained conscious of being a people apart from their gentile, or non-Jewish, neighbors, Jewish communities could not avoid cultural interchange with the societies within which they were settled.

Cultural exchange also contributed significantly to the development of a new form of Buddhist belief and devotion: the *Mahayana* sect. This school moved radically away from the Buddha's original teachings, which refused to consider such notions as personal immortality, by offering the promise of salvation. This message attracted many people suffering from the chaos of the breakdown of the first Afro-Eurasian Ecumene. Toward the middle of the first century B.C.E., Mahayana Buddhist ideas began to enter China, and in the centuries that followed, Buddhism in its many different forms swept through East Asia.

▼▼▼

Hinduism: The Way of Devotion

In one of the *Bhagavad Gita*'s most famous scenes (which does not appear in the excerpt quoted in Chapter 3, source 17), Krishna, an incarnation of the god Vishnu, teaches Arjuna that *bhakti,* or unconditional devotion to a god, is one of several *yogas* (paths of selfless, god-focused action) by which a person can win release from the cycle of rebirth. Such a path to liberation appealed to many low-caste and casteless persons (as well as many women), who found strict and selfless conformity to the laws of dharma (the Yoga of Karma) unattractive. It also appealed to persons who lacked the temperament or leisure to attain release from the shackles of matter through asceticism, study of the sacred scriptures, and meditation. The Yoga of Devotion, in which the individual passionately adored a savior god, offered a promise of immediate liberation to everyone.

In the Gupta Age (320–ca. 550 C.E.) and thereafter, there was an increasing tendency among many Hindus to reduce the myriad divine personifications of Brahman, the One, to three: Brahma the Creator, Vishnu the Preserver, and Shiva the Destroyer. Of this trinity, *Brahma* (not to be confused with *Brahman*) was the least widely worshiped because he was perceived as a remote kingly god who, after completing the process of creation, had retired from concerning himself with worldly affairs. Hindus widely adored Vishnu and Shiva, however, and they became two of the great gods of Asia. The cult of Shiva was especially popular in Southeast Asia, where he merged with several local native deities and was even adopted by some Buddhist sects.

Those Hindus who concentrated their worship on Vishnu or Shiva did not deny the existence of the many other divine and semidivine personalities who were part of the traditional pantheon of India. They simply chose Shiva or Vishnu as gods of special devotion because each, in his way, was a loving personification of the totality of Divine Reality. Vishnu's worshipers, for example, believed that he had selflessly blessed and taught humanity on a number of critical occasions in descents (*avataras*) from Heaven. On each occasion he took on either human or animal form and intervened on behalf of the forces of goodness to redress the equilibrium between good and evil. In fact, Vishnu's worshipers regarded the Buddha as one of Vishnu's nine chief avataras. Of all his various incarnations, however, the warriors Krishna and Rama enjoyed the widest devotional popularity. As Lord Krishna exemplified in the *Bhagavad Gita,* Vishnu's emergence into this world provided humanity with a model of divine perfection. By offering such a god exclusive and unqualified devotion, a worshiper hoped to share in that perfection.

This religious development of bhakti, which met so many of the needs of members of India's lower castes and social levels, helped Hinduism to counter successfully the challenge of Buddhism, especially that of the Mahayana school. It is no simple coincidence that the Gupta Age was a period of Hindu Renaissance, during which Hinduism gained considerable ground against Buddhism. Indeed, by 1500 C.E. Buddhism, as a religion with an identity separate from Hinduism, had largely disappeared from the land of its origin.

Vishnu, Destroyer of Sin
▼▼▼

44 ▾ *THE VISHNU PURANA*

Between approximately 300 and 1000 C.E. a new sacred literature known as the *Puranas* (stories of ancient times) developed to give voice to bhakti. Composed by anonymous authors for popular consumption, each of the eighteen major Puranas is a long, rambling collection of myth and folklore that brings home to its largely unsophisticated audience the central message that a particular god — Brahma, Vishnu, or Shiva — deserves worship without reservation. The following selection comes from the closing lines of the *Vishnu Purana*.

QUESTIONS FOR ANALYSIS

1. What power does the very name of *Vishnu* have?
2. What traditional avenues to liberation are referred to in this passage, and how does worship of Vishnu allow one to bypass or transcend them?
3. How does Vishnu, of and by himself, encompass all the powers of the Hindu trinity? How is he equated with Brahman, the World Soul?
4. Was the author of this passage a monotheist? Please explain your answer.
5. How, if at all, does the theological message of this Purana represent a departure from the spirit that pervades *The Laws of Manu* (Chapter 5, Source 38)?

I have related to you this Purana, which is equal to the Vedas[1] in sanctity, and by hearing which all faults and sins whatever are expiated. . . .

By hearing this, all sins are at once obliterated. In this also the glorious Hari[2] has been revealed, the cause of the creation, preservation, and destruction of the world; the soul of all things, and himself all things: by the repetition of whose name man is undoubtedly liberated from all sins, which fly like wolves that are frightened by a lion. The repetition of his name with devout faith is the best remover of all sins, destroying them as fire purifies the metal from the dross. The stain of the Kali age,[3] which ensures to men sharp punishments in hell,[4] is at once effaced by a single invocation of Hari. He who is

---

[1]Chapter 2, source 11.
[2]Another name for Vishnu.
[3]The Kali Age receives its name from Kali, goddess of destruction and consort of Shiva. This period comprises three hundred sixty thousand years of evil and is the last stage in a cycle of four eternally repetitive ages. Following dissolution of the Kali Age, a period of new birth and virtue will commence because the universe, although periodically de-

stroyed by Shiva, is eternal. The authors of the Puranas assumed they were living in a Kali Age.
[4]There are many hells (one Purana enumerates twenty-one) where the servants of Yama, god of death, punish persons for their social sins, especially sins against caste restrictions. This punishment is not eternal; eventually each soul is reborn into a lower caste, or life form, depending on the weight of one's karma.

all that is, the whole egg of Brahma[5] . . . he who is all things, who knows all things, who is the form of all things, being without form himself, and of whom whatever is, from mount Meru[6] to an atom, all consists — he, the glorious Vishnu, the destroyer of all sin — is described in this Purana. By hearing this Purana an equal recompense is obtained to that which is derived from the performance of an Asvamedha sacrifice,[7] or from fasting at the holy places. . . . This Purana is the best of all preservatives for those who are afraid of worldly existence, a certain alleviation of the sufferings of men, and remover of all imperfections. . . . Whoever hears this great mystery, which removes the contamination of the Kali, shall be freed from all his sins. He who hears this every day acquits himself of his daily obligations to ancestors, gods and men. . . . What marvel therefore is it that the sins of one who repeats the name of Achyuta[8] should be wiped away? Should not that Hari be heard of, whom those devoted to acts[9] worship with sacrifices continually as the god of sacrifice; whom those devoted to meditation[10] contemplate . . . , who, as the gods, accepts the offerings addressed to them; the glorious being who is without beginning or end; . . . who is the abode of all spiritual power; in whom the limits of finite things cannot be measured;

and who, when he enters the ear, destroys all sin?

I adore him, that first of gods, Purushottama,[11] who is without end and without beginning, without growth, without decay, without death; who is substance that knows not change. I adore that ever inexhaustible spirit, who assumed sensible qualities;[12] who, though one, became many; who, though pure, became as if impure, by appearing in many and various shapes; who is endowed with divine wisdom, and is the author of the preservation of all creatures. I adore him, who is the one conjoined essence and object of both meditative wisdom and active virtue; who is watchful in providing for human enjoyments; who is one with the three qualities;[13] who, without undergoing change, is the cause of the evolution of the world; who exists of his own essence, ever exempt from decay. I constantly adore him, who is entitled heaven, air, fire, water, earth, and ether; who is the bestower of all the objects which give gratification to the senses; who benefits mankind with the instruments of fruition; who is perceptible, who is subtle, who is imperceptible. May that unborn, eternal Hari, whose form is manifold, and whose essence is composed of both nature and spirit, bestow upon all mankind that blessed state which knows neither birth nor decay!

---

[5]All creation.
[6]The central mountain of the earth and the home of the gods.
[7]A horse sacrifice, which was a carryover from Aryan times.
[8]*The Unfallen One,* another of Vishnu's titles.
[9]Those who seek moksha (release) through the Yoga of Karma.

[10]Those who seek release through the Yoga of Knowledge.
[11]Another name for Vishnu — the sacrificial substance from which the world was created (see "The Hymn to Purusha," Chapter 2, source 11).
[12]Who had many incarnations, or avataras, such as Krishna (Chapter 3, source 17).
[13]Creation, preservation, destruction.

Shiva, Auspicious Destroyer
▼▼▼

45 ▾ *SHIVA NATARAJA*

Many people, especially those whose religions spring from the Southwest Asian tradition of ethical monotheism, might find it hard to accept the notion that a god whose primary function is destruction and death is regarded as a loving deity. Yet *Shiva,* the name of this destroyer god, means "auspicious." Indeed, contradiction is central to the cult of Shiva. He is celebrated as the divine patron of ascetics and other holy persons and is often portrayed as deep in meditation, with matted hair and covered with ashes — signs of the holy ascetic. At the same time, he is celebrated as a deity with an insatiable sexual appetite and is often portrayed as a sensuous lover.

The artifact illustrated here is a bronze statue of *Shiva Nataraja* (Lord of the Dance) from the Chola kingdom of southern India (ca. 850–1250), an area of fervent devotion to Shiva. The statue represents the god engaged in an ecstatic cosmic dance, by which he brings to an end one of the cosmos's cycles of time and ushers in a new era. The statue's symbols offer numerous clues to how his worshipers perceive Shiva. Here he is dancing within a circle of fire. His hair is piled up in a crownlike style; flowing from the sides of his head are strands of hair intertwined with flowers and forming the shape of wings. His upper-left hand holds a devouring flame; his upper-right hand clasps a drum for beating out the endless rhythm of the universe. The lower-right arm is entwined by a cobra, but the hand is raised in the silent "fear not" gesture. (Compare this with the Buddha's right hand in Chapter 5, sources 41 and 42.) The lower-left hand points to his raised left foot as a sign of release from the bonds of the material world. The other foot is planted firmly on the writhing body of Apasamara, the demon of ignorance and heedlessness.

QUESTIONS FOR ANALYSIS

1. What double function does fire serve, especially in an agricultural society?
2. Keeping in mind your answer to question 1 and also the fact that Shiva uses a drum to beat out the rhythm of the universe, what do you think the circle of fire and the flame in his left hand represent?
3. If fire presents a double message, what other symbols in this statue give a similar double message? Consider particularly Shiva's body language.
4. Consider Shiva's hair. According to one tradition, the sacred River Ganges, the Mother of India, flows from Shiva's head. What do this tradition and the manner in which the god's hair is represented suggest about this deity?
5. Why do you think the artist has depicted Shiva with four arms instead of the standard two?
6. We saw in source 44 that Vishnu's devotees believe that their savior god exercises all of the primary functions of the Godhead: creation, destruction, regeneration, preservation, and release. Can you find the appropriate symbols in this statue that illustrate a similar belief on the part of Shiva's followers?
7. Consider the demon of ignorance. How would an ignorant person regard death? What do you think Shiva's triumph over this demon represents?

Shiva Nataraja

▼▼▼

Mahayana Buddhism:
A Religion of Infinite Compassion

Asoka's Buddhism (Chapter 5, source 37) was idealistic, but it was also practical. He endeavored to make the Law of Righteousness a living reality for his people. Withdrawal from the world to live the life of a mendicant monk who sought Nirvana through meditation was not for Asoka. While he revered and patronized Buddhist monks, he chose to practice social activism based on his understanding of Buddhist principles. Moreover, by sending missionaries to neighboring and distant regions he affirmed his belief in Buddhism's universality. As his edicts indicate, Asoka also did not abandon belief in the gods or a heavenly hereafter.

All of the qualities of Asoka's Buddhism became more pronounced in the generations that followed. Eventually they contributed to the emergence of a new interpretation of Buddhism known as *Mahayana,* or the "Great Vehicle." The title is metaphorical: Mahayana sectarians picture their form of Buddhism as a great ferry, which, under the guidance of enlightened pilots known as *Bodhisattvas,* carries all of humanity simultaneously across the river of life to salvation on the opposite shore.

Conversely, Mahayanists term the older, more traditional form of Buddhism *Hinayana,* or the "Small Vehicle." The image is of a one-person raft because Hinayana Buddhism centers on the single *arahat,* or "perfected disciple," who individually attains Enlightenment and Nirvana through solitary meditation, normally within a monastic setting. Followers of this form of Buddhism — which today predominates in the island nation of Sri Lanka and several countries of mainland Southeast Asia, especially Burma and Thailand — generally dislike the term *Hinayana,* because it implies inferiority, and call their sect *Theravada* (the Teaching of the Elders).

Evidence indicates that Mahayana Buddhism emerged in northwest India during the first or second century of the Common Era and probably did so in part as a result of certain Southwest Asian influences, primarily the notion of savior deities. According to Mahayana belief, Siddhartha Gautama the Buddha was not unique. There have been many Buddhas who lived before and after Gautama and who now preside over countless heavens that serve as way stations to Nirvana. Additionally, there are infinite numbers of Bodhisattvas. The title *Bodhisattva* is Sanskrit and means "an enlightened being." Although they have attained Enlightenment, these compassionate saints delay Nirvana in order to lead all humanity to salvation, drawing upon the countless merits they have accumulated in their perfect lives of selflessness to achieve this task. Those whom they save become, in turn, Bodhisattvas, who then delay their entry into Nirvana in order to help others. Through this pyramid of selfless compassion, ultimately all humanity will cross together into Nirvana, a state of perfect bliss. This comforting, unexclusive doctrine was destined to become the basis of a world religion, and during the first millennium of the Common Era it spread throughout most of East Asia.

Perceiver of the World's Sounds:
A Universal Bodhisattva

▼▼▼

46 ▼ *THE LOTUS SUTRA*

When faced with disaster on the high seas, the Chinese pilgrim-monk Faxian sought the protection of *Guanshiyin* (Chapter 5, source 43). Better known as *Guanyin,* this Bodhisattva was the Chinese version of *Avalokitesvara,* whose name means "Perceiver of the World's Sounds." Avalokitesvara makes his initial appearance in one of the most influential and beloved of all the sacred texts of the Mahayana doctrine, *The Lotus Sutra.* We do not know when or where the book was composed or in what Indian or Central Asian language the now lost original appeared; we do know that its first Chinese translation was made in 255 C.E. A later translation of 406, however, became the standard version in which it was read throughout China and in areas within the Chinese cultural orbit. Our excerpt comes from that fifth-century Chinese text.

The lotus, or water lily, is one of the most common Buddhist symbols of Nirvana (Chapter 5, source 41), chosen because this flower, rooted in mud, rises through stagnant water to free itself in purity and beauty. In a similar manner, *The Lotus Sutra* describes the ten cosmic levels of existence, from hell to Nirvana. On the ninth level, just below the state of Buddhahood, dwell the Bodhisattvas, who serve to alleviate the sufferings of others and to ferry them to Nirvana. Among them is Perceiver of the World's Sounds (or Cries).

QUESTIONS FOR ANALYSIS

1. What does one do to attain this Bodhisattva's help?
2. How will this Bodhisattva assist his devotees?
3. What conclusions do you draw from your answers regarding the message of Mahayana Buddhism and its appeal?
4. Compare this doctrine with Bhakti (sources 44–45). Which strike you as more significant, the differences or the similarities, and what conclusions follow from your answer?
5. Compare this document with Faxian's account of Gupta India (Chapter 5, source 39). In what ways do they both present evidence of the relationship that existed between Brahminical Hinduism and Buddhism? What was that relationship, and what inferences do you draw from your answer?

At that time the Bodhisattva Inexhaustible Intent immediately rose from his seat, bared his right shoulder, pressed his palms together and, facing the Buddha, spoke these words: "World-Honored One, this Bodhisattva Perceiver of the World's Sounds — why is he called Perceiver of the World's Sounds?"

The Buddha said to Bodhisattva Inexhaustible Intent: "Good man, suppose there are immeasurable hundreds, thousands, ten thousands, millions of living beings who are undergoing various trials and suffering. If they hear of this Bodhisattva Perceiver of the World's Sounds and single-mindedly call his name, then at once he will perceive the sound of their voices and they will all gain deliverance from their trials.

"If someone, holding fast to the name of Bodhisattva Perceiver of the World's Sounds, should enter a great fire, the fire could not burn him. This would come about because of this Bodhisattva's authority and supernatural power. If one were washed away by a great flood and called upon his name, one would immediately find himself in a shallow place.

"Suppose there were a hundred, a thousand, ten thousand, a million living beings who, seeking for gold, silver, lapis lazuli, seashell, agate, coral, amber, pearls, and other treasures, set out on the great sea. And suppose a fierce wind should blow their ship off course and it drifted to the land of rakshasa demons.[1] If among those people there is even just one who calls the name of Bodhisattva Perceiver of the World's Sounds, then all those people will be delivered from their troubles with the rakshasas. This is why he is called Perceiver of the World's Sounds.

"If a person who faces imminent threat of attack should call the name of Bodhisattva Perceiver of the World's Sounds, then the swords and staves wielded by his attackers would instantly shatter into so many pieces and he would be delivered.

"Though enough yakshas[2] and rakshasas to fill all the thousand-millionfold world should try to come and torment a person, if they hear him calling the name of Bodhisattva Perceiver of the World's Sounds, then these evil demons will not even be able to look at him with their evil eyes, much less do him harm.

"Suppose there is a person who, whether guilty or not guilty, has had his body imprisoned in fetters and chains, cangue and lock. If he calls the name of Bodhisattva Perceiver of the World's Sounds, then all his bonds will be severed and broken and at once he will gain deliverance.

"Suppose, in a place filled with all the evil-hearted bandits of the thousand-millionfold world, there is a merchant leader who is guiding a band of merchants carrying valuable treasures over a steep and dangerous road, and that one man shouts out these words: 'Good men, do not be afraid! You must single-mindedly call on the name of Bodhisattva Perceiver of the World's Sounds. This Bodhisattva can grant fearlessness to living beings. If you call his name, you will be delivered from these evil-hearted bandits!' When the band of merchants hear this, they all together raise their voices, saying, 'Hail to the Bodhisattva Perceiver of the World's Sounds!' And because they call his name, they are at once able to gain deliverance. Inexhaustible Intent, the authority and supernatural power of the Bodhisattva and Mahasattva[3] Perceiver of the World's Sounds are as mighty as this!

"If there should be living beings beset by numerous lusts and cravings, let them think with constant reverence of Bodhisattva Perceiver of the World's Sounds and then they can shed their desires. If they have great wrath and ire, let them think with constant reverence of Bodhisattva Perceiver of the World's Sounds and then they can shed their ire. If they have great ignorance and stupidity, let them think with constant reverence of Bodhisattva Perceiver of the World's Sounds and they can rid themselves of stupidity.

"Inexhaustible Intent, the Bodhisattva Perceiver of the World's Sounds possesses great authority and supernatural powers, as I have described, and can confer many benefits. For this reason, living beings should constantly keep the thought of him in mind.

"If a woman wishes to give birth to a male child, she should offer obeisance and alms to Bodhisattva Perceiver of the World's Sounds and

---

[1]A race of evil divine beings, but they also serve as protectors of Buddhism.
[2]Nature forces and forest deities, very much like the elves and leprechauns of the West. They are both good and evil.

[3]A Sanskrit title that means "Great Being."

then she will bear a son blessed with merit, virtue, and wisdom. And if she wishes to bear a daughter, she will bear one with all the marks of comeliness, one who in the past planted the roots of virtue and is loved and respected by many persons.

"Inexhaustible Intent, the Bodhisattva Perceiver of the Worlds Sounds has power to do all this. If there are living beings who pay respect and obeisance to Bodhisattva Perceiver of the World's Sounds, their good fortune will not be fleeting or vain. Therefore living beings should all accept and uphold the name of Bodhisattva Perceiver of the World's Sounds.

"Inexhaustible Intent, suppose there is a person who accepts and upholds the names of as many Bodhisattvas as there are sands in sixty-two million Ganges, and for as long as his present body lasts, he offers them alms in the form of food and drink, clothing, bedding and medicines. What is your opinion? Would this good man or good woman gain many benefits, or would he not?"

Inexhaustible Intent replied, "They would be very many, World-Honored One."

The Buddha said: "Suppose also that there is a person who accepts and upholds the name of Bodhisattva Perceiver of the World's Sounds and even just once offers him obeisance and alms. The good fortune gained by these two persons would be exactly equal and without difference. For a hundred, a thousand, ten thousand, a million kalpas[4] it would never be exhausted or run out. Inexhaustible Intent, if one accepts and upholds the name of Bodhisattva Perceiver of the World's Sounds, he will gain the benefit of merit and virtue that is as immeasurable and boundless as this!"

Bodhisattva Inexhaustible Intent said to the Buddha, "World-Honored One, Bodhisattva Perceiver of the World's Sounds — how does he come and go in this saha[5] world? How does he preach the Law for the sake of living beings? How does the power of expedient means apply in his case?"

The Buddha said to Bodhisattva Inexhaustible Intent: "Good man, if there are living beings in the land who need someone in the body of a Buddha in order to be saved, Bodhisattva Perceiver of the World's Sounds immediately manifests himself in a Buddha body and preaches the Law for them. If they need someone in a pratyekabuddha's[6] body in order to be saved, immediately he manifests a pratyekabuddha's body and preaches the Law to them. If they need a voice-hearer to be saved, immediately he becomes a voice-hearer and preaches the Law for them. If they need King Brahma[7] to be saved, immediately he becomes King Brahma and preaches the Law for them. If they need the lord Shakra[8] to be saved, immediately he becomes the lord Shakra and preaches the Law for them. If they need the heavenly being Freedom to be saved, immediately he becomes the heavenly being Freedom and preaches the Law for them. If they need the heavenly being Great Freedom to be saved, immediately he becomes the heavenly being Great Freedom and preaches the Law for them. If they need a great general of heaven to be saved, immediately he becomes a great general of heaven and preaches the Law for them. If they need Vaishravana[9] to be saved, immedi-

---

[4]One day of the god Brahma, which equals four billion human years.

[5]A Sanskrit word that means "endurance"; it refers to the present life of suffering.

[6]A solitary sage of the Theravada doctrine whose life is that of one "who walks alone." This anti-Bodhisattva, having reached Enlightenment, passes into Nirvana without heeding the woes of others.

[7]The Hindu god of creation; in Mahayana Buddhist teachings he is a protective deity who lives in one of the four meditation heavens and rules the saha world (note 5).

[8]*The Powerful Lord,* one of Indra's titles (Chapter 2, source 11); this god of thunder became a protector deity in Mahayana teachings.

[9]In the Hindu pantheon, this is Agni, a vedic god of fire and sacrifice. In the Mahayana Buddhist cosmology, he is one of the Four Heavenly Kings and protects the north, the place from which the Buddha expounds the Law.

ately he becomes Vaishravana and preaches the Law for them. If they need a petty king to be saved, immediately he becomes a petty king and preaches the Law for them. If they need a rich man to be saved, immediately he becomes a rich man and preaches the Law for them. If they need a householder to be saved, immediately he becomes a householder and preaches the Law for them. If they need a chief minister to be saved, immediately he becomes a chief minister and preaches the Law for them. If they need a Brahmin to be saved, immediately he becomes a Brahmin and preaches the Law for them. If they need a monk, a nun, a layman believer, or a laywoman believer to be saved, immediately he becomes a monk, a nun, a layman believer, or a laywoman believer and preaches the Law for them. If they need the wife of a rich man, of a householder, a chief minister, or a Brahmin to be saved, immediately he becomes those wives and preaches the Law for them. If they need a young boy or a young girl to be saved, immediately he becomes a young boy or a young girl and preaches the Law for them. If they need a heavenly being, . . . a human or a nonhuman being to be saved, immediately he becomes all of these and preaches the Law for them. If they need a vajra-bearing[10] god to be saved, immediately he becomes a vajra-bearing god and preaches the Law for them.

"Inexhaustible Intent, this Bodhisattva Perceiver of the World's Sounds has succeeded in acquiring benefits such as these and, taking on a variety of different forms, goes about among the lands saving living beings. For this reason you and the others should single-mindedly offer alms to Bodhisattva Perceiver of the World's Sounds. This Bodhisattva and Mahasattva Perceiver of the World's Sounds can bestow fearlessness on those who are in fearful, pressing or difficult circumstances. That is why in this saha world everyone calls him Bestower of Fearlessness."

---

[10]A thunderbolt-wielding god.

The Bodhisattva Image
▼▼▼
47 ▼ *THREE BODHISATTVAS*

As befit a religion that preached the message of universal salvation, Mahayana Buddhism developed a strong tradition of spreading the word through every available medium. In China this meant mass printing of the sacred texts during the era of the Tang Dynasty (618–907). The oldest extant printed book known today is a Chinese copy of *The Diamond Sutra,* which dates from 868. But sutras were not enough. People, especially those who were illiterate, needed artistic representations of the Bodhisattvas to whom they prayed. Statues and paintings of Bodhisattvas became fixtures throughout lands in which the Mahayana doctrine took root, and as the following three statues demonstrate, images of the Bodhisattvas took many different forms.

The first statue is of Perceiver of the World's Sounds, whom we saw in source 46. Called *Avalokitesvara* in India, the home of his origin, this Bodhisattva had several different manifestations; one of these was as an androgynous young man, and he carried that image to China, where he was known as *Guanshiyin* or, more commonly, *Guanyin.* In China, Perceiver of the World's Sounds underwent a sex change. Probably because Guanyin assumed the dual functions of making women fertile and protecting them in childbirth, this Bodhisattva increasingly was portrayed as a woman. The two images, male and female, coexisted for a while, but the female won out by the beginning of the twelfth century. Whether called Guanyin or *Kannon,* her Japanese name, she became the most widely beloved and prayed to Bodhisattva in East Asia. A pure and benevolent spirit, she was the gateway to the Pure Land, or Western Paradise, a heavenly way station of bliss on the road to Nirvana.

This particular Guanyin is a gilded bronze statuette from the early years of the Sui Dynasty (589–618). Standing on a lotus blossom and wearing an ornate gown, jewelry, and a tasseled crown, she holds a flask of heavenly dew in her right hand. In her left hand Guanyin bears a willow sprig. A touch of the willow sprinkled with the dew cures all physical and spiritual disorders.

The second statue comes from the *Khmer* kingdom (802–1406), located in the Southeast Asian land of Cambodia. The temple complexes in the Khmer capital at Angkor, which reached their heights of splendor in the twelfth and thirteenth centuries, show the profound influence of Hindu culture, but they also display strong Mahayanist elements. Our statue is a late-twelfth-century representation of the Bodhisattva *Hevajra* and displays the world view of a branch of Mahayana Buddhism known as *Tantrism.* Tantrism, which originated in Hindu beliefs and practices, emphasizes magic and esoteric rituals. Beyond that it stresses the doctrine of *nondualism,* a rejection of the notion that apparently contradictory elements — such as life and death, female and male, goodness and evil — are truly opposed to one another. Tantric Buddhism is particularly prevalent in Tibet, and this statue is markedly Tibetan in its overall form, but its Indian influences are equally apparent. Here we see an eight-faced Hevajra, with four legs (only seven faces and two legs are visible in the picture) and sixteen arms. In each hand he holds a skull, and he dances above a corpse. Significantly, that corpse lies on a lotus blossom.

The third statue, carved in 1343, is of *Arapacana* and comes from the island of Java. He sits in the lotus position of meditation (see Chapter 1, source 9, seal 6) on a giant lotus flower. Wielding the sword of interior knowledge above his tiered crown, he clutches in his left hand the book of wisdom (*The Sutra of the Perfection of Insight*). Surrounding him are more lotuses and four lesser Bodhisattvas, who serve as his constant companions.

QUESTIONS FOR ANALYSIS

1. Consider Guanyin's dress, posture, facial expression, and implements. What do they combine to tell us about this Bodhisattva?
2. Review *The Lotus Sutra.* Is this statue true to the spirit and message of that sutra? If so, how?
3. What do Hevajra's multiple limbs and faces seem to connote?
4. Consider Hevajra in the light of Shiva Nataraja (source 45). Do they seem to present the same or similar messages? If so, does that message have anything to do with nondualism?

5. Consider Arapacana. What does he appear to be doing? In answering this, consider his posture, his facial expression, his special sword, and the book that he holds.
6. Compare the three Bodhisattvas. What do their similarities and differences suggest about Mahayana beliefs and devotion?

Guanyin

Hevajra

Arapacana

Rabbinical Judaism

In 66 C.E. the Jews of Palestine broke out in general rebellion against Roman occupation, and it took the Roman armies seven bloody years to root out the last vestiges of insurgency. In the process, Jerusalem and its Temple were destroyed in the year 70. Again in 132 C.E. another Jewish revolt against Roman authority flared up, and when it was finally suppressed in 135, the rebuilt remnants of ancient Jerusalem had been transformed into a Roman military camp that was closed to Jewish habitation. Long before the destruction of the Temple and their sacred city, Jews had established prosperous communities throughout the Greco-Roman, Persian, and Arabic Worlds. After these two unsuccessful rebellions, however, the Jewish flight from Palestine reached the proportions of a folk migration. The Great Dispersion, or *Diaspora,* was underway. For nineteen hundred years, Jews would be strangers in a variety of foreign lands — a people without a homeland.

In spite of these travails, Judaism survived as a living faith and culture because wherever Jews settled, they remained faithful to the memory of their special Covenant with God and their dream of returning to the Promised Land. Moreover, despite its innate conservatism, born of a need to maintain contact with the ways of the past, Judaism continued to be flexible. Jews proved adaptable to a variety of alien settings, and over the centuries Judaism continued its historical development in response to the needs of its various scattered communities.

The primary agents responsible for cementing dispersed Jewish communities together and keeping alive Judaism's distinctive traditions were its religious teachers, or *rabbis.* The destruction of the Temple in Jerusalem occasioned a shift in religious emphasis and leadership. The old priesthood that had performed Temple sacrifices lost its primacy, giving way to rabbis, who presided over congregations that met to pray and study in *synagogues.* Unlike the priests of old, rabbis did not inherit their positions by virtue of their ancestry; they achieved prominence because of their reputations for piety and mastery of the Law. In the course of the first five centuries of the Common Era, rabbis, especially groups of them residing in Palestine and Babylon, articulated a vision of Judaism that recognized only prayer and righteous conduct as legitimate forms of communication with the Divine. There were no heavenly saviors and no magical rituals. This was to become the core of mainstream Judaism down to the present.

A Defense of the Law

▼▼▼

48 ▼ *Flavius Josephus, AGAINST APION*

Joseph ben Matthias (37 or 38–ca. 100), known to his Roman patrons as *Flavius Josephus,* is the most important eyewitness to the history of the Jewish people during the first century C.E. Born into a distinguished priestly family in Jerusalem, Josephus received a sound education in Jewish traditions and Greek culture. At the outbreak of the revolt against Roman occupation in 66 C.E., Josephus became leader of the Jewish forces in the north. Following an early defeat and capture at the hands of the Romans, Josephus went over to the enemy and became an advisor to two successive Roman generals, Vespasian and his son Titus. Vespasian became emperor in 69, leaving the final stages of the siege and capture of Jerusalem to Titus. Titus not only conquered and destroyed Jerusalem, he succeeded his father as emperor in 79. Following the war, Josephus was brought to

Rome, where he was granted citizenship, lodged in the private household of his imperial patron, and provided with a generous pension. It was in this setting that he wrote, in Greek, a history of the Jewish War, a work flattering to the Romans but one that also attempted to present a sympathetic account of Jewish suffering and heroism. Following Titus's death in 81, Josephus found another Roman patron and continued to write on Jewish history and tradition. His *Jewish Antiquities* traces the story of his people from creation to the eve of the rebellion. More so than his earlier work, the *Antiquities* clearly rests on the argument that Judaism deserves an honored place within the Greco-Roman Ecumene. Josephus's last work was a spirited defense of Judaism entitled *Against Apion*. Written in the last decade of the first century, the work answered the anti-Jewish slanders made by many Greco-Roman critics, especially an Alexandrian grammarian named *Apion*. In our excerpt, which appears at the end of his tract, Josephus expounds on the Law of Moses. That law is the body of religious regulations contained within the first five books of the Bible, books ascribed to the authorship of Moses and known collectively as the *Torah* (the Law).

QUESTIONS FOR ANALYSIS

1. How does Josephus compare the Law of Moses with Greek law and philosophy? What is his point? What is his apparent purpose?
2. What is his apparent reason for stating that Judaism is a *theocracy?*
3. According to Josephus, what role does the Law play in a Jew's life?
4. "Josephus compared the particularism of the Greeks with the universalism of the Jews, thereby implicitly arguing that Jews, more than Greeks, were true citizens of the Roman Commonwealth." Comment on and evaluate this statement.

Now, I maintain that our legislator[1] is the most ancient of all legislators in the record of the whole world. Compared with him, you Lycurguses[2] and Solons,[3] . . . and all who are held in such high esteem by the Greeks appear to have been born but yesterday. Why, the very word "law" was unknown in ancient Greece. Witness Homer, who nowhere employs it in his poems. In fact, there was no such thing in his day; the masses were governed by maxims not clearly defined and by the orders of royalty, and continued long afterwards the use of unwritten customs, many of which were from time to time altered to suit

particular circumstances. On the other hand, our legislator, who lived in the remotest past (that, I presume, is admitted even by our most unscrupulous detractors), proved himself the people's best guide and counselor; and after framing a code to embrace the whole conduct of their life, induced them to accept it, and secured, on the firmest footing, its observance for all time.

Let us consider his first magnificent achievement. When our ancestors decided to leave Egypt and return to their native land, it was he who took command of all those myriads and brought them safely through a host of formidable

---

[1]Moses (see Chapter 2, source 14).
[2]Lycurgus was the ninth-century B.C.E. lawgiver of Sparta.

[3]Solon (ca. 638–ca. 559 B.C.E.) was an Athenian constitutional reformer.

difficulties. . . . Throughout all this he proved the best of generals, the sagest of counselors, and the most conscientious of guardians. He succeeded in making the whole people dependent upon himself, and, having secured their obedience in all things, he did not use his influence for any personal aggrandizement. No; at the very moment when leading men assume absolute and despotic power and accustom their subject to a life of extreme lawlessness, he, on the contrary, having reached that commanding position, considered it incumbent on him to live piously and to provide for his people an abundance of good laws, in the belief that this was the best means of displaying his own virtue and of ensuring the lasting welfare of those who had made him their leader. With such noble aspirations and such a record of successful achievements, he had good reason for thinking that he had God for his guide and counselor. Having first persuaded himself that God's will governed all his actions and all his thoughts, he regarded it as his primary duty to impress that idea upon the community; for to those who believe that their lives are under the eye of God all sin is intolerable. Such was our legislator; no charlatan or imposter, as slanderers unjustly call him, but one such as the Greeks boast of having had in Minos[4] and later legislators. . . .

There is endless variety in the details of the customs and laws which prevail in the world at large. To give but a summary enumeration: some peoples have entrusted the supreme political power to monarchies, other to oligarchies,[5] yet others to the masses. Our lawgiver, however, was attracted by none of these forms of polity, but gave to his constitution the form of what — if a forced expression be permitted — may be termed a "theocracy," placing all sovereignty and authority in the hands of God. To Him he persuaded all to look, as the author of all blessings, both those which are common to all mankind, and those which they had won for themselves by prayer in the crises of their history. He convinced them that no single action, no secret thought, could be hid from Him. He represented Him as One, uncreated and immutable to all eternity; in beauty surpassing all mortal thought, made known to us by His power, although the nature of His real being passes knowledge.

That the wisest of the Greeks learned to adopt these conceptions of God from principles with which Moses supplied them, I am not now concerned to urge; but they have borne abundant witness to the excellence of these doctrines, and to their consonance with the nature and majesty of God. In fact, Pythagoras, Anaxagoras, Plato, the Stoics[6] who succeeded him, and indeed nearly all the philosophers appear to have held similar views concerning the nature of God. These, however, addressed their philosophy to the few, and did not venture to divulge their true beliefs to the masses who had their own preconceived opinions; whereas our lawgiver, by making practice square with precept, not only convinced his own contemporaries, but so firmly implanted his belief concerning God in their descendants to all future generations that it cannot be moved. The cause of his success was that the very nature of his legislation made it [always] far more useful than any other; for he did not make religion a department of virtue, but the various virtues — I mean, justice, temperance, fortitude, and mutual harmony in all things between the members of the community — departments of religion. Religion governs all our actions and occupations and speech; none of these things did our lawgiver leave unexamined or indeterminate.

All schemes of education and moral training fall into two categories; instruction is imparted in the one case by precept, in the other by practical exercising of the character. All other legis-

---

[4]A legendary king of Crete.
[5]Governments ruled by small factions.
[6]Pythagoras was a Greek philosopher and mathematician of the sixth century B.C.E. Anaxagoras (ca. 500–428 B.C.E.) was a Greek philosopher and astronomer. For Plato, see Chapter 4, source 30. The Stoics were a Hellenistic school of philosophy founded in Athens by Zeno (ca. 335–ca. 263 B.C.E.).

lators, differing in their opinions, selected the particular method which each preferred and neglected the other. Thus the Lacedaemonians[7] and Cretans employed practical, not verbal, training; whereas the Athenians and nearly all the rest of the Greeks made laws enjoining what actions might or might not be performed, but neglected to familiarize the people with them by putting them into practice.

Our legislator, on the other hand, took great care to combine both systems. He did not leave practical training in morals inarticulate; nor did he permit the letter of the law to remain inoperative. Starting from the very beginning with the food of which we partake from infancy and the private life of the home, he left nothing, however insignificant, to the discretion and caprice of the individual. What meats a man should abstain from, and what he may enjoy; with what persons he should associate; what period would be devoted respectively to strenuous labor and to rest — for all this our leader made the Law the standard and rule, that we might live under it as under a father and master, and be guilty of no sin through wilfulness or ignorance.

For ignorance he left no pretext. He appointed the Law to be the most excellent and necessary form of instruction, ordaining, not that it should be heard once for all or twice or on several occasions, but that every week men should desert their other occupations and assemble to listen to the Law and to obtain a thorough and accurate knowledge of it, a practice which all other legislators seem to have neglected. . . .

To this cause above all we owe our admirable harmony. Unity and identity of religious belief, perfect uniformity in habits and customs, produce a very beautiful concord in human character. Among us alone will be heard no contradictory statements about God, such as are common among other nations, not only on the lips of ordinary individuals under the impulse of some passing mood, but even boldly propounded by philosophers; some putting forward crushing arguments against the very existence of God, others depriving Him of His providential care for mankind. Among us alone will be seen no difference in the conduct of our lives. With us all act alike, all profess the same doctrine about God, one which is in harmony with our Law and affirms that all things are under His eye. Even our womenfolk and dependents would tell you that piety must be the motive of all our occupations in life. . . .

Our earliest imitators were the Greek philosophers, who, though ostensibly observing the laws of their own countries, yet in their conduct and philosophy were Moses' disciples, holding similar views about God, and advocating the simple life and friendly communion between man and man. But that is not all. The masses have long since shown a keen desire to adopt our religious observances; and there is not one city, Greek or barbarian, nor a single nation, to which our custom of abstaining from work on the seventh day has not spread, and where the fasts and the lighting of lamps and many of our prohibitions in the matter of food are not observed. Moreover, they attempt to imitate our unanimity, our liberal charities, our devoted labor in the crafts, our endurance under persecution on behalf of our laws. The greatest miracle of all is that our Law holds out no seductive bait of sensual pleasure,[8] but has exercised this influence through its own inherent merits; and, as God permeates the universe, so the Law has found its way among all mankind. Let each man reflect for himself on his own country and his own household, and he will not disbelieve what I say. It follows, then, that our accusers must either condemn the whole world for deliberate malice in being so eager to adopt the bad laws of a foreign country in preference to the good laws of their own, or else give up their grudge against us.

---

[7]The Spartans (see Chapter 4, source 28).

[8]Jews and Christians alleged that pagan religious festivals were occasions for drinking, excessive eating, and sexual license. There was quite a bit of truth to the charge.

A Commentary on the Law
▼▼▼

49 ▼ *THE BABYLONIAN TALMUD*

The *Talmud,* which means "Instruction" or "Learning," is a collection of post-biblical laws, customs, moral teachings, and edifying stories compiled in Palestine and Mesopotamia during the first six centuries of the Common Era. So far as Rabbinical Judaism is concerned, it is second in authority only to the Tanakh, or Bible. Indeed, the Talmud *is* Rabbinical Judaism, inasmuch as it preserves the oral law and traditions of the early synagogues, where learned sages interpreted the Law of Moses in ways that accorded with changing circumstances. Even more important, the Talmud became and remains the basis for interpretation of a living Law that regulates all aspects of Jewish life. Rather than being the final word on a legal question, the Talmud is the starting point for learned debate.

The Talmud consists of two major divisions. The *Mishnah* (Repetition or Study), which was edited around 200 C.E. in Palestine, is a compendium of rabbinical teachings regarding various aspects of the Law. The *Gemara* (Explanation or Teaching) is actually two different collections of commentaries on the Mishnah. An earlier, shorter, and less authoritative edition was completed in Palestine sometime before 400 C.E. A larger and richer edition was completed sometime before 600 C.E. in Babylonia, the Mesopotamian region of the Sassanid Empire. When combined with the Mishnah, the former is known as the *Palestinian Talmud,* and the latter is known as the *Babylonian Talmud.*

Our selection, which comes from the Babylonian Talmud, illustrates the type of debate that Talmudic scholars engaged in. The point of law under consideration here is the duty of every Jew to marry and raise a family. The Mishnah sets out the problem by first stating the traditional Jewish understanding of the obligation and its biblical foundation. It then informs the reader of the ways in which the two major schools of early rabbinical thought, the Beit Shammai and the Beit Hillel, interpreted the obligation. The Mishnah then presents a second traditional Jewish opinion regarding the duty of procreation and a commentary on that notion by Rabbi Yohanan ben Beroka, one of the early rabbinical sages. Following this comes the commentary of the Gemara.

QUESTIONS FOR ANALYSIS

1. Compare the Mishnah's citation of the opinions of the Beit Shammai and the Beit Hillel with those of the Gemara. What do your findings suggest about the nature of Talmudic law?
2. The Beit Shammai and the Beit Hillel were two sometimes rival schools of Talmudic thought. One was considered more pragmatic and liberal than the other. Which was which?

3. The Gemara cites Rabbi Joshua's opinion, with which the Mishnah does not agree. Why do you think it included Rabbi Joshua's view? What does your answer suggest about the nature and purpose of the Gemara?
4. Note the aphorisms, or proverbs, that suddenly appear in the midst of the Gemara as apparent non sequiturs (e.g., "Do not be aggrieved . . ."). What do they suggest about this collection?
5. What does the story of Ben Azzai suggest, and why do you think it was preserved?
6. Note how these rabbis cite scripture to support their arguments. What does this suggest about their view of the Bible and their use of it?
7. What is the main weight of opinion regarding marriage and procreation, and what does this suggest about Judaism?

A person should not abstain from carrying out the obligation to "be fruitful and multiply"[1] unless he already has two children. The Beit Shammai[2] ruled: This means two sons, and the Beit Hillel[3] ruled: A son and a daughter, because it is written: "Male and female He created them."[4] The duty of procreation applies to a man, but not to a woman. R. Yohanan b. Beroka said: Concerning both it is written: "And God blessed them and said to them: Be fruitful and multiply."[5]

MISHNAH

This means that if he has children he may abstain from the duty of procreation but he may not abstain from the duty of living with a wife. This supports the view of R. Nahman who reported a ruling in the name of Samuel,[6] that even though a person has many children, he may not remain without a wife, as it is written: "It is not good for a man to be alone."[7] Others held the view that if he had children, he may abstain from the duty of procreation and he may also abstain from the duty of living with a wife. Shall we say that this contradicts what was reported by R. Nahman in the name of Samuel? No. If he has no children, he is to marry a woman capable of

having a child, but if he already has children, he may marry a woman who is incapable of having children.

Elsewhere it was taught: R. Nathan said: According to the Beit Shammai, a person satisfies the obligation to "be fruitful and multiply" if he has a son and a daughter, and according to the Beit Hillel if he has a son or a daughter. Said Rava: What is the reason for the view of the Beit Hillel? It is written: "He created it not to be a waste, He formed it to be inhabited,"[8] and [by having a son or a daughter] he has already contributed to making it a place of habitation.

It was stated: If a person had children while he was an idolator, and was later converted [to Judaism], R. Yohanan said that he has already fulfilled the duty of procreation but Resh Lakish said that he has not fulfilled it, because when a person is converted he is like a born-again child.

The Mishnah does not agree with the view of R. Joshua, for it was taught that R. Joshua stated: If a person married in his youth he is also to marry in his old age; if he had children in his youth, he is also to have children in his old age, for it is written: "Sow your seed in the morning and do not withdraw your hand in the evening, for you

---

[1]The Bible, Genesis, 1:28.
[2]Literally, "the house of Shammai." This is a reference to the school that followed the teachings of Rabbi Shammai, a teacher who lived at the turn of the millennium — the late first century B.C.E. and the early first century C.E.
[3]Along with Shammai, Hillel (ca. 70 B.C.E.–ca. 10 C.E.) was the dominant interpreter of the Torah, or Law, of his day. Like Shammai, he had his school of followers.
[4]The Bible, Genesis, 5:2.
[5]The Bible, Genesis, 1:28.
[6]A prophet of the eleventh century B.C.E. Citing Samuel as the source gives the opinion greater authority.
[7]The Bible, Genesis, 2:18.
[8]The Bible, Isaiah, 45:18.

do not know which will prosper, this or that, or whether both alike will be good."[9]

Said R. Tanhum in the name of R. Hanilai: A person who is without a wife is without joy, without blessing, without good. Without joy — as it is written: "You shall rejoice, you and your household";[10] without blessing — as it is written: "That a blessing may rest on your house"[11] ["house" in such a context has generally been interpreted to mean one's wife]; without good — as it is written: "It is not good for a man to be alone."[12] In Palestine they said: He is without Torah,[13] and without protection [from the ravages of life]. Without Torah — as it is written: "In truth, I have no one to help me [a wife], and sound wisdom [Torah] is driven from me";[14] without protection — as it is written: "A woman protects a man."[15] R. b. Ila said: He is without peace — as it is written: "And you shall know that your tent [when presided over by one's wife] is at peace, and you will visit your habitation and you will not sin."[16]

Said R. Joshua b. Levi: A person who knows his wife to be a God-fearing woman and he does not have marital relations with her is a sinner, as it is written: "And you shall visit your habitation [a euphemism for having relations with one's wife] and you will not sin."

The rabbis taught: When one loves his wife as himself, and honors her more than himself, and trains his sons and daughters in the right path and arranges for their marriage at a young age — concerning such a person does the verse say: "And you shall know that your tent is at peace."

Said R. Eleazar: A man without a wife is not a complete man, as it is written: "Male and female created He them, and He called their name *adam,* 'man.'"[17]

Turn away your eyes from the charms of another man's wife, lest you be trapped in her net. Do not join in fellowship with her husband, to drink with him wine and strong drink, for through the appearance of a beautiful woman have many been destroyed, and a mighty host are all her slain.

Do not be aggrieved about tomorrow's troubles for you do not know what a day will bring forth. Tomorrow may come, and you may be no more. You will thus have worried about a world that is not yours.

Keep away multitudes from your house, do not bring everyone to your house.

Many are well-wishers, but disclose your secret only to one in a thousand.

It was taught: R. Eliezer said: A person who does not share in propagating the race is as though he were guilty of bloodshed, for it is written: "Whoever sheds the blood of a person, by man shall his blood be shed,"[18] and following this is the verse "and you be fruitful and multiply."[19] R. Jacob said: It is as though he diminished the divine image, for it is written: "For in the image of God He made man."[20] Ben Azzai said: It is as though he shed blood, and diminished the divine image, for after both the reference to bloodshed and the divine we have the admonition: "And you be fruitful and multiply." They said to Ben Azzai [who was unmarried]: Some preach well and practice well, some act well but do not preach well, but you preach well but do not act well. Ben Azzai answered them: What can I do, I am addicted to the study of the Torah. The continuity of the world can be assured through others.

Other Sages say: He causes the divine presence to depart from Israel. Thus it is written: "[I will keep my covenant] to be God to you and to your descendants after you."[21] When there are descendants after you, the divine presence will be with them, but when there are not descendants after you, with whom will the divine presence be? With sticks and stones?

[9]The Bible, Ecclesiastes, 11:6.
[10]The Bible, Deuteronomy, 14:26.
[11]The Bible, Ezekiel, 44:30.
[12]The Bible, Genesis, 2:18.
[13]The Law, the first five books of the Bible ascribed to Moses' authorship (see source 48).
[14]The Bible, Job, 6:13.
[15]The Bible, Jeremiah, 31:22.
[16]The Bible, Job, 5:24.
[17]The Bible, Genesis, 5:2.
[18]The Bible, Genesis, 9:6.
[19]The Bible, Genesis, 9:7.
[20]The Bible, Genesis, 9:7.
[21]The Bible, Genesis, 17:7.

Chapter 7

▼▼▼

Christianity

Conquering the World for Christ

Mainstream Jewish thought perceived no meaningful distinction between church and state because Judaism's special Covenant with God bound it body and soul to the Lord of the universe. Jews therefore believed that, as God's people, they had been given a sanctified homeland. When they were dispossessed of that inheritance and scattered among the gentiles, they believed it was because of their sins. They further believed that should they reform their ways and fully observe their holy Covenant with God, they would regain sovereign possession of Palestine. By right, this Holy Land and its Chosen People should be ruled according to the Law given them by God through Moses and interpreted by their rabbis (Chapter 6, sources 48–49).

Not all Jewish sects, however, accepted this interpretation of the Covenant. One such dissident element was a small body of religious Jews who gathered around a prophet from Nazareth called *Joshua* or, in Greek, *Jesus* (ca. 4 B.C.E.–ca. 30 C.E.). The heart of Jesus' message was that the promised messianic Kingdom of God was at hand. The *Messiah* (the anointed one) — God's deliverer, whose coming the prophets had foretold — was generally expected to be a political and military leader who would reestablish Israel as a free state. Jesus, to the contrary, expanding upon certain themes in the teachings of Second Isaiah (Chapter 3, source 22), preached that the Messiah would usher in a spiritual age of universal judgment and redemption, whereby God's holy reign would extend to all lands and peoples.

As his ministry developed, Jesus became convinced he was the Messiah. Although he claimed "My kingdom is not of this earth," local Roman and Jewish authorities were disquieted by the threat to the establishment that Jesus and his followers seemed to offer, and they conspired successfully to execute him by crucifixion. Jesus' followers believed, however, that he rose from the dead, appeared to a number of his friends, and then ascended to Heaven with the promise of returning soon to sit in judgment of all humanity. Believing that his resurrection proved Jesus' messiahship, his disciples proceeded to spread the *Gospel* (Good News) of redemption.

At first these disciples preached only to Palestinian Jews. Within a short time, however, they spread the faith throughout the entire Roman Empire and beyond, welcoming both Jew and gentile to receive the New Covenant proclaimed by Jesus. Before the end of the first century C.E., *Christians* (called so because of Jesus' title *Christos,* which is Greek for *Messiah*) had established the faith in every major city of the Roman Empire and had penetrated the Parthian Empire, non-Roman Africa, Arabia, and the west coast of India. In the early fourth century Christianity was adopted as the state religion of the Axumite Kingdom of Ethiopia, became the favored religion of the Roman Emperor Constantine I (r. 306–337), and took root among a number of German tribes beyond the northeast frontiers of the Roman Empire. In the seventh century a group of dissident Christians known as *Nestorians* established themselves in western China. This otherworldly faith was waging a successful campaign of spiritual conquest in a fair portion of the Afro-Eurasian World.

▼▼▼

The Foundations of Christianity

In the course of Christianity's first century of existence, its followers had to define the religion to which they gave their allegiance. Just as important, they had to confront the issue of what Christianity was not: Were they Jews? Were they members of some new mystery religion? Were they something else? If something else, what set their religion apart from Judaism and all of the other religions that flourished within the Greco-Roman World? In essence, what did they believe, and how should they organize themselves?

In resolving these issues, Christians had the guidance of several great teachers. First and foremost, of course, was Jesus himself. His call for spiritual perfection was the foundation of the Christian faith and has remained so for almost two thousand years. Following Jesus' departure from the world, his followers had to grapple with many still unresolved questions: Who was Jesus? What was his relationship with God and humanity? What was the nature of the community he had left behind? Among the many leaders who tried to answer these questions, none was more influential than Paul of Tarsus, who laid down the basic theological framework for this emerging church.

Becoming Spiritually Perfect
▼▼▼

50 ▼ *THE GOSPEL OF ST. MATTHEW*

Tradition ascribes authorship of the Gospels, the four major accounts of Jesus of Nazareth's life and teachings, to authors known as Matthew, Mark, Luke, and John. The early Christian Church believed that Matthew had been one of Jesus' twelve *apostles,* or major companions, and accepted his Gospel as the authoritative remembrances of a divinely inspired author. Modern scholarship dates the work to the period around 85 or 90 C.E., or approximately fifty-five to sixty years after Jesus' ministry. Its author appears to have been a Christian of Antioch in Syria and possibly a disciple of the Apostle Matthew but probably not the apostle himself. The author clearly was trained in the Jewish rabbinical tradition but was equally comfortable with the Greek language and Hellenistic culture, and he seems to have addressed his Gospel to a cosmopolitan Christian community made up of former Jews and gentiles.

The central theme of the Gospel of Matthew is that Jesus is the Messiah, the fulfillment of the promises made by God through Abraham, Moses, and the prophets. More than that, as the promised Messiah, Jesus is the Son of God. For Matthew, Second Isaiah was the greatest of the prophets, the one who had most clearly foretold Jesus' mission of salvation and who had preached that the universal reign of the Lord was imminent (Chapter 3, source 22). In the following selection Matthew presents what is commonly known as the *Sermon on the Mount.* Here Jesus instructs his followers about what the Kingdom of God requires of all its members. In all likelihood, what Matthew presents is not a verbatim account of a specific sermon that Jesus delivered on some mountainside but a distillation of Jesus' core moral and theological teachings. As you read this excerpt, keep in mind that Jesus lived in the environment that produced Rabbinical Judaism and was himself considered a rabbi, or teacher.

QUESTIONS FOR ANALYSIS

1. Jesus establishes priorities for his followers. What are they?
2. In what ways does Jesus emphasize the spiritual relationship of each believer to God?
3. How does Jesus regard Judaism and especially the Law of Moses? In what ways does he claim that his teachings complete, or perfect, the Law of Moses?
4. What does Matthew mean when he states that Jesus taught with authority and was not like the scribes? Why does Jesus question the authority of the scribes and Pharisees? What is the presumed basis of Jesus' authority?
5. To whom would Jesus' message especially appeal? Why?
6. Compare the message and spirit behind the Sermon on the Mount with that of the Buddha's First Sermon on the Law (Chapter 3, source 19). Which

strike you as more pronounced, their differences or similarities? What do you conclude from your answer?

Seeing the crowds, he went up on the mountain, and when he sat down his disciples came to him. And he opened his mouth and taught them, saying:

"Blessed are the poor in spirit, for theirs is the kingdom of heaven.

"Blessed are those who mourn, for they shall be comforted.

"Blessed are the meek, for they shall inherit the earth.

"Blessed are those who hunger and thirst for righteousness, for they shall be satisfied.

"Blessed are the merciful, for they shall obtain mercy.

"Blessed are the pure in heart, for they shall see God.

"Blessed are the peacemakers, for they shall be called sons of God.

"Blessed are those who are persecuted for righteousness' sake, for theirs is the kingdom of Heaven.

"Blessed are you when men revile you and persecute you and utter all kinds of evil against you falsely on my account. Rejoice and be glad, for your reward is great in Heaven, for so men persecuted the prophets who were before you. . . .

"Think not that I have come to abolish the law and the prophets; I have come not to abolish them but to fulfill them. For truly, I say to you, till Heaven and earth pass away, not an iota, not a dot, will pass from the law until all is accomplished. Whoever then relaxes one of the least of these commandments and teaches men so, shall be called least in the kingdom of Heaven; but he who does them and teaches them shall be called great in the kingdom of Heaven. For I tell you, unless your righteousness exceeds that of the scribes and the Pharisees,[1] you will never enter the kingdom of Heaven.

"You have heard that it was said to the men of old, 'You shall not kill; and whoever kills shall be liable to judgment.' But I say to you that every one who is angry with his brother shall be liable to judgment; whoever insults his brother shall be liable to the council,[2] and whoever says, 'You fool!' shall be liable to the hell of fire. So if you are offering your gift at the altar, and there remember that your brother has something against you, leave your gift there before the altar and go; first be reconciled to your brother, and then come and offer your gift. . . . You have heard that it was said, 'An eye for an eye and a tooth for a tooth.' But I say to you, Do not resist one who is evil. But if any one strikes you on the right cheek, turn to him the other also. . . . You have heard that it was said, 'You shall love your neighbor and hate your enemy.' But I say to you, Love your enemies and pray for those who persecute you, so that you may be sons of your Father who is in Heaven; for he makes his sun rise on the evil and on the good, and sends rain on the just and on the unjust. For if you love those who love you, what reward have you? . . . You, therefore, must be perfect, as your heavenly Father is perfect. . . .

---

[1]The scribes were nonpriestly professionals who copied, interpreted, and applied the oral traditions that supplemented written biblical Law. The Pharisees were members of a Jewish religious party who stressed that all of this nonscriptural, oral law had to be observed as equally and as fully as the written Law of Moses. Rabbinical Judaism largely sprang out of the scribal and pharisaical traditions. For example, Shammai and Hillel were both Pharisees (Chapter 6, source 49).

[2]The Sanhedrin, Judaism's chief religious and judicial body.

"And in praying do not heap up empty phrases as the Gentiles do; for they think that they will be heard for their many words. Do not be like them, for your Father knows what you need before you ask him. Pray then like this:

Our Father who art in Heaven.
Hallowed be thy name.
Thy kingdom come,
Thy will be done,
    On earth as it is in Heaven.
Give us this day our daily bread;
And forgive us our debts,
    As we also have forgiven our debtors
And lead us not into temptation,
    But deliver us from evil.

For if you forgive men their trespasses, your heavenly Father also will forgive you; but if you do not forgive men their trespasses, neither will your Father forgive your trespasses. . . .

"Do not lay up for yourselves treasures on earth, where moth and rust consume and where thieves break in and steal, but lay up for yourselves treasures in Heaven, where neither moth nor rust consumes and where thieves do not break in and steal. For where your treasure is, there will your heart be also. . . . Therefore do not be anxious, saying, 'What shall we eat?' or 'What shall we drink?' or 'What shall we wear?' For the Gentiles seek all these things; and your heavenly Father knows that you need them all. But seek first his kingdom and his righteousness, and all these things shall be yours as well. . . .

"Judge not, that you be not judged. For with the judgment you pronounce you will be judged, and the measure you give will be the measure you get. . . .

And when Jesus finished these sayings, the crowds were astonished at his teaching, for he taught them as one who had authority, and not as their scribes.

The Path to Righteousness: The Law or Faith?

▼▼▼

51 ▾ St. Paul, *THE EPISTLE TO THE ROMANS*

Our earliest Christian sources are not the Gospels but rather the *epistles,* or letters, that St. Paul (ca. 3 B.C.E.–64 or 67 C.E.) wrote to a number of Christian communities. Paul, or to give him his Hebrew name, *Saul,* was a Hellenized Jew and rabbinical scholar from Tarsus in Asia Minor who has often been called *the second founder of Christianity.* Prior to his becoming a Christian, Paul was a member of the Jewish elite of the eastern Mediterranean. A Roman citizen, which was rare for Jews of his day, he studied under the leading pharisaical rabbi of his day, became a noted Pharisee himself, and probably was elevated to membership in the Sanhedrin, Judaism's supreme religious and judicial body. Converted dramatically to Christianity by a blinding revelation while traveling to Damascus in Syria in the pursuit of Christians whom he was persecuting, Paul became the leading opponent of certain Christian conservatives who wished to keep Christianity within the boundaries of Judaism. From roughly 47 to his death in Rome in either 64 or 67 (ancient authorities differ on the date), Paul was an indefatigable missionary, converting gentiles and Jews alike throughout the Mediterranean region. Most important of all, Paul transformed Jesus' messianic message into a faith centering on Jesus as Lord and Savior.

Paul developed his distinctive theology in his epistles, his only extant writings. Although each epistle was addressed to a specific group of Christians and often dealt with local issues, they were revered as authoritative pronouncements of general interest for all believers. As a result, copies were circulated, and in time some of his letters (as well as some Paul never composed but that were ascribed to him) were incorporated into the body of scriptural books known to Christians as the *New Testament* (the *Old Testament* being the pre-Christian, or Jewish, portion of the Bible).

Around the year 57, probably while residing in Corinth, Greece, Paul planned to establish a mission in Spain and decided to make Rome his base of operations. In preparation, he wrote to the Christians at Rome to inform them of his plans and to instruct them in the faith. The result was the *Epistle to the Romans,* the most fully articulated expression of Paul's theology of salvation.

QUESTIONS FOR ANALYSIS

1. According to Paul, who was Jesus?
2. This epistle centers on the issue of how one becomes righteous in the eyes of God. What role does faith play in putting one right with God? Faith in what or whom?
3. According to Paul, the former Pharisee and member of the Sanhedrin, can the Law of Moses or any other body of law put one right with God? Why or why not?
4. For Paul, what two virtues, or qualities, must dominate a Christian's life?
5. What do you infer from the evidence about the role of women in the early Church?
6. Like Second Isaiah (Chapter 3, source 22), Paul believes that God has a master plan for all humanity. How does Paul's understanding of that plan differ from that of his sixth-century B.C.E. predecessor?
7. Compare this epistle with the Sermon on the Mount. Do they agree, disagree, or complement one another?
8. What parallels can you discover between Christian devotion to Jesus, as taught by Paul, and similar contemporary forms of piety and belief in the Hindu and Buddhist traditions? In answering this question, consider the sources in Chapter 6.

Paul, a servant of Jesus Christ, called to be an apostle,[1] set apart for the Gospel of God which he promised beforehand through his prophets in the holy scriptures, the Gospel concerning his Son, who was descended from David[2] according to the flesh and designated Son of God in power according to the Spirit of holiness by his resurrection from the dead, Jesus Christ our Lord, through whom we have received grace and apostleship to bring about obedience to the faith

---

[1] Paul was not one of the original twelve apostles, Jesus' closest companions. He claimed apostolic status because he believed he had been miraculously called and converted by the Risen Christ, who appeared to him in a vision.

[2] The prophetic tradition maintained that the Messiah would be descended from the line of King David, Israel's greatest monarch, who flourished around 1000 B.C.E. Consequently, Christian Jews stressed Jesus' Davidic lineage.

for the sake of his name among all the nations, including yourselves who are called to belong to Jesus Christ;

To all God's beloved in Rome, who are called to be saints: . . . I am eager to preach the Gospel to you also who are in Rome.

For I am not ashamed of the Gospel: it is the power of God for salvation to every one who has faith, to the Jew first and also to the Greek.[3] For in it the righteousness of God is revealed through faith for faith; as it is written, "He who through faith is righteous shall live." . . . For we hold that a man is justified[4] by faith apart from works of law.[5] Or is God the God of Jews only? Is he not the God of gentiles also? Yes, of gentiles also, since God is one; and he will justify the circumcised[6] on the ground of their faith and the uncircumcised because of their faith. . . . The promise to Abraham[7] and his descendants, that they should inherit the world, did not come through the Law but through the righteousness of faith. If it is the adherents of the Law who are to be the heirs, faith is null and the promise is void. . . . That is why it depends on faith, in order that the promise may rest on grace and be guaranteed to all his descendants — not only to the adherents of the law but also to those who share the faith of Abraham, for he is the father of us all, as it is written, "I have made you the father of many nations." . . .

Therefore, since we are justified by faith, we have peace with God through our Lord Jesus Christ. Through him we have obtained access to this grace in which we stand, and we rejoice in our hope of sharing the glory of God. . . . God shows his love for us in that while we were yet sinners Christ died for us. Since, therefore, we are now justified by his blood, much more shall we be saved by him from the wrath of God. For if while we were enemies we were reconciled to God by the death of his Son, much more, now that we are reconciled, shall we be saved by his life. . . . There is therefore now no condemnation for those who are in Christ Jesus. For the law of the Spirit of life in Christ Jesus has set me free from the law of sin and death. . . .

If you confess with your lips that Jesus is Lord and believe in your heart that God raised him from the dead, you will be saved. For man believes with his heart and so is justified, and he confesses with his lips and so is saved. The scripture says, "No one who believes in him will be put to shame." For there is no distinction between Jew and Greek; the same Lord is Lord of all and bestows his riches upon all who call upon him. For, "every one who calls upon the name of the Lord will be saved." . . .

I appeal to you therefore, brethren, by the mercies of God, to present your bodies as a living sacrifice, holy and acceptable to God, which is your spiritual worship. . . . Let love be genuine; hate what is evil, hold fast to what is good; love one another with brotherly affection; outdo one another in showing honor. Never flag in zeal, be aglow with the Spirit, serve the Lord. Rejoice in your hope, be patient in tribulation, be constant in prayer. Contribute to the needs of the saints, practice hospitality.

Bless those who persecute you; bless and do not curse them. Rejoice with those who rejoice, weep with those who weep. Live in harmony with one another; do not be haughty, but associate with the lowly; never be conceited. Repay no one evil for evil, but take thought for what is noble in the sight of all. If possible, so far as it depends upon you, live peaceably with all. Beloved, never avenge yourselves, but leave it to the wrath of God; for it is written, "Vengeance is mine, I will repay, says the Lord." No, "if your enemy is hungry, feed him; if he is thirsty, give him drink; for

---

[3]*Greek* means any non-Jew, or gentile, because Greek was the common tongue of educated people in the eastern half of the Roman Empire.
[4]Made just, or righteous, in the eyes of God.
[5]The Law of Judaism.

[6]The Law of Moses prescribes circumcision for all Jewish males; gentiles are, therefore, the *uncircumcised.*
[7]The ancient patriarch from whom all Jews were descended and with whom YHWH entered into a covenant.

by so doing you will heap burning coals upon his head." Do not be overcome by evil, but overcome evil with good. . . .

Owe no one anything, except to love one another; for he who loves his neighbor has fulfilled the Law. The commandments, "You shall not commit adultery, You shall not kill, You shall not steal, You shall not covet," and any other commandment, are summed up in this sentence, "You shall love your neighbor as yourself." Love does no wrong to a neighbor; therefore love is the fulfilling of the Law. . . .

I commend to you to our sister Phoebe, a deaconess of the church at Cenchreae,[8] that you may receive her in the Lord as befits the saints, and help her in whatever she may require from you, for she has been a helper of many and of myself as well.

Greet Prisca and Aquila,[9] my fellow workers in Christ Jesus, who risked their necks for my life, to whom not only I but also all the churches of the gentiles give thanks; greet also the church in their house.

---

[8]A community in the Greek Peloponnesus. *Deaconesses* and their male counterparts, *deacons,* were assistants to the *presbyters* (elders). Their duties consisted of baptizing, preaching, and dispensing charity.

[9]A married couple of Jewish-Christians from Asia Minor who figured prominently in the Church of Rome. Prisca was the wife; Aquila, the husband.

▼▼▼

Christianity and the Roman World

Roman authorities were generally tolerant of the diverse deities and religious practices of the empire's subjects. Normally all they required was that the various cults and their devotees not manifestly threaten public order and morality and that each religion help guarantee the gods' continued favor toward the state. Yet as far as many Romans were concerned, Christians violated those basic requirements because of their uncompromising monotheism and extreme sense of exclusivity.

Unyielding adherence to the Christian religion became a crime, at least theoretically punishable by death, from the age of Emperor Nero (r. 54–68) onward. Despite this, persecution of Christians was sporadic, local, and often halfhearted for almost the next two centuries. When persecutions occurred before the mid third century, it was usually only when provincial governors found themselves forced to bow to local sentiment in order to keep a discontented populace quiet. Crop failures and other natural disasters often seemed to demand a few Christian victims as propitiation to the gods. This changed in the year 250, when Emperor Decius embarked on a short but bitter empirewide attack on Christians.

In 303 the empire launched its last and greatest persecution of Christianity; the attack continued until 311, when Emperor Galerius, in the grips of a frightening disease, decided to strike a bargain with the Christian god. His edict of toleration granted Christians freedom of worship in exchange for their prayers for him. A few days after issuing the edict, Galerius was dead.

The following year, Constantine, a claimant to the imperial throne, was campaigning in Italy against a rival. According to one Christian author, on the eve of battle Constantine had a vision bidding him to put on his soldiers' shields the

Greek characters *Chi* (χ) and *Rho* (ρ), an ancient symbol of victory and the emblem of the Unconquered Sun, Constantine's favorite god. To Christians, however, this was Christ's monogram, representing as it did the first two letters of the Greek word *Christos* — Christ. Constantine obeyed his vision, and shortly thereafter he won a decisive victory, thereby becoming uncontested emperor in the West. For whatever reason, Emperor Constantine I (r. 306–337) ascribed his victory to Jesus Christ. In 313 he and his coemperor met at Milan, in northern Italy, and there reached an agreement regarding freedom of worship for all persons in the empire and recognition of the full legal status of each local Christian church. Christianity had weathered the storm of Roman persecution.

After the meeting at Milan, Constantine never wavered in his patronage of Christianity, and the consequences were momentous for both the empire and Christianity. A faith that commanded the belief of only about ten percent of the empire's population in 313 was, by century's end, the religion of the vast majority of city dwellers in the eastern Mediterranean, and it was making rapid advances among the region's rural populations. In the western half of the empire the progress of conversion was slower but steady.

Persecution and Deliverance
▼▼▼

52 ▼ *Eusebius of Caesarea,* ECCLESIASTICAL HISTORY

Eusebius (ca. 260–339 or 340), leader, or *bishop,* of the church of Caesarea in Palestine, was a prolific writer. His single most enduring work is his *Ecclesiastical History,* which traces the fortunes of the Christian Church from its earliest days to the early fourth century. This history has rightly earned Eusebius the title *Father of Church history,* inasmuch as it is the most complete and coherent account that we possess of the early Church's first three centuries.

Eusebius's careful scholarship, however, did not negate the *Ecclesiastical History*'s apologetical tone and theological message. Within its pages history is a cosmic contest between the forces of God and those of the Devil. On the one side are the patriarchs, prophets, and saints; on the other are the pagans, persecutors, latter-day Jews, and *heretical,* or wrong-believing, Christians. Although the Devil and his minions always lose, the righteous suffer considerably as they struggle against evil.

More than simply a scholar, Eusebius was active in the affairs of the early fourth-century Church and suffered in the process. He had been imprisoned during the era of the Great Persecution (303–311) and had seen many of his friends tortured and martyred. But he also lived to see the miracle of the Emperor Constantine's conversion to Christianity after the emperor's victory in 312. Following Eusebius's elevation to the bishopric of Caesarea around 313, this church leader came to enjoy the Christian emperor's patronage and friendship.

Earlier, before the onslaught of the Great Persecution, Eusebius had begun a detailed history of the Church down to his own day, completing the work in seven volumes around 303. The events of 312 and following, however, necessitated that he update his work. Consequently, he enlarged the *Ecclesiastical History* to ten books in order to include the history of Christian fortunes down to 324, thereby demonstrating the manner in which Divine Providence had once again triumphed over the forces of evil.

Our excerpts come from Book 5, an appendix to Book 8 entitled "The Martyrs of Palestine," and Book 10. Note the significant differences in tone and message between the first two excerpts and the third, which deals with Constantine's victory in 324 over Licinius, his former coemperor.

QUESTIONS FOR ANALYSIS

1. How did Eusebius distinguish between the history that he wrote and the history that pagan Greeks and Romans wrote? Why did he make the distinction?
2. Consider the second excerpt. Why do you think Eusebius dwells on the punishments that Christian confessors bore?
3. What does his description of the heroism of the two female martyrs suggest about Christian notions of the place of women in the Church?
4. Compare your answer to question 3 with your answer to question 5 of source 51. What conclusions do you reach?
5. How does Eusebius's treatment of the conflict between Constantine and Licinius appear to contradict the message of the first excerpt? Does it really? If not, why not?
6. Is there a new tone in this third excerpt? If so, what is it?
7. Does the third excerpt seem to hold out any promises? If so, what are they?
8. What do you imagine might be the historical ramifications of this new Christian imperial system? Reconsider your answer after you have studied sources 53 and 54.

Other writers of history record the victories of war and trophies won from enemies, the skill of generals, and the manly bravery of soldiers, defiled with blood and with innumerable slaughters for the sake of children and country and other possessions. But our narrative of the government of God will record in ineffaceable letters the most peaceful wars waged in behalf of the peace of the soul, and will tell of men doing brave deeds for truth rather than country, and for piety rather than dearest friends. It will hand down to imperishable remembrance the discipline and the much-tried fortitude of the athletes of religion, the trophies won from demons, the victories over invisible enemies, and the crowns placed upon their heads.

▼ ▼ ▼

Up to the sixth year[1] the storm had been incessantly raging against us. Before this time there had been a very large number of confessors[2] of religion in the so-called Porphyry quarry in

---

[1] The sixth year of the persecution, which began in the spring of 303.

[2] Those who confess, or proclaim and live, the faith in a heroic manner.

Thebais,[3] which gets its name from the stone found there.[4] Of these, one hundred men, lacking three, together with women and infants, were sent to the governor of Palestine. When they confessed the God of the universe and Christ, Firmilianus, who had been sent there as a governor in the place of Urbanus, directed, in accordance with the imperial command, that they should be maimed by burning the sinews of the ankles of their left feet, and that their right eyes with the eyelids and pupils should first be cut out, and then destroyed by hot irons to the very roots. And he then sent them to the mines in the province to endure hardships with severe toil and suffering.

But it was not sufficient that these only who suffered such miseries should be deprived of their eyes, but those natives of Palestine also, who were mentioned just above as condemned to pugilistic combat,[5] since they would neither receive food from the royal storehouse nor undergo the necessary preparatory exercises. Having been brought on this account not only before the overseers, but also before Maximinus himself,[6] and having manifested the noblest persistence in confession by the endurance of hunger and stripes, they received like punishment with those whom we have mentioned, and with them other confessors in the city of Caesarea. Immediately afterwards others who were gathered to hear the Scriptures read, were seized in Gaza,[7] and some endured the same sufferings in the feet and eyes; but others were afflicted with yet greater torments and with most terrible tortures in the sides. One of these, in body a woman, but in understanding a man, would not endure the threat of rape, and spoke directly against the tyrant who entrusted the government to such cruel judges. She was first scourged and then raised aloft on the stake, and her sides lacerated. As those appointed for this purpose applied the tortures incessantly and severely at the command of the judge, another, with mind fixed, like the former, on virginity as her aim, — a woman who was altogether mean in form and contemptible in appearance, but, on the other hand, strong in soul, and endowed with an understanding superior to her body, — being unable to bear the merciless and cruel and inhuman deeds, with a boldness beyond that of the combatants famed among the Greeks,[8] cried out to the judge from the midst of the crowd: "And how long will you thus cruelly torture my sister?" But he was greatly enraged and ordered the woman to be immediately seized. Thereupon she was brought forward and having called herself by the august name of the Savior, she was first urged by words to sacrifice, and as she refused she was dragged by force to the altar. But her sister continued to maintain her former zeal, and with intrepid and resolute foot kicked the altar, and overturned it with the fire that was on it. Thereupon the judge, enraged like a wild beast, inflicted on her such tortures in her sides as he never had on any one before, striving almost to glut himself with her raw flesh. But when his madness was satiated, he bound them both together, this one and her whom she called sister, and condemned them to death by fire. It is said that the first of these was from the country of Gaza; the other, by name Valentina, was of Caesarea, and was well known to many.

▼ ▼ ▼

Thanks for all things be given unto God the Omnipotent Ruler and King of the universe, and the greatest thanks to Jesus Christ the Savior and Redeemer of our souls, through whom we pray that peace may be always preserved for us firm and undisturbed by external troubles and

---

[3]The region around Thebes in Egypt.
[4]Slave labor in stone quarries and mines, which usually ended in death, was a common criminal penalty.
[5]They were condemned to fight as boxing gladiators in the circus.
[6]Maximin Daia, emperor in the East from 305 to 313.
[7]The southern coastal region of Palestine.
[8]Professional wrestlers and boxers (see Chapter 5, source 31).

troubles of the mind. Since in accordance with your wishes, my most holy Paulinus,[9] we have added the tenth book of the Church History to those which have preceded, we will inscribe it to you, proclaiming you as the seal of the whole work; and we will fitly add in a perfect number[10] the perfect panegyric upon the restoration of the churches, obeying the Divine Spirit which exhorts us in the following words: "Sing unto the Lord a new song, for he hath done marvelous things. His right hand and his holy arm hath saved him. The Lord hath made known his salvation, his righteousness hath he revealed in the presence of the nations."[11] And in accordance with the utterance which commands us to sing the new song, let us proceed to show that, after those terrible and gloomy spectacles which we have described, we are now permitted to see and celebrate such things as many truly righteous men and martyrs of God before us desired to see upon earth and did not see, and to hear and did not hear. But they, hastening on, obtained far better things, being carried to Heaven and the paradise of divine pleasure. But, acknowledging that even these things are greater than we deserve, we have been astonished at the grace manifested by the author of the great gifts, and rightly do we admire him, worshiping him with the whole power of our souls, and testifying to the truth of those recorded utterances, in which it is said, "Come and see the works of the Lord, the wonders which he hath done upon the earth; he removeth wars to the ends of the world, he shall break the bow and snap the spear in sunder, and shall burn the shields with fire."[12] Rejoicing in these things which have been clearly fulfilled in our day, let us proceed with our account.

The whole race of God's enemies was destroyed in the manner indicated, and was thus suddenly swept from the sight of men. So that again a divine utterance had its fulfillment: "I have seen the impious highly exalted and raising himself like the cedars of Lebanon; and I have passed by, and behold, he was not; and I have sought his place, and it could not be found."[13] And finally a bright and splendid day, overshadowed by no cloud, illuminated with beams of heavenly light the churches of Christ throughout the entire world. And not even those outside our communion[14] were prevented from sharing in the same blessings, or at least from coming under their influence and enjoying a part of the benefits bestowed upon us by God.

All men, then, were freed from the oppression of the tyrants, and being released from the former ills, one in one way and another in another acknowledged the defender of the pious to be the only true God. And we especially who placed our hopes in the Christ of God had unspeakable gladness, and a certain inspired joy bloomed for all of us, when we saw every place which shortly before had been desolated by the impieties of the tyrants reviving as if from a long and death-fraught pestilence, and temples again rising from their foundations to an immense height, and receiving a splendor far greater than that of the old ones which had been destroyed. But the supreme rulers also confirmed to us still more extensively the munificence of God by repeated ordinances in behalf of the Christians; and personal letters of the emperor were sent to the bishops, with honors and gifts of money. It may not be unfitting to insert these documents, translated from the Roman into the Greek tongue, at the proper place in this book, as in a sacred tablet, that they may remain as a memorial to all who shall come after us. . . .

To him, therefore, God granted, from Heaven above, the deserved fruit of piety, the trophies of victory over the impious, and he cast the guilty

---

[9]The bishop of Tyre, whom Eusebius especially admired.

[10]According to Pythagorean numerology, *10* is the perfect number because it is the sum of the four principal geometric numbers: *1, 2, 3,* and *4.*

[11]The Bible, Psalms, 98:1–2.

[12]Psalms, 46:8–9.

[13]Psalms, 37:35–36.

[14]Non-Christians and Christian heretics.

one with all his counselors and friends prostrate at the feet of Constantine. For when Licinius[15] carried his madness to the last extreme, the emperor, the friend of God, thinking that he ought no longer to be tolerated, acting upon the basis of sound judgement, and mingling the firm principles of justice with humanity, gladly determined to come to the protection of those who were oppressed by the tyrant, and undertook, by putting a few destroyers out of the way, to save the greater part of the human race. For when he had formerly exercised humanity alone and had shown mercy to him who was not worthy of sympathy, nothing was accomplished; for Licinius did not renounce his wickedness, but rather increased his fury against the people that were subject to him, and there was left to the afflicted no hope of salvation, oppressed as they were by a savage beast. Wherefore, the protector of the virtuous, mingling hatred for evil with love for good, went forth with his son Crispus,[16] a most beneficent prince, and extended a saving right hand to all that were perishing. Both of them, father and son, under the protection, as it were, of God, the universal King, with the Son of God, the Savior of all, as their leader and ally, drew up their forces on all sides against the enemies of the Deity and won an easy victory; God having prospered them in the battle in all respects according to their wish. Thus, suddenly, and sooner than can be told, those who yesterday and the day before breathed death and threatening were no more, and not even their names were remembered, but their inscriptions and their honors suffered the merited disgrace. And the things which Licinius with his own eyes had seen come upon the former impious tyrants he himself likewise suffered, because he did not receive instruction nor learn wisdom from the chastisements of

his neighbors, but followed the same path of impiety which they had trod, and was justly hurled over the same precipice. Thus he lay prostrate.

But Constantine, the mightiest victor, adorned with every virtue of piety, together with his son Crispus, a most God-beloved prince, and in all respects like his father, recovered the East which belonged to them; and they formed one united Roman empire as of old, bringing under their peaceful sway the whole world from the rising of the sun to the opposite quarter, both north and south, even to the extremities of the declining day. All fear therefore of those who had formerly afflicted them was taken away from men, and they celebrated splendid and festive days. Everything was filled with light, and those who before were downcast beheld each other with smiling faces and beaming eyes. With dances and hymns, in city and country, they glorified first of all God the universal King, because they had been thus taught, and then the pious emperor with his God-beloved children. There was oblivion of past evils and forgetfulness of every deed of impiety; there was enjoyment of present benefits and expectation of those yet to come. Edicts full of clemency and laws containing tokens of benevolence and true piety were issued in every place by the victorious emperor. Thus after all tyranny had been purged away, the empire which belonged to them was preserved firm and without a rival for Constantine and his sons alone. And having obliterated the godlessness of their predecessors, recognizing the benefits conferred upon them by God, they exhibited their love of virtue and their love of God, and their piety and gratitude to the Deity, by the deed which they performed in the sight of all men.

---

[15]Licinius had been coemperor since 308. In 313 he and Constantine allied, with Constantine taking the western half of the empire, and in that same year they jointly issued an edict of religious toleration. In 316 Constantine attacked Licinius's lands, on the pretext that Licinius was persecuting Christians, and confiscated a major portion of the eastern half of the empire. In 324 Constantine returned to complete the job, on the same pretext. After capturing Licinius and uniting the entire empire under his control,

Constantine had his former colleague murdered within a year. Circumstances thus forced Eusebius to excise earlier complimentary allusions to Licinius from his last edition of the *Ecclesiastical History*.

[16]Crispus was Constantine's eldest son and had held the title of *Caesar* since 317. He served with distinction in the war of 324, commanding Constantine's naval forces. For reasons unknown, Constantine ordered his execution in 326.

The Imperial Religion

▼▼▼

53 ▼ CHRIST THE REDEEMER

Early Christian artists generally depicted Jesus as either a lamb or as a youthful and beardless Good Shepherd. When Christianity became the emperor's religion, Christian artists had to create new iconographical symbols in order to incorporate Christ into the imperial culture. After all, the emperor was, in theory, neither a sacrificial lamb nor a humble and mild shepherd.

This *mosaic* (a mural composed of pieces of colored stone, glass, and precious metal), which dates from around the year 500, is located in the archbishop's chapel at Ravenna, a city in northeast Italy that served as the western capital of the Roman Empire from 402 to 476 and thereafter continued to be Italy's most prominent political center into the eighth century. During the fifth century the archbishops of Ravenna, often imperial appointees, rivaled the popes of Rome in power and prestige.

Here Christ the Redeemer of the World is dressed in the full military uniform of a Roman emperor — golden armor, a purple cloak with a shoulder clasp bearing three pendants to signify imperial rank, and campaign boots. Underneath his feet are a lion and a snake, representing two biblical quotations. The Book of Psalms declares, "You shall tread on the lion and the adder; the young lion and the dragon you shall trample under feet." In the Gospel of Luke, Jesus tells his disciples, "Behold, I have given you power to tread on snakes and scorpions and to overcome all the power of the Enemy." The open book, symbolizing either the Gospels or the Book of Life, which contains the names of all the redeemed, reads, "I am the Way, the Truth, and Life," a statement ascribed to Jesus in the Gospel of John.

QUESTIONS FOR ANALYSIS

1. Consider some of the symbols not commented on in the introduction: How does Christ carry his cross? Do you find any significance in that posture? Describe Christ's facial expression. Again, do you find any significance here?
2. Based on your study of all of the mosaic's symbols, what do you conclude is the message of this piece of art?
3. Consider this mosaic in the light of Eusebius's *Ecclesiastical History* (source 52). Which strike you as more significant, the similarities or differences in tone and message? What do you conclude from your answer?
4. Compare this mosaic with Hejevara (source 47) and Shiva Nataraja (source 45). What common triumph do these three savior deities claim, and what do their parallel victories suggest?

Christ the Redeemer

The Origins of Christian Monasticism
▼▼▼

54 ▼ St. Ephraem of Edessa,
THE LIFE OF ST. MARY THE HARLOT

During the fourth and fifth centuries many pious men and women sought escape from the new Christian-imperial order and what they perceived to be a corrupt and decaying society by going into the wastelands of Egypt, Syria-Palestine, and Anatolia. These *Desert Elders* included such colorful and unconventional characters as Abbot John the Dwarf, Abbot Moses the Black, and Mary the Harlot, the heroine of the present story. Despite their many differences, they shared a number of characteristics. Chief among them was a desire to live the spirit of the Gospels in a totally uncompromising manner.

This flight to the desert became the foundation of Christian monasticism. The first Desert Elders were usually hermits (also known as *anchorites*), who elected to live solitary lives in their desert refuges. The desert oases could support only a limited number of hermitages, however, and in time many former hermits chose to join together into communities. Those who elected to live communally were known as *cenobites*. By the end of the sixth century cenobitic communities became the Christian monastic norm, but they never totally displaced hermits. Moreover, the lives and legends of the first desert hermits continued to inspire Christian monasticism through the ages. Whether anchorite or cenobite, Christian monks of every variety have universally claimed that their ways of life continue the tradition of the flight to the desert.

Our source comes from the pen of a Syrian anchorite and scholar, St. Ephraem of Edessa (d. 373), a friend of the monk Abraham, who figures so prominently in this tale. Although Ephraem, much like Abraham, preferred the solitude of his monastic cell to the bustle of the world, late in his life he left his monastic isolation in order to found and preside over a hospital that cared for the victims of a plague that was devastating the region around Edessa, a site located in the southeastern region of modern Turkey. When the plague passed, he returned to his hermitage.

The story that Ephraem tells revolves around two well-known fourth-century holy people, Abraham and his niece Mary. Upon being orphaned, Mary joined her paternal uncle as an anchorite. After twenty years of monastic austerity, Mary was seduced by a monk who visited her uncle under the pretense of seeking religious instruction. In her horror and shame, she fled the hermitage and joined a brothel in a distant city. After several years had passed, Abraham had a vision of where his niece was and left his cell in disguise to rescue her. The rest of the tale illustrates why these eccentric holy people, who were a small percentage of the population, became folk heroes of such magnitude that they, more than any other single group, were responsible for turning Christianity into a mass religion.

QUESTIONS FOR ANALYSIS

1. Mary, when reminded of her former monastic life, suddenly realizes how lonely she is, even though she has left her hermitage for a city. What is Ephraem's message?
2. How, if at all, does this story reflect the message of the Sermon on the Mount?
3. In his Epistle to the Romans (source 51), Paul writes of the primacy of love over all other religious obligations. In what ways do Abraham's actions during his rescue of Mary illustrate this principle?
4. The desert hermits have often been characterized as self-centered dropouts. Judging from this story, is that how their society perceived them? Please explain your answer.
5. The pre-Christian Greco-Roman World had tended to think and worship in terms of holy places, such as temples and natural sites sacred to various deities. During the fourth and fifth centuries, Christian holy people — who, it was believed, possessed special religious powers — began replacing holy spaces as the new focal point of people's religious imagination. How does this story illustrate that development?
6. Compare Abraham's treatment of Mary with the Buddha's treatment of his aunt (Chapter 3, source 20). Which strike you as more pronounced, the parallels or the differences? What do you conclude from your answer?

Abraham went forth to battle the Evil One and, once he had defeated him, to achieve the greater victory of bringing his niece home again. When he arrived at the city, he entered the tavern where she worked as a prostitute and anxiously looked around, glancing this way and that way, hoping to see her. Time went by, and he still had not caught sight of her. Finally, he addressed the innkeeper in a joking manner: "They tell me, my friend," he said, "that you have an excellent 'working girl' here. If it is all right with you, I would like to have a look at her."

The innkeeper . . . replied that everything he had heard was true. She was unusually beautiful. . . . The old man asked her name and was told they called her *Mary.* Beaming merrily, he then said: "Come on, bring her in and show her to me, and let me buy her a fine dinner, for I have heard her praises sung everywhere." So they called her. When she came in and the holy old man saw her in her prostitute's clothes, his entire body came close to collapsing in grief. How-

ever, he hid his heartache behind the facade of a cheerful face and heroically held back the tears that welled up in his eyes, lest the young woman recognize him and flee.

As they sat down and drank their wine, this magnificent old man began to joke around with her. She rose, put her arms around his neck, and teased him with kisses. As she was kissing him, she smelled the fragrant austerity that his lean body exuded, and she thought back to the days when she had lived as an ascetic. Struck as though a spear had pierced her soul, she began to weep. Unable to bear the pain in her heart, she cried out: "Ah, the pain at being alone and unhappy."

The innkeeper was amazed and asked: "What is troubling you, Mary, that suddenly you burst out into this sorrowful lament? You have been here two years to the day, and no one in that time ever heard a sigh or sad word from you. I have no idea of what has overcome you."

The young woman replied: "I would have been happy had I died three years ago." . . .

The holy old man then produced the gold coin he had brought with him and gave it to the inn-keeper, saying: "Now, friend, make us a good dinner, so that I can have some fun with the young woman. I have come a long distance in my love for her." O divinelike wisdom! O wise understanding of the spirit! O remarkable discretion for the sake of salvation! During fifty years of abstinence he had never tasted bread; now without hesitation he eats meat to save a lost soul. . . . Marvel at such madness, such a reversal of form, when an upright, wise, discreet, and prudent man becomes a reckless fool in order to snatch a soul from the jaws of the lion, and set free a captive. . . .

Once they had feasted, the young woman began to tease him to come to her room to lie with her. "Let us go," he said. Entering the room, he saw a high bed prepared for them, and immediately he sat on it in a light-hearted manner.

What should I call you, O perfect athlete of Christ?[1] I really do not know. Should I say you are continent or incontinent, wise or foolish, discreet or reckless? During the fifty years of your monastic profession you have slept on a straw mat. How is it that you can so indifferently climb onto such a bed? The long journey with its many stops along the way, your eating meat and drinking wine, your entering a brothel — you have done all of this in order to praise and glorify Christ by saving a soul. On our part, if we have to say one useful word to a neighbor, we are upset by the prospect of the task. . . .

"Come close to me, Mary," said the old man. When she was next to him, he took her by the hand, as though to kiss her. Then taking off his hat, and with a voice cracking with tears, he said: "Mary, my daughter, do you not know me? My heart, was I not the one who raised you? . . . Who was it who destroyed you? Where is that angelic garb you used to wear?[2] Where is your chastity? Your tears? Your vigils? Your bed on the ground? My daughter, how did you fall from the height of heaven into this pit? Why, when you lapsed into sin, did you not tell me? Why did you not come to me then and there? I would have done your penance for you, so also would have my beloved friend Ephraem.[3] Why did you desert me and bring this intolerable sorrow on me? For who is sinless, except God Himself? . . . Have pity on my old age. Grieve for the burden placed on my white head. I beg you. Get up and come home with me. Do not be afraid. A human is given to slipping, but if one falls down swiftly, one can also rise again swiftly with God's help. God does not desire a sinner's death but, rather, that the sinner is healed and lives."

She replied: "If you are sure that I can do penance and that God will accept my atonement, I will come as you request." . . . And they rose up and went away, . . . and so the blessed Abraham, his heart filled with joy, journeyed along the road with his niece.

When they arrived home, he placed her in the inner cell that had previously been his, and he remained in the outer cell.[4] She, clad in a hair shirt, resided there in humility of soul, weeping in her heart and through her eyes, disciplining herself with vigils and the stern burden of abstinence, . . . ceaselessly calling on God and bewailing her sin but with a sure hope of pardon. . . . And God the compassionate, who desires that no person perishes but that all come to repentance, so accepted her penance that after three years He restored many ill people to health through her prayers. Crowds flocked to her, and she would pray to God for their healing, and her prayers were granted.

The blessed Abraham, after living for another ten years in this earthly life, and seeing her

---

[1]Abraham. Monastic ascetics were often called *athletes* because they were involved in painful competition (*agonia* in Greek) for spiritual perfection.
[2]Her simple, rough-spun monastic robe.
[3]Probably Ephraem of Edessa.

[4]Originally she had inhabited the outer cell, or room. Being closer to the world, she had fallen into sin. In his greater solitude, Abraham had been unaware of what was happening to Mary and, for several days, was not even aware of her flight. He was now going to be her buffer against the world.

blessed repentance, and giving glory to God, rested in peace in his seventieth year. . . . Mary lived another five years, ever more devoutly disciplining her life and persevering night and day in tearful and sorrowful prayer to God, so that many a person passing by that place at night and hearing her grief-filled voice would be turned to weeping and add his tears to hers. When the hour of her sleeping came, in which she was taken from this life, all that saw her gave glory to God for the look of happiness on her face.

▼▼▼

Religious Exchange and Interchange

The Judaic roots of Christianity are quite clear, as sources 50 and 51 illustrate. Less obvious, perhaps, are the influences of late antiquity's mystery religions (see Chapter 5, source 34), such as *Gnosticism,* on the development of Christian belief and expression. Equally often overlooked is Christianity's impact on other religions of salvation, most notably *Manichaeism.* As the following sources illustrate, cultural syncretism was a two-way street during Christianity's formative years.

Gnostic Christianity:
The Secret Knowledge of Jesus

▼▼▼

55 ▼ *THE GOSPEL OF THOMAS*

In 1945 two Egyptian farmers unearthed a jar containing some fifty-two early Christian texts written in Coptic, the common tongue of late ancient Egypt. Known collectively as the *Nag Hammadi Library,* the texts, most of which were previously unknown, shed new light on an important but little understood branch of early Christianity known as the *Gnostics.*

Gnosticism is an all-encompassing term for a widespread, Hellenistic religious philosophy that was based on the belief that salvation is attainable through a secret, mystical knowledge, which is called *gnosis* in Greek. Gnosticism predated Christianity, and it manifested itself in many different varieties. There was no single, all-encompassing Gnostic Church. Rather, there were many different Gnostic sects, most of which were pagan, but there were even Jewish Gnostics. Notwithstanding its largely pagan associations, Gnosticism made inroads into early Christianity and influenced its development. Ultimately rejected as *heretics,* or "wrong believers," by the mainstream Christian Church, Gnostic Christians suffered the fate of having their core teachings condemned and their books largely destroyed.

For that reason alone, the discovery of the Nag Hammadi Library excited scholarly interest. Of all the recovered texts, the one that drew the most attention was *The Gospel of Thomas.* Ascribed to the authorship of Jesus' twin brother, the Apostle Judas Thomas, and composed during the second century C.E. or earlier, the gospel has no narrative; it simply consists of 113 sayings of Jesus. The reader who knows the four canonical Gospels of Matthew, Mark, Luke, and John will recognize some familiar passages. Many of the sayings, however, will seem foreign, possibly even strange. Cumulatively, the sayings portray Jesus as a purely spiritual, noncorporeal savior who imparts to a select few a secret wisdom that will enable them to discover within themselves the divine spark of heavenly light. Although the Gnostic vision did not become mainstream Christian theology, Gnosticism was one of many forces that left a mark on Christianity as it took shape within the late Hellenistic World.

QUESTIONS FOR ANALYSIS

1. How and where does one gain this knowledge, or *gnosis,* and how difficult is it to attain?
2. What does saying 22 seem to mean? Does it help to study it while keeping in mind the messages of the statues of *Shiva Nataraja* and *Hevajra* (Chapter 6, sources 45 and 47)?
3. Sayings 49 and 50 are overtly Gnostic. What do they suggest about Gnostic beliefs?
4. What does saying 70 mean?
5. What does saying 75 mean?
6. Compare saying 113 with *The Life of St. Mary the Harlot* (source 54). What conclusions do you reach?
7. Compare these sayings with the biblical passages cited in the notes. What do you infer from this comparison?
8. Compare the message contained in these sayings with the selections from the *Upanishads* (Chapter 2, source 16). What conclusions follow from this comparative analysis?

Prologue

These are the secret sayings that the living Jesus[1] spoke and Judas Thomas the Twin[2] recorded.

Saying 1

He said, "Whoever finds the interpretation of these sayings will not taste death."

Saying 2

Jesus said, "Let one who seeks not stop seeking until one finds.

When one finds, one will be disturbed.

When one is disturbed, one will be amazed, and will reign over all."

Saying 3

Jesus said, "If your leaders say to you, 'Behold, the kingdom is in the sky,' then the birds in the sky will get there before you. If they say to you, 'It is in the sea,' then the fish will get there before you.

"Rather, the kingdom is inside you and outside you.[3] When you know yourselves, then you will be known, and will understand that you are

---

[1]Jesus, who offered the life of *gnosis.*
[2]According to a Syriac Christian tradition, Jesus had a twin brother, Judas Thomas.

[3]The Kingdom of God begins with knowledge of self and of God.

children of the living Father. But if you do not know yourselves, then you live in poverty, and embody poverty." . . .

Saying 9

Jesus said, "Behold, the sower went out, took a handful of seeds, and scattered them. Some fell on the road, and the birds came and ate them. Others fell on rock, and they did not take root in the soil or produce any heads of grain. Others fell among thorns, and the thorns choked the seeds and worms consumed them. Still others fell on good soil, and brought forth a good crop: it yielded sixty per measure and one hundred twenty per measure."[4] . . .

Saying 22

Jesus saw some babies nursing. He said to his disciples, "These nursing babies are like those who enter the kingdom."[5]

They said to him, "Then shall we enter the kingdom as babies?"

Jesus said to them,
> "When you make the two into one,
> when you make the inner like the outer
>   and the outer like the inner,
>   and the upper like the lower,
> when you make male and female into a
>   single one,
>   so that the male will not be male
>   and the female will not be female,
> when you make eyes replacing an eye,
>   a hand replacing a hand,
>   a foot replacing a foot,
>   and an image replacing an image,
> then you will enter the kingdom." . . .

Saying 36

Jesus said, "Do not worry, from morning to evening and from evening to morning, about what you will wear."[6] . . .

Saying 39

Jesus said, "The Pharisees and the scribes have taken the keys to knowledge and have hidden them. They have not entered, nor have they allowed those who want to enter to do so. As for you, be as clever as snakes and as innocent as doves." . . .

Saying 49

Jesus said,
> "Blessed are those who are alone and chosen:
>   you will find the kingdom.
> For you have come from it, and you will
>   return there again."

Saying 50

Jesus said, "If some say to you, 'Where have come from?' say to them, 'We have come from the light,
>   where the light came into being by itself,
>   established itself,
>   and appeared in an image of light.'
"If they say to you, 'Are you the light?' say,
>   'We are its children,
>   and we are the chosen of the living Father.'
"If they ask you, 'What is the evidence of your Father in you?' tell them,
>   'It is motion and rest.'" . . .

Saying 54

Jesus said,
> "Blessed are the poor:
>   yours is the kingdom of heaven."[7] . . .

Saying 58

Jesus said,
> "Blessed is one who has suffered:
>   that one has found life."[8] . . .

Saying 68

Jesus said,

---

[4]Compare this with Matthew, 13:3–9; Mark, 4:3–9; and Luke, 8:5–8.
[5]Compare this with Matthew, 18:1–5; Mark, 9:33–37; and Luke, 9:46–48. Also compare Matthew 19:13–15; Mark, 10:13–16; and Luke, 18:15–17.

[6]Compare this with the Sermon on the Mount (source 50).
[7]Compare this with the Sermon on the Mount.
[8]Compare this with the Sermon on the Mount.

"Blessed are you when you are hated and
   persecuted,
and no one will discover the place where
   you have been persecuted."

Saying 69

Jesus said,
   "Blessed are those who have been persecuted
      in their hearts:
      they truly know the Father.
   "Blessed are those who are hungry,
      for the stomach of the famished will be
      filled."[9]

Saying 70

Jesus said,
   "If you bring forth what is within you,
      what you have will save you.
   If you do not have that within you,
      what you do not have within you will
         kill you." . . .

Saying 75

Jesus said,
   "I am the light that is over all things.
   I am all:
      all came forth from me,
      and all attained to me.
   Split a piece of wood,
      and I am there.
   Pick up a stone,
      and you will find me there." . . .

Saying 113

Simon Peter[10] said to them, "Let Mary leave us,
because women are not worthy of life."

   Jesus said, "Behold, I shall guide her so as to
make her male, that she too may become a living spirit like you men.[11] For every woman who
makes herself male will enter the kingdom of
heaven."

---

[9]Compare sayings 68 and 69 with the Sermon on the Mount.
[10]An apostle. In the tradition of the Gospels of Matthew,
Mark, and Luke, Simon Peter was the leader of the apostles.

[11]The male (heavenly) principle must replace totally the
female (earthly) principle.

Manichaeism: Enlightening the World
▼▼▼
56 ▼ *THE PARABLE ABOUT THE WORLD-OCEAN*

Gnosticism and mainstream Christianity parted ways, but the Gnostic search for
spiritual knowledge did not end there. In the third century C.E. a Persian prophet
from Babylonia named *Mani* (216–276) founded a gnostic religion that claimed a
worldwide mission. Drawing deeply from Christian, Jewish, Hindu, Buddhist,
and Zoroastrian sources, Mani articulated a Religion of Light whose message was
aimed not at a small group of select initiates but at all of humanity. Indeed,
Manichaeism became a major world religion, despite attempts to suppress it. Initially Manichaeism made major inroads into the Greco-Roman World, but the
Christian Roman Empire fought back and essentially ousted this gnostic faith
from the West before the sixth century was over. Manichaeism likewise enjoyed
early success in Mesopotamia and Iran, but persecution by the Zoroastrian Sassanid
Empire and the later triumph of Islam combined to produce a similar eclipse of
Manichaeism in the land of its birth.

   Regardless of these setbacks, Manichaeism did not die an early death. It traveled east along the Silk Road, making deep inroads in Central Asia and gaining a

firm foothold in China, where it proved to be a strong rival to Buddhism and lasted into early modern times. By the late seventeenth century very few living vestiges of Manichaeism remained in Central and East Asia, but certainly it had enjoyed a long life in those areas touched by the eastern portions of the Silk Road. This longevity was due in large part to Manichaean missionaries, who were willing and able to take this religion, which had sprung largely from Christian, Jewish, and Zoroastrian roots, and translate it into terms understandable to Central and East Asians. For example, Manichaeism's Jesus the Messiah, a savior who will return to earth, became identified with the Buddha Maitreya, a Mahayana Buddha of the future.

Babylonia was a religiously complex region in the third century. The fact that Mani was raised in a Gnostic Christian sect that maintained strong connections with Judaism hints at the religious syncretism that pervaded Mesopotamia. At age twenty-four Mani began his public preaching. Claiming direct revelation from Jesus of Light, the divine, supreme revealer of the truth of the Light, Mani maintained that his revelation completed that of three predecessors who had preached true religion: the Buddha, Zoroaster, and Jesus the Messiah, a fully divine historical being who was separate from Jesus of Light.

The essence of Mani's teaching was that there are two coeternal and coequal principles, Light and Darkness. *Light* is harmony and peace; *Darkness* is disorder and strife. Originally separated from one another, Light and Darkness came into conflict when Darkness attempted to possess Light for itself. Darkness's swallowing of part of the realm of Light led to the creation of the universe and humanity, in whom sparks of divine light reside within bodies that are ruled by Darkness. Humanity is now called upon to take part in the cosmic struggle. Once all the lost light is recovered, Darkness will be reduced to impotence, Light will reign supreme, and the universe will end.

The following document was written in the language of the people of the Central Asiatic state that the Chinese knew as *Kangju* (Chapter 5, source 40, note 5) and the Greco-Roman West called *Sogdiana.* Sogdian merchants who traveled the Silk Road, once the silk trade had resumed in the sixth century, proved to be especially fervent missionaries of Manichaeism, which they introduced to Turkish tribes far to the east. One such tribe was the *Uighurs,* who moved from the Mongolian steppes to the oasis towns along the branch of the Silk Road that skirted the northern fringes of the forbidding Taklamakan Desert (also called the *Tarim Basin*). In the mid ninth century the Uighurs established a partially Manichaean state centered on the caravan city of Turfan, and it was probably there that some Uighur scribe copied this text, which was discovered at Turfan in the early twentieth century.

The text takes the form of a *parable,* or extended metaphor. In it Mani's revelation is likened to the world-ocean into which all other rivers (previous religions) flow. If we read the parable carefully, we can discover several of Manichaeism's more important doctrines. Please note that words in parentheses are editorial explanations; words in brackets have been supplied by the editor to fill in the broken text.

QUESTIONS FOR ANALYSIS

1. According to the parable, is salvation possible outside of the Manichaean Church?
2. What does the Manichaean Church demand of all its members?
3. What is especially demanded of the elect?
4. Which of these articles reveal(s) the Gnostic elements within Manichaeism?
5. What is the daily work of the Manichaean Church?

And the wonderful Religion of the Apostle [is similar] to the world-ocean [in ten ways].

{First}: It is wise (full of wisdom), and no one knows nor can estimate its wisdom . . . , nor the quantity and [number] of its sermons and explanations; and no one can comprehend it. The former religions are similar to the small waters which arise in [different places]. . . . [But] the religion of the Apostles which [is similar] to the great world-ocean can be [seen] in the whole world and in every place. And it is ripe to be presented in [the darkness] in a most open manner and to be proclaimed in all languages. And [one can] find the explanation and systematization (?) of all wisdom in it.

Second: The other shore that no one [knows] is the fragrant, wonderful Paradise that the living beings [on earth], apart from the elect and the [auditors],[1] do not perceive and will never comprehend.

Third: The [waters] of the world-ocean have one taste, and the other waters have different tastes and appearances, but its own taste does not change. That is [the] deep wisdom of the Law and the commandments of the Religion, and the sweet, wonderful words that are preached.

The fine parables and [their] explanations [and] interpretations, the rich and wholly pure [practice] of [its] mode of life, the noble exercise of its good customs, the humble . . . change of mind which the Religion shows (suggests) to [men], teaching and instructing (them). . . . But it itself has not been instructed by anyone in anything.

Fourth: The world-ocean absorbs the bodies . . . and does not reject anyone. These are the mighty [spirits?] and men; and [whoever] of these comes to the Church of the Apostle is absorbed [by the Church], for it does not reject anyone. Rather, according to the order of its Law and commandments, it gives them their [places]. And as many as approach it [repeatedly], in order to enter it, [all] of them have their places either amongst the auditors or the elect. And they all do their works according to their rank, their zeal and their strength. And [the Religion] does not make . . . and honor . . . , and out of love it does not shout out loud. And however many of these people may be mighty, nothing takes it by surprise, nor does it rejoice, for it remains placid and tranquil at all times. [Thus] it is like the world-ocean.

---

[1]The Manichaean Church divided its members into the *elect* and the *auditors,* or "hearers." The elect were the chosen few who led lives of great asceticism and provided leadership in the Church. Because of their purity they were the earthly agents for the release of captive Light. The hearers were the mass of Manichaean believers who served the elect. Whereas the soul of the elect returns directly to the Kingdom of Light upon death, the soul of the hearer must still go through a series of reincarnations, first in a series of luminous fruits and then in the form of an elect. How soon this last incarnation happens depends on the quality of the hearer's service to the elect.

Fifth: The Religion of the Apostle [is] without stain, (being) clean and pure and holy; and it immediately refuses to retain those men who are confused and immoral and [have] filthy thoughts, men who are like corpses, excrements and diverse (forms of) pollution. It tosses them back onto the shore.

Sixth: When an elect one sees another elect one face to face, or an auditor sees [another] auditor, then the pure, loving gaze gives rise to great joy among them. And [so] great blessing comes upon them, and like light it appears in the faces of the light gods and becomes visible.

Seventh: The many great, strong bipeds and otherwise fashioned wonderful beings and animals [that are born] in the world-ocean are [like] the elect that behave quite differently from the world. And [they] bear the burden and the heavy load of the Law and endure great pain and suffering. And they always accept personally, what no man in the whole world would bear or take upon himself.

Eighth: In the world-ocean, . . . varied priceless pearls and beautiful, miraculous jewels are born which are not born in [any] deep [place] (in the earth). Never can this be comprehended and never can it be seen. This reflects the difference between the two places, the good and the evil one, and the self-realization of the soul which is not born in a learned place.[2] It (that wisdom) can never be attained except in [the Religion] and in the Law and in the commandments of the Apostle.

Ninth: The strong one[3] and the demon[4] of the world-ocean that shakes the whole world-ocean when it rises (in the tide) is the Nous[5] of the Religion, which is in the [whole] Church, shaking the bodies (of men). It (the Nous) seizes (them) mightily and draws out [the light] (they have accumulated), this being the daily work (of the men) of the Religion. [That light] ascends daily from the whole body of the elect to the light [chariots] (the Sun and the Moon); and the gods in command of these chariots draw it up [and] constantly send it on to the world of Paradise.

Tenth: All roaring and thundering waters that flow into the ocean, that then become still and stop roaring, are the adherents of [other] religions and men of worldly wisdom [and] eloquent men who remain [mere] creators of words, believing themselves to be wise. But when they come to the door of the Religion of the Apostle, they all become silent and their (own) words silence them. And now they do [not] exalt themselves (any more), and henceforth they do not dare to make any more speeches [and] dare not say anything.

[Here] ends the story about the Religion and the world-ocean.

---

[2]Worldly learning stands in contrast to the knowledge of the soul that one receives from the Manichaean religion.
[3]A metaphorical term for the *tide.*
[4]According to Manichaean cosmology, the tide, or "ocean giant," arises as a consequence of demonic substances poured into the ocean. This is positive, however, because the turbulence purifies the waters of the ocean.

[5]A Greek term that means *Divine Intelligence. Nous* is an emanation of Jesus of Light and carries out his redemptive role. Nous is the father of all true religious leaders and enters the world through their teachings. It is Nous that imparts knowledge of the divine origin of the soul, and this knowledge brings with it liberation from Darkness.

The Foundations of Islamic Life

Like the Buddha and Jesus, Muhammad was a teacher who spoke rather than wrote his message. But also like Buddhism and Christianity, following its Messenger's death Islam quickly became a religious culture centered on a body of sacred texts, and it has remained so to the present. Islam's text without equal is the *Qur'an* (the Recitations), which Muslims believe contains, word for word, absolutely everything that God revealed to Muhammad and nothing else. As the full and final revelation of God, the Qur'an encompasses everything that any human needs to know. Its verses, each a poetically perfect proclamation from Heaven, are both doctrine and law, governing essentially every aspect of a Muslim's life. Islam without the Qur'an is unimaginable.

A second source of guidance for most Muslims is *al-Hadith* (Tradition), a vast body of transmitted stories of what the Prophet said or did or what was said or done in his presence and therefore approved by him. Unlike the Qur'an, these stories, individually known as *hadiths* (tales or instructions), are not assembled in a single, absolutely accepted text. Rather, there are many collections of Hadith, some more authoritative than others, some even largely dismissed as spurious. Most Muslims believe that authentic hadiths enshrine the *sunna* (the beaten track), or traditions, of the Prophet and the first Islamic community and thereby provide perfect models for behavior in all aspects of life, especially those not expressly covered in the precepts of the Qur'an.

The Word of God

▼▼▼

57 ▼ THE QUR'AN

As long as the Prophet was alive, there was no compelling reason to set his words down in some definitive form. However, following Muhammad's sudden death in 632, Caliph Abu Bakr ordered one of the Prophet's companions, Zayd ibn Thabit, to collect, from oral and written sources, all of Muhammad's inspired utterances. Subsequently, Caliph Uthman (r. 644–656) promulgated an official collection of these Recitations and ordered all other versions destroyed.

The Qur'an quickly became (and remains) the basis of every pious Muslim's education. As Islam spread beyond Arab ethnic boundaries, Muslims all over the world learned Arabic in order to study and recite, usually from memory, the sacred *surahs* (chapters) of this holy book. Because of the Qur'an's centrality to Islam, Arabic literacy became the hallmark of Muslims from sub-Saharan West Africa to Southeast Asia.

The following excerpts come from the second of the Qur'an's one hundred fourteen surahs. Known as "The Cow" (*al-Baqarah*), because portions of it tell the story of how the ancient Israelites had sacrificed a cow to God, this surah illustrates several of Islam's major doctrinal tenets, religious obligations, and moral principles. It also deals with the connections between Islam and the faiths of Judaism and Christianity.

QUESTIONS FOR ANALYSIS

1. What evidence is there that Muhammad was having difficulty converting Jewish and Christian Arabs?
2. How does the Qur'an portray Jews and Christians, and what is Islam's relationship with these two faiths?
3. What are the basic tenets of faith enjoined on all Muslims?
4. What are a Muslim's basic moral obligations?
5. What specific religious rites and practices must every observant Muslim perform?
6. How are Muslims to deal with people who attack them?
7. "For members of the Islamic community, there is no distinction between what one believes and the manner in which one lives and conducts one's affairs." After reading these passages from the Qur'an, do you agree or disagree that this is a central Islamic principle?
8. Compare these passages with the readings from Second Isaiah (Chapter 3, source 22) and the Sermon on the Mount (Chapter 7, source 50). Which strike you as more significant, the similarities or the differences in message and tone? What do you conclude from your answer?

Those unbelievers of the People of the Book[1]
and the idolaters[2] wish not that any good
should be sent down upon you from your
    Lord;
but God singles out for His mercy whom he
    will;
    God is of bounty abounding. . . .

Many of the People of the Book wish they
    might
restore you as unbelievers, after you have
    believed,
in the jealousy of their souls, after the truth
has become clear to them; yet do you pardon
and be forgiving, till God brings His
    command;
truly God is powerful over everything.
And perform the prayer, and pay the alms;[3]

whatever good you shall forward to your souls'
    account,
you shall find it with God; assuredly God
    sees the things you do.
And they say, "None shall enter Paradise
except that they be Jews or Christians."
Such are their fancies. Say: "Produce your
    proof, if you speak truly."
Nay, but whosoever submits his will to God,
being a good-doer, his wage is with his Lord,
and no fear shall be on them, neither shall
    they sorrow.

The Jews say, "The Christians stand not on
    anything";
the Christians say, "The Jews stand not on
    anything";
yet they recite the Book. So too the ignorant

---

[1]Jews and Christians, who have their own sacred scriptures from God through such prophets as Moses and Jesus.
[2]Pagans who worship idols.

[3]The *zakat*, or obligatory alms-payment, which supports poor people within the Islamic community.

say the like of them. God shall decide
between them on the Day of Resurrection
  touching their differences.
And who does greater evil than he who bars
God's places of worship, so that His Name
be not rehearsed in them, and strives to
  destroy them?
Such men might never enter them, save in
  fear;
for them is degradation in the present world,
and in the world to come a mighty
  chastisement.

To God belong the East and the West;
whithersoever you turn, there is the
  Face of God;
  God is All-embracing, All-knowing. . . .

Children of Israel,[4] remember My blessing
wherewith I blessed you, and that I have
preferred you above all beings. . . .

And when his Lord tested Abraham[5]
with certain words, and he fulfilled them.
He said, "Behold, I make you a leader
for the people." Said he, "And of my seed?"
He said "My covenant shall not reach
  the evildoers."
And when We appointed the House[6] to be
a place of visitation for the people,
  and a sanctuary,
and: "Take to yourselves Abraham's station
for a place of prayer." And We made covenant
with Abraham and Ishmael,[7] "Purify
My House for those that shall go about it

and those that cleave to it, to those who bow
  and prostrate themselves."[8] . . .

When his Lord said to him, "Surrender,"
he said, "I have surrendered me to
  the Lord of all Being."
And Abraham charged his sons with this
and Jacob[9] likewise: "My sons, God has
  chosen for you the religion;
see that you die not
  save in surrender."[10]

Why, were you witnesses, when death came
to Jacob? When he said to his sons,
"What will you serve after me?" They said,
"We will serve thy God and the God of thy
  fathers
Abraham, Ishmael, and Isaac, One God;
  to Him we surrender."
That is a nation that has passed away;[11]
there awaits them that they have earned,
and there awaits you that you have earned;
you shall not be questioned concerning
  the things they did.

And they say, "Be Jews or Christians and
you shall be guided." Say thou: "Nay, rather
the creed of Abraham, a man of pure faith;
  he was no idolater."
Say you: "We believe in God, and
in that which has been sent down on us
and sent down on Abraham, Ishmael,
Isaac and Jacob, and the Tribes,[12]
and that which was given to Moses and Jesus
and the Prophets, of their Lord; we

---

[4]Jews — the offspring of Israel, or Jacob, the son of Isaac and grandson of Abraham.

[5]According to both Arabic and Jewish traditions, Abraham (ca. 1800 B.C.E.) was the father of both the Arabic and Jewish people.

[6]The Ka'bah, a cube-shaped shrine at the heart of the Great Mosque of Mecca. Associated with both Adam and Abraham, it is the focal point of a Muslim's daily prayer and the sacred spot around which pilgrims on *hajj* (note 19) circulate in a series of ritual ceremonies.

[7]Both Islamic and Jewish tradition see Ishmael, the son of Abraham and half-brother of Isaac (from whom the Jews are descended), as the forefather of the Arabs.

[8]Purify it from idols, whose worship Muslims consider to be the worst of all possible sins. Muhammad cleansed the Ka'bah of its idols following his triumphant reentry into Mecca in 630.

[9]See note 4.

[10]By surrendering to God, Abraham and his sons and grandsons were Muslims.

[11]Jews (the progeny of Jacob) who surrender to God, and are Muslims by reason of that submission, no longer exist.

[12]The Twelve Tribes of the Israelites whom Moses led out of Egypt.

make no division between any of them, and
    to Him we surrender."
And if they believe in the like of that you
believe in, then they are truly guided; but if
they turn away, then they are clearly in
    schism;[13]
God will suffice you for them; He is
    the All-hearing, the All-knowing;
the baptism of God; and who is there
that baptizes fairer than God?[14]
    Him we are serving.
Say: "Would you then dispute with us
concerning God, who is our Lord
and your Lord? Our deeds belong to us,
and to you belong your deeds; Him
    we serve sincerely. . . .

It is not piety, that you turn your faces
    to the East and to the West.[15]
    True piety is this:
to believe in God, and the Last Day,
the angels, the Book, and the Prophets,
to give of one's substance, however cherished,
    to kinsmen, and orphans,
the needy, the traveler, beggars,
    and to ransom the slave,
to perform the prayer,[16] to pay the alms.
And they who fulfill their covenant
when they have engaged in a covenant,
    and endure with fortitude
    misfortune, hardship, and peril,
these are they who are true in their faith,
    these are the truly godfearing. . . .

O believers, prescribed for you is
the Fast,[17] even as it was prescribed for
those that were before you — haply you
    will be godfearing —

for days numbered; and if any of you
be sick, or if he be on a journey,
then a number of other days. . . .

And fight in the way of God with those
who fight with you, but aggress not: God
    loves not the aggressors.
And slay them wherever you come upon them,
and expel them from where they expelled you;
persecution is more grievous than slaying.
But fight them not by the Holy Mosque[18]
until they should fight you there;
then, if they fight you, slay them —
such is the recompense of unbelievers —
but if they give over, surely God is
All-forgiving, All-compassionate.
Fight them, till there is no persecution
and the religion is God's; then if they
give over, there shall be no enmity
    save for evildoers.
The holy month for the holy month;
holy things demand retaliation.
Whoso commits aggression against you,
do you commit aggression against him
like as he has committed against you;
and fear you God, and know that God is
    with the godfearing.

And expend in the way of God;
and cast not yourselves by your own hands
into destruction, but be good-doers; God
    loves the good-doers.

Fulfill the Pilgrimage[19] and the Visitation
unto God; but if you are prevented,
then such offering as may be feasible. . . .
And when you have performed your holy rites
remember God, as you remember your fathers
or yet more devoutly. . . .

---

[13]*Schism* means "separation." They have separated themselves from Islam.

[14]Here the Qur'an juxtaposes the Christian sacrament of baptism, the ceremony of initiation into the Christian faith, with God's baptism of the Word.

[15]In prayer.

[16]The ritual prayer performed five times daily by all observant Muslims.

[17]The annual fast during the month of Ramadan, when observant Muslims refrain from all food, drink, and other physical pleasures from sunrise to sunset.

[18]The Great Mosque of Mecca (see also note 6).

[19]All adult Muslims who are able to make the journey must embark on the *hajj,* or pilgrimage to Mecca, at least once before death (see source 62).

God
there is no god but He, the
Living, the Everlasting.
Slumber seizes Him not, neither sleep;
to Him belongs
all that is in the heavens and the earth.
Who is there that shall intercede with Him
save by His leave?
He knows what lies before them and
what is after them,
and they comprehend not anything of
His knowledge save such as He
wills.
His Throne comprises the heavens and
earth;
the preserving of them oppresses Him not;
He is the All-high, the All-glorious.

No compulsion is there in religion.
Rectitude has become clear from error.
So whosoever disbelieves in idols
and believes in God, has laid hold of
the most firm handle, unbreaking; God is
All-hearing, All-knowing.

God is the Protector of the believers;
He brings them forth from the shadows
into the light. . . .

Those who believe and do deeds of
righteousness,
and perform the prayer, and pay the alms —
their wage awaits them with their Lord,
and no fear shall be on them, neither shall
they sorrow. . . .

God charges no soul save to its capacity;
standing to its account is what it has earned,
and against its account what it has merited.

Our Lord,
take us not to task
if we forget, or make mistake.
Our Lord,
charge us not with a load such
as Thou didst lay upon those before us.
Our Lord,
do Thou not burden us
beyond what we have the strength to bear.
And pardon us,
and forgive us,
and have mercy on us;
Thou art our Protector.
And help us against the people
of the unbelievers.

The Tales of Tradition
▼▼▼

58 ▼ *Imam Nawawi,*
GARDENS OF THE RIGHTEOUS

Although earlier Muslims, such as Malik ibn-Anas (d. 795), had collected stories about the Prophet, it was not until about two centuries after Muhammad's death that Muslim scholars began to catalogue systematically the traditions that circulated about the Prophet and his first followers. The most important individual in this effort was the Persian legal scholar Ismail al-Bokhari (810–870), who reportedly collected some six hundred thousand tales (undoubtedly many were variations of common themes) and memorized more than two hundred thousand of them. From this vast body of material he identified a little over seven thousand tales as genuine, which he then preserved. The second great editor of Hadith was Bokhari's younger contemporary, Abul Husain Muslim (819–875), whose collection is almost identical to Bokhari's. Slightly less important than the work of these two scholarly giants were the collections of Abu Daud (d. 889), al-Tirmidhi (d. 892), Ibn Majah (d. 896), and al-Nisai (d. 915). The combined efforts of these six individuals are known as the *Sahih Sitta* (*The Six Authentic Compilations*).

The sheer bulk of these canonical texts, as well as the discrepancies among them and the existence of many other less universally accepted compendia of such tales, necessitated continued editing and digesting of Muslim tradition by legions of Islamic jurists and religious scholars in every generation. One of the most significant of these later scholars was the Syrian *imam* (religious teacher) Nawawi (1233–1278), whose *Gardens of the Righteous* provided an analytical digest of the spiritual values enshrined in *The Six Authentic Compilations* and several lesser collections of Hadith.

As the following texts show, Nawawi's usual method of exposition was to set out a relevant passage or series of passages from the Qur'an and then to list a number of variant stories and sayings, largely as remembered by the Prophet's Companions, that illustrate the spiritual message contained in that qur'anic text.

QUESTIONS FOR ANALYSIS

1. Which virtues do these selections emphasize? Which of these are also part of the Judeo-Christian tradition?
2. The Arabic word used for *striving* in both the Qur'an and Hadith is *jihad*, which is often translated as "holy war." In the light of these excerpts, does this translation seem correct and complete?
3. What gives Hadith its authority, since, unlike the Qur'an, Muslims do not regard it as the literal word of God?
4. How does Hadith allow for a certain diversity within the context of religious uniformity?
5. "Hadith is a living commentary on the Qur'an, insofar as it makes explicit all that is implicit in that book." What does this statement mean? Does it appear to be a fair statement of how a Muslim would regard Hadith?
6. What picture emerges of the place of women in Muslim society? Compare the status of Muslim women with that of Hindu women as illustrated in the *Laws of Manu* (Chapter 5, source 38). Which are more striking, the differences or the parallels? What do you conclude from your answer?

ON MAKING PEACE BETWEEN PEOPLE

Allah, the Exalted, has said:

Most of their conferrings together are devoid of good, except such as enjoin charity, or the promotion of public welfare or of public peace (4.115).

Reconciliation is best (4.129).

Be mindful of your duty to Allah and try to promote accord between yourselves (8.2).

All believers are brothers; so make peace between your brothers (49.11).

Abu Hurairah relates that the Honorable Prophet said: Charity is incumbent upon every human limb every day on which the sun rises. To bring about just reconciliation between two contestants is charity. Helping a person to mount his animal, or to load his baggage on to it is charity. A good word is charity. Every step taken towards the mosque for *salat*[1] is charity. To remove anything from the street that causes inconvenience is charity (Bokhari and Muslim).

Umm Kulthum relates that she heard the Honorable Prophet say: He who brings about peace between people and attains good or says that which is good is not a liar (Bokhari and Muslim). Muslim's version adds: I did not hear him let people have a latitude in what they said except in three situations: war, making peace, and talk between husband and wife.

ON THE SUPERIORITY OF THE POOR AND WEAK AMONG MUSLIMS

Allah, the Exalted, has said:

Continue thy companionship with those who call on their Lord, morning and evening, seeking His pleasure, and look not beyond them (18.29).

Haritha ibn Wahb relates that he heard the Honorable Prophet say: Shall I tell you who are the dwellers of Paradise? It is every weak one who is accounted weak and is looked down upon, who if he takes an oath relying upon Allah He would fulfill it. Now shall I tell you who are the denizens of the Fire? It is every ignorant, impertinent, prideful, and arrogant one (Bokhari and Muslim). . . .

Usamah relates that the Honorable Prophet said: I stood at the gate of Paradise and observed that the generality of those who entered it were the lowly. The wealthy had been held back from

it. Then those condemned to the Fire were ordered to it and I stood at the gate of the Fire and observed that the generality of those who entered it were women (Bokhari and Muslim).

ON KIND TREATMENT OF ORPHANS, GIRLS, THE WEAK, THE POOR, AND THE LOWLY

Allah, the Exalted, has said:

Continue to be kindly gracious towards the believers (15.89).

Continue thy companionship with those who call on their Lord, morning and evening, seeking His pleasure, and look not beyond them, for if thou dost that thou wouldst be seeking the values of this life (18.29).

Oppress not the orphan and chide not him who asks (93.10–11).

Knowest thou him who rejects the faith? That is the one who drives away the orphan and urges not the feeding of the poor (107.2–4). . . .

Abu Hurairah relates that the Honorable Prophet said: He who exerts himself on behalf of widows and the indigent is like one who strives[2] in the cause of Allah; and the narrator thinks he added: and like the guardian who never retreats, and like one who observes the fast and does not break it (Bokhari and Muslim). . . .

Anas relates that the Honorable Prophet said: He who brings up two girls through their childhood will appear on the Day of Judgment attached to me like two fingers of a hand (Muslim). . . .

Ayesha[3] relates: A poor woman came to me with her two daughters. I gave her three dates. She gave one to each girl and raised the third to her own mouth to eat. The girls asked her for it. So she broke it into two parts and gave one to each of the girls. I was much struck by her ac-

---

[1]Ritual prayer. Observant Muslims pray five times daily and on Friday attend community prayer services at a *mosque.*
[2]*Jihad* (see question 2).

[3]The daughter of Abu Bakr, the first caliph; she was one of the Prophet's favorite wives and a major source of hadiths.

tion and mentioned what she had done to the Honorable Prophet. He said: Allah appointed Paradise for her in consequence of it; or he said: Allah freed her from the Fire[4] on account of it.

Abu Shuraih Khuwailad ibn Amr Khuza'i relates that the Honorable Prophet said: Allah, I declare sinful any failure to safeguard the rights of two weak ones; orphans and women (Nisai).

ON A HUSBAND'S RIGHT CONCERNING HIS WIFE

Allah, the Exalted, has said:

Men are appointed guardians over women, because of that in respect of which Allah has made some of them excel others, and because the men spend their wealth. So virtuous women are obedient and safeguard, with Allah's help, matters the knowledge of which is shared by them with their husbands (4.35). . . .

Ibn Umar relates that the Honorable Prophet said: Every one of you is a steward and is accountable for that which is committed to his charge. The ruler is a steward and is accountable for his charge, a man is a steward in respect of his household, a woman is a steward in respect of her husband's house and his children. Thus everyone of you is a steward and is accountable for that which is committed to his charge (Bokhari and Muslim).

Abu Ali Talq ibn Ali relates that the Honorable Prophet said: When a man calls his wife for his need, she should go to him even if she is occupied in baking bread (Tirmidhi and Nisai). . . .

Umm Salamah relates that the Honorable Prophet said: If a woman dies and her husband is pleased with her she will enter Paradise (Tirmidhi).

Mu'az ibn Jabal relates that the Honorable Prophet said: Whenever a woman distresses her husband his mate from among the *houris*[5] of Paradise says to her: Allah ruin thee, do not cause him distress for he is only thy guest and will soon part from thee to come to us (Tirmidhi).

Usamah ibn Zaid relates that the Honorable Prophet said: I am not leaving a more harmful trial for men than woman (Bokhari and Muslim).

ON STRIVING IN THE CAUSE OF ALLAH

Allah, the Exalted, has said:

Fight the idolators all together, as they fight you all together, and know that Allah is with the righteous (9.36). . . .

Allah has purchased of the believers their persons and their belongings in return for the promise that they shall have Paradise, for they fight in the cause of Allah and they slay the enemy or are themselves slain. This is a promise that He has made incumbent upon Himself as set out in the Torah, and the Gospel and the Qur'an; and who is more faithful to his promises than Allah? Rejoice, then, in the bargain that you have made with Him; that indeed is the supreme triumph (9.111). . . .

O ye who believe, shall I guide you to a commerce that will deliver you from a painful chastisement? It is that you believe in Allah and His Messenger, and strive in the cause of Allah with your belongings and your persons, that is the better for you, did you but know. He will forgive you your sins and will admit you to gardens beneath which rivers flow, and to pure and pleasant dwellings in Gardens of Eternity. That is the supreme triumph (61.11–14). . . .

Anas relates that the Honorable Prophet said: To be occupied in the cause of Allah a morning or evening is better than the world and all it contains (Bokhari and Muslim). . . .

---

[4]Hell.

[5]Beautiful virgins who serve the saved in Paradise.

Sahl ibn Sa'ad relates that the Honorable Prophet said: Patroling the frontier for a day is better than the world and all it contains. Your being allotted a strip in Paradise no wider than your horse-whip is better than the world and all it contains. Being occupied with striving in the cause of Allah for a morning or an evening is better than the world and all it contains (Bokhari and Muslim). . . .

Fuzalah ibn Ubaid relates that the Honorable Prophet said: Death puts an end to all action, except in the case of one who patrols the frontier in the cause of Allah, for his activity continues to grow till the Day of Judgment and he is shielded against the trials of the grave (Abu Daud and Tirmidhi).

Uthman relates that he heard the Honorable Prophet say: Patroling the frontier for a day in the cause of Allah is better than a thousand days of other good works (Tirmidhi). . . .

Abu Bakr ibn Abu Musa Ash'ari relates that he heard his father say in the face of the enemy: The Honorable Prophet said: The gates of Paradise are under the shadow of swords. Thereupon a man of lowly condition stood up and inquired: Abu Musa, did you indeed hear the Honorable Prophet say that? He answered: Yes. The man then turned towards his companions and saluted them in farewell. He then broke the scabbard of his sword and threw it away and walked with his sword into the enemy ranks and fought till he was killed (Muslim).

Abdullah ibn Jubair relates that the Honorable Prophet said: The Fire will not touch one whose feet are covered with dust in striving for the cause of Allah (Bokhari). . . .

Anas relates that the Honorable Prophet said: He who supplicates sincerely for martyrdom is granted it, even though he is not slain (Muslim).

Abu Hurairah relates that the Honorable Prophet said: A martyr does not suffer when he is slain anymore than one of you suffers from being bitten by an ant (Tirmidhi). . . .

Abu Hurairah relates that the Honorable Prophet said: He who observes the fast for a day in the cause of Allah will find that Allah has dug a moat between him and the Fire as wide as the distance between heaven and earth (Tirmidhi).

Abu Hurairah relates that the Honorable Prophet said: He who dies without having fought in the cause of Allah and without having thought of it in his mind dies with one characteristic of hypocrisy within him (Muslim). . . .

Abu Hurairah relates that a man asked the Honorable Prophet's permission to travel and he told him: The travel for my people is striving in the cause of Allah, the Lord of honor and glory (Abu Daud). . . .

Anas relates that the Honorable Prophet said: Strive against the idolators with your belongings, your persons and your tongues (Abu Daud).

▼▼▼

Variety and Unity in Islam

Ideally, Islam is a single community united in its submission and service to God. In fact, however, it has been fragmented into a wide variety of sects and schools. Chief among these are the *Sunni* and *Shi'ite* traditions and various forms of *Sufi* mysticism.

Despite these divisions, Muslims have maintained a degree of unity because of the centrality of the Qur'an in the life of every practicing Muslim, regardless of sect, and most Muslims' acceptance of certain fundamental religious obligations. Most basic of all are the Five Pillars of Islam: to say with absolute conviction,

"There is no God but God, and Muhammad is the Prophet of God"; to offer prescribed prayers at five stipulated times during the day; to give alms in charity to poorer members of the Islamic community; to fast from sunrise to sunset during the month of Ramadan; and to make a pilgrimage to Mecca at least once in one's lifetime. Some Muslims add a sixth pillar, *jihad,* which is understood in many different senses (source 58, question 2).

God's Martyrs: The Party of Ali
▼▼▼
59 ▼ *Ibn Babawayh al-Saduq,*
CREED CONCERNING THE IMAMS

The Six Authentic Compilations preserve traditions sacred to that majority element of Islam known as *Sunni* Muslims, who claim to follow the correct path (*sunna*) of tradition as it evolved from the day of the Prophet and his Companions to the present. Underlying the Sunni self-image is the belief that God's community is *infallible,* which means that it can never err. Consequently, the practices and institutions of mainstream Islam are always correct. Another major faction of Islam, which claims its own Hadith as the authentic record of the words and actions of the Prophet and his closest Companions, is the *Shi'at Ali,* or "Party of Ali." Members of this branch of Islam, known popularly as *Shi'ites,* today comprise almost all of Iran's population, are a slight majority in Iraq, and also inhabit portions of Syria, Lebanon, and the Indian subcontinent.

The Shi'ite break with other Muslims dates back to the mid seventh century. Partisans of Ali, Muhammad's cousin and son-in-law, managed to have him installed as fourth caliph (r. 656–661) following the murder of Caliph Uthman (r. 644–656). Many of Uthman's followers did not recognize Ali, however, and civil war ensued. The result was Ali's eventual assassination in 661, establishment of the rival Umayyad Dynasty in the caliphate (661–750), and the martyrdom in 680 of Ali's son, al-Husayn, the Prophet's sole surviving grandson. Supporters of the family of Ali, who included many of the original Muslims of Medina, refused to accept the Umayyads as rightful successors of the Prophet. Following the patriarchal traditions of the desert, they claimed that only a member of Muhammad's family could succeed him as *imam,* or religious leader, of Islam. The result was a schism in Islam, and to this day the annual commemoration of al-Husayn's martyrdom is the most sorrowful event on the Shi'ite religious calendar.

Often persecuted as religious dissidents and driven underground, the Shi'ites evolved a theology of history. They not only traced the rightful succession of leadership over the community of Islam from Muhammad and Ali through a number of subsequent imams, whom the Sunnis did not accept as legitimate, but they also developed the notion of a messianic *hidden imam,* or *Mahdi* (the Guided One). According to this religious vision, the imams who followed Muhammad were infallible teachers who spoke with the same authority as the Prophet. This line of earthly imams ended, however, at an early point in time. (Here the various Shi'ite sects disagree as to who was the last visible imam.) The imamate, however, was not destroyed. Rather, the last visible imam had, through the power of God, withdrawn from human sight into a state of *occultation,* or spiritual concealment. There he would remain until some future time, when he would reappear as the Mahdi to gather his faithful, persecuted followers around him, usher in a Muslim holy age, and herald the Last Judgment.

The largest of all Shi'ite sects is the *Twelver Shia,* which developed around the year 900. These Shi'ites, who predominate in Iran, accept a line of twelve infallible imams, divinely appointed from birth, and believe that the twelfth and last of these visible imams disappeared in the late ninth century.

The following selection from the *creed,* or statement of belief, of Muhammad ibn Ali ibn Babawayh — known as *Sheik al-Saduq* (d. 991), one of the greatest of the early Twelver theologians — illustrates several major Twelver beliefs.

QUESTIONS FOR ANALYSIS

1. Who is Muhammad al-Qa'im, and what will he accomplish?
2. What happened to the Prophet Muhammad and each of the first eleven Imams?
3. What is *taqiya,* and why is it obligatory for a Shi'ite? In what ways does a follower of the imams follow the model of al-Qa'im by practicing taqiya?
4. How does al-Suduq view Sunnis? Can you find any suggestion that Shi'ites believe they possess a secret religious truth denied Sunnis? If so, what would be the source of that truth?
5. Shi'ites are said to see themselves as the persecuted, righteous remnant of Islam. Is there any evidence in this document to support such a conclusion? Please explain your answer.

Our belief concerning the number of the prophets is that there have been one hundred and twenty-four thousand prophets and a like number of plenipotentiaries. Each prophet had a plenipotentiary to whom he gave instructions by the command of God. And concerning them we believe that they brought the truth from God and their word is the word of God, their command God's command, and obedience to them obedience to God. . . .

The leaders of the prophets are five (on whom all depends): Noah, Abraham, Moses, Jesus, and Muhammad. Muhammad is their leader . . . he confirmed the (other) apostles.

It is necessary to believe that God did not create anything more excellent than Muhammad and the Imams. . . . After His Prophet,[1] the proofs of God for the people are the Twelve Imams. . . .

We believe that the Proof of Allah in His earth and His viceregent among His slaves in this age of ours is the Upholder [*al-Qa'im*] [of the law of God], the Expected One, Muhammad ibn al-Hasan al-Askari.[2] He it is concerning whose

---

[1] The Prophet Muhammad.

[2] The twelfth imam. Al-Hasan al-Askari, the eleventh imam, died around January 1, 874. Twelvers believe that he was succeeded by a young son, Muhammad al-Qa'im (the Upholder of God's Law), who went into concealment around 878. *Muhammad ibn al-Hasan al-Askari* means "Muhammad, the son of al-Hasan al-Askari."

name and descent the Prophet was informed by God, and he it is who WILL FILL THE EARTH WITH JUSTICE AND EQUITY JUST AS IT IS NOW FULL OF OPPRESSION AND WRONG. He it is whom God will make victorious over the whole world until from every place the call to prayer is heard and religion will belong entirely to God, exalted be He. He is the rightly guided *Mahdi* about whom the prophet gave information that when he appears, Jesus, son of Mary, will descend upon the earth and pray behind him.[3] We believe there can be no other *Qa'im* than him; he may live in the state of occultation[4] (as long as he likes); were it the space of the existence of this world, there would be no *Qa'im* other than him.

Our belief concerning prophets, apostles, Imams, and angels is that they are infallible . . . and do not commit any sin, minor or major . . . he who denies infallibility to them in any matter . . . is a *kafir,* an infidel. . . .

Our belief concerning the Prophet [Muhammad] is that he was poisoned by Jews during the expedition to Khaybar. The poison continued to be noxious until he died of its effects.

1. Imam: And the Prince of Believers [Ali], on whom be peace, was murdered by . . . Ibn Muljam al-Muradi, may God curse him, and was buried in Ghari.
2. Imam: Hasan ibn Ali,[5] on whom be peace, was poisoned by his wife Ja'da bint Ash'ath of Kinda, may God curse her and her father.
3. Imam: Husayn ibn Ali[6] was slain at Karbala.

His murderer was Sinan ibn-Anal al-Nakha'i, may God curse him and his father. . . .

▷   Al-Saduq then lists the fourth through eleventh imams and identifies the murderer of each.

And verily the Prophet and Imams, on whom be peace, had informed the people that they would be murdered. He who says that they were not has given them the lie and has imputed falsehood to God the Mighty and Glorious.

Our belief concerning *taqiya* [permissible dissimulation of one's true beliefs] is that it is obligatory, and he who forsakes it is in the same position as he who forsakes prayer. . . . Now until the time when the Imam al-Qa'im appears, *taqiya* is obligatory and it is not permissible to dispense with it. He who does . . . has verily gone out of the religion of God. And God has described the showing of friendship to unbelievers as being possible only in the state of *taqiya.*

And the Imam Ja'far[7] said, "Mix with enemies openly but oppose them inwardly, so long as authority is a matter of question."[8] . . . And he said, "He who prays with hypocrites [Sunnis], standing in the first row, it is as though he prayed with the Prophet standing in the first row." And he said, "Visit their sick and attend their funerals and pray in their mosques." . . .

Our belief concerning the Alawiya [descendants of Ali] is that they are the progeny of the Messenger of God and devotion to them is obligatory.

---

[3]Sunni and Shi'ite Muslims believe that the return to earth of the prophet and Messiah Jesus (see source 57) will signal the Last Judgment.
[4]Invisible to earthly eyes.

[5]Hasan, the son of (*ibn*) Ali, was Ali's elder son.
[6]Al-Husayn, Ali's younger son.
[7]The sixth imam.
[8]As long as there are Sunni rulers.

God's Vice-Regent on Earth

▼▼▼

60 ▼ Abu'l-Hasan Ali al-Mawardi, BOOK OF THE PRINCIPLES OF GOVERNMENT

Until the capture of Baghdad in 1258 by Mongol forces and the death of the last legitimate Abbasid caliph, Sunni Muslims, who constituted the majority of the followers of Islam, looked to their caliphs for leadership. For Abu Bakr, the first caliph, and his first three successors, who ruled Islam from Medina (632–661), the title meant that its holder was Muhammad's deputy and served as first among equals within the Muslim community. The Umayyad caliphs, however, who ruled from Damascus in Syria (661–750), altered the nature of the caliphate by claiming the title *khalifat Allah* (God's Deputy). The implication was that whoever disobeyed them was an enemy of God and an unbeliever. The Abbasids, ruling from Baghdad (750–1258), expanded this tradition, assumed the title *Shadow of God on Earth,* and transformed the caliphate into a Persian-style autocracy.

In the following document, Abu'l-Hasan Ali al-Mawardi (d. 1058), a jurist and political philosopher who resided in Baghdad, describes the office and qualities of the ideal Sunni caliph. His use of the term *imam* for the caliph stems from the fact that, beginning in the reign of Caliph al-Mahdi (r. 775–785), the Abbasids claimed that the Prophet conferred the office of imam on his uncle Abbas, the Abbasids' direct ancestor. This claim, as well as the caliph's assuming the throne name *al-Mahdi* (the guided one; see source 59), was motivated, at least partially, by the Abbasids' desire to counter the charismatic appeal of their Shi'ite rivals. It also served as a way of demonstrating the Abbasids' piety, thereby distancing themselves from their predecessors, the Umayyads, who had a reputation for irreligiosity.

Al-Mawardi's treatise must be understood within the context of the caliph of Baghdad's eleventh-century position. The Shi'ite ruler of Egypt also claimed the title *caliph,* and in Muslim Spain there was a second rival caliph from the revived Umayyad Dynasty. Local Muslim princes in Southwest Asia were becoming independent of Abbasid control, and in Baghdad a Persian Shi'ite family known as the *Buyids* had gained control over the caliph and issued directives in his name. Far from being the absolute ruler of the worldwide empire of Islam, the Shadow of God on Earth was now a shadow of former Abbasid greatness.

QUESTIONS FOR ANALYSIS

1. How does al-Mawardi describe the ideal Sunni caliph and his office? What are his most important attributes? What are his chief duties?
2. Does al-Mawardi emphasize more the caliph's duties or his powers and prerogatives? What do you infer from your answer?

3. What is the caliph's relationship, in theory, with the Muslim community at large?
4. Which of Muhammad's special powers or functions are not attributed to the caliph? What do you infer from your answer?
5. How does the Sunni caliph, or imam, differ from the Shi'ite imam (source 59)? What do you infer from your answer?
6. The introduction informs us of the eleventh-century political-religious context in which al-Mawardi composed this treatise. How, if at all, does al-Mawardi seem to argue against those realities?

The office of Iman was set up in order to replace the office of Prophet in the defense of the faith and the government of the world. . . . There is disagreement as to whether this obligation [to elect an Imam] derives from reason or from Holy Law.[1] One group says it derives from reason, since it is in the nature of reasonable men to submit to a leader who will prevent them from injuring one another and who will settle quarrels and disputes, for without rulers men would live in anarchy and heedlessness like benighted savages. . . .

Another group says that the obligation derives from the Holy Law and not from reason, since the Imam deals with matters of Holy Law. . . . All that reason requires is that a reasonable man should refrain from mutual injury and conflict with his neighbor and act equitably in mutual fairness and good relations, conducting himself in accordance with his own reason, and not with someone else's. But it is the Holy Law which intervenes to entrust these affairs to its religious representative. God said, "O you who believe, obey God, obey the Prophet, and obey those among you who are in authority" [Qur'an, iv, 62]. He thus explicitly enjoined us to obey those among us who are in authority, and they are the Imams who hold sway over us. . . .

The conditions of eligibility for the Imamate are seven:

1. Rectitude in all respects.
2. The knowledge to exercise personal judgment in cases and decisions.
3. Soundness of hearing, sight, and tongue so that he may deal accurately with those matters which can only be attained by them.
4. Soundness of limb so that he has no defect which would prevent him from moving freely and rising quickly.
5. The discernment needed to govern the subjects and conduct public affairs.
6. The courage and vigor to defend the lands of Islam and to wage holy war against the enemy.
7. Descent, that is to say, he must be of the tribe of Quraysh.[2] . . .

The duties of the Imam in the conduct of public affairs are ten:

1. To maintain the religion according to established principles and the consensus of the first generation of Muslims. If an innovator appears or if some dubious person deviates from it, the Imam must clarify the proofs of religion to him, expound that

---

[1] *Shari'a*, or "the Way," is the sacred law of Islam and is based principally on the Qur'an and Hadith. Sacred Law encompasses a Muslim's entire life. Islam has no priests. Its religious leaders are the *ulama* (the learned), and among the ulama, the jurists who interpret Shari'a hold a special position of prominence.

[2] The Arabs of Mecca and the Prophet's own tribe.

which is correct, and apply to him the proper rules and penalties so that religion may be protected from injury and the community safeguarded from error.

2. To execute judgments given between litigants and to settle disputes between contestants so that justice may prevail and so that none commit or suffer injustice.

3. To defend the lands of Islam and to protect them from intrusion so that people may earn their livelihood and travel at will without danger to life or property.

4. To enforce the legal penalties for the protection of God's commandments from violation and for the preservation of the rights of his servants from injury or destruction.

5. To maintain the frontier fortresses with adequate supplies and effective force for their defense so that the enemy may not take them by surprise, commit profanation there, or shed the blood, either of a Muslim or an ally.

6. To wage holy war [*jihad*] against those who, after having been invited to accept Islam, persist in rejecting it, until they either become Muslims or enter the Pact [*dhimma*][3] so that God's truth may prevail over every religion.

7. To collect the booty and the alms in conformity with the prescriptions of the Holy Law, as defined by explicit texts and by independent judgment, and this without terror or oppression.

8. To determine the salaries and other sums due from the treasury, without extravagance and without parsimony, and to make payment at the proper time, neither in advance nor in arrears.

9. To employ capable and trustworthy men and appoint sincere men for the tasks which he delegates to them and for the money which he entrusts to them so that the tasks may be competently discharged and the money honestly safeguarded.

10. To concern himself directly with the supervision of affairs and the scrutiny of conditions so that he may personally govern the community, safeguard the faith, and not resort to delegation in order to free himself either for pleasure or for worship, for even the trustworthy may betray and the sincere may deceive. God said, "O David,[4] we have made you our viceregent[5] [*khalifa*] on earth; therefore, judge justly among men and do not follow your caprice, which will lead you astray from God's path" [Qur'an, *xxxviii, 25*]. In this, God was not content with delegation, but required a personal performance and did not excuse the following of passions, which, He says, lead astray from His path, and this, though He considered David worthy to judge in religion and to hold His viceregency. This is one of the duties of government of any shepherd. The Prophet of God, may God bless and save him, said, "You are all shepherds, and you are all answerable for your flocks." . . .

---

[3]See source 63.
[4]King of Israel circa 1000 B.C.E.

[5]A *viceregent* is the deputy of a ruler or sovereign.

Sufi Mysticism

▼▼▼

61 ▼ *Abu Hamid Muhammad al-Ghazali,* THE ALCHEMY OF HAPPINESS

Islam enjoins all its faithful to live a life centered on God. Those who have taken this injunction most literally, to the point of seeking mystical union with the Divine, are known as *Sufis.* The term's origins are obscure. It might derive from the rough wool (*suf*) clothes worn by Sufi ascetics; it could also refer to the reputed purity (*safa*) of their lives. Whatever the etymology of their title, Sufis have been part of Islam from its early days.

As is often the case with mystics and similar holy people, Sufis, although few in number, enjoyed widespread popularity among the masses and, like their Christian monastic counterparts (Chapter 7, source 54), proved to be great ambassadors of the faith. Also like the Christian desert hermits, Sufi mystics were more than just a little disturbing to many theologians, jurists, and state builders. Sufi emphasis on one's attaining a personal relationship, and even union, with God by means of a variety of meditative exercises struck many Muslim traditionalists as extremely suspicious. Sufis, however, had a champion in the person of Abu Hamid Muhammad al-Ghazali (1058–1111), Islam's most brilliant and respected theologian. This Persian Sunni managed in both his life and writings to create a synthesis of Sufi devotion and Sunni tradition and intellectualism. As a result, Sufis became more acceptable to Islam's learned religious teachers.

The following excerpts come from al-Ghazali's *The Alchemy of Happiness,* a treatise composed in the final years of his life. The title derives from al-Ghazali's contention that the mystic, by turning away from carnal pleasures in favor of contemplating Eternal Beauty, finds Heaven while still on earth and is transmuted from base matter into spiritual gold.

QUESTIONS FOR ANALYSIS

1. According to al-Ghazali, what is the key element in a person's spiritual transformation?
2. Why does al-Ghazali claim that Muslims do not have a monopoly on eternal life with God?
3. Consider the central message of this selection. Is it consistent with the messages of the Qur'an and Hadith? What do you conclude from your answer?
4. Is the message of this selection consistent with the tone and message of al-Mawardi's treatise (source 60)? What do you conclude from your answer?
5. Assuming al-Ghazali reflects mainstream Sufi thought, how do you imagine most Sufis would understand the religious duty of jihad (source 58, question 2)?

6. How do you imagine most Sufis would react to the issues that separated Shi'ites and Sunnis?
7. Compare these excerpts to Jesus' Sermon on the Mount (Chapter 7, source 50). Which seem more striking, the differences or the similarities? What do you conclude from that answer?

ON THE LOVE OF GOD

O traveler on the way and seeker after the love of God! know that the love of God is a sure and perfect method for the believer to attain the object of his desires. It is a highly exalted station of rest, during the journey of the celestial traveler. It is the consummation of the desires and longings of those who seek divine truth. It is the foundation of the vision of the beauty of the Lord.

The love of God is of the most binding obligation upon every one. It is indeed the spirit of the body, and the light of the eye. The Prophet of God declares that the faith of the believer is not complete, unless he loves God and his Prophet more than all the world besides. The Prophet was once asked, what is faith? He replied, "It is to love God and his Prophet more than wife, children, and property." And the Prophet was continually in the habit of praying, "O my God! I ask for your love, I ask that I may love whomsoever loves you, and that I may perform whatsoever your love makes incumbent upon me."

On the resurrection day all sects will be addressed by the name of the prophet whom each followed, "O people of Moses! O people of Jesus! O people of Muhammad!" even to all the beloved servants of God, and it will be proclaimed to them, "O Friends and beloved of God, come to the blessed union and society of God! Come to Paradise and partake of the grace of your beloved!" When they hear this proclamation, their hearts will leap out of their places, and they will almost lose their reason. Yahya ben Moa'z says, "It is better to have as much love of God, even if only as much as a grain of mustard seed, than seventy years of devotion and obedience without love." Hassan of Basra says, "Whoever knows God, will certainly love him, and whoever knows the world, will shun it."

O you who seek the love of God! know that this love is founded upon two things: one is Beauty, and the other is Beneficence. Beauty acts as a cause to produce love, because the being, the attributes and the works of God possess beauty, and every one loves that which is beautiful. There is a tradition which says "Verily, God is beautiful and he loves beauty." And the Prophet says, "Desire to transact your affairs with those who have beautiful countenances." It is on this account that the spirit in man has been created in accordance with the image of beauty, so that whenever it either hears or sees anything beautiful, it may have a propensity towards it, and seek for communion with it. . . .

O inquirer after the love of God! The love of God exists in every heart, though it lies concealed, just as fire exists in the flint stone, until it is drawn out. If you take the steel of desire and affection into your hands, and with it strike the heart, you obtain fire by the means, and your soul will be filled with light. The malice, deceitfulness, hatred, vileness, envy, and strife that are in the heart will be burned up, and it will be freed and purified from sensual perturbations. But if you are careless and do nothing and pass several days without seeking, the heart will again become like fire covered over with ashes, which by remaining a long time unused will finally be extinguished. So at last the heart becomes encased with sensual impurities and with the blackness of the passions, and is no longer capable of being enlightened with the light of truth. Our refuge is in God!

O, faithful friend, you who are worthy to be loved! Know, that the love of God is a standard that leads to victory. Whoever seeks refuge under it, will be a sovereign in two worlds, and lord of a throne at the king's court. This love is a universal solvent to secure happiness. Whoever secures it, is richer than in the possession of both worlds. God is always rich. . . . The heart which bears no traces of the love of God, is like a dead corpse, which knows nothing of its own spirit.

An African Pilgrim to Mecca
▼▼▼

62 ▼ *Mahmud Kati,*
THE CHRONICLE OF THE SEEKER

Despite their differences, all Muslims accept certain basic beliefs, such as the Oneness of God, and perform a number of common religious obligations that serve as powerful forces for Islamic unification. Among these is the pilgrimage, or *hajj,* to Mecca. Every Muslim adult is expected, unless it is impossible, to travel once in a lifetime to Mecca, arriving during the sacred month of *Dhu-al-Hijja,* and join a vast multitude of other pilgrims in a mass celebration of devotional activities. Here Muslims of all sects, races, and social levels mingle without distinction and join in affirming the unity of the family of Islam.

The following document describes the famous pilgrimage that Mansa (King) Musa (Moses) of Mali (r. 1312–1327) made to Mecca in 1324–1325. The sheer size of Mansa Musa's entourage and the generosity this king of sub-Saharan West Africa exhibited to Muslims along the route guaranteed that the memory of his pilgrimage would not be lost. Several written accounts exist. This particular record is ascribed to the family of Mahmud Kati (1468?–1593), a native scholar and Islamic judge of Timbuktu. Kati, who according to tradition lived for one hundred twenty-five years, began to compose his history around 1519 and continued it until his death almost seventy-five years later. His sons and grandsons carried on his labors, bringing the story of Islam in West Africa down to 1655. As was the case with all contemporary writers in that region of the world, Kati and his family composed the work in Arabic.

QUESTIONS FOR ANALYSIS

1. What does Mansa Musa's alleged reason for undertaking the pilgrimage suggest about the hajj and pilgrimages in general?
2. How did his going on pilgrimage make Mansa Musa a better Muslim? What does this suggest about the role of hajj?
3. Is there any evidence in this story to suggest that Islam, though a world religion, still retained strong Arabic connections and flavor? Please explain your answer.
4. What impact did Mansa Musa's hajj have on the traditions and shared historical memory of Mali?

5. What evidence is there that this particular story was composed in its final form by one of Kati's successors?
6. What evidence suggests that the author used a source dated earlier than the end of the fifteenth century?
7. What role did oral tradition apparently play in sub-Saharan West African society?

We shall now relate some of what we have been able to discover about the history of the Mali-koy Kankan Musa.[1]

This Mali-koy was an upright, godly, and devout sultan.[2] His dominion stretched from the limits of Mali as far as Sibiridugu, and all the peoples in these lands, Songhay[3] and others, obeyed him. Among the signs of his virtue are that he used to emancipate a slave every day, that he made the pilgrimage to the sacred house of God,[4] and that in the course of his pilgrimage he built the great mosque of Timbuktu[5] as well as the mosques of Dukurey, Gundam, Direy, Wanko, and Bako.

His mother Kankan was a native woman, though some say she was of Arab origin. The cause of his pilgrimage was related to me as follows by the scholar Muhammad Quma, may God have mercy on him, who had memorized the traditions of the ancients. He said that the Mali-koy Kankan Musa had killed his mother, Nana Kankan, by mistake. For this he felt deep regret and remorse and feared retribution. In expiation he gave great sums of money in alms and resolved on a life-long fast.

He asked one of the ulama[6] of his time what he could do to expiate this terrible crime, and he replied, "You should seek refuge with the Prophet of God, may God bless and save him. Flee to him, place yourself under his protection, and ask him to intercede for you with God, and God will accept his intercession. That is my view.

Kankan Musa made up his mind that very day and began to collect the money and equipment needed for the journey. He sent proclamations to all parts of his realm asking for supplies and support and went to one of his shaykhs[7] and asked him to choose the day of his departure. "You should wait," said the shaykh, "for the Saturday which falls on the twelfth day of the month. Set forth on that day, and you will not die before you return safe and sound to your residence, please God."

He therefore delayed and waited until these two coincided, and it was not until nine months later that the twelfth of the month fell on a Saturday. He set forth when the head of his caravan had already reached Timbuktu, while he himself was still in his residence in Mali.

Since that time travelers of that people believe it is lucky to set out on a journey on a Saturday which falls on the twelfth of a month. It has become proverbial that when a traveler returns in a bad state, they say of him, "Here is one who did not set out on the Mali-koy's Saturday of departure!"

Kankan Musa set out in force, with much money and a numerous army. A scholar told me that he heard from our shaykh, the very learned qadi[8] Abu'l-Abbas Sidi Ahmad ibn Ahmad ibn

---

[1]Titles meaning "King of Mali, Lord Musa."
[2]An Arabic term meaning "one who wields authority."
[3]Songhay lay to the east of Mali and centered on the trading city of Gao. Mansa Musa's armies conquered Gao around 1325, and Mali maintained control over Songhay until about 1375. By the late fifteenth century Songhay had replaced Mali as West Africa's major sub-Saharan trading kingdom and held this position of primacy until it was conquered in 1591 by invaders from Morocco.

[4]The *Ka'bah* in Mecca, Islam's holiest site.
[5]Timbuktu was the major trading city of the Kingdom of Mali from 1325 to 1433. Its mosque school became the chief center of Muslim learning in sub-Saharan West Africa.
[6]Religious authorities by virtue of their learning (see source 60, note 1).
[7]An Arabic title of respect meaning "elder."
[8]An Islamic judge.

...ad, may God have mercy on ...d with him, that on the day ...li ibn al-Qadir[10] left for Twat, ...e was going on the pilgrim-...sked how many persons were ...d was told that the total num-...the pasha had with him was about eighty. God is great! Praise be to God!," said the qadi. "Everything in the world grows less. When Kankan Musa left here to go on pilgrimage he had with him 8,000 men. The Askia Muhammad[11] made the pilgrimage later with 800 men, that is, one-tenth of that. Third after them came 'Ali ibn 'Abd al-Qadir, with 80 men, one-tenth of 800." And he added, "Praise be to God, other than Whom there is no God! 'Ali ibn 'Abd al-Qadir did not even achieve his purpose."

Kankan Musa went on his journey, about which there are many stories. Most of them are untrue and the mind refuses to accept them. One such story is that in every town where he stopped on Friday between here and Egypt he built a mosque on that very day. It is said that the mosques of Gundam and Dukurey were among those he built. Both at lunch and at dinner, from when he left his residence until he returned, he ate fresh fish and fresh vegetables.

I was told that his wife, called Inari Konte, went with him, accompanied by 500 of her women and serving women.

Our shaykh, the Mori Bukar ibn Salih, . . . may God have mercy on him, told me that Kankan Musa took forty mule-loads of gold with him when he went on his pilgrimage and visited the tomb of the Prophet.[12]

It is said that he asked the skaykh of the noble and holy city of Mecca, may Almighty God protect it, to give him two, three, or four *sharifs*[13] of the kin of the Prophet of God, may God bless him and save him, to go with him to his country, so that the people of these parts might be blessed by the sight of them and by the blessing of their footsteps in these lands. But the shaykh refused, it being generally agreed that such things should be prevented and refused out of respect and regard for the noble blood of the *sharifs* and for fear lest one of them fall into the hands of the infidels and be lost or go astray. But he persisted in his request and urged them very strongly, until the shaykh said, "I will not do it, but I will neither command nor forbid it. If anyone wishes, let him follow you. His fate is in his own hands, I am not responsible."

The Mali-koy then sent a crier to the mosques to say, "Whoever wishes to have a thousand *mithqals*[14] of gold, let him follow me to my country, and the thousand is ready for him." Four men of the tribe of Quraysh[15] came to him, but it is claimed that they were freedmen[16] of Quraysh and not real Qurayshis. He gave them 4,000, 1,000 each,[17] and they followed him, with their families, when he returned to his country.

When the Mali-koy reached Timbuktu on his way back, he collected ships and small boats on which he transported their families and luggage, together with his own women, as far as his country, for the riding animals were too exhausted to use. When the ships, carrying the *sharifs* from Mecca, reached the town of Kami, the Dienné-koy[18] . . . attacked the ships and plundered all that they contained. They took the *sharifs* ashore and revolted against the Mali-koy. But when the people of the ships told them about the *sharifs* and informed them of their high station, they attended them, and installed them in a nearby place called Shinshin. It is said that the *sharifs* of the town of Kay are descended from them.

---

[9]A Turkish title meaning "chief."
[10]Governor of Timbuktu, 1628–1632.
[11]Askia (Emperor) Muhammad Ture the Great (r. 1492–1528), Lord of Songhay. The askia undertook his pilgrimage in 1495–1496, accompanied by Mahmud Kati, who was one of his chief advisers.
[12]The Prophet's tomb is in Medina.
[13]An Arabic title meaning "exalted one."

[14]A weight of precious metal that varied by region.
[15]The tribe of the Prophet.
[16]Freed former slaves, therefore Qurayshis by adoption, not birth.
[17]He gave each of four men one thousand mithqals of gold.
[18]The lord of Dienné, technically one of Mansa Musa's vassals.

This is the end of the story of the pilgrimage of the Mali-koy Kankan Musa. . . .

As for Mali, it is a vast region and an immense country, containing many towns and villages. The authority of the Sultan of Mali extends over all with force and might. We have heard the common people of our time say that there are four sultans in the world, not counting the supreme sultan,[19] and they are the Sultan of Baghdad,[20] the Sultan of Egypt, the Sultan of Bornu,[21] and the Sultan of Mali.

---

[19]The Ottoman sultan of Constantinople.
[20]The last caliph of Baghdad died in 1258.

[21]A West African trading rival of Songhay located in the region of Lake Chad, along the border of modern Chad and Nigeria.

▼▼▼

Islam and Unbelievers

Source 57's excerpts from the Qur'an remind Muslims of the heritage that they share with the People of the Book — namely, Jews and Christians. Yet the Qur'an also threatens eternal hell fire for all who perversely refuse to become Muslims, including Jews and Christians who remain obstinate in their rejection of Islam. Source 58's excerpts from Hadith remind Muslims that the followers of Islam share the security of belonging to a community that, at least in the ideal, is fully integrated and supportive of all its members, even the poorest and weakest. Hadith also enjoins upon all Muslims the service of *jihad,* or holy struggle, in the name of God, and that includes struggling against unbelievers who do not belong to that community. But what about the unbelievers, or *infidels,* who submit to Islam's secular authority but remain outside the community of Muslim faithful? How should and, more importantly, *did* Muslim rulers deal with their non-Muslim subjects, both People of the Book and those outside the Judeo-Christian tradition? As the following sources suggest, the answer is not a simple one.

The *Dhimma:* A Contract with the People of the Book

▼▼▼

63 ▼ *THE PACT OF UMAR*

One vexing question that faced conquering Muslim armies in the early seventh century was how to deal with their non-Muslim subjects, particularly Jews and Christians. The following document, which purports to be the pact of peace offered by Caliph Umar I (r. 634–644) to the Christians of Syria around 637, was apparently written down in its present form in the ninth century, but it is supposedly based on the account of an early Muslim who died in 697. Most Western scholars, however, believe the pact is an anachronism that essentially reflects ninth-century realities because it is too restrictive for the quite tolerant age of Islam's first four caliphs (632–661) and the Umayyad Dynasty (661–750) that followed. Whatever its origins, the pact represented by this document is an excellent example of the *dhimma,* or contract of protection, offered to subject non-Muslims throughout most of premodern Islamic history. The non-Muslims who lived under this compact were known as *dhimmis* and generally paid a *jizya,* or poll tax (a tax levied on a person rather than on property), as a token of their submission to the authority of Islam.

QUESTIONS FOR ANALYSIS

1. Why do you think that non-Muslims were prohibited from teaching their children the Qur'an?
2. Why were dhimmis forbidden to use the very phrases and modes of dress employed by Muslims? Or even to adopt Muslim surnames?
3. How restrictive were these rules so far as the practice of Christianity was concerned?
4. Should dhimmis break this pact or even be perceived as breaking it, what was the threatened consequence?
5. What was the purpose of this pact?
6. How would you characterize the dhimma and the status of dhimmis?
7. Large numbers of Christians, Jews, Zoroastrians, Hindus, and others in regions conquered by Islam ultimately converted to Islam. Does this pact provide any evidence of one reason for some of the conversions? If so, what?

In the name of God, the Merciful, the Compassionate! This is a writing to Umar from the Christians of *such and such a city.* When you[1] marched against us,[2] we asked of you protection for ourselves, our posterity, and our co-religionists; and we made this stipulation with you that we will not erect in our city or the suburbs any new monastery, church, cell, or hermitage;[3] that we will not repair any of such buildings that might fall into ruins, or renew those that might be situated in the Muslim quarters of the town; that we will not refuse the Muslims entry into our churches either by night or by day; that we will open the gates wide to passengers and travelers; that we will receive any Muslim traveler into our houses and give him food and lodging for three nights; that we will not harbor any spy in our churches or houses or conceal any enemy of the Muslims.[4]

That we will not teach our children the Qur'an; that we will not make a show of the Christian religion or invite anyone to embrace it; that we will not prevent any of our kinsmen from embracing Islam, if they so desire. That we will honor the Muslims and rise up in our assemblies when they wish to take their seats; that we will not imitate them in our dress, either in the cap, turban, sandals, or parting of the hair; that we will not make use of their expressions of speech[5] or adopt their surnames; that we will not ride on

---

[1]Muslims.
[2]The Christians of Syria.
[3]The dwelling of a Christian hermit, or monk (see Chapter 7, source 54).

[4]Several of these ordinances were taken directly from earlier imperial Roman laws regarding non-Christians.
[5]Muslims greet one another with certain qur'anic verses and similar affirmations of their faith.

saddles or gird on swords or take to ourselves arms or wear them or engrave Arabic inscriptions on our rings; that we will not sell wine;[6] that we will shave the front of our heads; that we will keep to our own style of dress, wherever we might be; that we will wear belts around our waists.[7]

That we will not display the cross[8] upon our churches or display our crosses or our sacred books in the streets of the Muslims or in their marketplaces; that we will strike the clappers in our churches lightly;[9] that we will not recite our services in a loud voice when a Muslim is present; that we will not carry palm-branches[10] or our

images[11] in pro
burial of our d
carry lighted c
lims or their m
any slaves who
sion of Muslir
that we will no

All this we
ourselves and
protection from
late any of the c
we forfeit your
to treat us as enemies and rebels.

---

[6]Muslims are forbidden to drink wine.

[7]Dhimmis wore leather or cord belts; Muslims wore silk and other types of cloth belts.

[8]Islam greatly reveres Jesus the Messiah (source 57) but denies that he died on the cross.

[9]Christian churches could not ring bells; the faithful were summoned to prayer by wooden clappers.

[10]On Palm Sunday, the Sunday that precedes Easter. This public procession commemorates Jesus' triumphal entry into Jerusalem.

[11]Islam has traditionally looked upon the use of sacred images as *idolatry,* or the worship of idols. As far as Muslims are concerned, idolatry is a grave offense against God.

The Jewish Community
of Twelfth-Century Baghdad

▼▼▼

64 ▼ *Benjamin of Tudela, BOOK OF TRAVELS*

Benjamin ben Jonah of Tudela provides the best eyewitness account of twelfth-century Jewish life in Europe, Asia, and North Africa. This Jewish traveler, about whom we know so little, departed his native northern Spain around 1159 and spent the next thirteen or fourteen years visiting several hundred Jewish communities from the Mediterranean to possibly as far east as India. Benjamin possibly was a merchant, but whatever he was and whatever his primary purpose was for traveling, he took detailed notes on the Jewish communities that he visited and even some that he only heard about. For example, he informs us that the scattered remnants of Israel were flourishing in China.

In the following excerpt Benjamin describes the quality of life for Jews under Muslim rule in Baghdad, the capital of the Abbasid caliphate (source 60).

QUESTIONS FOR ANALYSIS

1. Who was Daniel the son of Hisdai, and what function did he serve under the caliph?

on a map the region supposedly under the Head of the Captivity's ...hority. What does this suggest about the extent of the Jewish Diaspora (Chapter 6)?

3. What was the status of Jews within the lands ruled by the caliph, and how would you characterize Muslim-Jewish relations in the reign of al-Abbasi?

4. Despite their status, the Jews of Baghdad referred to their leader as *Head of the Captivity,* a term that brings to mind the earlier Babylonian Captivity (Chapter 3, source 22). What does this term suggest about the Jews' vision of their present status and their hopes for the future?

5. What aspects of Baghdad's Jewish community most interested Rabbi Benjamin, and what does his interest in them suggest about the reasons Diaspora Judaism managed to flourish as a religion and a culture?

Baghdad [is] . . . the royal residence of the Caliph Emir al-Muminin al-Abbasi[1] of the family of Muhammad.[2] He is at the head of the Muslim religion, and all the kings of Islam obey him; he occupies a similar position to that held by the pope over the Christians.[3] He has a palace in Baghdad three miles in extent, wherein is a great park with all varieties of trees, fruit-bearing and otherwise, and all manner of animals. . . . There the great king, al-Abbasi the Caliph holds his court, and he is kind unto Israel, and many belonging to the people of Israel are his attendants; he knows all languages, and is well versed in the Law of Israel. He reads and writes the holy language [Hebrew]. . . . He is truthful and trusty, speaking peace to all men. . . .

In Baghdad there are about forty thousand Jews, and they dwell in security, prosperity, and honor under the great Caliph, and among them are great sages, the heads of Academies engaged in the study of the Law. In this city there are ten Academies.[4] . . . And at the head of them all is Daniel the son of Hisdai, who is styled "Our Lord the Head of the Captivity of all Israel." He possesses a book of pedigrees going back as far as David, King of Israel.[5] The Jews call him "Our Lord, Head of the Captivity," and the Muslims call him "Saidna ben Daoud,"[6] and he has been invested with authority over all the congregations of Israel at the hands of the Emir al-Muminin, the Lord of Islam. For thus Muhammad[7] commanded concerning him and his descendants; and he granted him a seal of office over all the congregations that dwell under his rule, and ordered that every one, whether Muslim or Jew, or belonging to any other nation in his dominion, should rise up before him and salute him, and that any one who should refuse to rise up should receive one hundred stripes.[8]

And every fifth day when he goes to pay a visit to the great Caliph, horsemen, gentiles as well as Jews, escort him, and heralds proclaim in advance, "Make way before our Lord, the son of David, as is due unto him," the Arabic words being "Amilu tarik la Saidna ben Daud." He is mounted on a horse, and is attired in robes of

[1]Also known as *al-Mustanjid* (r. 1160–1170).
[2]The Abbasids were descended from the Prophet's uncle Abbas.
[3]The bishop of Rome, who served as head of the Christian Church in the West (see Chapter 10, sources 86, 88, and 89).
[4]Academies for the study of scripture and the Talmud (Chapter 6, source 49). These scholars served as the rabbis, or religious teachers and judges, of their community.

[5]King of Israel around 1000 B.C.E.
[6]The Lord son of David.
[7]Not the Prophet Muhammad but possibly al-Abbasi's predecessor, Muhammad el-Moktafi.
[8]A public flogging, in which the person receives one hundred blows.

silk and embroidery with a large turban on his head. . . . Then he appears before the Caliph and kisses his hand, and the Caliph rises and places him on a throne which Muhammad had ordered to be made for him, and all the Muslim princes who attend the court of the Caliph rise up before him. And the Head of the Captivity is seated on his throne opposite to the Caliph, in compliance with the command of Muhammad. . . . The authority of the Head of the Captivity extends over all the communities of Shinar,[9] Persia, Khurasan[10] and Sheba which is El-Yemen,[11] and Diyar Kalach[12] and the land of Aram Naharaim,[13] and over the dwellers in the mountains of Ararat[14] and the land of the Alans.[15] . . . His authority extends also over the land of Siberia,[16] and the communities in the land of the Togarmim[17] unto the mountains of Asveh and the land of Gurgan, the inhabitants of which are called Gurganim who dwell by the river Gihon, and these are the Girgashites who follow the Christian religion.[18] Further it extends to the gates of Samarkand,[19] the land of Tibet, and the land of India. In respect of all these countries the Head of the Captivity gives the communities power to appoint Rabbis and Ministers who come unto him to be consecrated and to receive his authority. They bring him offerings and gifts from the ends of the earth. He owns hospices, gardens, and plantations in Babylon,[20] and much land inherited from his fathers, and no one can take his possessions from him by force. He has a fixed weekly revenue arising from the hospices of the Jews, the markets and the merchants, apart from that which is brought to him from far-off lands. The man is very rich, and wise in the Scriptures as well as in the Talmud, and many Israelites dine at his table every day.

At his installation, the Head of the Captivity gives much money to the Caliph, to the Princes, and to the Ministers. On the day that the Caliph performs the ceremony of investing him with authority, he rides in the second of the royal carriages, and is escorted from the palace of the Caliph to his own house with timbrels and fifes. The Exilarch[21] appoints the Chiefs of the Academies by placing his hand upon their heads, thus installing them in their office. The Jews of the city are learned men and very rich.

In Baghdad there are twenty-eight Jewish Synagogues, situated either in the city itself or in al-Karkh on the other side of the Tigris; for the river divides the metropolis into two parts. The great synagogue of the Head of the Captivity has columns of marble of various colors overlaid with silver and gold, and on these columns are sentences of the Psalms[22] in golden letters. And in front of the ark are about ten steps of marble; on the topmost step are the seats of the Head of the Captivity and of the Princes of the House of David. The city of Baghdad is twenty miles in circumference, situated in a land of palms, gardens and plantations, the like of which is not to be found in the whole land of Shinar.

---

[9]Southern Mesopotamia (ancient Sumer and Akkad).
[10]Northeastern Iran.
[11]Southern Arabia, the presumed land of the tenth-century B.C.E. queen of Sheba, who visited Israel's King Solomon (the Bible, 1 Kings, 10:1–13).
[12]Anatolia (modern Turkey).
[13]Northern Mesopotamia (modern northern Syria).
[14]Armenia.
[15]An Indo-European people inhabiting the Caucasus mountain region of Georgia.
[16]He probably means Iberia, not Siberia. If the reference is to Iberia, he does not mean the Iberian Peninsula, where the modern nations of Spain and Portugal are located, but rather the land that today roughly corresponds to the nation of Georgia (note 15).

[17]One of a number of people of the central Euphrates in biblical times (the Bible, Genesis, 10:3).
[18]Apparently, he means the African Christian civilizations of the Sudan (Kush) and Ethiopia (Chapter 11, source 95). Gihon was one of the four biblical rivers of the Garden of Eden and usually refers to the Nile. The Girgashites were one of the seven people who inhabited Canaan before its conquest by the Hebrews under Joshua.
[19]A major city that today is located in Uzbekistan, in Central Asia.
[20]The region around Baghdad.
[21]The ruler of the exile — Daniel the son of Hisdai.
[22]Sacred hymns that constitute one of the books of the Bible.

Fourteenth-Century Hindu *Dhimmis*
▼▼▼
65 ▼ THE DEEDS OF SULTAN FIRUZ SHAH

As we shall see in Chapter 9 (source 78), around the year 1000 Turkish Muslim raiders out of Afghanistan began pushing into northwest India, where they set up a base of operations in Lahore, which is located in the modern nation of Pakistan. Around the year 1200 another Muslim Turkish group of warlords, also out of Afghanistan, swept through north central India. In the course of the next one hundred fifty years this second wave of Turks established the *Sultanate of Delhi.* At its height in the early fourteenth century, this Islamic state controlled, in varying degrees, almost the entire Indian subcontinent, except for the southernmost areas.

Firuz Shah Tughluq, who reigned from 1351 to 1388, enjoyed the reputation of being the most pious, humane, and generous of the sultans of Delhi. Toward the end of his life he prepared an account of the accomplishments in which he took the greatest pride. In the following excerpts he details the manner in which he carried out his duties toward his subjects, of whom only a minority were Muslims.

QUESTIONS FOR ANALYSIS

1. How did Firuz Shah see his responsibilities toward Sunni Muslims?
2. How did he treat Shi'ites?
3. How did Firuz Shah treat his Hindu subjects? Did he seem to have any sense of responsibility on their behalf? If so, what sort of responsibility?
4. Compare his treatment of his Hindu subjects with the Pact of Umar (source 63). What do you conclude from your analysis?
5. Compare Firuz Shah's treatment of Hindus with the way in which he dealt with Shi'ites. What conclusions follow from your analysis?
6. What did Firuz Shah believe were his greatest responsibilities and achievements? What conclusions follow from your answer?
7. Reconsider your answer to question 7 of source 63 in the light of this document. Has the present document confirmed your earlier inferences or caused you to modify them? Please explain your answer.

Praises without end, and infinite thanks to that merciful Creator who gave to me his poor abject creature Firuz. . . . His impulse for the maintenance of the laws of His religion, for the repression of heresy, the prevention of crime, and the prohibition of things forbidden; who gave me also a disposition for discharging my lawful duties and my moral obligations. My desire is that, to the best of my human power, I should recount and pay my thanks for the many blessings He has bestowed upon me, so that I may be found among the number of His grateful servants. First

I would praise Him because when irreligion and sins opposed to the Law prevailed in Hindustan,[1] and men's habits and dispositions were inclined towards them, and were averse to the restraints of religion, He inspired me His humble servant with an earnest desire to repress irreligion and wickedness, so that I was able to labor diligently until with His blessing the vanities of the world, and things repugnant to religion, were set aside, and the true was distinguished from the false.

In the reigns of former kings[2] the blood of many Muslims had been shed, and many varieties of torture employed. Amputation of hands and feet, ears and noses; tearing out the eyes, pouring molten lead into the throat, crushing the bones of the hands and feet with mallets, burning the body with fire, driving iron nails into the hands, feet, and bosom, cutting the sinews, sawing men asunder; these and many similar tortures were practiced. The great and merciful God made me, His servant, hope and seek for His mercy by devoting myself to prevent the unlawful killing of Muslims, and the infliction of any kind of torture upon them or upon any men. . . .

By God's help I determined that the lives of Muslims and true believers should be in perfect immunity, and whoever transgressed the Law should receive the punishment prescribed by the book[3] and the decrees of judges. . . .

The sect of Shi'as . . . had endeavored to make proselytes.[4] They wrote treatises and books, and gave instruction and lectures upon the tenets of their sect, and traduced and reviled the first chiefs of our religion (on whom be the peace of God!). I seized them all and I convicted them of their errors and perversions. On the most zealous I inflicted punishment, and the rest I visited with censure and threats of public punishment. Their books I burnt in public, and so by the grace of God the influence of this sect was entirely suppressed. . . .

The Hindus and idol-worshipers had agreed to pay the money for toleration, and had consented to the poll tax,[5] in return for which they and their families enjoyed security. These people now erected new idol temples in the city and the environs in opposition to the Law of the Prophet which declares that such temples are not to be tolerated. Under Divine guidance I destroyed these edifices, and I killed those leaders of infidelity who seduced others into error, and the lower orders I subjected to stripes and chastisement, until this abuse was entirely abolished. . . . I forbade the infliction of any severe punishment on the Hindus in general, but I destroyed their idol temples, and instead thereof raised mosques. . . . Where infidels and idolaters worshiped idols, Muslims now, by God's mercy, perform their devotions to the true God. Praises of God and the summons to prayer are now heard there, and that place which was formerly the home of infidels has become the habitation of the faithful, who there repeat their creed and offer up their praises to God. . . .

In former times it had been the custom to wear ornamented garments, and men received robes as tokens of honor from kings' courts. Figures and devices were painted and displayed on saddles, bridles, and collars, on censers, on goblets and cups, and flagons, on dishes and ewers, in tents, on curtains and on chairs, and upon all articles and utensils. Under Divine guidance and favor I ordered all pictures and portraits to be removed from these things, and that such articles only should be made as are approved and recognized by the Law. Those pictures and portraits which were painted on the doors and walls of palaces I ordered to be effaced.[6]

Formerly the garments of great men were gen-

---

[1]The north central region of India inhabited largely by Hindus.
[2]Muhammad ben Tughluq (r. 1325–1351), his predecessor, had been noted for his cruelty.
[3]Shari'a, or Sacred Law, according to the dictates of the Qur'an.

[4]Converts.
[5]The jizya.
[6]Most Muslims regard the representation of human or animal figures to be blasphemy.

erally made of silk and gold brocades, beautiful but unlawful. Under Divine guidance I ordered that such garments should be worn as are approved by the Law of the Prophet, and that choice should be made of such trimmings of gold brocade, embroidery, or braiding as did not exceed four inches in breadth. Whatever was unlawful and forbidden by, or opposed to, the Law was set aside.

Among the gifts which God bestowed upon me, His humble servant, was a desire to erect public buildings. So I built many mosques and colleges and monasteries, that the learned and the elders, the devout and the holy, might worship God in these edifices, and aid the kind builder with their prayers. The digging of canals, the planting of trees, and the endowing with lands are in accordance with the directions of the Law. The learned doctors of the Law of Islam have many troubles; of this there is no doubt. I settled allowances upon them in proportion to their necessary expenses, so that they might regularly receive the income. . . .

For the benefit of travelers and pilgrims resorting to the tombs of illustrious kings and celebrated saints,[7] and for providing the things necessary in these holy places, I confirmed and gave effect to the grants of villages, lands, and other endowments which had been conferred upon them in olden times. In those cases where no endowment or provision has been settled, I made an endowment, so that these establishments might for ever be secure of an income, to afford comfort to travelers and wayfarers, to holy men and learned men. May they remember those ancient benefactors and me in their prayers.

I was enabled by God's help to build a . . . hospital, for the benefit of every one of high or low degree, who was suddenly attacked by illness and overcome by suffering. Physicians attend there to ascertain the disease, to look after the cure, to regulate the diet, and to administer medicine. The cost of the medicines and the food is defrayed from my endowments. All sick persons, residents and travelers, gentle and simple, bond and free, resort thither; their maladies are treated, and, under God's blessing, they are cured. . . .

I encouraged my infidel subjects to embrace the religion of the Prophet, and I proclaimed that every one who repeated the creed[8] and became a Muslim should be exempt from the jizya, or poll-tax. Information of this came to the ears of the people at large, and great numbers of Hindus presented themselves, and were admitted to the honor of Islam. Thus they came forward day by day from every quarter, and, adopting the faith, were exonerated from the jizya, and were favored with presents and honors. . . .

Whenever a person had completed the natural term of life and had become full of years, after providing for his support, I advised and admonished him to direct his thoughts to making preparation for the life to come, and to repent of all things which he had done contrary to the Law and religion in his youth; to wean his affections from this world, and to fix them on the next. . . .

My object in writing this book has been to express my gratitude to the All-bountiful God for the many and various blessings He has bestowed upon me. Secondly, that men who desire to be good and prosperous may read this and learn what is the proper course. There is this concise maxim, by observing which, a man may obtain God's guidance: Men will be judged according to their works, and rewarded for the good that they have done.

---

[7]The tombs of Sufi saints, around whom cults of veneration had grown.

[8]"There is no God but God; Muhammad is the Deputy of God."

Part Three

▾▾▾

Continuity, Change, and Interchange:
500–1500

Hinduism, Buddhism, Confucianism, Greek rationalism, imperial systems of government and bureaucracy, Christianity, and many other major world traditions were firmly in place by 500 C.E., and despite changes, they remained integral elements of global civilization for the next thousand years and beyond. The continuity of culture, especially in China and India, is one of the major features of the period 500 to 1500. A Chinese of the Han Dynasty would have found much that was familiar in *Ming* China (1368–1644), and while Islam was making an important impact on northern India after 1000, Hindu culture continued to flourish and develop along lines that reached back at least to Indo-Aryan antiquity. At the same time, this millennium witnessed radical changes from which even the essentially conservative societies of China and India were not immune.

Many of these changes were due to the movement and interchange of people. Germans and other fringe groups infiltrated the western regions of the Roman Empire, thereby serving as a major factor in the radical transformation of society in Western Europe. The rise and spread of Islam in the seventh and eighth centuries created a new cultural bloc that stretched from western North Africa and Spain to Central Asia. The later movement of Turkish and Mongol nomads out of Central Asia resulted in empires that severely strained but also richly cross-pollinated virtually all of Eurasia's older civilized societies. Hindu, Chinese, and Arab merchants greatly influenced the development of civilization in Southeast Asia, their common meeting ground. It is almost impossible to exaggerate the impact China had on the development of Korean and Japanese cultures. The *Byzantine* World became the model and civilizer of the Eastern Slavs, most notably the Russians. Western Christian Europe expanded into Ireland, Scandinavia, Germany, the lands of the Baltic Sea, Poland, and Hungary. By 1500 Christianity, in both its Latin and Byzantine forms, provided spiritual direction to Europeans from Iceland to the Volga. Long before 1500 major portions of sub-Saharan Africa had become integral parts of the Muslim world, and toward the end of the fifteenth century Europeans were making their presence known along the African coast.

Of all Eurasia's civilizations, Western Europe underwent the most radical changes during this thousand-year period. Out of the chaos that ensued following the collapse of Roman society in the West, a new civilization emerged: Western Christian Europe. By 1100 it was an aggressive, expansionistic power, as the crusades bear witness. Despite a number of crises in the fourteenth century, which occasioned a momentary retrenchment, Western Europe never abandoned its spirit of expansion. In 1492 it was ready to resume explorations across the Atlantic. The eventual result was the virtual destruction of almost all Amerindian cultures and their absorption into the fabric of European civilization.

Chapter 9

▼▼▼

Asia

Change in the Context of Tradition

Asia was home to the world's oldest and most complex civilizations, and as such, its deeply rooted cultures were the most tradition bound. Even Asia's newer civilizations, such as Japan, exhibited an innate conservatism, in part because they had borrowed so heavily from their well-established neighbors.

Change, of course, comes to all societies, old and new, and Asia was no exception. Occasionally, it arrived in dramatic fashion, as in the destruction of the Abbasid caliphate in 1258 or the establishment of the hated *Yuan* Dynasty (1264–1368) in China. More often than not, however, change arrived clothed in the guise of tradition. Even *Kubilai Khan,* Mongol emperor of China (r. 1260–1294), adopted a Chinese name for his dynasty, performed the Confucian imperial rites, and tried to reestablish the civil service examination system. When in 1192 Minamoto Yoritomo (1147–1199) transferred all real political and military power to himself as *shogun,* he left Japan's imperial court and structure in place and allowed local lords to retain a good measure of their old feudal autonomy.

A reverence for tradition did not mean a lack of dynamism. The great urban centers of Asia — Baghdad, Cambay, Delhi, Hangzhou, Nara — were prosperous and cosmopolitan. China in the eleventh century had several cities with populations of a million or more, and the volume of commerce in those urban centers eventually necessitated the creation of imperially guaranteed paper money. Economic prosperity also meant artistic patronage, and as a result artistic expression flourished from Southwest Asia to Japan. As European travelers learned, the riches of Asia were no empty fable.

▼▼▼

Japan: Creating a Distinctive Civilization

Composed of four main islands, Japan's closest continental neighbor is Korea, which at its closest point is still about one hundred twenty miles away across a stretch of often tempestuous water. This insularity has benefited Japan to the point that it is close enough to the East Asian mainland to receive the stimulation of foreign ideas but far enough away to be free to choose what it wishes to adopt from abroad. The result is a culturally homogenous Japanese civilization that has its distinctive identity but that also clearly has been the beneficiary of influences from across the Sea of Japan.

The Japanese spoken language is distantly related to Korean but unrelated to Chinese, suggesting that the ancestors of the historical Japanese originated in lands northeast of China and migrated down into the Korean peninsula, from where they sailed into the archipelago of islands that make up Japan. There they slowly displaced the islands' original inhabitants, including the *Ainu,* who are physically quite different from the Japanese. It is not at all clear when this migration took place, but sometime after 300 B.C.E. the Japanese emerged as a identifiable culture. It was only in the period around the end of the fourth century B.C.E. that agriculture based on rice cultivation arrived from South China, probably by way of Korea. Given Korea's proximity and earlier historical development, it is not at all surprising that the peninsula proved to be a major conduit for early cultural imports from mainland East Asia. Around 200 C.E. the Japanese were practicing iron metallurgy, a Chinese process received from Korea.

Japan's first identifiable state arose no earlier than the third century C.E., when the chieftains of a clan devoted to the sun goddess established their hegemony on the Yamato Plain in the western regions of the island of Honshu. To the Chinese, Japan in this period was the rustic land of *Wa,* which they represented by an ideograph that meant "dwarf." The Japanese themselves were illiterate until, as the story goes, a Korean scribe named Wani arrived in 405 C.E. to offer instruction in Chinese script, which the Japanese quickly adapted to their language. In the mid sixth century a Chinese form of Mahayana Buddhism made its way to Japan from Korea, and in 646 it was officially acknowledged as the religion of the aristocracy. The coming of Buddhism sharpened the desire of Japan's leaders to adopt Chinese culture, and during the seventh and eighth centuries the imperial court of Japan dispatched large numbers of sons of noblemen to China's imperial court at Chang'an, where they could observe the governmental system of the *Tang Dynasty* (618–907) firsthand before returning home to assume important official positions. These visitors to Chang'an brought back with them not only the forms of Chinese government but also some of the spirit that infused Chinese culture. Confucianism, Buddhism, and Daoism were woven into the fabric of Japanese civilization during these centuries of tutelage. What is more, many Chinese tastes, artistic styles, and artifacts were adopted.

Never, however, did these Chinese influences destroy native Japanese culture. The religion of *Shinto* (the way of the gods), Japan's original animistic religion, is a good example. Shinto remained a vital force within Japanese culture, despite attempts by some Japanese leaders to suppress it as a backward religion. Just as important, clan descent and inherited status remained vital social and political determinants in Japan. Unlike China, whose tightly organized government was increasingly in the hands of a professional class of scholars, Japan's society and government were still controlled by feudal clan lords and hereditary aristocrats. Japan experimented with but chose not to adopt the Chinese civil service examinations.

In 794 Emperor Kammu moved his capital from *Nara,* which had been modeled physically upon the Tang capital at Chang'an, to *Heian-kyo* (later known as *Kyoto*) in order to end what seemed to him to be a slavish imitation of everything Chinese. Tang China was now in turmoil, and it was a good time to modify and even discard some aspects of Chinese culture that earlier Japanese Sinophiles (lovers of all things Chinese) had adopted so enthusiastically. During the *Heian Period* (794–1185) the culture of the imperial court soared to unprecedented levels of refinement, and Japanese civilization reached a level of mature independence it would never relinquish. The Japanese became more selective in their assimilation of Chinese influences and increasingly discovered inspiration for creative expression in their own land and people.

The Constitution of Prince Shotoku
▼▼▼
66 ▼ *CHRONICLES OF JAPAN*

Japan is unique in the fact that a single imperial dynasty has reigned over the land and its people for the past 1,700 years. This family, known as the *Sun Line,* claims descent from the sun goddess Ameterasu through her great-great-grandson Jimmu Tennu (Divine Warrior), the mythic first emperor of Japan, who, according to legend, began to rule in 660 B.C.E. The historical truth is less grand. The *Yamato* clan, which became the Sun Line, seems to have established its dominance in western Japan no earlier than the third century C.E. Whatever the origins of their dynasty, the range of the Yamato clan's authority grew in the course of its first several centuries of state building, thanks to fortunate alliances, conquests, and the development of a literate bureaucracy. By the sixth century the Yamato emperors and empresses had become living symbols of Japanese religious and cultural unity. However, even though it claimed divine origins and, by virtue of that claim, held a monopoly on the imperial throne, the Yamamoto family could not control several of Japan's powerful clan chieftains. Indeed, the opposite was more the case. Several powerful clans vied to control the imperial family.

One of the most powerful of Japan's late-sixth-century clans, or *uji,* was the Soga family headed by Soga no Umako. In addition to struggling successfully against the rival Nakatomi and Mononobe clans for influence over the imperial court, Soga no Umako supported the policy of actively welcoming Chinese influences on a massive scale into Japan as a way of increasing the power of this island empire.

After engineering the assassination of one emperor, Soga no Umako chose a woman, Empress Suiko (r. 592–628), as nominal ruler. To guide her along proper lines, Soga designated an imperial prince to serve as regent. Under the direction of this crown prince, known as *Shotoku* (Sovereign Moral Power), Japan embarked on a course of deliberate cultural borrowing that was unprecedented in history. In 604 Prince Shotoku issued the so-called *Constitution of Seventeen Articles,* which laid out the ideological basis for the reforms that he, Empress Suiko, and Soga no Umako were championing.

Our knowledge of Shotoku's constitution comes from the *Nihongi,* or *Chronicles of Japan,* one of Japan's two oldest collections of legend and history. Composed in its final form in 720, the *Nihongi* traces the history of Japan back to the mythological age of the gods. By the time the *Nihongi* reaches the sixth century C.E., its narrative has largely left the realm of myth and become more reliable history.

QUESTIONS FOR ANALYSIS

1. What kind of constitution is this? Is it a code of institutional rules and regulations, or is it something else? What does your answer suggest?
2. What does this constitution allow you to infer about Shotoku's ideals and goals?
3. Review Chapter 4. What Confucian elements do you find in this document? What about Daoist elements? Legalist elements?
4. What central principles of Chinese political philosophy do you see in this document? (See Chapters 1 and 4.)
5. What native, or non-Chinese, elements do you find in this document? What do they suggest about Japanese society?

The Prince Imperial in person prepared for the first time laws. There were seventeen clauses as follows: —

1. Harmony is to be valued, and an avoidance of wanton opposition to be honored. All men are influenced by class-feelings, and there are few who are intelligent. Hence there are some who disobey their lords and fathers, or who maintain feuds with the neighboring villages. But when those above are harmonious and those below are friendly, and there is concord in the discussion of business, right views of things spontaneously gain acceptance. Then what is there which cannot be accomplished!

2. Sincerely reverence the three treasures. The three treasures: the Buddha, the Law, and the Priesthood,[1] are the final refuge . . . and are the supreme objects of faith in all countries. What man in what age can fail to reverence this law? Few men are utterly bad. They may be taught to follow it. But if they do not go to the three trea-

---

[1] The Buddha, the Law of Dharma, and the Sangha (order of male and female monks) are the three treasures, or key elements, of Buddhism (see Chapter 3, sources 19 and 20).

sures, how shall their crookedness be made straight?

3. When you receive the Imperial commands, fail not scrupulously to obey them. The lord is Heaven, the vassal is Earth. Heaven overspreads, and Earth upbears. When this is so, the four seasons follow their due course, and the powers of Nature obtain their efficacy. If the Earth attempted to overspread, Heaven would simply fall in ruin. Therefore is it that when the lord speaks, the vassal listens; when the superior acts, the inferior yields compliance. Consequently when you receive the Imperial commands, fail not to carry them out scrupulously. Let there be a want of care in this matter, and ruin is the natural consequence.

4. The Ministers and functionaries should make decorous behavior their leading principle, for the leading principle of the government of the people consists in decorous behavior. If the superiors do not behave with decorum, the inferiors are disorderly: if inferiors are wanting in proper behavior, there must necessarily be offenses. Therefore it is that when lord and vassal behave with propriety, the distinctions of rank are not confused: when the people behave with propriety, the Government of the Commonwealth proceeds of itself. . . .

6. Chastise that which is evil and encourage that which is good. This was the excellent rule of antiquity. Conceal not, therefore, the good qualities of others, and fail not to correct that which is wrong when you see it. Flatterers and deceivers are a sharp weapon for the overthrow of the State, and a pointed sword for the destruction of the people. Sycophants are also fond, when they meet, of speaking at length to their superiors on the errors of their inferiors; to their inferiors, they censure the faults of their superiors. Men of this kind are all wanting in fidelity to their lord, and in benevolence toward the people. From such an origin great civil disturbances arise.

7. Let every man have his own charge, and let not the spheres of duty be confused. When wise men are entrusted with office, the sound of praise arises. If unprincipled men hold office, disasters and tumults are multiplied. In this world, few are born with knowledge: wisdom is the product of earnest meditation. In all things, whether great or small, find the right man, and they will surely be well managed: on all occasions, be they urgent or the reverse, meet but with a wise man, and they will of themselves be amenable. In this way will the State be lasting and the Temples of the Earth and of Grain will be free from danger. Therefore did the wise sovereigns of antiquity seek the man to fill the office, and not the office for the sake of the man. . . .

10. Let us cease from wrath, and refrain from angry looks. Nor let us be resentful when others differ from us. For all men have hearts, and each heart has its own leanings. Their right is our wrong, and our right is their wrong. We are not unquestionably sages, nor are they unquestionably fools. Both of us are simply ordinary men. How can any one lay down a rule by which to distinguish right from wrong? For we are all, one with another, wise and foolish, like a ring which has no end. Therefore, although others give way to anger, let us on the contrary dread our own faults, and though we alone may be in the right, let us follow the multitude and act like them.

11. Give clear appreciation to merit and demerit, and deal out to each its sure reward or punishment. In these days, reward does not attend upon merit, nor punishment upon crime. You high functionaries who have charge of public affairs, let it be your task to make clear rewards and punishments. . . .

15. To turn away from that which is private, and to set our faces toward that which is public — this is the path of a Minister. Now if a man is influenced by private motives, he will assuredly feel resentments, and if he is influenced by resentful feelings, he will assuredly fail to act harmoniously with others. If he fails to act harmoniously with others, he will assuredly sacrifice the public interests to his private feelings. When resentment arises, it interferes with order, and is subversive of law. . . .

16. Let the people be employed [in forced labor] at seasonable times. This is an ancient and excellent rule. Let them be employed, therefore, in the winter months, when they are at leisure. But from Spring to Autumn, when they are engaged in agriculture or with the mulberry trees,[2] the people should not be so employed. For if they do not attend to agriculture, what will they have to eat? If they do not attend to the mulberry trees, what will they do for clothing?

17. Decisions on important matters should not be made by one person alone. They should be discussed with many. But small matters are of less consequence. It is unnecessary to consult a number of people. It is only in the case of the discussion of weighty affairs, when there is a suspicion that they may miscarry, that one should arrange matters in concert with others, so as to arrive at the right conclusion.

---

[2]The cultivation of silk worms, which ate mulberry leaves. The technique of silk production was an import from China.

An Aristocratic Woman in Eleventh-Century Japan
▼▼▼
67 ▼ *Murasaki Shikibu, DIARY*

When Prince Shotoku died in 622, the process of restructuring Japan along Chinese lines was far from complete, but the foundation had been laid. The next stage in Japan's adoption of Chinese values and modes of imperial administration was the *Taika,* or Great Transformation, that began in 645, ironically with the wholesale destruction of the Soga clan by a cabal of pro-Chinese reformers.

The centralized administrative system established in the Great Transformation failed, however, to function as intended, and by the mid ninth century true power in the provinces rested in the hands of local clan chiefs and a new element, Buddhist monasteries (see source 68). The Taika government continued to appoint provincial governors, who theoretically administered their regions in the name of the emperor, but most governors resided in the imperial court at Kyoto, far away from their areas of nominal responsibility. The court itself became an increasingly elegant setting for emperors and empresses, who were regarded as sacred beings and theoretically stood at the summit of all power. The elaborate ceremony that surrounded these people, who claimed to rule the world, masked, at least at close hand, the fact that effective power lay elsewhere.

While the imperial court was increasingly losing touch with the center of political authority, a group of aristocratic women at court were developing Japan's first native literature. Unlike many of Japan's Confucian scholars, who continued to study the Chinese classics along fairly rigid lines established a millennium earlier in a foreign land, these court women gave free play in their prose and poetry to their imaginations, emotions, and powers of analysis.

Japan's greatest literary artist of the Heian period was Murasaki Shikibu (ca. 978–ca. 1015), a lady-in-waiting at the court of Second Empress Akiko. Her masterpiece is the massive *The Tale of Genji,* a romance whose subtle psychological insights and realistic portraits of life have earned for it universal recognition as the single greatest piece of classical Japanese literature and one of the world's immortal novels. Focusing on the love affairs and emotions of Prince Genji, the work brilliantly captures the changing moods of people and nature.

Like many other imperial ladies-in-waiting, Lady Murasaki kept a diary in which she recorded — with the same level of insight, sensitivity, and narrative ability she displayed in *The Tale of Genji* — her observations on court life and her deepest reflections.

QUESTIONS FOR ANALYSIS

1. What was expected of court women? How did male aristocrats look upon and treat women of their class? As equals? As servants? As ornaments? As something else?
2. What did this aristocratic society think of literary accomplishment? How important was Chinese literature to Japanese literary artists?
3. What does this diary tell us about the level of refinement and sophistication among Japan's aristocracy? What does it suggest about the Japanese sense of beauty?
4. How Confucian was Lady Murasaki in her values and way of life? Does the diary contain any non-Confucian tones? What do you infer from your answers to these two questions?
5. What seems to be Lady Murasaki's view of women in general and herself in particular?
6. Compare Murasaki Shikibu's vision of what it means to be a woman with that of Madame Ban Zhao (Chapter 5, source 36). What do you conclude from that comparison?

As the autumn season approaches the Tsuchimikado[1] becomes inexpressibly smile-giving. The tree-tops near the pond, the bushes near the stream, are dyed in varying tints whose colors grow deeper in the mellow light of evening. The murmuring sound of waters mingles all the night through with the never-ceasing recitation of sutras[2] which appeal more to one's heart as the breezes grow cooler.

The ladies waiting upon her honored presence are talking idly. The Queen hears them; she must find them annoying, but she conceals it calmly. Her beauty needs no words of mine to praise it, but I cannot help feeling that to be near so beautiful a queen will be the only relief from my sorrow.[3] So in spite of my better desires [for a religious life] I am here. Nothing else dispels my grief — it is wonderful! . . .

I can see the garden from my room beside the entrance to the gallery. The air is misty, the dew is still on the leaves. The Lord Prime Minister is walking there; he orders his men to cleanse the

---

[1] The residence of Prime Minister Fujiwara Michinaga, father of Second Empress Akiko, who has returned to her father's home to give birth to Prince Atsusada.

[2] Buddhist texts.

[3] Her husband, whom she had married in 999, had died in 1001. It is now 1007.

brook. He breaks off a stalk of omenaishi [flower maiden], which is in full bloom by the south end of the bridge. He peeps in over my screen! His noble appearance embarrasses us, and I am ashamed of my morning [not yet painted and powdered] face. He says, "Your poem on this! If you delay so much the fun is gone!" and I seize the chance to run away to the writing-box, hiding my face —

Flower-maiden in bloom —
Even more beautiful for the bright dew,
Which is partial, and never favors me.

"So prompt!" said he, smiling, and ordered a writing-box to be brought for himself.
His answer:

The silver dew is never partial.
From her heart
The flower-maiden's beauty.

One wet and calm evening I was talking with Lady Saisho. The young Lord[4] of the Third Rank sat with the misu[5] partly rolled up. He seemed maturer than his age and was very graceful. Even in light conversation such expressions as "Fair soul is rarer than fair face" come gently to his lips, covering us with confusion. It is a mistake to treat him like a young boy. He keeps his dignity among ladies, and I saw in him a much-sought-after romantic hero when once he walked off reciting to himself:

Linger in the field where flower-maidens
are blooming
And your name will be tarnished with tales
of gallantry.

Some such trifle as that sometimes lingers in my mind when really interesting things are soon forgotten — why? . . .

On the fifth night the Lord Prime Minister celebrated the birth.[6] The full moon on the fif-

teenth day was clear and beautiful. Torches were lighted under the trees and tables were put there with rice-balls on them. Even the uncouth humble servants who were walking about chattering seemed to enhance the joyful scene. All minor officials were there burning torches, making it as bright as day. Even the attendants of the nobles, who gathered behind the rocks and under the trees, talked of nothing but the new light which had come into the world, and were smiling and seemed happy as if their own private wishes had been fulfilled. . . .

This time, as they chose only the best-looking young ladies, the rest who used to tie their hair on ordinary occasions to serve the Queen's dinner wept bitterly; it was shocking to see them. . . .

To serve at the Queen's dinner eight ladies tied their hair with white cords, and in that dress brought in Her Majesty's dining-table. The chief lady-in-waiting for that night was Miya-no-Naishi. She was brilliantly dressed with great formality, and her hair was made more charming by the white cords which enhanced her beauty. I got a side glance of her when her face was not screened by her fan.[7] She wore a look of extreme purity. . . .

The court nobles rose from their seats and went to the steps [descending from the balcony]. His Lordship the Prime Minister and others cast da.[8] It was shocking to see them quarreling about paper. Some others composed poems. A lady said, "What response shall we make if some one offers to drink saké with us?"[9] We tried to think of something.

Shijo-no-Dainagon is a man of varied accomplishments. No ladies can rival him in repartee, much less compete with him in poetry, so they were all afraid of him, but this evening he did not give a cup to any particular lady to make her compose poems. Perhaps that was because

---

[4]The prime minister's son Yorimichi, who was sixteen years old.
[5]A bamboo curtain used to hide distinguished persons from view.
[6]Of his imperial grandson.

[7]Women were expected to hide their faces behind fans.
[8]A game of dice.
[9]Thereby challenging the person to compose an impromptu poem.

he had many things to do and it was getting late. . . .

The Great Adviser[10] is displeased to be received by ladies of low rank, so when he comes to the Queen's court to make some report and suitable ladies to receive him are not available, he goes away without seeing Her Majesty. Other court nobles, who often come to make reports, have each a favorite lady, and when that one is away they are displeased, and go away saying to other people that the Queen's ladies are quite unsatisfactory. . . .

Lady Izumi Shikibu[11] corresponds charmingly, but her behavior is improper indeed. She writes with grace and ease and with a flashing wit. There is fragrance even in her smallest words. Her poems are attractive, but they are only improvisations which drop from her mouth spontaneously. Every one of them has some interesting point, and she is acquainted with ancient literature also, but she is not like a true artist who is filled with the genuine spirit of poetry. Yet I think even she cannot presume to pass judgment on the poems of others.

The wife of the Governor of Tamba Province is called by the Queen and Prime Minister Masa Hira Emon. Though she is not of noble birth, her poems are very satisfying. She does not compose and scatter them about on every occasion, but so far as we know them, even her miscellaneous poems shame us. Those who compose poems whose loins are all but broken, yet who are infinitely self-exalted and vain, deserve our contempt and pity.

Lady Seishonagon.[12] A very proud person. She values herself highly, and scatters her Chinese writings all about. Yet should we study her closely, we should find that she is still imperfect. She tries to be exceptional, but naturally persons of that sort give offense. She is piling up trouble for her future. One who is too richly gifted, who indulges too much in emotion, even when she ought to be reserved, and cannot turn aside from anything she is interested in, in spite of herself will lose self-control. How can such a vain and reckless person end her days happily?

▷ Here there is a sudden change from the Court to her own home.

Having no excellence within myself, I have passed my days without making any special impression on anyone. Especially the fact that I have no man who will look out for my future makes me comfortless. I do not wish to bury myself in dreariness. Is it because of my worldly mind that I feel lonely? On moonlight nights in autumn, when I am hopelessly sad, I often go out on the balcony and gaze dreamily at the moon. It makes me think of days gone by. People say that it is dangerous to look at the moon in solitude, but something impels me, and sitting a little withdrawn I muse there. In the wind-cooled evening I play on the koto,[13] though others may not care to hear it. I fear that my playing betrays the sorrow which becomes more intense, and I become disgusted with myself — so foolish and miserable am I. . . .

A pair of big bookcases have in them all the books they can hold. In one of them are placed old poems and romances. They are the homes of

---

[10]Fujiwara Michitaka, the prime minister's brother.
[11]One of Japan's greatest poets; she was no relation to Murasaki Shikibu. As do the Chinese, the Japanese place the family name first. Moreover, *Shikibu* was not Lady Murasaki's true given name, and it was not Lady Izumi's either. Polite society considered it improper to record the personal names of aristocratic women. *Shikibu* actually was a reference to an office that Lady Murasaki's father held, and *Murasaki,* which means "purple," might be a pun. She was descended from the Fujiwara clan, and the word *fuji* means "wisteria," a purple flower.

[12]One of the leading literary figures of her day and a rival of Murasaki Shikibu. Lady Seishonagon served at the court of the first empress, who was a rival of her cousin, the second empress.
[13]A stringed instrument.

worms which come frightening us when we turn the pages, so none ever wished to read them. [Perhaps her own writings, she speaks so slightingly of them.] As to the other cabinet, since the person[14] who placed his own books [there] no hand has touched it. When I am bored to death I take out one or two of them; then my maids gather around me and say: "Your life will not be favored with old age if you do such a thing! Why do you read Chinese? Formerly even the reading of sutras was not encouraged for women." They rebuke me in the shade [i.e., behind my back]. I have heard of it and have wished to say, "It is far from certain that he who does no forbidden thing enjoys a long life," but it would be a lack of reserve to say it [to the maids]. Our deeds vary with our age and deeds vary with the individual. Some are proud [to read books], others look over old cast-away writings because they are bored with having nothing to do. It would not be becoming for such a one to chatter away about religious thoughts, noisily shaking a rosary.[15] I feel this, and before my women keep myself from doing what otherwise I could do easily. But after all, when I was among the ladies of the Court I did not say what I wanted to say either, for it is useless to talk with those who do not understand one and troublesome to talk with those who criticize from a feeling of superiority.[16] Especially one-sided persons are troublesome. Few are accomplished in many arts and most cling narrowly to their own opinion.

---

[14]Her deceased husband, who had been a scholar of Chinese literature.

[15]Literally "a garland of roses," the rosary is an aid to prayer. Consisting of beads strung together in a circle, it allows a person to count prayers. Created by Hindus, the rosary spread among Buddhists and later to Muslims and Christians.

[16]But this diary was intended for publication!

The Ideal Samurai

▼▼▼

68 ▾ *CHRONICLE OF THE GRAND PACIFICATION*

While imperial courtiers at Kyoto composed exquisite poems that extolled the beauty of nature, Japan's warlords were engaged in carving out independent principalities backed by the might of their private armies of *samurai* (those who serve). Between 1180 and 1185 a conflict known as the *Gempei War* devastated the heartland of the main island of Honshu as the mighty Taira and Minimoto clans fought for control of the imperial family and its court. In 1185 the Minimoto house destroyed the Taira faction, thereby becoming the supreme military power in Japan.

Rather than seizing the imperial office for himself, the leader of the victorious Minimoto family accepted the title of *shogun,* or imperial commander-in-chief, and elected to rule over a number of military governors from his remote base at *Kamakura,* while a puppet emperor reigned at Kyoto. This feudal system, known as the *bakufu* (tent headquarters), shaped the politics and culture of Japan for centuries to come.

Toward the early fourteenth century the Kamakura Shogunate began to show signs of weakening, which in turn encouraged Emperor Go-Daigo (r. 1318–1336) to lead a coup in an attempt to destroy the shogunate and reestablish the primacy of the emperor. This rebel emperor became the nucleus of a full-scale feudal uprising by wide numbers of dissatisfied warlords, samurai, and warrior-monks. The warrior-monks were members of great landholding Buddhist monasteries, which already for many centuries had been centers of independent political, economic, and military power. The rebellion resulted in the destruction of Kamakura and the death of its last shogun.

Go-Daigo's victory was brief, however. Within a few years he was deposed by another warlord, who installed his own emperor and received back from him the title of shogun, thereby establishing the *Ashikaga Shogunate* (1338–1573). Japanese government and society, therefore, continued to be dominated by its feudal warriors.

The story of the last several years of the Kamakura Shogunate is recorded in the pages of the *Taiheiki,* or *Chronicle of the Grand Pacification.* Composed by a number of largely anonymous Buddhist monks between about 1333 and maybe as late as 1370, this chronicle recounts the battles and intrigues of the period 1318–1333. Its title refers to Go-Daigo's momentarily successful attempt to destroy, or "pacify," the shogunate.

Our excerpt tells the story of the defense in 1331 of Akasaka castle by Kusunoki Masashige, one of the emperor's most fervent supporters. This was a dark moment for the imperial forces. The emperor, along with many followers, had recently been captured at Kasagi, a fortified monastic temple. The imperial cause needed a victory, even a moral one, and this heretofore obscure warrior was about to provide new hope with his inspired defense of this stronghold.

Killed in 1333 in a battle he knew he could not win, Masashige has been revered through the centuries as a paragon of samurai virtues. The *kamikaze* (divine wind) suicide pilots whom Japan launched against the U.S. Navy in 1945 were called "chrysanthemum warriors" in reference to the Kusunoki family's flowered crest.

QUESTIONS FOR ANALYSIS

1. Why do the warriors assaulting Akasaka hope that Kusunoki will be able to hold out for at least one day? What does this suggest?
2. Bravery is naturally expected of all warriors, but which other samurai virtues does Kusunoki Masashige exemplify?
3. Which samurai virtues do his foes exhibit? In what ways did they show themselves to be less than ideal warriors?
4. Thinking their enemy dead, the shogun's warriors pause to remember Kusunoki Masashige. What does this suggest?
5. Based on this account, what picture emerges of the ideals and realities of fourteenth-century Japanese feudal warfare?

No man of the mighty host from the distant eastern lands was willing to enter the capital, so sorely were their spirits mortified because Kasagi castle had fallen.[1] . . . All took their way instead toward Akasaka castle, where Kusunoki Hyoe Masashige was shut up. . . .

When these had passed beyond the Ishi River, they beheld the castle. Surely this was a stronghold of hasty devising! The ditch was not a proper ditch, and there was but a single wooden wall, plastered over with mud. Likewise in size the castle was not more than one hundred or two hundred yards around, with but twenty or thirty towers within, made ready in haste. Of those who saw it, not one but thought:

"Ah, what a pitiable spectacle the enemy presents! Even if we were to hold this castle in one hand and throw, we would be able to throw it! Let us hope that in some strange manner Kusunoki will endure for at least a day, that by taking booty and winning honor we may obtain future rewards."

Drawing near, the three hundred thousand riders[2] got down from their horses, one after another, jumped into the ditch, stood below the towers, and competed to be the first to enter the castle.

Now by nature Masashige was a man who would "scheme in his tent to defeat an enemy a thousand leagues distant," one whose counsels were as subtle as though sprung from the brain of Chenping or Zhang Liang.[3] Wherefore had he kept two hundred mighty archers within the castle, and had given three hundred riders to his brother Shichiro and Wada Goro Masato outside in the mountains. Yet the attackers, all unwitting, rushed forward together to the banks of the ditch on the four sides, resolved to bring down the castle in a single assault.

Then from tower tops and windows the archers shot furiously with arrowheads aligned together, smiting more than a thousand men in an instant. And greatly amazed, the eastern warriors said:

"No, no! From the look of things at this castle, it will never fall in a day or two. Let us take time before going against it, that we may establish camps and battle-offices and form separate parties."

They drew back from the attack a little, took off their horses' saddles, cast aside their armor, and rested in their camps.

In the mountains Kusunoki Shichiro and Wada Goro said, "The time is right." They made two parties of the three hundred horsemen, came out from the shelter of the trees on the eastern and western slopes with two fluttering banners, whereon were depicted the chrysanthemum and water crest of the Kusunoki house, and advanced quietly toward the enemy, urging their horses forward in the swirling mist.

The attackers hesitated doubtfully.

"Are they enemies or friends?" they thought.

Then suddenly from both sides the three hundred attacked, shouting, in wedge-shaped formations. They smote the center of the three hundred thousand horsemen spread out like clouds or mist, broke into them in all directions, and cut them down on every side. And the attackers' hosts were powerless to form to give battle, so great was their bewilderment.

Next within the castle three gates opened all together, wherefrom two hundred horsemen galloped forth side by side to let fly a multitude of arrows from bows pulled back to the utmost limits. Although the attackers were a mighty host, they were confounded utterly by these few enemies, so that they clamored aloud. Some mounted tethered horses and beat them with their stirrups, seeking to advance; others fixed arrows to unstrung bows and tried vainly to shoot. Two or three men took up a single piece of armor and disputed it, pulling against each

---

[1]This force of Kamakura supporters from the east was dispirited because it had arrived too late to participate in the capture of Kasagi.

[2]The *Taiheiki* grossly exaggerates the number of pro-Kamakura fighters.

[3]Two ministers of the first Han emperor of China. The quotation is from Ban Gu and Ban Zhao's *History of the Former Han Dynasty*.

other. Though a lord was killed, his vassals knew nothing of it; though a father was killed, his sons aided him not, but like scattered spiders they retreated to the Ishi River. For half a league along their way there was no space where a foot might tread, by reason of their abandoned horses and arms. To be sure, great gains came suddenly to the common folk of Tojo district![4]

Perhaps the proud eastern warriors thought in their hearts that Kusunoki's strategy could not be despised, since blundering unexpectedly they had been defeated in the first battle. For though they went forth against Handa and Narahara,[5] they did not seek to attack the castle again quickly, but consulted together and made a resolution, saying:

"Let us remain awhile in this place, that led by men acquainted with the home provinces we may cut down trees on the mountains, burn houses, and guard thereby against warriors waiting in reserve to fall upon us. Then may we attack the castle with tranquil spirits."

But there were many . . . who had lost fathers and sons in the fighting. These roused themselves up, saying:

"What is the use of living? Though we go alone, let us gallop forth to die in battle!"

And thereupon all the others took heart as well, and galloped forward eagerly.

Now Akasaka castle might not be attacked easily on the east, where terraced rice fields extended far up the mountainside. But on three sides the land was flat; likewise there was but a single ditch and wall. All the attackers were contemptuous, thinking, "No matter what demons may be inside, it cannot be much of an affair." When they drew near again, they went forward quickly into the ditch to the opposite bank, pulled away the obstacles and made ready to enter. Yet within the castle there was no sound.

Then the attackers thought in their hearts:

"As it was yesterday, so will it be today. After wounding many men with arrows to confuse us,

they will send other warriors to fight in our midst."

They counted out a hundred thousand riders to go to the mountains in the rear, while the remaining two hundred thousand compassed the castle round about like thickly growing rice, hemp, bamboo, or reeds. Yet from within the castle not an arrow was released, nor was any man seen.

At last the attackers laid hold of the wall on the four sides to climb over it, filled with excitement. But thereupon men within the castle cut the ropes supporting that wall, all at the same time, for it was a double wall, built to let the outside fall down. More than a thousand of the attackers became as though crushed by a weight, so that only their eyes moved as the defenders threw down logs and boulders onto them. And in this day's fighting more than seven hundred of them were slain.

Unwilling to attack again because of the bitterness of the first two days of fighting, for four or five days the eastern hosts merely besieged the castle from camps hard by. Truly were they without pride, to watch thus idly from a nearby place! How mortifying it was that men of the future would make a mock of them, saying, "Although the enemy were no more than four or five hundred persons shut up in a flatland castle not five hundred yards around, the hosts of the eight eastern provinces would not attack them, but shamefully laid down a siege from a distance!"

At last the attackers spoke among themselves, saying:

"Previously we attacked in the fierceness of our valor, not carrying shields or preparing weapons of assault, wherefore we suffered unforeseen injury. Let us go against them now with a different method."

All commanded the making of shields with toughened hide on their faces, such as might not be smashed through easily, and with these up-

---

[4]Commoners scavenged battlefields.

[5]Settlements near Akasaka.

held they went against the castle once more, saying:

"There can be no difficulty about jumping across to the wall, since the banks are not high, nor is the ditch deep. Yet will not this wall also drop down upon us?"

They spoke with fearful hearts, reluctant to seize upon the wall lightly. All went down into the water of the ditch, laid hold upon the wall with grapnels, and pulled at it. But when the wall was about to fall, those within the castle took ladles with handles ten or twenty feet long, dipped up boiling water, and poured it onto them. The hot water passed through the holes in their helmet tops, ran down from the edges of their shoulder-guards, and burned their bodies so grievously that they fled panic-stricken, throwing down their shields and grapnels. How shameful it was! Although no man of them was slain, there were as many as two or three hundred persons who could not stand up from the burns on their hands and feet, or who lay down with sick bodies.

So it was that whenever the attackers advanced with new devisings, those within the castle defended against them with changed stratagems. Wherefore in consultation together the attackers said, "From this time on, let us starve them, for we can do no other." They forbore utterly to do battle, but only built towers in their camps, lined up obstacles, and laid down a siege.

Soon the warriors in the castle grew weary of spirit, since there was no diversion for them. Nor was their food sufficient, since Kusunoki had built the castle in haste. The battle having begun and the siege commenced, within twenty days the stores were eaten up; nor did food remain for more than four or five days.

Then Masashige spoke a word to his men, saying:

"In various battles of late have we overreached the foe, whose slain are beyond counting, but these things are as nothing in the eyes of so mighty a host. Moreover, the castle's food is eaten up, and no other warriors will come to deliver us.

"Assuredly I will not cherish life in the hour of need, from the beginning having been steadfast for His Majesty's sake. . . . But the true man of courage 'is cautious in the face of difficulties, and deliberates before acting.'[6] I will flee this castle for a time, causing the enemy to believe that I have taken my life, so that they may go away rejoicing. When they are gone I will come forward to fight; and if they return I will go deep into the mountains. When I have harassed the eastern hosts four or five times in this manner, will they not grow weary? This is a plan for destroying the enemy in safety. What are your views?"

All agreed, "It ought to be so."

Then quickly within the castle they dug a mighty hole seven feet deep, filling it with twenty or thirty bodies of the slain (who were fallen down dead into the ditch in great numbers), whereon they piled up charcoal and firewood. And they awaited a night of pouring rain and driving wind.

Perhaps because Masashige had found favor in the sight of heaven, suddenly a harsh wind came raising the sand, accompanied by a rain violent enough to pierce bamboo. The night was exceedingly dark, and all the enemy in their camps were sheltered behind curtains. This indeed was the awaited night!

Leaving a man in the castle to light a blaze when they were fled away safely five or six hundred yards, the defenders cast off their armor, assumed the guise of attackers, and fled away calmly by threes and fives, passing in front of the enemy battle-offices and beside enemy sleeping places.

It came about that the eyes of an enemy fell upon Masashige, where he passed before the stables of Nagasaki. The man challenged him, saying, "What person passes before

---

[6]A quotation from Confucius's *Analects* (Chapter 4, source 24).

this battle-office in stealth, not announcing himself?"

In haste Masashige passed beyond that place, calling back, "I am a follower of the grand marshal who has taken the wrong road."

"A suspicious fellow indeed!" thought the man. "Assuredly he is a stealer of horses! I shall shoot him down."

He ran up close and shot Masashige full in the body. But although the arrow looked to have driven deep at the height of the elbow-joint, it turned over and flew back again without touching the naked flesh.

Later, when that arrow's track was observed, men saw that it had struck an amulet wherein was preserved the *Kannon Sutra,*[7] which Masashige had trusted and read for many years. Its arrowhead had stopped in the two-line poem, "Wholeheartedly praising the name." How strange it was!

When in this manner Masashige had escaped death from a certain-death arrowhead, he fled to a safe place more than half a league distant. And looking back he saw that the warrior had lighted fires in the castle's battle-offices, faithful to his covenant.

The hosts of the attackers were seized with amazement at the sight of the flames.

"Aha! The castle has fallen!" they shouted exultantly. "Let no man be spared! Let none escape!"

When the flames died away, they saw a mighty hole inside the castle, piled up with charcoal, wherein lay the burned bodies of many men. And then not a man of them but spoke words of praise, saying:

"How pitiful! Masashige had ended his life! Though he was an enemy, his was a glorious death, well befitting a warrior."

---

[7]A sutra, or Buddhist holy book, dedicated to the female Bodhisattva *Kannon,* the Japanese counterpart of Guanyin (see Chapter 6, sources 46 and 47).

China: The Ages of Tang and Song

The period from 500 to 1500 witnessed a variety of momentous developments in China: renewed imperial greatness, philosophical and technological innovation, economic expansion and a rapidly growing population, new modes of artistic expression, conquest by Mongol invaders, and eventual recovery and retrenchment. Through it all, Chinese civilization managed to retain intact its basic institutions and way of life.

The Time of Troubles that followed the fall of the house of Han was over by the end of the sixth century, and under the *Tang Dynasty* (618–907) China was again a great imperial power, with a restored Confucian civil service firmly in power. At the end of the seventh century China's borders reached to Korea and Manchuria in the northeast, to Vietnam in the south, and to the Aral Sea in the western regions of Central Asia, where China met the new Islamic Empire. The almost simultaneous creation of these two empires in Asia resulted in a dramatic increase of traffic along the Silk Road. Foreign goods, precious metals, peoples, and ideas flowed into China's cities. As a consequence, Tang China enjoyed the richest, most cosmopolitan culture on the face of the earth, until its empire began to deteriorate after the mid eighth century. Between 755 and 763 China was torn apart by a rebellion led by An Lushan, a military governor of Turkic descent. In the wake of the devastation, Tang imperial strength rapidly disintegrated, and with it went an earlier openness of spirit to outside influences. Fifty-three years of disunity followed Tang's official collapse in 907, but, in fact, the previous half century of nominal Tang rule had been equally anarchic.

The *Song Dynasty* (960–1279) eventually reunited most of the Chinese heartland, but geographically and militarily Song China was a truncated shadow of former Tang greatness. Despite its external weakness, however, China under the Song achieved levels of political stability, economic prosperity, technological advancement, and cultural maturity that were unequaled anywhere else on earth at the time. By the mid eleventh century the production of printed books had become such an important industry that artisans were experimenting with moveable type — four hundred years before the introduction of a similar printing process in Europe. The thousands of books and millions of pages printed in Song China are evidence that a remarkably high degree of its population was literate. In addition to this dramatic rise in basic literacy, there were significant developments in advanced philosophy. Intellectuals reinvigorated Confucian thought by injecting into it metaphysical concepts borrowed from Buddhism and Daoism. This new Study of the Way, or *Neo-Confucianism,* provided fresh philosophical insights clothed in traditional forms and enabled Confucianism to topple Buddhism from its position of intellectual preeminence.

The fine arts also reached new levels of achievement. Landscape painting, particularly during the period known as *Southern Song* (1127–1279), expressed in two dimensions the mystical visions of Daoism and Chan Buddhism. On a three-dimensional plane, the craft of porcelain making became a high art, and large numbers of exquisitely delicate pieces of fine *chinaware* were traded from Japan to East Africa.

Advanced ships and navigational aids enabled Chinese traders to take to the sea in unprecedented numbers, especially in the direction of Southeast Asia, thereby transforming their homeland into the world's greatest merchant marine power of its day. Rapidly maturing strains of rice were introduced from Champa in Southeast Asia, making it possible to feed a population that exceeded one hundred million, about double that of the Age of Tang. Although most of this massive population was engaged in traditional, labor-intensive agriculture, some Chinese were employed in industries (such as mining, iron and steel production, and textile manufacture) that used advanced technologies unequaled anywhere else in the world.

Song's age of greatness was brought to a close by Mongol invaders, who by 1279 had joined all of China to the largest land empire in world history. Mongol rule during what is known as the *Yuan Dynasty* (1264–1368) was unmitigated military occupation. Both the Mongols and the many foreigners whom they admitted into their service essentially exploited and oppressed the Chinese. Although the Mongols encouraged agriculture and trade, few Chinese benefited from a prosperity that was largely confined to a small circle of landlords.

By the mid fourteenth century China was in rebellion, and in 1368 a commoner, Zhu Yuanzhang, reestablished native rule in the form of the *Ming Dy-*

nasty (1368–1644). This new imperial family restored Chinese prestige and influence in East Asia to levels enjoyed under Tang and provided China with stability and prosperity until the late sixteenth century. Under the Ming traditional Chinese civilization attained full maturity. Toward the middle of the Age of Ming, however, China reluctantly established relations with seaborne Western European merchants and missionaries, and the resultant challenge of the West would result, centuries later, in major transformations in Chinese life.

Chapters 12 and 13 will deal with the Yuan and Ming Eras. For the moment we will concentrate on Tang and Song, two of China's most celebrated Golden Ages.

Open to the World: Christianity in Tang China

▼▼▼

69 ▾ *Bishop Adam, THE CHRISTIAN MONUMENT*

The revived Silk Road provided missionaries, as well as merchants, with a convenient route into the heart of Tang China. In 635 a *Nestorian* Christian bishop from Persia named Aluoben (Abraham?) arrived in Chang'an, China's capital city. In the fifth century the Nestorian Christians of Syria, who drew a sharp distinction between the human and divine natures of Jesus, had been declared heretics (deviant believers) by the imperial Roman Church. The charges of heresy were motivated more by political considerations than theological doctrine, but the result was no less devastating. The Nestorians were effectively denied a place within the imperial Christian Church that looked to Constantinople and Rome as its twin centers of authority. Moving east, the Nestorians found a home in the Sassanid Empire of Persia. Despite sporadic persecution by the Sassanid *shahs,* or emperors, who promoted Zoroastrianism as the state religion, Nestorianism flourished in Sassanid Persia's two major cultural centers: Mesopotamia (also called *Babylonia*) and Iran. From there Nestorian Christian ideas traveled farther east to the Turkic peoples of Inner Asia and finally to China. Bishop Aluoben was not the first Nestorian to reach China, but he is the first of whom we have any record.

Aluoben was fortunate that he arrived in the reign of Tang Taizong (r. 626–649), the second Tang emperor. Of mixed Chinese and Turko-Mongol descent, Tang Taizong was open to novelties from the western steppes, including Buddhism, Manichaeism (Chapter 7, source 56), and Nestorian Christianity. Under the emperor's protection, Aluoben established a monastery, which initially housed twenty-one monks, probably all of them Persians.

In 781 a scholar-bishop named Adam, who also bore the Chinese name Jing Jing, composed a short history of the early fortunes of the Nestorian Church in China. Under the patronage of a prominent Chinese-born Nestorian of Persian descent named Yazdbozid, whose Chinese name was Yisi, Adam's history was then inscribed on a nine-foot-high stone memorial that bears the heading "A Monument Commemorating the Propagation of the Daqin (Syrian) Luminous Religion in the Middle Kingdom (China)." Interestingly, Yazdbozid, who apparently was Adam's father, was an assistant bishop in the Nestorian Church and had formerly served as a high-ranking general in the Chinese army and an imperial civil official. The career of this Christian priest, warrior, and civil servant of Persian heritage nicely illustrates the cosmopolitanism of early Tang, in which non-Chinese were called to the imperial service. Yazdbozid is also a symbol of the Nestorian Church's eighth-century political connections, which gave it a measure of influence in Tang China.

That good fortune did not last, however. By tying its fortunes to the patronage of the Tang emperors, this minor foreign religion suffered irreversible losses when the empire waged an assault on foreign religions between 840 and 846. Although some small communities possibly survived, Nestorian Christianity essentially disappeared in China by the late tenth century. It would only reappear in the twelfth and thirteenth centuries, brought in from Central Asia by various Turkic tribes that had adopted the faith. But it would suffer a second eclipse in the fourteenth century with the rise of the antiforeign Ming Dynasty (1368–1644).

Regardless of future reverses, the Nestorian community's *Christian Monument* celebrates an age when China was open to foreign innovations, including this faith from Southwest Asia.

QUESTIONS FOR ANALYSIS

1. Review source 23 in Chapter 4. How does Adam borrow Daoist imagery and terms to describe Nestorian Christianity? Why do you think he does so?
2. What Buddhist and Confucian overtones can you find in this memorial? How and why does Adam use them?
3. What reasons did Emperor Tang Taizong give for allowing this new religion into his empire? What does your answer suggest about the man and his reign?
4. How does the memorial deal with the issue of its reverses under Empress Wu? What do you infer from your answer?
5. What do those assaults on Nestorian Christianity suggest to you?
6. How does the memorial describe its imperial patrons? What do you infer from your answer?
7. At the apex of the monument is an ornate engraved cross, which rises from a white cloud, a symbol of Daoism, and beneath the cloud is a Buddhist lotus blossom. In light of the text of the memorial, what do you think this carved image means?

But, at any rate, "The *Way*" would not have spread so widely had it not been for the Sage,[1] and the Sage would not have been so great were it not for "The *Way*." Ever since the Sage and "The *Way*" were united to gather as the two halves of an indentured deed would agree,[2] then the world became refined and enlightened.

---

[1] Emperor Tang Taizong.

[2] Just as the two copies of a legal contract executed in duplicate would agree in all respects.

When the accomplished Emperor Taizong began his magnificent career in glory and splendor over the (recently) established dynasty[3] and ruled his people with intelligence, he proved himself to be a brilliant Sage.

And behold there was a highly virtuous man named Aluoben in the Kingdom of Daqin.[4] Auguring (of the Sage, i.e., Emperor) from the azure sky,[5] he decided to carry the true Sutras[6] (of the True Way) with him, and observing the course of the winds, he made his way (to China) through difficulties and perils. Thus in the ninth year of the period named Zhenguan (635 C.E.) he arrived at Chang'an.[7] The Emperor dispatched his Minister, Duke Fang Xuanling, with a guard of honor, to the western suburb to meet the visitor and conduct him to the Palace. The Sutras (Scriptures) were translated in the Imperial Library. (His Majesty) investigated "The *Way*" in his own forbidden apartments,[8] and being deeply convinced of its correctness and truth, he gave special orders for its propagation.

In the twelfth year of the Zhenguan Period (638 C.E.) in the seventh month of Autumn, the following Imperial Rescript was issued: —

"'The Way' had not, at all times and in all places, the selfsame name; the Sage had not, at all times and in all places, the selfsame human body. (Heaven) caused a suitable religion to be instituted for every region and clime so that each one of the races of mankind might be saved. Bishop Aluoben of the kingdom of Daqin, bringing with him the Sutras and Images,[9] has come from afar and presented them at our Capital. Having carefully examined the scope of his teaching, we find it to be mysteriously spiritual and of silent operation. Having observed its principal and most essential points, we reached the conclusion that they cover all that is most important in life. Their language is free from perplexing expressions; their principles are so simple that they 'remain as the fish would remain even after the net (of the language) were forgotten.' This Teaching is helpful to all creatures and beneficial to all men. So let it have free course throughout the Empire."

Accordingly, the proper authorities built a Daqin monastery in the Yining Ward[10] in the Capital and twenty-one priests were ordained and attached to it. The virtue of the honored House of Zhou had died away;[11] (the rider on) the black chariot had ascended to the West.[12] But (virtue revived) and "The *Way*" was brilliantly manifested again at the moment when the Great Tang began its rule, whilst the breezes of the Luminous (Religion) came eastward to fan it.[13] Immediately afterwards, the proper officials were again ordered to take a faithful portrait of the Emperor, and to have it copied on the walls of the monastery. The celestial beauty appeared in its variegated colors, and the dazzling splendor illuminated the Luminous "portals" (i.e., congregation). The sacred features (lit., foot-prints) (thus preserved) conferred great blessing (on the monastery), and illuminated the Church for evermore. . . .

---

[3]A great warrior even in his teens, Tang Taizong (his given name was Li Shimin) was the driving force that toppled the short-lived *Sui Dynasty* (581–618) and placed his father, Li Yuan, on the throne as first Tang emperor. His father later abdicated the throne in Li Shimin's favor.

[4]Syria. We should not take it literally. Aluoben came from the West with a religion that was shaped in Syria. Thus Iran, Mesopotamia, and Syria are all lumped together under this term.

[5]He discovered in the heavens signs of the Sage Emperor.

[6]The Bible.

[7]Tang China's capital, Chang'an (known today as Xi'an), was the largest and richest city in the world in the seventh century.

[8]The private imperial chambers.

[9]Artistic representations, or *icons*, of Jesus and the saints.

[10]The name of a street in the western part of the city.

[11]Rule by virtue, as established in the early Zhou Dynasty (Chapter 1, source 5) and later taught by Confucius (Chapter 4, source 24), had departed long before the rise of Tang.

[12]According to one tradition, when the virtue of the Eastern Zhou Dynasty failed (770–256 B.C.E.), Laozi, the founder of Daoism (Chapter 4, source 23), abandoned China in disgust. He went west (or ascended to the Western Heaven) in a chariot drawn by a black ox, thereby leaving China without a moral guide. The Tang Dynasty shared Laozi's family name, *Li,* and claimed descent from him.

[13]Laozi had gone west (note 12); now the Way was returning from the West.

The great Emperor Gaozong (650–683 C.E.) succeeded most respectfully to his ancestors; and giving the True Religion the proper elegance and finish, he caused monasteries of the Luminous Religion to be founded in every prefecture. Accordingly, he honored Aluoben by conferring on him the office of the Great Patron and Spiritual Lord of the Empire. The Law (of the Luminous Religion) spread throughout the ten provinces, and the Empire enjoyed great peace and concord. Monasteries were built in many cities, whilst every family enjoyed the great blessings (of Salvation).

During the period of Shengli (698–699 C.E.),[14] the Buddhists, taking advantage of these circumstances, and using all their strength raised their voices (against the Luminous Religion) in the Eastern Zhou,[15] and at the end of the Xiandian Period (712 C.E.)[16] some inferior scholars[17] ridiculed and derided it, slandering and speaking against it in the Western Hao.[18] But there came the Head-priest (or Archdeacon) Luohan,[19] Bishop Jilie,[20] and others, as well as Noblemen from the "Golden" region[21] and the eminent priests who had forsaken all worldly interests. All these men co-operated in restoring the great fundamental principles and united together to re-bind the broken ties.

The Emperor Xuanzong,[22] who was surnamed "the Perfection of the Way," ordered the Royal prince, the King of Ningguo and four other Royal princes to visit the blessed edifices (i.e., monastery) personally and to set up altars therein. Thus the "consecrated rafters" which had been temporarily bent, were once more straightened and strengthened, whilst the sacred foundation-stones which for a time had lost the right position were restored and perfected. In the early part of the period Tianbao (742 C.E.) he gave orders to his general Gao Lishi to carry the faithful portraits of the Five Emperors[23] and to have them placed securely in the monastery, and also to take the Imperial gift of one hundred pieces of silk with him. Making the most courteous and reverent obeisance to the Imperial portraits, we feel as though "we were in a position to hang on to the Imperial bow and sword, in case the beard of the Dragon should be out of reach."[24] Although the solar horns[25] shine forth with such dazzling brilliance, yet the gracious Imperial faces are so gentle that they may be gazed upon at a distance less than a foot.

In the third year of the same period (744 C.E.) there was a priest named Jihe[26] in the Kingdom of Daqin. Observing the stars, he decided to engage in the work of conversion; and looking toward the sun (i.e., eastward), he came to pay court to the most honorable Emperor. The Imperial orders were given to the Head-priest (Archdeacon) Luohan, priest Pulun[27] and others, seven in

---

[14]One of several periods in the reign of Empress Wu, who ruled the empire in her own name from 690 to 705. She had gained effective control over the state around 654, but at first used several puppet emperors to mask her power.

[15]Empress Wu changed the name of her short-lived dynasty to *Zhou* and moved her primary capital east to Luoyang, the capital city of the ancient Eastern Zhou Dynasty (770–256 B.C.). She declared Buddhism the official state religion in 691 and seems to have encouraged persecution of Christianity, although persecution did not become an articulated state policy. In 698 a mob sacked the Nestorian church in Luoyang.

[16]The last year of disorder following Empress Wu's retirement in 705.

[17]Probably Confucians but possibly Daoists. Maybe both.

[18]*Hao* was the name of Chang'an when it was the capital of the Western Zhou Dynasty (ca. 1100–771 B.C.). Hostile crowds attacked and violated the monastery in the Yining Ward, which Tang Taizong had patronized.

[19]Abraham.

[20]Gabriel?

[21]From the West, the source of so much gold and silver that flowed into Tang China by virtue of China's favorable balance of trade.

[22]Under Emperor Xuanzong (r. 712–756) Tang China reached the heights of its greatness and prosperity (see source 70, note 3).

[23]The legendary Five Sage Emperors, who established the foundations of Chinese civilization in predynastic times.

[24]Although the emperor (the dragon) might be far away, his power extends to the monastery.

[25]The radiance emanating from the faces of the Five Sage Emperors.

[26]George.

[27]Paul?

all, to perform services to cultivate merit and virtue with this Bishop Jihe in the Xingqing Palace. Thereupon the monastery-names, composed and written by the Emperor himself, began to appear on the monastery gates; and the front-tablets to bear the Dragon-writing (i.e., the Imperial hand-writing).[28] The monastery was resorted to by (visitors) whose costumes resembled the shining feathers of the king-fisher bird whilst all (the buildings) shone forth with the splendor of the sun. The Imperial tablets hung high in the air and their radiance flamed as though vying with the sun. The gifts of the Imperial favor are immense like the highest peak of the highest mountains in the South, and the food of its rich benevolence is as deep as the depths of the Eastern sea.

There is nothing that "The *Way*" cannot effect (through the Sage); and whatever it effects, it is right of us to define it as such (in eulogy). There is nothing that the Sage cannot accomplish (through "The *Way*"); and whatever He accomplishes, it is right we should proclaim it in writing (as the Sage's work).

---

[28]The emperor composed an inscription to be fixed above the monastery's door. Almost all public buildings in China had similar inscriptions.

Troubles in Late Tang
▼▼▼

70 ▼ *Du Fu, POEMS*

The Chinese consider the eighth century their golden age of classical poetry. Among the century's many great poets, three are universally recognized as China's preeminent poetic geniuses: the Buddhist Wang Wei (699–759), the Daoist Li Bo (701–762), and the Confucian Du Fu (712–770). Despite their differences in personality and perspective, they knew, deeply respected, and genuinely liked one another. Of the three, the Chinese most esteem Du Fu, primarily for the tone of compassion for the downtrodden that pervades his poetry.

Du Fu himself knew adversity. Despite his extraordinary erudition, he was denied a position of public responsibility and spent much of his adult life as an impoverished wanderer and farmer. He lived to see one of his children die of starvation and suffered through the destruction of General An Lushan's rebellion (755–763), a civil war from which the Tang regime never recovered. Despite these adversities, Du Fu never lost his love for humanity or his belief in the innate goodness of the common person.

QUESTIONS FOR ANALYSIS

1. According to Du Fu, what costs have the Chinese paid for their empire? Has it been worth it? What does he think of military glory?
2. From a Confucian perspective, what is wrong with eighth-century China?
3. Can you find any Daoist sentiments in these poems?
4. What do the second and third poems tell us about the economic and social consequences of An Lushan's rebellion?

5. In what ways do the first two poems seem to suggest that Du Fu believed that the Tang emperor might be losing the Mandate of Heaven (Chapter 1, source 5)?

6. One of the prime virtues of Confucianism is *ren,* which is best translated as "humaneness." The character for this word is composed of two elements: the signs for *person* and *two.* In what ways do these poems, especially the third poem, exemplify the qualities of *ren*?

BALLAD OF THE WAR CHARIOTS

The jingle of war chariots,
Horses neighing, men marching,
Bows and arrows slung over hips;
Beside them stumbling, running
The mass of parents, wives and children
Clogging up the road, their rising dust
Obscuring the great bridge at Hsienyang;
Stamping their feet, weeping
In utter desperation with cries
That seem to reach the clouds;

Ask a soldier: Why do you go?
Would simply bring the answer:
Today men are conscripted often;
Fifteen-year-olds sent up the Yellow River
To fight; men of forty marched away
To colonize the western frontier;
Village elders take young boys,
Do up their hair like adults
To get them off; if they return
It will be white with age, but even then
They may be sent off to the frontier again;

Frontiers on which enough blood has flowed
To make a sea, yet our Emperor still would
Expand his authority! Have you not heard
How east of Huashan[1] many counties
Are desolate with weeds and thorns?
The strongest women till the fields,
Yet crops come not as well as before;

Lads from around here are well known
For their bravery, but hate to be driven
Like dogs or chickens; only because
You kindly ask me do I dare give vent
To grievances; now for instance
With the men from the western frontier
Still not returned, the government
Demands immediate payment of taxes,
But how can we pay when so little
Has been produced?

Now, we peasants have learnt one thing:
To have a son is not so good as having
A daughter who can marry a neighbor
And still be near us, while a son
Will be taken away to die in some
Wild place, his bones joining those
That lie bleached white on the shores
Of Lake Kokonor,[2] where voices of new spirits
Join with the old, heard sadly through
The murmur of falling rain.

THINKING OF OTHER DAYS

In those prosperous times
Of the period of Kai Yuan,[3]
Even a small county city
Would be crowded with the rich;
Rice flowed like oil and both
Public and private granaries
Were stuffed with grain; all

---

[1] The land back home, east of the western frontier.
[2] A lake west of the Great Wall.

[3] A title of Emperor Xuanzong (r. 712–756). Also known as *Minghuang,* or Brilliant Monarch, he was the last effective Tang emperor and a great patron of the arts. The rebellion of General An Lushan broke out during the last years of his forty-four-year reign.

Through the nine provinces
There were no robbers on
The roads; traveling from home
Needless to pick an auspicious
Day to start; everywhere carriages
With folk wearing silk or brocade;
Farmers ploughed, women picked
Mulberries, nothing that did
Not run smoothly; in court
Was a good Emperor for whom
The finest music was played;
Friends were honest with each other
And for long there had been
No kind of disaster; great days with
Rites and songs, the best of other times,
Laws the most just; who could
Have dreamed that later a bolt
Of silk would cost ten thousand
Cash? Now the fields farmers
Tilled have become covered
With bloodshed; palaces at Loyang[4]
Are burnt, and temples to
The imperial ancestors are full
Of foxes and rabbit burrows!
Now I am too sad to ask
Questions of the old people,
Fearing to hear tales
Of horror and strife;
I am not able, but yet

The Emperor[5] has given me
A post, I hoping that he
Can make the country
Rise again like King Xuan
Of Zhou,[6] though for myself
I simply grieve that now age
And sickness take their toll.

ON ASKING MR. WU
FOR THE SECOND TIME

Do please let your neighbor
Who lives to the west of you
Pick up the dates in front of
Your home; for she is a woman
Without food or children; only
Her condition brings her to
This necessity; surely she
Ought not to fear you, because
You are not a local man, yet
It would be good of you to try
And help her, and save her
Feelings; so do not fence off
Your fruit; heavy taxation is
The cause of her misery; the
Effect of war on the helpless
Brings us unending sorrow.

---

[4]The auxiliary capital and one of China's most sacred and ancient cities.
[5]Xuanzong's son and successor.

[6]The last effective king of the Western Zhou Dynasty; he spent most of his reign (827–781 B.C.E.) fighting defensive wars against non-Chinese to the north.

The Dao of Agriculture in Song China
▼▼▼
71 ▼ *Chen Pu, THE CRAFT OF FARMING*

China has continually faced the problem of producing sufficient food to meet the needs of an expanding population. During the Song Era the Chinese met this challenge with reasonable success, despite a dramatic increase in population. This success was partially due to an activist agenda by the central government, which encouraged land reclamation through tax incentives and published illustrated handbooks that promoted up-to-date agricultural technology. The following selections from a popular treatise written in 1149 by the otherwise unknown Chen

Pu provide insight into the manner in which Song China approached the problem of feeding itself adequately.

QUESTIONS FOR ANALYSIS

1. What does Chen Pu assume is more scarce, and consequently more valuable, labor or land? What do you infer from your answer?
2. Chen Pu focuses on several key elements that contributed to Song China's success in feeding its people. What are they?
3. Traditional Chinese agriculture has often been characterized as *family market gardening*. What do you think this term means? Does this treatise support such a characterization?
4. According to Chen Pu, what qualities set the superior farmer apart from all others?
5. It has been said that this treatise focuses more on producing a superior farmer than a superior farm. What does this mean, and do you agree? If you agree, what do you find so distinctly Chinese about such a goal?
6. In what way is this treatise a combination of agricultural science, folk wisdom, Confucian learning, and Daoist ideology? Can you find any Legalist elements or influences in the essay?
7. Some have characterized this work as an essay on the Dao of farming. What do they mean? Do you agree? Why or why not?

FINANCE AND LABOR

All those who engage in business should do so in accordance with their own capacity. They should refrain from careless investment and excessive greed, lest in the end they achieve nothing. . . . In the farming business, which is the most difficult business to manage, how can you afford not to calculate your financial and labor capacities carefully? Only when you are certain that you have sufficient funds and labor to assure success should you launch an enterprise. Anyone who covets more than he can manage is likely to fall into carelessness and irresponsibility. . . . Thus, to procure more land is to increase trouble, not profit.

On the other hand, anyone who plans carefully, begins with good methods, and continues in the same way can reasonably expect success and does not have to rely on luck. The proverb says, "Owning a great deal of emptiness is less desirable than reaping from a narrow patch of land." . . . For the farmer who is engaged in the management of fields, the secret lies not in expanding the farmland, but in balancing finance and labor. If the farmer can achieve that, he can expect prosperity and abundance. . . .

PLOWING

Early and late plowing both have their advantages. For the early rice crop,[1] as soon as the reaping is completed, immediately plow the fields and expose the stalks to glaring sunlight. Then

---

[1]Rice became a central part of the Chinese diet in the Song Era, thanks to the introduction of early ripening, drought-resistant strains from Southeast Asia. These new seeds made it possible to grow the crop in areas that previously had been unsuitable for rice cultivation.

add manure and bury the stalks to nourish the soil. Next, plant beans, wheat, and vegetables to ripen and fertilize the soil so as to minimize the next year's labor. In addition, when the harvest is good, these extra crops can add to the yearly income. For late crops, however, do not plow until spring. Because the rice stalks are soft but tough, it is necessary to wait until they have fully decayed to plow satisfactorily. . . .

THE SIX KINDS OF CROPS

There is an order to the planting of different crops. Anyone who knows the right timing and follows the order can cultivate one thing after another, and use one to assist the others. Then there will not be a day without planting, nor a month without harvest, and money will be coming in throughout the year. How can there then be any worry about cold, hunger, or lack of funds?

Plant the nettle-hemp in the first month. Apply manure in intervals of ten days and by the fifth or sixth month it will be time for reaping. The women should take charge of knotting and spinning cloth out of the hemp.

Plant millet in the second month. It is necessary to sow the seeds sparsely and then roll cart wheels over the soil to firm it up; this will make the millet grow luxuriantly, its stalks long and its grains full. In the seventh month the millet will be harvested, easing any temporary financial difficulties.

There are two crops of oil-hemp. The early crop is planted in the third month. Rake the field to spread out the seedlings. Repeat the raking process three times a month and the hemp will grow well. It can be harvested in the seventh or the eighth month.

In the fourth month plant beans. Rake as with hemp. They will be ripe by the seventh month.

In mid-fifth month plant the late oil-hemp. Proceed as with the early crop. The ninth month will be reaping time.

After the 7th day of the seventh month, plant radishes and cabbage.

In the eighth month, before the autumn sacrifice to the god of the earth, wheat can be planted. It is advisable to apply manure and remove weeds frequently. When wheat grows from the autumn through the spring sacrifices to the god of the earth, the harvest will double and the grains will be full and solid.

The *Book of Poetry* says, "The tenth month is the time to harvest crops." You will have a large variety of crops, including millet, rice, beans, hemp, and wheat and will lack nothing needed through the year. Will you ever be concerned for want of resources? . . .

FERTILIZER

At the side of the farm house, erect a compost hut. Make the eaves low to prevent the wind and rain from entering it, for when the compost is exposed to the moon and the stars, it will lose its fertility. In this hut, dig a deep pit and line it with bricks to prevent leakage. Collect waste, ashes, chaff, broken stalks, and fallen leaves and burn them in the pit; then pour manure over them to make them fertile. In this way considerable quantities of compost are acquired over time. Then, whenever sowing is to be done, sieve and discard stones and tiles, mix the fine compost with the seeds, and plant them sparsely in pinches. When the seedlings have grown tall, again sprinkle the compost and bank it up against the roots. These methods will ensure a double yield.

Some people say that when the soil is exhausted, grass and trees will not grow; that when the qi[2] is weak, all living things will be stunted;

---

[2]Vital energy or material force. *Qi* was a construct of *Neo-Confucian* philosophers, who envisioned a cosmos in which all entities are composed of *li* (its principle or pattern) and *qi* (its driving force). Neo-Confucianism was developed in the Song Era, in part as a response to the challenge presented by Buddhism, whose metaphysical speculations threatened to overshadow China's more down-to-earth philosophical traditions. Whereas Confucius and his early classical followers focused exclusively on human relations, the Neo-Confucians constructed a cosmological system that encompassed the universe.

and that after three to five years of continuous planting, the soil of any field will be exhausted. This theory is erroneous because it fails to recognize one factor: by adding new, fertile soil, enriched with compost, the land can be reinforced in strength. If this is so, where can the alleged exhaustion come from?

WEEDING

The *Book of Poetry* says, "Root out the weeds. Where the weeds decay, there the grains will grow luxuriantly." The author of the *Record of Ritual* also remarks, "The months of mid-summer are advantageous for weeding. Weeds can fertilize the fields and improve the land." Modern farmers, ignorant of these principles, throw the weeds away. They do not know that, if mixed with soil and buried deep under the roots of rice seedlings, the weeds will eventually decay and the soil will be enriched; the harvest, as a result, will be abundant and of superior quality. . . .

CONCENTRATION

If something is thought out carefully, it will succeed; if not, it will fail; this is a universal truth. It is very rare that a person works and yet gains nothing. On the other hand, there is never any harm in trying too hard.

In farming it is especially appropriate to be concerned about what you are doing. Mencius said, "Will a farmer discard his plow when he leaves his land?" Ordinary people will become idle if they have leisure and prosperity. Only those who love farming, who behave in harmony with it, who take pleasure in talking about it and think about it all the time will manage it without a moment's negligence. For these people a day's work results in a day's gain, a year's work in a year's gain. How can they escape affluence?

Thirteenth-Century Hangzhou
▼▼▼
72 ▼ *A RECORD OF MUSINGS ON THE EASTERN CAPITAL*

When Jurchen steppe people overran all of northern China in the early twelfth century and established the rival Jin Dynasty (1115–1234) with its capital at Beijing, the Song imperial court moved from its capital at Kaifeng to the port city of *Hangzhou,* just south of the Yangzi River. From here the Song ruled over the southern remnants of their mutilated empire until Mongols captured the city in 1276.

Southern Song (1127–1279) presided over territory that in the age of Tang had been a pestilential borderland. By the twelfth century, however, it was China's most densely populated region and the newest hub of Chinese culture. Its heart was Hangzhou, which was more than merely an administrative center. In the thirteenth century it was home to well over one million people (some estimates reach as high as two and one-half million), who inhabited an area of seven to eight square miles, making it the largest and richest city in the world.

The following account, composed anonymously in 1235, describes the city and its residents.

QUESTIONS FOR ANALYSIS

1. How prosperous and varied does the city's economy appear to be?
2. What adjectives would you use to characterize this city?
3. Compare life in Hangzhou with that in a modern metropolis, such as New York or Los Angeles. What would a modern urban dweller or visitor recognize as familiar in this thirteenth-century city?

MARKETS

During the morning hours, markets extend from Tranquility Gate of the palace all the way to the north and south sides of the New Boulevard. Here we find pearl, jade, talismans, exotic plants and fruits, seasonal catches from the sea, wild game — all the rarities of the world seem to be gathered here. The food and commodity markets at the Heavenly-View Gate, River Market Place, Central Square, Ba Creek, the end of Superior Lane, Tent Place, and Universal Peace Bridge are all crowded and full of traffic.

In the evening, with the exception of the square in front of the palace, the markets are as busy as during the day. The most attractive one is at Central Square, where all sorts of exquisite artifacts, instruments, containers, and hundreds of varieties of goods are for sale. In other marketplaces, sales, auctions, and exchanges go on constantly. In the wine shops and inns business also thrives. Only after the fourth drum[1] does the city gradually quiet down, but by the fifth drum, court officials already start preparing for audiences and merchants are getting ready for the morning market again. This cycle goes on all year round without respite. . . .

On the lot in front of the wall of the city building, there are always various acting troupes performing, and this usually attracts a large crowd. The same kind of activity is seen in almost any vacant lot, including those at the meat market of the Great Common, the herb market at Charcoal Bridge, the book market at Orange Grove, the vegetable market on the east side of the city,

and the rice market on the north side. There are many more interesting markets, such as the candy center at the Five Buildings, but I cannot name them all.

COMMERCIAL ESTABLISHMENTS

In general, the capital attracts the greatest variety of goods and has the best craftsmen. For instance, the flower company at Superior Lane does a truly excellent job of flower arrangement, and its caps, hairpins, and collars are unsurpassed in craftsmanship. Some of the most famous specialties of the capital are the sweet-bean soup at the Miscellaneous Market, the pickled dates of the Ge family, the thick soup of the Guang family at Superior Lane, the fruit at the Great Commons marketplace, the cooked meats in front of Eternal Mercy Temple, Sister Song's fish broth at Penny Pond Gate, the juicy lungs at Flowing Gold Gate, the "lamb rice" of the Zhi family at Central Square, the boots of the Peng family, the fine clothing of the Xuan family at Southern Commons, the sticky rice pastry of the Zhang family, the flutes made by Gu the Fourth, and the Qiu family's Tatar whistles at the Great Commons.

WINE SHOPS

Among the various kinds of wine shops, the tea-and-food shops sell not only wine, but also various foods to go with it. However, to get seasonal delicacies not available in these shops, one

---

[1]The night was divided into five *watches,* each of which was signaled by a drumbeat.

should go to the inns, for they also have a menu from which one can make selections. The pastry-and-wine shops sell pastries with duckling and goose fillings, various fixings of pig tripe, intestines and blood, fish fat and spawn; but they are rather expensive. The mansion-style inns are either decorated in the same way as officials' mansions or are actually remodeled from such mansions. The garden-style inns are often located in the suburbs, though some are also situated in town. Their decoration is usually an imitation of a studio-garden combination. Among other kinds of wine shops are the straight ones which do not sell food. There are also the small retail wine shops which sell house wine as well as wine from other stores. Instead of the common emblem — a painted branching twig — used by all other winehouses, they have bamboo fences and canvas awnings. To go drinking in such a place is called "hitting the cup," meaning that a person drinks only one cup; it is therefore not the most respectable place and is unfit for polite company.

The "luxuriant inns" have prostitutes residing in them, and the wine chambers are equipped with beds. At the gate of such an inn, on top of the red gardenia lantern, there is always a cover made of bamboo leaves. Rain or shine, this cover is always present, serving as a trademark. In other inns, the girls only keep the guests company. If a guest has other wishes, he has to go to the girl's place. . . .

The expenses incurred on visiting an inn can vary widely. If you order food, but no drinks, it is called "having the lowly soup-and-stuff," and is quite inexpensive. If your order of wine and food falls within the range of 100–5,000 cash,[2] it is called a small order. However, if you ask for female company, then it is most likely that the girls will order the most expensive delicacies. You are well advised to appear shrewd and experienced, so as not to be robbed. One trick, for instance, in ordering wines is to give a large order, of, say, ten bottles, but open them one by one. In the end, you will probably have used only five or six bottles of the best. You can then return the rest. . . .

TEAHOUSES

In large teahouses there are usually paintings and calligraphies by famous artists on display. In the old capital,[3] only restaurants had them, to enable their patrons to while away the time as the food was being prepared, but now it is customary for teahouses as well to display paintings and the like. . . .

Often many young men gather in teahouses to practice singing or playing musical instruments. To give such amateur performances is called "getting posted."

A "social teahouse" is more of a community gathering place than a mere place that sells tea. Often tea-drinking is but an excuse, and people are rather generous when it comes to the tips.

There is a special kind of teahouse where pimps and gigolos hang out. Another kind is occupied by people from various trades and crafts who use them as places to hire help, buy apprentices, and conduct business. These teahouses are called "trade heads."

"Water teahouses" are in fact pleasure houses, the tea being a cover. Some youths are quite willing to spend their money there, which is called "dry tea money." . . .

SPECIALTY STORES

The commercial area of the capital extends from the old Qing River Market to the Southern Com-

---

[2]The basic unit of currency was the *cash,* a copper coin with a square hole in the middle. These were strung together in groups of hundreds and thousands. Late in the century, the government was circulating bank notes, backed by gold and silver, ranging in value from one thousand to one hundred thousand cash coins.

[3]Kaifeng, which was captured in 1126.

mons on the south and to the border on the north. It includes the Central Square, which is also called the Center of Five Flowers. From the north side of the Five Buildings to South Imperial Boulevard, there are more than one hundred gold, silver, and money exchanges. On the short walls in front of these stores, there are piles of gold, silver, and copper cash: these are called "the money that watches over the store." Around these exchanges there are also numerous gold and silversmiths. The pearl marts are situated between the north side of Cordial Marketplace and Southtown Marketplace. Most deals made here involve over 10,000 cash. A score of pawnshops are scattered in between, all owned by very wealthy people and dealing only in the most valuable objects.

Some famous fabric stores sell exquisite brocade and fine silk which are unsurpassed elsewhere in the country. Along the river, close to the Peaceful Ford Bridge, there are numerous fabric stores, fan shops, and lacquerware and porcelain shops. Most other cities can only boast of one special product; what makes the capital unique is that it gathers goods from all places. Furthermore, because of the large population and busy commercial traffic, there is a demand for everything. There are even shops that deal exclusively in used paper or in feathers, for instance.

WAREHOUSES

In Liu Yong's (ca. 1045) poem on Qiantang, we read that there were about ten thousand families residing here; but that was before the Yuanfeng reign (1078–1085). Today, having been the "temporary capital" for more than a hundred years,[4] the city has over a million households. The suburbs extend to the south, west, and north; all are densely populated and prosperous in commerce as well as in agriculture. The size of the suburbs is comparable to a small county or prefecture,

and it takes several days to travel through them. This again reflects the prosperity of the capital.

In the middle of the city, enclosed by the Northern Pass Dam, is White Ocean Lake. Its water spreads over several tens of *li*.[5] Wealthy families have built scores of warehouse complexes along this waterfront. Each of these consists of several hundred to over a thousand rooms for the storage needs of the various businesses in the capital and of traveling merchants. Because these warehouses are surrounded by water, they are not endangered by fires or thieves, and therefore they offer a special convenience.

HUSTLERS

Some of these hustlers are students who failed to achieve any literary distinction. Though able to read and write, and play musical instruments and chess, they are not highly skilled in any art. They end up being a kind of guide for young men from wealthy families, accompanying them in their pleasure-seeking activities. Some also serve as guides or assistants to officials on business from other parts of the country. The lowliest of these people actually engage themselves in writing and delivering invitation cards and the like for brothels. . . .

There are also professional go-betweens, nicknamed "water-treaders," whose principal targets are pleasure houses, where they flatter the wealthy young patrons, run errands for them, and help make business deals. Some gather at brothels or scenic attractions and accost the visitors. They beg for donations for "religious purposes," but in fact use the money to make a living for themselves and their families. If you pay attention to them, they will become greedy; if you ignore them, they will force themselves on you and will not stop until you give in. It requires art to deal with these people appropriately.

---

[4]The Song emperors never gave up hope of recovering Kaifeng and the northern part of the empire. Kaifeng thus remained the official capital, and Hangzhou was designated only *temporary capital*.

[5]A *li* is a bit more than one-third of a mile.

▼▼▼

Buddhism in East Asia: Acceptance, Rejection, and Accommodation

Buddhism began to spread out of India and into East Asia about the same time that the Mahayana doctrine was transforming the teachings of the Buddha into a popular religion (Chapter 6, sources 46 and 47). Following branches of the Silk Road out of northwest India, Mahayana Buddhism traveled through Central Asia and into the heartland of northern China, reaching the Middle Kingdom as early as the reign of Emperor Han Mingdi (58–75 C.E.). Buddhism initially made little progress in China because some of its practices, such as monasticism and celibacy (rejection of marriage), and its basic otherworldliness ran counter to two primary Chinese qualities: emphasis on the centrality of the family and preoccupation with this world. The few early inroads Buddhism made in China occurred largely because some Chinese initially were able to equate it with Daoism, whereby they perceived Nirvana to be the equivalent of the Daoist principle of active nonaction (*wuwei*), and they translated *Dharma* (the Law of Righteousness) as *Dao* (the Way). In the time of troubles that followed the collapse of Later Han in 220 C.E., however, Buddhism, especially in its Mahayana form, achieved its own place as a religious doctrine offering comfort in the face of affliction.

From China, Buddhist ideas were introduced into Korea by the fourth century, into Japan in the sixth, and later into Tibet, Mongolia, and northern regions of Southeast Asia. In each of these regions, Mahayana Buddhism took deep root and became a living part of its host civilization. As the following sources suggest, however, the story of Buddhism's spread through East Asia was not a simple one. As it traveled, Buddhism absorbed local ideas and styles, which in turn were passed on to a neighboring culture, which then adapted the received ideas and styles to suit its own needs and perceptions (for example, see Chapter 5, sources 41 and 42). Yet even when adapted to a preexisting culture, Buddhist ideas and ways could and did face local resistance, especially in China. Despite resistance, even solidly secular China was forced to come to grips with Buddhist metaphysics, and despite several attempts to suppress the religion, China assimilated Buddhism's basic concepts, deities, rituals, artistic motifs, and festivals into its everyday culture. Along with Confucianism, Daoism, and Legalism, Buddhism became one of the major pillars of Chinese civilization.

A Conflict of Values:
Foreign Religions in Late Tang China
▼▼▼

73 ▼ *Han Yu, MEMORIAL ON BUDDHISM, and Emperor Tang Wuzong, PROCLAMATION ORDERING THE DESTRUCTION OF THE BUDDHIST MONASTERIES*

Chinese Buddhism reached its high point of popularity and influence during the early years of the Tang Dynasty. Buddhist monasteries and sects proliferated, and the Tang imperial court often patronized Buddhism in one form or another during its first two centuries of power. However, because so many aspects of Buddhism were at variance with the traditional culture of China, especially Confucian values, conflict was almost inevitable.

One of the leaders in the Confucian counterattack on Buddhism was the classical prose stylist and poet Han Yu (768–824), who in 819 composed a polemic against Buddhism. Presented as a memorandum, or *memorial,* to Emperor Tang Xianzong on the subject of the emperor's veneration of a relic of the Buddha's finger, Han Yu's elegant and witty essay so enraged the emperor that initially he wanted to execute the author. Eventually, the emperor contented himself with banishing his impudent civil servant to a frontier outpost. Our first document is that essay, the celebrated *Memorial on Buddhism,* which occasioned Han Yu's fall from imperial favor.

A champion of rationalism, Han Yu wished to suppress religious Daoism as well as Buddhism. Stimulated by the example of Buddhism and by the same political turmoil that had aided the rise in popularity of the Mahayana faith in China, Daoism had evolved during the early centuries C.E. into an organized religion that promised immortality. Ironically, it was due to the influence of Daoist priests that Emperor Tang Wuzong initiated a policy of state suppression of a number of foreign religious establishments in 842, which culminated with his famous *Proclamation Ordering the Destruction of Buddhist Monasteries* of 845. The emperor died seven months after issuing the order, and with his death the full force of the edict was relaxed. Nonetheless, substantial damage had already been done to the institutional structures of Buddhism as well as Nestorian Christianity and other foreign faiths that had infiltrated China during the cosmopolitan reign of Early Tang.

Buddhist monasteries were especially hard hit by the state-ordered closures, and Chinese Buddhism consequently suffered a major reversal of fortune, so far as its possessions and political power were concerned. However, Buddhism remained strong at the popular level, especially a form of Mahayana devotion known as the *Pure Land Sect,* which centered on devotion to two deities: *Amitabha,* the Buddha of Infinite Light, who presided over the Western Paradise; and his chief assistant, the Bodhisattva Guanyin, who reigned as the goddess of mercy (Chapter 6, sources 46 and 47). Moreover, Buddhism increasingly merged with folk magic, Daoism, and Confucianism to become part of a uniquely Chinese religious complex.

QUESTIONS FOR ANALYSIS

1. How does Han Yu imply that emperors who have espoused Buddhism have lost the Mandate of Heaven (Chapter 1, source 5)?
2. What aspect of Buddhism most repels Han Yu?
3. In Han Yu's mind, what are the social, cultural, and political dangers of Buddhism?
4. Exactly what does the imperial proclamation command, and what does it *not* say? For example: Does the proclamation suppress only Buddhist monasteries? Does it forbid people to believe in foreign religions? Does it order the persecution of any individuals?
5. On what ideological basis does it order the suppression of monasteries and temples? Is there any evidence to suggest that maybe there were also political and economic reasons for closing down and confiscating these establishments? Please explain your answer.
6. Is there any evidence to suggest that the person who drafted the imperial proclamation had read or been influenced by Han Yu's *Memorial?* Again, please explain your answer.

MEMORIAL ON BUDDHISM

Your servant submits that Buddhism is but one of the practices of barbarians which has filtered into China since the Later Han. In ancient times there was no such thing. . . . In those times the empire was at peace, and the people, contented and happy, lived out their full complement of years. . . . The Buddhist doctrine had still not reached China, so this could not have been the result of serving the Buddha.

The Buddhist doctrine first appeared in the time of the Emperor Ming[1] of the Han Dynasty, and the Emperor Ming was a scant eighteen years on the throne. Afterwards followed a succession of disorders and revolutions, when dynasties did not long endure. From the time of the dynasties Song, Qi, Liang, Chen, and Wei,[2] as they grew more zealous in the service of the Buddha, the reigns of kings became shorter. There was only the Emperor Wu of the Liang who was on the throne for forty-eight years. First and last, he thrice abandoned the world and dedicated himself to the service of the Buddha. He refused to use animals in the sacrifices in his own ancestral temple. His single meal a day was limited to fruits and vegetables. In the end he was driven out and died of hunger. His dynasty likewise came to an untimely end. In serving the Buddha he was seeking good fortune, but the disaster

---

[1]Han Mingdi (58–75 C.E.).
[2]Five fairly short-lived dynasties of the troubled fourth through sixth centuries. The next document also mentions the Song, Qi, and Liang Dynasties. (See Chapter 5, source

41 for additional information on the Northern Wei Dynasty's patronage of Buddhism.) The Wei, who were foreign conquerors, apparently used Buddhism's universal message as an ideological buttress for their rule.

that overtook him was only the greater. Viewed in the light of this, it is obvious that the Buddha is not worth serving.

When Gaozu[3] first succeeded to the throne of the Sui,[4] he planned to do away with Buddhism, but his ministers and advisors were short-sighted men incapable of any real understanding of the Way of the Former Kings, or of what is fitting for past and present; they were unable to apply the Emperor's ideas so as to remedy this evil, and the matter subsequently came to naught — many the times your servant has regretted it. I venture to consider that Your Imperial Majesty, shrewd and wise in peace and war, with divine wisdom and heroic courage, is without an equal through the centuries. When first you came to the throne, you would not permit laymen to become monks or nuns or Daoist priests,[5] nor would you allow the founding of temples or cloisters. It constantly struck me that the intention of Gaozu was to be fulfilled by Your Majesty. Now even though it has not been possible to put it into effect immediately, it is surely not right to remove all restrictions and turn around and actively encourage them.

Now I hear that by Your Majesty's command a troupe of monks went to Fengxiang[6] to get the Buddha-bone, and that you viewed it from a tower as it was carried into the Imperial Palace; also that you have ordered that it be received and honored in all the temples in turn. Although your servant[7] is stupid, he cannot help knowing that Your Majesty is not misled by this Buddha, and that you do not perform these devotions to pray for good luck. But just because the harvest has been good and the people are happy, you are complying with the general desire by putting on for the citizens of the capital this extraordinary spectacle which is nothing more than a sort of theatrical amusement. How could a sublime intelligence like yours consent to believe in this sort of thing?

But the people are stupid and ignorant; they are easily deceived and with difficulty enlightened. If they see Your Majesty behaving in this fashion, they are going to think you serve the Buddha in all sincerity. All will say, "The Emperor is wisest of all, and yet he is a sincere believer. What are we common people that we still should grudge our lives?" Burning heads and searing fingers by the tens and hundreds, throwing away their clothes and scattering their money, from morning to night emulating one another and fearing only to be last, old and young rush about, abandoning their work and place; and if restrictions are not immediately imposed, they will increasingly make the rounds of temples and some will inevitably cut off their arms and slice their flesh in the way of offerings. Thus to violate decency and draw the ridicule of the whole world is no light matter.

Now the Buddha was of barbarian origin. His language differed from Chinese speech; his clothes were of a different cut; his mouth did not pronounce the prescribed words of the Former Kings,[8] his body was not clad in the garments prescribed by the Former Kings. He did not recognize the relationship between prince and subject, nor the sentiments of father and son. Let us suppose him to be living today, and that he come to court at the capital as an emissary of his country. Your Majesty would receive him courteously. But only one interview in the audience chamber, one banquet in his honor, one gift of

---

[3]Literally "high (or great) ancestor," an honorific title bestowed posthumously on several Chinese emperors. This high ancestor was Li Yuan (r. 618–626), the first Tang emperor (see source 69, note 3).

[4]The Sui Dynasty (581–618) reunited China in 589.

[5]By the second century C.E. a polytheistic Daoist Church, which practiced congregational worship, preached immortality, and utilized drugs and magic, had emerged as a significant force.

[6]A western city.

[7]Han Yu.

[8]The legendary Sage Emperors, who supposedly laid the basis of Chinese civilization before the rise of the Xia Dynasty (Chapter 1, source 5).

clothing, and he would be escorted under guard to the border that he might not mislead the masses.

How much the less, now that he has long been dead, is it fitting that his decayed and rotten bone, his ill-omened and filthy remains, should be allowed to enter in the forbidden precincts of the Palace? Confucius said, "Respect ghosts and spirits, but keep away from them."[9] The feudal lords of ancient times, when they went to pay a visit of condolence in their states, made it their practice to have exorcists go before with rush-brooms and peachwood branches to dispel unlucky influences. Only after such precautions did they make their visit of condolence. Now without reason you have taken up an unclean thing and examined it in person when no exorcist had gone before, when neither rush-broom nor peachwood branch had been employed. But your ministers did not speak of the wrong nor did the censors call attention to the impropriety; I am in truth ashamed of them. I pray that Your Majesty will turn this bone over to the officials that it may be cast into water or fire, cutting off for all time the root and so dispelling the suspicions of the empire and preventing the befuddlement of later generations. Thereby men may know in what manner a great sage acts who a million times surpasses ordinary men. Could this be anything but ground for prosperity? Could it be anything but a cause for rejoicing?

If the Buddha has supernatural power and can wreak harm and evil, may any blame or retribution fittingly fall on my person. Heaven be my witness: I will not regret it. Unbearably disturbed and with the utmost sincerity I respectfully present my petition that these things may be known.

Your servant is truly alarmed, truly afraid.

PROCLAMATION ORDERING THE DESTRUCTION OF THE BUDDHIST MONASTERIES

We learn that there was no such thing as Buddhism prior to the Three Dynasties, i.e., Xia, Yin, and Zhou.[10] After the dynasties of Han and Wei, the Image-Teaching[11] gradually began to flourish. And once established in that degenerate age, this strange custom prevailed far and wide, and now the people are soaked to the bone with it. Just now the national spirit begins to be spoiled unconsciously by it; and, leading the heart of the people astray, it has put the public in worse condition than ever. In the country — throughout the nine provinces, and among the mountains and fields as well as in both the capitals — the number of priests is daily increasing and the Buddhist temples are constantly winning support.

Wasting human labor in building, plundering the people's purse by golden decorations, neglecting both husband and wife by their vigil-keeping, no teaching is more harmful than this Buddhism. In breaking the laws of the country and injuring the people, none can surpass this Buddhism. Moreover, if a farmer neglects his field, many suffer the pangs of starvation from his negligence; if a woman neglects her silk-worm culture, many suffer the calamity of being frozen to death through her negligence. Now there are at present so many monks and nuns that to count them is almost impossible. They all depend on farming for their food, and upon silk-worms for their clothing!

"The public monasteries and temples, as well as private chapels and shrines, are innumerable; and all of them so gigantic and imposing that they vie with the Imperial Palace in splendor! In

---

[9]From *The Analects*. (See Chapter 4, source 24, for similar Confucian aphorisms.)
[10]China's first three dynasties (Chapter 1, source 5). *Yin* is another name for the Late Shang Dynasty.

[11]Buddhism, which used statues and paintings of Buddhas and Bodhisattvas for veneration and instruction.

Dynasties Jin (317–420 C.E.) and Song (420–476 C.E.), Qi (479–501 C.E.), and Liang (502–557 C.E.), the resources of this Empire were exhausted and the country gradually declined, while its manners and customs became flippant and insincere, solely because of this Buddhism.

"Our Imperial ancestor Taizong[12] put an end to confusion and disorder by his arms, and built up the glorious Middle Kingdom and governed his people by his accomplished learning and culture. The right of 'the pen' (i.e., peaceful rule or civic administration) and 'the sword' (i.e., war) belongs to the State, and they are the two weapons wherewith to govern the Empire. How dare the insignificant Teaching of the Western Lands compete with ours? During the periods of Zhenguan and Gaiyuan,[13] things were bettered once for all, but the remnants were smouldering, and poverty began to grow bigger and wider and threatened to set the country ablaze!

"After closely examining the examples set by our Imperial predecessors, We have finally decided to put an end to such conspicuous evils. Do you, Our subjects at home and abroad, obey and conform to Our sincere will. If you send in a Memorial suggesting how to exterminate these evils which have beset Us for many Dynasties, We shall do all We can to carry out the plan. Know that We yield to none in fulfilling the laws of Our predecessors and in trying to be helpful to Our people and beneficial to the public.

"Those 4,600 monasteries supported by the Government shall be confiscated and, at the same time, 260,500 nuns and priests shall return to the secular life so that they may be able to pay the taxes. We shall also confiscate 40,000 private temples with the fertile and good lands amounting to several tens of millions of acres; and emancipate 150,000 slaves and make them into free, tax-paying people. Examining into the teaching from the foreign lands in the Empire, We have discovered that there are over 3,000 monks from Daqin[14] and Muhufu;[15] and these monks also shall return to the lay life. They shall not mingle and interfere with the manners and customs of the Middle Kingdom.

"More than a hundred thousand idle, lazy people and busy bodies have been driven away, and numberless beautifully decorated useless temples have been completely swept away. Hereafter, purity of life shall rule Our people and simple and non-assertive rules prevail, and the people of all quarters shall bask in the sunshine of Our Imperial Influence. But this is only the beginning of the reforms. Let time be given for all, and let Our will be made known to every one of Our subjects lest the people misunderstand Our wish."

---

[12]See source 69.
[13]The official names of the reigns of Emperor Tang Taizong (r. 626–649) and Emperor Tang Xuanzong (r. 712–756), the dynasty's two greatest rulers.

[14]From Syria. A reference to Nestorian Christianity (see source 69).
[15]A reference to Zoroastrians from Persia (see Chapter 3, source 21).

Zen Buddhism in Japan

▼▼▼

74 ▾ Dogen, ON LIFE AND DEATH

Whereas Pure Land Buddhism's mass popularity survived Late Tang's assault on the Teaching of the Western Lands, *Chan* (meditation) Buddhism remained popular with the educated elite. Chan was introduced into China from India in the early sixth century. There it fused with Daoism to become a thoroughly sinicized Buddhist sect by the late seventh century. For Chan practitioners, meditation was not an avenue to insight; it *was* insight. Disdaining all learning and logic,

Chan masters sought to lead their students to a state in which they suspended all normal forms of reasoning and intuitively grasped the Buddha nature that lies within each person and thing. This Enlightenment, or Awakening, would be a blinding and unexpected flash that could be triggered by any nonrational activity or external stimulus: contemplating a rock or the jolt of a clap of thunder. To prepare their students for this moment of Awakening, Chan masters presented them with puzzles for meditation that had no logical answers. One of the classic conundrums Chan students wrestled with was What is the sound of one hand clapping?

Because Chan monks mostly remained aloof from imperial patronage in the Early Tang Era, their sect suffered far less than others in the persecutions of the mid ninth century. In the following era of the Song Dynasty (960–1279), Chan continued to exhibit great intellectual and artistic vitality, and it thus deeply influenced Song art, literature, and philosophy. During the age of Song, Chan Buddhism also took root in Japan due to the efforts of two Japanese masters who had studied in China: Eisei (1141–1215) and Dogen (1200–1253). Characteristically, the Japanese converted this import, which they pronounced *Zen,* into something distinctly Japanese.

Zen's austerity and discipline, as well as its emphasis on intuitive action as opposed to logical thought, appealed to Japan's feudal warrior class, the emerging samurai (source 68). Many fused Zen philosophy to their military skills, attempting to break down the artificial and logical duality between warrior and weapon. For example, a form of archery in which the archer sought to become one with the bow and arrow became part of Zen training. The archer did not consciously aim; instead, the arrow projected itself from the bow into the target. In a similar manner, Zen profoundly influenced all other forms of Japanese culture, especially its sense of beauty and proper ceremony. The tea ceremony becomes a moment of Zen meditation and potential Awakening, as one intuits how a common herb and a lump of clay are things of comfort and serene beauty. The Buddha-reality of a refreshing beverage and the delicately fashioned cup that holds it is revealed to the person open to receiving the insight.

One of the pioneers of the tea ceremony was Dogen, who, on a visit to China in 1222, brought with him a potter to study the art of Chinese porcelain. The potter later established a thriving center for the production of tea vessel ceramics in Japan. In the following sermon, Dogen talks not about tea but about life and death, important issues to a Zen master but no more so than the proper preparation and drinking of tea. Here Dogen addresses the issue of how both life and death are equally expressions of Buddha-reality.

QUESTIONS FOR ANALYSIS

1. What does Dogen mean when he states that one should neither renounce nor covet life and death?
2. What does he mean when he states that life and death must be regarded as identical to Nirvana?

3. Is Buddhahood something to be attained in another life? Is it even something to be achieved? What do your answers mean?
4. Reread Laozi in Chapter 4, source 23. Can you find any Daoist elements in Dogen's thought?
5. Why would the Zen approach to life and death be especially attractive to a warrior? Can you see any germs of a code of warrior conduct in this philosophy?
6. Would Dogen agree with the saying "Do not anticipate, be"? Please explain your answer.

"Since there is Buddhahood in both life and death," says Kassan, "neither exists." Jozan says, "Since there is no Buddhahood in life or death, one is not led astray by either." So go the sayings of the enlightened masters, and he who wishes to free himself of the life-and-death bondage must grasp their seemingly contradictory sense.

To seek Buddhahood outside of life and death is to ride north to reach Southern Etsu or face south to glimpse the North Star. Not only are you traveling the wrong way on the road to emancipation, you are increasing the links in your karma-chain. To find release you must begin to regard life and death as identical to Nirvana, neither loathing the former nor coveting the latter.

It is fallacious to think that you simply move from birth to death. Birth, from the Buddhist point of view, is a temporary point between the preceding and the succeeding; hence it can be called birthlessness. The same holds for death

and deathlessness. In life there is nothing more than life, in death nothing more than death: we are being born and are dying at every moment.

Now, to conduct: in life identify yourself with life, at death with death. Abstain from yielding and craving. Life and death constitute the very being of Buddha. Thus, should you renounce life and death, you will lose; and you can expect no more if you cling to either. You must neither loathe, then, nor covet, neither think nor speak of these things. Forgetting body and mind, by placing them together in Buddha's hands and letting him lead you on, you will without design or effort gain freedom, attain Buddhahood.

There is an easy road to Buddhahood: avoid evil, do nothing about life-and-death, be merciful to all sentient things, respect superiors and sympathize with inferiors, have neither likes nor dislikes, and dismiss idle thoughts and worries. Only then will you become a Buddha.

▼▼▼

Southwest Asia: Crossroads of the Afro-Eurasian World

Of all the significant developments that took place in Southwest Asia during this thousand-year period, the two most far reaching were the rise and spread of Islam and the arrival of Turkish, European, and Mongol invaders after 1000 C.E. By approximately 750 C.E. Islam was firmly in control of most of Southwest Asia, except for the Anatolian peninsula, which remained the heart of the East Roman, or *Byzantine,* Empire until late in the eleventh century, when Muslim Turkish forces began the process of transforming this land into Turkey. Seljuk and Ottoman Turks, European crusaders, Mongols, and the armies of Timur the Lame would invade and contest Southwest Asia for much of the period from 1000 to 1500.

Around the early sixteenth century a clear pattern emerged. Most of Europe's Christian crusaders had been expelled from the eastern Mediterranean, except for their precarious possession of a handful of island strongholds, such as Cyprus and Crete; the Mongol Empire was only a fading memory; and Timur the Lame's empire had crumbled upon his death in 1405. Two Turkish Muslim empires dominated Southwest Asia: the Shi'ite Safavids of Persia and the Sunni Ottomans, whose base of power was Anatolia but who also controlled Syria-Palestine, Egypt, and western Arabia and were driving deeply into Europe's Balkan peninsula. Although these two empires would quarrel viciously for control of Islam and Sunnis and Shi'ites would continue to shed one another's blood, Turkish domination of Southwest Asia was secure for the foreseeable future. European attempts to counter the Turkish menace by launching new crusades in the eastern Mediterranean generally proved feeble, and the Ottomans' and Safavids' pastoral cousins on the steppes of Inner Asia were becoming less of a threat to the stability of Eurasia's civilizations.

The Arrival of the Turks
▼▼▼

75 ▼ *Al-Jahiz,*
THE MERITS OF THE TURKS AND OF THE IMPERIAL ARMY AS A WHOLE

Early in the ninth century the caliphs of Baghdad (Chapter 8, source 60) addressed the problem of creating a loyal army by enlisting foreign slaves and mercenaries, many of whom came from various tribes of Turkic-speaking, pastoral peoples across the frontier in the steppes of Inner Asia. As aliens, the Turks had no ties to the various factions that threatened the caliph's power. To the contrary, they were initially dependent upon the caliph, their lord and paymaster. In a short time, however, these Turkish warriors converted to Islam and became powers behind the throne. Already by the mid ninth century some Turkish officers were playing important roles in the selection of caliphs. From that point on the caliphs and their ministers became increasingly dependent on various Turkish elements in the army, and it was almost an anticlimax when Tughril-Beg, leader of a tribe of Turks known as the *Seljuks,* entered Baghdad on December 19, 1055, to be recognized formally as *sultan* (governor) and to have his name mentioned in Friday prayers after that of the caliph. Civil and military authority now lay in the hands of Turkish sultans, and the caliph retained only religious and ceremonial functions. Under the Seljuks, Islam quickly expanded into Byzantine Anatolia, thereby precipitating a Western Christian response — the crusades (source 76 and Chapter 10, sources 91 and 92).

Two centuries earlier, a resident of the port city of Basra in southern Iraq, Abu Uthman Amr ibn Bahr (776–869) — better known by his nickname *al-Jahiz* (the Goggle-Eyed) — composed a study of the Turks, in which he attempted to place these recent converts to Islam in a favorable light. Many cultivated Arabs and Persians despised the so-called barbarians from Central Asia and resented their growing power. Al-Jahiz, one of the most popular and gifted essayists of his day and always a voice of reason and moderation, attempted to counter those attitudes. A person of largely African lineage, al-Jahiz was possibly influenced to take this public stand by the prejudice he had apparently suffered because of his dark skin.

QUESTIONS FOR ANALYSIS

1. What does al-Jahiz's essay tell us about the equestrian and military qualities of the Turks and, by extension, of other pastoral peoples from Inner Asia? Does this portrait help explain the role played in Eurasian history by the horse nomads?
2. How, according to the essayist, do the Turks resemble the Arabs of the Prophet's day?
3. Given these qualities, what special value do the Turks offer Muslim society?
4. Does al-Jahiz seem to believe that the Turks are capable of being civilized and becoming more than just warriors? If so, what? On what do you base your answer?
5. How, if at all, does this essay reveal the cosmopolitan perspective of ninth-century Iraq?

THE TURK AS A HORSEMAN

A Kharijite[1] at close quarters relies entirely on his lance. But the Turks are as good as the Kharijites with the lance, and in addition, if a thousand of their horsemen are hard-pressed they will loose all their arrows in a single volley and bring down a thousand enemy horsemen. No body of men can stand up against such a test.

Neither the Kharijites nor the Bedouins[2] are famous for their prowess as mounted bowmen. But the Turk will hit from his saddle an animal, a bird, a target, a man, a couching animal, a marker post or a bird of prey stooping on its quarry. His horse may be exhausted from being galloped and reined in, wheeled to right and left,

and mounted and dismounted: but he himself goes on shooting, loosing ten arrows before the Kharijite has let fly one. He gallops his horse up a hillside or down a gully faster than the Kharijite can make his go on the flat.

The Turk has two pairs of eyes, one at the front and the other at the back of his head. . . .

They train their horsemen to carry two or even three bows, and spare bowstrings in proportion. Thus in the hour of battle the Turk has on him everything needful for himself, his weapon and the care of his steed. As for their ability to stand trotting, sustained galloping, long night rides and cross-country journeys, it is truly extraordi-

---

[1]One of the earliest sects to break off from the main body of Islam; the Kharijites were noted as fierce warriors.

[2]Arab nomads of Arabia, North Africa, and the eastern Mediterranean.

nary. In the first place the Kharijite's horse has not the staying-power of the Turk's pony; and the Kharijite has no more than a horseman's knowledge of how to look after his mount. The Turk, however, is more experienced than a professional farrier,[3] and better than a trainer at getting what he wants from his pony. For it was he who brought it into the world and reared it from a foal; it comes when he calls it, and follows behind him when he runs. . . .

If the Turk's daily life were to be reckoned up in detail, he would be found to spend more time in the saddle than on the ground.

The Turk sometimes rides a stallion, sometimes a brood mare. Whether he is going to war, on a journey, out hunting or on any other errand, the brood mare follows behind with her foals. If he gets tired of hunting the enemy he hunts waterfowl. If he gets hungry, jogging up and down in the saddle, he has only to lay hands on one of his animals. If he gets thirsty, he milks one of his brood mares. If he needs to rest his mount, he vaults on to another without so much as putting his feet to the ground.

Of all living creatures he is the only one whose body can adapt itself to eating nothing but meat. As for his steed, leaves and shoots are all it needs; he gives it no shelter from the sun and no covering against the cold.

As regards ability to stand trotting, if the stamina of the border fighters, the posthorse outriders,[4] the Kharijites and the eunuchs[5] were all combined in one man, they would not equal a Turk.

The Turk demands so much of his mount that only the toughest of his horses is equal to the task; even one that he had ridden to exhaustion, so as to be useless for his expeditions, would outdo a Kharijite's horse in staying power, and no Tukhari pony could compare with it.

The Turk is at one and the same time herdsman, groom, trainer, horse-dealer, farrier and rider: in short, a one-man team.

When the Turk travels with horsemen of other races, he covers twenty miles to their ten, leaving them and circling around to right and left, up on to the high ground and down to the bottom of the gullies, and shooting all the while at anything that runs, crawls, flies or stands still. The Turk never travels like the rest of the band, and never rides straight ahead. On a long, hard ride, when it is noon and the halting-place is still afar off, all are silent, oppressed with fatigue and overwhelmed into weariness. Their misery leaves no room for conversation. Everything round them crackles in the intense heat, or perhaps is frozen hard. As the journey drags on, even the toughest and most resolute begin to wish that the ground would open under their feet. At the sight of a mirage or a marker post on a ridge they are transported with joy, supposing it to be the halting-place. When at last they reach it, the horsemen all drop from the saddle and stagger about bandy-legged like children who have been given an enema, groaning like sick men, yawning to refresh themselves and stretching luxuriously to overcome their stiffness. But your Turk, though he has covered twice the distance and dislocated his shoulders with shooting, has only to catch sight of a gazelle or an onager[6] near the halting-place, or put up a fox or a hare, and he is off again at a gallop as though he had only just mounted. It might have been someone else who had done that long ride and endured all that weariness.

At the gully the band bunches together at the bridge or the best crossing-place; but the Turk,

---

[3]A blacksmith.
[4]Mounted attendants who rode along side a carriage and, as needed, exchanged horses at post stations along the route.

[5]Castrated slaves who performed domestic services. According to ninth-century Arabic folklore, eunuchs endured long horse rides especially well — possibly as a consequence of their mutilation.
[6]A speedy wild ass of Central Asia.

digging his heels into his pony, is already going up the other side like a shooting star. If there is a steep rise, he leaves the track and scrambles straight up the hillside, going where even the ibex[7] cannot go. To see him scaling such slopes anyone would think he was recklessly risking his life: but if that were so he would not last long, for he is always doing it. . . .

NATIONAL CHARACTERISTICS

Know that every nation, people, generation or tribe that shows itself outstanding in craftsmanship or pre-eminent in eloquence, the various branches of learning, the establishment of empires or the art of war, only attains the peak of perfection because God has steered it in that direction and given it the means and the special aptitudes appropriate to those activities. Peoples of varying habits of thought, different opinions and dissimilar characters cannot attain perfection unless they fulfill the conditions needed to carry on an activity, and have a natural aptitude for it. Good examples are the Chinese in craftsmanship, the Greeks in philosophy and literature, the Arabs in fields that we mean to deal with in their proper place . . . and the Turks in the art of war. . . .

The Chinese for their part are specialists in smelting, casting and metalworking, in fine colors, in sculpture, weaving and drawing; they are very skillful with their hands, whatever the medium, the technique or the cost of the materials. The Greeks are theoreticians rather than practitioners, while the Chinese are practitioners rather than theoreticians; the former are thinkers, the latter doers.

The Arabs, again, were not merchants, artisans, physicians, farmers — for that would have degraded them —, mathematicians or fruit-farmers — for they wished to escape the humiliation of the tax; nor were they out to earn or amass money, hoard possessions or lay hands on other people's; they were not of those who make their living with a pair of scales; . . . they were not poor enough to be indifferent to learning, pursued neither wealth, that breeds foolishness, nor good fortune, that begets apathy, and never tolerated humiliation, which was dishonor and death to their souls. They dwelt in the plains, and grew up in contemplation of the desert. They knew neither damp nor rising mist, neither fog nor foul air, nor a horizon bounded by walls. When these keen minds and clear brains turned to poetry, fine language, eloquence and oratory, to physiognomy and astrology, genealogy, navigation by the stars and by marks on the ground, . . . to horse-breeding, weaponry and engines of war, to memorizing all that they heard, pondering on everything that caught their attention and discriminating between the glories and the shames of their tribes, they achieved perfection beyond the wildest dreams. Certain of these activities broadened their minds and exalted their aspirations, so that of all nations they are now the most glorious and the most given to recalling their past splendors.

It is the same with the Turks who dwell in tents in the desert and keep herds: they are the Bedouins of the non-Arabs. . . . Uninterested in craftsmanship or commerce, medicine, geometry, fruit-farming, building, digging canals or collecting taxes, they care only about raiding, hunting, horsemanship, skirmishing with rival chieftains, taking booty and invading other countries. Their efforts are all directed towards these activities, and they devote all their energies to these occupations. In this way they have acquired a mastery of these skills, which for them take the place of craftsmanship and commerce and constitute their only pleasure, their glory and the subject of all their conversation. Thus have they become in the realm of warfare what the Greeks are in philosophy, the Chinese in craftsmanship, and the Arabs in the fields we have enumerated.

---

[7]An Asian mountain goat.

The Arrival of the Franks

▼▼▼

76 ▼ *Usamah ibn Munqidh,*
THE BOOK OF REFLECTIONS

In 1095 Pope Urban II (r. 1088–1099) attempted to harness the martial values of Europe's warrior classes to service to the Church by calling for a holy war against Islam in the eastern Mediterranean, specifically to assist the Christian empire of Constantinople in its struggles with the Seljuk Turks and to liberate Jerusalem and other sites in the Holy Land. Christian Western Europeans had been fighting Islam intermittently since the eighth century, when Muslim armies had invaded the Iberian Peninsula and conquered the Visigothic kingdom of Spain. During the eleventh century the struggles between Christian and Islamic forces in Iberia had heated to a flashpoint whereby the *Reconquista,* or Christian reconquest, of the entire peninsula was well underway by midcentury, although the process would not be completed until 1492. It was against this background that Pope Urban set in motion an expedition known as the *First Crusade* (1096–1101).

That crusade inaugurated close to five hundred years of Western Christian involvement in the lands of the *Levant,* or eastern Mediterranean. Moreover, the crusades launched Western Europe on its first great age of overseas colonization. The later transoceanic voyages of Columbus, da Gama, and those who followed were in many ways a continuation of the crusade tradition.

From an eastern Mediterranean perspective, however, the crusades were barbarian invasions. Princess Anna Comnena of Constantinople (Chapter 10, source 91) characterized these Western coreligionists as unstable, greedy for money, and always ready to break their word. Imagine what the Muslims thought.

One of the most telling commentaries on crusader behavior in Syria-Palestine comes from the memoirs of Usamah ibn Munqidh (1095–1188), an Arab warrior and gentleman of Syria. Born in the year in which the First Crusade was called, Usamah lived long enough to see Jerusalem reconquered in 1187 by his friend and patron Saladin, sultan of Egypt and Syria. Late in life, sometime past his ninetieth birthday, Usamah undertook the narration of his memoirs. His descriptions of the *Franks* (as all Westerners were called in the Levant), collectively constitute only a small portion of this amiably rambling work. They are, however, some of the autobiography's most fascinating and insightful sections.

QUESTIONS FOR ANALYSIS

1. What does Usamah identify as the major deficiencies of the Franks?
2. Does he acknowledge any virtues or positive qualities on their part? If so, what?
3. *Acculturation* is the process of one ethnic group's adopting the cultural traits of another. Can you find any evidence of this phenomenon in Usamah's account?

4. Can you discover any evidence of friendly, or at least peaceful, relations between the crusaders and the Muslims of Syria-Palestine? To what do you ascribe such relations?

5. Despite such relations, what were the elements that separated crusaders and Muslims?

6. What is the general tone and overall message of Usamah's commentary on the Franks?

7. Review source 75. Now compose al-Jahiz's commentary on these stories.

AN APPRECIATION OF THE FRANKISH CHARACTER

Their Lack of Sense

Mysterious are the works of the Creator, the author of all things! When one comes to recount cases regarding the Franks, he cannot but glorify Allah (exalted is he!) and sanctify him, for he sees them as animals possessing the virtues of courage and fighting, but nothing else; just as animals have only the virtues of strength and carrying loads. I shall now give some instances of their doings and their curious mentality.

In the army of King Fulk,[1] son of Fulk, was a Frankish reverend knight who had just arrived from their land in order to make the holy pilgrimage[2] and then return home. He was of my intimate fellowship and kept such constant company with me that he began to call me "my brother." Between us were mutual bonds of amity and friendship. When he resolved to return by sea to his homeland, he said to me:

> My brother, I am leaving for my country and I want you to send with me your son (my son, who was then fourteen years old, was at that time in my company) to our country, where he can see the knights and learn wisdom and chivalry. When he returns, he will be like a wise man.

Thus there fell upon my ears words which would never come out of the head of a sensible man; for even if my son were to be taken captive, his captivity could not bring him a worse misfortune than carrying him into the lands of the Franks. However, I said to the man:

> By your life, this has exactly been my idea. But the only thing that prevented me from carrying it out was the fact that his grandmother, my mother, is so fond of him and did not this time let him come out with me until she exacted an oath from me to the effect that I would return him to her.

Thereupon he asked, "Is your mother still alive?" "Yes," I replied. "Well," said he, "disobey her not." . . .

Newly Arrived Franks Are Especially Rough: One Insists That Usamah Should Pray Eastward

Everyone who is a fresh emigrant from the Frankish lands is ruder in character than those who have become acclimatized and have held long association with the Muslims. Here is an illustration of their rude character.

---

[1]Fulk, count of Anjou and king of Jerusalem (r. 1131–1143).

[2]To the Holy Land. A *pilgrimage* is a religious journey (often for penitential purposes) to a sacred site. (See Chapter 8, source 62, for an example of the Islamic hajj, or pilgrimage.) Because crusaders fought for the Holy Land, they were considered pilgrims by the Roman Church and were accorded all the benefits of pilgrimage.

Whenever I visited Jerusalem I always entered the Aqsa Mosque,[3] beside which stood a small mosque which the Franks had converted into a church. When I used to enter the Aqsa Mosque, which was occupied by the Templars, who were my friends, the Templars would evacuate the little adjoining mosque so that I might pray in it. One day[4] I entered this mosque, repeated the first formula, "Allah is great," and stood up in the act of praying, upon which one of the Franks rushed on me, got hold of me and turned my face eastward saying, "This is the way you should pray!" A group of Templars hastened to him, seized him, and repelled him from me. I resumed my prayer. The same man, while the others were otherwise busy, rushed once more on me and turned my face eastward, saying, "This is the way you should pray!" The Templars again came in to him and expelled him. They apologized to me, saying, "This is a stranger who has only recently arrived from the land of the Franks and he has never before seen anyone praying except eastward." Thereupon I said to myself, "I have had enough prayer." So I went out and have ever been surprised at the conduct of this devil of a man, at the change in the color of his face, his trembling and his sentiment at the sight of one praying towards the *qiblah*.[5]

Another Wants to Show to a Muslim God as a Child

I saw one of the Franks come to al-Amir[6] Mu'in-al-Din (may Allah's mercy rest upon his soul!) when he was in the Dome of the Rock[7] and say

to him, "Do you want to see God as a child?" Mu'in-al-Din said, "Yes." The Frank walked ahead of us until he showed us the picture of Mary with Christ (may peace be upon him!) as an infant in her lap. He then said, "This is God as a child." But Allah is exalted far above what the infidels say about him! . . .

Their Judicial Trials: A Duel

I attended one day a duel in Nablus between two Franks. The reason for this was that certain Muslim thieves took by surprise one of the villages of Nablus. One of the peasants of that village was charged with having acted as guide for the thieves when they fell upon the village. So he fled away. The king sent and arrested his children. The peasant thereupon came back to the king and said, "Let justice be done in my case. I challenge to a duel the man who claimed that I guided the thieves to the village." The king then said to the tenant who held the village in fief, "Bring forth someone to fight the duel with him." The tenant went to his village, where a blacksmith lived, took hold of him and ordered him to fight the duel. The tenant became thus sure of the safety of his own peasants, none of whom would be killed and his estate ruined.

I saw this blacksmith. He was a physically strong young man, but his heart failed him. He would walk a few steps and then sit down and ask for a drink. The one who had made the challenge was an old man, but he was strong in spirit and he would rub the nail of his thumb against that of the forefinger in defiance, as if he was not

---

[3]The mosque of al-Aqsa is located on the Temple Mount, the site where the ancient temples of Solomon and Herod the Great had been located. Following the crusader capture of Jerusalem in 1099, the mosque had been converted into a palace of the Latin king of Jerusalem. Subsequently, King Baldwin II (r. 1118–1131) handed over a portion of this mosque-palace to a community of knights, who proposed to live a semimonastic life while defending the Christian kingdom of Jerusalem. As a consequence, this new elite fighting force became known as the *Knights of the Temple*, or simply the *Templars*.

[4]Around 1140.

[5]The niche in every mosque that indicates the direction of Mecca, toward which all Muslims pray. Depending on where

a mosque is in relation to Mecca, the *qiblah* can point in any direction of the compass. In Christian Europe, however, it was the custom to build altars so that the priest and worshipers standing before them faced east, the general direction of Jerusalem from western Europe. Ironically, the church of the Holy Sepulcher, the site in Jerusalem in whose direction European Christians prayed, lies about four hundred yards northwest of al-Aqsa.

[6]*Amir* (commander) was a title bestowed on military leaders and local lords.

[7]Also located on the Temple Mount, this late-seventh-century octagonal Islamic shrine is located above the rock tip of Mount Moriah, the site which tradition identifies as the Holy of Holies of the Temple of Solomon.

worrying over the duel. Then came the viscount, i.e., the lord of the town, and gave each one of the two contestants a cudgel and a shield and arranged the people in a circle around them.

The two met. The old man would press the blacksmith backward until he would get him as far as the circle, then he would come back to the middle of the arena. They went on exchanging blows until they looked like pillars smeared with blood. The contest was prolonged and the viscount began to urge them to hurry, saying, "Hurry on." The fact that the smith was given to the use of the hammer proved now of great advantage to him. The old man was worn out and the smith gave him a blow which made him fall. His cudgel fell under his back. The smith knelt down over him and tried to stick his fingers into the eyes of his adversary, but could not do it because of the great quantity of blood flowing out. Then he rose up and hit his head with the cudgel until he killed him. They then fastened a rope around the neck of the dead person, dragged him away and hanged him. The lord who brought the smith now came, gave the smith his own mantle, made him mount the horse behind him and rode off with him. This case illustrates the kind of jurisprudence and legal decisions the Franks have — may Allah's curse be upon them!

Ordeal by Water

I once went in the company of al-Amir Mu'in-al-Din (may Allah's mercy rest upon his soul!) to Jerusalem. We stopped at Nablus. There a blind man, a Muslim, who was still young and was well dressed, presented himself before al-amir carrying fruits for him and asked permission to be admitted into his service in Damascus.[8] The amir consented. I inquired about this man and was informed that his mother had been married to a Frank whom she had killed. Her son used to practice ruses against the Frankish pilgrims and cooperate with his mother in assassinating them. They finally brought charges against him and tried his case according to the Frankish way of procedure.

They installed a huge cask and filled it with water. Across it they set a board of wood. They then bound the arms of the man charged with the act, tied a rope around his shoulders and dropped him into the cask, their idea being that in case he was innocent, he would sink in the water and they would then lift him up with the rope so that he might not die in the water; and in case he was guilty, he would not sink in the water. This man did his best to sink when they dropped him into the water, but he could not do it. So he had to submit to their sentence against him — may Allah's curse be upon them! They pierced his eyeballs with red-hot awls.

Later the same man arrived in Damascus. Al-Amir Mu'in-al-Din (may Allah's mercy rest upon his soul!) assigned him a stipend large enough to meet all his needs and said to a slave of his, "Conduct him to Burhan-al-Din al-Balkhi (may Allah's mercy rest upon his soul!) and ask him on my behalf to order somebody to teach this man the Qur'an and something of Muslim jurisprudence." . . .

A Frank Domesticated in Syria Abstains from Eating Pork

Among the Franks are those who have become acclimatized and have associated long with the Muslims. These are much better than the recent comers from the Frankish lands. But they constitute the exception and cannot be treated as a rule.

Here is an illustration. I dispatched one of my men to Antioch[9] on business. There was in Antioch at that time al-Ra'is Theodoros Sophianos,[10] to whom I was bound by mutual ties of amity. His influence in Antioch was supreme. One day he said to my man, "I am invited by a

---

[8]One of the two major Muslim-held cities in Syria.
[9]The chief Christian city of Syria, which fell to the crusaders in 1098.

[10]The name indicates he was a Byzantine Greek.

friend of mine who is a Frank. You should come with me so that you may see their fashions." My man related the story in the following words:

> I went along with him and we came to the home of a knight who belonged to the old category of knights who came with the early expeditions of the Franks. He had been by that time stricken off the register and exempted from service, and possessed in Antioch an estate on the income of which he lived. The knight presented an excellent table, with food extraordinarily clean and delicious. Seeing me abstaining from food, he said, "Eat, be of good cheer! I never eat Frankish dishes, but I have Egyptian women cooks and never eat except their cooking. Besides, pork never enters my home."[11]

I ate, but guardedly, and after that we departed.

As I was passing in the market place, a Frankish woman all of a sudden hung to my clothes and began to mutter words in their language, and I could not understand what she was saying. This made me immediately the center of a big crowd of Franks. I was convinced that death was at hand. But all of a sudden that same knight approached. On seeing me, he came and said to that woman, "What is the matter between you and this Muslim?" She replied, "This is he who has killed my brother Hurso." This Hurso was a knight in Afamiyah who was killed by someone of the army of Hamah. The Christian knight shouted at her saying, "This is a bourgeois [i.e., a merchant] who neither fights nor attends a fight." He also yelled at the people who had assembled, and they all dispersed. Then he took me by the hand and went away. Thus the effect of that meal was my deliverance from certain death.

---

[11]Islamic law prohibits the eating of pork, which Muslims consider to be an unclean food.

Sinbad's First Voyage
▼▼▼
77 ▾ *A THOUSAND AND ONE ARABIAN NIGHTS*

Reading sources 75 and 76 in isolation might give us the impression that war was the primary reality of this thousand-year period of Southwest Asian history. That would be an incorrect conclusion. It is true that many different empire builders and invaders marched across this crossroad of the Afro-Eurasian World, and in the process they destroyed and altered much. Equally true, however, was the fact that villages, towns, and cities prospered in large numbers, fed by the productive activities of peasants, artisans, and merchants alike. Farming, craft production, and even large-scale industrial manufacture contributed to a healthy economy, but all these activities paled in comparison with the economic impact of commerce, particularly transit trade. Evidence suggests that Southwest Asian production of commodities for export declined from the eleventh century onward, whereas trade in manufactured goods produced elsewhere — primarily China, India, and Western Europe — rose appreciably. Added to this was a booming trade in the raw materials of Africa and Southeast Asia, including slaves, ivory, and gold from Africa and exotic woods and spices from the eastern islands of the Indian Ocean. Merchants who engaged in long-distance commerce could become rapidly wealthy and rise to positions of eminence within their cities.

This was especially the case with the merchants of Iraq. One ninth-century Arab geographer described Iraq as "the center of the world, the navel of the earth." Iraq's centrality, and its consequent prosperity, was a function of its lying at the head of the Persian Gulf. The Persian Gulf afforded the merchants of Baghdad and Basra access to the Indian Ocean and the rich markets of the Indian Ocean and the South China Sea. The potential for wealth was great for any Iraqi merchant who was sufficiently enterprising, courageous, skilled, and lucky. Danger, however, lay around every corner, as the following tale from *A Thousand and One Arabian Nights* suggests.

A Thousand and One Arabian Nights is one of the most celebrated collections of stories in the world. Loosely arranged around the theme of a series of nightly stories — told by Shahrazad in order to forestall decapitation by the order of her disturbed husband, Shahriyar, king of India and China — *The Arabian Nights* is a rich pastiche of Persian, Arabic, Greco-Roman, Indian, and Egyptian fables and legends. Its core is a now lost ancient Persian collection known as *A Thousand Tales,* which tenth-century Arab commentators tell us was similarly structured around Queen Shahrazad's ingenious filibuster. This Persian work served as the matrix around which numerous anonymous Arab storytellers wove additional tales, especially out of the rich folk traditions of Iraq and Egypt, to create by the fourteenth century *The Arabian Nights* as we more or less know it today.

A major Arab addition to this constantly changing treasury of tales was the Sinbad cycle: seven stories that related the merchant voyages of one of literature's most celebrated adventurers. In the course of his seven voyages into the Indian Ocean, Sinbad narrowly escaped death at the hands of pirates and cannibals, monster birds and huge serpents, storms and whirlpools, and the murderous one-eyed Cyclops and the Old Man of the Sea. In his travels he discovered such fabled places as the valley of diamonds, the land where living people were buried alive with their deceased spouses, and the ivory-rich elephant burying ground. Not only did he survive to tell his tales, but each voyage left him wealthier than before.

Doubtless, the professional storytellers who recounted the adventures of this fictional merchant-sailor deliberately employed hyperbolic flights of fancy because their purpose was to present thrilling entertainment. Yet the more fantastic elements within the stories also hint at some of the ways in which the world of the Indian Ocean was viewed from the perspective of Iraq.

QUESTIONS FOR ANALYSIS

1. How did an Arab merchant of modest means undertake the expense of outfitting a ship and filling it with cargo?
2. What do the goods that Sinbad brought back with him suggest about the nature of commerce in the Indian Ocean?
3. Consider the wonders that Sinbad reported. What do they suggest about the level of Arab knowledge of the more distant regions of the Indian Ocean? What do they suggest about Arab attitudes toward the eastern Indian Ocean?

4. It has been said that this tale illustrates the ambivalence of the Iraqi world toward the vast region of the Indian Ocean. Do you agree? Why or why not?
5. What might we infer from this story about the role and status of merchants in Arabic society?

I dissipated the greatest part of my paternal inheritance in the excesses of my youth; but at length, seeing my folly, I became convinced that riches were not of much use when applied to such purposes as I had employed them in; and I moreover reflected that the time I spent in dissipation was of still greater value than gold, and that nothing could be more truly deplorable than poverty in old age. I recollected the words of the wise Solomon, which my father had often repeated to me, that it is better to be in the grave than poor. Feeling the truth of all these reflections, I resolved to collect the small remains of my patrimony and to sell my goods by auction. I then formed connections with some merchants who had negotiations by sea, and consulted those who appeared best able to give me advice. In short, I determined to employ to some profit the small sum I had remaining, and no sooner was this resolution formed than I put it into execution. I went to Basra,[1] where I embarked with several merchants in a vessel which had been equipped at our united expense.

We set sail and steered toward the East Indies by the Persian Gulf, which is formed by the coast of Arabia on the right, and by that of Persia on the left, and is commonly supposed to be seventy leagues[2] in breadth in the widest part; beyond this gulf the Western Sea, or Indian Ocean, is very spacious, and is bounded by the coast of Abyssinia,[3] extending in length four thousand five hundred leagues to the island of Vakvak.[4] I was at first rather incommoded with what is termed sea-sickness, but I soon recovered my health; and from that period I have never been subject to that malady. In the course of our voyage we touched at several islands, and sold or exchanged our merchandise. One day, when in full sail, we were unexpectedly becalmed before a small island appearing just above the water, and which, from its green color, resembled a beautiful meadow. The captain ordered the sails to be lowered, and gave permission to those who wished it to go ashore, of which number I formed one. But during the time that we were regaling ourselves with eating and drinking, by way of relaxation from the fatigues we had endured at sea, the island suddenly trembled, and we felt a severe shock.

They who were in the ship perceived the earthquake in the island, and immediately called to us to re-embark as soon as possible, or we should all perish, for what we supposed to be an island was no more than the back of a whale. The most active of the party jumped into the boat, whilst others threw themselves into the water to swim to the ship: as for me, I was still on the island, or, more properly speaking, on the whale, when it plunged into the sea, and I had only time to seize hold of a piece of wood which had been brought to make a fire with. Meantime the captain, willing to avail himself of a fair breeze which had sprung up, set sail with those who had reached his vessel, and left me to the mercy of the waves. I remained in this situation the whole of that day and the following night; and on the

---

[1]Basra, located at the northern tip of the Persian Gulf and connected to Baghdad by the Tigris River, is Iraq's entryway to the Persian Gulf and Indian Ocean.
[2]A league is three miles.
[3]The horn of Africa: the region of the modern nations of Ethiopia and Somalia.
[4]Possibly a reference to Sumatra.

return of morning I had neither strength nor hope left, when a breaker happily dashed me on an island. The shore was high and steep, and I should have found great difficulty in landing, had not some roots of trees, which fortune seemed to have furnished for my preservation, assisted me. I threw myself on the ground, where I continued, more than half dead, till the sun rose.

Although I was extremely enfeebled by the fatigues I had undergone, I tried to creep about in search of some herb or fruit that might satisfy my hunger. I found some, and had also the good luck to meet with a stream of excellent water, which contributed not a little to my recovery. Having in a great measure regained my strength, I began to explore the island, and entered a beautiful plain, where I perceived at some distance a horse that was grazing. I bent my steps that way, trembling between fear and joy, for I could not ascertain whether I was advancing to safety or perdition. I remarked, as I approached, that it was a mare tied to a stake: her beauty attracted my attention; but whilst I was admiring her, I heard a voice underground of a man, who shortly after appeared, and coming to me, asked me who I was. I related my adventure to him; after which he took me by the hand and led me into a cave, where there were some other persons, who were not less astonished to see me than I was to find them there.

I ate some food which they offered me; and having asked them what they did in a place which appeared so barren, they replied that they were grooms to King Mihrage, who was the sovereign of that isle, and that they came every year about that time with some mares belonging to the king, for the purpose of having a breed between them and a sea-horse which came on shore at that spot. They tied the mares in that manner, because they were obliged almost immediately, by their cries, to drive back the sea-horse, otherwise he began to tear them in pieces. As soon as the mares were with foal they carried them back, and these colts were called sea-colts, and set apart for the king's use. To-morrow, they

added, was the day fixed for their departure, and if I had been one day later I must certainly have perished, because they lived so far off that it was impossible to reach their habitations without a guide.

Whilst they were talking to me, the horse rose out of the sea as they had described, and immediately attacked the mares. He would then have torn them to pieces, but the grooms began to make such a noise that he let go his prey, and again plunged into the ocean.

The following day they returned to the capital of the island with the mares, whither I accompanied them. On our arrival, King Mihrage, to whom I was presented, asked me who I was, and by what chance I had reached his dominions; and when I had satisfied his curiosity, he expressed pity at my misfortune. At the same time, he gave orders that I should be taken care of and have everything I might want. These orders were executed in a manner that proved the king's generosity, as well as the exactness of his officers.

As I was a merchant, I associated with persons of my own profession. I sought, in particular, such as were foreigners, as much to hear some intelligence of Baghdad, as with the hope of meeting with some one whom I could return with; for the capital of King Mihrage is situated on the sea-coast, and has a beautiful port, where vessels from all parts of the world daily arrive. I also sought the society of the Indian sages, and found great pleasure in their conversation; this, however, did not prevent me from attending at court very regularly, nor from conversing with the governors of provinces, and some less powerful kings, tributaries of Mihrage, who were about his person. They asked me a thousand questions about my country; and I, on my part, was not less inquisitive about the laws and customs of their different states, or whatever appeared to merit my curiosity.

In the dominions of King Mihrage there is an island called Cassel. I had been told that in that island there was heard every night the sound of cymbals, which had given rise to the sailors' opinion, that al-Dajjal[5] had chosen that spot for his residence. I felt a great desire to witness these wonders, and during my voyage I saw some fish of one and two hundred cubits in length,[6] which occasion much fear, but do no harm; they are so timid that they are frightened away by beating on a board. I remarked also some other fish that were not above a cubit long, and whose heads resembled that of an owl.

After I returned, as I was standing one day near the port, I saw a ship come toward the land; when they had cast anchor, they began to unload its goods, and the merchants, to whom they belonged, took them away to their warehouses. Happening to cast my eyes on some of the packages, I saw my name written, and, having attentively examined them, I concluded them to be those which I had embarked in the ship in which I left Basra. I also recollected the captain; but as I was persuaded that he thought me dead, I went up to him, and asked him to whom those parcels belonged. "I had on board with me," replied he, "a merchant of Baghdad, named Sinbad. One day, when we were near an island, at least such it appeared to be, he, with some other passengers, went ashore on this supposed island, which was no other than an enormous whale, that had fallen asleep on the surface of the water. The fish no sooner felt the heat of the fire they had lighted on its back, to cook their provisions, than it began to move and flounce about in the sea. The greatest part of the persons who were on it were drowned, and the unfortunate Sinbad was one of the number. These parcels belonged to him, and I have resolved to sell them, that, if I meet with any of his family, I may be able to return them the profit I shall have made of the principal." "Captain," said I then, "I am that Sinbad, whom you supposed dead, but who is still alive, and these parcels are my property and merchandise."

When the captain of the vessel heard me speak thus, he exclaimed, "Great God! whom shall I trust? There is no longer truth in man. I with my own eyes saw Sinbad perish; the passengers I had on board were also witnesses of it; and you have the assurance to say that you are the same Sinbad? what audacity! At first sight you appeared a man of probity and honor, yet you assert an impious falsity to possess yourself of some merchandise which does not belong to you." "Have patience," replied I, "and have the goodness to listen to what I have to say." "Well," said he, "what can you have to say? speak, and I will attend." I then related in what manner I had been saved, and by what accident I had met with King Mihrage's grooms, who had brought me to his court.

He was rather staggered at my discourse, but was soon convinced that I was not an impostor; for some people arriving from his ship knew me, and began to congratulate me on my fortunate escape. At last he recollected me himself, and embracing me, "Heaven be praised," said he, "that you have thus happily avoided so great a danger; I cannot express the pleasure I feel on the occasion. Here are your goods, take them, for they are yours, and do with them as you like." I thanked him, and praised his honorable conduct, and by way of recompense I begged him to accept part of the merchandise, but that he refused.

I selected the most precious and valuable things in my bales, as presents for King Mihrage. As this prince had been informed of my misfortunes, he asked me where I had obtained such rare curiosities. I related to him the manner in which I had recovered my property, and he had the complaisance to express his joy on the occasion; he accepted my presents, and gave me others of far greater value. After that, I took my leave of him, and re-embarked in the same ves-

---

[5]The *deceiver* or *imposter;* al-Dajjal is the false messiah who, according to Muslim belief, will appear shortly before Jesus returns to earth to usher in the end of time. Jesus will destroy al-Dajjal, and the Day of Judgment will follow.

[6]A cubit varies from seventeen to twenty-two inches.

sel, having first exchanged what merchandise remained with that of the country, which consisted of aloes and sandal-wood,[7] camphor,[8] nutmegs, cloves, pepper, and ginger. We touched at several islands, and at last landed at Basra, from whence I came here, having realized about a hundred thousand sequins.[9] I returned to my family, and was received by them with the joy which a true and sincere friendship inspires. I purchased slaves of each sex, and bought a magnificent house and grounds. I thus established myself, determined to forget the disagreeable things I had endured, and to enjoy the pleasures of life. . . .

I had resolved after my first voyage, to pass the rest of my days in tranquility at Baghdad. . . . But I soon grew weary of an idle life; the desire of seeing foreign countries, and carrying on some negotiations by sea returned: I bought some merchandise, which I thought likely to answer in the traffic I meditated; and I set off a second time with some merchants, upon whose probity I could rely. We embarked in a good vessel, and having recommended ourselves to the care of the Almighty, we began our voyage. . . .

▷ And so the second voyage begins.

---

[7]Both are woods noted for their aromatic and medicinal properties.

[8]A medicinal drug and aromatic made from camphor wood.
[9]Gold coins.

▼▼▼

India: Continuity and Change

Invasions from Central Asia by a nomadic people known as the *Hunas,* or White Huns, precipitated the collapse of the Gupta Empire (Chapter 5, source 39) around the middle of the sixth century. Northern India was again politically fragmented, but Hindu culture, having reached maturity in the Gupta period, continued to develop vigorously. Indeed, the history of classical India is largely the story of cultural continuity and evolution, in which political events and their chronology have little relevance. The one significant exception to this rule in the period 500–1500 was the coming of Islam. Its impact was profound and permanent.

Early in the eighth century, Arabs conquered the northwest corner of the Indian subcontinent, a region known as *Sind,* but advanced no farther. While Hindu civilization moved to its own rhythms, neighboring Muslims traded with it and freely borrowed whatever they found useful and nonthreatening to their Islamic faith. This included India's decimal mathematics and the so-called Arabic system of numeration, so named by Europeans because they learned this arithmetical system secondhand from Arab merchants, who transformed it into a tool of the marketplace. After millennia of contemplating the reality of Nothingness, Hindu civilization during the Gupta Era formulated the principal of *zero* as a positive numerical value, and India's Arab neighbors happily adopted the concept and passed it on.

Islam did not make a significant impact on Indian life until the appearance of the Turks. These recent converts to the faith, whose origins lay in Central Asia, conducted a series of raids out of Afghanistan between 986 and 1030. After a respite of about one hundred fifty years, they turned to conquest. In 1192 the army of Muhammad of Ghor crushed a coalition of Indian princes, and the whole

Ganges basin lay defenseless before his generals. By 1206 the Turkish sultanate of Delhi dominated all of northern India, and by 1327 it had extended its power over virtually the entire peninsula. Although these Turkish sultans lost the south to the Hindu state of Vijayanagar (1336–1565), they controlled India's northern and central regions until the arrival of other Muslim conquerors: first, Timur the Lame's plundering horde in 1398; then Babur, who established the great Mughal Dynasty (1526–1857), which ruled most of India until the mid eighteenth century.

As the modern Muslim states of Pakistan and Bangladesh bear witness, Islam became an important element in Indian society, but in the end Hinduism prevailed as the way of life for the majority of the Indian subcontinent's people. The coming and going of armies destroyed the vital remnants of Buddhist monasticism in mainland India, although it continued to flourish on the island of Ceylon (Sri Lanka). Nothing, however, could root out the hold that the many varieties of Hindu belief and custom had upon Indian life.

Islam and Hindu Civilization: Cultures in Conflict
▼▼▼

78 ▼ Abu'l Raihan al-Biruni, *DESCRIPTION OF INDIA*

At the end of the tenth century Sultan Mahmud of Ghazana (r. 998–1030), who proudly bore the titles the *Sword of Islam* and *the Image Breaker,* began a series of seventeen raids through the Khyber Pass and into India from his base just south of Kabul in modern Afghanistan. This Turkish lord made no serious attempt at conquering all of India, but he did incorporate into his lands part of the subcontinent's northwestern region of Punjab (an area that today is part of the Islamic state of Pakistan). For a century and a half after Mahmud's death, Islam penetrated no farther into India, but the precedent of Islamic jihad against infidel Hindus had been established.

The riches that Mahmud accumulated from his plunder and destruction of Hindu temples (he is reputed to have carried off six and a half tons of gold from one expedition alone) enabled him to turn his otherwise remote, mountain-ringed capital of Ghazana into a major center of Islamic culture. Scholars and artists from all over Southwest Asia gathered at Mahmud's court. Many came willingly; others were forced to come. In 1017 Mahmud conquered the Central Asian Islamic state of Khwarazm, located west of Ghazana and just south of the Aral Sea. The conqueror brought back many of Khwarazm's intellectuals and artisans to his capital, including the Iranian scholar Abu'l Raihan al-Biruni (973–ca. 1050).

Known to subsequent generations as *al-Ustadh* (the Master), al-Biruni was primarily an astronomer, mathematician, and linguist, but his wide-ranging interests and intellect involved him in many other fields of inquiry. For thirteen years following his capture, al-Biruni served Mahmud, probably as court astrologer, and traveled with him into India's Punjab region. Here, apparently, al-Biruni spent the bulk of his period of service to Mahmud. Shortly after his lord's death in 1030, al-Biruni completed his *Description of India,* an encyclopedic account of Indian civilization, especially Hindu science. The following excerpts come from the book's opening pages, in which the author deals with the essential differences that separate Hindus from Muslims.

QUESTIONS FOR ANALYSIS

1. According to al-Biruni, what separates Muslims from Hindus?
2. Where in previous sources have we seen the Hindu notions of purity and *mleccha?* By what other names or terms do you know this phenomenon?
3. What impact did eighth-century Islam have on India?
4. What impact did Mahmud and his father have on India?
5. Al-Biruni presents a critique of Hindu science and compares it with Greek science (and implicitly with Islamic science). In so doing, he faults Hindu scientists for certain basic failings. What are they? (Review Chapter 6, source 45.) What basic Hindu visions of reality might have influenced a scientific tradition that followed a path different from that of the Greeks and the Muslims?
6. What is the general tone of this entire excerpt, and what do you infer from it?
7. Review the autobiography of Sultan Firuz Shah (Chapter 8, source 65). Now compose his commentary on this excerpt.

ON THE HINDUS IN GENERAL, AS AN INTRODUCTION TO OUR ACCOUNT OF THEM.

Before entering on our exposition, we must form an adequate idea of that which renders it so particularly difficult to penetrate to the essential nature of any Indian subject. The knowledge of these difficulties will either facilitate the progress of our work, or serve as an apology for any shortcomings of ours. For the reader must always bear in mind that the Hindus entirely differ from us in every respect, many a subject appearing intricate and obscure which would be perfectly clear if there were more connection between us. The barriers which separate Muslims and Hindus rest on different causes.

First, they differ from us in everything which other nations have in common. And here we first mention the language, although the difference of language also exists between other nations. . . .

Secondly, they totally differ from us in religion, as we believe in nothing in which they believe, and *vice versa.* On the whole, there is very little disputing about theological topics among themselves; at the utmost, they fight with words, but they will never stake their soul or body or their property on religious controversy. On the contrary, all their fanaticism is directed against those who do not belong to them — against all foreigners. They call them *mleccha, i.e.* impure, and forbid having any connection with them, be it by intermarriage or any other kind of relationship, or by sitting, eating, and drinking with them, because thereby, they think, they would be polluted. They consider as impure anything which touches the fire and the water of a foreigner; and no household can exist without these two elements. Besides, they never desire that a thing which once has been polluted should be purified and thus recovered, as, under ordinary circumstances, if anybody or anything has become unclean, he or it would strive to regain the state of purity. They are not allowed to receive anybody who does not belong to them, even if he wished it, or was inclined to their religion. This, too, renders any connection with them quite impossible, and constitutes the widest gulf between us and them.

In the third place, in all manners and usages they differ from us to such a degree as to frighten their children with us, with our dress, and our ways and customs, and as to declare us to be devil's breed, and our doings as the very opposite of all that is good and proper. By the way, we must confess, in order to be just, that a similar depreciation of foreigners not only prevails among us and the Hindus, but is common to all nations towards each other. I recollect a Hindu who wreaked his vengeance on us for the following reason: —

Some Hindu king had perished at the hand of an enemy[1] of his who had marched against him from our country. After his death there was born a child to him, which succeeded him, by the name of Sagara. On coming of age, the young man asked his mother about his father, and then she told him what had happened. Now he was inflamed with hatred, marched out of his country into the country of the enemy, and plentifully satiated his thirst of vengeance upon them. After having become tired of slaughtering, he compelled the survivors to dress in our dress, which was meant as an ignominious punishment for them. When I heard of it, I felt thankful that he was gracious enough not to compel us to Indianise ourselves and to adopt Hindu dress and manners. . . .

But then came Islam;[2] the Persian empire perished, and the repugnance of the Hindus against foreigners increased more and more when the Muslims began to make their inroads into their country; for Muhammad Ibn al-Qasim entered Sind[3] . . . and conquered the cities of Bahmanwa and Mulasthana, the former of which he called *Al-mansura,* the latter *Al-ma'mura.* He entered India proper, and penetrated even as far as Kanauj, marched through the country of Gandhara, and on his way back, through the confines of Kashmir,[4] sometimes fighting sword in hand, sometimes gaining his ends by treaties, leaving to the people their ancient belief, except in the case of those who wanted to become Muslims. All these events planted a deeply rooted hatred in their hearts.

Now in the following times no Muslim conqueror passed beyond the frontier of Kabul and the river Sind until the days of the Turks, when they seized the power in Ghazna under the Samani dynasty, and the supreme power fell to the lot of Sabuktagin. This prince chose the holy war as his calling, and therefore called himself *al-Ghazi.*[5] In the interest of his successors he constructed, in order to weaken the Indian frontier, those roads on which afterwards his son Mahmud marched into India during a period of thirty years and more. God be merciful to both father and son! Mahmud utterly ruined the prosperity of the country, and performed there wonderful exploits, by which the Hindus became like atoms of dust scattered in all directions, and like a tale of old in the mouth of the people. Their scattered remains cherish, of course, the most inveterate aversion towards all Muslims. This is the reason, too, why Hindu sciences have retired far away from those parts of the country conquered by us, and have fled to places which our hand cannot yet reach, to Kashmir, Benares,[6] and other places. And there the antagonism between them and all foreigners receives more and more

---

[1] Apparently a Hindu enemy who had used the land beyond the Khyber Pass as a refuge and point from which to attack.
[2] The initial rise of Islam in the seventh century.
[3] In 711.

[4] The mountainous northwestern region that separates the modern nations of Pakistan and India.
[5] "The holy warrior."
[6] A city on the Ganges River in central northeast India; it is a sacred site of both Hindu and Buddhist pilgrimage.

nourishment both from political and religious sources.

In the fifth place, there are other causes, the mentioning of which sounds like satire — peculiarities of their national character, deeply rooted in them, but manifest to everybody. We can only say, folly is an illness for which there is no medicine, and the Hindus believe that there is no country but theirs, no nation like theirs, no kings like theirs, no religion like theirs, no science like theirs. They are haughty, foolishly vain, self-conceited, and stolid. They are by nature niggardly in communicating that which they know, and they take the greatest possible care to withhold it from men of another caste among their own people, still much more, of course, from any foreigner. According to their belief, there is no other country on earth but theirs, no other race of man but theirs, and no created beings besides them have any knowledge of science whatsoever. . . . If they traveled and mixed with other nations, they would soon change their mind, for their ancestors were not as narrow-minded as the present generation is. One of their scholars, Varahamihira,[7] in a passage where he calls on the people to honor the Brahmins, says: *"The Greeks, though impure, must be honored, since they were trained in sciences and therein excelled others. What, then, are we to say of a Brahmin, if he combines with his purity the height of science?"* In former times, the Hindus used to acknowledge that the progress of science due to the Greeks is much more important than that which is due to themselves. But from this passage of Varahamihira alone you see what a self-lauding man he is, while he gives himself airs as doing justice to others. . . .

The heathen Greeks, before the rise of Christianity, held much the same opinions as the Hindus; their educated classes thought much the same as those of the Hindus; their common people held the same idolatrous views as those of the Hindus. Therefore I like to confront the theories of the one nation with those of the other simply on account of their close relationship, not in order to correct them. For that which is not *the truth*[8] does not admit of any correction and all heathenism, whether Greek or Indian, is in its heart and soul one and the same belief, because it is only a deviation *from the truth*. The Greeks, however, had philosophers who, living in their country, discovered and worked out for them the elements of science, not of popular superstition, for it is the object of the upper classes to be guided by the results of science, while the common crowd will always be inclined to plunge into wrong-headed wrangling, as long as they are not kept down by fear of punishment. Think of Socrates when he opposed the crowd of his nation as to their idolatry and did not want to call the stars gods! At once eleven of the twelve judges of the Athenians agreed on a sentence of death, and Socrates died faithful to the truth.[9]

The Hindus had no men of this stamp both capable and willing to bring sciences to a classical perfection. Therefore you mostly find that even the so-called scientific theorems of the Hindus are in a state of utter confusion, devoid of any logical order, and in the last instance always mixed up with the silly notions of the crowd, *e.g.* immense numbers, enormous spaces of time, and all kinds of religious dogmas, which the vulgar belief does not admit of being called into question. . . . I can only compare their mathematical and astronomical literature, as far as I know it, to a mixture of pearl shells and sour dates, or of pearls and dung, or of costly crystals and common pebbles. Both kinds of things are equal in their eyes, since they cannot raise themselves to the methods of a strictly scientific deduction.[10]

---

[7]An astronomer and astrologer of the early sixth century (ca. 505); he was one of Gupta India's greatest scientists.
[8]The true faith of Islam.
[9]See Chapter 4, source 30. Al-Biruni's facts regarding the trial of Socrates are not correct.

[10]That is, logical argumentation, especially according to the system created by Aristotle, a Greek scientist-philosopher of the fourth century B.C.E. Aristotle's logic, which had a profound impact on both Islamic and Western science and philosophical thought, was based on the principle of contradiction: An entity cannot simultaneously be and not be.

The Perfect Wife

▼▼▼

79 ▾ *Dandin,* TALES OF THE TEN PRINCES

India's earliest known prose fiction dates from the sixth and seventh centuries, and the first acknowledged master of this art form was Dandin, who lived around 600. His *Tales of Ten Princes* is an ingenious interweaving of numerous subplots and stories around the central theme of the adventures of Prince Rajavahana. All of these stories celebrate the three things Dandin believed all people hold most dear in life: virtue, wealth, and love. As such, they illustrate the other side of the Hindu vision of the physical world. Although one of the basic insights of Hindu religion is that all material existence is transitory and unreal, as a practical matter Hindus accept *kama* (delight in the sensual pleasures of life) and *artha* (pursuit of riches and power) as valid human responses to the attractions of this world. Like many of the stories told by Dandin, the following vignette sheds light on everyday life and values.

QUESTIONS FOR ANALYSIS

1. What qualities does the ideal wife possess?
2. What does a man expect to receive in an ideal marriage? What is he expected to give in return?
3. Compare this story with the view of women provided by *The Laws of Manu* (Chapter 5, source 38). Are they similar or different? Together, what do they allow us to infer about the role and status of women in Hindu society?

"In the land of the Dravidians[1] is a city called Kanci. Therein dwelt the very wealthy son of a merchant, by name Saktikumara. When he was nearly eighteen he thought: 'There's no pleasure in living without a wife or with one of bad character. Now how can I find a really good one?' So, dubious of his chance of finding wedded bliss with a woman taken at the word of others, he became a fortune-teller, and roamed the land with a measure of unhusked rice tied in the skirts of his robe; and parents, taking him for an interpreter of birthmarks, showed their daughters to him. Whenever he saw a girl of his own class, whatever her birthmarks, he would say to her: 'My dear girl, can you cook me a good meal from this measure of rice?' And so, ridiculed and rejected, he wandered from house to house.

"One day in the land of the Sibis, in a city on the banks of the Kaveri, he examined a girl who was shown to him by her nurse. She wore little jewelry, for her parents had spent their fortune, and had nothing left but their dilapidated mansion. As soon as he set eyes on her he thought: 'This girl is shapely and smooth in all her members. Not one limb is too fat or too thin, too short or too long. Her fingers are pink; her hands are marked with auspicious lines — the barleycorn, the fish, the lotus, and the vase; her ankles are shapely; her feet are plump and the veins are not prominent; her thighs curve smoothly; her knees can barely be seen, for they merge into her rounded thighs; her buttocks are dimpled and

---

[1]The dark-skinned people of the south, whose language differs radically from that of the northerners.

round as chariot wheels; her naval is small, flat, and deep; her stomach is adorned with three lines; the nipples stand out from her large breasts, which cover her whole chest; her palms are marked with signs which promise corn, wealth, and sons; her nails are smooth and polished like jewels; her fingers are straight and tapering and pink; her arms curve sweetly from the shoulder, and are smoothly jointed; her slender neck is curved like a conch-shell; her lips are rounded and of even red; her pretty chin does not recede; her cheeks are round, full and firm; her eyebrows do not join above her nose, and are curved, dark, and even; her nose is like a half-blown sesamum flower; her wide eyes are large and gentle and flash with three colors, black, white, and brown; her brow is fair as the new moon; her curls are lovely as a mine of sapphires; her long ears are adorned doubly, with earrings and charming lotuses, hanging limply; her abundant hair is not brown, even at the tips, but long, smooth, glossy, and fragrant. The character of such a girl cannot but correspond to her appearance, and my heart is fixed upon her, so I'll test her and marry her. For one regret after another is sure to fall on the heads of people who don't take precautions!' So, looking at her affectionately, he said, 'Dear girl, can you cook a good meal for me with this measure of rice?'

"Then the girl glanced at her old servant, who took the measure of rice from his hand and seated him on the veranda, which had been well sprinkled and swept, giving him water to cool his feet. Meanwhile the girl bruised the fragrant rice, dried it a little at a time in the sun, turned it repeatedly, and beat it with a hollow cane on a firm flat spot, very gently, so as to separate the grain without crushing the husk. Then she said to the nurse, 'Mother, goldsmiths can make good use of these husks for polishing jewelry. Take them, and, with the coppers you get for them, buy some firewood, not too green and not too dry, a small cooking pot, and two earthen dishes.'

"When this was done she put the grains of rice in a shallow, wide-mouthed, round-bellied mortar, and took a long and heavy pestle of acacia-wood, its head shod with a plate of iron. . . . With skill and grace she exerted her arms, as the grains jumped up and down in the mortar. Repeatedly she stirred them and pressed them down with her fingers; then she shook the grains in a winnowing basket to remove the beard, rinsed them several times, worshiped the hearth, and placed them in water which had been five times brought to the boil. When the rice softened, bubbled, and swelled, she drew the embers of the fire together, put a lid on the cooking pot, and strained off the gruel. Then she patted the rice with a ladle and scooped it out a little at a time; and when she found that it was thoroughly cooked she put the cooking pot on one side, mouth downward. Next she damped down those sticks which were not burnt through, and when the fire was quite out she sent them to the dealers to be sold as charcoal, saying, 'With the coppers that you get for them, buy as much as you can of green vegetables, ghee,[2] curds, sesamum oil, myrobalans[3] and tamarind.'[4]

"When this was done she offered him a few savories. Next she put the rice-gruel in a new dish immersed in damp sand, and cooled it with the soft breeze of a palm-leaf fan. She added a little salt, and flavored it with the scent of the embers; she ground the myrobalans to a smooth powder, until they smelt like a lotus; and then, by the lips of the nurse, she invited him to take a bath. This he did, and when she too had bathed she gave him oil and myrobalans (as an unguent).

"After he had bathed he sat on a bench in the paved courtyard, which had been thoroughly sprinkled and swept. She stirred the gruel in the two dishes, which she set before him on a piece of pale green plantain leaf, cut from a tree in the courtyard. He drank it and felt rested and happy, relaxed in every limb. Next she gave him two ladlefuls of the boiled rice, served with a little ghee and condiments. She served the rest of the rice with curds, three spices (mace, cardamom,

---

[2]Clarified butter.
[3]Edible seed from the so-called Indian almond tree.

[4]A pungent spice.

and cinnamon), and fragrant and refreshing buttermilk and gruel. He enjoyed the meal to the last mouthful.

"When he asked for a drink she poured him water in a steady stream from the spout of a new pitcher — it was fragrant with incense, and smelt of fresh trumpet-flowers and the perfume of full-blown lotuses. He put the bowl to his lips, and his eyelashes sparkled with rosy drops as cool as snow; his ears delighted in the sound of the trickling water; his rough cheeks thrilled and tingled at its pleasant contact; his nostrils opened wide at its sweet fragrance; and his tongue delighted in its lovely flavor, as he drank the pure water in great gulps. Then, at his nod, the girl gave him a mouthwash in another bowl. The old woman took away the remains of his meal, and he slept awhile in his ragged cloak, on the pavement plastered with fresh cowdung.

"Wholly pleased with the girl, he married her with due rites, and took her home. Later he neglected her awhile and took a mistress, but the wife treated her as a dear friend. She served her husband indefatigably, as she would a god, and never neglected her household duties; and she won the loyalty of her servants by her great kindness. In the end her husband was so enslaved by her goodness that he put the whole household in her charge, made her sole mistress of his life and person, and enjoyed the three aims of life — virtue, wealth, and love. So I maintain that virtuous wives make their lords happy and virtuous."

A Sati's Sacrifice
▼▼▼
80 ▾ *VIKRAMA'S ADVENTURES*

One of the many myths regarding premodern Indian history is that a majority of widows performed ritual suicide by self-immolation on their late husbands' funeral pyres, and those who refused to go willingly to their deaths were forced into the flames. In point of fact, it was rare for widows to join their recently deceased husbands in death in ancient India. Indeed, it was only during the Gupta Era, when female remarriage began to be discouraged and even prohibited, that the practice began to become something of a tradition. Even then, death by burning was not the fate of the vast majority of widows in that or any subsequent period. There were, however, enough incidents of widow suicide and murder to shock British colonial administrators, who took over direct management of India in the mid nineteenth century and managed to suppress the practice fairly effectively.

Another myth shared by Western observers is that Indians call this practice *suttee*. There is no such word. *Suttee* is a British misunderstanding and mispronunciation of *sati,* which means "a virtuous woman." According to the social-religious traditions that supported the practice of widow burning, a widow, no matter her caste, could not remarry, for this would entail her breaking her marriage vow and endangering her husband's spiritual welfare. She was expected to live out her life in severe austerity, shunned by all but her children, in the hope of remarrying her husband in some future incarnation. If she were especially virtuous, she would choose to join her deceased husband sooner rather than later and end her present life on his funeral day. Undoubtedly, some satis committed suicide willingly. Probably far greater numbers were forced by their husbands' relatives, for social and economic reasons, to perform this ultimate act of loyalty.

Our text, which sheds some light on this act of sacrifice, comes from an anonymous collection of stories recounting the adventures and wisdom of the semilegendary King Vikrama, or Vikramaditya, who might have lived around 58 B.C.E. The stories, as we have received them, were probably collected between the eleventh and thirteenth centuries.

QUESTIONS FOR ANALYSIS

1. Can a widow who refuses to immolate herself achieve moksha (release)?
2. What proprietary interest do the families to which the sati belongs have in her sacrifice?
3. What impact does her act have on her husband's soul? On her own?
4. What social and psychological factors make suicide appear so attractive?
5. Compare this story with the preceding one told by Dandin. In what ways was the wife in that story a sati? What does she have in common with this sati?
6. "By her perfect selflessness, a sati perfects and redeems her husband." What does this anonymous statement mean? How, if at all, do both this and Dandin's story illustrate that attitude?
7. Some commentators have argued that these two stories are predicated upon the assumption that wives and husbands fulfill one another, and without the other, each is incomplete. Do you agree with this analysis? Why or why not? In addressing this question, you might want to review *The Laws of Manu* (Chapter 5, source 38).

Once King Vikrama, attended by all his vassal princes, had ascended his throne. At this time a certain magician came in, and blessing him with the words "Live forever!" said: "Sire, you are skilled in all the arts; many magicians have come into your presence and exhibited their tricks. So today be so good as to behold an exhibition of my dexterity." The king said: "I have not time now; it is the time to bathe and eat. Tomorrow I will behold it." So on the morrow the juggler came into the king's assembly as a stately man, with a mighty beard and glorious countenance, holding a sword in his hand, and accompanied by a lovely woman; and he bowed to the king. Then the ministers who were present, seeing the stately man, were astonished, and asked: "O hero, who are you, and whence do you come?" He said: "I am a servant of Great Indra;[1] I was cursed once by my lord, and was cast down to earth; and now I dwell here. And this is my wife. Today a great battle has begun between the gods and the Daityas [demons], so I am going thither. This King Vikramaditya treats other men's wives as his sisters, so before going to the battle I wish to leave my wife with him." Hearing this the king also was greatly amazed. And the man left his wife with the king and delivered her over to him, and sword in hand flew up into heaven. Then a great and terrible shouting was heard in the sky: "Ho there, kill them, kill them, smite them, smite them!" were the words they heard. And all the people who sat in the court, with upturned faces, gazed in amazement. After this, when a moment had passed by, one of the man's arms, holding his sword and stained with blood, fell from the sky into the king's assembly. Then all

---

[1]Chapter 2, source 11.

the people, seeing it, said: "Ah, this great hero has been killed in battle by his opponents; his sword and one arm have fallen." While the people who sat in the court were even saying this, again his head fell also; and then his trunk fell too. And seeing this his wife said: "Sire, my husband, fighting on the field of battle, has been slain by the enemy. His head, his arm, his sword, and his trunk have fallen down here. So, that this my beloved may not be wooed by the heavenly nymphs, I will go to where he is. Let fire be provided for me." Hearing her words the king said: "My daughter, why will you enter the fire? I will guard you even as my own daughter; preserve your body." She said: "Sire, what is this you say? My lord, for whom this body of mine exists, has been slain on the battlefield by his foes. Now for whose sake shall I preserve this body? Moreover, you should not say this, since even fools know that wives should follow their husbands. For thus it is said:

1. Moonlight goes with the moon, the lightning clings to the cloud, and women follow their husbands; even fools know this.

And so, as the learned tradition has it:

2. The wife who enters into the fire when her husband dies, imitating Arundhati [a star, regarded as the wife of one of the Seven Rishis (the Dipper), and as a typical faithful spouse) in her behavior, enjoys bliss in heaven.

3. Until a wife burns herself in the fire after the death of her husband, so long that woman can in no way be permanently freed from the body.

4. A woman who follows after her husband shall surely purify three families: her mother's, her father's, and that into which she was given in marriage.

And so:

5. Three and a half crores[2] is the number of the hairs on the human body; so many years shall a wife who follows her husband dwell in heaven.

6. As a snake-charmer powerfully draws a snake out of a hole, so a wife draws her husband

upward [by burning herself] and enjoys bliss with him.

7. A wife who abides by the law of righteousness [in burning herself] saves her husband, whether he be good or wicked; yes, even if he be guilty of all crimes.

Furthermore, O king, a woman who is bereft of her husband has no use for her life. And it is said:

8. What profit is there in the life of a wretched woman who has lost her husband? Her body is as useless as a banyan tree in a cemetery.

9. Surely father, brother, and son measure their gifts; what woman would not honor her husband, who gives without measure?

Moreover:

10. Though a woman be surrounded by kinsfolk, though she have many sons, and be endowed with excellent qualities, she is miserable, poor wretched creature, when deprived of her husband.

And so:

11. What shall a widow do with perfumes, garlands, and incense, or with manifold ornaments, or garments and couches of ease?

12. A lute does not sound without strings, a wagon does not go without wheels, and a wife does not obtain happiness without her husband, not even with a hundred kinsfolk.

13. Woman's highest refuge is her husband, even if he be poor, vicious, old, infirm, crippled, outcast, and stingy.

14. There is no kinsman, no friend, no protector, no refuge for a woman like her husband.

15. There is no other misery for women like widowhood. Happy is she among women who dies before her husband.

Thus speaking she fell at the king's feet, begging that a fire be provided for her. And when the king heard her words, his heart being tender with genuine compassion, he caused a pyre to be erected of sandalwood and the like, and gave her leave. So she took leave of the king, and in his presence entered the fire together with her husband's body.

---

[2]A *crore* is ten million; therefore, thirty-five million.

Chapter 10

▼▼▼

Two Christian Civilizations

Byzantium and Western Europe

Contrary to popular belief, the Roman Empire was not a European civilization nor did the Romans think of themselves as Europeans. It is true, of course, that the city of Rome was located in Italy, which is a European peninsula, and a portion of its empire lay in lands that later became part of the community known as Europe. Nevertheless, the Roman Empire was essentially a Mediterranean civilization that encompassed the coastlands and peoples of three continents: Africa, Asia, and Europe. As such, it was a Hellenistic civilization (Chapter 5, sources 31–34), with all of the cultural variety that the term suggests.

During the period from roughly 235 to 600 C.E. this Mediterranean civilization underwent a transformation. Many modern historians have characterized this era as the period of "the decline and fall of the Roman Empire," but this phrase and all that it connotes misses the mark. Rome and its empire did not fall in the sense of a sudden collapse. What happened was more subtle and profound. The Roman Empire, which embraced the cultures of so many diverse peoples, was metamorphosed over a period of centuries into three new civilizations: Byzantium, Europe, and Islam.

Islam originated in Arabia, a land beyond the boundaries of the Roman Empire, and in the mid eighth century it established its capital at Baghdad, in the heart of the former Persian Empire. Nevertheless, by conquering the lands of Syria-Palestine, all of North Africa, and most of the Iberian Peninsula, Islam inherited a good deal of Hellenistic culture, including Greek science and philosophy, and in that sense it was a heir of the Roman Empire. We have already studied Islam in Chapters 8 and 9, and it needs no further comment here. Byzantium and Europe, Rome's other two heirs, are another matter. It is to these two new civilizations that we now must turn.

The civilization that we term *Byzantium* receives its name from the eastern Mediterranean city of that name (*Byzantion* in Greek; *Byzantium* in Latin), which Emperor Constantine the Great (Chapter 7, source 52) transformed into the capital of the newly Christianized Roman Empire in 330. The fact that Constantine chose to locate *New Rome,* as he styled the city, in the East is testimony to the increasing unimportance of the West to the fourth-century empire. Although the city came to be called *Constantinople* (Constantine's city), modern scholars favor using the older name — *Byzantium* — to delineate the civilization that centered on this East Roman capital. Actually, the *Byzantines* never called themselves anything other than *Romaioi* (Romans). From the early fourth century to 1453, when the city and its empire finally succumbed to the advances of the Ottoman Turks, Constantinople was the center of an empire and a civilization whose members viewed it as the legitimate heir of Roman imperial traditions. In fact, however, already by the late sixth century, Byzantium had become a distinctive civilization — a Greek-speaking civilization that retained many Hellenistic qualities but that also developed many new forms of expression and organization.

This new civilization resulted from the fusion of three key elements. First there were the traditions of the late Roman Empire, in which the emperor had been transformed into an autocratic ruler along the lines of the Persian *shahs,* or emperors. Then there was *Eastern Orthodox Christianity. Orthodox* is a Greek term that means "correct thinking," and in this context it means the time-honored traditions of eastern Mediterranean Christianity, which included folk practices as well as the teachings of theologians and church councils. The third element was the cultural heritage of the Hellenistic past, itself a fusion of Greek, western Asiatic, and Egyptian elements.

Although Byzantium was an empire, with definite boundaries that expanded and contracted over the centuries, as a civilization it transcended political boundaries. Byzantine traditions deeply influenced the cultures of a number of neighboring peoples, especially the Russians, Bulgars, and Serbs. In a real sense, even after the Byzantine Empire collapsed in the face of Ottoman Turkish assaults, its civilization lived on, in somewhat altered form, among such Christian Orthodox cultures as Russia, Bulgaria, and Serbia.

The story in the western half of the Roman Empire was different. Continuities were less evident, and dramatic changes were more the norm. Whereas the empire's eastern half evolved somewhat gently into a new cultural synthesis, the western half experienced a painful process of political breakdown and sweeping cultural transformation.

Toward the end of the fourth century C.E., pressures on Rome's western frontiers become intolerable, and the western portion of the empire rapidly slid toward its unforeseen end, defeated and transformed by fringe peoples who came from beyond the borders of the Rhine and Danube Rivers. By the end of the sixth century, precious little of the western half of the Roman world was still ruled by imperial Roman authority. More profoundly, these newcomers played a key role in transforming culture in the West, thereby helping to usher out the old Greco-Roman order and to lay the basis for a new civilization that many historians call *The First Europe.*

One of the enduring clichés favored by writers of history textbooks is that Europe emerged out of a fusion of three elements: the remnants of Greco-Roman civilization; Latin, or Western, Christianity; and the culture and vigor of the fringe peoples who migrated into the western regions of the late Roman Empire. As is true of so many commonplace notions, there is a good deal of truth to this statement, but it is not the complete story. These three elements differed radically from one another in many essential ways, and it took centuries for them to fuse into something resembling a coherent civilization. Even when they had achieved a level of integration, their differences continued to infuse tensions into this emerging European civilization. And those tensions became identifying characteristics of the new, dynamic order developing in the West. That dynamism eventually drove Europe into competition with Islam and Byzantium — competition that would have global consequences.

▼▼▼

Byzantium and Its Neighbors

Some eighteenth-century European historians considered Byzantine civilization merely an unoriginal and degenerate fossilization of late antiquity, but nothing could be farther from the truth. Although the Byzantines saw their state as a living continuation of the Roman Empire, by the late sixth century Constantinople had become the matrix of a new civilization that persisted and largely flourished down to 1453, when finally the city of Constantinople fell to Ottoman Turkish forces. To be sure, over those nine hundred years Byzantium experienced inevitable fluctuations in fortune and creativity, but, by and large, Byzantine civilization was noted throughout its long history for economic prosperity and cultural brilliance.

The first of the following sources illustrates Byzantine imperial culture in the age of Emperor Justinian I (r. 527–565), arguably the most important transitional figure in the history of Byzantium. The second source sheds light on one of Byzantium's ages of special vitality, the era of Emperor Basil II (r. 976–1025). The third source reflects one of the most important characteristics of Byzantine imperial policy: intense regulation of a vigorous economy. Such a vital and prosperous empire could not avoid exerting a powerful influence on its neighbors. The fourth source reveals one significant consequence of Byzantium's gravitational pull.

Two Imperial Portraits: Justinian and Theodora
▼▼▼
81 ▼ *THE MOSAICS OF SAN VITALE*

The age of Justinian I (r. 527–565) was pivotal in the history of the Eastern Roman Empire. A sincerely but narrowly pious man, who took seriously his duties as God-anointed emperor, Justinian promoted the cause of Christian orthodoxy in a cosmopolitan empire that contained large numbers of variant Christian beliefs and ways of interpreting the faith. The result was deep alienation, especially among Egyptian and Syrian subjects of the empire, and a consequent weakness that Islamic Arab forces exploited in the next century as they conquered Syria-Palestine, Egypt, and North Africa.

The last of the emperors of Constantinople to speak Latin as his native tongue, Justinian also attempted to reconquer the West from the various Germanic tribes that had divided it into competing kingdoms. Justinian's forces invaded Italy in 535 in order to wrest it from the Ostrogoths, who had controlled the peninsula since the late fifth century. The war that ensued was protracted, bitter, and destructive. When fighting finally ceased in 553 the Ostrogoths had been eliminated as a recognizable culture, and Rome's aristocratic families likewise had disappeared from the historical record. Cities, towns, and countryside alike were in ruin. Fifteen years later, in 568, new Germanic invaders, the Lombards, carved out their own kingdom in northern Italy and several smaller, semiindependent states in parts of central and southern Italy, thereby denying Byzantium control over the entire peninsula. In effect, Justinian's attempt at reconquest enjoyed only limited, short-term success. Its major accomplishment was transforming Rome and much of Italy into a war-ravaged backwater and stripping the eastern empire of much needed resources. After Justinian's age, the Greek-speaking emperors and people of Constantinople were forced to look less to the West and more toward their eastern, southern, and northern borders, thereby accelerating the impact of Asian influences on Byzantium's cultural development.

For all of his large-scale miscalculations, however, Justinian ranks as one of Byzantium's greatest emperors; indeed, he often is referred to as *Justinian the Great,* the last Roman and first Byzantine emperor. A measure of that greatness is seen in the portrait mosaics of Justinian and Empress Theodora at the church of San Vitale in Ravenna, Italy.

Created in 548 following the capture of Ravenna by imperial troops, the two mosaics flank the altar of the church. High above the altar is a mosaic of Christ in Glory. Below and to his right is Justinian's mosaic; opposite and to Christ's left is Theodora's mosaic. In Justinian's mosaic we see the crowned emperor, his head surrounded by a *nimbus,* or *halo,* a sign of sacred power. He wears imperial purple and gold and carries, as an offering, the eucharistic bread, which a priest will transform at mass into the Body of Christ. On his left are four individuals: three churchmen and what appears to be a court official (the person in the background). One of the clerics is Maximian, archbishop of Ravenna; his name appears over his head, he holds a cross, and he wears around his shoulders an archbishop's *pallium,* a long, white cloth with an embroidered cross. There also are two priests. One priest holds a book of Gospels (every mass has a gospel reading from the same side of the altar on which Justinian's mosaic is located); the other holds an incense burner. On the emperor's right stand two high-ranking imperial officials and six members of the imperial bodyguard, known as the Praetorian Guard. One of the guardsmen displays a shield with the *chi-rho* monogram: the Greek letters χ (Chi) and ρ (Rho), which when combined represent the word *Christos* (Christ). Empress Theodora, Justinian's wife, also appears with a crown, imperial purple and gold robes, and a halo. In her hands is a golden, bejeweled cup containing the eucharistic wine, which a priest will transform at mass into the Blood of Christ. On her left are seven court ladies, in descending order of rank; the one closest to her wears the purple of the imperial family. Two high-ranking civil officials stand on her right. One pulls back a curtain to reveal a baptismal font, the fountain in which persons are baptized into the Church.

QUESTIONS FOR ANALYSIS

1. Theodora's mosaic places her into a definite space: an imperial palace (or possibly a church). Justinian's mosaic lacks any spatial points of reference. Does this seem significant? If so, how do you interpret this lack of place?

2. Two titles borne by the emperor of Constantinople were *isapostolos* (peer of the Apostles) and *autokrator* (sole ruler of the world). Does Justinian's mosaic symbolize either or both of these titles? Please be specific in your answer.

3. Based on these two mosaics, please describe the place that Empress Theodora apparently held within the empire. What was her theoretical position? What do you think were her actual powers? As always, be as specific as possible.

4. "The Byzantine emperor was perceived as the living image of God on earth, insofar as his imperial majesty was a pale reflection of the Glory of God. As
("Questions for Analysis" continue on page 322.)

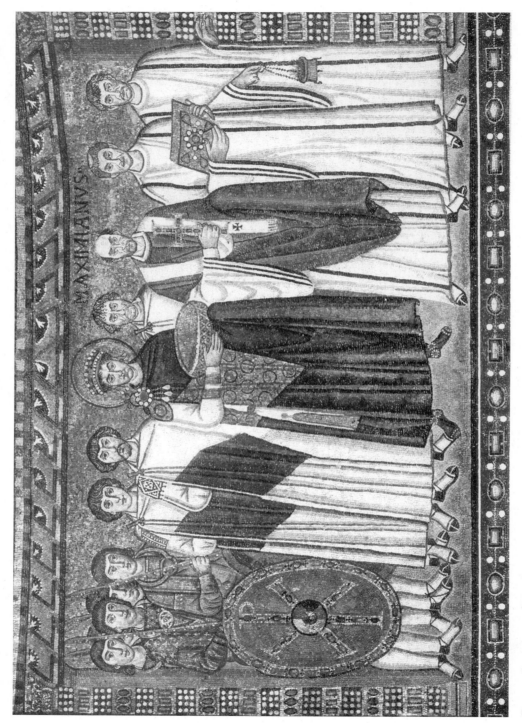

Emperor Justinian and His Court

Empress Theodora and Her Court

such, he was the link between the Roman Christian people and their God."
In light of these mosaics, what do you think of this anonymous statement?
Please be specific.

5. Compare this mosaic with *Christ the Redeemer* (Chapter 7, source 53),
   another Ravenna mosaic, which had been created half a century earlier.
   What inferences do you draw?

Emperor Basil II and the Apogee of Byzantine Power

▼▼▼

82 ▼ *Michael Psellus, THE CHRONOGRAPHIA*

The history of Byzantium is characterized by peaks and troughs. The pattern of
triumph, decline, and recovery repeated itself continuously until Byzantium's
collapse in the mid fifteenth century. One key to understanding this cycle is the
power invested in the emperor (and occasionally the empress). Rarely does an
individual single-handedly have a radical effect on the historical course of an
empire or any other large institution, but autocratic monarchs could and did play
inordinately important roles in the unfolding of Byzantine fortunes. One of the
most significant of Byzantium's emperors was Basil II (r. 976–1025), who dominated an age of Byzantine greatness. In fact, many historians see his reign as the
political, military, and cultural apogee of Byzantine civilization.

Late in the eleventh century, Michael Psellus (1018–after 1081?) — a monk,
scholar, and politician — composed the *Chronographia* (*Chronicle*), a series of
imperial character sketches covering the period from the start of the reign of
Basil II through that of Michael VII (r. 1071–1078). As far as Psellus was concerned, the empire's history was largely driven by the ways in which individual
emperors and empresses responded to the challenges and temptations of office.
In the following excerpt Psellus describes the qualities that he believed allowed
Basil II to rule so successfully.

QUESTIONS FOR ANALYSIS

1. What picture of Basil II emerges from this sketch?
2. According to Psellus, which of the emperor's personal qualities aided his
   success? How so?
3. Based on your reading of Psellus, what factors seem to have contributed
   most to Byzantium's power in the age of Basil II?
4. Based on this account, what inferences can you draw about the nature of
   Byzantine imperial government?

In his dealings with his subjects, Basil behaved with extraordinary circumspection. It is perfectly true that the great reputation he built up as a ruler was founded rather on terror than on loyalty. As he grew older and became more experienced he relied less on the judgment of men wiser than himself. He alone introduced new measures, he alone disposed his military forces. As for the civil administration, he governed, not in accordance with the written laws, but following the unwritten dictates of his own intuition, which was most excellently equipped by nature for the purpose. Consequently he paid no attention to men of learning: on the contrary, he affected utter scorn — towards the learned folk, I mean. It seems to me a wonderful thing, therefore, that while the emperor so despised literary culture, no small crop of philosophers and orators sprang up in those times. One solution of the paradox, I fancy, is that the men of those days did not devote themselves to the study of letters for any ulterior purpose: they cultivated literature for its own sake and as an end in itself, whereas the majority nowadays do not approach the subject of education in this spirit, but consider personal profit to be the first reason for study. Perhaps I should add, that though gain is the object of their zeal for literature, if they do not immediately achieve this goal, then they desist from their studies at once. Shame on them!

However, we must return to the emperor. Having purged the empire of the barbarians,[1] he dealt with his own subjects and completely subjugated them too — I think 'subjugate' is the right word to describe it. He decided to abandon his former policy, and after the great families had been humiliated and put on an equal footing with the rest, Basil found himself playing the game of power-politics with considerable success. He surrounded himself with favorites who were neither remarkable for brilliance of intellect, nor of noble lineage, nor too learned. To them were entrusted the imperial rescripts, and with them he was accustomed to share the secrets of state. However, since at that time the emperor's comments on memoranda or requests for favor were never varied, but only plain, straightforward statements (for Basil, whether writing or speaking, eschewed all elegance of composition) he used to dictate to his secretaries just as the words came to his tongue, stringing them all together, one after the other. There was no subtlety, nothing superfluous, in his speech.

By humbling the pride or jealousy of his people, Basil made his own road to power an easy one. He was careful, moreover, to close the exit-doors on the monies contributed to the treasury. So a huge sum of money was built up, partly by the exercise of strict economy, partly by fresh additions from abroad. Actually, the sum accumulated in the imperial treasury reached the grand total of 200,000 talents.[2] As for the rest of his gains, it would indeed be hard to find words adequately to describe them. All the treasures amassed in Iberia and Arabia, all the riches found among the Celts or contained in the land of the Scyths[3] — in brief, all the wealth of the barbarians who surround our borders — all were gathered together in one place and deposited in the emperor's coffers. In addition to this, he carried off to his treasure-chambers and sequestrated there, all the money of those who rebelled against him and were afterwards subdued. And since the

---

[1]Basil had defeated several claimants to the imperial throne, along with their foreign allies. Also, between 990 and 995, he all but destroyed Bulgarian power in the north central regions of his empire, thereby earning the sobriquet *Bulgar-slayer*.

[2]A *talent* was a weight of precious metal that varied according to time and place.

[3]In this context, *Iberia* means the land of Georgia near the Caucasus Mountains of Southwest Asia and not the Iberian Peninsula, where modern Portugal and Spain are located. The *Scyths* were a horse-riding, warrior people, who dominated the region north of the Black Sea from about 700 to around 100 B.C.E. and entered into Greco-Roman lore as archetypes of steppe-dwelling barbarians. In this context, the land of the Scyths means the steppe region of Eastern Europe and Central Asia.

vaults of the buildings made for this purpose were not big enough, he had spiral galleries dug underground, after the Egyptian style, and there he kept safe a considerable proportion of his treasures. He himself took no pleasure in any of it: quite the reverse indeed, for the majority of the precious stones, both the white ones (which we call pearls) and the colored brilliants, far from being inlaid in diadems or collars, were hidden away in his underground vaults. Meanwhile Basil took part in his processions and gave audience to his governors clothed merely in a robe of purple, not the very bright purple, but simply purple of a dark hue, with a handful of gems as a mark of distinction. As he spent the greater part of his reign serving as a soldier on guard at our frontiers and keeping the barbarians from raiding our territories, not only did he draw nothing from his reserves of wealth, but even multiplied his riches many times over.

On his expedition against the barbarians,[4] Basil did not follow the customary procedure of other emperors, setting out at the middle of spring and returning home at the end of summer. For him the time to return was when the task in hand was accomplished. He endured the rigors of winter and the heat of summer with equal indifference. He disciplined himself against thirst. In fact, all his natural desires were kept under stern control, and the man was as hard as steel. He had an accurate knowledge of the details of army life, and by that I do not mean the general acquaintance with the composition of his army, the relative functions of individual units in the whole body, or the various groupings and deployments suited to the different formations. His experience of army matters went further than that: the duties of the *protostate,* the duties of the *bemilochites,*[5] the tasks proper to the rank immediately junior to them — all these were no mysteries to Basil, and the knowledge stood him in good stead in his wars. Accordingly, jobs appropriate to these ranks were not devolved on others, and the emperor, being personally conversant with the character and combat duties of each individual, knowing to what each man was fitted either by temperament or by training, used him in this capacity and made him serve there.

Moreover, he knew the various formations suited to his men. Some he had read of in books, others he devised himself during the operations of war, the result of his own intuition. He professed to conduct his wars and draw up the troops in line of battle, himself planning each campaign, but he preferred not to engage in combat personally. A sudden retreat might otherwise prove embarrassing. Consequently, for the most part he kept his troops immobile. He would construct machines of war and skirmish at a distance, while the maneuvering was left to his light-armed soldiers. Once he had made contact with the enemy, a regular military liaison was established between the different formations of the Roman army. The whole force was formed up like a solid tower, headquarters being in touch with the cavalry squadrons, who were themselves kept in communication with the light infantry, and these again with the various units of heavy-armed foot. When all was ready, strict orders were given that no soldier should advance in front of the line or break rank under any circumstance. If these orders were disobeyed, and if some of the most valiant or daring soldiers did ride out well in front of the rest, even in cases where they engaged the enemy successfully, they could expect no medals or rewards for valor when they resumed. On the contrary, Basil promptly discharged them from the army, and they were punished on the same level as common criminals. The decisive factor in the achievement of victory was, in his opinion, the massing of troops in one coherent body, and for this reason alone he believed the Roman armies to be invincible. The careful inspections he made before battle used to aggravate the soldiers and they abused him openly, but the emperor met their scorn with

---

[4]His campaign against the Bulgars (note 1).

[5]Both were junior officer ranks in the army.

common sense. He would listen quietly, and then, with a gay smile, point out that if he neglected these precautions, their battles would go on for ever.

Basil's character was two-fold, for he readily adapted himself no less to the crises of war than to the calm of peace. Really, if the truth be told, he was more of a villain in wartime, more of an emperor in time of peace. Outbursts of wrath he controlled, and like the proverbial 'fire under the ashes,' kept anger hid in his heart, but if his orders were disobeyed in war, on his return to the palace he would kindle his wrath and reveal it. Terrible then was the vengeance he took on the miscreant. Generally, he persisted in his opinions, but there were occasions when he did change his mind. In many cases, too, he traced crimes back to their original causes, and the final links in the chain were exonerated. So most defaulters obtained forgiveness, either through his sympathetic understanding or because he showed some other interest in their affairs. He was slow to adopt any course of action, but never would he willingly alter the decision, once it was taken. Consequently, his attitude to friends was unvaried, unless perchance he was compelled by necessity to revise his opinion of them. Similarly, where he had burst out in anger against someone, he did not quickly moderate his wrath. Whatever estimate he formed, indeed, was to him an irrevocable and divinely-inspired judgment.

Economic Regulation
▼▼▼
83 ▼ *THE BOOK OF THE EPARCH*

Byzantium inherited from the fourth-century Roman Empire a system of close governmental regulation of essential industries, trades, and services, and it retained that policy for more than a thousand years. As far as the Byzantine government was concerned, it was just as necessary to the well-being of the empire for the state to control the economy as it was for it to direct foreign relations.

In the age of the Macedonian Dynasty (867–1056), when Byzantium was at the peak of its power and prosperity, the city of Constantinople had at least twenty-two different occupational guilds, all of which were directly supervised by the city's chief civil official, the *eparch,* or prefect. Sometime during the tenth century an anonymous editor compiled in twenty-two chapters a collection of regulations regarding Constantinople's guilds. Known as *The Book of the Eparch,* this compendium illustrates clearly the ways in which the government attempted to direct the economy.

QUESTIONS FOR ANALYSIS

1. What obligations did these regulations lay upon bankers?
2. What obligations did they lay upon grocers?
3. Grocers were prohibited from engaging in certain commercial practices, and their profit margin was strictly set by law. What philosophy lay behind such regulations?

4. What do you infer from the severity of the penalties imposed on bankers and grocers who engaged in illegal economic activities?
5. Considering the tone of these laws, what do you think was the likelihood that a significant number of people engaged in prohibited economic practices? Explain your answer.
6. According to one historian, "Byzantium's economic regulations transformed its merchants and artisans into quasi civil officials and imposed police duties on them." Based on your reading of this source, do you agree or disagree? Why?

THE BANKERS

1. Anyone who wishes to be nominated as a banker must be vouched for by respected and honest men who will guarantee that he will do nothing contrary to the ordinances; to wit, that he will not pare down, or cut, or put false inscriptions on *nomismata*[1] or *miliarisia,*[2] or set one of his own slaves in his place at his bank if he should happen to be occupied with some temporary duties, so that no trickery may thereby enter into the business of the profession. If anyone is caught in such practices, he shall be punished by the amputation of his hand.

2. The money-changers shall report to the prefect the forgers who station themselves in the squares and streets in order to prevent them from indulging in illegal practices. If they know of such and fail to report them, they shall suffer the aforementioned punishment.

3. The money-changers shall make no deduction from the value of an unadulterated *miliarision* which bears the genuine royal stamp, but shall accept it as equivilent to twenty-four *obols.*[3] However, if the condition of the coin is otherwise, it must be valued accordingly.[4] Those who disregard this injunction shall be scourged, shorn, and suffer confiscation.

4. Each banker shall keep two assistants to sort his coins. He must go surety for these, so that if one of them is detected acting contrary to the ordinances both he and the one who appointed him shall suffer the aforesaid penalties.

5. Any money-changer who receives a counterfeited *nomisma* or *miliarision,* and fails to report it to the prefect together with its possessor, shall be scourged, shorn, and banished.

6. The bankers must not give their subordinates account books or coins and station them in the squares and streets in order to receive the profit accruing from their activities. Even on occasions of distribution of largesses[5] or the performance of services for the emperor they shall not go away and abandon their banks. If anyone is caught doing so, he shall be beaten, shorn, and suffer confiscation. . . .

THE GROCERS

1. The grocers shall open their shops in the square and streets throughout the whole city so that the necessities of life may easily be found. They shall sell meat, pickled fish, meal, cheese, honey, olive oil, green vegetables of all sorts, butter, solid and liquid pitch, cedar resin, hemp, flax, plaster, pottery vessels, bottles, nails, and

---

[1]Gold coins. *Nomismata* is the plural form of *nomisma.*
[2]Silver coins. *Miliarisia* is the plural form of *miliarision.* Twelve miliarisia equaled one nomisma.
[3]Bronze coins.

[4]The value of a coin derived from its true weight of silver or gold. Worn or defaced coins were worth less than full-weight coins.
[5]When money or goods were distributed to the city's populace in the emperor's name.

all the other things sold by a bar-balance and not by twin scales. They are forbidden to engage in the trades of the perfumers, or soap-makers, or linen merchants, or tavern keepers, or butchers even in the slightest degree. If anyone is found acting contrary to these regulations, he shall be scourged, shorn, and banished.

2. If any grocer has in his possession weights or measures not marked with the seal of the prefect, or if he pares down gold coins, or if he withdraws from circulation *nomismata* of four or two quarters bearing the genuine imperial stamp, he shall be beaten, shorn, and banished.

3. If a grocer is caught cheating another in a purchase and raising the price agreed upon, he shall be fined ten *nomismata*.[6] Likewise one who exhibits his wares outside his shop on the Lord's

Day or on another Holy Day[7] shall undergo the same penalty.

4. The grocers shall keep watch upon the imports that pertain to them, so that, if anyone not enrolled in their guild stores these up against a time of scarcity, he may be denounced to the prefect and called to account by him.

5. The grocers shall sell their goods in small quantities at a profit of two *miliarisia* on the *nomisma*.[8] If a calculation of their authorized gains shows that they are making a larger profit, they shall be scourged, shorn, and forced to give up this trade.

6. If any one of them secretly or openly raises the rental of another, he shall suffer the aforesaid penalty.

---

[6]The equivalent of the tax charged a fully laden ship leaving Constantinople; it could ruin an average small trader.

[7]Sunday is the Lord's Day; other holy days would be days of special religious commemoration, such as Epiphany (January 6), when the three magi visited the infant Jesus, and Good Friday (the day commemorating Jesus' crucifixion).
[8]See notes 1 and 2.

Bringing Christianity to the Rus'

▼▼▼

84 ▼ *THE RUSSIAN PRIMARY CHRONICLE*

Under the leadership of emperors like Basil II (source 82), the Eastern Roman, or Byzantine, Empire defended itself against a number of pagan enemies on its northern frontiers, eventually converting many of them to Eastern Orthodox Christianity. The most notable example of Constantinople's successful blending of imperial foreign policy with Christian missionary fervor was its conversion, beginning in the late tenth century, of the Rus' of Kiev, a people of mixed Scandinavian and Slavic origins. The leader who took the fateful step that resulted in the rather rapid Christianization of the Rus' was Prince Vladimir I of Kiev (r. 978–1015). For his successful efforts in converting his people to Orthodox Christianity, Vladimir is venerated as a saint in the Russian Orthodox Church.

The following account, which blends fact and fiction into a charming pastiche, presents Vladimir's conversion from a Kievan perspective. Compiled by a single monastic author around 1113 from earlier written sources and oral traditions, *The Russian Primary Chronicle* is the single most important source for the history of the state of Kiev from the mid ninth to the early twelfth century.

QUESTIONS FOR ANALYSIS

1. The tale of Prince Vladimir's study of various religions might not be literally true, but what deeper truth does it reveal about why Byzantine Christianity was so attractive to the Rus' and other pagans on the empire's frontiers?
2. What did Vladimir gain from his conversion?
3. What did the Byzantine Empire gain from Vladimir's conversion?
4. This account was composed by a Kievan monk in the early twelfth century. Judging from the tone of the chronicle, how deeply had Byzantine Christianity penetrated Kievan culture in a little over a century?

6495 (987).[1] Vladimir summoned together his boyars[2] and the city-elders, and said to them, "Behold, the Bulgars[3] came before me urging me to accept their religion. Then came the Germans and praised their own faith;[4] and after them came the Jews.[5] Finally the Greeks[6] appeared, criticizing all other faiths but commending their own, and they spoke at length, telling the history of the whole world from its beginning. Their words were artful, and it was wondrous to listen and pleasant to hear them. They preach the existence of another world. 'Whoever adopts our religion and then dies shall arise and live forever. But whosoever embraces another faith, shall be consumed with fire in the next world.' What is your opinion on this subject, and what do you answer?" The boyars and the elders replied, "You know, oh Prince, that no man condemns his own

possessions, but praises them instead. If you desire to make certain, you have servants at your disposal. Send them to inquire about the ritual of each and how he worships God."

Their counsel pleased the prince and all the people, so that they chose good and wise men to the number of ten, and directed them to go first among the Bulgars and inspect their faith. The emissaries went their way, and when they arrived at their destination they beheld the disgraceful actions of the Bulgars and their worship in the mosque;[7] then they returned to their country. Vladimir then instructed them to go likewise among the Germans, and examine their faith, and finally to visit the Greeks. They thus went into Germany, and after viewing the German ceremonial, they proceeded to Tsar'grad,[8] where they appeared before the emperor.[9] He inquired

---

[1] By Byzantine reckoning, the world was created in 5508 B.C.E. Consequently, the year 987 C.E. was the 6,495th year since Creation.

[2] Rus' nobles.

[3] The Bulgars of the Volga, a Turkic people who had inhabited the upper Volga since about the fifth century C.E. (see source 82). Vladimir had spread Rus' power all the way to the valley of the Volga.

[4] Both the Roman papacy and the Western emperors, who also happened to be the kings of Germany, were actively attempting to convert the Rus' of Kiev and Novgorod to Roman Catholic Christianity at this time.

[5] These Jews were the Khazars, a Turkic people who inhabited the region between the Black and Caspian Seas. The Khazars embraced Judaism toward the middle of the eighth century, possibly under the influence of Jewish refugees from Persia.

[6] The Byzantines. To outsiders, such as the Rus' and Western Europeans, all Byzantines were *Greeks,* and Byzantium was simply *Greece,* even though the heart of the empire lay in Asiatic Anatolia. The reason for this was simple: Byzantines spoke Greek and continued the cultural traditions of Eastern Hellenism.

[7] A Muslim place of communal worship (see Chapter 8). Unlike the Bulgars of the Balkans, who had accepted Eastern Orthodox Christianity, the Volga Bulgars were Muslims.

[8] *The Imperial City* — the Russian term for *Constantinople.*

[9] Basil II (source 82).

on what mission they had come, and they reported to him all that had occurred. When the emperor heard their words, he rejoiced, and did them great honor on that very day.

On the morrow, the emperor sent a message to the patriarch[10] to inform him that a Russian delegation had arrived to examine the Greek faith, and directed him to prepare the church and the clergy, and to array himself in his sacerdotal robes, so that the Rus' might behold the glory of the God of the Greeks. When the patriarch received these commands, he bade the clergy assemble, and they performed the customary rites. They burned incense, and the choirs sang hymns. The emperor accompanied the Rus' to the church, and placed them in a wide space, calling their attention to the beauty of the edifice, the chanting, and the pontifical services and the ministry of the deacons, while he explained to them the worship of his God. The Rus' were astonished, and in their wonder praised the Greek ceremonial. Then the Emperors Basil and Constantine[11] invited the envoys to their presence, and said, "Go hence to your native country," and dismissed them with valuable presents and great honor.

Thus they returned to their own country, and the prince called together his boyars and the elders. Vladimir then announced the return of the envoys who had been sent out, and suggested that their report be heard. He thus commanded them to speak out before his retinue. The envoys reported, "When we journeyed among the Bulgars, we beheld how they worship in their temple, called a mosque, while they stand ungirt. The Bulgar bows, sits down, looks hither and thither like one possessed, and there is no happiness among them, but instead only sorrow and a dreadful stench. Their religion is not good. Then we went among the Germans, and saw them performing many ceremonies in their temples; but we beheld no glory there. Then we went to Greece, and the Greeks led us to the edifices where they worship their God, and we knew not whether we were in heaven or on earth. For on earth there is no such splendor or such beauty, and we are at a loss how to describe it. We only know that God dwells there among men, and their service is fairer than the ceremonies of other nations. For we cannot forget that beauty. Every man, after tasting something sweet, is afterward unwilling to accept that which is bitter, and therefore we cannot dwell longer here." Then the boyars spoke and said, "If the Greek faith were evil, it would not have been adopted by your grandmother Olga[12] who was wiser than all other men." Vladimir then inquired where they should all accept baptism, and they replied that the decision rested with him.

After a year had passed, in 6496 (988), Vladimir proceeded with an armed force against Kherson, a Greek city,[13] and the people of Kherson barricaded themselves therein. Vladimir halted at the farther side of the city beside the harbor, a bowshot from the town, and the inhabitants resisted energetically while Vladimir besieged the town. Eventually, however, they became exhausted, and Vladimir warned them that if they

---

[10]The patriarch of Constantinople, at this moment Nicholas II (r. 979–991), was the chief bishop of the Byzantine Church. He was usually an imperial appointee, and his authority should not be equated with that of the pope of Rome.
[11]The future Emperor Constantine VIII (r. 1025–1028), Basil II's brother and successor.
[12]Olga, widow of Prince Igor and regent of Kiev from 945 to 964, accepted Christian baptism, apparently several years before she traveled to Constantinople in 957. Her conversion and her ties with Byzantium laid the foundation for her grandson's work in introducing Christianity to the Rus'. The Russian Orthodox Church venerates her as Saint Olga.

[13]Kherson was a Byzantine city located in the Crimea, the peninsula that juts into the northern regions of the Black Sea and the object of fierce competition between the Kievans and the Byzantines.

did not surrender, he would remain on the spot for three years. When they failed to heed this threat, Vladimir marshalled his troops and ordered the construction of an earthwork in the direction of the city. While this work was under construction, the inhabitants dug a tunnel under the city-wall, stole the heaped-up earth, and carried it into the city, where they piled it up in the center of the town. But the soldiers kept on building, and Vladimir persisted. Then a man of Kherson, Anastasius by name, shot into the Rus' camp an arrow on which he had written, "There are springs behind you to the east, from which water flows in pipes. Dig down and cut them off." When Vladimir received this information, he raised his eyes to heaven and vowed that if this hope was realized, he would be baptized. He gave orders straightway to dig down above the pipes, and the water-supply was thus cut off. The inhabitants were accordingly overcome by thirst, and surrendered.

Vladimir and his retinue entered the city and he sent messages to the Emperors Basil and Constantine, saying, "Behold, I have captured your glorious city. I have also heard that you have an unwedded sister. Unless you give her to me to wife, I shall deal with your own city as I have with Kherson." When the emperors heard this message they were troubled, and replied, "It is not proper for Christians to give in marriage to pagans. If you are baptized, you shall have her to wife, inherit the kingdom of God, and be our companion in the faith. Unless you do so, however, we cannot give you our sister in marriage." When Vladimir learned their response, he directed the envoys of the emperors to report to the latter that he was willing to accept baptism, having already given some study to their religion, and that the Greek faith and ritual, as described by the emissaries sent to examine it, had pleased him well. When the emperors heard this report, they rejoiced, and persuaded their sister

Anna to consent to the match. They then requested Vladimir to submit to baptism before they should send their sister to him, but Vladimir desired that the princess should herself bring priests to baptize him. The emperors complied with his request, and sent forth their sister, accompanied by some dignitaries and priests. Anna, however, departed with reluctance. "It is as if I were setting out into captivity," she lamented; "better were it for me to die at home." But her brothers protested, "Through your agency God turns the land of Rus' to repentance, and you will relieve Greece from the danger of grievous war. Do you not see how much harm the Rus' have already brought upon the Greeks? If you do not set out, they may bring on us the same misfortunes." It was thus that they overcame her hesitation only with great difficulty. The princess embarked upon a ship, and after tearfully embracing her kinfolk, she set forth across the sea and arrived at Kherson. The natives came forth to greet her, and conducted her into the city, where they settled her in the palace.

By divine agency, Vladimir was suffering at that moment from a disease of the eyes, and could see nothing, being in great distress. The princess declared to him that if he desired to be relieved of this disease, he should be baptized with all speed, otherwise it could not be cured. When Vladimir heard her message, he said, "If this proves true, then of a surety is the God of the Christians great," and gave order that he should be baptized. The bishop of Kherson, together with the princess's priests, after announcing the tidings, baptized Vladimir, and as the bishop laid his hand upon him, he straightway received his sight. Upon experiencing this miraculous cure, Vladimir glorified God, saying, "I have now perceived the one true God." When his followers beheld this miracle, many of them were also baptized.

Western Europe:
The Emergence of a New Civilization

Although Byzantine cultural influences spread beyond the territorial limits of the Eastern Roman Empire (as we saw in source 84), Byzantium was largely a civilization centered upon a single empire. In the West, to the contrary, a new civilization arose that was not identified with any single political entity, even though the West created its own empire in the year 800 and then recreated it in 962. Despite having its own *Holy Roman Empire,* as it was later called, European civilization was politically pluralistic and was never tied to any single state.

If any single entity commanded the loyalties of all or most Europeans, it was the Roman Church, which was centered upon the person and office of the *pope* of Rome. The pope, whose title means "father" in Latin, was bishop of the city of Rome and claimed authority over all of Christendom, not just the Western Church, by virtue of being the heir of St. Peter. According to arguments first put forward in the fourth century, Christ had given St. Peter, the leader of the Apostles, "the keys of the Kingdom of Heaven" and therefore authority over the entire Church. Peter later became the first bishop of Rome, and it was as bishop of Rome that he exercised his God-given authority over Christendom. When he died in office, all his power passed to his successor, and it continued to be handed on to each successive bishop of Rome. This vision of church history, which received a fair amount of acceptance in the West, failed to convince Christians in the East, including those who looked to Constantinople for spiritual guidance. Indeed, popes discovered that their claims did not go uncontested, even in the West. The fact that Europe was creating itself as a civilization meant that it was host to many contradictions and internal tensions, many of which proved to be dynamic, driving forces.

In many respects, youthful, dynamic Europe was an ever-expanding culture in the period from roughly 500 to 1500. By the year 1000 European civilization stretched from the southern coastline of Greenland in the west to Poland, Serbia, and Bohemia in the east and from Scandinavia in the north to portions of the Iberian Peninsula in the south. By 1500 it encompassed the entire Iberian Peninsula and was being carried across the Atlantic to the Americas by Spaniards and Portuguese.

Yet this dynamism was certainly not obvious during the early centuries in which European civilization was taking shape. With the passing of Roman imperial order, Western Europeans were thrown back on their own resources and forced to create new social and political structures and a new civilization. As noted earlier, in fashioning this civilization, Westerners melded together three elements: the vestiges and memories of Roman civilization; the moral and organizational leadership of the Roman Catholic Church; and the vigor and culture of the various fringe peoples who carved out kingdoms in Europe from the fifth century onward. The single act that most vividly symbolizes the new order that emerged from that fusion was Pope Leo III's crowning of Charles the Great (*Charlemagne*) as Roman emperor on Christmas Day, 800.

Charles the Great's empire, which never included all of the West, was short lived, and Europe was again thrown on the defensive as it was invaded by new fringe peoples during the ninth and tenth centuries. Around the year 900 the European West certainly seemed the least promising of Rome's three successor civilizations. Its manifest political and economic weaknesses and general low level of learning stood in stark contrast to the magnificence of Byzantium and Islam. While its two more powerful siblings enjoyed ages of great prosperity, cultural efflorescence, and wide-ranging influence, Western Christendom was forced to fight for its very existence. But fight it did, and it prevailed. Indeed, as backward and endangered as this society appears to have been during an era often called *The Early Middle Ages* (500–1000), these centuries were the formative period of a tenacious, revolutionary civilization — a new civilization whose technology, ideas, and institutions would in time transform the world. All of this lay in the distant future, but by 1000 Western Europe had survived its crises and entered an era of rapid growth and prosperity. It was ready to take its place as a major civilization and power alongside Islam and Byzantium. Europe was now in an era known as *The High Middle Ages* (1000–1300), a period of intensive creativity and expansion.

As the following six sources illustrate, the process by which Europe created a new civilization was never easy, but it was productive.

Charlemagne: Europe's First Emperor

▼▼▼

85 ▼ Einhard, THE LIFE OF CHARLES THE GREAT

Charles the Great, or Charlemagne, king of the Franks and the Lombards and emperor in the West, ruled a major portion of continental Europe for close to half a century (768–814). During his lifetime, Charles's efforts to expand the boundaries of Christendom and impose an order based on his understanding of Christian principles won him a reputation that extended all the way to the court of Caliph Harun al-Rashid in Baghdad. His *Carolingian* (the family of Charles) successors, however, were less fortunate and probably less able. In 843 Charles's three grandsons divided the empire into three kingdoms, signaling continental Europe's return to political pluralism. As Carolingian unity and order began to crumble, Westerners fondly looked back on Charles's reign as a golden age. It was an age that was never recaptured, although many later emperors and kings tried.

One of Charles's many accomplishments was his patronage of scholarship on a modest but historically significant scale, a phenomenon often referred to as the *Carolingian Renaissance.* One of the scholars congregating at Charles's court was Einhard (ca. 770–840), a Frankish intellectual who arrived at Charles's court at

Aachen, or Aix-la-Chappelle, in the 790s. Einhard was vastly talented in a wide variety of areas. As an architect, he supervised the construction of Charles's church at Aachen. He also served Charles as an ambassador and was a poet of considerable skill. In all likelihood, he also became in 796 the head of Charles's court school — a school for clerics and the sons of Frankish nobles. Needless to say, Einhard came to know Charles quite well during the last two decades of the emperor's life. Following Charles's death, Einhard served as private secretary to Charles's son and successor, Emperor Louis the Pious (r. 813–840), but retired in 830.

Early in his retirement years, probably between 830 and 833, Einhard undertook the task of writing a biography of Charles the Great. Basing this life of his late emperor, patron, and friend on the *Lives of the Twelve Caesars* by the Roman historian Suetonius (ca. 69–140), Einhard implicitly argued that Charlemagne had been more than the equal of the early exemplars of Roman imperial greatness. Beyond that, Einhard set out to instruct Emperor Louis on the qualities that an effective Christian-Frankish emperor should have, at the very moment in which family quarrels were pulling Louis's empire apart.

In the following excerpts Einhard describes Charles's Saxon wars, his relations with his children, his love of learning, his character and piety, his relations with the Roman papacy (with special attention paid toward his imperial acclamation in 800), and Louis's imperial coronation in 813.

QUESTIONS FOR ANALYSIS

1. According to this excerpt, what were Charles's most sterling qualities? Which of them probably contributed to the success of Charles's reign? Which of them contributed to the legend of Charlemagne the emperor-hero?

2. What light, if any, do these excerpts shed on Charles's patronage of learning?

3. Einhard's statement that Charles initially had an aversion to the imperial title has puzzled some historians. From other sources we know that on Christmas Day, 800, Pope Leo, perhaps to Charles's surprise, placed a crown on the Frankish king's head, and the assembled people in St. Peter's basilica acclaimed Charles emperor. Compare these facts with Einhard's treatment of that day, and also compare that Roman ceremony with the manner in which Louis the Pious was made emperor. Can you now think of any reason why Charles might have been displeased thirteen years earlier? (Note that Charles never returned to Rome after leaving in 801.)

4. Compare Charlemagne with Basil II (source 82). How did their styles of ruling and policies differ? Can we infer anything from those differences regarding their respective empires? If so, what?

No war ever undertaken by the Frankish nation was carried on with such persistence and bitterness, or cost so much labor, because the Saxons,[1] like almost all the tribes of Germany, were a fierce people, given to the worship of devils and hostile to our religion, and did not consider it dishonorable to transgress and violate all law, human and divine. Then there were peculiar circumstances that tended to cause a breach of peace every day. Except in a few places, where large forests or mountain-ridges intervened and made the boundaries certain, the line between ourselves and the Saxons passed almost in its whole extent through an open country, so that there was no end to the murders, thefts, and arsons on both sides. In this way the Franks became so embittered that they at last resolved to make reprisals no longer, but to come to open war with the Saxons.

Accordingly, war was begun against them, and was waged for thirty-three successive years[2] with great fury; more, however, to the disadvantage of the Saxons than of the Franks. It could doubtless have been brought to an end sooner, had it not been for the faithlessness of the Saxons. It is hard to say how often they were conquered, and, humbly submitting to the king, promised to do what was enjoined upon them, gave without hesitation the required hostages, and received the officers sent them from the king. They were sometimes so much weakened and reduced that they promised to renounce the worship of devils and to adopt Christianity; but they were no less ready to violate these terms than prompt to accept them, so that it is impossible to tell which came easier to them to do; scarcely a year passed from the beginning of the war without such changes on their part. But the king did not suffer his high purpose and steadfastness — firm alike in good and evil fortune — to be wearied by any fickleness on their part, or to be turned from the task that he had undertaken; on the contrary, he never allowed their faithless behavior to go unpunished, but either took the field against them in person, or sent his counts with an army to wreak vengeance and exact righteous satisfaction.[3] At last, after conquering and subduing all who had offered resistance, he took ten thousand of those who lived on the banks of the Elbe, and settled them, with their wives and children, in many different bodies here and there in Gaul and Germany.[4] The war that had lasted so many years was at length ended by their acceding to the terms offered by the king; which were renunciation of their religious customs and the worship of devils, acceptance of the sacraments[5] of the Christian religion, and union with the Franks to form one people. . . .

The plan that he adopted for his children's education was, first of all, to have both boys and girls instructed in the liberal arts, to which he also turned his own attention. As soon as their years admitted, in accordance with the custom of the Franks, the boys had to learn horsemanship, and to practice war and the chase, and the girls to familiarize themselves with cloth-making, and to handle distaff and spindle, that they might not grow indolent through idleness, and he fostered in them every virtuous sentiment. . . . He was so careful of the training of his sons and daughters that he never took his meals without them when he was at home, and never made a journey without them; his sons would ride at his side, and his daughters follow him, while a number of his bodyguard, detailed for their protection, brought up the rear. . . .

Charles was temperate in eating, and particularly so in drinking, for he abominated drunkenness in anybody, much more in himself and those of his household; but he could not easily abstain from food, and often complained that fasts injured his health. He very rarely gave entertainments, only on great feastdays, and then

---

[1] A Germanic people who lived in the region beyond the Frankish kingdom's northeastern frontier.
[2] 772 to 804, or thirty-two years.
[3] Charles's armies undertook at least eighteen separate campaigns in Saxony. Most did not result in any significant pitched battles. Rather, the campaigns consisted of Frankish pacification efforts in the face of Saxon guerrilla warfare and stubborn attempts to retain their culture.
[4] In 804.
[5] The key rites, or ceremonies, of the Christian Church.

to large numbers of people. His meals ordinarily consisted of four courses, not counting the roast, which his huntsmen used to bring in on the spit; he was more fond of this than of any other dish. While at table, he listened to reading or music. The subjects of the readings were the stories and deeds of olden time: he was fond, too, of St. Augustine's books, and especially of the one entitled *The City of God.*[6] He was so moderate in the use of wine and all sorts of drink that he rarely allowed himself more than three cups in the course of a meal.

Charles had the gift of ready and fluent speech, and could express whatever he had to say with the utmost clearness. He was not satisfied with ability to use his native language merely, but gave attention to the study of foreign ones, and in particular was such a master of Latin that he could speak it as well as his native tongue; but he could understand Greek better than he could speak it. He was so eloquent, indeed, that he might have been taken for a teacher of oratory. He most zealously cherished the liberal arts, held those who taught them in great esteem, and conferred great honors upon them. He took lessons in grammar from the deacon[7] Peter of Pisa, at that time an aged man.[8] Another deacon, Albin of Britain, otherwise called Alcuin, a man of Saxon birth,[9] who was the greatest scholar of the day, was his teacher in other branches of learning.[10] The king spent much time and labor with him

studying rhetoric,[11] dialectic,[12] and especially astronomy. He learned to make calculations, and used to investigate with much curiosity and intelligence the motions of the heavenly bodies. He also tried to write, and used to keep tablets and blanks in bed under his pillow, that at leisure hours he might accustom his hand to form the letters; however, as he began his efforts late in life, and not at the proper time, they met with little success.

He cherished with the greatest fervor and devotion the principles of the Christian religion, which had been instilled into him from infancy. Hence it was that he built the beautiful basilica[13] at Aix-la-Chapelle, which he adorned with gold and silver and lamps, and with rails and doors of solid brass.[14] He had the columns and marbles for this structure brought from Rome and Ravenna, for he could not find such as were suitable elsewhere.[15] He was a constant worshiper at this church as long as his health permitted, going morning and evening, even after nightfall, besides attending mass.[16] He took care that all the services there conducted should be held in the best possible manner, very often warning the sextons[17] not to let any improper or unclean thing be brought into the building, or remain in it. He provided it with a number of sacred vessels of gold and silver, and with such a quantity of clerical robes that not even the door-keepers, who filled the humblest office in the church, were

---

[6]*The City of God,* by St. Augustine (354–430), was one of the most influential (and often misunderstood) books of Europe's Early Middle Ages. It attempts to explain the course of human history by placing it within the context of humanity's God-directed, spiritual destiny.

[7]A cleric who ranks just below a priest.

[8]When Charles captured Pavia, the Lombard capital, in 774, he found the grammarian Peter of Pisa teaching there and prevailed upon him to travel to the land of the Franks to serve at the royal court as a teacher.

[9]A Saxon in the sense of the Saxons who invaded Britain in the fifth century and were converted to Christianity in the seventh century. Actually, Alcuin was an Angle, a member of another Germanic tribe that invaded Britain in the fifth century.

[10]Called *Ealhwine* in his native Anglian and *Albinus* in Latin, *Alcuin* was a product of the intellectual milieu of Northumbria in England, one of early eighth-century Western Christendom's major centers of learning. He served as the

headmaster of Charles's palace school from 782 until his retirement in 796.

[11]The study of the elements of language, literature, and oratory.

[12]The art of critical reasoning and argumentation based on analysis of the meanings of words and the veracity of arguments and conclusions.

[13]A church constructed on the rectangular architectural plan of late Roman public halls.

[14]All that remains of this great complex is Charles's octagonal private chapel, which now serves as a chapel in the cathedral of Aachen.

[15]Many came from the former palace of the then defunct *exarch* of Ravenna, the chief Byzantine official in Italy from the mid sixth century to the mid eighth century.

[16]The central religious ceremony of the Roman Church, which commemorates Jesus' death and sacrifice.

[17]Persons charged with the church's maintenance.

obliged to wear their everyday clothes when in the performance of their duties. He took great pains to improve the church reading and singing, for he was well skilled in both, although he neither read in public nor sang, except in a low tone and with others.

He was very active in aiding the poor, and in that open generosity which the Greeks call alms; so much so, indeed, that he not only made a point of giving in his own country and his own kingdom, but when he discovered that there were Christians living in poverty in Syria, Egypt, and Africa, at Jerusalem, Alexandria, and Carthage, he had compassion on their wants, and used to send money over the seas to them. The reason that he earnestly strove to make friends with the kings beyond seas was that he might get help and relief to the Christians living under their rule.[18] He cared for the church of St. Peter the Apostle[19] at Rome above all other holy and sacred places, and heaped high its treasury with a vast wealth of gold, silver, and precious stones. He sent great and countless gifts to the popes; and throughout his whole reign the wish that he had nearest his heart was to re-establish the ancient authority of the city of Rome under his care and by his influence, and to defend and protect the church of St. Peter, and to beautify and enrich it out of his own store above all other churches. Nevertheless, although he held it in such veneration, only four times[20] did he repair to Rome to pay his vows and make his supplications during the whole forty-seven years that he reigned.

When he made his last journey thither, he had also other ends in view. The Romans had inflicted many injuries upon the Pontiff Leo, tearing out his eyes and cutting out his tongue,[21] so that he had been compelled to call upon the king for help. Charles accordingly went to Rome,[22] to set in order the affairs of the Church, which were in great confusion, and passed the whole winter there. It was then that he received the titles of Emperor and Augustus, to which he at first had such an aversion that he declared that he would not have set foot in the church the day that they were conferred, although it was a great feast-day, if he could have foreseen the design of the pope. He bore very patiently with the jealousy which the Roman emperors[23] showed upon his assuming these titles, for they took this step very ill; and by dint of frequent embassies and letters, in which he addressed them as brothers, he made their haughtiness yield to his magnanimity,[24] a quality in which he was unquestionably much their superior. . . .

Towards the close of his life,[25] when he was broken by ill-health and old age, he summoned Louis, king of Aquitania,[26] his only surviving son by Hildegard, and gathered together all the chief men of the whole kingdom of the Franks in a solemn assembly. He appointed Louis, with their unanimous consent,[27] to rule with himself over the whole kingdom, and constituted him heir to the imperial name; then, placing the diadem upon his son's head, he bade him be proclaimed Emperor and Augustus. This step was hailed by all present with great favor, for it really seemed as if God had prompted him to it for the kingdom's good; it increased the king's[28] dignity, and struck no little terror into foreign nations.

---

[18]In 799 Charles sent an ambassador to Jerusalem to inquire about the conditions of the Christians living there. During the first decade of the ninth century Charles exchanged several embassies with Caliph Harun al-Rashid, presumably because Charles was interested in the well-being of the many Christians living under the caliph's rule.

[19]The pope of Rome claims to be the deputy, or vicar, of St. Peter, prince of the apostles, to whom Jesus gave governance of the Church.

[20]774, 781, 787, and 800.

[21]Pope Leo III (r. 795–816) was attacked on April 25, 799, by factional opponents, including members of the family of the previous pope, Hadrian I. Although an attempt was made to blind him and cut out his tongue, thereby rendering him incapable of serving as a priest, the attackers failed.

[22]Charles arrived on November 24, 800.

[23]In Constantinople.

[24]In 812 Emperor Michael I (r. 811–813) recognized Charles's imperial title in exchange for Venice and some territory in the Balkans.

[25]813.

[26]A region in modern southwest France.

[27]The consent of all leading Frankish nobles was needed to *ratify* a royal succession.

[28]Louis.

A Papal Portrait: Leo III and Charles the Great

▼▼▼

86 ▾ A LATERAN PALACE MOSAIC

Pope Leo III (r. 795–816) was lavish in the money he spent beautifying papal Rome, and one of his more ambitious building projects was adding two massive state reception halls to the papal residence known as the *Lateran Palace*. In the fashion of the day, the interiors of each hall were covered with mosaics. One pictured a seated St. Peter flanked by two kneeling figures: Pope Leo and King Charles. Inasmuch as the mosaic was completed sometime between 798 and April 799, Charles undoubtedly saw this artistic interpretation of papal-Frankish relations on his fateful last visit to Rome in 800/801 (source 85). We can only wonder what he thought of it.

Lateran Palace Mosaic

Time badly deteriorated the mosaic, and a heavy-handed attempt at restoration in 1743 completed the process of destruction. What we see in this mid-eighteenth-century replacement copy is St. Peter, the keys to the Kingdom of Heaven on his lap, handing a pallium (source 81) to Pope Leo and a lance with attached battle standard to King Charles. The pallium that Leo receives is the sign of authority worn by popes and archbishops. Note that Peter, who is dressed in clerical robes, wears one. Both the pope and the king have square nimbuses, or haloes, conventional signs that they are especially sanctified or powerful people who are still living; Peter has a round nimbus, a sign of canonized sainthood. The four Latin inscriptions read (from top to bottom and left to right as we view the mosaic): "Saint Peter"; "Most Holy Lord Pope Leo"; "To Lord King Charles"; and "Blessed Peter, You Give Life to Pope Leo and You Give Victory to King Charles."

QUESTIONS FOR ANALYSIS

1. Is there anything significant about Leo's position on St. Peter's right and Charles's position on his left? Explain your answer.
2. What do you make of the fact that it is *Peter* who gives Charles the lance and not Jesus or some other manifestation of God?
3. What is the message of this mosaic?
4. Review source 85. Now compose Charles the Great's commentary on the mosaic.
5. Review source 81. Now compose a Byzantine commentary on the mosaic.

The Feudal Perspective
▼▼▼
87 ▼ THE SONG OF ROLAND

In the wake of the collapse of Charles the Great's short-lived empire, Europeans produced a variety of military and political expedients that allowed them to get on with the task of building a civilization. By the year 1000 warrior-landholders in Northwest Europe had evolved a system of governance and military organization that modern historians term *feudalism*. Like Japan's *samurai* (source 68), the feudal *vassal* (both terms mean "one who serves") was a warrior who served a lord and enjoyed in return a variety of political, social, and economic benefits. One of the major reasons a soldier became a vassal was to receive a *fief* (*feudum* in Latin, hence the term *feudalism*) as payment for services rendered. Originally, this fief, or *fee,* was anything of value, but increasingly it became a grant of land that the vassal ruled in the lord's name. During the eleventh century these fiefs tended to become hereditary, passing to the vassal's oldest surviving male heir. Therefore, feudal soldiers, who several generations earlier had generally been hired thugs in the employ of warlords, were becoming landed nobles. In the process they articulated a set of shared values that became known as the *Code of*

Chivalry. Ideally, these principles and customs governed the life and conduct of the *chevalier,* or mounted knight. Reality, however, often diverged from the ideal.

One of the earliest and most popular literary articulations of the chivalric code is the anonymous *Song of Roland,* an epic *chanson de geste* (song of heroic deeds). Composed in Old French around 1100, the *Song of Roland* is saturated with the ideology of the French warrior class at the time of the First Crusade (source 91). This narrative poem, which relates the legendary last battle of Count Roland and his companions, is loosely based on a minor disaster suffered by Charlemagne in 778. While his army was returning from an expedition in northern Spain, Christian Basques ambushed and wiped out his baggage train and rear guard in the mountain pass of Roncesvalles. Among the fallen was Roland, duke of the Breton frontier. We know little else about this skirmish or the historical Roland. However, when Roland reemerges several centuries later, he has been transformed into Charlemagne's nephew and the greatest champion in the emperor's holy war against Islam: The Basque bandits have become an enormous Muslim army. Charlemagne, who was only thirty-six at the time of the ambush and twenty-two years shy of his eventual coronation as emperor, has been metamorphosed into a Moses-like patriarch more than two hundred years old, who rules as God's sole agent on earth over a united Christian world. He, his nephew, and his nephew's companions are now Frenchmen, even though there had been no France or French culture in Charlemagne's day. Likewise, feudalism was in its infancy when Charles the Great's Frankish kingdom served as western Christendom's focal point, yet the *Song of Roland* assumes a society pervaded by feudal relationships and values.

The story revolves around the themes of feudal loyalty and honor. Roland has unwittingly offended his stepfather, Ganelon, who in revenge enters into a conspiracy with the Saracen (Muslim) king, Marsilion, to deliver up Roland and the rest of the flower of French knighthood. Ganelon then arranges for Roland to command the emperor's rear guard, knowing that the Saracens plan to ambush it and that Roland will be too proud to sound his horn for reinforcements. Such is the case. Despite the entreaties of Oliver, his closest friend, Roland does not sound the horn until the battle is lost and twenty thousand Christian soldiers lie dead. The emperor returns too late to prevent his nephew's death but manages to exact revenge by destroying all Muslim forces in Spain and consigning Ganelon to death by torture. Our selection describes the opening and final stages of Roland's last fight.

QUESTIONS FOR ANALYSIS

1. Consider the words and actions of Roland, Oliver, and Turpin, and from them draw up a list of the Code of Chivalry's components. Do you see any potentially contradictory values or practices?
2. How does the author express the salvation of Roland's soul in feudal terms?
3. This poem was composed around the time of the First Crusade. What does it allow us to infer about Western Europe's crusade ideology?

4. Students often confuse feudal vassals with *serfs,* the semifree tenant farmers who worked the estates of Europe's landed lords. What evidence is there in this poem that by the mid eleventh century feudal vassals were enjoying a status far higher than that of peasants?
5. Which of these two warriors, Roland or Oliver, would Kusunoki Masashige (Chapter 9, source 68) admire more? Why?
6. Compare this poem with the *Taiheiki* (*Chronicle of the Grand Pacification*). Which values do these two warrior societies share? Can you discern any significant differences between the two? What role does religion play in each? Are those roles similar or different? What does your answer suggest?
7. Compose Usamah ibn Munqidh's commentary on the *Song of Roland* (see Chapter 9, source 76). Keep in mind that he also was a warrior.

The pagans[1] arm themselves with Saracen[2] coats of triple-layered chain mail.[3] They buckle on helmets made in Saragossa[4] and strap on swords of Viennese steel. Their shields are handsome, and their lances, crafted in Valencia,[5] are tipped with white, blue, and scarlet streamers. They leave behind their pack mules and riding horses and, mounting their war-horses, ride forth in tight formation. The day is fair and the sun bright, and all their gear glistens in the light. To add to the splendor, they sound a thousand trumpets. So great is the clamor, the sound carries to the Franks.[6]

Upon hearing it, Oliver says to Count Roland: "Sir comrade, I think we are now going to battle the Saracens." Roland answers: "May God so grant it. If we make a stand here for our monarch, we are only doing what is expected of good men. A man ought to be willing to suffer pain and loss for his lord. He should endure extremes of heat and cold and should be ever ready to lose hide and hair in his lord's service. Let each of us now be sure to strike hard blows, so that no bard may sing ill of us in his songs. Pagans are wrong,

and Christians are right. On my part, I will not set a bad example."

Oliver says: "The heathen army is massive, and our numbers are few. Roland, my good friend, sound your horn. Charles will hear it and return with his whole army." Roland replies: "That would be a foolish act, for by so doing I would lose all fame in sweet France. I prefer to strike hard blows with Durendal,[7] so that its blade is bloodied right up to the hilt. These foul pagans made a mistake in coming to this mountain pass. I pledge that they have not long to live."

"Roland, my comrade, blow your horn. Charles will hear it, return with his army, and the king and his barons will aid us." Roland answers: "God forbid that my family be shamed by my actions or any dishonor fall on fair France. No, I will fight with Durendal, the good sword girded here at my side, and you will see its blade fully reddened. The pagans asked for trouble when they gathered their army. I pledge that all of them will die." . . .

Oliver says: "I see no shame here. I have seen the Saracens of Spain, they cover the hills and

---

[1]The Muslims. At the time of the First Crusade, European Christians were generally ignorant of the fact that Muslims are monotheists and therefore not pagans.
[2]Originally, *Saracen* was a term the Romans used to designate an inhabitant of Arabia; later, it became a general Western synonym for *Muslim.*
[3]A knee-length garment of interconnected iron rings (chain mail) that protected the torso and thighs.

[4]A city in northeast Spain that Christian forces captured from Islam in 1118.
[5]A region in eastern Spain.
[6]The Christian army.
[7]The name of Roland's sword.

valleys, the scrubland and the plains. Numerous are the ranks of this hostile people, and we are but a small band of comrades." Roland answers: "This only inflames my desire. May God and His angels forbid that France should suffer any loss because of me. I would rather die than dishonor myself. The more we act like warriors, the more the emperor loves us."

Roland is valiant, Oliver is wise, and both are courageous. Once armed and on their horses, they would rather die than flee the battlefield. . . .

Close at hand is Archbishop Turpin.[8] He now spurs his horse to the crest of a knoll and delivers a sermon to the Franks: "Lord barons, Charles placed us here, and it is a man's duty to die for his monarch. Now help defend Christianity. It is certain you will have to fight, for here are the Saracens. Confess your sins and beg God's mercy. For the salvation of your souls, I will absolve your sins. Should you die, you will die as holy martyrs, and you will have exalted seats in Paradise." The Franks dismount and kneel, and the archbishop blesses them. As their penance,[9] he commands them to use their swords.

▷ Despite a courageous stand, the rear guard is overwhelmed.

Count Roland, aware of the great slaughter of his men, turns to Oliver, saying: "Noble comrade, for God's sake, what do you think? See how many good men lie on the ground. We ought to weep for sweet France, the fair, that has lost such barons. Ah, my king and friend, would that you were here now! Oliver, my brother, what should we do? How shall we send the king news of this?" "I do not know," says Oliver, "but I would prefer to die than dishonor myself." Then Roland says: "I will blow my horn, and Charles, as he crosses the mountains, will hear it. I swear that the Franks will return." Oliver then replies: "That would be shameful for you to do and would dishonor your family. It would be a disgrace they would carry to their graves. You would not blow the horn when I told you to do so, now I advise you not to sound it. To do so now would be useless." . . .

Roland asks: "Why are you angry with me?" Oliver answers: "Comrade, you have no one to blame but yourself. Valor tempered by wisdom is not foolishness, and prudence is better than pride. Because of your folly these Franks have died. Never again will King Charles enjoy our service. Had you taken my advice, my lord Charles would have been here, and this battle would have ended differently. King Marsilion would have been captured or killed. Your valor, Roland, has been our undoing. We shall never again fight for the great Emperor Charles, who will have no equal till the end of time. Now you must die, and France will be shamed by its loss. Today our loyal friendship will be ended; before night falls we will be sorrowfully parted."

The archbishop, hearing them quarrel, goads his horse with spurs of pure gold, rides to them, and rebukes them both, saying: "Sir Roland, and you, Sir Oliver, in God's name, I pray you, stop this strife. Your horn will give us little help now, yet it is better if you blow it. Should the king come, he will avenge us, and the pagans will not depart from here rejoicing. Our Frankish comrades will dismount and find us dead and mutilated. They will lay us on stretchers placed on the backs of pack mules and will mourn us in sorrow and pity. They will bury us in churches, so that our corpses are not eaten by wolves, swine, and dogs."

"Sir, you speak well and correctly," says Roland. Whereupon he sets his horn to his lips and blows

---

[8]Archbishop of the church of Reims and, along with Roland and Oliver, one of the Twelve Peers of France. *Peer* means "equal"; these twelve champions were socially the emperor's equals by virtue of their birth, prowess, and worth to him. Although a priest, Turpin is also a fighter.

[9]After receiving absolution of one's sins from God through the agency of a priest, the penitent was required by the priest to perform some penitential act as a token of contrition. Depending on the severity of the sins forgiven, the act could range from saying simple prayers to making a pilgrimage to the Holy Land.

it with all his might. . . . A good thirty leagues away they hear it resound. Charles and his whole army hear it, and the king remarks: "Our men are engaged in battle." . . . With anguish and deep torment, Count Roland blows his horn with all his might, to the point that bright blood spurts out of his mouth, and the vessels of his brain are ruptured. . . .

Roland knows his time is over. . . . He has laid himself down beneath a pine tree, his face turned toward Spain. He begins to remember many things: all the lands he has conquered, sweet France, the noble lineage from which he is descended, and Charlemagne, his lord, who raised him in his own household. He cannot keep back

his tears and sighs. But not forgetting himself, he confesses his sins and begs God's mercy: "Father, You who are truth itself, who raised Lazarus from the dead[10] and saved Daniel from the lions,[11] preserve my soul from all the dangers that beset it because of the sins I have committed throughout my life." He holds out his right glove to God, and Saint Gabriel[12] takes it from his hand. His head sinks down to rest on his arm. With clasped hands he meets his end. God sends down His cherubim[13] and Saint Michael,[14] who saves us from the perils of the sea, and with them comes Saint Gabriel, and they carry the soul of the count to paradise.

---

[10]A friend whom Jesus raised from the dead.
[11]A Jewish prophet protected by God while in a lion's den.
[12]An archangel and messenger of God.
[13]An order of angels.

[14]St. Michael the Archangel, a warrior saint. The island monastery of Mont-Saint-Michel off the Breton coast is dedicated to St. Michael.

Bringing Christianity to the Magyars
▼▼▼

88 ▼ *Pope Sylvester II,*
LETTER TO ST. STEPHEN OF HUNGARY

The Rus' of Kiev began to adopt Byzantine forms of Christian culture shortly before the year 1000 (source 84), just about the same time that the *Hungarians* were embracing Western European forms of Christian culture. The Hungarians (or *Magyars,* as they called themselves) entered Europe as invaders during the late ninth and early tenth centuries. A Finno-Ugric pastoral people out of the Great Steppes of Eurasia, the Hungarians were terrifying as they swept into the eastern portions of the disintegrating Carolingian Empire. Characterized by one Western churchman as an "exceedingly ferocious people, . . . crueler than any beast," these fierce horsemen inspired the prayer "Lord, preserve us from the arrows of the Hungarians."

The Magyars continued to be a menace until King Otto I of Saxony (the future Emperor Otto I) inflicted a crushing defeat upon them at the Battle of the Lechfeld in southern Germany in 955. Soon thereafter they settled down in a region defined by the Middle Danube and the Pannonian Plain, a land they transformed into Hungary. They also began receiving Christian missionaries, especially from Saxony, the land and people to which Charlemagne's armies and missionaries had earlier brought Christianity. Ironically, Saxony was now the heart of a revived Western Empire.

The first three Saxon emperors were enthusiastic patrons of this missionary work in Hungary, especially the young and idealistic Otto III (r. 983–1002). Otto III, who variously styled himself as *servant of the Apostles* and *servant of Jesus Christ,* envisioned a Christian empire in which pope and emperor worked harmoniously to create a society permeated by Christian principles. To that end, he appointed to the papacy Gerbert of Aurillac, a monk and the foremost scholar of his day. Gerbert, the first person from the kingdom of France to advance to the papal throne, assumed the name *Sylvester II* (r. 999–1003).

The name was highly significant. The first Sylvester had been bishop of Rome in the time of Constantine the Great, and according to tradition, it was Sylvester I (r. 314–335) who had converted and baptized the Roman emperor. Also according to tradition (and a forged eighth-century document known as *The Donation of Constantine*), Emperor Constantine I had conferred on Pope Sylvester I authority over Rome, Italy, and "the lands of the West," just before he transferred his capital to Constantinople. There was no truth to these legends, although they were almost universally believed in the West. On his part, Otto III dismissed *The Donation of Constantine* as a fraud but probably believed that Sylvester I and Constantine had worked together closely. Therefore, Gerbert's assumption of the name *Sylvester* was a token of his determination to work alongside this latter-day Constantine to create a Christian commonwealth on earth, and that included supporting the empire's missionary activities among the Slavs, Scandinavians, and Magyars.

On their part, the Hungarian leaders, beginning with Duke Géza (r. 972–997), were more than willing to accept Western forms of Christianity, but they wanted no part of German overlordship. As part of his program of welcoming missionaries while keeping Otto's empire at arm's length, Géza's son Vajk (r. 997–1038), who changed his name to *Stephen* (which means "crown" in Greek), submitted his land and people directly to papal overlordship. In return, he was invested as king on Christmas Day, 1000, with a crown sent him by Pope Sylvester II. (Note the parallel with Charlemagne's coronation in 800.) For his successful efforts in converting his people to Catholic Christianity, King Stephen was declared a saint in 1083.

The document that follows is Pope Sylvester's letter of 1000, in which he officially conferred the title of *king* on Stephen. Never before had a pope bestowed a royal title on anyone.

QUESTIONS FOR ANALYSIS

1. What relationship did this letter establish between Hungary and the papacy? What relationship did it establish between the king of Hungary and the pope?
2. What powers and honors did the grant confer on the king?
3. Based on your answers to the preceding questions, what do you conclude were, to Stephen's mind, the benefits to be gained from accepting the crown from the pope? Why you think Pope Sylvester made this grant?

4. Otto III approved the pope's action. What do you think Otto might have had in mind?

5. In the late eleventh century and following, the papacy interpreted Sylvester's granting of a crown as an important precedent. How do you think these later popes viewed the act?

6. Compare King Stephen, Prince Vladimir (source 84), and their respective alliances with Rome and Constantinople. What is similar? What is different? Which strike you as more significant, the similarities or the differences? What do you conclude from your answer?

Sylvester, bishop, servant of the servants of God, to Stephen, king of the Hungarians, greeting and apostolic benediction. Your ambassadors, especially our dear brother, Astricus, bishop of Colocza,[1] were received by us with the greater joy and accomplished their mission with the greater ease, because we had been divinely forewarned to expect an embassy from a nation still unknown to us. . . . Surely, according to the apostle: "It is not of him who wills nor of him who runs, but of God who shows mercy";[2] and according to the testimony of Daniel: "He changes the times and the seasons; he removes kings and sets up kings; he reveals the deep and secret things; he knows what is in the darkness";[3] for in him is that light which, as John teaches, "lights every man who comes into the world."[4] Therefore we first give thanks to God the Father, and to our Lord Jesus Christ, because he has found in our time another David,[5] and has again raised up a man after his own heart to feed his people Israel, that is, the chosen race of the Hungarians. Secondly, we praise you for your piety toward God and for your reverence for this Apostolic See,[6] over which, not by our own merits, but by the mercy of God, we now preside.

Finally, we commend the liberality you have shown in offering to St. Peter yourself and your people and your kingdom and possessions by the same ambassadors and letters. For by this deed you have clearly demonstrated that you already are what you have asked us to declare you.[7] But enough of this; it is not necessary to commend him whom God himself has commended and whose deeds openly proclaim to be worthy of all commendation. Now therefore, glorious son, by the authority of omnipotent God and of St. Peter, the prince of apostles, we freely grant, concede, and bestow with our apostolic benediction all that you have sought from us and from the Apostolic See; namely, the royal crown and name, the creation of the metropolitanate of Gran,[8] and of the other bishoprics.[9] Moreover, we receive under the protection of the holy Church the kingdom which you have surrendered to St. Peter, together with yourself and your people, the Hungarian nation; and we now give it back to you and to your heirs and successors to be held, possessed, ruled, and governed. And your heirs and successors, who shall have been legally elected by the nobles, shall duly offer obedience and reverence to us and to our successors in their own

---

[1]The bishopric of Kalocsa in central Hungary. Stephen transformed it from a bishopric to an archbishopric. A *bishop* was the head of a regional church, whereas an *archbishop* supervised subordinate bishops (see notes 8 and 9).
[2]The Bible, Epistle to the Romans, 9:16.
[3]The Bible, Book of Daniel, 2:21-22.
[4]The Bible, Gospel of John, 1:9.
[5]The king who ruled ancient Israel as its model king from around 1000 to 961 B.C.E.
[6]The Roman papacy.

[7]A king.
[8]The archbishopric (metropolitanate) of Esztergom, called *Gran* in German. Esztergom was Stephen's capital. Its bishop was now, by Sylvester's act, the *primate,* or chief archbishop, of the Hungarian Church. By transforming Esztergom into a primatial archdiocese, Pope Sylvester made Hungary ecclesiastically independent of Germany.
[9]Eleventh-century Hungary had two archbishops and eight *suffragan,* or subordinate, bishops.

persons or by ambassadors, and shall confess themselves the subjects of the Roman Church,[10] who does not hold her subjects as slaves, but receives them all as children. They shall persevere in the catholic faith and the religion of our Lord and Savior Jesus Christ, and strive always to promote it. And because you have fulfilled the office of the apostles in preaching Christ and propagating his faith, and have tried to do in your realm the work of us and of our clergy, and because you have honored the same prince of apostles above all others, therefore by this privilege we grant you and your successors, who shall have been legally elected and approved by the Apostolic See, the right to have the cross borne before you as a sign of apostleship,[11] after you have been crowned with the crown which we send and according to the ceremony which we have committed to your ambassadors. And we likewise give you full power by our apostolic au-

thority to control and manage all the churches of your realm, both present and future, as divine grace may guide you, as representing us and our successors. All these things are contained more fully and explicitly in that general letter which we have sent by our messenger to you and to your nobles and faithful subjects. And we pray that omnipotent God, who called you even from your mother's womb to the kingdom and crown, and who has commanded us to give you the crown which we had prepared for the duke of Poland,[12] may increase continually the fruits of your good works, and sprinkle with the dew of his benediction this young plant of your kingdom, and preserve you and your realm and protect you from all enemies, visible and invisible, and, after the trials of the earthly kingship are past, crown you with an eternal crown in the Kingdom of Heaven.

---

[10]Stephen and his successors have become the pope's nominal vassals and Hungary is their fief, given back to them by the pope. By this act of symbolic submission, Stephen and his heirs gain papal protection.

[11]The kings of Hungary claimed the title *Apostolic King* into the twentieth century.

[12]Duke Boleslaw the Mighty of Poland (r. 992–1025), an active patron of Christian missionary work, desired a royal crown and had reason to believe he would receive it around the year 1000. He remained a ducal vassal of the emperor, however, until 1024, when he finally received his royal crown from the papacy.

A Conflict of Authorities
▼▼▼

89 ▾ *FOUR DOCUMENTS FROM THE INVESTITURE CONTROVERSY*

The *Investiture Controversy,* which raged from 1075 to 1122, was a struggle between the papacy and the Western Empire, an empire that Otto I (known as *the Great*) had recreated in 962 but that essentially encompassed only Germany and northern Italy. The controversy ostensibly centered on the issue of laylords investing high-ranking church leaders with their offices and the symbols of their spiritual powers — in effect, turning them into vassals (source 87). However, the issues were far more complex than that.

The immediate background to the Investiture Controversy lay in successful attempts to free the Roman papacy from the control of local Roman factions and to reform the moral life of the Roman clergy, especially of the pope. Emperor Henry III (r. 1039–1056) played a major role in this reformation from 1046 until his death in 1056. During that decade he appointed four successive reform-minded popes from the ranks of the German clergy. His death at a youthful age and the succession of a child as king of Germany created a power vacuum that allowed more radical clerical reformers to take increasing control of the now reformed papacy. The radicals blamed lay control of the Church and its priests for what they perceived to be the moral degeneracy of Christendom. Their argument was simple: The laity, by virtue of its immersion in the corruption of this world, corrupted clerics whenever and wherever it controlled them, even when the laypeople were pious emperors. The situation was ripe for confrontation when the young Henry IV (r. 1056–1106) came of age and endeavored to assert traditional imperial rights over the Church, and the situation reached a point of crisis when one of the radical reformers, a man named Hildebrand, assumed the papal throne as *Gregory VII* (r. 1073–1085).

The first document, known as the *Dictatus Papae* (*The Pope's Proclamation*), appeared in the official collection of Pope Gregory's correspondence for March 1075 under the title "What Is the Power of the Roman Pontiffs?" It is clearly not a letter. The best informed opinion is that, in the normal course of events, each of the twenty-seven assertions in this list would have been supported by citations from the Bible and other authoritative sources. It was, in other words, the outline of a proposed collection of *canons* (church laws and traditions) that never was published. As sketchy as it is, the document provides good insight into the program and mindset of the papal party as the situation was beginning to heat up but before the controversy became full blown.

The second document is a letter of January 24, 1076, that Henry IV sent to Pope Gregory in response to the pope's letter of December 1075, in which Gregory had warned Henry to fall into line and to obey papal mandates regarding papal attempts to reform the Church or else be ready to suffer the consequences. Henry's reply, which was drafted at a council of imperial church leaders that Henry had convened at Worms, was the opening salvo in what became a half century war of words and swords.

The third document is Gregory's first *excommunication* (exclusion from the Church) and deposition of King Henry in February 1076. With his authority in the empire seriously undermined by this excommunication, Henry performed penance before the pope in January 1077 at the northern Italian fortress of Canossa and was readmitted into the Church, but soon thereafter he fell to quarrelling with the pope again. In March 1080 Gregory declared Henry once again excommunicated and deposed from his royal office.

Gregory's thundering proclamations could not prevent Henry from capturing Rome in 1084 and installing his own antipope. Pope Gregory, however, escaped capture and went into exile south of Rome, where he died, reportedly proclaiming "I have loved Righteousness and hated iniquity, and, therefore, I die in exile." Surely this was the confident cry of triumph of a self-professed martyr.

Gregory's confidence that his position would prevail was not as misplaced as it might first appear. Despite Henry's apparent victory, the controversy dragged on between the papal reform party, which elected its own successor to Gregory VII, and the imperial party and its antipope. Finally, with both sides exhausted, Henry IV's son and successor, Henry V (r. 1106–1125), entered into a peace treaty with

Pope Calixtus II (r. 1119–1124), which history knows as the *Concordat of Worms of 1122*. The concordat, which is our fourth and last document, settled the issue over which the two parties had struggled so bitterly for so long. Or did it?

QUESTIONS FOR ANALYSIS

1. What powers does Gregory claim over other clerics in the *Dictatus Papae?* What powers does he claim over princes?
2. Based on your answers to question 1, what do you conclude was Gregory's vision of the pope's place in Christendom?
3. What charges does Henry IV bring against Pope Gregory VII, and what does Henry do about them?
4. The *Dictatus Papae* and King Henry's letter of January 1076 reveal two views of how the earthly Church functions. What are those views, and how, if at all, do they differ?
5. Consider the tone of Gregory's letter that excommunicates and deposes Henry and its implied world view. What insight does that letter give you into the mind and personality of Pope Gregory?
6. What issues did the Concordat of Worms settle? Were there any important issues that it did not address? All things considered, how successfully did the concordat resolve the basic issues of the Investiture Controversy?
7. Review source 81. Now compose a Byzantine emperor's commentary on these documents.

DICTATUS PAPAE

1. That the Roman church was established by God alone.
2. That the Roman pontiff alone is rightly called universal.[1]
3. That he alone has the power to depose and reinstate bishops.
4. That his legate,[2] even if he be of lower ecclesiastical rank, presides over bishops in council, and has the power to give sentence of deposition against them.
5. That the pope has the power to depose those who are absent.[3]

6. That, among other things, we ought not to remain in the same house with those whom he has excommunicated.
7. That he alone has the right, according to the necessity of the occasion, to make new laws, to create new bishoprics. . . .
8. That he alone may use the imperial insignia.[4]
9. That all princes shall kiss the foot of the pope alone.
10. That his name alone is to be recited in the churches.

---

[1] The term *Roman Pontiff* refers to the pope. This sentence means that the pope alone has universal authority over all churches.
[2] A papal representative who possesses delegated papal power.
[3] From a council. And the pope can do so without giving them a hearing.

[4] A claim based on an eighth-century forgery known as *The Donation of Constantine* (see the introduction to source 88). According to the forged donation, Constantine ceded to Pope Sylvester I the prerogative of wearing all imperial insignia, as well as giving him dominion over Rome, Italy, and all the western regions.

11. That the name applied to him belongs to him alone.[5]
12. That he has the power to depose emperors.
13. That he has the right to transfer bishops from one see[6] to another when it becomes necessary.
14. That he has the right to ordain as a cleric anyone from any part of the church whatsoever.
15. That anyone ordained by him may rule [as bishop] over another church. . . .
16. That no general synod[7] may be called without his order.[8]
17. That no action of a synod and no book shall be regarded as canonical[9] without his authority.
18. That his decree can be annulled by no one, and that he can annul the decrees of anyone.
19. That he can be judged by no one.
20. That no one shall dare to condemn a person who has appealed to the Apostolic See.[10]
21. That the important cases of any church whatsoever shall be referred to the Roman Church.
22. That the Roman Church has never erred and will never err to all eternity, according to the testimony of the holy scriptures.
23. That the Roman pontiff who has been canonically ordained[11] is made holy by the merits of St. Peter. . . .
24. That by his command or permission subjects may accuse their rulers.
25. That he can depose and reinstate bishops without the calling of a synod.

26. That no one can be regarded as catholic who does not agree with the Roman Church.
27. That he has the power to absolve subjects from their oath of fidelity to wicked rulers.

▼ ▼ ▼

THE LETTER OF HENRY IV TO GREGORY VII, JANUARY 24, 1076

Henry, king not by usurpation, but by the holy ordination of God, to Hildebrand, not pope, but false monk.

This is the salutation which you deserve, for you have never held any office in the Church without making it a source of confusion and a curse to Christian men instead of an honor and a blessing. To mention only the most obvious cases out of many, you have not only dared to touch the Lord's anointed, the archbishops, bishops, and priests; but you have scorned them and abused them, as if they were ignorant servants not fit to know what their master was doing. This you have done to gain favor with the vulgar crowd. You have declared that the bishops know nothing and that you know everything; but if you have such great wisdom you have used it not to build but to destroy. Therefore we believe that St. Gregory, whose name you have presumed to take, had you in mind when he said: "The heart of the prelate is puffed up by the abundance of subjects, and he thinks himself more powerful than all others."[12] All this we have endured because of our respect for the papal office, but you have mistaken our humility for fear, and have dared to

---

[5]He alone may bear the title *pope*. By tradition, the patriarch of Alexandria (in Egypt) also bore the title.
[6]The seat, or place of residence and authority, of a bishop.
[7]A general, or *ecumenical,* council (also called a general *synod*), in which high-ranking clerics representing the entire Church meet and settle important matters, especially regarding doctrine. Such councils are considered infallible, because they speak and act under the inspiration of God the Holy Spirit.
[8]Between 325 and 870 eight ecumenical councils convened. Each was held in the East under the authority of the emperor. As far as the Byzantine Church was (and is) con-

cerned, the last ecumenical council met at Constantinople between 869 and 870. The West, however, has another view: In a moment of strength following the Concordat of Worms (see p. 350), the papacy would call its own ecumenical council, the First Lateran Council in 1123.
[9]Legal according to church (canon) law.
[10]The Roman papacy — the bishopric, or *see,* of the Apostle (Peter).
[11]Legally elected and consecrated.
[12]Pope St. Gregory the Great (r. 590–604), *The Pastoral Rule.*

make an attack upon the royal and imperial authority[13] which we received from God. You have even threatened to take it away, as if we had received it from you, and as if the empire and kingdom were in your disposal and not in the disposal of God. Our Lord Jesus Christ has called us to the government of the empire, but he never called you to the rule of the Church. This is the way you have gained advancement in the Church: through craft you have obtained wealth; through wealth you have obtained favor, the power of the sword; and through the power of the sword, the papal seat, which is the seat of peace;[14] and then from the seat of peace you have expelled peace. For you have incited subjects to rebel against their prelates by teaching them to despise the bishops, their rightful rulers. You have given to laymen the authority over priests, whereby they condemn and depose those whom the bishops have put over them to teach them.[15] You have attacked me, who, unworthy as I am, have yet been anointed to rule among the anointed of God, and who, according to the teaching of the fathers, can be judged by no one save God alone, and can be deposed for no crime except infidelity. For the holy fathers in the time of the apostate Julian did not presume to pronounce sentence of deposition against him, but left him to be judged and condemned by God.[16] St. Peter himself said: "Fear God, honor the king" [1 Pet. 2:17]. But you, who fear not God, have dishonored me, whom He has established. St. Paul, who said that even an angel from heaven should be accursed who taught any other than the true doctrine, did not make an exception in your favor, to permit you to teach false doctrines. For he says: "But though we, or an angel from heaven, preach any other gospel unto you than

that which we have preached unto you, let him be accursed" [Gal. 1:8]. Come down, then, from that apostolic seat which you have obtained by violence; for you have been declared accursed by St. Paul for your false doctrines and have been condemned by us and our bishops for your evil rule. Let another ascend the throne of St. Peter, one who will not use religion as a cloak of violence, but will teach the life-giving doctrine of that prince of the apostles. I, Henry, king by the grace of God, with all my bishops, say unto you: "Come down, come down, and be accursed through all the ages."

GREGORY VII'S FIRST EXCOMMUNICATION AND DEPOSITION OF HENRY IV

St. Peter, prince of the apostles, incline your ear to me, I beseech you, and hear me, your servant, whom you have nourished from my infancy and have delivered from my enemies who hate me for my fidelity to you. You are my witness, as are also my mistress, the mother of God, and St. Paul your brother, and all the other saints, that your holy Roman church called me to its government against my own will, and that I did not gain your throne by violence; that I would rather have ended my days in exile than have obtained your place by fraud or for worldly ambition. It is not by my efforts, but by your grace, that I am set to rule over the Christian world which was specially entrusted to you by Christ. It is by your grace and as your representative that God has given to me the power to bind and to loose in heaven and in earth. Confident of my integrity and authority, I now declare in the name of omnipotent God,

---

[13]Actually, Henry had not yet been crowned emperor by the pope. He was only king of Germany and emperor-elect.
[14]Henry claims that Gregory had usurped the papal throne. There had been a slight irregularity when Gregory was elected pope. The people of Rome enthusiastically acclaimed the popular Hildebrand as pope before the cardinals, the official electors, had voted. The cardinals then elected Hildebrand pope, and he assumed the name *Gregory VII.*

[15]A reference to the fact that Gregory and other radical reformers within the papal party had called upon Europe's laity to reject sinful bishops and priests.
[16]A reference to Emperor Julian the Apostate (r. 361–363), who rejected Christianity and attempted to reinstate state worship of the ancient Greco-Roman deities.

the Father, Son, and Holy Spirit, that Henry, son of the emperor Henry, is deprived of his kingdom of Germany and Italy; I do this by your authority and in defense of the honor of your church, because he has rebelled against it. He who attempts to destroy the honor of the Church should be deprived of such honor as he may have held. He has refused to obey as a Christian should, he has not returned to God from whom he had wandered, he has had dealings with excommunicated persons, he has done many iniquities, he has despised the warnings which, as you are witness, I sent to him for his salvation, he has cut himself off from your Church, and has attempted to rend it asunder; therefore, by your authority, I place him under the curse. It is in your name that I curse him, that all people may know that you are Peter, and upon your rock the Son of the living God has built his Church, and the gates of hell shall not prevail against it.

THE CONCORDAT OF WORMS

The Oath of Calixtus II

Calixtus, bishop, servant of the servants of God, to his beloved son, Henry, by the grace of God emperor of the Romans,[17] Augustus.

We hereby grant that in Germany the elections of the bishops and abbots who hold directly from the crown shall be held in your presence, such elections to be conducted canonically and without simony[18] or other illegality. In the case of disputed elections you shall have the right to decide between the parties, after consulting with the archbishop of the province and his fellow-bishops. You shall confer the regalia[19] of the office upon the bishop or abbot elect by the scepter,[20] and this shall be done freely without exacting any payment from him; the bishop or abbot elect on his part shall perform all the duties that go with the holding of the regalia.

In other parts of the empire the bishops shall receive the regalia from you in the same manner within six months of their consecration, and shall in like manner perform all the duties that go with them. The undoubted rights of the Roman Church, however, are not to be regarded as prejudiced by this concession. If at any time you shall have occasion to complain of the carrying out of these provisions, I will undertake to satisfy your grievances as far as shall be consistent with my office. Finally, I hereby make a true and lasting peace with you and with all of your followers, including those who supported you in the recent controversy.

The Oath of Henry V

In the name of the holy and undivided Trinity.

For the love of God and his holy church and of Pope Calixtus, and for the salvation of my soul, I, Henry, by the grace of God, emperor of the Romans, Augustus, hereby surrender to God and his apostles, Sts. Peter and Paul, and to the holy Catholic Church, all investiture by ring and staff.[21] I agree that elections and consecrations shall be conducted canonically and shall be free from all interference. I surrender also the possessions and regalia of St. Peter which have been seized by me during this quarrel, or by my father in his lifetime, and which are now in my possession, and I promise to aid the Church to recover such as are held by any other persons. I restore also the possessions of all other churches and princes, clerical or secular, which have been taken away during the course of this quarrel, which I have, and promise to aid them to recover such as are held by any other persons.

Finally, I make true and lasting peace with Pope Calixtus and with the holy Roman Church and with all who are or have ever been of his party. I will aid the Roman Church whenever my help is asked, and will do justice in all matters in regard to which the Church may have occasion to make complaint.

---

[17]Pope Paschal II had crowned Henry V as emperor in 1111 during a time of momentary accord.
[18]The sin of buying or selling anything sacred, including a priestly office.
[19]Delegated royal powers.

[20]The emperor (or king of Germany) could invest the new *prelate* (literally, "one set before," therefore, a high-ranking cleric) with secular powers by touching him (or her, in the case of an imperial abbess) with the imperial scepter.
[21]The symbols of a prelate's office.

The Merchants of Southampton

▼▼▼

90 ▼ *ORDINANCES OF THE MERCHANT GUILD OF SOUTHAMPTON*

One constant refrain among Western European visitors to Constantinople was that no one back home could imagine the city's magnitude and splendor. This was no exaggeration for much of the period from 330 to 1453. During the reign of Basil II, Constantinople probably had a million inhabitants, and it numbered about four hundred thousand dwellers around 1200, despite a period of economic recession. By comparison, Western Europe in 1200 had quite a few towns, but their populations were modest. Most could boast only three to six thousand inhabitants. Most of Europe's cities were also small by eastern Mediterranean standards. Europe had maybe twenty cities that could each claim about twenty-five to fifty thousand people and probably fewer than a dozen larger cities, such as Milan and Paris, with populations of fifty to one hundred thousand. Certainly no European city could rival Constantinople for sheer wealth, size, or grandeur.

Size and raw wealth, however, were not the whole story. The period from roughly 1050 to about 1300 was one of rapid growth and prosperity for Western Europe. This age witnessed an urban explosion, in which numerous towns and small cities sprang up, often in areas that had recently been forest or marginal land. These new urban settings served as centers of vibrant trade, industry, learning, and religious change. And those who dwelt in them, the *bourgeoisie*, became one of the West's major dynamic forces, despite their relatively small numbers.

Towns and townspeople served as effective counterweights to the feudal nobility. While early medieval society usually saw its members engaged in three primary tasks — prayer, fighting, and agricultural labor — European society from the eleventh century onward fostered an emerging class of free men and women who, unhampered by the servile bonds of serfdom, were employed in commerce and production. These bourgeoisie were not only personally free but also enjoyed a large measure of self-government. At the very least, a town would secure from the local lord or king a *charter of liberties,* which limited the extent to which any external authority could intervene in its fiscal, political, and judicial affairs. Indeed, some towns and cities, especially in northern Italy, went further and became independent of all outside control. For example, while contemporary Song China's prosperous and far more numerous urban dwellers also possessed personal freedom, their cities were not self-governing but were instead centers of imperial administration. It was only in far less developed Europe that cities and towns, of modest size by Asian standards, achieved a degree of corporate independence, thereby challenging successfully the dominance of Europe's landed feudal nobility.

In the mid twelfth century, Southampton, a port town on England's southeast shore, became part of a major trading network. Carrying prime English wool to French markets, Southampton's merchants returned with agricultural products, especially western France's wines. Sailing northeast to the textile centers of the

Low Countries (modern Belgium), Southampton's merchants exchanged wool for manufactured cloth and a wide variety of luxury goods.

Southampton's profitable commerce became the impetus for the rise to power of its *guild* (professional association) of merchants, which took the lead in securing from the king the town's charter of limited self-government. The following document, which lists the rules of Southampton's merchant guild, reflects the inner workings and power of a fairly typical late-thirteenth-century guild of merchants.

QUESTIONS FOR ANALYSIS

1. How did the guild regulate entry into its membership? Why do you think it did so? How did the guild protect its members?
2. How did the guild regulate trade? Why do you think it did so?
3. Consider items 13, 14, 16, and 22. What police and judicial powers does the guild claim over nonmembers? What do you infer from your answer?
4. Consider items 1, 27, 32, and 35. By what right does the guild mandate the type of officers who will govern Southampton, their duties, and the manner in which municipal elections will be held? Who do you think serves as the borough's chief alderman? Why have you reached that conclusion?
5. What do your answers to the above questions suggest about the guild's power and place in the community?
6. Compare this charter with *The Book of the Eparch* (source 83). Each regulates economic activity, but they do so in different ways. How do they differ? What do those differences suggest about their respective economic, social, and political environments?

1. In the first place, there shall be elected from the merchant guild, and established, an alderman,[1] a steward,[2] a chaplain,[3] four skevins,[4] and an usher.[5] And it is to be known that whosoever shall be alderman shall receive from each one entering into the guild fourpence,[6] the steward, twopence; the chaplain, twopence; and the usher, one penny. And the guild shall meet twice a year: that is to say, on the Sunday next after St. John the Baptist's day,[7] and on the Sunday next after St. Mary's day.[8] . . .

9. And when a guildsman dies, his eldest son or his next heir shall have the seat of his father, or of his uncle, if his father was not a guildsman, and of no other one; and he shall give nothing for his seat. No husband can have a seat in the guild by right of his wife, nor demand a seat by right of his wife's ancestors.

10. And no one has the right or power to sell or give his seat in the guild to any man; and the son of a guildsman, other than his eldest son, shall enter into the guild on payment of

---

[1]Literally, "the senior man."
[2]The official in charge of the guild's property.
[3]A priest.
[4]Attendants. Originally, they had minor functions, but they evolved into a body of four elders.

[5]The doorkeeper and sergeant-at-arms.
[6]Two hundred forty pence make one pound sterling.
[7]June 24.
[8]December 8.

ten shillings,[9] and he shall take the oath of the guild.

11. And if a guildsman shall be imprisoned in England in time of peace, the alderman with the steward and with one of the skevins shall go, at the cost of the guild, to procure the deliverance of the one who is in prison.

12. And if any guildsman strikes another with his fist and is convicted thereof, he shall lose the guild until he shall have bought it back for ten shillings, and taken the oath of the guild again like a new member. And if a guildsman strikes another with a stick, or a knife, or any other weapon, whatever it may be, he shall lose the guild and the franchise,[10] and shall be held as a stranger until he shall have been reconciled to the good men of the guild and has made recompense to the one whom he has injured, and has paid a fine to the guild of twenty shillings;[11] and this shall not be remitted.

13. If any one does an injury, who is not of the guild, and is of the franchise[12] or strikes a guildsman and is reasonably convicted, he shall lose his franchise and go to prison for a day and a night.

14. And if any stranger or any other who is not of the guild nor of the franchise strikes a guildsman, and is reasonably convicted thereof, let him be in prison two days and two nights, unless the injury is such that he should be more severely punished.

15. And if a guildsman reviles or slanders another guildsman, and a complaint of it comes to the alderman, and if he is reasonably convicted thereof, he shall pay two shillings fine to the guild, and if he is not able to pay he shall lose the guild.

16. And if anyone who is of the franchise speaks evil of a guildsman, and is convicted of

this before the alderman, he shall pay five shillings for a fine or lose the franchise.

17. And no one shall come to the council of the guild if he is not a guildsman. . . .

19. And no one of the city of Southampton shall buy anything to sell again in the same city, unless he is of the merchant guild or of the franchise. And if anyone shall do so and is convicted of it, all which he has so bought shall be forfeited to the king; and no one shall be quit of custom unless he proves that he is in the guild or in the franchise, and this from year to year.

20. And no one shall buy honey, fat, salt herrings, or any kind of oil, or millstones, or fresh hides, or any kind of fresh skins, unless he is a guildsman: nor keep a tavern for wine, nor sell cloth at retail, except in market or fair days;[13] nor keep grain in his granary beyond five quarters, to sell at retail, if he is not a guildsman; and whoever shall do this and be convicted shall forfeit all to the king. . . .

22. If any guildsman falls into poverty and has not the wherewithal to live, and is not able to work or to provide for himself, he shall have one mark[14] from the guild to relieve his condition when the guild shall sit.[15] No one of the guild nor of the franchise shall claim another's goods for his by which the custom of the city shall be injured. And if any one does so and is convicted, he shall lose the guild and the franchise; and the merchandise so claimed shall be forfeited to the king. . . .

24. And anyone who is of the merchant guild shall share in all merchandise which another guildsman shall buy or any other person, whosoever he is, if he comes and demands part and is there where the merchandise is bought, and also if he gives satisfaction to the seller and gives security for his part. But no one who is not a guilds-

---

[9]Twelve pence (note 6) make one shilling, and ten shillings constitute one-half pound sterling.

[10]Membership in the borough. From an Old French term meaning "endowed with freedom."

[11]One pound sterling (see notes 6 and 9).

[12]A *burgess,* or town member, of Southampton (see note 10).

[13]Weekly or twice-weekly market days were when farmers and fishermen brought food into the town for sale. Fairs were seasonal and substantially larger markets, at which foreign merchants were welcome.

[14]One-half pound of silver; it could support an early thirteenth-century family modestly for about half a year.

[15]Its semiannual meetings (see article 1).

man is able or ought to share with a guildsman, without the will of the guildsman.

25. And if any guildsman or other of the city refuse a part to the guildsman in the manner above said, he[16] shall not buy or sell in that year in the town, except his food. . . .

27. It is provided that the chief alderman of the town, or the bailiffs[17] and the twelve sworn men,[18] shall give attention to the merchants as well strangers as private men, as often as it shall be required, to see that they have sufficient security for their debts, and recognizance[19] from their debtors; and the day of this shall be enrolled before them, so that if the day is not kept, on proof by the creditor, the debtor should be then distrained[20] according to the recognizance which he has made, in lands and chattels, to give satisfaction according to the usage of the town, without any manner of pleading, so that the men of the town should not have damage by the default of payment of the debtors aforesaid.

28. And if any guildsman for any debt which he may owe will not suffer himself to be distrained, or when he has been distrained, shall break through, or make removal or break the king's lock,[21] and be convicted thereof, he shall lose his guildship until he has bought it again for twenty shillings, and this each time that he offends in such manner. And he shall be none the less distrained until he has made satisfaction for the debt he owes; and if he will not submit to justice as aforesaid and be thereof convicted, he shall go to prison for a day and a night like one who is against the peace; and if he will not submit to justice let the matter be laid before the king and his council in manner aforesaid. . . .

32. Every year, on the morrow of St. Michael,[22] shall be elected by the whole community of the town, assembled in a place provided, to consider the estate and treat of the common business of the town — then shall be elected by the whole community, twelve discreet men to execute the king's commands, together with the bailiffs, and to keep the peace and protect the franchise, and to do and keep justice to all persons, as well poor as rich, natives or strangers, all that year; and to this they shall be sworn in the form provided. And these twelve discreet men shall choose the same day two discreet men from among themselves and the other profitable and wise men to be bailiffs for the ensuing year, who shall take care that the customs shall be well paid; and they shall receive their jurisdiction the day after Michaelmas, as has been customary. And this shall be done from year to year, so that the bailiffs shall be renewed every year, and the twelve aforesaid, if there is occasion. The same shall be done as to clerk and sergeants of the city, in making and removing. . . .

35. The common chest[23] shall be in the house of the chief alderman or of the steward, and the three keys of it shall be lodged with three discreet men of the aforesaid twelve sworn men, or with three of the skevins, who shall loyally take care of the common seal, and the charters and the treasure of the town, and the standards, and other muniments of the town; and no letter shall be sealed with the common seal, nor any charter taken out of the common-chest but in the presence of six or twelve sworn men, and of the alderman or steward; and nobody shall sell by any kind of measure or weight that it is not sealed, under forfeiture of two shillings. . . .

---

[16]The person who refused to share.
[17]Officers of the town who maintained law and order; supervised markets, weights, and measures; registered debts; and kept customs and tax records (see article 32).
[18]See article 32.
[19]An obligation of record that is entered into before a magistrate or judge and often secured with a bond (a pledge of money or goods to guarantee performance).
[20]Compelled.
[21]The royal seal on his goods that have been taken as security.
[22]September 30, the day after the feast of St. Michael.
[23]Of the borough.

Byzantium and the West: The Dividing of Christendom

Many history textbooks continue to perpetuate the myth that the Churches of Constantinople and Rome entered into clear and permanent *schism,* or separation, in 1054, when the patriarch of Constantinople and representatives of the pope hurled mutual curses of damnation and excommunication at one another's church. In fact, nothing of the sort happened. It is true that, following a heated argument, several papal envoys laid a sentence of excommunication on the patriarch and his supporters. But they did so on their own initiative, and their attack was largely aimed at one man — Patriarch Michael Cerularius. It is also true that Byzantine church officials responded in kind by excommunicating the offending Western churchmen. But the Byzantine Church officially refused to believe that the legates were true representatives of the pope or the Western Church. The point is that this celebrated incident of 1054 was not the *cause* of a visible rift between these two branches of Christendom. It was, however, one of many *symptoms* of a growing alienation between the two Christian cultures.

The factors that led to the division between the Churches of Catholic Rome and Orthodox Constantinople were rooted in centuries of political separation and cultural estrangement. The process began as early as the fourth century and accelerated as time went on. Not until the latter half of the eleventh century, however, when the reformed papacy promoted its agenda of transforming Christian society under its own leadership, did the differences between the Byzantine and Western visions of the world and the Church begin to become apparent.

One expression of the new papal self-confidence was its attempt to marshal the military vigor of the West in a series of holy wars known as the *crusades.* As early as 1074 news of Seljuk Turkish victories over Byzantine forces moved Pope Gregory VII to propose publicly that he lead an army of fifty thousand volunteers to rescue these Christian siblings in the East. The Investiture Controversy prevented him from realizing this dream, but the reformed papacy never forgot the project. His successor once removed, Pope Urban II (r. 1088–1099), responded to overtures from Emperor Alexius I (r. 1081–1118) for help in raising troops for the Byzantine army by calling upon the warrior class of the West, and especially of the pope's own French homeland, to march eastward to rescue their fellow Christians from Islam and to liberate Jerusalem from the infidel. The pope's appeal, which he enunciated for the first time on November 27, 1095, provided the impetus for the First Crusade (1096–1101).

By transforming this simple request from Emperor Alexius for assistance in raising mercenary soldiers for the imperial army into a call for a mass expedition of holy warriors, Pope Urban unleashed the vigor of emerging Europe upon an unsuspecting eastern Mediterranean world. In all probability, the pope believed that by succoring the Christians of the East, the crusaders would help heal the religious differences between Byzantium and the West — differences that were becoming increasingly apparent to both parties by this time. In an act of ultimate Christian charity — putting their lives at risk for fellow Christians — the crusaders (the very name means "cross bearers") would usher in a new age of harmony and peace. At least, that was the dream. As the following two sources suggest, however, the crusaders brought not peace but a sword. And that sword severed Christendom.

The West and the First Crusade from a Byzantine Perspective

▼▼▼

91 ▼ Anna Comnena, THE ALEXIAD

The response to Urban's idealistic appeal was astounding. Between 1096 and 1101 three major waves of crusaders left Europe for the Holy Land; altogether, maybe as many as one hundred thirty thousand men, women, and children participated, of whom probably only about ten percent were professional warriors. Urban set in motion a phenomenon that was to engage much of Europe's energy for the next several centuries and would touch all levels of European society. What is more, the crusades would have a profound impact on the immediate and long-range histories of Islam, Byzantium, and ultimately the world. Arguably, their effects are still being felt today.

The following document, which reflects a twelfth-century Byzantine view of Western Europe and its crusaders, comes from the pen of Anna Comnena (1083–after 1148), daughter of Emperor Alexius I. Anna, who had received an extensive education in classical Greek literature and thought, undertook to write the history of her father's eventful reign following the death of her husband in 1137. The fact that she entitled the work the *Alexiad,* in imitation of Homer's epic poem the *Iliad,* clearly indicates the view she held of her father's place in history. Anna's protestations of historical objectivity notwithstanding, this is partisan history, but its very partisanship allows us to see the world through Byzantine eyes.

In the first selection Anna comments on the Investiture Controversy (source 89), a struggle that provided the domestic background to the First Crusade. Although it was much more than just an instance of papal muscle flexing, on one important level Urban's call for the First Crusade was an assertion of papal moral supremacy over Emperor Henry IV, with whom the pope was locked in ideological battle. The second selection deals with the arrival on Byzantine soil in 1096 of the lead elements of the First Crusade.

QUESTIONS FOR ANALYSIS

1. What does Anna Comnena think of Pope Gregory VII's actions in the Investiture Controversy?

2. What does she think of the Roman papacy's claims?
3. To her mind, who is the Church's chief priest, and what is the source of his authority?
4. Compose her commentary on the first three documents from the Investiture Controversy in source 89.
5. What was Princess Anna's view of the Western crusaders?
6. The age of the crusades witnessed a growing estrangement between the societies of Western Europe and Byzantium. Judging from Anna's account, what do you think contributed to that rift?

Meanwhile, an event occurred which is worth relating, as it, too, contributed to this man's [Emperor Alexius] reputation and good fortune. . . . Now it happened that the pope of Rome[1] had a difference with Henry, king of Germany.[2] . . . The pope is a very high dignitary, and is protected by troops of various nationalities. The dispute between the king and the pope was this: the latter accused Henry of not bestowing livings[3] as free gifts, but selling them for money,[4] and occasionally entrusting archbishoprics to unworthy recipients,[5] and he also brought further charges of a similar nature against him. The king of Germany on his side indicted the pope of usurpation, as he had seized the apostolic chair without his consent.[6] Moreover, he had the effrontery to utter reckless threats against the pope, saying that if he did not resign his self-elected office, he should be expelled from it. . . . When these words reached the pope's ears, he vented his rage upon Henry's ambassadors; first he tortured them inhumanly, then clipped their hair with scissors, and sheared their beards with a razor, and finally committed a most indecent outrage upon them,

which transcended even the insolence of barbarians, and so sent them away. My womanly and princely dignity forbids my naming the outrage inflicted on them, for it was not only unworthy a high priest, but of anyone who bears the name of a Christian. I abhor this barbarian's idea, and more still the deed, and I should have defiled both my pen and my paper had I described it explicitly.[7] But as a display of barbaric insolence, and a proof that time in its flow produces men with shameless morals, ripe for any wickedness, this alone will suffice, if I say, that I could not bear to disclose or relate even the tiniest word about what he did. And this was the work of a high priest. Oh, justice! The deed of the supreme high priest! nay, of one who claimed to be the president of the whole world, as indeed the Latins assert and believe, but this, too, is a bit of their boasting. For when the imperial seat was transferred from Rome hither to our native Queen of Cities, and the senate, and the whole administration, there was also transferred the arch-hieratical primacy.[8] And the emperors from the very beginning have given the supreme right

---

[1]Pope Gregory VII.
[2]Henry IV. As king of Germany, Henry was also emperor-elect of the Western Roman Empire.
[3]A *living*, also known as a *prebend,* was the income a cleric received to support him in his clerical office and duties.
[4]The papacy claimed that lay rulers, such as Henry, were guilty of the sin of *simony* — the selling of sacred clerical offices and other holy items.
[5]According to the papal reformers, this was another abuse of the system known as *lay investiture,* and some radical reformers, such as Gregory VII, called upon pious laypeople to throw out unworthy clerics who had been invested in their offices by lay rulers. (Review source 89, especially note 15.)

[6]See source 89, note 14. By tradition, the pope-elect applied for imperial approval of his election.
[7]Anna seems to imply that Gregory had the envoys castrated. There is no credible evidence of his having abused Henry's legates in this manner.
[8]Chief *patriarch* of the universal Church (see note 9).

to the episcopacy[9] of Constantinople, and the Council of Chalcedon emphatically raised the bishop of Constantinople to the highest position, and placed all the dioceses of the inhabited world under his jurisdiction.[10] There can be no doubt that the insult done to the ambassadors was aimed at the king who sent them; not only because he scourged them, but also because he was the first to invent this new kind of outrage. For by his actions, the pope suggested, I think, that the power of the king was despicable, and by this horrible outrage on his ambassadors that he, a demi-god, as it were, was treating with a demi-ass! The pope consequently, by wreaking his insolence on the ambassadors, and sending them back to the king in the state I have mentioned, provoked a very great war.

▾ ▾ ▾

Before he[11] had enjoyed even a short rest, he heard a report of the approach of innumerable Frankish[12] armies. Now he dreaded their arrival for he knew their irresistible manner of attack, their unstable and mobile character and all the peculiar natural and concomitant characteristics which the Frank retains throughout; and he also knew that they were always agape for money, and seemed to disregard their truces readily for any reason that cropped up. For he had always heard this reported of them, and found it very true. However, he did not lose heart, but prepared himself in every way so that, when the occasion called, he would be ready for battle. And indeed the actual facts were far greater and more terrible than rumor made them. For the whole of the West and all the barbarian tribes which dwell between the further side of the Adriatic and the pillars of Heracles,[13] had all migrated in a body and were marching into Asia through the intervening Europe, and were making the journey with all their household. . . . And they were all so zealous and eager that every highroad was full of them. And those Frankish soldiers were accompanied by an unarmed host more numerous than the sand or the stars, carrying palms and crosses on their shoulders; women and children, too, came away from their countries.[14] And the sight of them was like many rivers streaming from all sides, and they were advancing towards us through Dacia[15] generally with all their hosts. . . .

The incidents of the barbarians approach followed in the order I have described, and persons of intelligence could feel that they were witnessing a strange occurrence. The arrival of these multitudes did not take place at the same time nor by the same road (for how indeed could such masses starting from different places have crossed the straits of Lombardy all together?). Some first, some next, others after them and thus successively all accomplished the transit, and then marched through the continent. Each army was preceded, as we said, by an unspeakable number of locusts; and all who saw this more than once recognized them as forerunners of the Frankish armies.

---

[9]Another term for *bishopric*. A *bishop* was the chief priest of a city or large town and its surrounding lands. An *archbishop* was the bishop of a major city and exercised authority over a number of subordinate, or suffragan, bishops. A *patriarch* was the bishop of such an exceptionally important city that he claimed authority over vast areas and large numbers of subordinate archbishops and bishops. The question was, Who was the chief patriarch of the Church — the bishop of Rome or the bishop of Constantinople?

[10]Wrong. The Ecumenical Council of Chalcedon of 451 (see source 89, notes 7 and 8, for a definition of *ecumenical council*) stipulated in canon (regulation) 28 that the bishop of Constantinople enjoyed a primacy of honor second only to that of the bishop of Rome because Constantinople was the *New Rome*.

[11]Emperor Alexius.

[12]*Frank* was a term used in the eastern Mediterranean to refer to any Westerner (see Chapter 9, source 76).

[13]The Strait of Gibraltar.

[14]This, the first wave of the crusade, was the so-called (and misnamed) *Peasants' Crusade of 1096*.

[15]Hungary and Romania.

Byzantium and the Fourth Crusade from a Western Perspective

▼▼▼

92 ▼ *Gunther of Pairis,* *A CONSTANTINOPOLITAN HISTORY*

As Anna Comnena's account suggests, from the Byzantine perspective the crusades were nothing less than barbarian invasions from the West. Before the First Crusade ended, Latin and Greek Christians had already clashed on the field of battle, although these initial skirmishes were not terribly serious (except to the people who died in them). During the twelfth century, as Latin fortunes suffered a number of reverses in the Holy Land, two additional major crusades were sent eastward: the Second Crusade (1147–1149) and the Third Crusade (1189–1192). Each further exacerbated Latin-Byzantine relations by engendering increasingly sharp conflicts and misunderstandings.

Following the Muslim recapture of Jerusalem in 1187 and the failure of the Third Crusade to retake the holy city, the West was eager to strike back at Islam. In the early thirteenth century a force made up largely of French warriors and Venetian sailors planned to strike at Islam by capturing Alexandria in Egypt, thereby relieving pressure on the embattled Latin settlements in the Holy Land. That particular assault never took place. Rather, circumstances led the army and fleet of the Fourth Crusade (1202–1204) to Constantinople, where the crusaders became embroiled in a dynastic power struggle between rival imperial claimants. Eventually the crusaders attacked Constantinople on April 12, 1204, and captured it the following day. After three days of brutal looting, the crusaders settled down and established the Latin Empire of Constantinople (1204–1261).

The Byzantines regained their capital city in 1261, but their empire was by then largely a shadow of its former self. Just as significant, the events of 1204 caused the final and, until today, irreconcilable rupture between the Roman Catholic and Eastern Orthodox branches of Christianity.

One of the participants in the April 1204 looting of Constantinople was Martin, abbot of the Cistercian monastery of Pairis, which was located in the Vosges mountains of German-speaking Alsace. Upon his return to Pairis in 1205, Martin commissioned one of the monastery's brothers, Gunther, to compose an account of the abbot's adventures on the crusade. Gunther (ca. 1150?–after 1210?), already an accomplished scholar and poet, took this opportunity to construct the *Hystoria Constantinopolitana* (*A Constantinopolitan History*), a masterpiece of artfully intermingled prose and poetry, written to reveal the ways of God to humanity.

In the following two selections Gunther uses prose and poetry to pass judgment on Constantinople, to explain the reasons, both human and divine, behind the crusaders' decision to travel to that city in 1203, and to justify the assault of April 1204. The first selection appears at midpoint in Gunther's history; here, at the pivotal moment in his story, the author stops to reflect on the meaning of what is about to unfold. The second selection serves as a poetic explanation of why and how the crusaders attacked the Christian city of Constantinople.

QUESTIONS FOR ANALYSIS

1. According to Gunther, do either the crusaders or God hate the Byzantines or wish to destroy them? Please explain your answer.
2. According to Gunther, why did God will the crusader capture of Constantinople?
3. Based on your answers to questions 1 and 2, what do you conclude was Gunther's attitude toward Greek Christians? Please explain your answer.
4. According to Gunther, in what ways were the crusaders' motives to go to Constantinople a mixture of piety and greed? What does this suggest about crusader motives in general? Does Gunther judge them severely for this? Again, please explain your answer.
5. Elsewhere in her *Alexiad,* Anna Comnena characterizes the Western crusaders as unstable, greedy for money, and always ready to break their word. Compose her commentary on Gunther's history.
6. What do the excerpts from Anna Comnena and Gunther of Pairis suggest about relations between these two Christian cultures in the age of the crusades? What attitudes and beliefs separated them?

Now the series of events which had led our people to this constraining crisis[1] can be condensed as follows. When the royal youth Alexius (as was mentioned above)[2] came to the encampment accompanied by messengers and a letter from King Philip[3] and after he had deeply moved the princes of our army through his personal entreaties and extravagant promises, everyone gradually began, as we said, to lean in his favor and toward support of his case. This tendency was encouraged by various factors: first, out of consideration for the influence of King Philip, who was imploring our people so urgently on his behalf; next, because it seemed to them right (if they could effect it) to restore the kingdom's legitimate heir to his throne, from which he had been cruelly deposed; then also because of the youth's entreaties and his promises that, if he were restored, he would be able, both then and afterward, to offer significant assistance to all pilgrims.[4] Moreover, it helped that they knew that this very city was rebellious and offensive to the Holy Roman

---

[1]The crisis that forced the crusaders to attack Constantinople in April 1204.

[2]Prince Alexius Angelos sought help in the West to restore his deposed father, Isaac II (r. 1185–1195 and 1203). Isaac had been deposed, blinded, and imprisoned by his brother, the current emperor, Alexius III (r. 1195–1203). When the crusade army restored Isaac to the throne in 1203, the crusaders insisted that Prince Alexius be made coemperor. Alexius IV (r. 1203–1204) was killed in an anticrusader palace coup, and his death precipitated the eventual April attack on the city.

[3]Philip of Swabia, king of Germany (r. 1197–1208), was Prince Alexius's brother-in-law and supported the young man's overtures to the crusade army for help.

[4]A *pilgrim* is someone who undertakes a religious journey (*pilgrimage*) to a sacred place. Usually this is done for penitential reasons (see Chapter 8, source 62). Crusaders were considered to be pilgrims of a special sort — armed pilgrims who were atoning for their sins by journeying to and liberating Jerusalem — and they enjoyed all of the special privileges the Church accorded pilgrims.

Church,[5] and they did not think its conquest by our people would displease very much either the supreme pontiff[6] or even God. Also, the Venetians, whose fleet they were using, were particularly urging it, partly in hope of the promised money (for which that race is extremely greedy) and partly because their city, supported by a large navy, was, in fact, arrogating to itself sovereign mastery over that entire sea. Through the union of all of these factors and, perhaps, of others, it happened that all unanimously found in favor of the young man and promised him their aid.

Yet there was also, we believe, another far older and more powerful reason than all of these, namely, the decision of Divine Goodness, which so arranged, through this pattern of events, that this people, proud because of its wealth, should be humbled by their very pride and recalled to the peace and concord of the Holy Catholic Church. It certainly seemed proper that this people, which otherwise could not be corrected, should be punished by the death of a few[7] and the loss of those temporal goods with which it had puffed itself up; that a pilgrim people should grow rich on spoils from the rich and the entire land pass into our power; and that the Western Church, illuminated by the inviolable relics of which these people had shown themselves unworthy, should rejoice forever.[8] It is, in any case, significant that the oft-mentioned city, which had always been faithless to pilgrims,[9] following (by God's will) a change of citizenry, will remain faithful and supportive and render us aid in fighting the barbarians and in capturing and holding the Holy Land — an aid that is more significant because of its closer proximity. Anyway, all of these matters would be unsettled had that people been conquered by persons of another faith, heathen or heretic, or (what would have been most disastrous) had it been forced to convert to their error. Therefore, I believe these considerations, surely hidden from us, yet manifest to Him who foresees all, were of utmost importance to God. It was because of them that those monumental and miraculous events, of which we shall speak, were conducted to their outcome along a fixed but secret path.

▾ ▾ ▾

Break in! Now, honored soldier of Christ,
　Break in!
Break into the city which Christ has given to
　the conqueror.
Imagine for yourself Christ, seated on a
　gentle ass,[10]
The King of Peace, radiant in countenance,
　leading the way.
You fight Christ's battles. You execute Christ's
　vengeance,
By Christ's judgment. His will precedes your
　onslaught.
Break in! Rout menaces; crush cowards; press
　on more bravely;

---

[5]From the Western perspective, the Greek Church had broken away from obedience to papal authority. From the Byzantine perspective, the pope claimed powers that rightly belonged to the entire Church, which was guided by the Orthodox emperor and the community of all right-believing bishops.

[6]Pope Innocent III (r. 1198–1216). Pope Innocent had forbidden the diversion to Constantinople because he feared the crusade army would be destroyed in the process, and he also did not want to see the blood of Greek Christians shed. However, the crusader leaders knew he was no admirer of Byzantium. Even while he was telling representatives from the crusade army that the army must not go to Constantinople, the pope expressed the sentiment that he wished the city could be captured without bloodshed by some Catholic (Western Christian) people.

[7]Gunther maintains, wrongly, that only a handful of Greeks died in the battles of April 1204.

[8]Among the objects seized in the sack of the city, the holy relics of the saints and especially of Jesus (such as his Shroud, or burial cloth) were highly prized. Abbot Martin piously looted a church and brought home a treasure trove of relics, which Gunther ironically referred to as "the spoils of sacred sacrilege."

[9]From the Western perspective, Constantinople had worked actively to ruin the Second and Third Crusades. In fact, the Byzantines had little sympathy for the crusades or the crusaders.

[10]According to the Gospels of Matthew, Mark, and Luke, Jesus entered Jerusalem in triumph seated on a donkey. Christians commemorate this event on Palm Sunday, the Sunday preceding Easter.

Shout in thundering voice; brandish iron, but
  spare the blood.
Instill terror, yet remember they are brothers.
Whom you overwhelm, who by their guilt
  have merited it for sometime.
Christ wished to enrich you with the
  wrongdoers' spoils,
Lest some other conquering people despoil
  them.
Behold, homes lie open, filled with enemy
  riches,
And an ancient hoard will have new masters.

Yet you, meanwhile, curbing heart and hand,
Postpone and disdain the pillage of goods until
  the right moment!
Throw yourself on the timorous; press firmly
  upon the conquered;
Do not allow the fatigued to recover and
  regain strength.
Immediately upon the enemy's expulsion from
  the entire city,
There will be time for looting; it will be
  proper to despoil the conquered.

Chapter 11

▼▼▼

Africa and the Americas

As we saw in Chapter 5, toward the end of the first century B.C.E. the dominant civilizations of Eurasia and North Africa were loosely linked through a series of trade networks and imperialistic adventures. The result was the first Afro-Eurasian Ecumene, or universal community, whose heyday extended down to about 200 C.E. The term itself is somewhat misleading, however, because most of Africa south of the Sahara Desert lay outside of this first ecumene of the so-called Old World, as Strabo's *Geography* (Chapter 5, source 32) showed.

The cultures of the so-called New World — the Americas — also did not participate in that first age of Afro-Eurasian linkage, nor in the second, which peaked between 1250 and 1350 (Chapter 12). A few adventurers and lost sailors from Africa and Eurasia undoubtedly stumbled across the lands of America prior to 1492, as was the case with a handful of Vikings who set up a short-lived colony in northern Newfoundland around 1000 C.E. Nevertheless, there is no convincing evidence that these occasional visitors established any meaningful links between the Americas and the outside world, nor is there reason to believe that they had any substantial impact on the development of Amerindian cultures. Prior to the late fifteenth century C.E., the American peoples developed their societies and civilizations in essential isolation from the lands that lay across the Pacific and Atlantic Oceans. Isolated though they might have been from the rest of the world, most Amerindian peoples were linked, although loosely, in an American Ecumene that made possible the spread of goods and cultural influences over vast expanses. Maize, for example, initially domesticated as early as 4000 B.C.E. in the highlands of central Mexico, had spread to Peru by 2000 B.C.E. and Canada by 1000 C.E.

Sub-Saharan Africa also had its early cultural and trade networks, which made possible a widespread diffusion of such technologies as agriculture and iron metallurgy and such ideas as the faith of Islam. Moreover, despite the continued growth of the Sahara Desert from around 2500 B.C.E. to the present, interior Africa has never been totally cut off from the rest of the Afro-Eurasian World, even in the most ancient times. However, the volume of traffic across the Sahara only began to achieve significant proportions after the introduction into North Africa of the Arabian, or single-humped, camel as a beast of burden during the early centuries C.E., ironically just as the first Afro-Eurasian Ecumene was beginning to break down due to crises in China and the Roman Empire. Conquest of western North Africa by Muslim Arabs in the seventh century provided another major boost to trans-Saharan trade, so that by about the year 1000 four major commercial routes connected the north with western sub-Saharan Africa. Gold, more than any other single item, drew the camel caravans of Berber and Arab traders to the inland kingdoms of West Africa's grasslands, but large numbers of slaves were also sold for transportation northward to markets throughout the Mediterranean and beyond. In return, western sub-Saharan Africans received salt, raw copper, fine horses, and such manufactured goods as tempered steel and even glassware from Venice.

Trade and the development of trade-based Islamic states in the western sub-Saharan grasslands constitute a major chapter in Africa's history, but they are not the whole story of what was happening during the millennium 500–1500 C.E. in this richly diverse continent. East Africa, especially its coastal region from Somalia to Tanzania, was linked to a shipping network of monsoon-driven vessels that sailed throughout the Indian Ocean and its adjacent waters — all the way to China. Commodities such as ivory and gold made their way from the interior of East Africa to ports on the Indian Ocean, where they joined such coastal raw materials as ambergris (a resin used in the production of perfumes) and mangrove timber. At these emporia, which dotted the islands off the coast, East Africa's goods were exchanged for pottery from China, glassware, and Indian textiles. In addition, captives taken in war and by raiding parties were brought to the coast, where they were sold to Arab slavers for exportation to the mines and plantations of Iraq. For better and for worse, Africa was increasingly becoming linked to the Eurasian world between 500 and 1500 C.E.

▼▼▼

Africa

Africa commands a special place in the history of humanity because it is the home of the earliest protohumans. Moreover, although experts heatedly debate the evidence, it seems likely that the earliest modern human, *Homo sapiens,* also evolved in tropical Africa about one hundred fifty thousand years ago. Nothing, short of the total destruction of humanity, will likely ever rival these historical firsts in scope, but Africa's place in human history hardly stopped there.

During the millennium under present consideration, Africa witnessed a number of important historical developments. Chief among these were the Bantu Expansion, the coming of Islam, the creation of trade empires in the western Sudan, the rise of a Swahili culture in East Africa, and the arrival of Europeans toward the end of this period.

The approximately four hundred fifty languages belonging to the *Bantu* linguistic family that are spoken today throughout most of the southern half of the continent are traceable to a common place of origin in West Africa, probably in present eastern Nigeria. Bantu speakers probably began spreading out of their ancestral homeland as early as three or four thousand years ago, aided by their skills in fishing and agriculture. In its later stages, this slow, almost imperceptible movement was aided by their iron-working skills. As they spread east and southward, the Bantu-speaking peoples introduced wherever they settled the crafts of farming and iron metallurgy. By the early centuries C.E. Bantu speakers had pushed as far south as the region today occupied by the nation of Zimbabwe. There, by the late thirteenth century, they constructed a gold-trade civilization centered on the now famous Great Zimbabwe stone citadel, from which the modern state took its name in 1979.

Another great migration that profoundly influenced Africa's history was the influx of Islam in the wake of the conquering Arab armies that swept through North Africa in the seventh century. These conquests, and the conversions that followed, transformed what had been Christian North Africa into an integral part of the Islamic world, thereby wrenching it out of the orbits of Constantinople and Rome and tying it culturally to Mecca, Damascus, and Baghdad.

From North Africa the faith and culture of Islam penetrated into the trade empires of the western grassland states south of the Sahara after 1000 C.E. The empires of Ghana (source 94), Mali (Chapter 8, source 62; Chapter 12, source 108), and Songhay became progressively more Islamic and therefore more closely tied to North Africa and the greater Muslim world beyond Africa by reason of a shared religious culture, as well as by commercial interests.

On the east coast of Africa a similar phenomenon was at work. In the ninth and tenth centuries Arab sailor-merchants established trading settlements far down the coast of East Africa. The culture that emerged from the interchange between the Arabic and East African peoples who traded and intermarried here is known as *Swahili* (from the Arabic *sahil*, "coast"). Like *Kiswahili*, the language of the region, Swahili culture was a coastal trade culture consisting of an indigenous Bantu base with strong Arabic influences. From about 1200 to the early sixteenth century, the port city of Kilwa, today located in the nation of Tanzania, served as the Swahili coast's main emporium.

Kilwa's commercial prominence along Africa's eastern shore ended with its sack and destruction by the Portuguese in 1505. With the arrival in force of the Portuguese, first on Africa's west coast in the fifteenth century (Chapter 12, source 111) and then on the east coast in the early sixteenth century, the age of direct European contact with sub-Saharan Africa had begun. We shall consider some of the consequences that followed from that interchange in Chapter 13, sources 114–116.

Despite the impact of Islam and Europe on Africa south of the Sahara, older ways of life usually proved resilient to influences from outside. Ethiopia, for example, successfully resisted Islamic and later Portuguese attempts at conquest and conversion, retaining its autonomy and ancient Christian culture (source 95). Likewise, the coastal states of West Africa retained their essentially African features, even as their leaders accepted the faith of Islam. Moreover, they maintained autonomy, extensive political authority, and widespread economic interests, even in the face of the European presence along their coastline.

The Land of Zanj: Tenth-Century East Africa

▼▼▼

93 ▼ *Abu'l-Hasan Ali al-Mas'udi, MEADOWS OF GOLD*

Ancient Greek and Roman geographers knew the coastal region of eastern Africa as *Azania*. The Arabs who traded along this coast knew it as the *Land of Zanj*, a name that survives in *Zanzibar*, an island that comprises part of the modern nation of Tanzania. Following the monsoon winds of the Indian Ocean, which blow toward East Africa between November and March, Arab merchants sailed from Oman and other regions of the Arabian Peninsula and visited trading ports that stretched southward from Mogadishu in Somalia to Sofala, which is located in the modern nation of Mozambique. At these trading centers, the Arabs met sailors from India and the islands of Southeast Asia as well as colonists from Arabia and Persia, many of whom had intermarried with Africans. Because of the presence of Arabic-speaking people along this coast, the Arab merchants who visited the region found little difficulty in conducting commerce, apart from the normal hazards of venturing long distances across treacherous ocean waters in small vessels. After acquiring their desired raw materials, Arab merchants returned home or else sailed to India, driven by monsoon winds that blow northeastward between April and October.

One of the earliest Arabic accounts of East African society and its trade comes from the pen of Abu'l-Hasan Ali al-Mas'udi (ca. 890–956), who visited the region in 915/916. In his masterwork of history and geography, *Meadows of Gold,* which he composed in 943, al-Mas'udi informs his reader of the Indian Ocean trade network, into which the Land of Zanj was interwoven, and of the people of interior East Africa, who fed that trade. How much of what he tells us about the people of Zanj is fact and how much is the stuff of distorted legend is open to question. What is clear and undisputed is the picture that al-Mas'udi draws of the African east coast's importance to foreign merchants.

QUESTIONS FOR ANALYSIS

1. What evidence does al-Mas'udi provide of the evolving Swahili culture of this region?
2. What are the dangers of the voyage to the Land of Zanj? What are the rewards?
3. Describe the ivory trade that originated in East Africa.
4. What does al-Mas'udi tell us about the culture of the Bantu people of the interior? Which elements seem the most believable? Why? Which seem the least believable? Why?
5. Review the story of Sinbad (Chapter 9, source 77). Does al-Mas'udi's account place the story into a clearer context? If so, what is that context?

The pilots of Oman[1] pass by the channel [of Berbera] to reach the island of Kanbalu,[2] which is in the Zanj sea.[3] It has a mixed population of Muslims and Zanj idolaters.[4] . . . The aforesaid Kanbalu is the farthest point of their voyages on the Zanj sea, and the land of Sofala and the Waqwaq,[5] on the edge of the Zanj mainland and at the end of this branch of the sea. The people of Siraf[6] also make this voyage, and I myself have sailed on this sea, setting off from Sanjar, the capital of Oman, in company with a number of Omani shipowners, among whom were Muhammad ibn al-Zaidbud and Jawhar ibn Ahmad surnamed Ibn Sirah, who was later lost at sea with his ship. My last voyage from Kanbalu to Oman was in A.H. 304[7] on the ship belonging to Ahmad and Abd al-Samad, who were the brothers of Abd al-Rahim ibn Ja'far al-Sirafi, a native of Mikan, which is a quarter of Siraf. They were both lost at sea with all their goods later on. The Amir[8] of

---

[1]The region of southeast Arabia that stretches along the entrance to the Persian Gulf.

[2]The island of Pemba.

[3]The region of the Indian Ocean that washes the eastern shore of Africa.

[4]Worshipers of idols. People who follow traditional religions.

[5]The Arabs normally used this term to refer only to the people of Malaysia, who speak a language that is related to the Malagasy tongue of Madagascar. Madagascar is a large island off the coast of East Africa and opposite Sofala; Malaysia is across the Indian Ocean in Southeast Asia (see note 19). In the present context, however, the term seems to refer to the people of interior Africa.

[6]A port on the Iranian shore of the Persian Gulf.

[7]A.H. is an abbreviation for a Latin term that means "in the year of the Hijra." Muhammad's hijra from Mecca to Medina, which began on July 16, 622, is the starting point of the Muslim calendar. Because the Muslim year is lunar, one cannot simply subtract six hundred twenty-two years from a date in the common calendar to arrive at its equivalent in the Muslim calendar. A.H. 304 equates to 915/916 C.E.

[8]An Arabic term that means "commander." Here it means "prince" or "governor."

Oman at the time of my last voyage was Ahmad ibn Hilal, son of a sister of al-Qital. I have sailed much on the seas, . . . but I do not know of one more dangerous than that of the Zanj, of which I have just spoken. . . .

The land of Zanj produces wild leopard skins. The people wear them as clothes, or export them to Muslim countries. They are the largest leopard skins and the most beautiful for making saddles. The sea of Zanj and that of Abyssinia[9] lie on the right of the sea of India, and join up. They also export tortoise-shell for making combs, for which ivory is likewise used. . . . As we have said, the Zanj and other Abyssinian peoples are spread about on the right bank of the Nile,[10] as far as the end of the Abyssinian sea. The Zanj are the only Abyssinian people[11] to have crossed the branch which flows out of the upper stream of the Nile into the sea of Zanj. They settled in that area, which stretches as far as Sofala, which is the farthest limit of land and the end of the voyages made from Oman and Siraf on the sea of Zanj. In the same way that the sea of China ends with the land of Japan, the sea of Zanj ends with the land of Sofala and the Waqwaq, which produces gold and many other wonderful things. It has a warm climate and is fertile. The Zanj capital is there[12] and they have a king called the *Mfalme*. This is the ancient name of their kings, and all the other Zanj kings are subject to him: he has 300,000 horsemen. The Zanj use the ox as a beast of burden, for they have no horses, mules or camels in their land, and do not know of their existence. Like all Abyssinians they do not know of snow or hail. Some of their tribes sharpen their teeth and are cannibals. The land of Zanj begins with the branch which leaves the upper Nile[13] and continues to the land of Sofala and Waqwaq. The villages stretch for 700 parasangs[14] and the same distance inland: the country is cut up into valleys, mountains and stony deserts. There are many wild elephants but no tame ones. The Zanj do not use them for war or anything else, but only hunt and kill them. When they want to catch them, they throw down the leaves, bark and branches of a certain tree which grows in their country: then they wait in ambush until the elephants come to drink. The water burns them and makes them drunk. They fall down and cannot get up: their limbs will not articulate. The Zanj rush upon them armed with very long spears, and kill them for their ivory. It is from this country that come tusks weighing fifty pounds and more. They usually go to Oman, and from there are sent to China and India. This is the chief trade route, and if it were not so, ivory would be common in Muslim lands.

In China the kings and military civil officers use ivory palanquins:[15] no officer or notable dares to come into the royal presence in an iron palanquin, and ivory alone can be used. Thus they seek after straight tusks in preference to the curved, to make the things we have spoken of. They also burn ivory before their idols and cense their altars with it, just as Christians use the Mary incense[16] and other perfumes. The Chinese make no other use of the elephant, and consider it un-

---

[9]Usually the term refers only to the land of Ethiopia, but al-Mas'udi seems to use it here to refer to all the east coast regions of sub-Saharan Africa (see note 11).

[10]Not the Nile. Maybe he means the Sabi River, which flows out of the Zimbabwe Plateau and reaches the ocean in the modern state of Mozambique.

[11]Apparently all black Africans are Abyssinians (see note 9).

[12]Probably the site, far up the Sabi River Valley, where the Shona state would construct the massive enclosures of Great Zimbabwe between 1200 and 1450.

[13]Al-Mas'udi is wrong again (see note 10). Several major rivers run into the Indian Ocean, but not one of them is the Nile. This river, which delineates the northern boundary of the Land of Zanj, might be the Juba River.

[14]A parasang, an ancient Persian unit of measurement, is three and a half miles.

[15]A covered liter carried on the shoulders of two or four persons.

[16]Incense (also known as frankincense) was a fragrant resin that Christians, Muslims, Jews, Zoroastrians, and many others burned in their places of worship. Here the author seems to refer to a particular grade of incense that was burned in Christian churches in honor of Mary, the Mother of Jesus.

lucky to use it for domestic purposes or war. This fear has its origin in a tradition about one of their most ancient military expeditions. In India ivory is much sought after.[17] It is used for the handles of daggers called *harari* or *harri* in the singular: and also for the curved sword-scabbards called *kartal,* in the plural *karatil,* but the chief use of ivory is making chessmen and backgammon pieces. . . .

In the land of Zanj the elephant lives about 400 years, according to what the people say, and they speak with certainty of having met an elephant so tall that it was impossible to kill it. . . . It is only in the land of Zanj and in India that elephants reproduce. . . .

Now let us return to our subject of the beginning of the chapter, the Zanj, the description of their country and of the other peoples of Abyssinia. The Zanj, although always busied hunting the elephant and collecting its ivory, make no use of it for domestic purposes. They use iron instead of gold and silver, just as they use oxen, as we said before, both for beasts of burden and for war. These oxen are harnessed like a horse and run as fast. . . .

To go back to the Zanj and their kings, these are known as *Wafalme,*[18] which means son of the Great Lord, since he is chosen to govern them justly. If he is tyrannical or strays from the truth, they kill him and exclude his seed from the throne; for they consider that in acting wrongfully he forfeits his position as the son of the Lord, the King of Heaven and Earth. They call God *Maliknajlu,* which means Great Lord.

The Zanj have an elegant language and men who preach in it. One of their holy men will often gather a crowd and exhort his hearers to please God in their lives and to be obedient to him. He explains the punishments that follow upon disobedience, and reminds them of their ancestors and kings of old. These people have no religious law: their kings rule by custom and by political expediency.

The Zanj eat bananas,[19] which are as common among them as they are in India; but their staple food is millet[20] and a plant called *kalari* which is pulled out of the earth like truffles. It is plentiful in Aden[21] and the neighboring part of Yemen[22] near to the town. It is like the cucumber of Egypt and Syria. They also eat honey and meat. Every man worships what he pleases, be it a plant, an animal or a mineral. They have many islands where the coconut grows: its nuts are used as fruit by all the Zanj peoples. One of these islands, which is one or two days' sail from the coast, has a Muslim population and a royal family. This is the island of Kanbalu of which we have already spoken.

---

[17]Despite the presence of elephants in India, Indian artisans preferred African ivory because of its texture and size.
[18]Apparently these are the kings mentioned above who are subordinate to the *Mfalme.*
[19]Migrants from Malaysia in Southeast Asia settled in Madagascar around the first century C.E. and brought with them plants and seeds from their homeland, including the banana (see note 5). From Madagascar the banana traveled into the tropical rain forests of continental Africa, where it flourished.

[20]A cereal.
[21]An Arabian port city that commands the entrance to the Red Sea.
[22]Southwest Arabia.

The Land of Ghana: Eleventh-Century Western Sudan

▼▼▼

94 ▼ Abu Ubaydallah al-Bakri, THE BOOK OF ROUTES AND REALMS

Located south of the Sahara Desert is a broad expanse of grasslands, or *savanna,* that stretches across the breadth of the African continent, from the Atlantic Ocean to the Red Sea. To the Arabs this region was known as *Bilad al-Sudan* (the country of the blacks). Arab and Berber merchants were especially interested in West Africa's Sudan because its inhabitants were advantageously located between the markets of North Africa and cultures farther south toward the tropical rain forests of the coast. From the southern peoples of the Niger and Senegal River Valleys the inhabitants of the savanna obtained gold and slaves, which they traded for manufactured goods, horses, and salt with Berber and Arab merchants, who arrived in camel caravans from the north. In time, this trans-Saharan commerce became the basis for the development of a series of large trading states in the region that connected West Africa's gold fields with the cities of Mediterranean North Africa.

One of the earliest important trading empires to emerge was *Ghana* (not to be confused with its modern namesake, the nation of Ghana), which was located essentially in territory encompassed today by the nations of Mauritania and Mali. The origins of Ghana as an organized entity are lost in the shadows of the past but go back at least as far as the fifth century C.E., when the introduction of the camel made it easier for outsiders to penetrate across the Sahara into the land of the *Soninke* people. Coming as traders and as raiders, the nomadic *Berber* people of the western Sahara apparently helped stimulate the formation of a Soninke kingdom organized for commerce and defense. In time that kingdom would become known as *Ghana* — a term that originated as a royal title. During the course of the eighth and ninth centuries Arab merchants inhabiting the coastal cities of North Africa began to enter the lucrative trans-Saharan trading system, thereby gaining direct access to the region they called *the land of gold* — a land then dominated by the well-established state of Ghana.

In 1067/1068 Abu Ubaydallah al-Bakri (d. 1094), a resident of the city of Cordova in what is today Spain but was then the Muslim land of *al-Andalus,* composed a detailed description of this fabled region. Although he never traveled to nearby Africa and probably never even left his native land, al-Bakri provides us with one of the most important sources for the early history of the western Sudan. As was the accepted practice among Muslim geographers of his era, al-Bakri drew heavily from the writings of predecessors, many of whose works are now otherwise lost, and he also interviewed merchants who had traveled to the area. These interviews made it possible for al-Bakri to present up-to-date information on Ghana at a crucial moment in its history.

During the latter portion of the eleventh century the rulers and leading families of Ghana were increasingly adopting the faith and attendant culture of Islam.

However, Muslims from the north brought not only the peaceful message of universal submission to the Word of God, they also brought war. A fundamentalist Islamic group of Berbers known as the *Almoravids* waged holy war, or jihad, against the Soninke of Ghana. It is unclear whether the Almoravids prevailed in this war, but apparently the conflict disrupted trade and weakened Ghana's economic base. In addition, the heartland of Ghana was becoming far less able to support its population, due to an environmental crisis brought about by overfarming and excessive grazing. Large numbers of farmers and townspeople were forced to move away. With these combined losses, the recently converted monarchs of Ghana lost their ability to hold together their loosely organized and still predominantly non-Islamic empire. By the early thirteenth century Ghana had disintegrated. Hegemony over the markets of the western Sudan briefly passed to the kingdom of *Sosso* and then to the state of *Mali,* which reached its greatest territorial extent under Mansa Musa (r. 1312–1327), whom we saw in Chapter 8 (source 62). We shall see Mali again in Chapter 12, source 108.

QUESTIONS FOR ANALYSIS

1. To whom did a monarch pass his royal power? What does this tradition of royal succession suggest about Ghanian society?
2. Describe the city of Ghana. What does its physical environment, especially its two centers, suggest about eleventh-century Ghanian culture?
3. How do we know that the empire of Ghana was not the only state in the western Sudan?
4. How would you characterize the authority and sources of power of the rulers of Ghana?
5. What role did Islam play in Ghanian society? What does your answer suggest about the way in which Islam entered the western Sudan?
6. What does the story of the conversion of the king of Malal suggest about the process of Islamization in the western Sudan?

Ghana is a title given to their kings; the name of the region is Awkar, and their king today, namely in the year 460,[1] is Tunka Manin. He ascended the throne in 455.[2] The name of his predecessor was Basi and he became their ruler at the age of 85. He led a praiseworthy life on account of his love of justice and friendship for the Muslims. At the end of his life he became blind, but he concealed this from his subjects and pretended that he could see. When something was put before him he said: "This is good" or "This is bad." His ministers deceived the people by indicating to the king in cryptic words what he should say, so that the commoners could not understand. Basi was a maternal uncle of Tunka Manin. This is their custom and their habit, that the kingship is inherited only by the son of the king's sister. He has no doubt that his successor is a son of his sister, while he is not certain that his son is in fact his own, and he is not convinced of the

---

[1] See source 93, note 7. The equivalent date in the common calendar is 1067/1068 C.E.

[2] 1063 C.E.

genuineness of his relationship to him. This Tunka Manin is powerful, rules an enormous kingdom, and possesses great authority.

The city of Ghana consists of two towns situated on a plain.[3] One of these towns, which is inhabited by Muslims, is large and possesses twelve mosques, in one of which they assemble for the Friday prayer. There are salaried imams and muezzins,[4] as well as jurists and scholars. In the environs are wells with sweet water, from which they drink and with which they grow vegetables. The king's town is six miles distant from this one and bears the name of Al-Ghaba.[5] Between these two towns there are continuous habitations. The houses of the inhabitants are of stone and acacia wood. The king has a palace and a number of domed dwellings all surrounded with an enclosure like a city wall. In the king's town, and not far from his court of justice, is a mosque where the Muslims who arrive at his court pray. Around the king's town are domed buildings and groves and thickets where the sorcerers of these people, men in charge of the religious cult, live. In them too are their idols and the tombs of their kings. These woods are guarded and none may enter them and know what is there. In them also are the king's prisons. If somebody is imprisoned there no news of him is ever heard. The king's interpreters, the official in charge of his treasury and the majority of his ministers are Muslims. Among the people who follow the king's religion[6] only he and his heir apparent (who is the son of his sister) may wear sewn clothes. All other people wear robes of cotton, silk, or brocade, according to their means. All of them shave their beards, and women shave their heads. The king adorns himself like a woman, wearing necklaces round his neck and bracelets on his forearms, and he puts on a high cap decorated with gold and wrapped in a turban of fine cotton. He sits in audience or to hear grievances against officials in a domed pavilion around which stand ten horses covered with gold-embroidered materials. Behind the king stand ten pages holding shields and swords decorated with gold, and on his right are the sons of the vassal kings[7] of his country wearing splendid garments and their hair plaited with gold. The governor of the city sits on the ground before the king and around him are ministers seated likewise. . . . When people who profess the same religion as the king approach him they fall on their knees and sprinkle dust on their heads, for this is their way of greeting him. As for the Muslims, they greet him only by clapping their hands.

Their religion is paganism and the worship of idols. When their king dies they construct over the place where his tomb will be an enormous dome of wood. Then they bring him on a bed covered with a few carpets and cushions and place him beside the dome. At his side they place his ornaments, his weapons, and the vessels from which he used to eat and drink, filled with various kinds of food and beverages. They place there too the men who used to serve his meals. They close the door of the dome and cover it with mats and furnishings. Then the people assemble, who heap earth upon it until it becomes like a big hillock and dig a ditch around it until the mound can be reached at only one place.

They make sacrifices to their dead and make offerings of intoxicating drinks.

On every donkey-load of salt when it is brought into the country their king levies one

---

[3]Imagine a city consisting of two separate, walled towns connected by a long, unwalled strip of private dwellings. This was probably the city of Koumbi-Saleh, whose ruins are located in the southern region of the modern nation of Mauritania. At its eleventh-century height, this double city probably held some twenty thousand people.

[4]*Imams* are religious teachers, and *muezzins* are the chanters who ascend the minarets, or towers, of the mosques and call the faithful to prayer five times daily.

[5]The term means *the forest* and refers to the sacred grove mentioned below. (For more on sacred groves, see source 96.)

[6]The king was not a Muslim. He followed the ancient religious ways of the Soninke people.

[7]Subordinate kings, or lords.

golden dinar,[8] and two dinars when it is sent out. From a load of copper the king's due is five mithqals,[9] and from a load of other goods ten mithqals. The best gold found in his land comes from the town of Ghiyaru, which is eighteen days' traveling distant from the king's town over a country inhabited by tribes of the Sudan whose dwellings are continuous.

The nuggets found in all the mines of his country are reserved for the king, only this gold dust being left for the people. But for this the people would accumulate gold until it lost its value. The nuggets may weigh from an ounce to a pound. It is related that the king owns a nugget as large as a big stone. . . .

The king of Ghana, when he calls up his army, can put 200,000 men[10] into the field, more than 40,000 of them archers. . . .

On the opposite bank of the Nil[11] is another great kingdom, stretching a distance of more than eight days' marching, the king of which has the title of *Daw.* The inhabitants of this region use arrows when fighting. Beyond this country lies another called Malal,[12] the king of which is known as *al-musulmani.*[13] He is thus called because his country became afflicted with drought one year following another; the inhabitants prayed for rain, sacrificing cattle till they had exterminated almost all of them, but the drought and the misery only increased. The king had as his guest a Muslim who used to read the Qur'an and was acquainted with the Sunna.[14] To this man the king complained of the calamities

that assailed him and his people. The man said: "O King, if you believed in God (who is exalted) and testified that He is One, and testified as to the prophetic mission of Muhammad (God bless him and give him peace) and if you accepted all the religious laws of Islam, I would pray for your deliverance from your plight and that God's mercy would envelop all the people of your country and that your enemies and adversaries might envy you on that account." Thus he continued to press the king until the latter accepted Islam and became a sincere Muslim. The man made him recite from the Qur'an some easy passages and taught him religious obligations and practices which no one may be excused from knowing. Then the Muslim made him wait till the eve of the following Friday,[15] when he ordered him to purify himself by a complete ablution, and clothed him in a cotton garment which he had. The two of them came out towards a mound of earth, and there the Muslim stood praying while the king, standing at his right side, imitated him. Thus they prayed for a part of the night, the Muslim reciting invocations and the king saying "Amen." The dawn had just started to break when God caused abundant rain to descend upon them. So the king ordered the idols to be broken and expelled the sorcerers from his country. He and his descendants after him as well as his nobles were sincerely attached to Islam, while the common people of his kingdom remained polytheists. Since then their rulers have been given the title of *al-musulmani.*

---

[8]A standard gold coin in the Islamic world that weighed 4.72 grams, or one mithqal (see note 9).

[9]A standard of weight equalling 4.72 grams.

[10]An apparent exaggeration. There was no regular standing Ghanian army; the various districts of the empire sent warriors as the occasion warranted.

[11]Muslim geographers of this era mistakenly believed that the Niger River was the western source of the Nile.

[12]A *Mandike* kingdom that probably was the nucleus of the later empire of Mali.

[13]"The Muslim."

[14]The traditions of Islam.

[15]The beginning of the Islamic day of rest and community worship.

The Land of Seyon:
Fourteenth-Century Ethiopia
▼▼▼
95 ▼ *THE GLORIOUS VICTORIES OF 'AMDA SEYON*

Ethiopia, a kingdom to the southeast of Kush, or Nubia (Chapter 1, source 9), in Africa's northeast highlands, looks out across the Red Sea to Yemen, the southern portion of the Arabian peninsula. Settlers from Yemen crossed these waters, perhaps as early as the seventh century B.C.E., and mixed with the indigenous inhabitants to produce a hybrid civilization whose language, *Ge'ez,* was essentially Semitic but contained significant Kushitic elements. Because of its strategic location astride a trade route that linked Egypt and the Mediterranean world with the markets of East Africa, Arabia, and India, Ethiopia flourished. A Greek shipping manual of the first century C.E. notes that Adulis, Ethiopia's port on the Red Sea, was northeast Africa's premier center for the ivory trade.

According to Ethiopian chronicles, in 333 C.E. King Ezana (r. 320–350) converted to Christianity and made it the official religion of his realm. In the years that followed the Ethiopian people gradually adopted the new faith. Like the Egyptians and Nubians to their north, the Ethiopians later adopted a type of Christianity known as *Monophysitism* (from the Greek words for "one nature"). This form of Christian belief, which arose in the fifth century, centered on a doctrine that de-emphasized Jesus' humanity to the point of maintaining that he had a single, divine nature. When the Churches of Constantinople and Rome condemned Monophysite teachings as heresy in 451, the Ethiopian Church was doctrinally cut off from these two centers of Christianity. The Arab-Muslim conquest of Egypt in the 640s further cut Ethiopia off from its Christian co-religionists in Byzantium and the West. In time, most of previously Christian Egypt converted to Islam, although its native Christians, known as *Coptic Christians,* remained a significant minority, as they are today. Egypt, the land that had introduced Christianity to Nubia and Ethiopia, was now an Islamic stronghold. On their part, Nubians and Ethiopians vigorously fought to retain their political autonomy and Christian identity in the face of Muslim pressure from Egypt. After the mid thirteenth century, however, Nubian resistance to Islam weakened. By the mid fourteenth century Nubia no longer had an independent Christian monarchy, and the Christian faith was fast losing out to Islam. By the sixteenth century Nubia's Christian population was a minority and would remain so down to the present.

Farther to the south, Ethiopia, fairly secure in its mountain strongholds, continued to hold out against Islam. The following document, composed by an eyewitness to the events, tells the story of how King 'Amda Seyon I (r. 1314–1344), whose throne name was *Gabra Masqal* (servant of the Cross), resisted an invasion in 1329 by Sabr ad-Din, the ruler of Ifat, a nearby Muslim principality. More than simply a monarch on the defensive, 'Amda Seyon was a militant expansionist, who in his thirty-year reign undertook a series of offensive operations against neighboring Islamic states and achieved significant success at their expense. Between 1320 and 1340 he managed to bring Ifat and other Islamic states of the highland plateau under the control of his expanding kingdom. As the chronicle points out, Sabr ad-Din was actually a tributary prince who revolted against 'Amda Seyon's authority.

QUESTIONS FOR ANALYSIS

1. What picture emerges of Muslim-Christian relations in fourteenth-century Ethiopia?
2. The Ethiopian-Christian attitude toward Jews and Judaism has been characterized as ambivalent (containing conflicting attitudes). Do you find in this source any evidence to support such a judgment? Please be specific in your answer.
3. Reread Eusebius of Caesarea's *Ecclesiastical History* (Chapter 7, source 52) and *The Song of Roland* (Chapter 10, source 87). Do you see any parallels between the tones and messages of those two sources and this document? What are they? What conclusions do you draw?

Let us write, with the help of our Lord Jesus Christ, of the power and the victory which God wrought by the hands of 'Amda Seyon king of Ethiopia, whose throne-name is Gabra Masqal. . . . Now the king of Ethiopia . . . heard that the king of the Rebels[1] had revolted, and in his arrogance was unfaithful to him, making himself great, like the Devil who set himself above his creator and exalted himself like the Most High. The king of the Rebels, whose name was Sabradin, was full of arrogance towards his lord 'Amda Seyon, and said, "I will be king over all the land of Ethiopia; I will rule the Christians according to my law, and I will destroy their churches." And having said this, he arose and set out and came to the land of the Christians, and killed some of them; and those who survived, both men and women, he took prisoner and converted them to his religion.

And after this he said, "I will nominate governors over the provinces of Ethiopia." . . . And he appointed governors over all the provinces of Ethiopia, even those which he had not been able to reach.

But the feet cannot become the head, nor the earth the sky, nor the servant the master. That perverse one, the son of a viper, of the seed of a serpent, the son of a stranger from the race of Satan, thought covetously of the throne of David[2] and said, "I will rule in Seyon,"[3] for pride en-

---

[1] The word *'elwan* can also be translated as "infidels" or "non-believers."

[2] The Ethiopian royal family, known as the *Solomonid Dynasty* (1270–1974), claimed descent from the union of the Queen of Sheba and King Solomon of Israel (r. ca. 962–922 B.C.E.), son of King David. (See the Bible, 1 Kings, 10:1–13, and 2 Chronicles, 9:1–12, for an account of the queen's visit to King Solomon.) According to Ethiopian tradition, Menelik, son of the Queen of Sheba and Solomon

and first king of Ethiopia, brought the Ark of the Covenant to Ethiopia, where it is still revered as the country's most sacred relic.

[3] The Ge'ez transliteration of *Zion*, one of Jerusalem's hills and a common symbolic term for Jerusalem and even the entire Holy Land. Here *Seyon* refers to Ethiopia because the Ethiopians claim partial Hebraic descent (note 2). *'Amda Seyon* means "pillar of Zion."

tered into his heart, as into the Devil his father. He said, "I will make the Christian churches into mosques for the Muslims, and I will convert to my religion the king of the Christians together with his people, and I will nominate him governor of one province, and if he refuses to be converted to my religion I will deliver him to the herdsmen . . . that they make him a herder of camels. As for the queen Zan Mangesa, the wife of the king, I will make her work at the mill." . . .

Saying this, he collected all the troops of the Muslims, and chose from among them the ablest and most intelligent. These in truth were not able and intelligent, but fools, men full of error, impostors who foretell the future by means of sand and take omens from the sun and moon and stars of heaven, who say, "We observe the stars," but they have knowledge only of evil, they have no knowledge of God, their knowledge is of men which fades and perishes, for as Saint Paul says, "God hath made foolish the wisdom of this world."[4]

Let us return to the original subject. This evil man then questioned the diviners, saying, "Now tell me, I pray you, shall we conquer when we fight with the king of the Christians?" And one of them rose, a prophet of darkness. . . .

When Sabradin the king of the Rebels examined him, this diviner answered him persuasively, saying, "Behold, the kingdom of the Christians is finished; it shall be given to us, and you shall reign in Seyon. Rise, make war on the king of the Christians, and conquering you shall rule him and his people." And all the diviners said likewise. So the Rebel king sent into all the lands of the Muslims and called together his troops, and formed them into three divisions: one division set out for the land of Amhara, another set out for the land of Angot, and he himself prepared for war and set out to invade Shoa where the king was, — the slave of slaves against the prince of princes, the tail of the dog against the head of

the lion, trusting in the false prediction that the Christian kingdom was come to an end.

As for us, we have heard and we know from the Holy Scriptures that the kingdom of the Muslims, established for but seven hundred years, shall cease to be at the proper time. But the kingdom of the Christians shall continue till the second coming of the Son of God, according to the words of Holy Scripture; and above all we know that the kingdom of Ethiopia shall endure till the coming of Christ, of which David prophesied saying "Ethiopia shall stretch her hands unto God."[5]

The messengers whom the king had sent to that Rebel returned to him the whole answer of the renegade, that rebel against righteousness. Hearing the insults of the evil man, the king called together his commanders. . . . He sent them forth to war against the evil Sabradin on the 24th day of Yakatit,[6] saying to them, "May God give you strength and victory, and may He help you." . . . And they fought with him and forced him out of his residence; and he fled before them. And they defeated him through the power of God. . . . And they pursued him till sunset; but he escaped them, going by a different road. God threw him down from his glory. . . .

Then the army of the king set forth and attacked the camp of the Rebel. They looted the rebel king's treasure houses and took gold and silver and fine clothes and jewels without number. They killed men and women, old men and children; the corpses of the slain filled a large space. And those who survived were made prisoners, and there were left none but those who had escaped with that evil man. But the soldiers could not find a place to camp because of the foul smell of the corpses; and they went to another place and made their camp there. . . .

The king, hearing that the Rebel had escaped, went into the tabernacle[7] and approached the altar; seizing the horns of the altar[8] he implored

---

[4]The Bible, I Corinthians 1:20.
[5]The Bible, Psalms 68:31.
[6]February 18, 1329.
[7]A tent used as a chapel in the king's camp.

[8]As was the fashion in ancient Israel, Ethiopian altars had horns on all four corners. Suppliants would grasp one while praying.

mercy of Jesus Christ saying, "Hear the petition of my heart and reject not the prayer of my lips, and shut not the gates of Thy mercy because of my sins, but send me Thy good angel to guide me on my road to pursue mine enemy who has set himself above Thy sheep and above Thy holy name." And having said this, he gave an offering to the church of colored hangings for the altar, and went out. Then he sent other troops, . . . cavalry and foot-soldiers, strong and skilled in war, powerful without comparison in warfare and battle; he sent their commander . . . to make war in the land of the renegades who are like Jews, the crucifiers,[9] . . . Because like the Jews, the crucifiers, they denied Christ, he sent troops to destroy and devastate them and subject them to the rule of Christ. . . .

The Rebel was filled with fear, and not knowing where to turn, for fear had taken possession of him, he sent to the queen[10] saying, "I have done wrong to my lord the king, I have wrought injustice against him, and it is better that I fall into his hands than into the hands of a stranger. I will come myself and surrender to him, that he may do what he will to me." Thereupon the queen went to tell the king the whole of the message from that Rebel Sabradin, whose acts, like his name 'broken judgment,'[11] consist of insults, mad rage, errors, contentions, and arrogance. When the king heard this message which the Rebel had sent to the queen, he was exceedingly angry, and said to the queen, "Do you send him a message and say: 'If you come, or if you do not come, it will not trouble me; but if you go to a distant country I will pursue you through the power of God. And if you go into a cave, or if you just run away, I will not leave you alone nor will I return to my capital till I have taken you.'"

Now when he received this message, Sabradin set out and came to the king, and stood before him. And the king asked him, saying, "Why have you behaved thus to me? The gifts which you formerly sent to me you have given to your servants; and the multitude of goods of silver and gold which I gave to the poor you have taken away. Those who traded with me you have bound in chains; and what is worse, you have aspired to the throne of my kingdom, in imitation of the Devil your father who wished to be the equal of his creator." When that Rebel heard these words of the king he was at a loss for an answer in the greatness of his fear, for he was afraid of the king's presence; and he answered, "Do with me according to your will." And immediately the soldiers who were on the left and right of the king stood forth in anger and said, "This man is not worthy of life, for he has burnt the churches of God, he has slain Christians, and those whom he did not kill he has compelled to accept his religion. Moreover he desired to ascend the high mountain of the kingdom." And some said, "Let us slay him with the edge of the sword"; others said, "Let us stone him to death"; and others again, "Let us burn him with fire that he may disappear from the earth." And they said to the king, "Think not, O king, that he comes to you honestly and freely, for he trusts in his magic art." And so saying, they lifted from his bosom and arm a talisman and revealed the form of his magic. Then said the king, "Can your talismans deliver you from my hands in which God has imprisoned you?" And he gave orders for his two hands to be bound with iron chains; he did not wish him to be killed, for he is merciful and forbearing. Thus was taken the Rebel in the net which he himself had woven, and in the snare which he himself had set. . . . After this the king sent news to the capital of his kingdom. . . . "There is good news for you: with the help of your prayers I have defeated my enemy who is also the enemy of Christ."

---

[9]The *Falashas,* or Ethiopian Jews, Kushitic people whose ancestors had intermarried with Jewish immigrants from Yemen. They are termed *crucifiers* here because of the notion that the Jews were responsible for Jesus' crucifixion.

[10]Queen Mangesa, wife of King 'Amda Seyon.
[11]A pun. In Ge'ez *sabara* means "break" and *dayn* means "judgment." Actually, the Arabic name *Sabr ad-Din* means "constant in the faith."

A Yoruba Woman of Authority?

▼▼▼

96 ▼ SEATED FEMALE FIGURE

Like the Ethiopians, the *Yoruba*-speaking peoples of West Africa, who inhabit the forestlands that stretch from the edge of the savanna to the coast, trace their ancestry back to Southwest Asia, specifically Mecca. Such oral traditions are suspect as historical evidence, since they might simply have arisen from a desire on the part of people converted to Islam well after 1200 C.E. to create for themselves an Arabic lineage. Whatever their origins, by the late fourteenth century the Yoruba people had established a number of independent kingdoms in a region encompassed today by the nations of Nigeria and Benin. One of the most important of these Yoruba kingdoms was *Oyo*. Although it reached its apogee as a regional power in the period 1600–1830, Oyo's foundations as a city-state go back much earlier. Its first capital city, Old Oyo, located near the Niger River, was founded sometime between 800 and 1000 C.E.

The Yoruba of Oyo and elsewhere were great artists as well as state builders. The town of Esie in Nigeria is the site of a collection of over a thousand soapstone carvings of human figures that have lain for centuries in a grove. (See source 94 for a description of Ghana's sacred groves.) Each carving is an individual portrait, and for this reason it seems reasonable to infer that each represents a prominent, probably deceased individual. The sculptures date to somewhere between 1100 and 1500 and seem to have come from either Old Oyo or the equally powerful Yoruba city-state of *Ife*.

The sculpture pictured here is twenty-six inches high and represents a seated woman holding a cutlass that rests against her right shoulder. Note her elaborate hairstyle, whose height equals that of her face, the three-stringed necklace, and the scarification of her face. This arrangement of scars is found equally on male and female effigies in the collection. The figure probably represents an *Iyalode* (mother in charge of external affairs), an important officer among the Yoruba. Although the specific functions of the Iyalode differed from kingdom to kingdom and from era to era, it is clear that they enjoyed wide-ranging political, social, economic, and even military powers. Simply stated, the Iyalode was a chief in her own right and one of the monarch's main lieutenants.

QUESTIONS FOR ANALYSIS

1. List and comment on all of the clues that lead us to infer that this figurine represents a woman of authority. What do you think each symbol of authority represents?
2. Compare this statue with the four statues in Chapter 5, source 41. What do all five statues have in common? What do those common characteristics suggest about the way in which authority is perceived and portrayed across cultures and time?

A Yoruba Woman of Authority?

▼▼▼

The Americas

The date of the arrival of the first humans in the Americas is highly disputed. Based on fragmentary, controversial evidence, some scholars believe that migrants from Asia crossed the Bering Strait into North America as early as thirty-seven thousand years ago and at least no later than twenty thousand years ago. Others reject these dates as too early, believing that America's first human inhabitants were big-game hunters who crossed across the Bering landbridge during the last glacial era around 10,000 B.C.E. Recent evidence of human habitation found at Monte Verde in Chile and dated to around 10,500 B.C.E. (or earlier) has introduced new excitement into the controversy. How long it took the ancestors of these early inhabitants of Chile to make their way from Alaska to South America remains a mystery.

The original peopling of the Americas was an epochal event (or series of events because it was probably achieved in successive waves of migration from East Asia), rivaled only in magnitude by the demographic shifts that took place following the arrival in force of Europeans and Africans after 1492. With the advent of European and African peoples and their diseases, the whole population structure of the Americas underwent massive changes.

During the many years that separated these two periods, the Americas witnessed a variety of other only slightly less monumental developments. One of the most consequential was the indigenous development of agriculture based on the cultivation of over one hundred different crops unknown to the peoples of Africa and Eurasia. Chief among these were maize (*corn* in American English), potatoes, tomatoes, peanuts, manioc, and various types of beans, peppers, and squashes. By the time the Europeans arrived, agriculture was practiced from the woodlands of eastern North America to the rain forests of the Amazon tropics. As elsewhere, agriculture imposed restrictions on the behavior and social patterns of the cultivators and also produced enough food in a sufficiently regular manner to allow for the growth of dense populations. One result was the rise of civilizations, first in Mexico and farther south in Meso- and South America and later in regions that are today part of the United States.

Three of the major civilizations of North America were the *Mississippian Mound Culture,* the *Hohokam,* and the *Anasazi*. Between 1050 and 1200 C.E. the Mississippian Mound Builders created the city of Cahokia at a site that today is in East St. Louis, Illinois. At its height, Cahokia supported a population of at least eleven thousand people and possibly as many as thirty thousand. The *Hohokam* (those who have vanished) of the Sonoran Desert produced a complex urban society based upon their ability to construct and maintain some three hundred miles of irrigation canals in the region of what is today Phoenix, Arizona. During the twelfth and thirteenth centuries the *Anasazi* (the ancient ones) of the Four Corners region of the American Southwest built cities in Chaco Canyon, New Mexico, and at Mesa Verde in Colorado, which today stand as silent testimony of their engineering skills. All three civilizations participated in widespread trade networks and were influenced by the earlier civilizations of Mexico. All three also passed away as urban cultures long before the arrival of Europeans, who could only marvel at the ruins they left behind.

Because they left no written records behind and abandoned their urban centers so long ago, these North American civilizations remain largely mysterious, despite the considerable work of archeologists over the past half century. The Maya, Aztec, and Inca peoples of farther south, however, were still identifiable cultures when European conquerors and missionaries arrived on the scene. Despite the best attempts of many Europeans to efface totally the presumed devilish cultures that they had discovered, the Maya, Aztec, and Inca civilizations would not be forgotten.

The sources that follow — the products of Amerindian and European authors — combine to shed light on four important American cultures that flourished between 500 and 1500 C.E.

The God Who Descended from the Mountains
▼▼▼
97 ▼ *A MOCHE CERAMIC*

To most educated people, pre-Columbian civilization in Peru is synonymous with the Inca culture of the Andean highlands. Actually, the Incas, whom the Spanish conquistadors met and conquered in the course of the sixteenth century C.E., were newcomers and only the most recent participants in what was already some two and a half thousand years of Peruvian civilization. More than one thousand years before the rise of the Inca Empire, a people we call the *Moche,* or *Mochica,* constructed a highly developed civilization along the coastal desert plain of northern Peru. This region is one of the driest places on earth, receiving an average of far less than an inch of annual rainfall. It is fed, however, by a number of rivers that rise in the towering Andes to the east and flow down to the Pacific Ocean. One of those rivers is the Rio Moche. The fertility of the Moche Valley allowed its inhabitants to carve out a powerful state and a distinctive civilization that was at the height of its creativity in the period 200–750 C.E.

Moche artisans perfected the craft of casting and alloying a variety of soft metals, allowing them to create some of the finest gold, silver, and copper artifacts ever produced in antiquity. The most distinctive and brilliant artistic products of this culture, however, were made from a humbler material — clay. The Moche people produced vast numbers of finely crafted ceramics — particularly effigy vessels that represented a wide variety of deities, humans, animals, plants, and structures — and large numbers of them have survived. More than ninety percent of all Moche art and craftwork uncovered by modern archeologists consists of these magnificent ceramics — all created without benefit of the potter's wheel.

No effigy pot, by itself, tells us much about Moche culture, but cumulatively they tell a compelling story of the daily lives, beliefs, and rituals of the people who created these earthenware masterpieces. Although a single example of Moche art might more easily confuse than illuminate, the artifact that appears here is an exception and provides some interesting insights into the Moche vision of the world.

Moche Effigy Pot

This vessel is molded into a stylized mountain, from which several deities emerge. In the center is a Moche god, who wears a sunrise headdress from which a snake's head projects, and he is flanked by two snakes. To his right is a were-jaguar, an individual possessing both jaguar and human characteristics (see Chapter 1, source 10). This individual, who seems to be a god (or a shaman who has taken on divine attributes), wears a living snake belt that curls beneath him.

QUESTIONS FOR ANALYSIS

1. Note the cave from which the god on the right (the center of the pot) emerges. What is his apparent relationship with the mountain?
2. Consider this same god's headdress. What is the message? (Keep in mind the geographic relationship of the mountains to the Moche Valley.)
3. Does the geographic situation of the Moche Valley provide any clue as to what the four snakes that flow from the mountain represent?
4. Based on your answers to questions 1–3, what do you conclude this god's main functions were?
5. What about the feline qualities of the god/shaman on the far left? What does he seem to represent? (In answering this question, you might want to refer back to Chapter 1, source 10.)
6. Consider the title of this source. Which of the two deities was the "god who descended from the mountains"? Why do you reach this conclusion?
7. Which of these two gods seems more remote and lofty? Why? Which seems more active and closer to humanity? Why? Which of these is the creator god? What are the apparent functions of the other god? Which deity was probably more loved and prayed to? Why?

Taino Culture
▼▼▼

98 ▼ *Ramón Pane,*
A REPORT CONCERNING THE
ANTIQUITIES OF THE INDIANS

In the autumn of 1493 Christopher Columbus embarked on his second voyage to the West with a seventeen-ship flotilla and about twelve hundred sailors and colonists. One of the adventurers was a missionary priest named Ramón Pane, about whom we know very little, other than that he was a native of the region of Catalonia and a member of the Hermits of St. Jerome, a Spanish religious congregation noted for its strict asceticism. On arriving in the Caribbean, Pane went to live among the Tainos of Española (Hispaniola) in order to convert them to Catholic Christianity. In the course of his labors, Pane mastered the Taino language and listened to their sacred hymns and epic tales. On orders from Columbus, Pane prepared a detailed report of Taino religious beliefs and practices and presented it to the admiral, probably in 1498 when Columbus returned to the Americas for the third time.

Pane's report, the first systematic study of any Native American culture by a European observer, is rich in detail and provides much information that would otherwise be lost to us. Unfortunately, the work went almost unnoticed by Pane's contemporaries, perhaps because most who read it had difficulty comprehending the sacred cosmology of the Tainos. Bartolomé de Las Casas, one of the most important sixteenth-century Spanish defenders of Amerindian rights, dismissed Pane as a simple-minded man whose description of Taino religious life was confused and of little worth. Happily, one person who did take the report seriously was Fernando Colón, Christopher Columbus's son, who included the whole text of Pane's study in his biography of his father, *History of the Admiral Christopher Columbus by His Son.* That history, however, was itself not taken seriously and remained unpublished at Fernando's death in 1539. In 1571 it was finally translated from Spanish into Italian and printed in Venice. While the translator seems to have done a reasonably good job on the biography, he had difficulty with the included report by Pane, as certain gaps in the translation indicate. To compound the problem, the original manuscript of Colón's work, along with Pane's original report, were lost about the same time that the translation was prepared. So far as Pane's report was concerned, this meant that all that remained were the flawed Italian translation and several earlier brief summaries of the report, one of which was by the unsympathetic and somewhat confused Las Casas.

Despite these problems, Pane's report is a valuable text for modern historians and anthropologists. Research has revealed that far from being a simple-minded individual who wrote down a jumble of ill-understood stories, Pane was a careful student of Taino culture who probably managed not only to get the stories right but also maintained something of the original tone of the sacred stories and songs that he heard. As such, he gives us a fascinating glimpse into the Taino world as it existed for centuries prior to the arrival of the Spaniards.

QUESTIONS FOR ANALYSIS

1. How did the Tainos remember and pass on their traditions?
2. What did they believe regarding the dead?
3. Who or what were *bohutís,* and what do the stories about them suggest about Taino culture? Please be specific in your answer.
4. Who or what were *cemis,* and what do the stories about them suggest about Taino culture? Please be specific in your answer.
5. Compare Pane's description of Taino culture with that of Columbus's letter of 1493 in the Prologue. Does Pane's report substantiate any of Columbus's observations? How, if at all, does Pane correct any of Columbus's observations?

The Relation of Fray[1] Ramón Concerning the Antiquities of the Indians, Which He, Knowing Their Language, Carefully Compiled by Order of the Admiral

I, Fray Ramón, a poor anchorite[2] of the Order of St. Jerome, write by order of the illustrious Lord Admiral, viceroy, and governor of the islands and mainland of the Indies what I have been able to learn concerning the beliefs and idolatry of the Indians, and the manner in which they worship their gods. Of these matters I shall give an account in the present treatise.

Each one adores the idols or *cemis*[3] that he has in his house in some special way and with some special rites. They believe that there is an immortal being in the sky whom none can see and who has a mother but no beginning. They call him Yocahu Vagua Maorocoti, and his mother Atabex, Yermaoguacar, Apito, and Zuimaco, which are five different names.[4] I write only of the Indians of the island of Española, for I know nothing about the other islands and have never seen them. These Indians also know whence they came and where the sun and moon had their beginning, and how the sea was made, and of the place to which the dead go. They believe that the dead people appear on the roads to one who walks alone, but when many go together, the dead do not appear. All this they were taught by their forebears, for they cannot read or count above ten. . . .

XII. *Their beliefs concerning the wanderings of the dead, of their appearance, and what they do.* They believe the dead go to a place called Coaybay, on one side of an island called Soraya. They say that the first to live there was one Maquetaurie Guayava, who was lord of Coaybay, home and dwelling place of the dead.

XIII. *Of the forms which they assign to the dead.* They say that during the day the dead live in seclusion, but at night walk about for recreation and eat of fruit called *guabaza,* which has the flavor of [the quince][5] and during the day is[6] . . . but at night is changed into fruit; and they have festivities and keep company with the living. The Indians have this method of identifying dead people: They touch the belly of a person with the hand, and if they do not find a navel, they say that person is *operito,* which means dead; for they say that dead persons have no navels. Sometimes one who does not take this precaution and lies with a woman of Coaybay is mocked; for when he holds her in his arms, she suddenly disappears and his arms are empty. They still believe this. When a person is alive, they call his spirit *goeiz;* when he is dead, *opia.* They say that this *goeiz* appears to them often, now in the shape of a man, now of a woman. They say there was a man who wished to fight with a spirit; but when he closed with it, it disappeared, and the man flung his arms about a tree from whose branches he hung. All of them, young and old, believe this; they also believe that the spirits appear to them in the shape of their father, mother, brothers, relatives, or in some other shape. The fruit that they believe the dead eat is the size of a peach. The dead do not appear to them by day, but only by night, and therefore one who walks about at night feels great fear.

XIV. *Whence come these beliefs and why they persist in them.* There are certain men among them, called *bohutís,* who practice great frauds upon the Indians, as shall be explained hereafter, to make

---

[1] *Fray* is Spanish for *Friar,* or "Brother" — a title accorded members of certain religious orders.
[2] A synonym for *hermit.*
[3] See the Prologue, note 15.
[4] The text is corrupted here, and the Italian translator provides only four names of the mother goddess. A summary of the Spanish text of Pane's report by the churchman Peter Martyr supplies the missing name: *Iella.*

[5] There is a gap in the Italian translation, but Peter Martyr's summary (note 4) provides the fruit — quince.
[6] Another gap in the Italian text.

them believe that they, the *bohutís,* speak with the dead and that they know all their deeds and secrets, and that when the Indians are ill they cure them. These deceptions I have seen with my own eyes, whereas the other things I told about I heard of only from others, especially from their principal men — because these men believe these fables more firmly than the others. Like the Moors,[7] they have their religion set forth in ancient chants by which they are governed, as the Moors are by their Scripture.[8] When they sing their chants, they play an instrument called *mayohavau* that is made of wood and is hollow, strong, yet very thin, an ell long and half as wide; the part which is played has the shape of a blacksmith's tongs, and the other end is like a club, so that it looks like a gourd with a long neck; this instrument is so sonorous that it can be heard a league and a half away.[9] To its accompaniment they sing their chants, which they know by heart; and their principal men learn from infancy to play it and sing to it, according to their custom. Now I shall tell many other things concerning the ceremonies and customs of these heathen.

XV. *Of how the* buhuitihus[10] *practice medicine, and what they teach the people, and of the deceptions they practice in their cures.* All the Indians of the island of Española have many different kinds of *cemis.* In some they keep the bones of their father, mother, relations, and forebears; these *cemis* are made of stone or wood. They have many of both kinds. There are some that speak, others that cause food plants to grow, others that bring rain, and others that make the winds blow. These simple, ignorant people, who know not our holy faith, believe that these idols or rather demons do all these things. When an Indian falls ill, they bring the *buhuitihu* to him. This doctor must observe a diet just like his patient and must assume the suffering expression of a sick man. He must also purge himself just as the sick man does, by snuffing a powder called *cohoba*[11] up his nose. This produces such intoxication that they do not know what they are doing; and they say many senseless things, declaring that they are speaking with the *cemis* and that the latter are telling him the cause of the illness.

XVI. *What these* buhuitihus *do.* When a *buhuitihu* goes to call upon a patient, before leaving his hut he takes some soot from a cooking pot, or some charcoal, and blackens his face in order to make the sick man believe whatever he may say about his sickness; then he takes some small bones and a little meat, wraps the whole in something so it will not fall out, and puts it in his mouth. Meanwhile the patient has been purged in the manner described above. Entering the sick man's hut, the doctor sits down, and all fall silent; if there are any children in the hut, they are put out so they will not interfere with the *buhuitihu's* work; only one or two of the principal men remain. Then the *buhuitihu* takes some *güeyo* herb,[12] . . . wide, and another herb, wrapped in an onion leaf four inches long (but the *güeyo* herb is what they all generally use), and taking it between his hands, he mashes it into a pulp; and then he puts it into his mouth at night so as to vomit anything harmful that he may have eaten. Then he begins to sing his chant and, taking up a torch, drinks the juice of that herb. This done, he is quiet for a time; then he rises, goes toward the sick man, who lies alone in the middle of the hut, and walks about him twice or as many

---

[7] North African and Spanish Muslims.
[8] The Qur'an.
[9] About four and a half miles.
[10] A variant of *bohutís* (Chapter XIV). The titles are used interchangeably throughout the Italian text. Peter Martyr's summary calls them *boitius,* and Las Casas variously records their title as *bohique* and *behique.* Apparently, *bohutí(s)* is more correct and as close as we will ever get to the original Taino word for these shamans.

[11] A hallucinogenic snuff made from the crushed seeds of the piptadenia tree.
[12] Another gap in the Italian translation.

times as he thinks proper. Then he stands in front of him and takes him by the legs, feeling of his body from the thighs to the feet, after which he draws his hands away forcefully, as if pulling something out. Then he goes to the door, shuts it, and speaks to it, saying: "Begone to the mountain, or the sea, or where you will"; then, after he has blown like one who blows chaff from his hand, he turns around, joins his hands together as if he were very cold, blows on his hands, and sucks in his breath as if sucking marrow from a bone, then sucks at the sick man's neck, or stomach, or shoulder, or cheeks, or the belly or some other part of the body. Having done this, he begins to cough and make a face as if he had eaten something bitter; then he spits into his hand the stone or bone or piece of meat that he put in his mouth at home or on the road. And if it is a piece of food, he tells the sick man, "You must know that you have eaten something that caused the sickness from which you suffer. See how I have taken it out of your body, where your *cemi* lodged it because you did not pray to him or build him a shrine or give him some land." If it is a stone, he says, "Take good care of it." Sometimes they believe these stones are good and help women in childbirth, and they take good care of them, wrapping them in cotton, placing them in small baskets, and putting food before them; they do the same with the *cemis* they have in their houses. On a holiday, when they have much food — fish, meat, or bread — they put some of each food in the house of the *cemi,* and next day they carry this food back to their huts after the *cemi* has eaten. But it would truly be a miracle if the *cemi* ate of that or anything else, for the *cemi* is a dead thing of stone or wood.

XVII. *How these physicians are sometimes paid back for their deceptions.* If the sick man should die in spite of having done all these things, and if he has many relations or one who is lord over a village and so can stand up to the *buhuitihu* or doctor (for men of small influence dare not contend with them), then those who wish to do the *buhuitihu* mischief do the following: First, in order to learn if the sick man died through the

doctor's fault, or because he did not observe the diet that the doctor prescribed for him, these relations take an herb which is called *güeyo,* whose leaves resemble those of the sweet basil, being thick and long; this herb is also called *zacón.* They squeeze the juice from the leaf, then cut the dead man's nails and the hair above his forehead, pound the nails and hair to a powder between two stones, mix this powder with the juice of the herb, and pour the mixture between the dead man's lips to find out from him if the doctor was the cause of his death and whether he observed his diet. They ask this of him many times, until at last he speaks as distinctly as if he were alive and answers all their questions, saying that the *buhuitihu* did not observe the diet, or was the cause of his death. They say that the doctor asks him if he is alive, and that he can speak very clearly; he replies that he is dead. After they have learned from him what they want to know, they return him to the grave from which they took him. They perform this sorcery in still another way. They take the dead man and make a great fire like that used for making charcoal, and when the wood has turned to live coals, they throw the body into that fierce blaze; then they cover it with earth, as the charcoal-burner does the charcoal, and leave it there as long as they think advisable. Then they ask him the same question as above. The dead man replies that he knows nothing. This they ask of him ten times, and ten times he replies in the same way. Again they ask him if he is dead, but he will speak only those ten times.

XVIII. *How the dead man's relatives avenge themselves when they have had a reply through the sorcery of the potions.* The dead man's relations assemble on a certain day and lie in wait for the said *buhuitihu,* give him such a thrashing that they break his legs, arms, and head, and leave him for dead. At night, they say, there come many different kinds of snakes — white, black, green, and many other colors — that lick the face and whole body of the physician whom the Indians have left for dead. This they do two or three nights in succession; and presently, they say, the bones of his body knit together again and mend. And he rises and walks rather slowly to his home. Those who meet him on the road say, "Were you not dead?" He replies that the *cemis* came to his aid in the shape of snakes. And the dead man's relations, very angry and desperate because they thought they had avenged the death of their kinsman, again try to lay hands on him; and if they catch him a second time, they pluck out his eyes and smash his testicles, for they say no amount of beating will kill one of these physicians if they do not first tear out his testicles.

How the dead man whom they have burned reveals what they wish to know, and how they take their vengeance. When they uncover the fire, the smoke rises until it is lost from sight, and when it leaves the furnace, it makes a chirping noise. Then it descends and enters the hut of the *buhuitihu* or doctor. If he did not observe the diet, he falls sick that very moment, is covered with sores, and his whole body peels. This they take for a sign that he did not observe his diet, and so they try to kill him in the manner described above. These are the sorceries they perform.

XIX. *How they make and keep their wooden or stone cemis.* They make the wooden *cemis* in this fashion. If a man walking along the way sees a tree moving its roots, he stops, filled with fear, and asks who it is. The tree replies, "Summon a *buhuitihu*, and he will tell you who I am." Then that man goes in search of a physician and tells him what he has seen. The sorcerer or warlock immediately runs toward that tree, sits down by it, and prepares a *cohoba* for it. . . . And having made the *cohoba*, he rises, and pronounces all its titles as if it were a great lord, and says to it: "Tell me who you are and what you are doing here, and what you want of me and why you summoned me. Tell me if you want me to cut you down, and if you wish to come with me, and how you want me to carry you; for I shall build a house for you and endow it with land." Then that *cemi* or tree, become an idol or devil, tells him the shape in which it wants to be made. And the sorcerer cuts it down and carves it into the shape that it has

ordered, builds a house for it and endows it with land; and many times a year he makes *cohoba* for it.

This *cohoba* is their means of praying to the idol and also of asking it for riches. When they wish to know if they will gain a victory over their enemies, they enter a hut to which only the principal men are admitted. And the lord is the first to make the *cohoba* and plays an instrument; and while he makes the *cohoba* none may speak. After he has finished his prayer he remains for some time with bowed head and arms resting on his knees; then he lifts his head, looks up to the sky, and speaks. All respond to him in a loud voice, and having spoken, they all give thanks; and he relates the vision he had while stupefied with the *cohoba* that he snuffed up his nose and that went to his head. He tells that he has spoken with the *cemi* and that they will gain the victory, or that their enemies will flee, or that there will be many deaths, or wars, or famines, or the like, or whatever comes to his addled head to say. One can imagine the state he is in, for they say the house appears to him to be turned upside-down and the people to be walking with their feet in the air. This *cohoba* they make not only for the *cemis* of stone and wood but also for the bodies of the dead, as told above.

There are different kinds of stone *cemis*. Some the doctors extract from bodies of sick people, and it is believed these are the best to induce childbirth in pregnant women. There are other *cemis* that speak; these have the shape of a large turnip with leaves that trail over the ground and are as long as the leaves of the caper bush; these leaves generally resemble those of the elm, others have three points: The natives believe they help the yucca grow. The root resembles that of the radish, and the leaf generally has six or seven points. I know not with what to compare it, because I have seen no plant like it in Spain or in any other country. The stalk of the yucca is as high as a man.

Now I shall tell of their beliefs concerning their idols and *cemis*, and how they are greatly deluded by them.

▷ Pane now narrates stories about a variety of famous cemis. The following two stories are typical.

XXII. *Concerning another* cemi *named Opiyel-guovirán, who belonged to a principal man named Cavavaniovavá, who had many vassals.* They say this *cemi* Opiyelguovirán had four legs, like a dog, and was made of wood, and frequently left his house by night and went into the woods. They would go in search of him, and bring him back to the house tied with cords, but he always returned to the woods. They say that when the Spaniards arrived on the island of Española, this *cemi* fled and went to a lagoon; they followed him there by his tracks, but never saw him again, and know nothing more of him. That is the story they tell, and faithfully do I tell it again.

[13]The Taino word for *chief,* which has spread to both the Spanish and English languages.

XXIII. *Concerning another* cemi *named Guabancex.* This *cemi* lived in the land of a principal cacique,[13] named Aumatex. It is a woman, and they say she has two other *cemis* for companions; one is a herald and the other is the collector and governor of the waters. They say that when Guabancex is angry, she raises the winds and water, throws down houses, and tears up the trees. They say this *cemi* is a woman and is made of stones of that country. Her herald, named Guatauba, carries out her orders by making the other *cemis* of the province help in raising wind and rain. Her other companion is named Coatrisquié; of him they say that he collects the waters in the valleys between the mountains and then lets them loose to destroy the countryside. The people hold this to be gospel truth.

Quiché Mayan Gods and Monarchs
▼▼▼
99 ▼ *THE BOOK OF THE COMMUNITY*

Among all the peoples of ancient America, only the Meso-Americans created systems of writing, although the Quechua-speaking people of the Andes, who carved out the Inca Empire, devised a system of record keeping by means of knotted strings that served almost as well (source 100). Of all the forms of writing used in Central America, the *Maya* had the most sophisticated, an exceedingly complex system based on a wide range of picture symbols, technically known as *glyphs,* that variously represented objects, concepts, and sounds. Unfortunately, Spanish missionaries, zealous to destroy all remnants of indigenous paganism, burned most of the books of the Maya. Only three preconquest Mayan books, and fragments of a fourth, survived the fires of the Spanish Catholic Inquisition. Nevertheless, three factors allow us to know more about the preconquest Maya than any other Amerindian civilization: (1) recently scholars broke the code of the Mayas' ancient written language, enabling historians to read most of their texts and engraved monuments; (2) the classical Maya left behind a rich archeological heritage, which is still being explored and interpreted; and (3) the Maya, as a people and culture, survive and even flourish today in Guatemala, Belize, and Mexico's Yucatan peninsula, preserving much of their past in their living traditions.

The document that appears here dates from shortly after the early sixteenth-century Spanish conquest of the *Quiché* Maya of Guatemala, the most powerful of the then existing Mayan states of Central America. The Maya, who had a shared culture but were never organized under a single central authority, had reached their classical heights between about 300 and 800 C.E. but by 900 had abandoned many of their cities and ceremonial centers. Yet even with the collapse of many of their states and urban centers, the Maya persisted as a culture and even built a few new cities. When the army of Pedro de Alvardo invaded the territory of the Quiché in 1524, it found a vigorous society that initially offered spirited resistance. Eventually, however, the Spaniards prevailed.

Faced with the threat of losing all memory of the Mayan way of life, an anonymous Quiché Indian, who was at least nominally a convert to Catholic Christianity, undertook to compile, in his native tongue, a collection of Mayan beliefs, traditions, and history down to 1550, because, as he noted, "The original book, written long ago, existed, but its sight is hidden to the searcher." The result was the *Popul Vuh, or Book of the Community.* The *Popul Vuh* remained hidden for about one hundred fifty years until it was discovered by a sympathetic Spanish priest, who was also a scholar of the Quiché culture. He transcribed the text from its manuscript, thereby preserving the original Quiché version, and translated it into Spanish, in order "to bring to light what had been among the Indians in the olden days [and] . . . to give information on the errors which they had in their paganism and which they still adhere to among themselves."

The following selection tells about *Tohil,* chief god of the Quiché Maya, and his relationship with the *Ahpop,* or Quiché monarch, in the era preceding the coming of the Spaniards.

QUESTIONS FOR ANALYSIS

1. What special functions did the ancient Quiché monarchs have? Why did the monarchs fast?
2. What were the mutual responsibilities of monarchs and subjects? What do they suggest about this society?
3. How was the Quiché state ruled? What does its having three royal houses suggest?
4. What did the people owe Tohil? What was expected in return?
5. How do we know that Tohil was a syncretic deity, whose manifestations and functions were drawn from a variety of sources? What does this suggest about the make-up of the Quiché state?
6. What evidence is there that the Quiché saw themselves as belonging to a single culture, despite their tribal divisions?
7. What allows us to infer that postclassical Quiché civilization was still vibrant?

We shall now tell of the House of the God. The house was also given the same name as the god. The Great Edifice of Tohil was the name of the Temple of Tohil, of those of Cavec.[1] . . .

Tzutuhá, which is seen in Cahbahá,[2] is the name of a large edifice in which there was a stone which all the lords of Quiché worshiped and which was also worshiped by all the tribes.

The people first offered their sacrifices before Tohil, and afterward went to pay their respects to the Ahpop and the Ahpop-Camhá.[3] Then they went to present their gorgeous feathers and their tribute before the king. And the kings whom they maintained were the Ahpop and the Ahpop-Camhá, who had conquered their towns.

Great lords and wonderful men were the marvelous kings Gucumatz and Cotuhá, the marvelous kings Quicab and Cavizimah.[4] They knew if there would be war, and everything was clear before their eyes; they saw if there would be death and hunger, if there would be strife. They well know that there was a place where it could be seen, that there was a book which they called the *Popol Vuh.*

But not only in this way was the estate of the lords great, great also were their fasts. And this was in recognition of their having been created, and in recognition of their having been given their kingdoms. They fasted a long time and made sacrifices to their gods. Here is how they fasted: Nine men fasted and another nine made sacrifices[5] and burned incense. Thirteen more men fasted, and another thirteen more made offerings and burned incense before Tohil. And while before their god, they nourished themselves only with fruits, with *zapotes, matasanos,* and *jocotes.* And they did not eat any *tortillas.* Now if

there were seventeen men who made sacrifice, or ten who fasted, the truth is they did not eat. They fulfilled their great precepts, and thus showed their position as lords.

Neither had they women to sleep with, but they remained alone, fasting. They were in the House of God, all day they prayed, burning incense and making sacrifices. Thus they remained from dusk until dawn, grieving in their hearts and in their breasts, and begging for happiness and life for their sons and vassals as well as for their kingdom, and raising their faces to the sky.

Here are their petitions to their god, when they prayed; and this was the supplication of their hearts:

"Oh, Thou, beauty of the day! Thou, Huracán;[6] Thou, Heart of Heaven and of Earth! Thou, giver of richness, and giver of the daughters and the sons! Turn toward us your power and your riches; grant life and growth unto my sons and vassals; let those who must maintain and nourish Thee multiply and increase; those who invoke Thee on the roads, in the fields, on the banks of the rivers, in the ravines, under the trees, under the vines.

"Give them daughters and sons. Let them not meet disgrace, nor misfortune, let not the deceiver come behind or before them. Let them not fall, let them not be wounded, let them not fornicate, nor be condemned by justice. Let them not fall on the descent or on the ascent of the road. Let them not encounter obstacles back of them or before them, nor anything which strikes them. Grant them good roads, beautiful, level roads. Let them not have misfortune, nor disgrace, through Thy fault, through Thy sorceries.

---

[1] The principal branch of the Quiché people.
[2] The name of the ceremonial center where the temple called *Tzutuha* was located.
[3] The Ahpop-Camhá was a coreigning subking. Both the Ahpop and Ahpop-Camhá came from the chief royal family of the Quiché people, the *Cavec.*

[4] Gucumatz and Cotuhá were Ahpop and Ahpop-Camhá during the fifth generation of the twelve generations of Cavec monarchs, who ruled the Quiché prior to the Spanish conquest. They were the first of a line of sorcerer kings. Quicab and Cavizimah were seventh-generation Cavec monarchs.
[5] Possibly human sacrifices.
[6] One of Tohil's names.

"Grant a good life to those who must give Thee sustenance and place food in Thy mouth, in Thy presence, to Thee, Heart of Heaven, Heart of Earth, Bundle of Majesty. And Thou, Tohil; Thou, Avilix;[7] Thou, Hacavitz,[8] Arch of the Sky, Surface of the Earth, the Four Corners, the Four Cardinal Points. Let there be but peace and tranquility in Thy mouth, in Thy presence, oh, God!"

Thus [spoke] the lords, while within, the nine men fasted, the thirteen men, and the seventeen men. During the day they fasted and their hearts grieved for their sons and vassals and for all their wives and their children when each of the lords made his offering.

This was the price of a happy life, the price of power, the price of the authority of the Ahpop, of the Ahpop-Camhá, of the Galel and of the Ahtzic-Vinac.[9] Two by two they ruled, each pair succeeding the other in order to bear the burden of the people of all the Quiché nation.

One only was the origin of their tradition and [one only] the origin of the manner of maintaining and sustaining, and one only, too, was the origin of the tradition and the customs of those of Tamub and Ilocab and the people of Rabinal and the Cakchiquel, those of Tziquinahá, of Tuhalahá and Uchabahá.[10] And there was but one trunk [a single family] when they heard there in Quiché what all of them were to do.

But it was not only thus that they reigned. They did not squander the gifts of those whom they sustained and nourished, but they ate and drank them. Neither did they buy them; they had won and seized their empire, their power, and their sovereignty.

And it was not at small cost, that they conquered the fields and the towns; the small towns and the large towns paid high ransoms; they brought precious stones and metals, they brought honey of the bees, bracelets, bracelets of emeralds and other stones, and brought garlands made of blue feathers, the tribute of all the towns. They came into the presence of the marvelous kings Gucumatz and Cotuhá, and before Quicab and Cavizimah,[11] the Ahpop, the Ahpop-Camhá, the Galel, and the Ahtzic-Vinac.

It was not little what they did, neither were few, the tribes which they conquered. Many branches of the tribes came to pay tribute to the Quiché; full of sorrow they came to give it over. Nevertheless, the [Quiché] power did not grow quickly. Gucumatz it was, who began the aggrandizement of the kingdom. Thus was the beginning of his aggrandizement and that of the Quiché nation.

---

[7]The god of Balam-Acab, one of the founders of the Quiché state.

[8]The god of the Ahau-Quiché, one of the three royal houses of the Quiché (see note 9).

[9]The Quiché had three royal houses. The Cavec supplied its two chief rulers (note 3). The Galel was a court official who was also king of the House of Nihaib; the Ahtzic-Vinac was head of the House of Ahau Quiché.

[10]Various Quiché tribes and regions.

[11]See note 4.

Governing the Inca Empire

▼▼▼

100 ▾ Pedro de Cieza de León, CHRONICLES

Because no society of South America developed a system of writing, there are no written records of South America's civilizations prior to the arrival of the Spaniards. Our best sources for their preconquest history are therefore archeological artifacts (source 97) and accounts composed by sixteenth- and early seventeenth-century Amerindian and Spanish writers, who labored to preserve the memory of a past in imminent danger of being lost forever. One such ethnohistorian was

Pedro de Cieza de León (1520–1554), who in 1535 arrived in the Americas as a teen-age soldier-adventurer and spent the next seventeen years trekking throughout South America, falling increasingly under the spell of the continent and its native peoples. As he traveled and fought, he constantly took detailed notes of all he had observed and experienced. Believing, as he noted, that "we and the Indians have the same origin," Cieza wrote with great sympathy for the many different Amerindian cultures he encountered, even though he seems never to have doubted the righteousness of the Spanish conquest and conversion of these peoples. Indeed, one of his primary reasons for recording his observations was that he considered it "right that the world know how so great a multitude of these Indians were brought into the sanctity of the Church."

Although Cieza's *Chronicles* describe many different native South American cultures, their greatest value to modern historians is the wealth of detail they provide of the Inca Empire and the *Quechua* Amerindians who had created it. Like the Aztecs of Mexico, far to their north, the Quechuas were recent arrivals on the scene who fashioned a civilization that borrowed heavily from a variety of preceding cultures. Also like the Aztec Empire, the Inca Empire was young, having taken shape during the reigns of Pachacuti (1438–1471) and his son Topac Yupanqui (1471–1493). As was also true in Mexico, its life was prematurely cut short by *conquistadores*.

In the following selection Cieza describes how the Inca monarchs governed an empire that covered about one-half million square miles, stretched some two thousand five hundred miles from end to end, and included anywhere from six to thirteen million people of different ethnic origins and languages.

QUESTIONS FOR ANALYSIS

1. What devices did the Incas use to govern their vast empire?
2. How did the Inca Empire manage to function without a system of writing?
3. From Cieza's perspective, what were the most admirable qualities of this empire?
4. What appear to have been the strengths of this empire? The weaknesses? Were the Incas aware of these shortcomings, and, if so, how did they attempt to counter them?

It is told for a fact of the rulers of this kingdom that in the days of their rule they had their representatives in the capitals of all the provinces, . . . for in all these places there were larger and finer lodgings than in most of the other cities of this great kingdom, and many storehouses. They served as the head of the provinces or regions, and from every so many leagues[1] around the tributes were brought to one of these capitals, and from so many others, to another. This was so well organized that there was not a village that did not know where it was to send its tribute. In all these capitals the Incas had temples of the sun, mints, and many silversmiths who did nothing

---

[1]A league is three miles.

but work rich pieces of gold or fair vessels of silver; large garrisons were stationed there, and, as I have said, a steward or representative who was in command of them all, to whom an accounting of everything that was brought in was made, and who, in turn, had to give one of all that was issued. And these governors could in no way interfere with the jurisdiction of another who held a similar post, but within his own, if there were any disorder or disturbance, he had authority to punish it[s perpetrators], especially if it were in the nature of a conspiracy or a rebellion, or failure to obey the Inca,[2] for full power resided in these governors. And if the Incas had not had the foresight to appoint them and to establish the *mitimaes*,[3] the natives would have often revolted and shaken off the royal rule; but with the many troops and the abundance of provisions, they could not effect this unless they had all plotted such treason or rebellion together. This happened rarely, for these governors who were named were of complete trust, all of them *Orejones*,[4] and most of them had their holdings, or *chacaras*, in the neighborhood of *Cuzco*,[5] and their homes and kinfolk. If one of them did not show sufficient capacity for his duties, he was removed and another put in his place.

When one of them came to Cuzco on private business or to see the Inca, he left a lieutenant in his place, not one who aspired to the post, but one he knew would faithfully carry out what he was ordered to do and what was best for the service of the Inca. And if one of these governors or delegates died while in office, the natives at once sent word to the Inca how and of what he had died, and even transported the body by the post road if this seemed to them advisable. The trib-

ute paid by each of these districts where the capital was situated and that turned over by the natives, whether gold, silver, clothing, arms, and all else they gave, was entered in the accounts of . . . [those] who kept the *quipus*[6] and did everything ordered by the governor in the matter of finding the soldiers or supplying whomever the Inca ordered, or making delivery to Cuzco; but when they came from the city of Cuzco to go over the accounts, or they were ordered to go to Cuzco to give an accounting, the accountants themselves gave it by the quipus, or went to give it where there could be no fraud, but everything had to come out right. Few years went by in which an accounting of all these things was not made. . . .

Realizing how difficult it would be to travel the great distances of their land where every league and at every turn a different language was spoken, and how bothersome it would be to have to employ interpreters to understand them, these rulers, as the best measure, ordered and decreed, with severe punishment for failure to obey, that all the natives of their empire should know and understand the language of Cuzco, both they and their women. This was so strictly enforced that an infant had not yet left its mother's breast before they began to teach it the language it had to know. And although at the beginning this was difficult and many stubbornly refused to learn any language but their own, the Incas were so forceful that they accomplished what they had proposed, and all had to do their bidding. This was carried out so faithfully that in the space of a few years a single tongue was known and used in an extension of more than 1,200 leagues, yet, even though this language was employed, they

---

[2] *Inca* means "sovereign lord," and in its strictest sense should be used only to refer to this civilization's god-kings. Today, however, historians customarily use the term loosely to refer to the civilization, its empire, and the Quechua people who created them.
[3] Literally, "those moved from one land to another." This was the systematic practice of resettling groups from one area of the empire to another. These resettled people would serve as a check on the loyalties of the natives of the region to which they had been transferred and would, in turn, be

kept in check by their new neighbors. This not only helped keep down rebellions and break down regional and ethnic differences within the empire, it also was a means of cultivating land that needed settlers.
[4] Literally in Spanish, "big ears." These were members of the ruling class, often of royal blood, who were distinguished by the large ear plugs they wore.
[5] The capital city of the empire.
[6] The Quechua system of record keeping by means of knotted strings that León describes later in this excerpt.

all spoke their own [languages], which were so numerous that if I were to list them it would not be credited. . . .

As the city of Cuzco was the most important in all Peru, and the Incas lived there most of the time, they had with them in the city many of the leading men of the country, the most intelligent and informed of all, as their advisers. For all agree that before they undertook anything of importance, they discussed it with these counselors, and submitted their opinion to that of the majority. And for the administration of the city, and that the highways should be safe and nowhere should offenses or thefts be committed, from among the most highly esteemed of them he [the Inca] appointed those whose duty it was to punish wrongdoers, and to this end they were always traveling about the country. The Incas took such care to see that justice was meted out that nobody ventured to commit a felony or theft. This was to deal with thieves, ravishers of women, or conspirators against the Inca; however, there were many provinces that warred on one another, and the Incas were not wholly able to prevent this.

By the river that runs through Cuzco justice was executed on those who were caught or brought in as prisoners from some other place. There they had their heads cut off, or were put to death in some other manner which they chose. Mutiny and conspiracy were severely punished, and, above all, those who were thieves and known as such; even their wives and children were despised and considered to be tarred with the same brush. . . .

We have written how it was ordered by the Incas that the statues be brought out at their feasts, and how they selected from the wisest among their men those who should tell what the life of their kings had been and how they had conducted themselves in the rule of their kingdoms, for the purpose I have stated. It should also be known that, aside from this, it was the custom among them, and a rule carefully observed, for each of them to choose during his reign three or four old men of their nation, skilled

and gifted for that purpose, whom they ordered to recall all that had happened in the province during the time of their reign, whether prosperous or adverse, and to make and arrange songs so that thereby it might be known in the future what had taken place in the past. Such songs could not be sung or proclaimed outside the presence of the Inca, and those who were to carry out this behest were ordered to say nothing referring to the Inca during his lifetime, but after he was dead, they said to his successor almost in these words: "Oh, mighty and powerful Inca, may the Sun and Moon, the Earth, the hills and trees, the stones and your forefathers guard you from misfortune and make you prosperous, happy, and blessed among all who have been born. Know that the things that happened to your predecessor were these." And saying this, with their eyes on the ground and heads hanging, with great humility they gave an account and report of all they knew, which they could do very well, for there were many among them of great memory, subtle wit, and lively intelligence, and abounding in knowledge, as those of us who are here and hear them can bear witness. After they said this, when the Inca had heard them, he sent for other of his old Indians whom he ordered to learn the songs the others bore in their memory, and to prepare new ones of what took place during the time of his reign, what was spent, what the provinces contributed, and put all this down in the quipus, so that after his death, when his successor reigned, what had been given and contributed would be known. And except on days of great celebration, or on the occasion of mourning and lament for the death of a brother or son of the Inca, for on such days it was permitted to relate their grandeur and their origin and birth, at no other time was it permitted to deal with this, for it had been forbidden by their lords, and if they did so, they were severely punished.

[The Indians] had a method of knowing how the tributes of food supplies should be levied on the provinces when the Lord-Inca came through with his army, or was visiting the kingdom; or, when nothing of this sort was taking place, what came into the storehouses and what was issued to the subjects, so nobody could be unduly burdened. . . . This involved the quipus, which are long strands of knotted strings, and those who were the accountants and understood the meaning of these knots could reckon by them expenditures or other things that had taken place many years before. By these knots they counted from one to ten and from ten to a hundred, and from a hundred to a thousand. On one of these strands there is the account of one thing, and on the other of another, in such a way that what to us is a strange, meaningless account is clear to them. In the capital of each province there were accountants whom they called *quipu-camayocs,* and by these knots they kept the account of the tribute to be paid by the natives of that district in silver, gold, clothing, flocks, down to wood and other more insignificant things, and by these same quipus at the end of a year, or ten, or twenty years, they gave a report to the one whose duty it was to check the account so exact that not even a pair of sandals was missing. . . .

The *Orejones* of Cuzco who supplied me with information are in agreement that in olden times, in the days of the Lord-Incas, all the villages and provinces of Peru were notified that a report should be given to the rulers and their representatives each year of the men and women who had died, and all who had been born, for this was necessary for the levying of the tributes as well as to know how many were available for war and those who could assume the defense of the villages. This was an easy matter, for each province at the end of the year had a list by the knots of the quipus of all the people who had died there during the year, as well as of those who had been born. At the beginning of the new year they came to Cuzco, bringing their quipus, which told how many births there had been during the year, and how many deaths. This was reported with all truth and accuracy, without any fraud or deceit. In this way the Inca and the governors knew which of the Indians were poor, the women who had been widowed, whether they were able to pay their taxes, and how many men they could count on in the event of war, and many other things they considered highly important.

As this kingdom was so vast, as I have repeatedly mentioned, in each of the many provinces there were many storehouses filled with supplies and other needful things; thus, in times of war, wherever the armies went they drew upon the contents of these storehouses, without ever touching the supplies of their confederates or laying a finger on what they had in their settlements. And when there was no war, all this stock of supplies and food was divided up among the poor and the widows. These poor were the aged, or the lame, crippled, or paralyzed, or those afflicted with some other diseases; if they were in good health, they received nothing. Then the storehouses were filled up once more with the tributes paid the Inca. If there came a lean year, the storehouses were opened and the provinces were lent what they needed in the way of supplies; then, in a year of abundance, they paid back all they had received. Even though the tributes paid to the Inca were used only for the aforesaid purposes, they were employed to advantage, for in this way their kingdom was opulent and well supplied.

No one who was lazy or tried to live by the work of others was tolerated; everyone had to work. Thus on certain days each lord went to his lands and took the plow in hand and cultivated the earth, and did other things. Even the Incas themselves did this to set an example, for everybody was to know that there should be nobody so rich that, on this account, he might disdain or affront the poor. And under their system there was none such in all the kingdom, for, if he had his health, he worked and lacked for nothing; and if he was ill, he received what he needed from the storehouses. And no rich man could deck himself out in more finery than the poor, or wear different clothing, except the rulers and headmen, who, to maintain their dignity, were allowed great freedom and privilege, as well as the *Orejones,* who held a place apart among all the peoples.

Part Four

⩗

Travel, Encounter, and Exchange: 1000–1700

Europe's late-fifteenth-century transoceanic explorations inaugurated a new stage of global interconnectedness by virtue of Columbus's sailing to the Americas. Yet in many respects the events of 1492 and following were a continuation of a process of long-range cultural exchange that had been gaining momentum throughout Eurasia and Africa since at least the opening of the Silk Road in the second century B.C.E. This process had its periods of retreat and retrenchment, as routes closed down due to any number of factors, but the overall pattern was one of growing interchange. The collapse of the Han, Kushana, and Roman empires dealt Silk Road traffic a severe setback after 200 C.E., but rising involvement in long-distance travel and trade on the part of China, Islam, and Byzantium after 600 C.E. revived the Silk Road and provided the impetus for opening up new land and water routes. Between about 1000 and 1400 C.E. long-distance interchange received a boost from the travels and state-building of some newcomers, most notably the Vikings, the Turks, the Western European "Franks," and the Mongols. To be sure, many of their travels and conquests were filled with wholesale destruction, yet these adventurers and empire builders also created new pathways for the transmission of cultures.

As important as these contacts were, none matched the historical significance of the transoceanic exchanges set in motion by Western Europe in the late fifteenth century. Earlier in that century, ships flying the flag of the small kingdom of Portugal began to probe the waters of Africa's west coast in the hope of reaching the source of Muslim North Africa's sub-Saharan gold trade and of contacting Prester John, the legendary Christian king believed by some to be living in Africa (Chapter 12, source 109). Although the Portuguese finally made contact with the ancient East African Christian civilization of Ethiopia (Chapter 11, source 95), they failed to convert it to Catholicism, and their missionaries were expelled in 1633. Despite occasional setbacks, Portuguese commercial ventures along the African coastline and beyond proved to be enormously lucrative. Having reached India in 1498, the Malay coast in 1511, and China in 1513, the Portuguese were soon bringing back to Europe spices, silks, dyes, and other exotic items and reaping huge profits. Because of fierce competition among the European states, other European nations sought to rival the Portuguese by seeking new oceanic routes to East and South Asia, a region that Europeans vaguely called *the Indies*. Columbus's voyage of 1492 was only the first of dozens of Spanish enterprises that established Spain as the dominant power not in Asia, as hoped, but in a New World: the Americas. The nations of northern Europe also joined in. The French, Dutch, English, Danes, and Swedes claimed lands in the western hemisphere, and the French, Dutch, and English successfully challenged and broke the early Portuguese monopoly in African and Asian trade. By 1600 the European presence was beginning to be felt around the globe.

This initial burst of European expansion affected the various societies that Europeans encountered in radically different ways. It had little impact on the ancient centers of civilization in South and East Asia, the rulers of which tolerated a limited amount of trade but were strong enough to prevent the Europeans from undermining their political power or the cultural traditions of their subjects. In contrast, the Amerindian civilizations of Mexico, Central America, and South America were all but wiped out by Spanish military conquests, economic exploitation, missionary activity, and the introduction of deadly new diseases. The story north of the Rio Grande was somewhat different. Some North American cultures were obliterated soon after the first arrival of Europeans. Most of the Amerindians of North America, however, faced similar threats of extinction only after 1600, when the French and English arrived in substantial numbers. Here the Native Americans' loss of territory and identity was generally not so sudden, but the process was no less painful and in the end the results were largely the same. In Africa, Europeans were unable to topple native rulers or impose their language and religion on most indigenous communities. Europeans largely remained on the coast, relying on Africans to bring them commodities for trade.

Tragically, in addition to gold and ivory, these commodities included human slaves. Indeed, for the first several centuries of direct European–West African contact, the slave trade dominated coastal commerce along Africa's western shores. Initially, the Portuguese shipped their African slaves to Europe and various Atlantic islands, where they primarily labored on sugar plantations. Then, in ever greater numbers, European entrepreneurs brought these workers-in-bondage to the plantations of the New World. There the Africans replaced the large numbers of Amerindian forced laborers who had died off and the far fewer numbers of transported European criminals and outcasts who had also succumbed to tropical diseases and abuse. Before it ended in the nineteenth century, the trans-Atlantic slave trade robbed millions of human beings of their freedom, dignity, and lives.

Chapter 12

▼▼▼

Adventurers, Merchants, Diplomats, Pilgrims, and Missionaries

A Half Millennium of Travel and Encounter: 1000–1500

The era from roughly 1000 to about 1500 witnessed large-scale movements of individuals and peoples across much of the Afro-Eurasian Ecumene, and it also witnessed direct contacts between the so-called Old World of Europe and the so-called New World of the Americas. The first of the recorded contacts between Europeans and Americans proved to be a dead end; the second, however, became an epochal event that set the history of the entire human community onto a new plane. Whereas the exploits of Scandinavian seafarers who reached the shores of North America around the year 1000 left no permanent imprint on either the Americas or Europe, the arrival of Spaniards in the Americas just before the year 1500 transformed both civilizations and, arguably, the world.

Long before Columbus and his Portuguese counterparts set sail, however, the Old Afro-Eurasian World was well on its way toward becoming the home of an increasingly interconnected human community. Turks out of the steppes of Central Asia converted to Islam and then spread their faith and culture into India, the Balkan region of southeastern Europe, and deeper into their traditional Central Asian homeland as they carved out and expanded a variety of states. In Western Europe, Scandinavian adventurers (known as *Vikings, Norse,* and *Northmen*) first pillaged and then settled in Ireland, England, western France, Iceland, and various other places. With the exception of the Scandinavians who settled in Russia and accepted Byzantine Christianity, the Vikings converted to Catholic Christianity, and during the eleventh century these new members of the faith of Rome became a sharp cutting edge of militant, expansionistic Western Christendom. Norse who had settled in France and had become *Norman* French expanded the boundaries of European Christendom into the Mediterranean. During the last half of the eleventh century Norman adventurers conquered southern Italy from the Byzantine Empire and Sicily from its Muslim overlords. These same Normans assaulted the Balkan possessions of the emperor at Constantinople and became an integral part of medieval Western Europe's most energetic and protracted overseas colonial adventure — the crusades in the Levant. Of all the catalysts of cultural exchange, the most explosive and impressive were the Mongols. In the course of the thirteenth century they created a Eurasian land empire that reached from the Pacific to Ukraine. After the initial shock of their conquests, they established a *Pax Mongolica* (Mongol Peace) that opened up lines of direct communication between East Asia and Western Europe. For about a century, people, goods, ideas, and even diseases traveled faster than ever before from one end of the Eurasian landmass to the other.

A number of factors combined by 1400 to sever most of the overland routes between Europe and China that had opened up in the thirteenth century. They included the onslaught of the Eurasian-wide pandemic of the Black Death; massive economic depression that affected lands and peoples throughout Eurasia; the breakup of the Mongol Empire around the middle of the fourteenth century; the disruption of the ancient Silk Road routes of Inner Asia by the armies of the Turkish conqueror Timur the Lame (Tamerlane) between 1369 and 1405; the increasing antipathy toward foreigners and foreign adventure shown by China's Ming Dynasty (r. 1368–1644); and the successes of the Ottoman Turks, who swept through Anatolia and the Balkans, finally capturing Constantinople in 1453.

To be sure, there was still a trickle of Western contact with Central, South, and East Asia in the early and mid fifteenth century. A handful of European merchants and adventurers even managed to reach the waters of the Indian Ocean by way of either the Red Sea or the Persian Gulf. Nevertheless, the heady days of regular mercantile and missionary contacts with the fabled land of *Cathay*, as China was called in the West, were now at an end — at least for the moment.

With the land routes now blocked, it fell to the kingdoms of Europe's Iberian Peninsula that had ports on the Atlantic to attempt contact by way of the ocean. The results of their attempts proved quite extraordinary. During the last decade of the fifteenth century Spain supported an enterprise that resulted in the European discovery of the Americas, and Portugal pushed into the Indian Ocean by way of Africa and also stumbled across Brazil in 1500.

▾▾▾

Pilgrims and Merchants before the Mongol Age

As we shall see in this chapter, the Mongol Empire established an environment conducive to long-distance travel and cultural interchange by providing an avenue across Eurasia from the Pacific Ocean to the Black Sea. We would be wrong, however, to think that long-distance travel and cultural interaction only occurred as the result of conquest and state building. Long before the rise of the Mongol Empire, hundreds of thousands, even millions, of anonymous men and women traveling as merchants, pilgrims, missionaries, diplomats, and curiosity seekers had already made long-distance travel and its consequent cultural exchanges an important historical phenomenon. This was especially true after 1000. Indian and Chinese merchants traveled into Southeast Asia, where they influenced the evolution of a hybrid culture that has been termed *Indo-Chinese*. Arabs and Berbers in camel caravans trekked across the desert to trade salt and manufactured goods for the gold, ivory, and slaves of sub-Saharan West Africa. Italian merchants established bases in the Black Sea on the western edge of Central Asia. African, Arab, Indian, Southeast Asian, Chinese, and even a few European sailors shared the waters of the Indian Ocean. Pilgrims of many different faiths often traveled great distances to worship at their holy sites. Muslim and Christian missionaries, motivated by devotion and love, labored among foreign peoples who they believed would be damned to hell without spiritual guidance. Envoys in the service of princes and spiritual leaders regularly carried important messages to faraway potentates, and some states, such as Genoa and Venice, even established resident ambassadors in distant lands. And then there were the curiosity seekers and adventurers, who simply traveled for the sheer joy and experience of it all. As the following two documents suggest, untold numbers of unknown people traveled about after the turn of the millennium and before the rise of the Mongol Empire, and they did so for a variety of reasons.

The Pilgrimage to Rome

▼▼▼

101 ▼ Benedict of St. Peter, THE MARVELS OF THE CITY OF ROME

Religious pilgrimage, whereby a devotee travels to a holy site in search of spiritual communion with the Sacred, is a universal religious practice. We have already seen the Muslim *hajj,* or pilgrimage to the holy city of Mecca (Chapter 8, source 62). In the midst of their Diaspora, or Great Dispersion, Jews held firm in their focus on their holy city — Jerusalem. Indeed, the pilgrimage to Jerusalem was understood on at least two levels. On the personal level, Jews as individuals were encouraged to undertake the sanctifying experience of journeying to the Holy City, where they could pray in the shadow of the ruins of the Temple. On a higher level, the prayers of these pilgrims and, indeed, the prayers of Jews all over the world were for the realization of the Ultimate Pilgrimage, the triumphal return of the Children of Israel to Jerusalem, an act of redemption for all Jews. Hinduism has never focused on a single, supremely sacred place, given its vision that there are an infinite number of paths to the One and an equally infinite number of manifestations of Divine Reality. Rather, its holy places of pilgrimage number in the thousands, each a reminder of Hinduism's ability to absorb comfortably a variety of cults. For the Buddhist pilgrim, such as Faxian (Chapter 5, sources 39 and 43), the most sacred places at which to worship are those sites in Nepal and northern India associated with the life of the Buddha. As Buddhism spread beyond India, however, it also acquired new sites of pilgrimage in the lands that adopted the faith, especially in its Mahayana form. Such a sacred place is Mount Wutai in China, which is the locus of the cult of Manjushri, the Bodhisattva of Wisdom. Christianity also has had its sites of pilgrimage down through the ages. For medieval Christians the chief sites were Jerusalem, to which, beginning in the late eleventh century, Western Christendom sent a new type of pilgrim — the armed pilgrim, or crusader — whose goal was to liberate the Holy City from the hands of unbelievers; Constantinople, a city holy to both Byzantine and Western Christians by reason of its vast numbers of sacred *relics* (the physical remains of saints and various objects associated with the life of Jesus, Mary his mother, and other holy individuals); Santiago de Compostela in northwest Spain, which purportedly holds the relics of St. James the Apostle; and Rome, the city that boasts having the relics of Saints Peter and Paul and numerous other early martyrs of the Church.

The medieval journey to Rome was not easy, and once arrived, the visitor faced life-threatening fevers from Rome's ambient swamps. Regardless, Rome attracted pilgrims from all over the Christian world and beyond. In 1203, for example, crusaders at Constantinople met an African who identified himself as the king of Christian Nubia and claimed he was on his way to Rome, after having made his pilgrimage to Jerusalem. In response to all of this pilgrim traffic, several enterprising authors composed guidebooks to the Eternal City on the Tiber.

The most popular of these was *The Marvels of the City of Rome,* written between 1140 and 1143 by Benedict, an otherwise unknown clerical official of St. Peter's basilica in Rome, a papal church that stood over the presumed burial site of the Apostle Peter. In his guidebook Benedict provides his readers with a systematic, anecdotally embellished tour through the city. Many of the stories he includes are fables and not sober history, but perhaps they reveal a deeper truth: the way in which twelfth-century Europeans perceived the present in relation to Rome's distant past.

QUESTIONS FOR ANALYSIS

1. Benedict begins his guidebook with a story concerning Emperor Octavian. What seems to be his purpose in leading off his tour with this story?
2. "The sites and stories Benedict included in his book suggest that he expected his pious pilgrim readers to pay attention to more than just the city's religious attractions." Please comment in detail on this statement. Do you agree or disagree? Why?
3. Do these excerpts have any unifying theme? If so, what is it?
4. Consider the holy relics listed in this account. What do they collectively suggest about the religious mindset of the people who venerated them?

THE VISION OF OCTAVIAN AND THE SIBYL'S ANSWER

In the time of Emperor Octavian[1] the senators,[2] seeing him to be of such great beauty that none could look into his eyes and of such great prosperity and peace that he made all the world render tribute to him, said to him, "We desire to worship you because the godhead is in you; for if it were not so all things would not prosper with you as they do." But he was reluctant and demanded a delay and called the Sibyl of Tibur[3] to him, and he repeated all that the senators had said. She begged for three days time, during which she kept a strict fast, and then answered him after the third day. "These things, lord emperor, shall surely come to pass:

> Token of doom: the earth shall drip with
>   sweat;
> From heaven shall come the king of
>   evermore,
> And present in the flesh shall judge the
>   world."

And the other verses that follow. And while Octavian diligently listened to the Sibyl, heaven opened, and a great brightness shone on him,

---

[1]Octavian, who became Caesar Augustus (r. 31 B.C.E.–14 C.E.), the first emperor of Rome (see Chapter 5, source 41). This story, as is true of most of Benedict's stories, has no basis in fact.

[2]In the age of the Roman Republic, which preceded the age of one-man rule ushered in by Octavian, control of the Roman state was usually in the hands of the Senate, an oligarchy of wealthy landed nobles. Even after Octavian's reforms, senators retained their ancient privileges and honors while losing most of their real power.

[3]A prophetess and priestess of the god Apollo (see note 37). Actually, she was known as the *Sibyl of Cumae.*

and he saw in heaven a virgin exceedingly fair standing on an altar holding a man-child in her arms. Octavian marveled greatly at this, and he heard a voice from heaven saying: "This is the Virgin who shall conceive the Savior of the World."[4] And again he heard another voice from heaven saying, "This is the altar of the Son of God." The emperor straightway fell to the ground and worshipped the Christ that should come. He showed this vision to the senators and they likewise marveled exceedingly. The vision took place in the chamber of Emperor Octavian where the Church of Santa Maria in Capitolio[5] is now and where the Friars Minor[6] are. Therefore it is called Santa Maria in Aracoeli.[7]

Another day when the people had decreed to call Octavian "Lord," he immediately stopped them with his gesture and glance. He did not allow himself to be called "Lord" even by his sons saying: "Mortal I am and [you] will not call me Lord." . . .

THE PANTHEON

In the times of the senators and consuls[8] the Prefect[9] Agrippa[10] with four legions of soldiers subjugated the Suevians, Saxons and other western nations[11] to the Roman Senate. The bell of the image of the kingdom of the Persians, which was on the Capitoline, rang when he returned. In the Temple of Jupiter and Moneta on the Capitoline[12] was an image of every kingdom of the world with a bell about its neck, and as soon as the bell

sounded they knew that the country was rebellious. The priest who was on watch that week, hearing the sound of the bell, therefore showed it to the senators. The senators gave the Prefect Agrippa responsibility for organizing this war. He initially denied that he was able to carry out so great a charge, but he was at length compelled, and he then asked permission to take counsel for three days.

During this period, one night, after too much thinking, he fell asleep, and there appeared to him a woman who said to him, "What are you doing, Agrippa? You are very deep in thought." He answered her, "Madam, I am." She said, "Comfort yourself and promise me if you shall win the victory to make me a temple such as I will show you." And he said, "I will make it." And she showed him in a vision a temple made after that fashion. And he said, "Madam, who are you?" And she said, "I am Cybele, the mother of the gods.[13] Bear libations[14] to Neptune,[15] who is a mighty god, so that he will help you and have this temple dedicated to my worship and Neptune's, because we will be with you, and you shall prevail."

Agrippa then arose with gladness and repeated in the Senate all of this conversation. He then went with a great array of ships and with five legions and overcame the Persians and put them under a yearly tribute to the Roman Senate. When he returned to Rome he built this temple and had it dedicated to the honor of Cybele, mother of the gods, and to the honor of Nep-

---

[4]The Virgin Mary and her son, Jesus.

[5]The Capitoline Hill was ancient Rome's religious center.

[6]The Friars Minor (Lesser Brothers), also known as the *Franciscans,* are an order of Catholic clergy. Inasmuch as the Franciscans were founded in the early thirteenth century and came into possession of the church mentioned here only in 1250, this clause, or even the entire sentence, could not have been written by Benedict. Such later insertions are known as *interpolations.*

[7]*Aracoeli* means "altar of Heaven." The church of the Aracoeli is dedicated to Mary, the Virgin Mother.

[8]*Consuls* were the chief magistrates of Republican Rome. Hence, this is the time before Caesar Augustus (see note 1).

[9]The office of *prefect* ranked just below that of consul in Republican Rome.

[10]A somewhat confused reference to Caesar Augustus's friend, son-in-law, general, and hand-picked heir, Marcus Agrippa (d. 12 B.C.E.). Agrippa died before he could succeed Caesar Augustus.

[11]A bit of twelfth-century Roman pride is revealed in this reference to the mythic subjugation of the Germanic Suevians, Saxons, and other western nations. Around 1140 the German emperor Conrad III, a Swabian (Suevian), was trying to assert imperial control over central Italy.

[12]This Capitoline temple was dedicated to Jupiter, Rome's chief deity, and Moneta, the goddess of prosperity.

[13]See Chapter 5, source 34.

[14]Wine to be poured out as an offering.

[15]The god of the sea.

tune, god of the sea, and to the honor of all the gods, and he called this temple the Pantheon. In honor of the same Cybele he made a gilded image, which he set upon the top of the temple above the opening and covered it with a magnificent roof of gilded brass.[16]

After many ages Pope Boniface, in the time of Phocas,[17] a Christian emperor, seeing that such a marvelous temple, dedicated to the honor of Cybele, mother of the gods, before which Christian people were often stricken by devils, prayed to the emperor to grant this temple to him so that, as it was dedicated to Cybele, mother of the gods, on the Calends of November,[18] he might consecrate it to the Blessed Mary, ever-virgin, who is the mother of all the saints, on the Calends of November. Caesar granted this to him, and the pope with the whole Roman people on the Calends of November dedicated the temple[19] and ordained that on that day the Roman pontiff should sing mass there, and the people should take the body and blood of Our Lord as they did on Christmas. On the same day all the saints with their mother, Mary ever-virgin, and the heavenly spirits should have a festival, and throughout the churches of the world the dead would have a sacrifice for the ransom of their souls. . . .

CONSTANTINE'S THREE GREAT CHURCHES OF ROME

During the days of Pope Silvester,[20] Constantine Augustus[21] built the Lateran Basilica,[22] which he adorned beautifully. He put there the Ark of the Covenant,[23] which Titus had carried from Jerusalem with many thousands of Jews,[24] and the Golden Candlestick of Seven Lamps with vessels for oil.[25] In the ark are these things: the golden emeralds, the mice of gold,[26] the Tablets of the Covenant,[27] the Rod of Aaron,[28] manna,[29] the barley loaves, the golden urn,[30] the coat with-

---

[16]This temple was originally constructed in 27 B.C.E. by Agrippa (see note 10) and dedicated to "all the deities," which is what the Greek phrase *pantheon* means. Emperor Hadrian (r. 117–138) totally rebuilt the structure between about 118 and 126 C.E., and that is the building described here with its massive, bronze-sheathed dome, which has a central opening to light the interior.

[17]Phocas was emperor of Constantinople from 602 to 610; Pope Boniface IV reigned from 608 to 615.

[18]The first day of November. Significantly, this is All Saints Day, which commemorates all of the Church's known and unknown saints. (See note 16 for an explanation of what *pantheon* means. See also note 19.)

[19]The dedication day was probably May 13, 610. However, because the Pantheon was now re-dedicated to Mary and All the Saints, November 1, which is the feast day of Mary and All the Saints (note 18), became a holy day that was special to the church of the Pantheon.

[20]Pope Silvester I (r. 314–335).

[21]Emperor Constantine I (see Chapter 7, source 52).

[22]The church of St. John in Lateran. Originally, a *basilica* was a large, rectangular public building, often used as a law court. With the acceptance of Christianity by the Roman state, many fourth- and fifth-century Christian churches were built along the lines of the basilica. In time, the term came to mean a special papal church.

[23]According to tradition, during their wandering in the desert, the Hebrews carried the two tablets of the Law, which YHWH had given Moses on Mount Sinai, in a gilded, portable chest known as the *Ark of the Covenant*. Later, in the tenth century B.C.E., they constructed the Temple in Jerusalem to house the Ark and its contents. The Ark was probably lost when the Chaldeans sacked Jerusalem and destroyed the First Temple in 586 B.C.E. However, the Ethiopian Christian Church claims to possess the original Ark of the Covenant.

[24]In 70 C.E. Roman troops under Titus, the son of Emperor Vespasian and a future emperor himself, captured and destroyed Jerusalem and its Third Temple.

[25]Known as the *Menorah,* this was a massive, seven-branched ceremonial candelabrum that was originally carried in the Ark and later brought to the Temple. The seven branches symbolized the seven days of creation. Carvings on the Arch of Titus show a Menorah (probably not the original one) being borne as booty in a triumphal procession in Rome. It was deposited in Rome's Temple of Peace and subsequently lost or destroyed.

[26]According to the First Book of Samuel, Chapters 5 and 6, when the Philistines captured and carried off the Ark of the Covenant, the inhabitants of the five Philistine city-states suffered grievous tumors, or *emerods.* In order to rid themselves of this affliction, they returned the Ark, along with ten magical offerings: five golden mice and five golden emerods, or carvings resembling tumors. So there never were any golden emeralds in the Ark.

[27]See note 23.

[28]The symbol of priestly authority borne by Aaron, Moses' brother and the high priest of the Hebrews during the Exodus.

[29]*Manna* was the food provided the Hebrews by YHWH while they wandered in the desert.

[30]YHWH commanded the Israelites to place within the Ark golden urns for wine offerings and consecrated "loaves of permanent offering" (the Bible, Exodus, 25: 29–30).

out seam,[31] the reed and garment of Saint John the Baptist,[32] and the tongs that Saint John the Evangelist was shorn with.[33] Moreover he also put in the basilica a ciborium[34] with pillars of porphyry.[35] And he set there four pillars of gilded brass, which the consuls of old had brought to the Capitoline from the Campo Marzio[36] and set in the Temple of Jupiter.

He also made, in the time of the pope and after his prayer, a basilica for the Apostle Peter before Apollo's Temple[37] in the Vatican.[38] The emperor first dug the foundation, and in reverence to the twelve apostles he carried out twelve basketsful of earth. Saint Peter's[39] body is kept as follows. He made a chest closed on all sides with brass and copper, which may not be moved, five feet of length at the head, five at the foot, on the right side five feet and on the left side five feet, five feet above and five feet below. And so he enclosed the body of the Blessed Peter.

He adorned the altar above in the fashion of an arch with bright gold. And he set there in front of the altar twelve pillars of glass, which he brought from Greece and which were from Apollo's Temple at Troy.[40] Moreover he set above the Blessed Apostle Peter's body a cross of pure gold weighing one hundred and fifty pounds.

On it is written: *Constantinus Augustus et Helena Augusta.*[41]

He also built a basilica for the Blessed Apostle Paul[42] on the Via Ostiense[43] and put his body in brass and copper just like the body of the Blessed Peter.

The same emperor, after he became a Christian and built these churches also gave to the Blessed Silvester a *Phrygium* [Tiara], and white horses, and all the *imperialia*[44] pertaining to the dignity of the Roman Empire. Then he went away to Byzantium. The pope, decorated with these gifts, went forth with Constantine as far as the Roman Arch, where they embraced and kissed each other, and so parted.[45] . . .

CONCLUSION

These and more temples and palaces of emperors, consuls, senators and prefects were inside this Roman city in the time of the heathen, as we have read in old chronicles, have seen with our own eyes, and have heard the ancient men tell of. In writing we have tried as well as we could to bring back to the human memory how great was their beauty in gold, silver, brass, ivory and precious stones.

---

[31]The garment that Jesus wore to his crucifixion.

[32]The staff (see Aaron's staff in note 28) and garment of coarse camel hair worn by this prophet, who was a cousin and precursor of Jesus.

[33]Objects of torture used on one of Jesus' Twelve Apostles and the purported author of the Gospel of St. John.

[34]A vaulted canopy that rises above an altar.

[35]A stone of purplish hue.

[36]"The Field of Mars," a broad, open space in which a large number of public gardens, baths, arenas, and theaters stood during imperial times.

[37]Although he was a major Greek deity, the Romans regarded Apollo as the fairly minor god of healing and prophecy (see note 3).

[38]The Vatican Hill, the site of a cemetery, lay across the Tiber and outside the walls of imperial Rome.

[39]According to tradition, the leader of the apostles and the first bishop of Rome, who was martyred in Rome and buried at the Vatican cemetery. The popes' claim to authority over the Church rests on their belief that they are Peter's successors.

[40]The ancient city sacked by the Greeks around 1260 B.C.E. and commemorated in the *Iliad* and the *Odyssey*. Romans claimed descent from refugees from Troy.

[41]"Emperor Constantine and Empress Helena." St. Helena was Constantine's mother.

[42]Chapter 7, source 51. According to tradition, Paul was martyred just outside Rome.

[43]The basilica of St. Paul Outside the Walls, which contains Paul's body, lies outside Rome on the road to the port city of Ostia.

[44]The special garments that serve as symbols of imperial office.

[45]In other words, Constantine gave Pope Silvester imperial authority over Rome and Italy when he left to reside in his new capital at Constantinople. This legend, which is known as the *Donation of Constantine,* has no basis in fact.

A Jewish Merchant Writes Home

▼▼▼

102 ▾ *A LETTER FROM THE CAIRO GENIZA*

We have already seen a reflection of Arab commercial activity in the Indian Ocean mirrored in the mythic story of Sinbad (Chapter 9, source 77). Indian Ocean commerce, however, was not confined to a single ethnic group. One group that played an active role was the Arabic-speaking Jewish community of Egypt, which served as an important intermediary in moving goods that originated in East and South Asia into the Mediterranean market. Those Jewish-Egyptian merchants who chose to deal directly with India sailed down the Red Sea, using Aden on the southern tip of Arabia as their midway point. From there they followed the trade winds to their Indian ports of call — usually the cities of the western coast. With luck, they returned home the next year, driven by the opposite trade winds. At a minimum, the merchant was away from home for two years. Often circumstances could extend that absence many more years.

A fairly large body of documents from the pens of these India traders from Egypt exists thanks to the discovery of the *Cairo Geniza*. A geniza is the place attached to a synagogue where discarded scraps of paper on which the name of God was or might have been written are deposited. In order to preserve them from profanation, these writings are subsequently buried. When unearthed, geniza collections are a rich treasure trove for the historian. What makes the Cairo Geniza especially valuable is the fact that a large percentage of its documents are primarily secular in nature: business letters, contracts, accounts, shipping bills, court records, and the like.

The document appearing here is a letter that dates from around 1204 in which an India trader writes to his wife back home in Cairo. Portions of the letter are missing, as the brackets in the present translation show. The modern editor and translator of this letter concludes that the letter's lack of an address and some other major missing parts indicate that the author of the letter probably never sent it to his wife, perhaps having second thoughts about its revealing frankness. Rather, he returned to Egypt safely, was reunited with his wife, and personally deposited the draft letter in the geniza. Whatever the truth, the fact is this letter is an important document because it clearly shows us the hazards and strains of long-distance commerce.

QUESTIONS FOR ANALYSIS

1. What sort of communications has Solomon had with his home? How do you know that?
2. What do those communications suggest?
3. What crisis has Solomon recently faced? How did he meet it? What do his actions suggest?
4. What domestic problems is Solomon facing? What do those problems suggest about the stresses of long-distance trade in the Indian Ocean?

In (Your name!)

A. Death of the Judge

Just is the Lord in all his ways, etc. (Psalm 145:17)

The righteous man has gone, etc. (Isaiah 51:1)

Comfort, comfort my people, etc. (Isaiah 40:1)

From their father who is yearning after them,[1] Solomon, son of Japheth, (may he) r(est in) E(den).[2]

I am able to express only a fraction of my grief over the passing away of my lord, the illustrious leader, *(his) h(onor), g(reatness, and) h(oliness), our master and teacher Manasse, the wise and prudent judge, whose demise has hurt the hearts and caused pain to the souls.*[3] *(May the) m(emory of the) r(ighteous) be b(lessed).* How deeply was I afflicted by his death and by his being taken away from those who relied on him. May God assign him a *place with the saints,* may he grant consolation to his mourners and heal their wounds and comfort them *in his great mercy.*

B. Escape of the Family from the Plague

Would I try to describe the extent of my feelings of longing and yearning for you all the time, my letter would become too long and the words too many. But He who knows the secrets of the heart has the might to bring about relief for each of us by uniting us in joy.

Your precious letters have arrived; I have read and scrutinized them, and was happy to learn from them that you are well and healthy and that you have escaped from those great terrors, the like of which have not been experienced for many generations.[4] Praise be to God for your deliverance and for granting you respite until you might be recompensed in a measure commensurate with your sufferings.

C. The Dedicated Husband

In your letters you alternately rebuke and offend me or put me to shame and use harsh words all the time. I have not deserved any of this. I swear by God, I do not believe that the heart of anyone traveling away from his wife has remained like mine, all the time during all the years — from the moment of our separation to the very hour of writing this letter — so constantly thinking of you and yearning after you and regretting to be unable to provide you with what I so much desire: your legal rights on every Sabbath[5] and holiday, and to fulfill all your wishes, great and small, with regard to dresses or food or anything else. And you write about me as if I had forgotten you and would not remember you had it not been for your rebukes, and as if, had you not warned me that the public would reprove me, I would not have thought of you. Put this out of your mind and do not impute such things to me. And if what you think or say about my dedication to you is the product of your mind, believing that words of rebuke will increase my yearning — no, in such a way God will not let me reach the fulfillment of my hope, although in my heart there is twice as much as I am able to write. But he is able to have us both reach compensation for our sufferings and then, when we shall be saved, we shall remember in what situation we are now.

D. Travel beyond the Coromandel Coast[6]

You rebuke me with regard to the ambergris.[7] You poor ones!!! Had you known how much

---

[1]The letter was intended primarily for his wife, but convention dictated that he not address her by name, lest the letter fall into a stranger's hands. Therefore, he addresses the letter to his children.

[2]Paradise.

[3]This judge was the spiritual leader of the Cairo community (see note 17).

[4]A reference to the famine and plague that devastated Egypt between 1201 and 1203.

[5]Talmudic law (Chapter 6, source 49) dictated that a scholar was to visit his wife once a week on the night of the Sabbath — namely, Friday night. This merchant considered himself a member of the class learned in the Law.

[6]The southeast coast of India. Few Jewish merchants from Egypt went to India's eastern coast. To sail to the Southeast Asian lands beyond it was extraordinary.

[7]A waxy substance that sperm whales expel and that is added to perfumes.

trouble and expenses I have incurred to get this ambergris for you, you would have said: there is nothing like it in the world. This is the story: After I was resurrected from the dead and had lost all that I carried with me I took a loan of [. . .] dinars[8] and traveled to countries beyond al-Ma'bar.[9] I checked my accounts and found [ ] with "the decimals."[10] I took them and paid to one of our coreligionists who traveled back from al-Ma'bar to Aden . . . and for it he bought for you [. . .].

E. Drunk but Pious

This was my way of life from the moment I left you until I arrived in Aden (and from there to India) and from India back to Aden:[11] Day and night I was constantly drinking, not of my free will,[12] but I conducted myself in an exemplary way[13] and if anyone poked fun in foul speech in my presence, I became furious with him, until he became silent, he and others. I constantly fulfilled what God knows, and cursed my soul by fasting during the days and praying during the nights. The congregations in Aden and in India often asked me to lead them in prayer, and I am regarded by them and regard myself as a pious man.

F. As to Divorce — The Choice Is Left to the Wife

Now in one of your letters you adjure me to set you free, then letters arrived from the old man[14] saying the same. Later Ma'āni b. al-Dajājī [15] met me and told me that you came to his house before he set out on his travel. You had given him nutmeg paste as collateral on a loan of 100 dirhems, but he released 20 dirhems[16] to you. Please let me know whether this is correct, in which case I shall return this sum to him. He reported also that you had asked him to return to you letters which your late father — may God have mercy on him — had sent with him, but he had said to you: "I have already packed them away on the boat." Then you said that these letters were not written with your consent and you asked him not to deliver them to me. On this Ma'āni had replied: The judge might have meanwhile sent a message demanding something from the elder,[17] in which case the delivery of these letters might be useful to him.

Now, if this[18] is your wish, I cannot blame you. For the waiting has been long. And I do not know whether the Creator will grant relief immediately so that I can come home, or whether matters will take time, for I cannot come home with nothing. Therefore I resolved to issue a writ which sets you free.[19] Now the matter is in your hand. If you wish separation from me, accept *the bill of repudiation* and you are free. But if this is not your decision and not your desire, do not lose these long years of waiting: perhaps relief is at hand and you will regret at a time when regret will be of no avail.

And please do not blame me, for I have never neglected you from the time when those things happened and made an effort to save you and me from people talking and impairing my honor. The refusal[20] was on your side, not on mine. I do not know whether this[21] is your decision or that of someone else, but after all this, please do not

---

[8]Arabic gold coins.

[9]The Coromandel Coast (see note 6).

[10]His abacus.

[11]Apparently he is now back in Aden.

[12]But out of the sorrow that came from his separation from his wife.

[13]Apparently he drank himself silly but avoided prostitutes.

[14]Her late father.

[15]Although his name was Arabic, this was a fellow Jewish merchant of Cairo. The Jews of Egypt spoke and wrote in Arabic.

[16]Usually spelled *dirham,* it is a silver coin that weighs a bit less than three grams.

[17]The writer of the present letter is "the elder." The judge is, presumably, her late father. Could he have been the late Manasse, whose death the writer laments at the beginning of the letter? It appears so.

[18]The divorce (setting her free) mentioned above.

[19]A conditional bill of repudiation, which becomes a valid divorce once she accepts it.

[20]Apparently an earlier offer of divorce when his stay away from home was becoming too long.

[21]Request for a divorce.

say, you or someone else: this is our reward from him and our recompense. All day long I have a lonely heart and am pained by our separation. I feel that pain while writing these lines. But the choice is with you; the decision is in your hand: if you wish to carry the matter through, do so; if you wish to leave things as they are, do so. But do not act after the first impulse. Ask the advice of good people and act as you think will be the best for you. May God inspire you with the right decision.

▼▼▼

Travel in the Age of the *Pax Mongolica*

Temujin (1167–1227), the Mongol lord who assumed the title *Chinggis* (Ghengis) *Khan* (universal lord) in 1206, believed he had a destiny to rule the world. He and his immediate successors, particularly his grandson Kubilai (1214–1294), actually came close to controlling all of Eurasia. Although the Mongols were stopped in Syria, in Southeast Asia, at the borders of India and Arabia, in Eastern Europe, and in the waters off Japan, by 1279 they had still managed to create the largest land empire in history.

Beginning around the time of the rule of Kubilai Khan (r. 1260–1294) and extending for more than half a century after his death, the Mongols ruled over their enormous empire in relative peace and good order. Mongol discipline and organization made it possible to travel between Europe and China with a fair degree of safety and speed. Indeed, large numbers of merchants, ambassadors, fortune seekers, missionaries, and other travelers journeyed in all directions across the Mongol Empire. This steppe landbridge between East Asia and Western Europe was severed after 1350, however, as the Mongol Empire broke up, and the opportunity for normal direct contact between the eastern and western extremities of Eurasia was lost for a century and a half.

Mongol Culture

▼▼▼

103 ▼ *William of Rubruck,*
JOURNEY TO THE LAND OF THE TARTARS

Between 1236 and 1241 Mongol forces under the command of Batu, grandson of Chinggis Khan, overran a number of Christian states in Eastern Europe and even briefly reached the Adriatic Sea. As word of the devastations wrought by the Mongols reached Western Europe, the West's level of anxiety rose appreciably. Although the Mongol westward advance was stopped in 1241 by the sudden death of Ogodei (r. 1229–1241), Chinggis Khan's son and successor as Great Khan, there was no guarantee that the Mongols would not soon resume their assault on European Christendom.

It was in that context that, beginning in 1245, the Roman papacy initiated a series of embassies to various Mongol khans in order to discover their designs regarding Western Europe and to convert them to Catholic Christianity. The hope was that if the Mongols became Christians, they would join the West in crushing Islam in a final, glorious crusade. This double dream of conversion and crusade never became a reality, but it did initiate a century of Roman Catholic relations with the Mongols and involvement by a number of extraordinary Franciscan and Dominican friars in the mission fields of Central and East Asia.

One of the earliest missionary-ambassadors to the Great Khan in East Asia was Brother William of Rubruck, a Franciscan priest. Between May 1253 and June 1255 Friar William traveled from Constantinople to the court of Mongke Khan (r. 1251–1259) at Karakorum in Mongolia and returned to the eastern Mediterranean. William's mission failed to convert the Great Khan, but it did result in a report that he submitted to King Louis IX of France of his adventures and observations while among the Mongols. An exceptionally observant individual, Brother William provides us with one of the most detailed accounts of mid-thirteenth-century Mongol society.

QUESTIONS FOR ANALYSIS

1. Mongol religion is generally categorized as *shamanistic*. Based on what Rubruck tells us about their religious practices, what do you think this term means?
2. Many people think of nomads as wanderers, who aimlessly travel about with their herds. What evidence does Rubruck provide to refute this misconception?
3. Consider the Mongols' attitude toward thunder. Why do you think these people of the steppes so feared it?
4. How would you characterize the status of women relative to men? In addressing this issue, consider the respective tasks of women and men and Mongol marriage customs.
5. On the basis of this account, how would you characterize Mongol society in the mid thirteenth century?

THE TARTARS[1] AND THEIR DWELLINGS

The Tartars have no abiding city. . . . Each captain, according to whether he has more or fewer men under him, knows the limits of his pasturage and where to feed his flocks in winter, summer, spring, and autumn, for in winter they come down to the warmer districts in the south, in summer they go up to the cooler ones in the north. They drive their cattle to graze on the

---

[1]Westerners mistakenly called the Mongols *Tartars*, a corruption of *Tatars*, the name of a tribe of steppe nomads who dwelled near the Mongols. *Tartar* seems to have been a deliberate pun. The classical Latin name for hell was *Tartarus*; hence, the Mongols were the "devil's horsemen."

pasture lands without water in winter when there is snow there, for the snow provides them with water.

The dwelling in which they sleep has as its base a circle of interlaced sticks, and it is made of the same material; these sticks converge into a little circle at the top and from this a neck juts up like a chimney; they cover it with white felt and quite often they also coat the felt with lime or white clay and powdered bone to make it a more gleaming white, and sometimes they make it black. The felt round the neck at the top they decorate with lovely and varied paintings. Before the doorway they also hang felt worked in multicolored designs; they sew colored felt onto the other, making vines and trees, birds, and animals. They make these houses so large that sometimes they are thirty feet across. . . .

In addition they make squares to the size of a large coffer out of slender split twigs; then over it, from one end to the other, they build up a rounded roof out of similar twigs and they make a little entrance at the front end; after that they cover this box or little house with black felt soaked in tallow or ewes' milk so that it is rain-proof, and this they decorate in the same way with multicolored handwork. Into these chests they put all their bedding and valuables; they bind them onto high carts which are drawn by camels so that they can cross rivers. These chests are never removed from the carts. When they take down their dwelling houses, they always put the door facing the south. . . .

The married women make for themselves really beautiful carts which I would not know how to describe for you except by a picture; in fact I would have done you paintings of everything if I only knew how to paint. A wealthy Mongol or Tartar may well have a hundred or two hundred such carts with chests. Baatu[2] has twenty-six wives and each of these has a large house, not counting the other small ones which are placed

behind the large one and which are, as it were, chambers in which their attendants live; belonging to each of these houses are a good two hundred carts. When they pitch their houses the chief wife places her dwelling at the extreme west end and after her the others according to their rank, so that the last wife will be at the far east end, and there will be the space of a stone's throw between the establishment of one wife and that of another. And so the orda[3] of a rich Mongol will look like a large town and yet there will be very few men in it.

One woman will drive twenty or thirty carts, for the country is flat. They tie together the carts, which are drawn by oxen or camels, one after the other, and the woman will sit on the front one driving the ox while all the others follow in step. If they happen to come on a bad bit of track they loose them and lead them across it one by one. They go at a very slow pace, as a sheep or an ox might walk.

When they have pitched their houses with the door facing south, they arrange the master's couch at the northern end. The women's place is always on the east side, that is, on the left of the master of the house when he is sitting on his couch looking toward the south; the men's place is on the west side, that is, to his right.

On entering a house the men would by no means hang up their quiver in the women's section. Over the head of the master there is always an idol like a doll or little image of felt which they call the master's brother, and a similar one over the head of the mistress, and this they call the mistress's brother; they are fastened on to the wall. Higher up between these two is a thin little one which is, as it were, the guardian of the whole house. The mistress of the house places on her right side, at the foot of the couch, in a prominent position, a goatskin stuffed with wool or other material, and next to it a tiny image turned toward her attendants and the women.

---

[2]Baatu or Batu (d. 1255/1256), grandson of Chinggis Khan and founder of the Golden Horde, the group of Mongols that conquered and ruled Russia.

[3]*Orda* is a Turkic word meaning "camp," from which we derive the word *horde*.

By the entrance on the women's side is still another idol with a cow's udder for the women who milk the cows, for this is the women's job. On the other side of the door toward the men is another image with a mare's udder for the men who milk the mares.

When they have foregathered for a drink they first sprinkle with the drink the idol over the master's head, then all the other idols in turn; after this an attendant goes out of the house with a cup and some drinks; he sprinkles thrice toward the south, genuflecting each time; this is in honor of fire; next toward the east in honor of the air, and after that to the west in honor of water; they cast it to the north for the dead. When the master is holding his cup in his hand and is about to drink, before he does so he first pours some out on the earth as its share. If he drinks while seated on a horse, before he drinks he pours some over the neck or mane of the horse. And so when the attendant has sprinkled toward the four quarters of the earth he returns into the house; two servants with two cups and as many plates are ready to carry the drink to the master and the wife sitting beside him upon his couch. If he has several wives, she with whom he sleeps at night sits next to him during the day, and on that day all the others have to come to her dwelling to drink, and the court is held there, and the gifts which are presented to the master are placed in the treasury of that wife. Standing in the entrance is a bench with a skin of milk or some other drink and some cups.

In the winter they make an excellent drink from rice, millet, wheat, and honey, which is clear like wine. Wine, too, is conveyed to them from distant regions. In the summer they do not bother about anything except cosmos.[4] Cosmos is always to be found inside the house before the entrance door, and near it stands a musician with his instrument. Our lutes and viols I did not see there but many other instruments such as are not known among us. When the master begins

to drink, then one of the attendants cries out in a loud voice "Ha!" and the musician strikes his instrument. And when it is a big feast they are holding, they all clap their hands and also dance to the sound of the instrument, the men before the master and the women before the mistress. After the master has drunk, then the attendant cries out as before and the instrument-player breaks off. Then they drink all round, the men and the women, and sometimes vie with each other in drinking in a really disgusting and gluttonous manner. . . .

THE FOOD OF THE TARTARS

As for their food and victuals I must tell you they eat all dead animals indiscriminately and with so many flocks and herds you can be sure a great many animals do die. However, in the summer as long as they have any cosmos, that is mare's milk, they do not care about any other food. If during that time an ox or a horse happens to die, they dry the flesh by cutting it into thin strips and hanging it in the sun and the wind, and it dries immediately without salt and without any unpleasant smell. Out of the intestines of horses they make sausages which are better than pork sausages and they eat these fresh; the rest of the meat they keep for the winter. From the hide of oxen they make large jars which they dry in a wonderful way in the smoke. From the hind part of horses' hide they make very nice shoes.

They feed fifty or a hundred men with the flesh of a single sheep, for they cut it up in little bits in a dish with salt and water, making no other sauce; then with the point of a knife or a fork especially made for this purpose — like those with which we are accustomed to eat pears and apples cooked in wine — they offer to each of those standing round one or two mouthfuls, according to the number of guests. Before the flesh of the sheep is served, the master first takes what

---

[4]More correctly *qumiz*, the Mongols' favorite alcoholic drink, which they fermented from mare's milk.

pleases him; and also if he gives anyone a special portion then the one receiving it has to eat it himself and may give it to no one else. But if he cannot eat it all he may take it away with him or give it to his servant, if he is there, to keep for him; otherwise he may put it away in his *captargac,* that is, a square bag which they carry to put all such things in: in this they also keep bones when they have not the time to give them a good gnaw, so that later they may gnaw them and no food be wasted.

THE DUTIES OF THE WOMEN AND THEIR WORK

It is the duty of the women to drive the carts, to load the houses onto them and to unload them, to milk the cows, to make the butter and *grut,*[5] to dress the skins and to sew them, which they do with thread made out of tendons. They split the tendons into very thin threads and then twist these into one long thread. They also sew shoes and socks and other garments. They never wash their clothes, for they say that that makes God angry and that it would thunder if they hung them out to dry; they even beat those who do wash them and take them away from them. They are extraordinarily afraid of thunder. At such a time they turn all strangers out of their dwellings and wrap themselves in black felt in which they hide until it has passed over. They never wash their dishes, but when the meat is cooked, they wash out the bowl in which they are going to put it with some boiling broth from the cauldron which they afterwards pour back. The women also make the felt and cover the houses.

The men make bows and arrows, manufacture stirrups and bits and make saddles; they build the houses and carts, they look after the horses and milk the mares, churn the cosmos, that is the mares' milk, and make the skins in which it is kept, and they also look after the camels and load them. Both sexes look after the sheep and goats, and sometimes the men, sometimes the women, milk them. They dress skins with the sour milk of ewes, thickened and salted.

When they want to wash their hands or their head, they fill their mouth with water and, pouring this little by little from their mouth into their hands, with it they wet their hair and wash their head.

As for their marriages, you must know that no one there has a wife unless he buys her, which means that sometimes girls are quite grown up before they marry, for their parents always keep them until they sell them. They observe the first and second degrees of consanguinity,[6] but observe no degrees of affinity; they have two sisters at the same time or one after the other. No widow among them marries, the reason being that they believe that all those who serve them in this life will serve them in the next, and so of a widow they believe that she will always return after death to her first husband. This gives rise to a shameful custom among them whereby a son sometimes takes to wife all his father's wives, except his own mother; for the orda of a father and mother always falls to the youngest son[7] and so he himself has to provide for all his father's wives who come to him with his father's effects; and then, if he so wishes, he uses them as wives, for he does not consider an injury has been done to him if they return to his father after death.

And so when anyone has made an agreement with another to take his daughter, the father of the girl arranges a feast and she takes flight to relations where she lies hid. Then the father declares: "Now my daughter is yours; take her wherever you find her." Then he searches for her with his friends until he finds her; then he has to take her by force and bring her, as though by violence, to his house.

---

[5] A sour curd cheese.
[6] Siblings and first cousins are prohibited from marrying one another.

[7] The youngest son of his chief wife.

Another View of Mongol Society

▼▼▼

104 ▾ Marco Polo, DESCRIPTION OF THE WORLD

No chapter on trans-Eurasian travel in the Mongol Age would be complete without a selection from Marco Polo (ca. 1253–1324), a Venetian who spent twenty years in East Asia, most of that time in the service of Kubilai Khan. Around 1260 Marco's father and uncle, Niccoló and Maffeo, both merchants from Venice, set sail for the Black Sea and from there made an overland trek to Khanbalik and the court of Kubilai. When they were preparing to return home, the Great Khan requested that they visit the pope and ask him to send one hundred missionary-scholars to Cathay. The Polos arrived at the crusader port of Acre (in modern Israel) in 1269 and in 1271 received a commission from Pope Gregory X (r. 1271–1276) to return to China with two Dominican friars. The two friars quickly abandoned the expedition, afraid of the dangers that awaited them, but Niccoló's seventeen-year-old son, Marco, was made of sterner stuff. The brothers Polo, now accompanied by young Marco, returned to Khanbalik. Here Marco entered the khan's service and for close to two decades traveled extensively over much of Kubilai's empire as one of the many foreign officials serving the Mongol, or *Yuan,* Dynasty (1260–1368).

In 1292 the three men set sail for the West by way of the Indian Ocean and arrived home in Venice in 1295. In 1298 Marco was captured in a war with Genoa and, while in prison, related his adventures to a writer of romances known as Rustichello of Pisa. Together they produced a rambling, often disjointed account of the sites, peoples, personalities, and events Marco had encountered in Asia. To be sure, the book probably exaggerates Polo's importance and service to the Great Khan, but there is no good reason to reject, as some modern writers have done, its basic historicity or the claim of its narrator to have visited and lived in China.

Despite its literary flaws and a self-puffery that was obvious even to fourteenth-century contemporaries, the book was widely translated and distributed throughout late medieval Europe. Its popularity was due in part to Marco's eye for ethnographic detail, as the book abounds with stories of customs that Westerners found fascinatingly different. In the following selections Polo, like Rubruck, tells his audience about Mongol culture.

Historical research generally consists of sifting through large amounts of textual evidence and comparing partial, and often even conflicting, accounts of an event in the hope of arriving at a reasonably true reconstruction of the past. No single source ever gives us a complete and unbiased view of whatever we are studying. Polo's and Rubruck's descriptions of Mongol society, when studied together, allow us to test each other's worth. When compared, they also provide evidence of some of the continuities and changes in Mongol society over the last half of the thirteenth century.

QUESTIONS FOR ANALYSIS

1. Draw two columns. In one, list all the significant details regarding Mongol culture provided by Rubruck. In the other, list those provided by Polo. Where are they in agreement? Are there any significant disagreements? What details are provided by only one witness?
2. Consider the points on which they seem to differ. Assuming each is an honest and observant reporter, how do you explain those differences?
3. Based on the exercise you have just done, what can you say with confidence about thirteenth-century Mongol culture?
4. Based on your reading of both sources, what would you conclude were the factors that contributed to the Mongols' success in forging and governing their empire?
5. Toward the end of his account, Polo provides a hint of one of the factors that would lead to the breakup of the Mongol Empire. What is it?
6. Do the Mongols seem to have changed significantly over the course of the thirteenth century?

It is their custom that the bodies of all deceased grand khans and other great lords from the family of Chinggis Khan are carried for internment to a great mountain called Altai.[1] No matter where they might die, even if it is a hundred days' journey away, they nevertheless are brought here for burial. It is also their custom that, in the process of conveying the bodies of these princes, the escort party sacrifices whatever persons they happen to meet along the route, saying to them: "Depart for the next world and there serve your deceased master." They· believe that all whom they kill in this manner will become his servants in the next life. They do the same with horses, killing all the best, so that the dead lord might use them in the next world. When the corpse of Mongke Khan[2] was transported to this mountain, the horsemen who accompanied it slew upward of 20,000 people along the way.

Now that I have begun speaking about the Tartars, I will tell you more about them. They never remain fixed in one location. As winter approaches they move to the plains of a warmer region in order to find sufficient pasturage for their animals. In summer they inhabit cool regions in the mountains where there is water and grass and their animals are free of the annoyance of gad-flies and other biting insects. They spend two or three months progressively climbing higher and grazing as they ascend, because the grass is not sufficient in any one spot to feed their extensive herds.

Their huts, or tents, are circular and formed by covering a wooden frame with felt. These they transport on four-wheeled carts wherever they travel, since the framework is so well put together that it is light to carry. Whenever they set their huts up, the entrance always faces south. They also have excellent two-wheeled vehicles so well covered with black felt that, no matter how long it rains, rain never penetrates. These are drawn by oxen and camels and serve to carry their wives, children, and all necessary utensils and provisions.

It is the women who tend to their commercial concerns, buying and selling, and who tend to all the needs of their husbands and households. The men devote their time totally to hunting,

---

[1]The Altai Mountain range is in eastern Mongolia.

[2]Mongke, or Mangu, ruled as Great Khan from 1251 to 1259.

hawking, and warfare. They have the best falcons in the world, as well as the best dogs. They subsist totally on meat and milk, eating the produce of their hunting, especially a certain small animal, somewhat like a hare, which our people call Pharaoh's rats,[3] which are abundant on the steppes in summer. They likewise eat every manner of animal: horses, camels, even dogs, provided they are fat. They drink mare's milk, which they prepare in such a way that it has the qualities and taste of white wine. In their language they call it *kemurs*.[4]

Their women are unexcelled in the world so far as their chastity and decency of conduct are concerned, and also in regard to their love and devotion toward their husbands. They regard marital infidelity as a vice which is not simply dishonorable but odious by its very nature. Even if there are ten or twenty women in a household, they live in harmony and highly praiseworthy concord, so that no offensive word is ever spoken. They devote full attention to their tasks and domestic duties, such as preparing the family's food, managing the servants, and caring for the children, whom they raise in common. The wives' virtues of modesty and chastity are all the more praiseworthy because the men are allowed to wed as many women as they please. The expense to the husband for his wives is not that great, but the benefit he derives from their trading and from the work in which they are constantly employed is considerable. For this reason, when he marries he pays a dowry to his wife's parents. The first wife holds the primary place in the household and is reckoned to be the husband's most legitimate wife, and this status extends to her children. Because of their unlimited number of wives, their offspring is more numerous than that of any other people. When a father dies, his son may take all of his deceased father's wives, with the exception of his own mother. They also cannot marry their sisters, but upon a brother's death they may marry their sisters-

in-law. Every marriage is solemnized with great ceremony.

This is what they believe. They believe in an exalted god of heaven, to whom they burn incense and offer up prayers for sound mind and body. They also worship a god called Natigay, whose image, covered with felt or other cloth, is kept in everyone's house. They associate a wife and children with this god, placing the wife on his left side and the children before him. . . . They consider Natigay as the god who presides over their earthly concerns, protecting their children, their cattle, and their grain. They show him great respect. Before eating they always take a fat portion of meat and smear the idol's mouth with it, as well as the mouths of his wife and children. Then they take some of the broth in which the meat has been cooked and pour it outside, as an offering. When this has been done they believe that their god and his family have had their proper share. The Tartars then proceed to eat and drink without further ceremony.

The rich among these people dress in gold cloth and silks and the furs of sable, ermine, and other animals. All their accouterments are expensive.

Their weapons are bows, iron maces, and in some instances, spears. The bow, however, is the weapon at which they are the most expert, being accustomed to use it in their sports from childhood. They wear armor made from the hides of buffalo and other beasts, fire-dried and thus hard and strong.

They are brave warriors, almost to the point of desperation, placing little value on their lives, and exposing themselves without hesitation to every sort of danger. They are cruel by nature. They are capable of undergoing every manner of privation, and when it is necessary, they can live for a month on the milk of their mares and the wild animals they catch. Their horses feed on grass alone and do not require barley or other grain. The men are trained to remain on horse-

---

[3]The brown marmot, a burrowing rodent of the steppes.

[4]*Qumiz* (see source 103, note 4).

back for two days and two nights without dismounting, sleeping in the saddle while the horse grazes. No people on the earth can surpass them in their ability to endure hardships, and no other people shows greater patience in the face of every sort of deprivation. They are most obedient to their chiefs, and are maintained at small expense. These qualities, which are so essential to a soldier's formation, make them fit to subdue the world, which in fact they have largely done.

When one of the great Tartar chiefs goes to war, he puts himself at the head of an army of 100,000 horsemen and organizes them in the following manner. He appoints an officer to command every ten men and others to command groups of 100, 1,000, and 10,000 men respectively. Thus ten of the officers who command ten men take their orders from an officer who commands 100; ten of these captains of a 100 take their orders from an officer in charge of a 1,000; and ten of these officers take orders from one who commands 10,000. By this arrangement, each officer has to manage only ten men or ten bodies of men. . . . When the army goes into the field, a body of 200 men is sent two days' march in advance, and parties are stationed on each flank and in the rear, to prevent surprise attack.

When they are setting out on a long expedition, they carry little with them. . . . They subsist for the most part on mare's milk, as has been said. . . . Should circumstances require speed, they can ride for ten days without lighting a fire or taking a hot meal. During this time they subsist on the blood drawn from their horses, each man opening a vein and drinking the blood. They also have dried milk. . . . When setting off on an expedition, each man takes about ten pounds. Every morning they put about half a pound of this into a leather flask, with as much water as necessary. As they ride, the motion violently shakes the contents, producing a thin porridge which they take as dinner. . . .

All that I have told you here concerns the original customs of the Tartar lords. Today, however, they are corrupted. Those who live in China have adopted the customs of the idol worshippers,[5] and those who inhabit the eastern provinces have adopted the ways of the Muslims.

---

[5]Buddhists.

A European Missionary in China
▼▼▼
105 ▼ John of Monte Corvino, *LETTER TO THE WEST*

Despite disappointment at the Mongols' reception of their early embassies to the Great Khan and his lieutenants, popes and kings in the West did not abandon hope of converting the Mongols to Roman Christianity and allying with them against Islam. On their part, various Mongol khans continued to flirt with the idea of joining with European Christian powers against a common Muslim foe.

In 1287 Arghun, *il-khan* of Persia (r. 1284–1291), a nephew and subordinate of the Great Khan, Kubilai (r. 1260–1294), sent a Nestorian Christian monk, Rabban (Master) Sauma (ca. 1230–1294) to the West, bearing letters for the pope, the kings of France and England, and the emperor of Constantinople, in which the Mongol prince offered to become a Christian in return for an alliance against a common enemy, the Muslim Mamluks of Egypt. The Mamluks had rolled back a Mongol invasion of Syria-Palestine with a decisive victory at 'Ayn Jalut in 1260, and they were on the threshold of capturing the last of the crusader strongholds in that same region. Arghun died before he or anyone else could act on the proposal, and in 1295 his successor embraced Islam, thereby ending any hope of a Mongol-European crusade in the Holy Land. Arghun's overtures, however, set in motion a remarkable adventure for one European missionary.

In response to Rabban Sauma's appearance in Rome in 1289, Pope Nicholas IV dispatched a Franciscan friar, John of Monte Corvino (1247–ca. 1328), to the Mongols with letters for Arghun and other khans farther to the east, including the khan of khans, Kubilai. Friar John had only just returned to Rome after having served as a missionary in Armenia and Mongol-controlled Persia between about 1280 and 1289. Apparently his report so impressed Pope Nicholas that the pope ordered John to return immediately to the Middle East and then to travel on to the Great Khan in northern China.

In 1291 John was in Tauris (modern Tabriz), Arghun's capital, but the il-khan died in March of that year, and between May and July of the same year the last crusader strongholds in the Holy Land fell to Muslim forces. With nothing further to be accomplished in Persia, John set out for the court of the Great Khan in China. Civil war among the Mongols delayed Friar John's journey across Central Asia and resulted in a detour to India, from where Friar John sent back to Rome a detailed report on India's native Christian communities. Due to this delay, John arrived at the Mongol capital of Khanbalik (modern Beijing) in 1295, a year after Kubilai's death. Making the best of his situation, John remained in China as a missionary.

In the course of his long stay in China, Friar John wrote two letters to his fellow Franciscans back home. In response, Pope Clement V appointed him archbishop of Khanbalik in 1307 and dispatched several assistant missionaries. The new archbishop remained at his post until his death around 1328, and Pope Benedict XII subsequently sent a replacement. Notwithstanding this effort, the Roman Catholic mission in China barely limped along. When the Mongols finally were expelled from China in 1368, European missionary activity in China ended and would not be revived until the coming of the Jesuits in the sixteenth century.

The following document is one of the letters that Friar John sent to the West from China. In it he relates his success working with the late King Kerguz, or George, leader of the Ongut Turks, whose family had intermarried with that of Chinggis Khan.

QUESTIONS FOR ANALYSIS

1. What problems did Friar John encounter?
2. How was Friar John able to gain most of his converts, and from which group(s) does he seem to have won most of his converts: the Turkic Nestorian Christians, the non-Christian Mongols, or the Chinese? What do you conclude from your answers?
3. What picture does John draw of the Mongol empire? How, if at all, has it changed since the days of Friar William of Rubruck (source 103)?

4. How easy or difficult was it to reach China from the West in at the end of the thirteenth century? Be specific in your answer.
5. What does this letter allow us to infer about European-Chinese contacts in during this period?
6. What does John's letter suggest about Mongol attitudes and policy toward Christians? How, if at all, have Mongol-European relations changed since the mid thirteenth century?

I, Friar John of Monte Corvino, of the Order of Friars Minor,[1] departed from Tauris, a city of the Persians, in the year of the Lord 1291, and proceeded to India. And I remained in the country of India, wherein stands the church of St. Thomas the Apostle,[2] for thirteen months, and in that region baptized in different places about one hundred persons. The companion of my journey was Friar Nicholas of Pistoia, of the Order of Preachers,[3] who died there, and was buried in the aforesaid church.

I proceeded on my further journey and made my way to Cathay,[4] the realm of the emperor of the Tatars[5] who is called the Grand Khan.[6] To him I presented the letter of our lord the pope, and invited him to adopt the Catholic faith of our Lord Jesus Christ, but he had grown too old in idolatry. However he bestows many kindnesses upon the Christians, and these two years past I am abiding with him.

The Nestorians, a certain body who profess to bear the Christian name, but who deviate sadly from the Christian religion, have grown so powerful in those parts that they will not allow a Christian of another ritual to have ever so small a chapel, or to publish any doctrine different from their own.[7]

To these regions there never came anyone of the apostles, nor yet of the disciples.[8] And so the aforesaid Nestorians, either directly or through others whom they bribed, have brought on me the sharpest of persecutions. For they got up stories that I was not sent by our lord the pope, but was a great spy and impostor; and after a while they produced false witnesses who declared that there was indeed an envoy sent with presents of immense value for the emperor, but that I had murdered him in India and stolen what he had in charge. And these intrigues and calumnies went on for some five years. And thus it came to pass that many a time I was dragged before the judgment seat with ignominy and threats of death. At last, by God's providence, the emperor, through the confessions of a certain individual, came to know my innocence and the malice of my adversaries; and he banished them with their wives and children.

In this mission I abode alone and without any associate for eleven years, but it is now going on for two years since I was joined by Friar Arnold, a German of the province of Cologne.[9]

I have built a church in the city of Khanbaliq, in which the king has his chief residence. This I completed six years ago; and I have built a

---

[1]Friars Minor, or Lesser Brothers, was the official title of the Franciscan Order.

[2]According to tradition, St. Thomas the Apostle had established a small Christian community on India's western coast in the late first century. Whatever the truth of that legend, Persian Nestorian Christians (Chapter 9, source 69) had established a well-organized Church in western India by the mid sixth century.

[3]Like the Friars Minor, members of the Order of Preachers (more popularly known as *Dominicans*) were *mendicant* (begging) friars. The Dominicans and the Franciscans equally served as the Church's most active missionary orders since their inception in the early thirteenth century.

[4]Northern China. The name *Cathay* is derived from the Khitan Tatars, whose state of Liao in northwest China flourished from 946 to 1125. They were the first power to transform Beijing into a capital city.

[5]Mongols, not Tatars (see source 103, note 1).

[6]Timur Khan (r. 1294–1307).

[7]For a description of the Nestorian Christian Church, see Chapter 9, source 69. (See also note 19 below.)

[8]In other words, Christianity was not introduced into China until after the Apostolic Age of the first and second centuries C.E.

[9]He dated the thirteen-year mission from 1291. See the letter's date.

belltower to it, and put three bells in it. I have baptized there, as well as I can estimate, up to this time some 6,000 persons; and if those charges against me of which I have spoken had not been made, I should have baptized more than 30,000. And I am often still engaged in baptizing.

Also I have gradually bought one hundred and fifty boys, the children of pagan parents, and of ages varying from seven to eleven, who had never learned any religion. These boys I have baptized, and I have taught them Greek and Latin after our manner. Also I have written out psalters for them, with thirty hymnaries and two breviaries.[10] By help of these, eleven of the boys already know our service, and form a choir and take their weekly turn of duty as they do in convents,[11] whether I am there or not. Many of the boys are also employed in writing out psalters[12] and other things suitable. His Majesty the emperor moreover delights much to hear them chanting. I have the bells rung at all the canonical hours,[13] and with my congregation of babes and sucklings I perform divine service,[14] and the chanting we do by ear because I have no service book with the notes.

A certain king of this part of the world, by name George, belonging to the sect of Nestorian Christians, and of the illustrious family of that great king who was called Prester John of India,[15] in the first year of my arrival here attached himself to me, and being converted by me to the truth of the Catholic faith, took the lesser orders,[16] and when I celebrated mass[17] he used to attend me wearing his royal robes. Certain others of the Nestorians on this account accused him of apostasy, but he brought over a great part of his people with him to the true Catholic faith, and built a church on a scale of royal magnificence in honor of our God, of the Holy Trinity,[18] and of our lord the pope, giving it the name of the *Roman Church.*

This King George six years ago departed to the Lord a true Christian, leaving as his heir a son scarcely out of the cradle, and who is now nine years old. And after King George's death his brothers, perfidious followers of the errors of Nestorius,[19] perverted again all those whom he had brought over to the church, and carried them back to their original schismatical creed.[20] And being all alone, and not able to leave his Majesty the khan, I could not go to visit the above-mentioned church, which is twenty days' journey distant.

Yet, if I could but get some good fellow-workers to help me, I trust in God that all this might be retrieved, for I still possess the grant which was made in our favor by the late King George before mentioned. So I say again that if it had not been for the slanderous charges which I have spoken of, the harvest reaped by this time would have been great!

Indeed if I had had but two or three comrades to aid me 'tis possible that the emperor khan

---

[10]Various prayer books.

[11]In *convents,* or houses where friars reside, in the West.

[12]Books of psalms, or songs, for use in church.

[13]The seven periods of prayer and reflection that mark the passing of each day.

[14]The *mass* and other liturgical ceremonies (see note 17).

[15]When premodern Europeans used the term *India* or *the Indies,* they usually meant Farther Asia and did not specifically refer to the subcontinent of India. Regarding *Prester John,* see source 109.

[16]The Roman Church recognizes seven clerical orders, or grades. King George was admitted to the four minor clerical orders below those of priest, deacon, and subdeacon.

[17]The mass is Catholic Christianity's central religious ceremony. Here the Eucharist is consecrated and consumed in commemoration of Jesus' sacrifice on the cross.

[18]Christians believe that God is three co-eternal, co-equal, distinct, and separate divine persons in one indivisible divine essence: God the Father, the Creator; God the Son, the Redeemer (who became the fully human and fully divine Jesus of Nazareth); and God the Holy Spirit, the Sanctifier and Illuminator, who dispenses grace and divine wisdom to God's people.

[19]An early fifth-century patriarch of Constantinople who was deposed in 431. The so-called errors of Nestorius and his followers revolved around their desire to draw a clear distinction between the divine and human natures of Jesus (see note 18). Consequently, they rejected the Byzantine and Roman practice of referring to Mary, the mother of Jesus, as *Theotokos* (the Mother of God).

[20]Those in *schism* are separated from the Church; a *creed* is a body of religious beliefs (from the Latin *credo* — "I believe").

would have been baptized by this time! I ask then for such brethren to come, if any are willing to come, such I mean as will make it their great business to lead exemplary lives. . . .

As for the road here I may tell you that the way through the land of the Goths[21] subject to the emperor of the Northern Tatars, is the shortest and safest; and by it the friars might come, along with the letter-carriers, in five or six months. The other route again is very long and very dangerous, involving two sea-voyages; the first of which is about as long as that from Acre to the province of Provence,[22] while the second is as long as from Acre to England. And it is possible that it might take more than two years to accomplish the journey that way.[23] But, on the other hand, the first-mentioned route has not been open for a considerable time, on account of wars that have been going on.

It is twelve years since I have had any news of the papal court, or of our order, or of the state of affairs generally in the West. Two years ago indeed there came hither a certain Lombard[24] . . . surgeon, who spread abroad in these parts the most incredible blasphemies about the court of Rome and our order[25] and the state of things in the West, and on this account I exceedingly desire to obtain true intelligence. I pray the brethren whom this letter may reach to do their possible to bring its contents to the knowledge of our lord the pope and the cardinals,[26] and the agents of the order at the court of Rome. . . .

I have myself grown old and grey, more with toil and trouble than with years; for I am not more than fifty-eight. I have got a competent knowledge of the language and character which is most generally used by the Tatars. And I have already translated into that language and character the New Testament and the psalter, and have caused them to be written out in the fairest penmanship they have; and so by writing, reading, and preaching, I bear open and public testimony to the Law of Christ. And I had been in treaty with the late King George, if he had lived, to translate the whole Latin ritual, that it might be sung throughout the whole extent of his territory; and while he was alive I used to celebrate mass in his church, according to the Latin ritual, reading in the before-mentioned language and character the words of both the preface and the canon.[27]

And the son of the king before-mentioned is called after my name, John; and I hope in God that he will walk in his father's steps.

As far as I ever saw or heard tell, I do not believe that any king or prince in the world can be compared to his majesty the khan in respect of the extent of his dominions, the vastness of their population, or the amount of his wealth. Here I stop.

Dated at the city of Khanbaliq in the kingdom of Cathay, in the year of the Lord 1305, and on the 8th day of January.

---

[21]He probably means the Alans, Christian Iranians who dwelt on the northern shores of the Black Sea. Undoubtedly, he is telling them to take the overland route across the steppes.

[22]From Israel to Mediterranean France. Acre was a major crusader port, which fell to the Mamluks in May 1291.

[23]The sea route would involve sailing down either the Red Sea or, more likely, the Persian Gulf into the Indian Ocean and from there proceeding across to India, then to Southeast Asia, and finally northward to a southern Chinese port.

[24]Lombardy is a region of north central Italy.

[25]There was a bitter conflict between Pope Boniface VIII and a radical, splinter sect known as the *Spiritual Franciscans.*

[26]*Cardinals* are the chief officials of papal government.

[27]The preface of the mass (note 17) is a series of opening prayers; the *canon,* or core, of the mass consists of the three central acts of the Eucharistic service: offertory, consecration, and communion. In other words, Friar John celebrated the Latin-rite mass in the language of King George's people.

Khmer Society in Chinese Eyes
▼▼▼

106 ▼ *Zhou Daguan,*
RECOLLECTIONS OF THE
CUSTOMS OF CAMBODIA

The Yuan emperors of China used foreign-born officials, such as Marco Polo, because of the high degree of mutual distrust and antipathy that existed between the old Confucian governing class and their new Mongol lords, but many Chinese did serve the Mongols faithfully. Among them was Zhou Daguan (d. after 1346), who spent nearly a year in the Khmer kingdom of Cambodia (Chapter 6, source 47) as a high-ranking member of an embassy sent by Kubilai Khan to secure the Cambodians' recognition of his overlordship.

When the successful legation returned home in 1297, Zhou Daguan set down his impressions of this land and its people. Although he modestly noted that "It goes without saying that the customs and the activities of the country cannot be completely known in so short a time," he was able to provide posterity with the single best contemporary account of Khmer society at the height of its cultural brilliance. In the following selections Zhou describes the land's cultural divisions, its economic activities, and the ceremony that attended the Khmer king.

QUESTIONS FOR ANALYSIS

1. According to Zhou, what kinds of hill people inhabited the regions outside of Cambodia's centers of civilization, and what was their relationship with town and village dwellers?
2. What other divisions existed within Khmer society?
3. What sort of market economy did Cambodia have? What were its major items of export and import? How would you characterize its trade with China?
4. Polo (source 104) notes that Mongol women took care of all commerce, and Zhou notes the same thing about Cambodian women. Does this seem significant? If so, what do you think it means?
5. From Zhou's perspective, why did Cambodia seem so "barbarous and strange"?
6. What does the evidence allow you to infer about Cambodia's overall relations with China?
7. Based on Zhou's description of royal ceremony, how would you characterize Khmer kingship?
8. Overall, what picture emerges of late-thirteenth-century Cambodia from these selections?

THE SAVAGES

There are two kinds of savages: those who know the language and are sold as slaves; the other are those who do not understand the language and could not adapt themselves to civilization. The latter have no permanent dwelling places, but, followed by their families, wander in the mountains carrying their few provisions in clay jars on their heads. If they find a wild animal, they will kill it with spears or bows and arrows, make a fire by striking stones together, cook the animal, eat it in common, and continue their wandering. Ferocious by nature, they use deadly poisons. Within their own band, they often kill one another. In recent times a few have started cultivating cardamom and cotton and weaving a cloth that is coarse and irregularly patterned.

SLAVES

Savages are brought to do the work of servants. When they are young and strong, they fetch a hundred pieces of cloth; old and weak, from thirty to forty. Wealthy families may have more than a hundred; even those of modest means have ten or twenty; only the poor have none at all. The savages inhabit the wild mountains and belong to a different race; they are called *zhuangs,* thieves. If, in a quarrel, a man calls another a *zhuang,* it is a deadly insult, so despised are the savages, who are considered to be subhuman. Brought to the city, they never dare appear on the street. They are forced to live in the space under the houses which are built on stilts and when they come up into the house to do their work, they must first kneel and make the proper obeisance, prostrating themselves before they can advance. They call their owners "father" and "mother." If they make a mistake, they are beaten. They take their punishment with bent head and without making the slightest movement.

THE LANGUAGE

This country has its own language. Even though the sounds are fairly similar, the people of Champa[1] and of Siam[2] do not understand it. . . . The officials have an official style for their deliberations; the scholars[3] speak in a literary manner; the Buddhist monks and Daoist priests[4] have their own language; and different villages speak differently. It is absolutely the same as in China.

PRODUCTS

Many strange trees are found in the mountains and in the clearings, herds of rhinoceros and elephants live, rare birds and many unusual animals are to be found. The most precious articles are the feathers of the kingfisher (valued in Canton to ornament gold jewelry), ivory, rhinoceros horn, and beeswax; cardamom and other forest products are more common.

The kingfisher is quite difficult to catch. In the thick woods are ponds and in the ponds are fish. The kingfisher leaves the forest to catch fish. Hidden under the leaves, by the side of the water, the Cambodian crouches. In a cage he has a female bird to attract the male and in his hand a small net. He waits until the bird comes and then catches him in his net. Some days he can catch as many as five; other days he waits vainly for a kingfisher.

Ivory is collected by the hill people. From a dead elephant one secures two tusks. Formerly it was thought that the elephant shed his tusks every year; this is not true. The ivory taken from an animal killed by a spear is the best. Then comes that which is found shortly after the animal has died a natural death; the least valued is that which is found in the mountains years after the death of the elephant.

Beeswax is found in rotted trees standing in the villages. It is produced by winged insects that have thin antlike waists. The Cambodians

---

[1]Central Vietnam.
[2]Thailand.

[3]These so-called scholars were probably Brahmin priests.
[4]Probably priests of Shiva and not Daoists.

take it away from the insects; a boatload can carry from two to three thousand honeycombs.

Rhinoceros horn that is white and veined is the most valued; the black variety is of inferior quality.

Cardamom is cultivated in the mountains by the savages. Pepper is also found occasionally. It climbs up bushes and entwines itself like a common weed. The green-blue variety is the most bitter.

TRADE

In Cambodia, women attend to trade. Even a Chinese who arrives there and takes a woman will profit greatly from her trading abilities. They do not have permanent stores, but simply spread a piece of mat on the ground. Everyone has her own spot. I have heard that they pay an official for the right to a location. In small transactions, one pays in rice, grain, Chinese goods, and, lastly, fabrics; in large transactions they use gold and silver.

In a general way, the country people are very naive. When they see a Chinese, they address him timidly, respectfully, calling him Fo — Buddha. As soon as they catch sight of him, they throw themselves on the ground and prostrate themselves. Lately some of them have cheated the Chinese and harmed them. This has happened to numbers of those who have gone into the villages.

CHINESE MERCHANDISE DESIRED IN CAMBODIA

I do not think that Cambodia produces either gold or silver; and what the Cambodians value most is Chinese silver and gold, then silks, lightly patterned in two-toned threads. After these items comes the pewter of Zhenzhou, lacquerware from Wenzhou, the blue porcelain of Quanzhou, mercury, vermilion, paper, sulphur, saltpeter, sandalwood, irisroot, musk, hemp cloth, umbrellas, iron pots, copper platters, sieves, wood combs,

and needles. That which they desire most of all is beans and wheat — but their exportation is forbidden.

THE ARMY

The troops go naked and barefoot. They hold a lance in their right hand and a shield in their left. The Cambodians have neither bows nor arrows, war machines nor bullets, helmets nor armor. It is said that in the war against the Siamese everyone was obliged to fight, but they had no knowledge of tactics or strategy.

THE PRINCE'S APPEARANCES IN PUBLIC

When the king leaves the palace, first comes the cavalry, leading his escort, followed by an array of standards, banners, and music. Next comes a troupe of palace girls, anywhere from three to five hundred, dressed in flowered material, their heads garlanded with flowers and holding large candles lighted even in broad daylight. After them come more palace girls bearing the royal utensils of gold and silver and an assortment of all kinds of ornaments whose usage I don't understand. Then come the palace girls who, armed with lance and shield, form the king's private bodyguard; they, too, form a troupe. They are followed by carriages ornamented in gold and drawn by goats and horses. Ministers and nobles mounted on elephants look straight ahead, while clustered around them are their many, many red parasols of rank. After them in palanquins, carriages, and on elephants come the king's wives and concubines; they have more than a hundred parasols decorated in gold. Behind them comes the king. Holding the precious sword, he stands on the royal elephant, whose tusks are encased in gold. More than twenty white parasols, gold-trimmed and with golden handles, surround him. A great many elephants form a cordon around the king and the cavalry guards him. . . .

Twice each day the king holds an audience to conduct the affairs of government. There is no set procedure. Whoever desires to see the king — either officials or any private person — sits on the ground and awaits him. After a little while, one hears, far off in the palace, distant music; outside they blow on conchs to announce his approach. I have heard that he uses only a gold palanquin and does not come from very far away. An instant later, two palace girls lift the curtain on the Golden Window and the king, sword in his hand, appears. All those present — ministers and people — clasp their hands together and beat their foreheads on the ground. As the sound of the conchs ceases, they can raise their heads. At the king's pleasure, they may approach and sit down on a lion skin, which is considered a royal object. When all matters are disposed of, the king retires, the two palace girls let the curtain fall; everyone rises. Thus one sees that, though this country is barbarous and strange, they do not fail to know what it is to be a king.

Advice for Merchants Traveling to Cathay
▼▼▼

107 ▾ Francesco Pegolotti, THE BOOK OF DESCRIPTIONS OF COUNTRIES

Around 1340 Francesco Balducci Pegolotti, an otherwise unknown agent of the Bardi banking house of Florence, composed a handbook of practical advice for merchants. Pegolotti, who had served the Bardi family's interests from London to Cyprus, drew upon his years of mercantile experience to produce a work filled with lists of facts and figures on such items as local business customs, the taxes and tariffs of various localities, and the relative values of different standards of weights, measures, and coinage. In other words, the book contained just about everything a prudent merchant would want to know before entering a new market. In addition to these catalogues of useful data, Pegolotti included a short essay of advice for merchants bound for China.

QUESTIONS FOR ANALYSIS

1. What evidence is there that Pegolotti himself had not traveled to Cathay?
2. Considering that his advice is not based on firsthand experience, how knowledgeable does he appear to be on the subject, and what does this suggest?
3. Consider Pegolotti's advice regarding the types of interpreters the merchant will need. What language skills suffice to carry on this trans-Eurasian business enterprise? What does this suggest about the markets of northern China?
4. When and where could the trip be especially hazardous? What does this suggest about the *Pax Mongolica?*
5. What overall impression does Pegolotti give us of this journey and its rewards?

THINGS NEEDFUL FOR MERCHANTS WHO DESIRE TO MAKE THE JOURNEY TO CATHAY

In the first place, you must let your beard grow long and not shave. And at Tana[1] you should furnish yourself with a dragoman.[2] And you must not try to save money in the matter of dragomen by taking a bad one instead of a good one. For the additional wages of the good one will not cost you so much as you will save by having him. And besides the dragoman it will be well to take at least two good menservants, who are acquainted with the Cumanian[3] tongue. And if the merchant likes to take a woman with him from Tana, he can do so; if he does not like to take one there is no obligation, only if he does take one he will be kept much more comfortably than if he does not take one. Howbeit, if he does take one, it will be well that she be acquainted with the Cumanian tongue as well as the men.

And from Tana traveling to Gittarchan[4] you should take with you twenty-five days' provisions, that is to say, flour and salt fish, for as to meat you will find enough of it at all the places along the road. And so also at all the chief stations noted in going from one country to another in the route, according to the number of days set down above, you should furnish yourself with flour and salt fish; other things you will find in sufficiency, and especially meat.

The road you travel from Tana to Cathay is perfectly safe, whether by day or by night, according to what the merchants say who have used it. Only if the merchant, in going or coming, should die upon the road, everything belonging to him will become the perquisite of the lord of the country in which he dies, and the officers of the lord will take possession of all. And in like manner if he die in Cathay. But if his brother be with him, or an intimate friend and comrade calling himself his brother, then to such a one they will surrender the property of the deceased, and so it will be rescued.

And there is another danger: this is when the lord of the country dies, and before the new lord who is to have the lordship is proclaimed; during such intervals there have sometimes been irregularities practiced on the Franks, and other foreigners. (They call "Franks" all the Christians of these parts from Romania[5] westward.) And neither will the roads be safe to travel until the other lord be proclaimed who is to reign in place of him who is deceased.

Cathay is a province which contains a multitude of cities and towns. Among others there is one in particular, that is to say the capital city, to which is great resort of merchants, and in which there is a vast amount of trade; and this city is called Cambalec.[6] And the said city has a circuit of one hundred miles, and is all full of people and houses and of dwellers in the said city. . . .

You may reckon also that from Tana to Sara[7] the road is less safe than on any other part of the journey; and yet even when this part of the road is at its worst, if you are some sixty men in the company you will go as safely as if you were in your own house.

Anyone from Genoa or from Venice, wishing to go to the places above-named, and to make the journey to Cathay, should carry linens with him, and if he visit Organci[8] he will dispose of these well. In Organci he should purchase sommi

---

[1]The modern city of Azov on the northeast coast of the Sea of Azov, which itself is an extension of the Black Sea. Tana was the farthest eastern point to which a person could sail from the Mediterranean.
[2]An interpreter fluent in Arabic, Persian, or Turkish.
[3]A Turkic people inhabiting the middle Volga.
[4]Modern Astrakhan, a city in the Volga delta, just north of the Caspian Sea.

[5]The European term for the Byzantine Empire.
[6]Khanbalik (City of the Khan), modern Beijing.
[7]Sarai on the Volga, the capital of the il-khans of Kipchak (also known as the *Golden Horde*), who ruled Russia and Kazakhstan.
[8]Urgench on the Oxus River in Central Asia.

of silver,[9] and with these he should proceed without making any further investment, unless it be some bales of the very finest stuffs which go in small bulk, and cost no more for carriage than coarser stuffs would do.

Merchants who travel this road can ride on horseback or on asses, or mounted in any way that they choose to be mounted.

Whatever silver the merchants may carry with them as far as Cathay the lord of Cathay will take from them and put into his treasury. And to merchants who thus bring silver they give that paper money of theirs in exchange. This is of yellow paper, stamped with the seal of the lord aforesaid. And this money is called balishi; and with this money you can readily buy silk and all other merchandise that you have a desire to buy. And all the people of the country are bound to receive it. And yet you shall not pay a higher price for your goods because your money is of paper. And of the said paper money there are three kinds, one being worth more than another, according to the value which has been established for each by that lord.

---

[9]Sommi were weights of silver. Each sommo was equivalent to five golden florins, the standard coin of Florence. Pegolotti calculated that the average merchant would carry merchandise worth about twenty-five thousand florins, and the expenses for the merchant, interpreter, and two personal servants would amount to a combined sixty to eighty sommi, or three to four hundred florins.

▼▼▼

Travel beyond the Mongol Ecumene

Sources 101 and 102 hint at the fairly high level of long-distance travel that took place across Eurasia well before the Age of the Mongol Peace. Both sources also suggest that religious motives and ties played major roles in that movement. What was true for Christianity and Judaism was even more true for the ecumenical community that called itself *Dar al-Islam* (the House of Islam). The family of Islam's very nature encouraged travel. Educated Muslims, no matter what their ethnic origins or native tongues, shared a sacred language — Arabic — and could communicate with one another. Muslims also shared the obligation of *hajj* (if at all possible). The pilgrimage routes that enabled African, Spanish, Iranian, Indian, and East Asian Muslims to travel to Arabia's holy sites served equally as important avenues of cultural and material exchange. Moreover, as noted in Chapter 11 and elsewhere, merchants spread Islam to such faraway regions as sub-Saharan Africa and the coastal lands of Southeast Asia. Once the faith had taken root, there was even more reason to maintain contact with these societies, many of which were so distant from Islam's Southwest Asian birthplace.

Muslims were not the only people who were involved in long-distance travel prior to the *Pax Mongolica* and continued to travel great distances after the breakup of the Mongol Empire. China and Western Europe had taken to the seas long before the rise of Chinggis Khan and continued their interests in seafaring and naval technology throughout the thirteenth and fourteenth centuries and beyond. Early in the fifteenth century Ming China sent seven massive naval expeditions into the Indian Ocean, and portions of several of those fleets reached the shores of East Africa and Arabia. Also in the fifteenth century, Western Europe, finding the overland routes to Cathay mostly blocked, began to seek sea routes to the Indies. The consequences of those explorations were astounding. Before the century was over Europeans had sailed to East Africa, India, and the Americas.

A Moroccan Visitor in Sub-Saharan Africa
▼▼▼

108 ▼ Ibn Battuta,
A DONATION TO THOSE
INTERESTED IN CURIOSITIES

The life and world travels of Abu 'Abdallah Muhammad ibn Battuta (1304–1369) provide eloquent testimony to the international cosmopolitanism of fourteenth-century Islam. Ibn Battuta was born into the religious upper class of Tangier, Morocco, where he received an education in Islamic law and Arabic literature. In 1325 he left home to make the first of what would be several pilgrimages to Mecca. In the course of the next three decades he visited Constantinople, Mesopotamia, Persia, India (where he resided and worked for seven years), Burma, Sumatra, Spain, Mali, and probably southern China. In all, his travels covered about seventy-five thousand miles, and most of his stops along the way were within the cultural confines of *Dar al-Islam,* where the sacred law of the Qur'an prevailed. In 1354 he returned to Morocco to stay and almost immediately began to narrate his experiences and observations to Ibn Juzayy, a professional scribe who fashioned these stories into one of the most popular forms of literature in the Muslim world: a *rihla,* or book of travels.

Before settling down and recording his adventures for posterity, Ibn Battuta embarked in early 1352 on his last great adventure, a trip by camel caravan to the West African kingdom of Mali in the Niger River region. Almost two years later he arrived back home with marvelous tales to tell of this Malinke-speaking land of gold, whose leaders had converted to Islam in the early thirteenth century.

QUESTIONS FOR ANALYSIS

1. What did Ibn Battuta admire most about these people? What did he find hardest to accept? Why?
2. Did Ibn Battuta understand fully all he encountered? Can you find any evidence of cultural or racial tension?
3. In what ways were the cultures of the people whom Ibn Battuta encountered a mixture of native African and Muslim elements?
4. How organized and controlled does the state of Mali appear to be?
5. Compare fourteenth-century Mali with eleventh-century Ghana (Chapter 11, source 94). What are their similarities and differences? Which seem more significant? What do you conclude from that answer?

6. **Based on a careful study of sources 94 and 96 of Chapter 11, as well as of this document, what inferences do you draw about the social status of women in sub-Saharan West Africa?**

Then we reached the town of Iwalatan . . . after a journey . . . of two whole months. It is the first district of the Sudan and the sultan's[1] deputy there is Farba Husayn. *Farba* means "deputy." When we arrived there the merchants[2] placed their belongings in an open space, where the Sudan[3] took over the guard of them while they went to the *farba*. He was sitting on a carpet under a *saqif*[4] with his assistants in front of him with lances and bows in their hands and the chief men of the Masufa[5] behind him. The merchants stood before him while he addressed them, in spite of their proximity to him, through an interpreter, out of contempt for them. At this I repented at having come to their country because of their ill manners and their contempt for white men.[6] I made for the house of Ibn Badda', a respectable man of Sala to whom I had written to rent a house for me. He had done so. Then the *mushrif*[7] (of Iwalatan), who is called the *manshaju*, invited those who had come with the caravan to receive his reception-gift (*diyafa*). I declined to go but my companions entreated me urgently, so I went with those who went. Then the *diyafa* was brought. It was *anili*[8] meal mixed with a little honey and yogurt which they had placed in half a gourd made into a kind of bowl. Those present drank and went away. I said to them: "Was it to this that the black man invited us?" They said; "Yes, for them this is a great banquet." Then I knew for certain that no good was to be expected from them and I wished to depart with the pilgrims of Iwalatan. But then I thought it better to go to see the seat of their king.

My stay in Iwalatan lasted about fifty days. Its inhabitants did me honor and made me their guest. Among them was the qadi[9] of the place Muhammad b. 'Abd Allah b. Yanumur and his brother the faqih[10] and teacher Yahya. The town of Iwalatan is extremely hot. There are a few little palm trees there in the shade of which they sow watermelons. . . . Mutton is abundant there and the people's clothes are of Egyptian cloth of good quality. Most of the inhabitants there belong to the Masufa, whose women are of surpassing beauty and have a higher status than the men.

THE MASUFA LIVING IN IWALATAN

These people have remarkable and strange ways. As for their men, they feel no jealousy. None of them traces his descent through his father, but from his maternal uncle, and a man's heirs are the sons of his sister only, to the exclusion of his own sons. This is something that I have seen nowhere in the world except among the Indian infidels in the land of Mulaybar, whereas these are Muslims who observe the prayer and study fiqh[11] and memorize the Qur'an. As for their women, they have no modesty in the presence of men and do not veil themselves in spite of their assiduity in prayer. If anybody wishes to marry one of them he may do so, but they do not travel with the husband, and if one of them wished to do so her family would prevent her.

The women there have friends and companions among the foreign men, just as the men have

---

[1]The sultan, or king, of Mali, for whom this was an outlying province.
[2]Berbers and Arabs from North Africa.
[3]Here this Arabic word, which means "blacks," refers to the local people and not to the region.
[4]A colonnade.
[5]A Berber people of the western Sahara.

[6]Merchants from North Africa: Berbers and Arabs.
[7]The sultan's overseer of the town's markets.
[8]Millet.
[9]An Islamic religious judge.
[10]A teacher of religion.
[11]Religion.

companions from among the foreign women. One of them may enter his house and find his wife with her man friend without making any objection. . . .

One day I went into the presence of Abu Muhammad Yandakan al-Masufi in whose company we had come and found him sitting on a carpet. In the courtyard of his house there was a canopied couch with a woman on it conversing with a man seated. I said to him: "Who is this woman?" He said: "She is my wife." I said: "What connection has the man with her?" He replied: "He is her friend." I said to him: "Do you acquiesce in this when you have lived in our country and become acquainted with the precepts of the Shar?"[12] He replied: "The association of women with men is agreeable to us and a part of good conduct, to which no suspicion attaches. They are not like the women of your country." I was astonished at his laxity. I left him, and did not return thereafter. He invited me several times but I did not accept.

When I resolved to travel to Mali . . . I hired a guide from the Masufa, since there is no need to travel in company because of the security of that road, and set off with three of my companions. . . .

Then we . . . arrived at the River Sansara, which is about ten miles from the capital of Mali. It is their custom to prevent people from entering it except by authorization. I had written before this to the white community . . . to ask them to rent a house for me. When I reached the afore-mentioned river I crossed it by the ferry without anybody preventing me. I arrived at the town of Mali, the seat of the king of the Sudan. . . .

THE SULTAN OF MALI

He is the sultan Mansa Sulayman.[13] *Mansa* means "sultan" and Sulayman is his name. He is a mi-

serly king from whom no great donation is to be expected. It happened that I remained for this period without seeing him on account of my illness. Then he gave a memorial feast for our Lord Abu 'l-Hasan[14] (may God be content with him) and invited the emirs and faqihs and the qadi and khatib,[15] and I went with them. They brought copies of the Qur'an and the Qur'an was recited in full. They prayed for our lord Abu 'l-Hasan (may God have mercy on him) and prayed for Mansa Sulayman. When this was finished I advanced and greeted Mansa Sulayman and the qadi and the khatib and Ibn al-Faqih told him who I was. He answered them in their language and they said to me: "The sultan says to you: 'I thank God.'" I replied: "Praise and thanks be to God in every circumstance."

THEIR TRIVIAL RECEPTION GIFT AND THEIR RESPECT FOR IT

When I departed the reception gift was sent to me and dispatched to the qadi's house. The qadi sent it with his men to the house of Ibn al-Faqih. Ibn al-Faqih hastened out of his house barefooted and came in to me saying: "Come! The cloth and gift of the sultan have come to you!" I got up, thinking that it would be robes of honor and money, but behold! it was three loaves of bread and a piece of beef fried in *gharti*[16] and a gourd containing yogurt. When I saw it I laughed, and was long astonished at their feeble intellect and their respect for mean things.

MY SPEAKING TO THE SULTAN AFTER THIS AND HIS KINDNESS TOWARDS ME

After this reception gift I remained for two months during which nothing was sent to me by the sultan and the month of Ramadan[17] came

---

[12]*Shari'a,* or Islamic Sacred Law.
[13]The brother of Mansa Musa (Chapter 8, source 62), Mansa Sulayman ruled Mali from 1341 to 1360.
[14]The late sultan of Morocco (r. 1331–1351).

[15]A public preacher at Friday mosque services.
[16]A vegetable oil.
[17]The month during which Muslims fast from sunrise to sunset.

in. Meanwhile I frequented the *mashwar* [council-place] and used to greet him and sit with the qadi and the khatib. I spoke with Dugha the interpreter, who said: "Speak with him, and I will express what you want to say in the proper fashion." So when he held a session at the beginning of Ramadan and I stood before him and said: "I have journeyed to the countries of the world and met their kings. I have been four months in your country without your giving me a reception gift or anything else. What shall I say of you in the presence of other sultans?" He replied: "I have not seen you nor known about you." The qadi and Ibn al-Faqih rose and replied to him saying: "He greeted you and you sent to him some food." Thereupon he ordered that a house be provided for me to stay in and an allowance to be allotted to me. Then, on the night of 27 Ramadan, he distributed among the qadi and the khatib and the faqihs a sum of money which they call *zakah*[18] and gave to me with them 33 1/3 mithqals.[19] When I departed he bestowed on me 100 mithqals of gold. . . .

THE SELF-DEBASEMENT OF THE SUDAN BEFORE THEIR KING AND THEIR SCATTERING OF DUST ON THEMSELVES BEFORE HIM AND OTHER PECULIARITIES

The Sudan are the humblest of people before their king and the most submissive towards him. They swear by his name, saying: *"Mansa Sulayman ki."* When he calls to one of them at his sessions in the pavilion which we have mentioned the person called takes off his clothes and puts on ragged clothes, and removes his turban and puts on a dirty *shashiyya*[20] and goes in holding up his garments and trousers half-way up his leg, and advances with submissiveness and humility. He then beats the ground vigorously with his two elbows, and stands like one performing a *rak'a*[21] to listen to his words.

If one of them addresses the sultan and the latter replies he uncovers the clothes from his back and sprinkles dust on his head and back, like one washing himself with water. I used to marvel how their eyes did not become blinded. . . .

WHAT I APPROVED OF AND WHAT I DISAPPROVED OF AMONG THE ACTS OF THE SUDAN

One of their good features is their lack of oppression. They are the farthest removed of people from it and their sultan does not permit anyone to practice it. Another is the security embracing the whole country, so that neither traveler there nor dweller has anything to fear from thief or usurper. Another is that they do not interfere with the wealth of any white man who dies among them, even though it be *qintar* upon *qintar*.[22] They simply leave it in the hands of a trustworthy white man until the one to whom it is due takes it. Another is their assiduity in prayer and their persistence in performing it in congregation and beating their children to make them perform it. If it is a Friday and a man does not go early to the mosque he will not find anywhere to pray because of the press of the people. It is their habit that every man sends his servant with his prayer-mat to spread it for him in a place which he thereby has a right to until he goes to the mosque. Their prayer-carpets are made from the fronds of the tree resembling the palm which has no fruit. Another of their good features is their dressing in fine white clothes on Friday. If any one of them possesses nothing but a ragged

---

[18]Alms distributed at the end of Ramadan.
[19]One *mithqal* was about 4.72 grams of gold.
[20]A skull cap.

[21]A set sequence of utterances and gestures that form the *salah*, or obligatory ritual prayer, that Muslims must engage in five times daily.
[22]"Weight upon weight" (i.e., a large amount of wealth).

shirt he washes it and cleanses it and attends the Friday prayer in it. Another is their eagerness to memorize the great Qur'an. They place fetters on their children if there appears on their part a failure to memorize it and they are not undone until they memorize it.

I went into the house of the qadi on the day of the festival and his children were fettered so I said to him: "Aren't you going to let them go?" He replied: "I shan't do so until they've got the Qur'an by heart!" One day I passed by a youth of theirs, of good appearance and dressed in fine clothes, with a heavy fetter on his leg. I said to those who were with me: "What has this boy done? Has he killed somebody?" The lad understood what I had said and laughed, and they said to me: "He's only been fettered so that he'll learn the Qur'an!"

One of their disapproved acts is that their female servants and slave girls and little girls appear before men naked, with their privy parts uncovered. During Ramadan I saw many of them in this state, for it is the custom of the *farariyya*[23] to break their fast[24] in the house of the sultan, and each one brings his food carried by twenty or more of his slave girls, they all being naked. Another is that their women go into the sultan's presence naked and uncovered, and that his daughters go naked. On the night of 25 Ramadan I saw about two hundred slave girls bringing out food from his palace naked, having with them two of his daughters with rounded breasts having no covering upon them. Another is their sprinkling dust and ashes on their heads out of good manners. . . . Another is that many of them eat carrion, and dogs, and donkeys.[25]

---

[23]Emirs, or chief men.
[24]The daily fast of the month of Ramadan ends at sunset (note 17).

[25]Unclean meat, according to qur'anic law.

A European View of the World

▼▼▼

109 ▼ John Mandeville, TRAVELS

If Ibn Battuta's *rihla* illustrates a cosmopolitan Muslim's vision of the world, a curious work ascribed to a largely unknown person named Sir John Mandeville illustrates the Western European view of that same globe. First appearing in Europe between 1356 and 1366, Mandeville's *Travels* purported to be the firsthand account of an English knight's trans-Eurasian adventures between 1322 and 1356, in which he claimed to have served both the sultan of Egypt and the Mongol khan of China. There is every good reason to believe this work is largely a fictional tour de force by a gifted author who masked his identity behind the pen name *John Mandeville* and whose expeditions were largely to European libraries, where he discovered quite a few travel books from which he borrowed liberally. There is some evidence that suggests Mandeville (or whatever his name was) traveled to the eastern Mediterranean, but he seems to have gone no farther east. The basic outline of Sir John's vividly described travels to the Indies and Cathay is plagiarized from the genuine travel account of the Franciscan missionary Odoric of Pordenone (ca. 1265–1331), who spent thirty-five years in Russia and Asia, including three years as an assistant to Archbishop John of Monte Corvino in Khanbalik (source 105). Mandeville amplified Friar Odoric's rather spare story by adding fables and tales from many other authors, by giving free rein to his own fertile imagination and sardonic wit, and by spicing his story with an impressive array of geographic and astronomical theories, many of them based on borrowed Arabic science.

No matter the book's questionable origins, Mandeville's *Travels,* written originally in French, was widely circulated and translated into almost every European language by 1400. Indeed, it became late medieval Europe's most popular travelogue in an age noted for its fascination with world travel. In many ways, it shaped Western Europeans' vision of the outside world on the eve of their overseas explorations. Therefore, even though Sir John did not travel to all of the regions he claimed to have visited, his work is historically important because it illustrates the manner in which Europeans of the fourteenth and fifteenth centuries viewed the lands and peoples beyond their frontiers. Indeed, in many ways Mandeville was instrumental in shaping that vision.

In the first selection Sir John deals with the shape and size of the earth. Most people today are unaware that the notion that medieval European scholars believed the world was flat is a modern myth created, tongue in cheek, by the American humorist and writer Washington Irving in the nineteenth century. In the second selection Mandeville shares his putative firsthand knowledge of the wondrous land of *Prester John,* descendant of the *Magi,* or the three wise kings from the East, who had visited the Christ Child. Prester John (John the priest), whose existence was firmly accepted in the West from the mid twelfth century onward, was the mythic priestly emperor of some supposedly lost Christian people. The Prester John myth was born partly out of rumors of actual distant Christian cultures — such as the Ethiopians of Africa, the Nestorians of Central and East Asia, and the St. Thomas Christians of India's west coast — and partly out of a crusading zeal to discover Christian allies in the war against Islam. As a consequence, European adventurers as late as the sixteenth century sought Prester John in Asia and Africa (source 111).

One thing to keep in mind as you read these excerpts is that many scholars have concluded that although Mandeville certainly meant to amuse his readers, his charming stories also had a serious purpose. These commentators argue that Mandeville often used his descriptions of the exotic peoples and places whom he had supposedly encountered as a way of subtly pointing out the shortcomings of his own Christian Europe.

QUESTIONS FOR ANALYSIS

1. What was John's view of the physical world? Be specific.
2. What do Mandeville's stories suggest about his attitudes toward alien customs and the world beyond Europe?
3. Many societies cherish a myth of a promised redeemer, or hero-to-come. How had the Christian West created in the mythic Prester John a person who represented the fulfillment of some of their deepest wishes?
4. In what ways, if at all, does Sir John seem to use these stories to point out his own society's flaws?

5. Reread the tale of Sinbad the Sailor (Chapter 9, source 77). Leaving details aside, can you discover any common themes between that tale and Mandeville's stories? What do those common motifs suggest to you?
6. Reread Columbus's letter of 1493 (Prologue). How had Mandeville prepared him to discover in the Caribbean evidence that he had landed on an island off the coast of Asia? Conversely, does Columbus's letter in any way shape the evidence to fit Mandeville's portrait of the world? Please explain your answers.

From India people go by the ocean sea by way of many islands and different countries, which it would be tedious for me to relate. Fifty-two days' journey from that land there is another large country called Lamary [Sumatra]. That land is extremely hot, so that the custom there is for men and women to walk about totally naked, and they scorn foreigners who wear clothes. They say that God created Adam and Eve naked, and no person, therefore, should be ashamed to appear as God made him, because nothing that comes from nature's bounty is foul. They also say that people who wear clothes are from another world, or else they are people who do not believe in God. They say that they believe in God who created the world and made Adam and Eve and everything else. Here they do not marry wives, since all the women are common to all men, and no woman forsakes any man. They say that it is sinful to refuse any man, for God so commanded it of Adam and Eve and all who followed when he said: "Increase and multiply and fill the earth."[1] Therefore, no man in that country may say: "This is my wife." No woman may say: "This is my husband." When they bear children, the women present them to whatever man they wish of those with whom they have had sexual relations. So also all land is held in common. What one man holds one year, another has another year, and everyone takes that portion which he desires. Also all the produce of the soil is held in common. This is true for grains and other goods as well. Nothing is held in private, nothing is locked up, and every person there takes what he wants without anyone saying "no." Each is as rich as the other.

There is, however, in that country an evil custom. They eat human flesh more happily than any other meat, this despite the fact that the land abounds in meats, fish, grains, gold, silver, and every other commodity. Merchants go there, bringing with them children to sell to the people of that country, and they purchase the children. If they are plump, they eat them immediately. If they are lean, they feed them until they fatten up, and then they eat them. They say this is the best and sweetest flesh in all the world.

In that land, and in many others beyond it, no one can see the Transmontane Star, known as the Star of the Sea, which is immoveable and stands in the north and is called the Lode Star.[2] They see, rather, another star, its opposite, which stands in the south and is called the Antarctic Star. Just as sailors here get their bearings and steer by the Lode Star, so sailors beyond those parts steer by the southern star, which we cannot see. So our northern star, which we call the Lode Star, cannot be seen there. This is proof that the earth and sea are round in shape and form. For portions of the heavens that are seen in one country do not appear in another. . . . I can prove that point by what I have observed, for I have been in parts of Brabant[3] and seen, by means of an astrolabe, that the Transmontane Star is 53 degrees in elevation. In Germany and Bohemia it is 58 degrees; and farther north it is 62 degrees and

---

[1]The Bible, Genesis, 1:22.
[2]Polaris, or the North Star, which guides mariners.

[3]A region between modern Belgium and the Netherlands.

some minutes high. I personally have measured it with an astrolabe. Understand that opposite the Transmontane Star is the other known as the Antarctic Star, as I have said. These two stars never move, and around them all the heavens revolve, just like a wheel about an axle. So those two stars divide the heavens into two equal parts, with as much above [the equator] as below. . . .

I say with certainty that people can encircle the entire world, below the equator as well as above,[4] and return to their homelands, provided they have good company, a ship, and health. And all along the way one would find people, lands, and islands. . . . For you know well that those people who live right under the Antarctic Star are directly underneath, feet against feet, of those who dwell directly under the Transmontane Star,[5] just as we and those who dwell under us[6] are feet to feet. For every part of the sea and the land has its opposite, which balances it, and it is both habitable and traversable. . . . So people who travel to India and the foreign isles girdle the roundness of the earth and the seas, passing under our countries in this hemisphere.

Something I heard as a youth has occurred to me often. A worthy man from our country departed some time ago to see the world. And so he passed through India and the islands beyond India, which number more than 5,000.[7] He traveled so far by sea and land and had so girdled the globe over the period of so many seasons that he found an island where he heard his own language being spoken. . . . He marveled at this, not knowing what to make of it. I conclude he had traveled so far by land and sea that he had encircled the entire globe, circumnavigating to the very frontier of his homeland. Had he traveled only a bit farther, he would have come to his own home. But he turned back, returning along the route

by which he had come. And so he spent a great deal of painful labor, as he acknowledged, when he returned home much later. For afterwards he went to Norway, where a storm carried him to an island. While on that island he discovered it was the island where earlier he had heard his own language spoken.[8] . . .

That could well be true, even though it might seem to simple-minded persons of no learning that people cannot travel on the underside of the world without falling off toward the heavens. That, however, is not possible, unless it is true that we also are liable to fall toward heaven from where we are on the earth. For whatever part of the earth people inhabit, above or below [the equator], it always seems to them that they are in a more proper position than any other folk. And so it is right that just as it seems to us that they are under us, so it seems to them that we are beneath them. For if a person could fall from the earth into the heavens, it is more reasonable to assume that the earth and sea, which are more vast and of greater weight, should fall into the heavens. But that is impossible. . . .

Although it is possible for a person to circumnavigate the world, nonetheless, out of a 1,000 persons, one might possibly return home. For, given the magnitude of the earth and the sea, a 1,000 people could venture forth and follow a 1,000 different routes. This being so, no person could plot a perfect route toward the place from where he left. He could only reach it by accident or the grace of God. For the earth is very large and is some 20,425 miles in circumference, according to the opinion of wise astronomers from the past, whose words I am not going to contradict, even though it seems to me, with my limited understanding and with all due respect, that it is larger.[9]

---

[4]Here Mandeville refutes a notion, accepted by classical Greco-Roman geographers, that the *antipodes,* or lands south of the equator, are uninhabitable due to their extreme heat.
[5]In other words, the South Pole is 180 degrees south of (or under) the North Pole.
[6]The place directly opposite on the globe.
[7]The islands of Southeast Asia.

[8]This story, especially in light of the passage that follows, seems to claim that the Englishman traveled south to India and the islands of Southeast Asia and then continued south across the South Pole and up the far side of the globe across the North Pole to Scandinavia; then he returned home by retracing his steps.
[9]Actually, it is closer to twenty-five thousand miles.

▼ ▼ ▼

This emperor, Prester John, commands a very large region and has many noble cities and fair towns in his realm, as well as many islands large and broad. For this land of India is divided into islands due to the great rivers that flow out of Paradise, dividing the land into many parts.[10] He also has many islands in the sea. . . . This Prester John has many kings and islands and many different peoples of various cultures subject to him. And this land is fertile and wealthy, but not as wealthy as the land of the Great Khan. For merchants do not as commonly travel there to purchase merchandise as they do to the land of the Great Khan, for it is too far to travel to. Moreover, people can find in that other region, the Island of Cathay, every manner of commodity that people need — gold cloth, silk, spices, and every sort of precious item. Consequently, even though commodities are less expensive in Prester John's island, nonetheless people dread the long voyage and the great sea-perils in that region. . . . Although one must travel by sea and land eleven or twelve months from Genoa or Venice before arriving in Cathay, the land of Prester John lies many more days of dreadful journey away. . . .

The Emperor Prester John always marries the daughter of the Great Khan, and the Great Khan likewise marries Prester John's daughter.[11] For they are the two greatest lords under heaven.

In Prester John's land there are many different things and many precious gems of such magnitude that people make vessels, such as platters, dishes, and cups, out of them. There are many other marvels there, so many, in fact, that it would be tiresome and too lengthy to put them down in a book . . . but I shall tell you some part.

This Emperor Prester John is Christian, as is a great part of his country as well. Yet they do not share all the articles of our faith. They believe fully in God, in the Son, and in the Holy Spirit. They are quite devout and faithful to one another, and they do not quarrel or practice fraud and deceit.

He has subject to him 72 provinces, and in every province there is a king. And these kings have kings under them, and all are tributaries to Prester John. And he has in his lordships many marvels. In his country is a sea that people call the Gravelly Sea.[12] It is all gravel and sand, without a drop of water, and it ebbs and flows in great waves, as other seas do, and never rests at any time. No one can cross that sea by ship or any other craft and, therefore, no one knows what land lies beyond that sea. Although it has no water, people find in it and on its banks plenty of good fish of a shape and size such as are found nowhere else, but they are tasty and delicious to eat. Three days journey from that sea are great mountains, out of which flows a great river that originates in Paradise. And it is full of precious stones, without a drop of water. . . . Beyond that river, rising toward the deserts, is a great gravel plain set between the mountains. On that plain everyday at sunrise small trees begin to grow, and they grow until mid-day, bearing fruit. No one dares, however, to eat the fruit, for it is like a deceptive phantom. After mid-day the trees decrease and reenter the earth, so that by sunset they are no longer to be seen. And they do this every day. And that is a great marvel. In that desert are many wild people who are hideous to look at, for they are horned and do not speak but only grunt like pigs. . . .

When Emperor Prester John goes into battle against any other lord, he has no banners borne before him. Rather, he has three crosses of fine gold, which are massive and very tall and encrusted with precious stones. Each cross is set in a richly adorned chariot. To guard each cross,

---

[10]According to John, the Terrestrial Paradise, from which Adam and Eve had been expelled, lies far to the east of Prester John's country; four rivers — the Ganges, Nile, Tigris, and Euphrates — flow out of that paradise and divide the major lands of the earth.

[11]This particular version of the Prester John myth seems to be a somewhat distorted reflection of the fact that many Mongol khans had Nestorian Christian wives.

[12]Apparently a garbled reference to the Gobi (Gravel) Desert of Central Asia.

there is a detail of 10,000 mounted men at arms and 100,000 men on foot, . . . and this number is in addition to the main body of troops. . . . When he rides out in peace time with a private entourage, he has borne before him only one wooden cross, unpainted and lacking gold, silver, or gems, as a remembrance that Jesus Christ suffered death on a wooden cross.[13] He also has borne before him a golden platter filled with earth, in token of the fact that his nobility, might, and flesh will all turn to earth. He also has borne before him a silver vessel full of great nuggets of gold and precious gems, as a token of his lordship, nobility, and might.

---

[13]Keep in mind that *crusade* means "to bear a cross."

Zheng He's Western Voyages
▼▼▼

110 ▼ Ma Huan, THE OVERALL SURVEY OF THE OCEAN'S SHORES

Vigorous expansionism characterized the early Ming Dynasty (1368–1644), particularly during the reign of Chengzu, known as the *Yongle Emperor* (r. 1402–1424). Between 1405 and 1421 this emperor sent out a series of six great fleets under the command of China's most famous admiral, a Muslim eunuch of Mongolian ancestry named Zheng He (1371–1435). If we can believe the records, several fleets carried in excess of twenty-seven thousand sailors, soldiers, and officials. The first expedition of 1405–1407 reportedly consisted of three hundred seventeen vessels, including sixty-two massive treasure ships, some of which were over four hundred feet long, more than one hundred fifty feet wide (imagine a ship larger than a football field), and around three thousand one hundred tons in weight. These armadas — as well as a seventh, which went out in 1431 and returned in 1433 — sailed through the waters of Southeast Asia and the Indian Ocean, visiting numerous ports of call in such faraway places as the Spice Islands, India, East Africa, and the Arabian Peninsula.

Following long-established Arab and Chinese sailing routes, these expeditions were certainly not voyages of exploration. Rather, their main purpose appears to have been the reassertion of Chinese prestige to the south and west. Like the expedition that Zhou Daguan joined a century earlier, these fleets were commissioned to accept the submission and tribute of the so-called barbarian rulers they encountered. A secondary purpose seems to have been to stimulate China's economy and strengthen its commercial position in South Asia, particularly in light of the fact that the armies of Timur the Lame had severed the old Silk Route.

Despite the psychological impact the fleets' show of strength had upon the people they visited (in one area of Thailand, Zheng He was remembered as a god), China would never dominate the Indian Ocean. After the Yongle Emperor's death, the imperial court did not follow through on what had begun so well. The reasons are not too difficult to discern. The cost of mounting the expeditions was prohibitively high. Moreover, the Confucian literarcy, with its traditional contempt for commerce and foreign cultures, was on the ascendance after the Yongle Emperor's death. Although Zheng He was allowed to lead a seventh expedition westward, it proved to be China's last moment of transoceanic greatness. The court called a halt to further overseas adventures. The fleet was allowed to decay, and China deliberately and effectively forgot much of the naval technology that had made it the world's greatest maritime power in the ages of Song and early Ming.

The following account describes various sites visited in the course of three of Zheng He's expeditions in western waters. Its author, Ma Huan (ca. 1380–after 1451), a Chinese Muslim, joined the fourth voyage (1413–1415) as an Arabic translator and upon his return transcribed his notes into book form. He later sailed on the sixth (1421–1422) and seventh (1431–1433) expeditions and amended his account accordingly, eventually publishing it in 1451.

QUESTIONS FOR ANALYSIS

1. What evidence is there that the emperor saw these expeditions as a way of extending Chinese influence abroad?
2. How did Zheng He use both diplomacy and military force to achieve this objective?
3. What evidence is there that these expeditions also served commercial purposes?
4. What evidence is there that a high level of international commerce existed in the Indian Ocean well before the coming of Zheng He's fleets?

THE COUNTRY OF MANLAJIA[1] (MALACCA)

From Zhan City[2] you go due south, and after traveling for eight days with a fair wind the ship comes to Longya strait,[3] after entering the strait you travel west; and you can reach this place in two days.

Formerly this place was not designated a "country"; and because the sea hereabouts was named "Five Islands," the place was in consequence named "Five Islands." There was no king of the country; and it was controlled only by a chief. This territory was subordinate to the jurisdiction of Xian Luo,[4] it paid an annual tribute of forty *liang*[5] of gold; and if it were not paid, then Xian Luo would send men to attack it.

In the seventh year of the Yongle period,[6] the Emperor ordered the principal envoy, the grand eunuch Zheng He, and others to assume command (of the treasure-ships), and to take the imperial edicts and to bestow upon this chief two silver seals, a hat, a belt and a robe. Zheng He set up a stone tablet and raised the place to a city; and it was subsequently called the "country of Manlajia." Thereafter Xian Luo did not dare to invade it.

---

[1] Malacca, a port on the west coast of the Malay Peninsula.
[2] In Champa (central Vietnam).
[3] The Singapore Strait.
[4] Thailand.
[5] About forty-eight ounces.
[6] 1409. This would be the third expedition (1409–1411).

The chief, having received the favor of being made king, conducted his wife and son, and went to the court at the capital[7] to return thanks and to present tribute of local products. The court also granted him a sea-going ship, so that he might return to his country and protect his land. . . .

Whenever the treasure-ships of the Central Country[8] arrived there, they at once erected a line of stockading, like a city-wall, and set up towers for the watchdrums at four gates; at night they had patrols of police carrying bells; inside, again, they erected a second stockade, like a small city-wall, within which they constructed warehouses and granaries; and all the money and provisions were stored in them. The ships which had gone to various countries[9] returned to this place and assembled; they marshaled the foreign goods and loaded them in the ships; then waited till the south wind was perfectly favorable. In the middle decade of the fifth moon they put to sea and returned home.[10]

Moreover, the king of the country made a selection of local products, conducted his wife and son, brought his chiefs, boarded a ship and followed the treasure-ships; and he attended at court and presented tribute. . . .

THE COUNTRY OF SUMENDALA[11] (SEMUDERA, LHO SEUMAWE)

The country of Sumendala is exactly the same country as that formerly named Xuwendana. This place is indeed the principal center of the Western Ocean. . . .

The king of the country of Sumendala had previously been raided by the "tattooed-face king" of Naguer; and in the fighting he received a poi-

soned arrow in the body and died. He had one son, who was young and unable to avenge his father's death. The king's wife made a vow before the people, saying "If there is anyone who can avenge my husband's death and recover his land, I am willing to marry him and to share with him the management of the country's affairs." When she finished speaking, a fisherman belonging to the place was fired with determination, and said "I can avenge him."

Thereupon he took command of an army and at once put the "tattooed-face king" to flight in battle; and later he avenged the former king's death when the "tattooed-face king" was killed. The people of the latter submitted and did not dare to carry on hostilities.

Whereupon the wife of the former king, failing not to carry out her previous vow, forthwith married the fisherman. He was styled "the old king," and in such things as the affairs of the royal household and the taxation of the land, everybody accepted the old king's decisions. In the seventh year of the Yongle period[12] the old king, in fulfillment of his duty, brought tribute of local products,[13] and was enriched by the kindness of Heaven;[14] and in the tenth year of the Yongle period[15] he returned to his country.

When the son of the former king had grown up, he secretly plotted with the chiefs, murdered his adoptive father the fisherman, usurped his position, and ruled the kingdom.

The fisherman had a son by his principal wife; his name was Suganla; he took command of his people, and they fled away, taking their families; and, after erecting a stockade in the neighboring mountains, from time to time he led his men in incursions to take revenge on his father's enemies. In the thirteenth year of the Yongle

---

[7]Nanjing (the southern capital). The Ming court moved from the seaport capital of Nanjing to inland Beijing (the northern capital) in 1421, signaling a shift in China's focus.

[8]China, the Middle Kingdom.

[9]Elements were detached from the main fleet and sent off on special missions.

[10]1433, the last expedition.

[11]Semudera on the north coast of the island of Sumatra and across the Strait of Malacca from Malaysia.

[12]1409.

[13]To the Ming court at Nanjing.

[14]The emperor.

[15]1412.

period[16] the principal envoy, the grand eunuch Zheng He, and others, commanding a large fleet of treasure-ships, arrived there; they dispatched soldiers who captured Suganla; and he went to the capital;[17] and was publicly executed. The king's son was grateful for the imperial kindness, and constantly presented tribute of local products to the court. . . .

At this place there are foreign[18] ships going and coming in large numbers, hence all kinds of foreign goods are sold in great quantities in the country.

In this country they use gold coins and tin coins. The foreign name for the gold coin is *dinaer*;[19] they use pale gold, seventy percent pure, for casting it. . . . The foreign name for the tin coin is *jiashi*,[20] and in all their trading they regularly use tin coins. . . .

THE COUNTRY OF GULI[21] (CALICUT)

This is the great country of the Western Ocean. . . .

In the fifth year of the Yongle period the court ordered the principal envoy, the grand eunuch Zheng He, and others to deliver an imperial mandate to the king[22] of this country and to bestow on him a patent conferring a title of honor, and the grant of a silver seal, also to promote all the chiefs and award them hats and belts of various grades.

So Zheng He went there in command of a large fleet of treasure-ships, and he erected a tablet with a pavilion over it and set up a stone which said, "Though the journey from this country to the Central Country is more than a hundred thousand *li*,[23] yet the people are very similar, happy and prosperous, with identical customs. We have here engraved a stone, a perpetual declaration for ten thousand ages."

The king of the country is a Nankun[24] man; he is a firm believer in the Buddhist religion[25] and he venerates the elephant and the ox.

The population of the country includes five classes, the Muslim people, the Nankun people, the Zhedi people, the Geling people, and the Mugua[26] people. . . .

The king has two great chiefs who administer the affairs of the country; both are Muslims. . . .

The people are very honest and trustworthy. Their appearance is smart, fine, and distinguished.

Their two great chiefs received promotion and awards from the court of the Central Country.

If a treasure-ship goes there, it is left entirely to the two men to superintend the buying and selling; the king sends a chief and a Zhedi Weinuoji[27] to examine the account books in the official bureau; a broker comes and joins them; and a high officer who commands the ships discusses the choice of a certain date for fixing prices. When the day arrives, they first of all take the silk embroideries and the open-work silks, and other such goods which have been brought there, and discuss the price of them one by one; and when the price has been fixed, they write out an agreement stating the amount of the price; this agreement is retained by these persons. . . .

---

[16]1415.
[17]Presumably Nanjing.
[18]Non-Chinese.
[19]From the Arabic *dinar*.
[20]The English would later transliterate this local word as "cash."
[21]Calicut on India's southwest coast (not to be confused with Calcutta in the northeast).
[22]1407. This was the second expedition (1407–1409). Although Zheng He was its nominal commander, he did not accompany it.

[23]A *li* is a bit more than a third of a mile.
[24]Upper class. He probably means a member of the Kshatriya, or warrior-ruler, caste.
[25]Incorrect; he was Hindu.
[26]These would be the four castes, or varnas.
[27]Probably an accountant.

THE COUNTRY OF HULUMOSI[28] (HORMUZ)

Setting sail from the country of Guli, you go towards the north-west; and you can reach this place after traveling with a fair wind for twenty-five days. The capital lies beside the sea and up against the mountains.

Foreign ships from every place and foreign merchants traveling by land all come to this country to attend the market and trade; hence the people of the country are all rich. . . .

The king of this country, too, took a ship and loaded it with lions, *qilin,*[29] horses, pearls, precious stones, and other things, also a memorial to the throne written on a golden leaf; and he sent his chiefs and other men, who accompanied the treasure-ships dispatched by the Emperor, which were returning from the Western Ocean; and they went to the capital and presented tribute.[30]

---

[28]Hormuz, an island off the coast of Iran and at the mouth of the Persian Gulf.
[29]A giraffe.

[30]This probably took place at the end of the seventh expedition.

The Origins of Portugal's Overseas Empire
▼▼▼

111 ▼ *Gomes Eannes de Azurara,* *CHRONICLE OF GUINEA*

At the same time that Zheng He's fleets were sailing majestically through the western seas and Muslim sailors dominated the coastal traffic of virtually every inhabited land washed by the Indian Ocean (except Australia), the Portuguese were tentatively inching down the west coast of Africa. From 1419 onward Prince Henry (1394–1460), third son of King John I (r. 1385–1433), almost annually sent out a ship or two in an attempt to push farther toward the sub-Saharan land the Portuguese called *Guinea;* only in 1434, however, did one of his caravels manage to round the feared Cape Bojador, along the western Sahara coast. Once this psychological barrier had been broken, the pace of exploration quickened. By 1460 Portuguese sailors had ventured as far south as modern Sierra Leone, an advance of about fifteen hundred miles in twenty-six years. Finally, Bartholomeu Dias rounded the southern tip of Africa in early 1488, and Vasco da Gama, seeking, in his words, "Christians and spices," dropped anchor off Calicut on May 20, 1498. Although Da Gama lost two of his four ships and many of his crew in this enterprise, Portugal was now in the Indian Ocean to stay.

Portugal's commercial empire was still over half a century in the future when, in 1452, Gomes Eannes de Azurara (ca. 1400–after 1472) began to compose a history of the life and work of Prince Henry "the Navigator," in so many ways the parent of an empire-to-be. Azurara's history details Portuguese explorations along the coast of West Africa down to 1448. He promised a sequel because Henry was still alive and actively promoting voyages to Africa when Azurara completed *The Chronicle of Guinea* in 1453. His other duties apparently intervened, and he never returned to the topic. Still, the chronicle he managed to write is a revealing picture of the spirit behind Portugal's first generation of oceanic exploration and colonialism.

In the following excerpts, Azurara explains why Prince Henry sponsored the expeditions and defends the consequent enslavement of West Africans. Trade in Guinean slaves, which became an integral part of Portugal's commercial imperialism, began in 1441 with the capture of ten Africans, and Azurara estimated that nine hundred twenty-seven West African slaves had come into Portugal by 1448. This humane man, who was disturbed by many aspects of this exploitation, could not foresee that between 1450 and 1500 roughly one hundred fifty thousand more Africans would enter Portugal as slaves, and over the next four centuries untold millions of so-called heathens would be transported out of Africa by European and Euro-American slavers.

QUESTIONS FOR ANALYSIS

1. What were Henry's motives? What seems to have been foremost in his mind: commercial, political, or religious gain or simple curiosity?
2. Some modern commentators argue that Europeans initially entered the African slave trade out of a sense of racial superiority. Based on this account, do you think Azurara would agree with that assessment? In other words, how does he justify the enslavement of Africans? Please be specific in your answer.
3. It has been said that Henry was a fifteenth-century crusader. From the evidence, does this seem to be a fair judgment? Why or why not?
4. Compare this document with Christopher Columbus's letter of 1493 (the Prologue). Do they seem to share a common spirit? If so, what is it?
5. Compare the purposes behind the Portuguese and Spanish explorations with those of Zheng He's expeditions. In what ways are do they differ, and to what do you ascribe those differences?

We imagine that we know a matter when we are acquainted with the doer of it and the end for which he did it. And since in former chapters we have set forth the Lord Infant[1] as the chief actor in these things, giving as clear an understanding of him as we could, it is meet that in this present chapter we should know his purpose in doing them. And you should note well that the noble spirit of this Prince, by a sort of natural constraint, was ever urging him both to begin and to carry out very great deeds. For which reason, after the taking of Ceuta[2] he always kept ships well armed against the Infidel, both for war, and because he had also a wish to know the land that lay beyond the isles of Canary and that Cape called Bojador, for that up to his time, neither by writings, nor by the memory of man, was known with any certainty the nature of the land beyond that Cape. Some said indeed that Saint Brendan[3] had passed that way; and there

---

[1] Prince Henry. An *infante* (feminine *infanta*) was any son of a Portuguese or Spanish monarch who was not an heir to the Crown.

[2] A Muslim naval base in Morocco, which Portugal captured in 1415.
[3] A wandering Irish monk of the sixth century.

was another tale of two galleys rounding the Cape, which never returned. But this does not appear at all likely to be true, for it is not to be presumed that if the said galleys went there, some other ships would not have endeavored to learn what voyage they had made. And because the said Lord Infant wished to know the truth of this — since it seemed to him that if he or some other lord did not endeavor to gain that knowledge, no mariners or merchants would ever dare to attempt it — (for it is clear that none of them ever trouble themselves to sail to a place where there is not a sure and certain hope of profit) — and seeing also that no other prince took any pains in this matter, he sent out his own ships against those parts, to have manifest certainty of them all. And to this he was stirred up by his zeal for the service of God and of the King Edward his Lord and brother,[4] who then reigned. And this was the first reason of his action.

The second reason was that if there chanced to be in those lands some population of Christians, or some havens, into which it would be possible to sail without peril, many kinds of merchandise might be brought to this realm, which would find a ready market, and reasonably so, because no other people of these parts traded with them, nor yet people of any other that were known; and also the products of this realm might be taken there, which traffic would bring great profit to our countrymen.

The third reason was that, as it was said that the power of the Moors in that land of Africa was very much greater than was commonly supposed, and that there were no Christians among them, nor any other race of men; and because every wise man is obliged by natural prudence to wish for a knowledge of the power of his enemy; therefore the said Lord Infant exerted him-

self to cause this to be fully discovered, and to make it known determinately how far the power of those infidels extended.

The fourth reason was because during the one and thirty years that he had warred against the Moors, he had never found a Christian king, nor a lord outside this land, who for the love of our Lord Jesus Christ would aid him in the said war. Therefore he sought to know if there were in those parts any Christian princes, in whom the charity and the love of Christ was so ingrained that they would aid him against those enemies of the faith.

The fifth reason was his great desire to make increase in the faith of our Lord Jesus Christ and to bring to him all the souls that should be saved, — understanding that all the mystery of the Incarnation, Death, and Passion of our Lord Jesus Christ was for this sole end — namely the salvation of lost souls — whom the said Lord Infant by his travail and spending would fain bring into the true path. For he perceived that no better offering could be made unto the Lord than this; for if God promised to return one hundred goods for one, we may justly believe that for such great benefits, that is to say for so many souls as were saved by the efforts of this Lord, he will have so many hundreds of rewards in the kingdom of God, by which his spirit may be glorified after this life in the celestial realm. For I who wrote this history saw so many men and women of those parts turned to the holy faith, that even if the Infant had been a heathen, their prayers would have been enough to have obtained his salvation. And not only did I see the first captives,[5] but their children and grandchildren as true Christians as if the Divine grace breathed in them and imparted to them a clear knowledge of itself.

---

[4]King Duarte (r. 1433–1438).

[5]West African slaves who had been captured and transported to Portugal by licensed slave hunters.

Chapter 13

▼▼▼

Transoceanic Encounters

1500–1700

Although aggressive expansion had already been part of the dynamics of European civilization for over seven hundred years, its transoceanic explorations from the late fifteenth century onward mark a turning point in the history not only of the West but of the entire world. Europe's push across wide expanses of ocean eventually became the single most important factor in the breakdown of regional isolation around the world and the creation of a true global community in the years after 1500.

The story is not simple. By 1700 Europeans had culturally and demographically altered forever large areas of the Americas, but they had yet to visit much of those two great continents. The major civilizations of East Asia were still successfully resisting most unwanted European influences, and European penetration of India's interior had hardly begun. At the end of the seventeenth century, Western exploration and direct exploitation of the regions of Africa beyond the coasts were even less advanced. Moreover, although it is easy from a twentieth-century perspective to see in its early transoceanic ventures the origins of Europe's eventual dominance of the world, this would not have been apparent to most people living during these two centuries. For every area into which Europeans were expanding their influence, there was another in which they were retreating or being rebuffed. For example, sixteenth- and seventeenth-century Europeans fearfully witnessed the advancing menace of the Ottoman Turks into Europe itself.

Under Sultan Suleiman II (r. 1520–1566), the Ottoman Empire became a major force to be reckoned with so far as Europe was concerned. In 1522 Suleiman's armies established control over the eastern Mediterranean by seizing the island of Rhodes. In 1526 the Turks destroyed a Hungarian army and within two decades controlled most of that Christian kingdom. By the autumn of 1529 Ottoman forces besieged Vienna but were forced to withdraw. The Ottoman Turks remained Europe's greatest challenger for the next two centuries, and many believed that the next time Ottoman soldiers advanced on Vienna they would not be stopped. Indeed, the siege of 1683 failed only by the slightest margin.

Equally impressive was the expansion of Chinese borders, especially during the reign of Emperor Kangxi (r. 1661–1722), when China took control of the island of Formosa (modern Taiwan), incorporated Tibet into its empire, finally turned the nomads of Mongolia into quiescent vassals, and entered into a border treaty with imperial Russia that inaugurated a long period of Sino-Russian peace. On its part, Russia carved out the largest land empire of its day through a steady process of exploration and colonization across Eurasia's eastern forests and steppes. In 1637 Russian pioneers reached the Pacific, and colonists were not far behind. Given this state of affairs, Western Europeans did not see expansion as a one-way street, nor did they see themselves as aggressors and the rest of the world as their victims.

▼▼▼

Europeans in the Americas

As Columbus's letter of 1493 indicates, Europeans almost instantly discovered that the world across the Atlantic contained exploitable sources of wealth (such as silver, gold, timber, and furs) and was capable of supporting large-scale agricultural production of such crops as sugar and tobacco, for which there was an eager European market. All these things seemed theirs for the taking, not only in the thinly populated regions of North America and eastern and southern South America, but even in the densely populated regions of Mexico, Peru, and the Caribbean.

The consequences of this attitude were catastrophic for America's indigenous peoples. By 1650 Spaniards and Portuguese ruled and exploited Mexico, the Caribbean, Central and South America, and southern portions of North America; the English, French, Dutch, and other Europeans had begun to settle the northern portions of North America's Atlantic coast and the St. Lawrence River Basin. In the wake of these European incursions, Native American political structures disintegrated, uncounted millions of Amerindians died, and traditional patterns of life and belief managed only a tenuous (but tenacious) survival.

While this sad story is true enough, it would be incorrect to say that the majority of the European colonists and the governments who supported them attempted to exterminate the Native Americans. Certainly most European colonists sought to exploit the Amerindians, and even the Amerindians' protectors sought to convert them to European religious beliefs, thereby offering the natives a form of cultural suicide. Moreover, there is no denying the fact that the European newcomers contained within their ranks a number of ruthless thugs who did not hesitate to brutalize and kill, sometimes on a large scale. Still, there is no credible evidence of any widespread attempts at *genocide,* or the systematic, state-sponsored annihilation of an entire people. Such a notion was inconsistent with the world view and aims of the European colonizers who, as we saw in Columbus's letter of 1493, sought souls to save and slaves for servitude.

Europeans might have lacked the intention of killing off millions of Native Americans, but they managed unintentionally to do so, as a consequence of the viruses, bacteria, and other parasites that they carried across the Atlantic in their bodies. What is more, when West African slaves were brought to the Caribbean to replace the native populations that were rapidly dying off, additional fatal diseases came into the Americas. Smallpox, measles, diphtheria, chicken pox, whooping cough, influenza, malaria, yellow fever — all of these and more became killers when introduced into populations that lacked genetic resistance, due to their thousands of years of isolation from the Afro-Eurasian world.

The Tainos, who greeted Columbus in 1492, numbered about one million in 1492; by 1530 they numbered a few thousand. In 1519, the year of Cortés's arrival, the population of Mexico was about twenty-one and one-half million people; in 1532 it had fallen to about sixteen million; at midcentury, following the epidemic of 1545–1548, it was possibly as low as two and one-half million. That is a ninety percent decrease in the short space of thirty years! No part of the Americas was untouched; even areas not visited personally by Europeans felt the devastating effects of killer epidemics. The Mississippian Mound Culture of North America seems to have disappeared as an identifiable entity in the mid sixteenth century as a result of European diseases that traveled along native trade routes to its population centers well before Europeans ever saw the magnificent mound complexes that this culture left behind as silent witnesses of its former greatness.

The first of the following two documents hints at the critical role played by the hidden ally of disease in the Spanish *conquistadors'* conquest of Mexico. It also suggests other factors that combined to give the Spaniards their victory. The second source reveals the devastating effects of simple greed on the part of Spanish entrepreneurs in Peru.

The Battle for Tenochtitlán: An Aztec Perspective

▼▼▼

112 ▼ *Bernardino de Sahagún,* *GENERAL HISTORY OF THE* *THINGS OF NEW SPAIN*

Bernardino de Sahagún (ca. 1499–1590), a member of the Franciscan Order, was one of the earliest Spanish missionaries in Mexico, arriving in 1529. He soon developed a keen interest in the culture of the natives of Mexico, for whom he had deep affection and respect. He mastered the *Nahuatl* language, spoken by the Aztecs and other central Mexican peoples, and in 1545 began a systematic collection of oral and pictorial information about the culture of the native Mexicans. The result was his *General History of the Things of New Spain,* the first major ethnographic work on any Native American society and our principal source of information about Mexican culture at the time of the Spanish conquest. Many Spaniards opposed his work because they believed his efforts to preserve the memory of native culture threatened their policy of exploiting and Christianizing the Amerindians. As a result, in 1578 his writings and notes were confiscated by royal decree and sent back to Spain, where they gathered dust in an archive until discovered and published in the nineteenth century.

The following selection comes from the twelfth and last book of the *General History.* Based on interviews Sahagún and his Amerindian assistants had with Aztecs who had experienced the conquest some twenty-five years earlier, Book Twelve, which exists in both Nahuatl and Spanish versions, recounts the conquest of Mexico from the time Cortés arrived on the Mexican coast in April 1519 until the days following the Aztecs' capitulation in August 1521. Although scholars hotly debate the exact role of Sahagún and his assistants in composing and organizing Book Twelve, most agree that it accurately portrays Aztec views and perceptions of the events that unfolded between 1519 and 1521.

Our excerpt, translated from the Nahuatl text, picks up the story in November 1519. By then the Spaniards had gained as allies the Tlaxcalans, the Aztecs' bitter enemies, and were leaving Cholula, an ancient city that the Spaniards and their allies had sacked because of its leaders' lack of cooperation. They were on their way to Tenochtitlán, the splendid Aztec capital on Lake Texcoco, for an anticipated meeting with the Aztec emperor, Moctezuma.

QUESTIONS FOR ANALYSIS

1. What does the source reveal about the motives of the Spaniards and their allies for their attack on the Aztecs?
2. What was Moctezuma's strategy to deal with the Spaniards? Why did it fail?
3. What impression did Spanish firearms and cannons have on the Aztecs? What evidence is there that the Aztecs adjusted their strategy to counter the Spanish weapons?
4. Aside from their firearms, what other military advantages did the Spaniards have over their opponents? How decisive do these other advantages seem to have been?
5. On several occasions the Aztecs routed the Spaniards. What explains these Aztec victories?
6. Why were the Aztecs eager to capture their enemies?
7. How did the Aztec view of war differ from that of the Spaniards?
8. What does the source reveal about Aztec religious beliefs, values, and practices?

And after the dying in Cholula, the Spaniards set off on their way to Mexico,[1] coming gathered and bunched, raising dust. . . .

Thereupon Moteuccoma[2] named and sent noblemen and a great many other agents of his . . . to go meet [Cortés] . . . at Quauhtechcac. They gave [the Spaniards] golden banners of precious feathers, and golden necklaces.

And when they had given the things to them, they seemed to smile, to rejoice and to be very happy. Like monkeys they grabbed the gold. It was as though their hearts were put to rest, brightened, freshened. For gold was what they greatly thirsted for; they were gluttonous for it, starved for it, piggishly wanting it. They came lifting up the golden banners, waving them from side to side, showing them to each other. They seemed to babble; what they said to each other was in a babbling tongue. . . .

Another group of messengers — rainmakers, witches, and priests — had also gone out for an encounter, but nowhere were they able to do anything or to get sight of [the Spaniards]; they did not hit their target, they did not find the people they were looking for, they were not sufficient. . . .

▷   Cortés and his entourage continue their march.

Then they set out in this direction, about to enter Mexico here. Then they all dressed and equipped themselves for war. They girded themselves, tying their battle gear tightly on themselves and then on their horses. Then they arranged themselves in rows, files, ranks.

Four horsemen came ahead going first, staying ahead, leading. . . .

Also the dogs, their dogs, came ahead, sniffing at things and constantly panting.[3]

By himself came marching ahead, all alone, the one who bore the standard on his shoulder. He came waving it about, making it spin, tossing it here and there. . . .

Following him came those with iron swords. Their iron swords came bare and gleaming. On their shoulders they bore their shields, of wood or leather.

The second contingent and file were horses carrying people, each with his cotton cuirass,[4] his leather shield, his iron lance, and his iron sword hanging down from the horse's neck. They came with bells on, jingling or rattling. The horses, the deer,[5] neighed, there was much neighing, and they would sweat a great deal; water seemed to fall from them. And their flecks of foam splatted on the ground, like soapsuds splatting. . . .

The third file were those with iron crossbows, the crossbowmen. Their quivers went hanging at their sides, passed under their armpits, well filled, packed with arrows, with iron bolts. . . .

The fourth file were likewise horsemen; their outfits were the same as has been said.

The fifth group were those with harquebuses,[6] the harquebusiers, shouldering their harquebuses; some held them [level]. And when they went into the great palace, the residence of the ruler, they repeatedly shot off their harquebuses. They exploded, sputtered, discharged, thundered, disgorged. Smoke spread, it grew dark with smoke, everyplace filled with smoke. The fetid smell made people dizzy and faint.

Then all those from the various altepetl[7] on the other side of the mountains, the Tlaxcalans, the people of Tliliuhquitepec, of Huexotzinco,

---

[1] *Mexico* throughout the text refers to Tenochtitlán, the capital of the Aztec Empire. *Mexica* refers to the people of Tenochtitlán and Tlatelolco, a large suburb of Tenochtitlán.
[2] One of several acceptable modern spellings of the Aztec emperor's name, including *Moctezuma, Motecuhzoma,* and *Montezuma.*
[3] Specially bred war dogs for use in combat.

[4] A piece of armor that covered the body from neck to waist.
[5] Having never before seen horses, some Aztecs considered them to be large deer.
[6] A heavy matchlock gun.
[7] The Nahuatl term for any sovereign state, especially the local ethnic states of central Mexico.

came following behind. They came outfitted for war with their cotton upper armor, shields, and bows, their quivers full and packed with feathered arrows, some barbed, some blunted, some with obsidian[8] points. They went crouching, hitting their mouths with their hands yelling, singing, . . . whistling, shaking their heads. . . .

▷ Cortés and his army entered Tenochtitlán in November 1519 and were amicably received by Moctezuma, who was nonetheless taken captive by the Spaniards. Cortés's army was allowed to remain in a palace compound, but tensions grew the following spring. Pedro de Alvarado, in command while Cortés left to deal with a threat to his authority from the governor of Cuba, became increasingly concerned for the Spaniards' safety as the people of Tenochtitlán prepared to celebrate the annual festival in honor of Huitzilopochtli, the warrior god of the sun.

And when it had dawned and was already the day of his festivity, very early in the morning those who had made vows to him[9] unveiled his face. Forming a single row before him they offered him incense; each in his place laid down before him offerings of food for fasting and rolled amaranth[10] dough. And it was as though all the youthful warriors had gathered together and had hit on the idea of holding and observing the festivity in order to show the Spaniards something, to make them marvel and instruct them.[11] . . .

When things were already going on, when the festivity was being observed and there was dancing and singing, with voices raised in song, the singing was like the noise of waves breaking against the rocks.

When it was time, when the moment had come for the Spaniards to do the killing, they came out equipped for battle. They came and closed off each of the places where people went in and out. . . . And when they had closed these exits,

they stationed themselves in each, and no one could come out any more. . . . Then they surrounded those who were dancing, going among the cylindrical drums. They struck a drummer's arms; both of his hands were severed. Then they struck his neck; his head landed far away. Then they stabbed everyone with iron lances and struck them with iron swords. They struck some in the belly, and then their entrails came spilling out. They split open the heads of some, they really cut their skulls to pieces, their skulls were cut up into little bits. And if someone still tried to run it was useless; he just dragged his intestines along. There was a stench as if of sulfur. Those who tried to escape could go nowhere. When anyone tried to go out, at the entryways they struck and stabbed him.

And when it became known what was happening, everyone cried out, "Mexica warriors, come running, get outfitted with devices, shields, and arrows, hurry, come running, the warriors are dying; they have died, perished, been annihilated, o Mexica warriors!" Thereupon there were war cries, shouting, and beating of hands against lips. The warriors quickly came outfitted, bunched together, carrying arrows and shields. Then the fighting began; they shot at them with barbed darts, spears, and tridents, and they hurled darts with broad obsidian points at them. . . .

▷ The fighting that ensued drove the Spaniards and their allies back to the palace enclave. Without a reliable supply of food and water, in July 1520, Cortés, who had returned with his power intact, led his followers on a desperate nocturnal escape from the city, but they were discovered and suffered heavy losses as they fled. They retreated to the other side of the lake, and the Aztecs believed the Spanish threat had passed.

---

[8]A volcanic glass that can be sharpened to a razor-sharp edge.
[9]Huitzilopochtli. As god of the sun, he needed daily sacrifices of human hearts and blood in order to rise from the east each morning.

[10]An image of the god was fashioned from amaranth seed flour and the blood of recently sacrificed victims.
[11]An integral part of the ceremony was the singing of hymns that extolled battle, blood, and honor on the field of conflict.

Before the Spanish appeared to us, first an epidemic broke out, a sickness of pustules.[12] . . . Large bumps spread on people; some were entirely covered. They spread everywhere, on the face, the head, the chest, etc. The disease brought great desolation; a great many died of it. They could no longer walk about, but lay in their dwellings and sleeping places, no longer able to move or stir. They were unable to change position, to stretch out on their sides or face down, or raise their heads. And when they made a motion, they called out loudly. The pustules that covered people caused great desolation; very many people died of them, and many just starved to death; starvation reigned, and no one took care of others any longer.

On some people, the pustules appeared only far apart, and they did not suffer greatly, nor did many of them die of it. But many people's faces were spoiled by it, their faces and noses were made rough. Some lost an eye or were blinded.

This disease of pustules lasted a full sixty days; after sixty days it abated and ended. When people were convalescing and reviving, the pustules disease began to move in the direction of Chalco.[13] And many were disabled or paralyzed by it, but they were not disabled forever. . . . The Mexica warriors were greatly weakened by it.

And when things were in this state, the Spaniards came, moving toward us from Tetzcoco. . . .

▷   Having resupplied his Spanish/Tlaxcalan army and having constructed a dozen cannon-carrying brigantines for use on the lake, Cortés resumed his offensive late in 1519. In April 1520 he reached Tenochtitlán and placed the city under a blockade.

When their twelve boats had come from Tetzcoco, at first they were all assembled at Acachinanco, and then the Marqués[14] moved to Acachinanco. He went about searching where the boats could enter, where the canals were straight, whether they were deep or not, so that they would not be grounded somewhere. But the canals were winding and bent back and forth, and they could not get them in. They did get two boats in; they forced them down the road coming straight from Xoloco. . . .

And the two boats came gradually, keeping on one side. On the other side no boats came, because there were houses there. They came ahead, fighting as they came; there were deaths on both sides, and on both sides captives were taken. When the Tenochca who lived in Coquipan saw this, they fled, fled in fear. . . . They took nothing at all with them, they just left all their poor property in fear, they just scattered everything in their haste. And our enemies[15] went snatching things up, taking whatever they came upon. Whatever they hit on they carried away, whether cloaks, lengths of cotton cloth, warrior's devices, log drums, or cylindrical drums.

The Tlatelolca fought in Çoquipan, in war boats. And in Xoloco the Spaniards came to a place where there was a wall in the middle of the road, blocking it. They fired the big guns at it. At the first shot it did not give way, but the second time it began to crumble. The third time, at last parts of it fell to the ground, and the fourth time finally the wall went to the ground once and for all. . . .

Once they got two of their boats into the canal at Xocotitlan. When they had beached them, then they went looking into the house sites of the people of Xocotitlan. But Tzilacatzin and some other warriors who saw the Spaniards immediately came out to face them; they came running after them, throwing stones at them, and they scattered the Spaniards into the water. . . .

When they got to Tlilhuacan, the warriors crouched far down and hid themselves, hugging the ground, waiting for the war cry, when there would be shouting and cries of encouragement. When the cry went up, "O Mexica, up and at

---

[12]Smallpox.
[13]A city on the southeast corner of Lake Texcoco.

[14]Cortés.
[15]The various Amerindian allies of the Spaniards.

them!" the Tlappanecatl Ecatzin, a warrior of Otomi[16] rank, faced the Spaniards and threw himself at them, saying, "O Tlatelolca warriors, up and at them, who are these barbarians? Come running!" Then he went and threw a Spaniard down, knocking him to the ground; the one he threw down was the one who came first, who came leading them. And when he had thrown him down, he dragged the Spaniard off.

And at this point they let loose with all the warriors who had been crouching there; they came out and chased the Spaniards in the passageways, and when the Spaniards saw it they, the Mexica, seemed to be intoxicated. Then captives were taken. Many Tlaxcalans, and people of Acolhuacan, Chalco, Xochimilco, etc.,[17] were captured. A great abundance were captured and killed. . . .

Then they took the captives to Yacacolco, hurrying them along, going along herding their captives together. Some went weeping, some singing, some went shouting while hitting their hands against their mouths. When they got them to Yacacolco, they lined them all up. Each one went to the altar platform where the sacrifice was performed.[18] The Spaniards went first, going in the lead; the people of the different altepetl just followed, coming last. And when the sacrifice was over, they strung the Spaniards' heads on poles on skull racks; they also strung up the horses' heads. They placed them below, and the Spaniards' heads were above them, strung up facing east.[19] . . .

▷ Despite this victory, the Aztecs could not overcome the problems of shortages of food, water, and warriors. In mid-July 1521 the Spaniards and their allies resumed their assault, and in early August the Aztecs decided to send into battle a quetzal-owl warrior, whose success or failure, it was believed, would reveal if the gods wished the Aztecs to continue the war.

And all the common people suffered greatly. There was famine; many died of hunger. They no longer drank good, pure water, but the water they drank was salty. Many people died of it, and because of it many got dysentery and died. Everything was eaten: lizards, swallows, maize straw, grass that grows on salt flats. And they chewed at . . . wood, glue flowers, plaster, leather, and deerskin, which they roasted, baked, and toasted so that they could eat them, and they ground up medicinal herbs and adobe bricks. There had never been the like of such suffering. The siege was frightening, and great numbers died of hunger. And bit by bit they came pressing us back against the wall, herding us together. . . . There was no place to go; people shoved, pressed and trampled one another; many died in the press. But one woman came to very close quarters with our enemies, throwing water at them, throwing water in their faces, making it stream down their faces.

And when the ruler Quauhtemoctzin[20] and the warriors Coyohuehuetzin, Temilotzin, Topantemoctzin, the Mixcoatlailotlac Ahuelitoctzin, Tlacotzin, and Petlauhtzin took a great warrior named Tlapaltecatl opochtzin . . . and outfitted him, dressing him in a quetzal-owl costume.[21] . . . "Let him wear it, let him die in it. Let him dazzle people with it, let him show them something; let our enemies see and admire it." When they put it on him he looked very frightening and splendid. And they ordered four [others] to come helping him, to accompany him. They gave him the darts of the devil,[22] darts of wooden rods with flint tips. And the reason they did this was

[16]Elite warriors bound by oath never to retreat.
[17]Amerindian allies of the Spaniards.
[18]Traditionally the sacrifice consisted of cutting the heart out of the victim.
[19]The direction of the god Huitzilopochtli (see note 9).
[20]Quauhtemoctzin was now the Aztec emperor, Moctezuma having died while in Spanish captivity.

[21]This rare bird had been sacred to the Maya and was equally sacred to the Aztecs. Its four iridescent blue-green tail feathers were highly prized.
[22]Battle darts sacred to Huitzilopochtli.

that it was as though the fate of the rulers of the Mexica were being determined.

When our enemies saw him, it was as though a mountain had fallen. Every one of the Spaniards was frightened; he intimidated them, they seemed to respect him a great deal. Then the quetzal-owl climbed up on the roof. But when some of our enemies had taken a good look at him they rose and turned him back, pursuing him. Then the quetzal-owl turned them again and pursued them. Then he snatched up the precious feathers and gold and dropped down off the roof. He did not die, and our enemies did not carry him off. Also three of our enemies were captured. At that the war stopped for good. There

was silence, nothing more happened. Then our enemies went away. It was silent and nothing more happened until it got dark.

And the next day nothing more happened at all, no one made a sound. The common people just lay collapsed. The Spaniards did nothing more either, but lay still, looking at the people. Nothing was going on, they just lay still. . . .

▷ Two weeks passed before the Aztecs capitulated on August 13, 1521, after a siege of over three months' duration.

The Mountain of Silver and the Mita System
▼▼▼
113 ▼ *Antonio Vazquez de Espinosa,*
COMPENDIUM AND DESCRIPTION OF THE WEST INDIES

Many of Columbus's dreams and promises for the lands he explored were never realized, but his vision that the inhabitants could be exploited proved all too correct. Queen Isabella was, by most accounts, disquieted by the idea of enslaving Amerindians, but forced labor came to the new Spanish colonies nevertheless, largely because it proved economically advantageous for the colonizers, especially on their plantations and in their mines.

In 1545 an Indian herder lost his footing on a mountain in Peru while chasing his llama, and to keep from falling, he grabbed a bush, which he pulled from the ground, revealing a rich vein of silver. This is the most widely told story about how the Spaniards learned of the world's richest silver mine, at Potosí. Located two miles above sea level in a cold, desolate region of modern Bolivia, Potosí became the site of the western hemisphere's first and greatest silver rush. Within four decades Potosí had a racially mixed population of one hundred sixty thousand inhabitants, making it the largest, wildest, gaudiest, and richest city in the New World. With one-fifth of all the silver extracted going directly to the Spanish crown, Potosí was a major reason the kings of Spain were able to launch a huge naval armada against England in 1588, carry on a crusade against the Ottoman Empire in the eastern Mediterranean, and send armies off to campaigns in France, the Low Countries, and Central Europe. The silver of Potosí also contributed significantly to massive inflation in Spain and, as the wealth filtered out of the Iberian Peninsula, throughout Western Europe.

The backbone of the Potosí operation was the *mita* system of labor, described in the following document by Antonio Vazquez de Espinosa (d. 1630), a Spanish Carmelite friar who abandoned an academic career to do missionary work in the Americas. He returned to Spain in 1622, where he wrote a half dozen books on the Americas and topics relating to priestly work. His best-known book is his *Compendium and Description of the West Indies,* an extensive summary of observations made during his travels through Mexico and Spanish South America.

In the first part of the selection that follows Espinosa describes the mine and facilities at Huancavelica for extracting mercury, a necessary element in the refining of silver. The second portion provides a wealth of details on the mining of silver at Potosí. Throughout the document, Espinosa presents insights into the functioning of the mita system of labor, which had its roots in the Inca Empire, when villages had been required to provide an annual quota of laborers for public works projects. The Spaniards continued the practice of enforced labor quotas, at first for public works and later for work in mines, factories, and fields owned by private individuals.

QUESTIONS FOR ANALYSIS

1. What was the range of annual wages for each laborer at Huancavelica? How did this amount of money compare with the annual salary of the royal hospital chaplain? How did the annual sum of their wages compare with the cost of tallow candles at Potosí? Compare the wages of the mita workers at Potosí with the wages paid those Amerindians who freely hired themselves out. What do you conclude from all these figures?
2. What were the major hazards of the work connected with the extraction and production of mercury and silver?
3. What evidence does Espinosa provide of Spanish concern for the welfare of the Amerindian workers? What evidence is there of unconcern? Where does the weight of the evidence seem to lie?
4. Wherever huge profits justify the risks, there will be people who function beyond the constraints of the law. What evidence does Espinosa provide of such a phenomenon in Spanish South America?
5. How did the mita system work?
6. What appears to have been the impact of the mita system on native Peruvian society?

And so at the rumor of the rich deposits of mercury . . . in the years 1570 and 1571, they started the construction of the town of Huancavelica de Oropesa in a pleasant valley at the foot of the range. It contains 400 Spanish residents, as well as many temporary shops of dealers in merchandise and groceries, heads of trading houses, and transients, for the town has a lively commerce. It has a parish church with vicar and curate,[1] a Dominican convent, and a Royal Hospital un-

---

[1] A parish priest and his assistant priest.

der the Brethren of San Juan de Diós for the care of the sick, especially Indians on the range; it has a chaplain with a salary of 800 pesos contributed by His Majesty; he is curate of the parish of San Sebastián de Indios, for the Indians who have come to work in the mines and who have settled down there. There is another parish on the other side of the town, known as Santa Ana, and administered by Dominican friars.

Every two months His Majesty sends by the regular courier from Lima[2] 60,000 pesos to pay for the mita of the Indians, for the crews are changed every two months, so that merely for the Indian mita payment [in my understanding of it] 360,000 pesos are sent from Lima every year, not to speak of much besides, which all crosses at his risk that cold and desolate mountain country which is the puna[3] and has nothing on it but llama ranches.

Up on the range there are 3,000 or 4,000 Indians working in the mine; it is colder up there than in the town, since it is higher. The mine where the mercury is located is a large layer which they keep following downward. When I was in that town (which was in the year 1616) I went up on the range and down into the mine, which at that time was considerably more than 130 stades[4] deep. The ore was very rich black flint, and the excavation so extensive that it held more than 3,000 Indians working away hard with picks and hammers, breaking up that flint ore; and when they have filled their little sacks, the poor fellows, loaded down with ore, climb up those ladders or rigging, some like masts and others like cables, and so trying and distressing that a man empty-handed can hardly get up them. That is the way they work in this mine, with many lights and the loud noise of the pounding and great confusion. Nor is that the greatest evil and difficulty; that is due to thievish and undisciplined superintendents. As that

great vein of ore keeps going down deeper and they follow its rich trail, in order to make sure that no section of that ore shall drop on top of them, they keep leaving supports or pillars of the ore itself, even if of the richest quality, and they necessarily help to sustain and insure each section with less risk. This being so, there are men so heartless that for the sake of stealing a little rich ore, they go down out of hours and deprive the innocent Indians of this protection by hollowing into these pillars to steal the rich ore in them, and then a great section is apt to fall in and kill all the Indians, and sometimes the unscrupulous and grasping superintendents themselves, as happened when I was in that locality; and much of this is kept quiet so that it shall not come to the notice of the manager and cause the punishment of the accomplices. . . .

This is how they extract the mercury. On the other side of the town there are structures where they grind up the mercury ore and then put it in jars with molds like sugar loaves on top of them, with many little holes, and others on top of them, flaring and plastered with mud, and a channel for it to drip into and pass into the jar or place where it is to fall. Then they roast the ore with a straw fire from the plant growing on the puna, like esparto grass, which they call ichu; that is the best sort of fire for the treatment of this ore. Under the onset of this fire it melts and the mercury goes up in vapor or exhalation until, passing through the holes in the first mold, it hits the body of the second, and there it coagulates, rests, and comes to stop where they have provided lodging for it; [but] if it does not strike any solid body while it is hot, it rises as vapor until it cools and coagulates and starts falling downward again. Those who carry out the reduction of this ore have to be very careful and test cautiously; they must wait till the jars are cold before uncovering them for otherwise they

---

[2]Lima was the capital city of the vice-royalty of Peru, one of the two major administrative units of Spanish America, covering all of Spanish South America, except for part of the Caribbean coast.

[3]A high, cold plateau.
[4]A *stade* was a measure of length, approximately an eighth of a mile.

may easily get mercury poisoning and if they do, they are of no further use; their teeth fall out, and some die. After melting and extracting the mercury by fire, they put it in dressed sheepskins to keep it in His Majesty's storehouses, and from there they usually transport it on llamaback to the port of Chincha, . . . where there is a vault and an agent appointed by the Royal Council, and he has charge of it there; then they freight it on shipboard to the port of San Marcos de Arica, from which it is carried by herds of llamas and mules to Potosí. In the treatment of the silver they use up every year more than 6,000 quintals,[5] plus 2,000 more derived from the ore dust, i.e., the silver and mercury which was lost and escaped from the first washing of the ore, made in vats. . . .

▼ ▼ ▼

The famous Potosí range, so celebrated all over the world for the great wealth which God has created unique in its bowels and veins, lies in the Province of the Charcas, 18 leagues from the city of Chuquisaca, which was later called La Plata, on account of the great richness of this range. It is in the midst of the Cordillera, and since that is high-altitude country, that region is usually colder than Germany, so much so that it was uninhabitable for the native tribes. . . . On account of the cold, not a fly, mosquito, or [any] other unpleasant creature can live there; there was no living thing on that waste but guanacos, vicuñas, ostriches, and vizcachas, which are characteristic of that cold country.

▼ ▼ ▼

According to His Majesty's warrant, the mine owners on this massive range have a right to the mita of 13,300 Indians in the working and exploitation of the mines, both those which have been discovered, those now discovered, and those which shall be discovered. It is the duty of the Corregidor of Potosí[6] to have them rounded up and to see that they come in from all the provinces between Cuzco over the whole of El Collao and as far as the frontiers of Tarija and Tomina;[7] this Potosí Corregidor has power and authority over all the Corregidors in those provinces mentioned; for if they do not fill the Indian mita allotment assigned each of them in accordance with the capacity of their provinces as indicated to them, he can send them, and does, salaried inspectors to report upon it, and when the remissness is great or remarkable, he can suspend them, notifying the Viceroy[8] of the fact.

These Indians are sent out every year under a captain whom they choose in each village or tribe, for him to take them and oversee them for the year each has to serve; every year they have a new election, for as some go out, others come in. This works out very badly, with great losses and gaps in the quotas of Indians, the villages being depopulated; and this gives rise to great extortions and abuses on the part of the inspectors toward the poor Indians, ruining them and thus depriving the . . . chief Indians of their property and carrying them off in chains because they do not fill out the mita assignment, which they cannot do, for the reason given and for others which I do not bring forward.

These 13,300 are divided up every 4 months into 3 mitas, each consisting of 4,433 Indians, to work in the mines on the range and in the 120 smelters in the Potosí and Tarapaya areas; it is a good league[9] between the two. These mita Indians earn each day, or there is paid each one for his labor, 4 reals.[10] Besides these there are others not under obligation, who are mingados or hire themselves out voluntarily: these each get from 12 to 16 reals, and some up to 24, accord-

---

[5]A measure of weight equaling anywhere from one hundred to one hundred thirty pounds.
[6]A district military leader.
[7]This region consisted of approximately one hundred thirty-nine Indian villages.

[8]Literally, "the royal deputy"; he was appointed by the crown to serve as chief military and civil administrator over a vast region.
[9]A league is three miles.
[10]A Spanish silver coin.

ing to their reputation of wielding the pick and knowing how to get the ore out. These mingados will be over 4,000 in number. They and the mita Indians go up every Monday morning to the locality of Guayna Potosí which is at the foot of the range; the Corregidor arrives with all the provincial captains or chiefs who have charge of the Indians assigned them, and he there checks off and reports to each mine and smelter owner the number of Indians assigned him for his mine or smelter; that keeps him busy till 1 P.M., by which time the Indians are already turned over to these mine and smelter owners.

After each has eaten his ration, they climb up the hill, each to his mine, and go in, staying there from that hour until Saturday evening without coming out of the mine; their wives bring them food, but they stay constantly underground, excavating and carrying out the ore from which they get the silver. They all have tallow candles, lighted day and night; that is the light they work with, for as they are underground, they have need of it all the time. The mere cost of these candles used in the mines on this range will amount every year to more than 300,000 pesos, even though tallow is cheap in that country, being abundant; but this is a very great expense, and it is almost incredible, how much is spent for candles in the operation of breaking down and getting out the ore.

These Indians have different functions in the handling of the silver ore; some break it up with bar or pick, and dig down in, following the vein in the mine; others bring it up; others up above keep separating the good and the poor in piles; others are occupied in taking it down from the range to the mills on herds of llamas; every day they bring up more than 8,000 of these native beasts of burden for this task. These teamsters who carry the metal do not belong to the mita, but are mingados — hired.

So huge is the wealth which has been taken out of this range since the year 1545, when it was discovered, up to the present year of 1628, which makes 83 years that they have been working and reducing its ores, that merely from the registered mines, as appears from an examination of most of the accounts in the royal records, 326,000,000 assay pesos have been taken out. At the beginning when the ore was richer and easier to get out, for then there were no mita Indians and no mercury process, in the 40 years between 1545 and 1585, they took out 111,000,000 of assay silver. From the year 1585 up to 1628, 43 years, although the mines are harder to work, for they are deeper down, with the assistance of 13,300 Indians whom His Majesty has granted to the mine owners on that range, and of other hired Indians, who come there freely and voluntarily to work at day's wages, and with the great advantage of the mercury process, in which none of the ore or the silver is wasted, and with the better knowledge of the technique which the miners now have, they have taken out 215,000,000 assay pesos. That, plus the 111 extracted in the 40 years previous to 1585, makes 326,000,000 assay pesos, not counting the great amount of silver secretly taken from these mines . . . to Spain, paying no 20 percent or registry fee,[11] and to other countries outside Spain; and to the Philippines and China, which is beyond all reckoning; but I should venture to imagine and even assert that what has been taken from the Potosí range must be as much again as what paid the 20 percent royal impost.

Over and above that, such great treasure and riches have come from the Indies in gold and silver from all the other mines in New Spain and Peru, Honduras, the New Kingdom of Granada, Chile, New Galicia, New Bizcaya, and other quarters since the discovery of the Indies, that they exceed 1,800 millions.

---

[11]The twenty percent registry fee was the royal tax on all New World silver.

▼▼▼

African Reactions
to the European Presence

Due mainly to the catastrophic decline of the Amerindian population, Spanish and Portuguese colonists increasingly turned to African slaves for labor in the sixteenth century. Portugal, which had begun to explore the west coast of Africa in 1418, was initially in an advantageous position to supply this human chattel. During the 1480s the Portuguese established fortified posts along West Africa's Gold Coast, where it traded with such coastal kingdoms as Benin for gold, slaves, and ivory. By 1500 some seven hundred kilos of gold and approximately ten thousand slaves were arriving annually in Lisbon from West Africa. While engaging in this trade, the Portuguese were also pushing down the coast. Finally, in 1487–1488 Bartolomeu Dias rounded the Cape of Good Hope, opening the east coast of Africa to direct Portuguese contact. Under the leadership of Francisco de Almeida (ca. 1450–1510), the Portuguese set up fortified trading posts along Africa's east coast, thereby successfully challenging Arab hegemony over East African trade.

The Portuguese led the way, but other European maritime powers were not far behind in establishing their presence in Africa. While the Spaniards concentrated on North Africa, capturing Tunis in 1535 and holding it until 1574, the English under John Hawkins instituted their own slave trade from West Africa to the New World between 1562 and 1568. After 1713, when England won the right of *asiento,* by which it was granted license to transport African slaves to the Spanish Americas, the English came to dominate the African slave trade. In 1595 the Dutch began to trade on the Guinea coast, and in 1652 they founded Cape Town on the southern tip of the continent. The first French forts in Africa appeared in 1626 on the island of Madagascar, which France annexed in 1686, and by 1637 the French were building numerous forts on West Africa's Gold Coast and exploring Senegal. Even the Prussians had a minor presence in West Africa by 1683.

Slaves and gold were the two major attractions for all these European powers on the African coasts, and many Africans were quite willing to deal in these commodities with the outside world. Arab and Berber traders had already been crossing the Sahara for centuries to purchase the goods of inner Africa, including millions of slaves. European merchants now simply opened a new door — a coastal door — to this lucrative, long-booming market.

Although Europeans were becoming a major presence along the coasts, their penetration of the interior would have to wait for a later age. The general social and political strength of most African regional kingdoms, the wide variety of debilitating and often deadly African diseases, against which Europeans had no immunities, and the absence of safe and fast inland transportation combined to block significant European thrust into the interior until the nineteenth century. The Europeans were thus forced to come largely as traders and not colonizers, and they had to negotiate with local African leaders for goods and slaves.

An African Voice of Protest

▼▼▼

114 ▾ *Nzinga Mbemba (Afonso I),*
LETTERS TO THE KING OF PORTUGAL

The largest state in central West Africa by 1500 was the kingdom of Kongo, stretching along the estuary of the Congo River in territory that today lies within the nations of Angola and Zaire. In 1483 the Portuguese navigator Diogo Cão made contact with Kongo and several years later visited its inland capital. When he sailed home he brought with him Kongo emissaries, whom King Nzinga a Kuwu dispatched to Lisbon to learn European ways. They returned in 1491, accompanied by Portuguese priests, artisans, and soldiers, who brought with them a wide variety of European goods, including a printing press. In the same year, the king and his son, Nzinga Mbemba, were baptized into the Catholic faith.

Around 1506 Nzinga Mbemba, whose Christian name was *Afonso,* succeeded his father and ruled until about 1543. Afonso promoted the introduction of European culture into his kingdom by adopting Christianity as the state religion (although most of his subjects, especially those in the hinterlands, remained followers of the ancient ways), imitating the etiquette of the Portuguese royal court, and using Portuguese as the language of state business. His son Henrique was educated in Portugal and returned to serve as West Africa's first native-born Roman Catholic bishop. European firearms, horses, and cattle, as well as new foods from the Americas, became common in Kongo, and Afonso dreamed of achieving a powerful and prosperous state through cooperation with the Europeans. By the time of his death, however, his kingdom was on the verge of disintegration, in no small measure because of the Portuguese. As many later African rulers were to discover, the introduction of European products and customs caused dissension and instability. Worse yet, Portuguese involvement in the slave trade undermined Afonso's authority and made his subjects restive.

In 1526 King Afonso wrote the following three letters to King João III of Portugal. The three documents are part of a collection of twenty-four letters that Afonso and his Portuguese-educated native secretaries dispatched to two successive kings of Portugal on a variety of issues. This collection is our earliest extant source of African commentary on the European impact.

QUESTIONS FOR ANALYSIS

1. According to King Afonso, what have been the detrimental effects of the Portuguese presence in his kingdom?
2. What do the letters reveal about the mechanics of the slave trade in the kingdom? Who participated in it?
3. What do the letters reveal about King Afonso's attitude toward slavery? Was he opposed to the practice in its entirety or only certain aspects of it?

4. What steps has the king taken to deal with the problems caused by the Portuguese? What do the letters suggest about the effectiveness of these steps?
5. How would you characterize Afonso's attitude toward the power and authority of the king of Portugal? Does he consider himself inferior to the Portuguese king or his equal?
6. Based on this evidence, what do you conclude was King Afonso's conception of the ideal relationship between the Portuguese and his kingdom?

Sir, Your Highness should know how our Kingdom is being lost in so many ways that it is convenient to provide for the necessary remedy, since this is caused by the excessive freedom given by your agents and officials to the men and merchants who are allowed to come to this Kingdom to set up shops with goods and many things which have been prohibited by us, and which they spread throughout our Kingdoms and Domains in such an abundance that many of our vassals, whom we had in obedience, do not comply because they have the things in greater abundance than we ourselves; and it was with these things that we had them content and subjected under our vassalage and jurisdiction, so it is doing a great harm not only to the service of God, but the security and peace of our Kingdoms and State as well.

And we cannot reckon how great the damage is, since the mentioned merchants are taking every day our natives, sons of the land and the sons of our noblemen and vassals and our relatives, because the thieves and men of bad conscience grab them wishing to have the things and wares of this Kingdom which they are ambitious of; they grab them and get them to be sold; and so great, Sir, is the corruption and licentiousness that our country is being completely depopulated, and Your Highness should not agree with this nor accept it as in your service. And to avoid it we need from those (your) King-

doms no more than some priests and a few people to teach in schools, and no other goods except wine and flour for the holy sacrament. That is why we beg of Your Highness to help and assist us in this matter, commanding your factors that they should not send here either merchants or wares, because it is *our will that in these Kingdoms there should not be any trade of slaves nor outlet for them.*[1] Concerning what is referred [to] above, again we beg of Your Highness to agree with it, since otherwise we cannot remedy such an obvious damage. Pray Our Lord in His mercy to have Your Highness under His guard and let you do forever the things of His service. I kiss your hands many times.

At our town of Kongo, written on the sixth day of July, João Teixeira[2] *did it in 1526.*
The King. Dom[3] *Affonso.*
  {On the back of this letter the following can be read:
  To the most powerful and excellent prince Dom João, King our Brother.}

▼ ▼ ▼

Moreover, Sir, in our Kingdoms there is another great inconvenience which is of little service to God, and this is that many of our people, keenly desirous as they are of the wares and things of your Kingdoms, which are brought here by your people, and in order to satisfy their voracious appetite, seize many of our people, freed and ex-

---

[1]The emphasis appears in the original letter.
[2]That is, wrote the letter. João Teixeira was probably a Kongo-born secretary who had been baptized and educated by Portuguese missionaries.

[3]Portuguese for "lord."

empt men, and very often it happens that they kidnap even noblemen and the sons of noblemen, and our relatives, and take them to be sold to the white men who are in our Kingdoms; and for this purpose they have concealed them; and others are brought during the night so that they might not be recognized.

And as soon as they are taken by the white men they are immediately ironed and branded with fire, and when they are carried to be embarked, if they are caught by our guards' men the whites allege that they have bought them but they cannot say from whom, so that it is our duty to do justice and to restore to the freemen their freedom, but it cannot be done if your subjects feel offended, as they claim to be.

And to avoid such a great evil we passed a law so that any white man living in our Kingdoms and wanting to purchase goods in any way should first inform three of our noblemen and officials of our court whom we rely upon in this matter, and these are Dom Pedro Manipanza and Dom Manuel Manissaba, our chief usher, and Gonçalo Pires our chief freighter, who should investigate if the mentioned goods are captives or free men, and if cleared by them there will be no further doubt nor embargo for them to be taken and embarked. But if the white men do not comply with it they will lose the aforementioned goods. And if we do them this favor and concession it is for the part Your Highness has in it, since we know that it is in your service too that these goods are taken from our Kingdom, otherwise we should not consent to this. . . .

▼ ▼ ▼

Sir, Your Highness has been kind enough to write to us saying that we should ask in our letters for anything we need, and that we shall be provided with everything, and as the peace and the health of our Kingdom depend on us, and as there are among us old folks and people who have lived for many days, it happens that we have continuously many and different diseases which put us very often in such a weakness that we reach almost the last extreme; and the same happens to our children, relatives and natives owing to the lack in this country of physicians and surgeons who might know how to cure properly such diseases. And as we have got neither dispensaries nor drugs which might help us in this forlornness, many of those who had been already confirmed and instructed in the holy faith of Our Lord Jesus Christ perish and die; and the rest of the people in their majority cure themselves with herbs and breads and other ancient methods, so that they put all their faith in the mentioned herbs and ceremonies if they live, and believe that they are saved if they die; and this is not much in the service of God.

And to avoid such a great error and inconvenience, since it is from God in the first place and then from your Kingdoms and from Your Highness that all the good and drugs and medicines have come to save us, we beg of you to be agreeable and kind enough to send us two physicians and two apothecaries and one surgeon, so that they may come with their drugstores and all the necessary things to stay in our kingdoms, because we are in extreme need of them all and each of them. We shall do them all good and shall benefit them by all means, since they are sent by Your Highness, whom we thank for your work in their coming. We beg of Your Highness as a great favor to do this for us, because besides being good in itself it is in the service of God as we have said above.

{Extracts from letter of King Afonso to the King of Portugal dated Oct. 18, 1526. By hand of Dom João Teixeira.}

Images of the Portuguese in the Art of Benin
▼▼▼
115 ▼ A BENIN-PORTUGUESE SALTCELLAR and A BENIN WALL PLAQUE

Over many centuries sub-Saharan Africans have produced some of the world's most impressive artworks, especially sculptures. Since at least 500 B.C.E. West African sculptors used clay, wood, ivory, and bronze to create a wide variety of works — masks, animal figures, ceremonial weapons, religious objects, and images of rulers and other important people — that were of central importance to their various cultures. In some regions bronze casting and ivory carving were royal monopolies carried on by highly trained professionals.

Such was the case in the kingdom of Benin, located on the west coast of tropical Africa in an area that today is part of Nigeria. The kingdom, created by a people known as the *Edo,* took shape around 1300, when a number of agricultural villages accepted the authority of an *oba,* or divine king, who ruled with a hierarchy of chiefs from the capital, Benin City. By the time the Portuguese arrived in 1485 Benin was a formidable military and commercial power and also a center of state-sponsored artistic activity. Ivory carvers and bronze casters were organized into hereditary guilds and resided in neighborhoods set aside for them in Benin City. They produced bronze heads, animal and human figures, pendants, plaques, musical instruments, drinking vessels, and armlets, all of which were used by their society's elites for ceremonial and personal purposes or were exchanged in trade.

The arrival of the Portuguese affected Benin's artistic development in two important ways. First, Portuguese merchants, unable to establish Benin as a major source of slaves, turned to other commodities, including artworks, as objects of trade. Benin ivory carvers received numerous commissions from Portuguese merchants to produce condiment sets, utensils, and hunting horns for sale in Europe. Second, the Portuguese also stimulated the production of artworks for use in Benin itself by providing Benin artists through trade an increased supply of copper, which was used in the alloys that were turned into plaques and sculptures.

The two works reproduced here provide an opportunity to appreciate the high quality of Benin art and to make some inferences about the attitudes of the people of Benin toward Europeans. The first item is an ivory carving crafted in the sixteenth or early seventeenth century and usually identified as a *salario,* or saltcellar. It depicts two Portuguese officials, flanked by two assistants. Above them is a Portuguese ship, with a man peering out of a crow's nest.

The second work, which also dates from the sixteenth or early seventeenth century, is a copper plaque, approximately eighteen inches high and designed to be hung on a wall in the oba's palace in Benin City. (We can see the holes on the top and bottom of the plaque where it was attached.) The central figure is the oba, shown holding a spear and shield. To his right stand two attendants. The one farther away holds a C-shaped iron bar, which was used as currency in trade;

A Benin-Portuguese Saltcellar

A Benin Wall Plaque

the figure closer to the oba holds an *eban,* a ceremonial sword. To the oba's left stands another attendant playing a flutelike musical instrument. The two figures in the background, on each side of the oba's head, represent Portuguese. In one hand, each figure holds a rectangular object, perhaps a glass mirror, and in the other hand, what appears to be a goblet. Most experts believe these objects represent items the Portuguese offered in trade for the goods of Benin.

QUESTIONS FOR ANALYSIS

1. In the saltcellar, notice what hangs around the standing figure's neck, what he holds in his hands, and his facial expression. What is the sculptor trying to communicate about this figure?
2. Why might this image of the Portuguese official have appealed to the European purchasers for whom the work was intended?
3. Consider the second item. What distinguishes the oba from the other figures in the plaque? Which details illustrate the oba's power and perhaps his divinity?
4. How does the representation of the Portuguese in the plaque differ from that of the saltcellar?
5. Compare the representation of the Portuguese official in the saltcellar with that of the oba in the plaque. Do you see any similarities? Which strike you as more significant, the similarities or the differences? What inferences do you draw from your answer?
6. What might we infer from these works about Portuguese-Benin relations and the attitudes of the people of Benin toward the Portuguese?

The Economics of the West African Slave Trade
▼▼▼

116 ▼ James Barbot,
A VOYAGE TO NEW CALABAR RIVER
IN THE YEAR 1699

Source 114 illustrates how an African king's attempt to control commerce between his subjects and the Portuguese was at least partially frustrated and how the slave trade had a number of tragic consequences for African society. This source offers another perspective. James Barbot, a French member of a late-seventeenth-century English slave-trading expedition to Ibani, describes trade negotiations with its king, William, in 1699. Ibani, or *Bonny,* as the English called it, was an island state in the Niger delta. By the late eighteenth century it was the principal slave market of the entire Guinea coast. One English captain, who sailed to Bonny between 1786 and 1800, estimated that at least twenty thousand slaves were bought and sold there annually. In this document we see how the trading system worked a century earlier.

QUESTIONS FOR ANALYSIS

1. How would you characterize trade at Bonny? Was it haphazard bartering? A well-developed system with specific currency? Something else?
2. How did the English benefit from the way in which trade was conducted?
3. What benefits did the king enjoy from this arrangement?
4. What was Barbot's attitude toward Ibani society?
5. How did the Ibani seem to regard the English?
6. What do the prices of the other commodities purchased by the English say about the relative value of one slave?
7. Who was the exploiter, and who was the exploited?
8. What does this account reveal about social structure in Ibani?

June 30, 1699, being ashore, had a new conference which produced nothing. Then Pepprell [Pepple], the king's brother, delivered a message from the king:

> He was sorry we would not accept his proposals. It was not his fault, since he had a great esteem and regard for the whites, who had greatly enriched him through trade. His insistence on thirteen bars[1] for male and ten for female slaves was due to the fact that the people of the country maintained a high price for slaves at their inland markets, seeing so many large ships coming to Bonny for them. However, to moderate matters and to encourage trade with us, he would be content with thirteen bars for males and nine bars and two brass rings for females, etc.

We offered thirteen bars for men and nine for women and proportionately for boys and girls, according to their ages. Following this we parted, without concluding anything further.

On July 1, the king sent for us to come ashore. We stayed there till four in the afternoon and concluded the trade on the terms offered them

the day before. The king promised to come aboard the next day to regulate it and be paid his duties. . . .

The second [of July]. . . . At two o'clock we fetched the king from shore, attended by all his *Caboceiros*[2] and officers, in three large canoes. Entering the ship, he was saluted with seven guns. The king had on an old-fashioned scarlet coat, laced with gold and silver, very rusty, and a fine hat on his head, but barefooted. All his attendants showed great respect to him and, since our arrival, none of the natives have dared to come aboard or sell the least thing, till the king adjusted trade matters.

We had again a long talk with the king and Pepprell, his brother, concerning the rates of our goods and his customs. This Pepprell was a sharp black and a mighty talking black, perpetually making objections against something or other and teasing us for this or that *dassy*[3] or present, as well as for drinks, etc. Would that such a one as he were out of the way, to facilitate trade. . . .

Thus, with much patience, all our affairs were settled equitably, after the fashion of a people who are not very scrupulous when it comes to

---

[1]Bars of iron (see source 115).
[2]A Portuguese term; here it means "chiefs and elders."

[3]A trade term meaning "gift."

finding excuses or objections for not keeping to the word of any verbal contract. For they do not have the art of reading and writing, and we therefore are forced to stand to their agreement, which often is no longer than they think fit to hold it themselves. The king ordered the public crier to proclaim permission to trade with us, with the noise of his trumpets, . . . we paying sixteen brass rings to the fellow for his fee. The blacks objected against our wrought pewter and tankards, green beads, and other goods, which they would not accept. . . .

We gave the usual presents to the king. . . . To Captain Forty, the king's general, Captain Pepprell, Captain Boileau, alderman Bougsbyu, my lord Willyby, duke of Monmouth, drunken Henry, and some others[4] two firelocks, eight hats, nine narrow Guinea stuffs. We adjusted with them the reduction of our merchandise into bars of iron, as the standard coin, namely: one bunch of beads, one bar; four strings of rings, ten rings each, one ditto; four copper bars, one ditto. . . . And so on *pro rata* for every sort of goods. . . .

The price of provisions and wood was also regulated. Sixty king's yams, one bar; one hundred and sixty slave's yams, one bar; for fifty thousand yams to be delivered to us. A butt[5] of water, two rings. For the length of wood, seven bars, which is dear, but they were to deliver it ready cut into our boat. For one goat, one bar. A cow, ten or eight bars, according to its size. A hog, two bars. A calf, eight bars. A jar of palm oil, one bar and a quarter.

We also paid the king's duty in goods; five hundred slaves, to be purchased at two copper rings a head.

---

[4]The king's chiefs and elders.

[5]A large cask.

▼▼▼

Chinese and Japanese Reactions to the West

China and Japan were no exception to the rule that most societies in Asia and Africa were able to successfully resist European efforts during the sixteenth and seventeenth centuries to impose trade on Western terms and Christianity. Although ultimately rebuffed by the Chinese and Japanese, European merchants and missionaries nonetheless had good reason to believe during the sixteenth century that their labors in East Asia would be richly rewarded.

Portuguese traders reached south China in 1513, opened trade at Guangzhou (Canton) in 1514, and established a permanent trading base in Macao in 1557. In 1542 the first Portuguese merchants reached Japan and soon were reaping healthy profits by carrying goods between China and Japan. Later in the century the Dutch and English successfully entered these East Asian markets. Roman Catholic Europeans, especially the Portuguese, energetically supported missionary efforts in China and Japan, usually in cooperation with the newly founded Society of Jesus, more popularly known as the *Jesuits*. Francis Xavier and other Jesuits began preaching in Japan in 1549, and by the early 1600s they had won approximately three hundred thousand converts to Christianity. Catholic missionary activities in China began later in 1583 and followed a somewhat different strategy: The Jesuits did less preaching to the common people and instead sought the support of Chinese intellectuals, government officials, and members of the imperial court. The Jesuits were moderately successful because they impressed Confucian scholars with their erudition, especially in mathematics and science, and the Chinese appreciated the missionaries' willingness to understand and respect China's culture.

For all their efforts, the economic benefits and religious gains the Westerners obtained were meager. Although the Chinese tolerated learned Jesuit missionaries, they viewed European merchants as boorish, overly aggressive, and purveyors of shoddy goods. Preferring to deal with Arabs and other foreigners, they limited trade with Europeans to Guangzhou and Macao and placed it under numerous restrictions. Missionary activity resulted in a few converts, but feuding among Catholic religious orders, staunch opposition from many Chinese officials, and the unwillingness of most Chinese, even converts, to abandon such ancient rites as ancestor worship weakened the enterprise. When in 1742 Pope Benedict XIV decreed that Chinese Catholics must abandon Confucianism, Emperor Qianlong expelled the missionaries and Chinese Christianity withered.

Although European efforts to win souls and trade had a more promising start in Japan, by the mid seventeenth century the Japanese had suppressed Christianity and restricted European trade to only one Dutch ship a year. This turn of events resulted from attempts by Japanese leaders to bring stability to Japan after a century of civil war and rebellion. Convinced that European merchants and missionaries had contributed to Japan's disorder, the government outlawed Christianity and essentially closed Japan to the outside world.

The Jesuits in China

▼▼▼

117 ▼ *Matteo Ricci, JOURNALS*

The most celebrated of the Jesuit scholar-missionaries to work in China was the Italian Matteo Ricci (1552–1610), who arrived in 1583. Father Ricci dazzled the Chinese literarchy with clocks, maps, and various types of scientific equipment, much of which he constructed himself. A gifted linguist, he composed over twenty-five works in Chinese on mathematics, literature, ethics, geography, astronomy, and, above all else, religion. He so impressed Confucian scholars that they accorded him the title *Doctor from the Great West Ocean.* In 1601 Emperor Wanli summoned Ricci to his court at Beijing and provided him with a subsidy to carry on his study of mathematics and astronomy. When Ricci died, the emperor donated a burial site outside the gates of the imperial city as a special token of honor.

During his twenty-seven years in China, Ricci kept a journal, with no thought of publishing it. Shortly after his death, however, a Jesuit colleague edited and published the journal, into which he incorporated a number of other, more official sources, and it became one of Europe's primary stores of information about China until the late eighteenth century, when accounts by European travelers to the Middle Kingdom became more common. In the following selection from that diary, Ricci tells of charges brought against certain Jesuits working at Nanchang. Here we can see some of the cultural barriers and attitudes that frustrated the Jesuits' efforts to accommodate Christianity to Chinese civilization.

QUESTIONS FOR ANALYSIS

1. What most offended the Confucians who brought charges against the Jesuits and their religion?
2. The Jesuits' association with Father Ricci seems to have favored them in the course of events. Why? What was there about Ricci that gave his Jesuit colleagues an aura of legitimacy?
3. Why did Ricci view the outcome as a Christian victory?
4. How do you think the Jesuits' Confucian opponents saw this confrontation and its resolution?
5. Imagine you are the Chief Justice, and you are preparing a report to the imperial court concerning your decision, the reasoning behind it, and what you believe will be its consequences. Compose that report.
6. Compare the charges brought against the Jesuits with Han Yu's *Memorial on Buddhism* and Emperor Tang Wuzong's *Proclamation Ordering the Destruction of the Buddhist Monasteries* (Chapter 9, source 73). Which are more striking, the differences or the similarities? What do you conclude from your answer?

During 1606 and the year following, the progress of Christianity in Nancian[1] was in no wise retarded. . . . The number of neophytes[2] increased by more than two hundred, all of whom manifested an extraordinary piety in their religious devotions. As a result, the reputation of the Christian religion became known throughout the length and breadth of this metropolitan city. . . .

Through the efforts of Father Emanuele Dias another and a larger house was purchased, in August of 1607, at a price of a thousand gold pieces. This change was necessary, because the house he had was too small for his needs and was situated in a flood area. Just as the community was about

to change from one house to the other, a sudden uprising broke out against them. . . .

At the beginning of each month, the Magistrates hold a public assembly . . . in the temple of their great Philosopher.[3] When the rites of the new-moon were completed in the temple, and these are civil rather than religious rites,[4] one of those present took advantage of the occasion to speak on behalf of the others, and to address the highest Magistrate present. . . . "We wish to warn you," he said, "that there are certain foreign priests in this royal city, who are preaching a law, hitherto unheard of in this kingdom,[5] and who are holding large gatherings of

---

[1]Nanchang, in the southern province of Kiangsi.
[2]New converts.
[3]Confucius.
[4]Ricci and his fellow Jesuits chose to regard all Confucian ceremonies, including those that honored the spirits of ancestors, as purely *civil rites,* rather than religious observances.

This allowed their converts to Catholic Christianity to continue to pay traditional devotion to deceased family members.
[5]Ricci (or his editor) consistently refers to China as a *kingdom,* even though it had an emperor, not a king.

people in their house." Having said this, he referred them to their local Magistrate, . . . and he in turn ordered the plaintiffs to present their case in writing, assuring them that he would support it with all his authority, in an effort to have the foreign priests expelled. The complaint was written out that same day and signed with twenty-seven signatures. . . . The content of the document was somewhat as follows.

> Matthew Ricci, Giovanni Soerio, Emanuele Dias, and certain other foreigners from western kingdoms, men who are guilty of high treason against the throne, are scattered amongst us, in five different provinces. They are continually communicating with each other and are here and there practicing brigandage on the rivers, collecting money, and then distributing it to the people, in order to curry favor with the multitudes. They are frequently visited by the Magistrates, by the high nobility and by the Military Prefects, with whom they have entered into a secret pact, binding unto death.
>
> These men teach that we should pay no respect to the images of our ancestors, a doctrine which is destined to extinguish the love of future generations for their forebears. Some of them break up the idols, leaving the temples empty and the gods to be pitied, without any patronage. In the beginning they lived in small houses, but by this time they have bought up large and magnificent residences. The doctrine they teach is something infernal. It attracts the ignorant into its fraudulent meshes, and great crowds of this class are continually assembled at their houses. Their doctrine gets beyond the city walls and spreads itself through the neighboring towns and villages and into the open country, and the people become so wrapt up in its falsity, that students are not following their course, laborers are neglecting their work, farmers are not cultivating their acres, and even the women have

no interest in their housework. The whole city has become disturbed, and, whereas in the beginning there were only a hundred or so professing their faith, now there are more than twenty thousand. These priests distribute pictures of some Tartar or Saracen,[6] who they say is God, who came down from heaven to redeem and to instruct all of humanity, and who alone, according to their doctrine, can give wealth and happiness; a doctrine by which the simple people are very easily deceived. These men are an abomination on the face of the earth, and there is just ground for fear that once they have erected their own temples, they will start a rebellion. . . . Wherefore, moved by their interest in the maintenance of the public good, in the conservation of the realm, and in the preservation, whole and entire, of their ancient laws, the petitioners are presenting this complaint and demanding, in the name of the entire province, that a rescript of it be forwarded to the King, asking that these foreigners be sentenced to death, or banished from the realm, to some deserted island in the sea. . . .

Each of the Magistrates to whom the indictment was presented asserted that the spread of Christianity should be prohibited, and that the foreign priests should be expelled from the city, if the Mayor saw fit, after hearing the case, and notifying the foreigners. . . . But the Fathers,[7] themselves, were not too greatly disturbed, placing their confidence in Divine Providence, which had always been present to assist them on other such dangerous occasions.

▷   Father Emanuele is summoned before the Chief Justice.

Father Emanuele, in his own defense, . . . gave a brief outline of the Christian doctrine. Then he showed that according to the divine law, the

---

[6]The reference is to Jesus Christ.

[7]The Jesuit fathers, or priests.

first be honored, after God, were a man's parents. But the judge had no mind to hear or to accept any of this and he made it known that he thought it was all false. After that repulse, with things going from bad to worse, it looked as if they were on the verge of desperation, so much so, indeed, that they increased their prayers, their sacrifices, and their bodily penances, in petition for a favorable solution of their difficulty. Their adversaries appeared to be triumphantly victorious. They were already wrangling about the division of the furniture of the Mission residences, and to make results doubly certain, they stirred up the flames anew with added accusations and indictments. . . .

The Mayor, who was somewhat friendly with the Fathers, realizing that there was much in the accusation that was patently false, asked the Magistrate Director of the Schools,[8] if he knew whether or not this man Emanuele was a companion of Matthew Ricci, who was so highly respected at the royal court, and who was granted a subsidy from the royal treasury, because of the gifts he had presented to the King. Did he realize that the Fathers had lived in Nankin[9] for twelve years, and that no true complaint had ever been entered against them for having violated the laws. Then he asked him if he had really given full consideration as to what was to be proven in the present indictment. To this the Director of the Schools replied that he wished the Mayor to make a detailed investigation of the case and then to confer with him. The Chief Justice then ordered the same thing to be done. Fortunately, it was this same Justice who was in charge of city affairs when Father Ricci first arrived in Nancian. It was he who first gave the Fathers permission,

with the authority of the Viceroy, to open a house there. . . .

After the Mayor had examined the charges of the plaintiffs and the reply of the defendants, he subjected the quasi-literati[10] to an examination in open court, and taking the Fathers under his patronage, he took it upon himself to refute the calumnies of their accusers. He said he was fully convinced that these strangers were honest men, and that he knew that there were only two of them in their local residence and not twenty, as had been asserted. To this they replied that the Chinese were becoming their disciples. To which the Justice in turn replied: "What of it? Why should we be afraid of our own people? Perhaps you are unaware of the fact that Matthew Ricci's company is cultivated by everyone in Pekin, and that he is being subsidized by the royal treasury. How dare the Magistrates who are living outside of the royal city expel men who have permission to live at the royal court? These men here have lived peacefully in Nankin for twelve years. I command," he added, "that they buy no more large houses, and that the people are not to follow their law." . . .

A few days later, the court decision was pronounced and written out . . . and was then posted at the city gates as a public edict. The following is a summary of their declaration. Having examined the cause of Father Emanuele and his companions, it was found that these men had come here from the West because they had heard so much about the fame of the great Chinese Empire, and that they had already been living in the realm for some years, without any display of ill-will. Father Emanuele should be permitted to practice his own religion, but it was not con-

---

[8]The director of the local Confucian academy was one of the Jesuits' chief opponents.

[9]Nanjing, the southern auxiliary capital.

[10]Those who are almost learned or learned to a limited degree. This is Ricci's term for the chief tormenters of the Jesuits in Nanchang. They were Confucian scholars who had passed the first and most basic of the three Confucian civil service examinations and thereby earned the title *Cultivated Talents*. By passing the first examination level, they

earned recognition simply as competent students. Hence, Ricci dismisses them as quasi-literati. Cultivated Talents were subject to periodic reexamination at that level and could lose their status and privileges. Only scholars who passed the second, or provincial, level examination and became *Elevated Men* attained a permanent rank and were eligible for appointment to one of the lower civil posts. Apparently the Cultivated Talents felt threatened by the Jesuits.

sidered to be the right thing for the common people, who are attracted by novelties, to adore the God of Heaven. For them to go over to the religion of foreigners would indeed be most unbecoming. . . . It would therefore seem to be . . . [in] . . . the best interests of the Kingdom, to . . . [warn] . . . everyone in a public edict not to abandon the sacrifices of their ancient religion by accepting the cult of foreigners. Such a movement might, indeed, result in calling together certain gatherings, detrimental to the public welfare, and harmful also to the foreigner, himself. Wherefore, the Governor of this district, by order of the high Magistrates, admonishes the said Father Emanuele to refrain from perverting the people, by inducing them to accept a foreign religion. The man who sold him the larger house is to restore his money and Emanuele is to buy a smaller place, sufficient for his needs, and to live there peaceably, as he has done, up to the present. Emanuele, himself, has agreed to these terms and the Military Prefects of the district have been ordered to make a search of the houses there and to confiscate the pictures of the God they speak of, wherever they find them. It is not permitted for any of the native people to go over to the religion of the foreigners, nor is it permitted to gather together for prayer meetings. Whoever does contrary to these prescriptions will be severely punished, and if the Military Prefects are remiss in enforcing them, they will be held to be guilty of the same crimes. To his part of the edict, the Director of the Schools added, that the common people were forbidden to accept the law of the foreigners, and that a sign should be posted above the door of the Father's residence, notifying the public that these men were forbidden to have frequent contact with the people.

The Fathers were not too disturbed by this pronouncement, because they were afraid that it was going to be much worse. In fact, everyone thought it was rather favorable, and that the injunction launched against the spread of the faith was a perfunctory order to make it appear that the literati were not wholly overlooked, since the Fathers were not banished from the city, as the literati had demanded. Moreover it was not considered a grave misdemeanor for the Chinese to change their religion, and it was not customary to inflict a serious punishment on those violating such an order. The neophytes, themselves, proved this when they continued, as formerly, to attend Mass.

The Seclusion of Japan

▼▼▼

118 ▼ *Tokugawa Iemitsu,*
CLOSED COUNTRY EDICT OF 1635 and
EXCLUSION OF THE PORTUGUESE, 1639

When the first Europeans reached Japan, they encountered a land plagued by civil war and rebellion. The authority of the *shoguns,* military commanders who had ruled Japan on behalf of the emperor since the twelfth century, was in eclipse, as the *daimyo* (great lords) fought for power. Turbulence ended toward the close of the sixteenth century, when three military heroes — Oda Nobunaga (1534–1582), Toyotomi Hideyoshi (1536–1598), and Tokugawa Ieyasu (1543–1616) — forced the daimyo to accept central authority. In 1603 the emperor recognized Tokugawa Ieyasu as shogun; the era of the Tokugawa Shogunate, which lasted to 1868, had begun.

Between 1624 and 1641 Iemitsu, grandson of Ieyasu and shogun from 1623 to 1651, issued edicts that closed Japan to virtually all foreigners. This was the culmination of policies begun under Toyotomi Hideyoshi, who had sought to limit contacts between Japanese and foreigners, especially Catholic missionaries. He and his successors viewed the missionaries' aggressive proselytizing as a potential source of social unrest and rebellion. The first document that follows, the most celebrated of Tokugawa Iemitsu's edicts, is directed to the two *bugyo,* or commissioners, of Nagasaki, a port city in southwest Japan and a center of Japanese Christianity; the second more specifically deals with the missionary activities of the Portuguese.

QUESTIONS FOR ANALYSIS

1. To what extent was the edict of 1635 directed against the activities of foreigners? To what extent was it directed against certain presumed antisocial activities by Japanese?
2. Much of the 1635 edict dealt with trade issues. What do the various trade provisions suggest about the shogun's attitude toward commerce?
3. What was the major purpose behind the 1635 edict?
4. What can you infer about the reasons for promulgating the 1639 edict?

CLOSED COUNTRY EDICT OF 1635

1. Japanese ships are strictly forbidden to leave for foreign countries.
2. No Japanese is permitted to go abroad. If there is anyone who attempts to do so secretly, he must be executed. The ship so involved must be impounded and its owner arrested, and the matter must be reported to the higher authority.
3. If any Japanese returns from overseas after residing there, he must be put to death.
4. If there is any place where the teachings of padres[1] is practiced, the two of you must order a thorough investigation.
5. Any informer revealing the whereabouts of the followers of padres must be rewarded accordingly. If anyone reveals the whereabouts of a high ranking padre, he must be given one hundred pieces of silver. For those of lower ranks, depending on the deed, the reward must be set accordingly.
6. If a foreign ship has an objection [to the measures adopted] and it becomes necessary to report the matter to Edo,[2] you may ask the Omura domain[3] to provide ships to guard the foreign ship. . . .
7. If there are any Southern Barbarians[4] who propagate the teachings of padres, or otherwise commit crimes, they may be incarcerated in the prison. . . .
8. All incoming ships must be carefully searched for the followers of padres.
9. No single trading city shall be permitted to purchase all the merchandise brought by foreign ships.

---

[1]Fathers (Catholic priests).
[2]Modern Tokyo, the seat of Tokugawa government.
[3]The area around Nagasaki.
[4]Westerners.

10. Samurai are not permitted to purchase any goods originating from foreign ships directly from Chinese merchants in Nagasaki.

11. After a list of merchandise brought by foreign ships is sent to Edo, as before you may order that commercial dealings may take place without waiting for a reply from Edo.

12. After settling the price, all white yarns[5] brought by foreign ships shall be allocated to the five trading cities[6] and other quarters as stipulated.

13. After settling the price of white yarns, other merchandise [brought by foreign ships] may be traded freely between the [licensed] dealers. However, in view of the fact that Chinese ships are small and cannot bring large consignments, you may issue orders of sale at your discretion. Additionally, payment for goods purchased must be made within twenty days after the price is set.

14. The date of departure homeward of foreign ships shall not be later than the twentieth day of the ninth month. Any ships arriving in Japan later than usual shall depart within fifty days of their arrival. As to the departure of Chinese ships, you may use your discretion to order their departure after the departure of the Portuguese *galeota*.[7]

15. The goods brought by foreign ships which remained unsold may not be deposited or accepted for deposit.

16. The arrival in Nagasaki of representatives of the five trading cities shall not be later than the fifth day of the seventh month. Anyone arriving later than that date shall lose the quota assigned to his city.

17. Ships arriving in Hirado[8] must sell their raw silk at the price set in Nagasaki, and are not permitted to engage in business transactions until after the price is established in Nagasaki.

You are hereby required to act in accordance with the provisions set above. It is so ordered.

EXCLUSION OF THE PORTUGUESE, 1639

1. The matter relating to the proscription of Christianity is known [to the Portuguese]. However, heretofore they have secretly transported those who are going to propagate that religion.

2. If those who believe in that religion band together in an attempt to do evil things, they must be subjected to punishment.

3. While those who believe in the preaching of padres are in hiding, there are incidents in which that country [Portugal] has sent gifts to them for their sustenance.

In view of the above, hereafter entry by the Portuguese *galeota* is forbidden. If they insist on coming [to Japan], the ships must be destroyed and anyone aboard those ships must be beheaded. We have received the above order and are thus transmitting it to you accordingly.

The above concerns our disposition with regard to the *galeota*.

Memorandum

With regard to those who believe in Christianity, you are aware that there is a proscription, and thus knowing, you are not permitted to let padres and those who believe in their preaching to come aboard your ships. If there is any violation, all of you who are aboard will be considered culpable. If there is anyone who hides the fact that he is a Christian and boards your ship, you may report it to us. A substantial reward will be given to you for this information.

This memorandum is to be given to those who come on Chinese ships. [A similar note to the Dutch ships.]

---

[5]Raw silk.
[6]The cities of Kyoto, Edo, Osaka, Sakai, and Nagasaki.

[7]A *galleon,* an ocean-going Portuguese ship.
[8]A small island in the southwest, not far from Nagasaki.

The Great Mughals and the West

Between 1526 and his death in 1530, the Turkish lord of Afghanistan, Babur, subdued north central India with a small, well-equipped army that enjoyed the advantage of firearms received from the Ottoman Turks. This new Muslim lord of Hindustan, a direct descendant of the Mongol Chinggis Khan and the Turk Timur the Lame, initiated India's *Mughal* (the Persian word for *Mongol*) Age and laid the base for the reign of his grandson Jalal ad-Din Akbar (r. 1556–1605), known to history as simply *Akbar* (the Great).

Akbar's empire encompassed only the northern half of the Indian subcontinent. His great-grandson Aurangzeb (r. 1658–1707), the last effective Mughal emperor, reigned over twice that amount of land, holding all the subcontinent except its southern tip and the island of Ceylon (modern Sri Lanka). Nevertheless, Akbar fully deserved to be known as the *Great Mughal,* a title awed European visitors to his court at Fatehpur-Sikri (the City of Victory) bestowed on him. From this court Akbar forged a centralized empire, which during his reign of more than a half century enjoyed prosperity and a fair level of peace between Hindus and Muslims. Although the Portuguese had established three major bases along the west Indian coast by 1535, Akbar was secure enough in his power to keep them and other Europeans at arm's length throughout the last half of the sixteenth century.

The European presence, however, increased in the seventeenth century. In 1603 the English East India Company — chartered on December 31, 1600, the last day of the sixteenth century — sent its first envoy to Akbar's court. After defeating a Portuguese squadron in 1639, the English established their first trading station at Madras on India's east coast and in 1661 acquired Bombay on the west coast. As Portuguese influence in India declined, other European maritime powers secured trading privileges in the Mughal Empire. The Dutch acquired several important sites on both coasts between 1640 and 1663; in 1664 France founded an East India Company, and several French trading bases followed. In time, the Dutch shifted their focus away from India to the islands of Southeast Asia, leaving the French and English to fight for control of the Indian markets.

Despite all these late-seventeenth-century incursions along India's coasts, Emperor Aurangzeb was able to hold the West and its merchants at bay for the most part, even dealing the English a military setback in the 1680s. In 1700 the directors of the English East India Company rejected as unrealistic the notion of acquiring additional territory or establishing colonies in India. The decline of Mughal authority in the eighteenth century, however, changed the situation substantially, and toward midcentury the French and British were engaged in armed struggle for control of Indian territory.

Dealing with the Faringis
▼▼▼

119 ▼ *Abul Fazl, AKBARNAMA*

Assisting Akbar in formulating and carrying out his largely successful policies of state was Abul Fazl (1551–1602), the emperor's chief adviser and confidant from 1579 until Abul Fazl's assassination at the instigation of Prince Salim, the future Emperor Jahangir (r. 1605–1627). Abul Fazl's death cut short his composition of the *Akbarnama,* a gigantic, laudatory history of Akbar's distinguished ancestors and the emperor's own reign. Before he was murdered, Abul Fazl carried his history to Akbar's forty-sixth year, creating a work universally regarded as one of the masterpieces of Mughal literature.

These thousands of pages of elegant Persian prose and poetry provide surprisingly few references to Akbar's or even India's relations with Europeans, or *Faringis* (Franks), as they were called at the Mughal court. This silence speaks eloquently of the level of early Mughal concern with these foreigners. The following excerpts constitute the work's major references to Europeans in India.

QUESTIONS FOR ANALYSIS

1. What aspects of European culture most fascinated Akbar?
2. What did he and Abul Fazl believe they could gain from the *Faringis?*
3. What did they believe they could offer the Europeans?
4. How did Akbar and Abul Fazl regard the Portuguese coastal bases?
5. What does the discussion with Padre Radif (Father Rodolfo) suggest about Akbar and Abul Fazl's attitudes toward the teachings of Europe's Christian missionaries?
6. Jesuit missionaries to Akbar's court often believed they were on the verge of converting him to Roman Catholicism. Why do you suppose they believed this? What evidence strongly indicates there was never any chance Akbar would become a Christian?
7. Compare these accounts of Muslim-Christian relations with the memoirs of Usamah (Chapter 9, source 76). Which strike you as more significant, the similarities or the differences? What do you conclude from your answer?

One of the occurrences of the siege[1] was that a large number of Christians came from the port of Goa[2] and its neighborhood to the foot of the sublime throne, and were rewarded by the bliss of an interview. Apparently they had come at the request of the besieged in order that the latter might make the fort over to them, and so convey themselves to the shore of safety. But when

---

[1]The siege of the west coast port of Surat in 1573 during Akbar's campaign in Gujarat (note 6). This successful expedition gave Akbar access to the sea. Through his conquests Akbar more than tripled the empire he had inherited.

[2]The chief Portuguese stronghold in India since 1510.

that crew saw the majesty of the imperial power, and had become cognizant of the largeness of the army, and of the extent of the siege-train they represented themselves as ambassadors and performed the *kornish*.[3] They produced many of the rarities of their country, and the appreciative Khedive[4] received each one of them with special favor and made inquiries about the wonders of Portugal and the manners and customs of Europe. It seemed as if he did this from a desire of knowledge, for his sacred heart is a storehouse of spiritual and physical sciences. But his . . . soul wished that these inquiries might be the means of civilizing this savage race.[5]

▾ ▾ ▾

One of the occurrences was the dispatch of Haji Habibu-llah Kashi to Goa. At the time when the country of Gujarat became included among the imperial dominions, and when many of the ports of the country came into possession, and the governors of the European ports became submissive,[6] many of the curiosities and rarities of the skilled craftsmen of that country became known to His Majesty. Accordingly the Haji,[7] who for his skill, right thinking and powers of observation was one of the good servants of the court, was appointed to take with him a large sum of money, and the choice articles of India to Goa, and to bring for His Majesty's delectation the wonderful things of that country. There were sent with him clever craftsmen, who to ability and skill added industry, in order that just as the wonderful productions of that country [Goa and Europe] were being brought away, so also might rare crafts be imported [into Akbar's dominions].

▾ ▾ ▾

One of the occurrences was the arrival [at court] of Haji Habibu-llah. It has already been mentioned that he had been sent to the port of Goa with a large sum of money and skillful craftsmen in order that he might bring to his country the excellent arts and rarities of that place. On the 9th he came to do homage, attended by a large number of persons dressed up as Christians and playing European drums and clarions. He produced before His Majesty the choice articles of that territory. Craftsmen who had gone to acquire skill displayed the arts which they had learned and received praises in the critical place of testing. The musicians of that territory breathed fascination with the instruments of their country, especially with the organ. Ear and eye were delighted and so was the mind.

▾ ▾ ▾

One night, the assembly in the 'Ibadatkhana[8] was increasing the light of truth. Padre Radif,[9] one of the Nazarene[10] sages, who was singular for his understanding and ability, was making points in that feast of intelligence. Some of the untruthful bigots[11] came forward in a blundering way to answer him. Owing to the calmness of the august assembly, and the increasing light of justice, it became clear that each of these was weaving a circle of old acquisitions, and was not following the highway of proof, and that the explanation of the riddle of truth was not present to their thoughts. The veil was nearly being stripped, once for all, from their procedure. They were ashamed, and abandoned such discourse, and applied themselves to perverting the words

---

[3]The act of obeisance.
[4]Akbar.
[5]The Portuguese.
[6]In 1573 Akbar conquered the northwest coastal region of Gujarat, where the Portuguese held the ports of Diu and Bassein. In theory, but not fact, these Portuguese bases were now under Akbar's control.
[7]Haji Habibu-llah. He bore the title *Haji* because he had completed the hajj, or pilgrimage, to Mecca (Chapter 8, source 62).

[8]*The House of Worship,* where Akbar held weekly Thursday-night discussions on theological issues with Muslim, Hindu, Zoroastrian, and Christian religious teachers.
[9]Father Rodolfo Acquaviva, a Jesuit missionary.
[10]Christian (a follower of Jesus of Nazareth).
[11]Here he refers to the *ulama,* Muslim religious teachers. Abul Fazl, who pursued a vigorous policy of religious and cultural toleration, considered the ulama to be narrow-minded hypocrites.

of the Gospels. But they could not silence their antagonist by such arguments. The Padre quietly and with an air of conviction said, "Alas, that such things should be thought to be true! In fact, if this faction have such an opinion of our Book, and regard the *Furqan* [the Qur'an] as the pure word of God, it is proper that a heaped fire be lighted. We shall take the Gospel in our hands, and the 'Ulama[12] of that faith shall take their book, and then let us enter that testing-place of truth. The escape of any one will be a sign of his truthfulness." The liverless and black-hearted fellows wavered, and in reply to the challenge had recourse to bigotry and wrangling. This cowardice and effrontery displeased Akbar's equitable soul, and the banquet of enlightenment was made resplendent by acute observations. Continually, in those day-like nights, glorious subtleties and profound words dropped from his pearl-filled mouth.

Among them was this: "Most persons, from intimacy with those who adorn their outside, but are inwardly bad, think that outward semblance, and the letter of Islam, profit without internal conviction. Hence we by fear and force compelled many believers in the Brahman [i.e., Hindu] religion to adopt the faith of our ancestors. Now that the light of truth has taken possession of our soul, it has become clear that in this distressful place of contrarieties [the world], where darkness of comprehension and conceit are heaped up, fold upon fold, a single step cannot be taken without the torch of proof, and that that creed is profitable which is adopted with the approval of wisdom. To repeat the creed, to remove a piece of skin [i.e., to become circumcised] and to place the end of one's bones on the ground [i.e., the head in adoration] from dread of the Sultan,[13] is not seeking after God.

▾ ▾ ▾

One of the occurrences was the appointing an army to capture the European ports.[14] Inasmuch as conquest is the great rule of princes, and by the observance of this glory-increasing practice, the distraction of plurality[15] places its foot in the peacefulness of unity, and the harassed world composes her countenance, the officers of the provinces of Gujarat and Malwa were appointed to this service under the leadership of Qutbu-d-din Khan on 18 Bahman, Divine month (February 1580). The rulers of the Deccan were also informed that the troops had been sent in that direction in order to remove the Faringis who were a stumbling-block in the way of the pilgrims to the Hijaz.[16]

---

[12]See note 11.
[13]Akbar.
[14]The ports of Diu and Bassein (note 6). This expedition was unsuccessful, and Abu Fazl tells us nothing more about it.
[15]The distraction of multiple rulers.

[16]Pilgrims to Mecca. (Mecca is located in the Hijaz, Arabia's west coast.) Many Muslim pilgrims complained that when embarking at Portuguese ports, they were forced to purchase letters of passage imprinted with images of Jesus and Mary. Orthodox Muslims consider such images blasphemous, and some Muslim ulama (note 11) went so far as to argue that it was better to forego the pilgrimage than to submit to such sacrilege.

Seventeenth-Century Commerce in India
▾▾▾
120 ▾ Jean-Baptiste Tavernier, TRAVELS IN INDIA

The increasing volume of French trade with seventeenth-century Mughal India attracted Jean-Baptiste Tavernier (1605–after 1689), a Parisian gem merchant, who arrived in India in 1640 on the first of five trips to the empire of the Great Mughal. Following his last voyage to India, which ended in 1668, Tavernier was able to live in wealthy semiretirement thanks to his profitable Eastern ventures.

In 1670 he purchased the title of *baron of Aubonne* and settled down to write his memoirs, probably from notes he had made during his career in the East.

His *Travels* covers a pivotal period in Mughal-European relations. French and English merchants were becoming increasingly important in India, even as cracks were beginning to appear in the Mughal Empire under Shah Jahan (r. 1627–1658) and Aurangzeb (r. 1658–1707), whose respective building programs (Shah Jahan constructed the Taj Mahal) and military campaigns placed severe strains on the economy and general well-being of Indian society. In the following selection, Tavernier details the manner in which the Mughal government attempted to control and profit from the Western merchants and the tactics some Europeans employed to circumvent these controls and raise their profit margins.

QUESTIONS FOR ANALYSIS

1. Why do you think the English and Dutch East India Companies paid a lower tariff on their imported goods and gold? What added to their costs of doing business in India, and why do you think they paid these extra expenses?

2. Did the European merchants take advantage of the Indian officials with whom they dealt? Did the Indian officials seem to resent or not want this business with the Europeans? What do your answers suggest?

3. Why do you think the officers of the Dutch and English East India Companies were treated as described? Why did they refuse to engage in smuggling? What do your answers suggest about relations between the Mughal government and these trading companies?

4. What does the story of the roast pig suggest?

5. Do you perceive any significant differences in Indian-European relations between the era of Akbar and the period described by Tavernier? If so, what are they? What do these changes suggest to you?

As soon as merchandise is landed at Surat[1] it has to be taken to the custom-house, which adjoins the fort. The officers are very strict and search persons with great care. Private individuals pay as much as four and five percent duty on all their goods; but as for the English and Dutch Companies, they pay less. But, on the other hand, I believe that, taking into account what it costs them in . . . presents, which they are obliged to make every year at court, the goods cost them nearly the same as they do private persons.

Gold and silver are charged two percent,[2] and as soon as they have been counted at the custom-house the Mintmaster removes them, and coins them into money of the country, which he hands over to the owner, in proportion to the amount and standard of the bullion. You settle with him, according to the nature of the amount, a day when he is to deliver the new coins, and for as many days as he delays to do so beyond the term agreed upon, he pays interest in proportion to the sum which he has received. The Indians are cunning and exacting in reference to coin and payments; for when money has been coined for three or four years it has to lose one-half percent,[3] and it continues in the same proportion

---

[1] A city on the west coast that served as India's main port of entry for Dutch, English, and French merchants and their goods at this time.

[2] For the Dutch and English East India Companies.

[3] The Indians discounted these gold coins by one-half of one percent because of the metal that had been rubbed off.

according to age, not being able, as they say, to pass through many hands without some diminution. . . .

As regards gold, the merchants who import it use so much cunning in order to conceal it, that but little of it comes to the knowledge of the customs' officers. The former do all they can to evade paying the customs, especially as they do not so much risk as in the custom-houses of Europe. For in those of India, when anyone is detected in fraud, he is let off by paying double, ten percent instead of five, the Emperor comparing the venture of the merchant to a game of hazard, where one plays double or quits.[4] However, for some time back this has been somewhat changed, and it is today difficult to compound with the customs' officers upon that condition. The Emperor has conceded to the English Captains that they shall not be searched when they leave their vessels to go on shore; but one day an English Captain, when going to Tatta,[5] one of the largest towns of India, a little above Sindi,[6] which is at the mouth of the river Indus, as he was about to pass, was arrested by the customs' guards, from whom he could not defend himself, and they searched him in spite of anything he could say. They found gold upon him; he had in fact already conveyed some in sundry journeys which he had made between his vessel and the town; he was, however, let off on payment of the ordinary duty. The Englishman, vexed by this affront, resolved to have his revenge for it, and he took it in a funny manner. He ordered a suckling-pig to be roasted, and to be placed with the grease in a china plate, covered with a napkin, and gave it to a slave to carry with him to the town, anticipating exactly what would happen. As he passed in front of the custom-house, where the Governor of the town, the Shah-bandar,[7] and the Master of the Mint were seated in a

divan, they did not fail to stop him, but the slave still advancing with his covered plate, they told his master that he must needs go to the custom-house, and that they must see what he carried. The more the Englishman protested that the slave carried nothing liable to duty, the less was he believed; and after a long discussion he himself took the plate from the hands of the slave, and proceeded to carry it to the custom-house. The Governor and the Shah-bandar thereupon asked him, in a sharp tone, why he refused to obey orders, and the Englishman, on his part, replied in a rage that what he carried was not liable to duty, and rudely threw the plate in front of them, so that the suckling-pig and the grease soiled the whole place, and splashed up on their garments. As the pig is an abomination to the Muslims, and by their Law they regard as defiled whatever is touched by it, they were compelled to change their garments, to remove the carpet from the divan, and to have the structure rebuilt, without daring to say anything to the Englishman, because the Shah-bandar and the Master of the Mint have to be careful with the Company,[8] from which the country derives so much profit. As for the Chiefs of the Companies, both English and Dutch, and their deputies, they are treated with so much respect that they are never searched when they come from their vessels; but they, on their part, do not attempt to convey gold in secret as the private merchants do, considering it beneath their dignity to do so. . . .

The English, seeing that the custom of searching them had been adopted, had recourse to little stratagems in order to pass the gold, and the fashion of wearing wigs having reached them from Europe, they bethought themselves of concealing . . . [gold coins] . . . in the nets of their wigs every time they left their vessels to go on shore.

---

[4]Tavernier writes elsewhere that another reason the Mughals had such a lenient policy in regard to smuggling was that qur'anic law forbids charging interest and tariffs, and they were troubled by the practice.

[5]A city in modern Pakistan.

[6]Better known as *Sind;* this harbor at the mouth of the Indus River gave its name to the whole northwest corner of India (today Pakistan).

[7]The Mughal commissioner in charge of merchants.

[8]The English East India Company.

Sources

Prologue

(1) Cecil Jane, ed. and trans., *Select Documents Illustrating the Four Voyages of Columbus,* 2 vols. (London: Hakluyt Society, 1930–1933), vol. 1, pp. 2–18. Reprinted by permission of David Higham Associates. (2) Anonymous woodcut of 1511.

Part One ▾ The Ancient World

Chapter 1

Source 1: Excerpts from *The Epic of Gilgamesh,* translated by Nancy K. Sandars (Penguin Classics, Second Revised Edition, 1972), copyright © N. K. Sandars, 1960, 1964, 1972, pp. 91–93, 102, 106–110, 111–114, 118. Reprinted by permission of Penguin Books UK.

Source 2: Chilperic Edwards, *The Hammurabi Code* (1904), pp. 23–80, passim. Reprinted without copyright by Kennikut Press, 1971.

Source 3: Miriam Lichtheim, *Ancient Egyptian Literature: A Book of Readings,* 3 vols. (University of California Press, 1973–1980), vol. 2 (1976), pp. 124–126. Reprinted by permission of the University of California Press.

Source 4: Miriam Lichtheim, *Ancient Egyptian Literature: A Book of Readings,* 3 vols. (University of California Press, 1973–1980), vol. 2 (1976), pp. 169–172. Reprinted by permission of the University of California Press.

Source 5: James Legge, trans., *The Sacred Books of China: The Texts of Confucianism,* in F. Max Mueller, ed., *The Sacred Books of the East,* 50 vols. (Oxford: Clarendon Press, 1879–1910), vol. 3, pp. 92–95.

Source 6: James Legge, trans., *The Book of Poetry* (New York: Paragon Book Reprint, 1967), pp. 16, 48, 99, 101–102, 300–301.

Source 7: Musée de l'Homme, Paris, France. Courtesy of Erich Lessing/Art Resource, NY.

Source 8: (1–6) Walter A. Fairservis, Jr., *The Roots of Ancient India: The Archaeology of Early Indian Civilization,* illustrated with drawings by Jan Fairservis (New York: Macmillan, 1971), pp. 276, 276, 279, 278, 274, 276. Copyright © 1971 by Walter A. Fairservis. Reprinted with the permission of Macmillan Publishing Company. (7–8) Courtesy of the British Museum, London. (9) Courtesy of the Ashmolean Museum, Oxford University, Oxford.

Source 9: (1) Courtesy of Hamlyn Publishing, London. (2) Sudan Archaeological Museum, Khartoum. Courtesy of Werner Forman Archive/Art Resource, NY.

Source 10: (1, 3, and 4) Courtesy of Dumbarton Oaks Research Library and Collections, Washington, D.C. (2) Man-Jaguar, Artist unknown — Olmec, Mexico. Tabasso, c. 1000–600 B.C. Courtesy of Los Angeles County Museum of Art; Gift of Constance McCormick Fearing.

Chapter 2

Source 11: (1) Ralph T. H. Griffith, trans., *The Hymns of the Rig Veda,* 4 vols. (Benares: E. J. Lazarus, 1889–1892), vol. 1, pp. 56–59. (2) Wendy D. O'Flaherty, ed. and trans., *The Rigveda: An Anthology* (Harmondsworth, England: Penguin Books, 1981), pp. 160–162. (3) Griffith, vol. 4, pp. 289–293.

Source 12: A. J. Andrea, trans., *The Odyssey of Homer.*

Sources 13, 14, and 15: *Revised Standard Version of the Bible.* Copyright © 1946, 1952, 1971 by the Division of Christian Education of the National Council of Churches of Christ in the USA. Used by permission. All rights reserved.

Chapter 3

Source 16: F. Max Mueller, trans., *The Upanishads,* in Mueller, ed., *The Sacred Books of the East,* 50 vols. (Oxford: Clarendon Press, 1879–1910), vol. 1, pp. 92, 104–105; vol. 15, pp. 173, 175–177, 168–169, passim.

Source 17: Tashinath Trmibak Telang, trans., *The Bhagavad Gita,* in F. Max Mueller, ed., *The Sacred Books of the East,* 50 vols. (Oxford: Clarendon Press, 1879–1910), vol. 8, pp. 43–46, 48–49, 51–52, 126–128, passim.

Source 18: Hermann Jacobi, trans., *Gaina Sutras,* in F. Max Mueller, ed., *The Sacred Books of the East,* 50 vols. (Oxford: Clarendon Press, 1879–1910), vol. 22, pp. 36, 81–87, 202–208, passim.

Source 19: (1) T. W. Rhys Davids and Hermann Oldenberg, trans., *Vinaya Texts,* in F. Max Mueller, ed., *The Sacred Books of the East,* 50 vols. (Oxford: Clarendon Press, 1879–1910), vol. 13, pp. 94–97, 100–102, passim. (2) Henry C. Warren, ed. and trans., *Buddhism in Translations* (Cambridge: Harvard University Press, 1896), pp. 117–122, passim (modernized).

Source 20: F. Max Mueller, ed., *The Sacred Books of the East,* 50 vols. (Oxford: Clarendon Press, 1879–1910), vol. 20, pp. 320–326.

Source 21: James Hope Moulton, Yasnas 43, 44, 45, in *Early Zoroastrianism* (London: Williams and Norgate, 1913), pp. 364–370, passim.

Source 22: *Revised Standard Version of the Bible.* Copyright © 1946, 1952, 1971 by the Division of Christian Education of the National Council of Churches of Christ in the USA. Used by permission. All rights reserved.

Chapter 4

Source 23: F. Max Mueller, ed., *The Sacred Books of the East,* 50 vols. (Oxford: Clarendon Press, 1879–1910), vol. 39, passim.

Source 24: James Legge, trans., *Confucian Analects, the Great Learning, and the Doctrine of the Mean,* in *Chinese Classics Series of the Clarendon Press* (Oxford: Clarendon Press, 1893), vol. 1. Reprinted without copyright by Dover in 1971.

Source 25: W. L. Liano, trans., *The Complete Works of Han Fei Tzu* (London: Arthur Probsthain, 1939), vol. 1, pp. 40, 45–47. Copyright © 1939. Used by permission of Arthur Probsthain.

Source 26: Yang Hsien-yi and Gladys Yang, *Records of the Historian* (Hong Kong: Commercial Press, 1974), pp. 170–172, 177–178. Copyright © 1974. Used by permission of Commercial Press (Hong Kong), Ltd.

Source 27: A. J. Andrea, trans.

Source 28: B. Jowett, trans., *Thucydides Translated into English* (Oxford: Clarendon Press, 1881), vol. 1, pp. 115–129, passim.

Source 29: "The Trojan Women" excerpt by Euripides from *Three Greek Plays: Prometheus Bound, Agamemnon, and The Trojan Women,* by Edith Hamilton, translator. Copyright 1937 by W. W. Norton & Company, Inc. , renewed © 1965 by Doris Fielding Reid. Reprinted by permission of W. W. Norton & Company, Inc.

Source 30: B. Jowett, trans., *The Dialogues of Plato,* 3rd ed., 5 vols. (Oxford: University Press, 1892), vol. 2, pp. 151–156.

Chapter 5

Source 31: (1) Villa Albani, Rome. Deutsches archäologisches Institut, Rome. Print courtesy of the New York Public Library from J. J. Pollitt, *Art in the Hellenistic Age* (Cambridge: Cambridge University Press, 1986), p. 72, plate 71. Used with permission. (2 and 4) Museo Nazionale Romano delle Terme, Rome, Italy. Courtesy of Alinari/Art Resource, NY. (3) Courtesy of The Metropolitan Museum of Art, Rogers Fund, 1909 (09.39).

Source 32: Horace L. Jones, trans., *The Geography of Strabo,* 8 vols. (New York: G. P. Putnam's Sons, 1917), vol. 1, pp. 451–455, 501–503, 277–385, passim.

Source 33: A. J. Andrea, trans., from Bruno Keil, ed., *Aelii Aristidis Smyrnaei quae supersunt omnia,* 2 vols. (Berlin: Weidmann, 1898), vol. 2, pp. 91–124, passim.

Source 34: A. J. Andrea, trans., from Lucius Apuleius, *Metamorphoses.*

Source 35: From *Records of the Grand Historian of China,* 2 vols. translated by Burton Watson. Copyright © 1961 by Columbia University Press. Reprinted with permission of the publisher.

Source 36: Nancy Lee Swann, trans., *Pan Chao: Foremost Woman Scholar of China* (New York: Century, 1932), pp. 82–90.

Source 37: *The Edicts of Asoka,* translated and edited by N. A. Nikam and Richard McKeon (University of Chicago Press, 1958). Reprinted by permission of The University of Chicago Press.

Source 38: G. Buehler, trans., *The Laws of Manu,* in F. Max Mueller, ed., *The Sacred Books of the East,* 50 vols. (Oxford: Clarendon Press, 1879–1910), vol. 25, pp. 24, 69, 84–85, 195–197, 260–326, 329–330, 343–344, 370–371, 402–404, 413–416, 420, 423, passim.

Source 39: James Legge, trans., *A Record of Buddhistic Kingdoms* (Oxford: Clarendon Press, 1886), pp. 42–45, 77–79.

Source 40: From *Records of the Grand Historian of China,* 2 vols. translated by Burton Watson. Copyright © 1961 by Columbia University Press. Reprinted with permission of the publisher.

Source 41: (1) Museo Nazionale Romano delle Terme, Rome, Italy. Courtesy of Alinari/Art Resource, NY. (2) Courtesy of Iraq Museum. (3) Courtesy of the University of Pennsylvania Museum, Philadelphia (neg. #S5-23340). (4) Courtesy of The Metropolitan Museum of Art, Kennedy Fund, 1926 (26.123).

Source 42: National Museum, Ho Chi Minh City, Vietnam. Photo courtesy of the Library of Congress from Louis Frédéric, *The Art of Southeast Asia* (New York: Harry N. Abrams, 1965), plate 250. Used with permission.

Source 43: Nancy Lee Swann, trans., *Pan Chao: Foremost Woman Scholar of China* (New York: Century, 1932), pp. 111–114. Reprinted with the permission of Gest Oriental Library, Princeton, NJ.

Part Two ▾ *Faith, Devotion, and Salvation: Great World Religions to 1500 C.E.*

Chapter 6

Source 44: H. W. Wilson, trans., *The Vishnu Purana,* 3rd ed. (Calcutta: Punthi Pustak, 1961), pp. 516–520, passim. Copyright © 1961. Used by permission of the publisher.

Source 45: National Museum, Madura, Tamil Nadu, India. Photo courtesy of Giraudon/Art Resource, NY.

Source 46: From *The Lotus Sutra* (pp. 298–302), translated by Burton Watson. Copyright © 1993 by Columbia University Press. Reprinted with permission of the publisher.

Source 47: (1) © Smithsonian Institution, 1986. Courtesy of the Freer Gallery of Art. Washington, D.C. 20560. Rights of reproduction and publication reserved (negative no. 79.51-1). (2) National Museum of Phnom Penh, Cambodia. Photo courtesy of the Library of Congress from Louis Frédéric, *The Art of Southeast Asia* (New York: Harry N. Abrams, 1965), plate 344. Used with permission. (3) Courtesy of the Staatliche Museen zu Berlin–Preußischer Kulturbesitz Museum für Indische Kunst.

Source 48: Reprinted by permission of the publishers and the Loeb Classical Library from Josephus: "The Life" and "Against Apion," Volume I (pp. 353, 355, 357, 359, 361, 365, 405, 407), translated by H. St. Thackeray, Cambridge, Mass.: Harvard University Press, 1926.

Source 49: Reprinted from *The Talmud: Selected Writings* (pp. 131–133), translated by Ben Zion Bokser. © 1989 by Baruch M. Bokser. Used by permission of Paulist Press.

Chapter 7

Sources 50 and 51: *Revised Standard Version of the Bible.* Copyright © 1946, 1952, 1971 by the Division of Christian Education of the National Council of Churches of Christ in the USA. Used by permission. All rights reserved.

Source 52: Arthur C. McGiffert, trans., in *A Select Library of Nicene and Post-Nicene Fathers,* 14 vols., 2nd series (Christian Literature, 1890), vol. 1, pp. 349–350, 369–370, 386–387 (modified).

Source 53: Museo Arcivescorile, Ravenna, Italy. Courtesy of Alinari/Art Resource, NY.

Source 54: A. J. Andrea, trans., from *Vitae Patrum.*

Source 55: From *The Secret Teachings of Jesus* (pp. 19–20, 23–24, 26–29, 32–33, 38, passim), by Marvin W. Meyer. Copyright © 1984 by Marvin W. Meyer. Reprinted by permission of Random House, Inc.

Source 56: Excerpt from *Gnosis on the Silk Road* (pp. 180–181), by Hans-Joachim Klimkeit. Copyright © 1993 by Hans-J. Klimkeit. Reprinted by permission of HarperCollins Publishers, Inc.

Chapter 8

Source 57: *The Koran Interpreted,* trans. Arthur J. Arberry, 2 vols. (London: George Allen and Unwin, 1955), vol. 1, pp. 41–46, 50–55, 65, 69, 71–72, passim. Reprinted by permission of HarperCollins Publishers, Ltd.

Source 58: Imam Nawawi, *Gardens of the Righteous,* trans. Muhammad Zafrulla Khan (London: Curzon Press, 1975), pp. 60–63, 65–66, 68–69, 220–224, 226–228, passim.

Source 59: Hasan ibn Yusuf, "Creed Concerning the Imams," in A. A. A. Fyzec, ed. and trans., *A Shi'ite Creed* (New Delhi: Oxford, 1942). Copyright © 1942. Used by permission of Oxford University Press, New Delhi.

Source 60: Bernard Lewis, ed., and trans., *Islam from the Prophet Muhammad to the Capture of Constantinople,* Volume I, *Politics and War,* Translation copyright © 1987 by Bernard Lewis. Used by permission of Oxford University Press, Inc.

Source 61: Abu Hamid Muhammad al-Ghazali, *The Alchemy of Happiness,* trans. Henry A. Homes (Albany, NY: J. Munsell, 1873), pp. 104–105, 113.

Source 62: Bernard Lewis, ed., and trans., *Islam from the Prophet Muhammad to the Capture of Constantinople,* Volume I, *Politics and War,* Translation copyright © 1987 by Bernard Lewis. Used by permission of Oxford University Press, Inc.

Source 63: T. W. Arnold, trans., *The Preaching of Islam,* 2nd ed. (London, 1913), pp. 57–59 (modified).

Source 64: Benjamin Ben Jonah, *The Itinerary of Benjamin of Tudela,* trans. Marcus N. Adler (London: H. Frowde, 1907), pp. 35–42, passim.

Source 65: H. M. Elliot and John Dowson, eds. and trans., *The History of India as Told By Its Own Historians,* 8 vols. (London: Truebner, 1867–1877), vol. 3, pp. 374–388, passim.

Part Three ▼ *Continuity, Change, and Interchange: 500–1500*

Chapter 9

Source 66: W. G. Aston, trans., *Nihongi: Chronicles of Japan from the Earliest Times to* A.D. *697,* 2 vols. (London: Kegan, Paul, Trench, Truebner, 1896), vol. 2, pp. 128–133.

Source 67: Annie Shepley Omori and Kochi Doi, trans., *Diaries of Court Ladies of Old Japan* (Boston: Houghton Mifflin, 1920), pp. 71–73, 86–87, 89–90, 130–134.

Source 68: *The Taiheiki: A Chronicle of Medieval Japan,* translated by Helen Craig McCullough. Copyright © 1959 by Columbia University Press. Reprinted with permission of the publisher.

Source 69: P. Y. Saeki, *The Nestorian Documents and Relics in China* (Tokyo: Maruzen, 1951), pp. 56–61 (modified).

Source 70: Tu Fu, *Selected Poems,* trans. Rewi Alley (Beijing: Foreign Languages Press, 1964), pp. 12–13, 131–132, 163.

Source 71: Agriculture: From Chen Pu, "On Farming," trans. Clara Yu. Reprinted with permission of The Free Press, a Division of Simon & Schuster, from *Chinese Civilization and Society: A Sourcebook,* by Patricia Buckley Ebrey, pp. 109–112. Copyright © 1981 by The Free Press.

Source 72: "The Attractions of the Capital," trans. Clara Yu, in *Chinese Civilization and Society: A Sourcebook,* by Patricia Buckley Ebrey (New York: Free Press, 1981), pp. 100–102, 104–105, passim.

Source 73: Han Yu's *Memorial,* from *Ennin's Travels in T'Ang China,* Edwin O. Reischauer, pp. 221–224. Copyright © 1955 by the Ronald Press Company. Reprinted by permission of John Wiley & Sons, Inc.

Source 74: Lucian Stryk, *World of the Buddha: A Reader* (Garden City, NY: Doubleday, 1968), pp. 364–365. Copyright © 1968 by Lucian Stryk. Used by permission of Grove Press, a division of Wheatland Corporation.

Source 75: Charles Pellat, *The Life and Works of Jahiz,* trans. D. M. Hawkes (Berkeley, CA: University of California Press, 1969), pp. 251, 257–258, 265–267, passim.

Source 76: Philip K. Hitti, trans., *Memoirs of an Arab-Syrian Gentleman* (Beirut: Khayats, 1964), pp. 161, 163–164, 167–170.

Source 77: *The Arabian Nights' Entertainments* (London: George Routledge, 1890), pp. 113–116.

Source 78: Edward C. Sachau, trans., *Alberuni's India* (Delhi, 1910), pp. 17–25, passim.

Source 79: Arthur L. Basham, *The Wonder That Was India* (New York: Grove Press, 1954), pp. 444–446. Reprinted by permission of Sidgwick & Jackson, a division of Pan Macmillan Ltd.

Source 80: Franklin Edgerton, ed. and trans., *Vikrama's Adventures,* 2 vols. (Cambridge, Mass.: Harvard University Press, 1926), vol. 1, pp. 228–230. Copyright © 1926 by Harvard University Press. Reprinted by permission.

Chapter 10

Source 81: (1 and 2) S. Vitale, Ravenna, Italy. Courtesy of Alinari/Art Resource, NY.

Source 82: *The Chronographia of Michael Psellus,* E. R. A. Sewter, trans. (New Haven: Yale University Press, 1953), pp. 23–27.

Source 83: A. E. R. Boak, trans., "The Book of the Prefect," *Journal of Economic and Business History, 1,* Harvard University Press, 1928–1929, pp. 605, 613–614. Reprinted with permission of Baker Library, Harvard Graduate School of Business.

Source 84: Samuel Hazard Cross and Olgerd P. Sherbowitz-Wetzor, trans., *The Russian Primary Chronicle* (Cambridge, Mass.: Mediaeval Academy of America), pp. 110–113. Reprinted by permission.

Source 85: Einhard, *The Life of Charlemagne,* trans. S. E. Turner (New York: Harper, 1880), pp. 26–28, 56–66, 69, passim.

Source 86: S. Giovanni in Laterano, Rome, Italy. Courtesy of Alinari/Art Resource, NY.

Source 87: A. J. Andrea, trans., *The Song of Roland.*

Source 88: Oliver J. Thatcher and Edgar H. McNeal, trans., *A Source Book for Mediaeval History* (New York: Charles Scribner's Sons, 1905), pp. 119–121 (modified).

Source 89: Oliver J. Thatcher and Edgar H. McNeal, trans., *A Source Book for Mediaeval History* (New York: Charles Scribner's Sons, 1905), pp. 136–138, 151–152, 155–156, 165–166. (The translation of the "Concordat of Worms" has been modified by A. J. Andrea based on his reading of the Latin text in the MGH, Leges, 2:75–76.)

Source 90: E. P. Cheney, trans., *University of Pennsylvania Translations and Reprints* (Philadelphia: University of Pennsylvania, 1897), vol. 2, no. 1, pp. 12–17.

Source 91: Elizabeth A. S. Dawes, trans., *The Alexiad of the Princess Anna Comena* (New York: Barnes and Noble, 1967), pp. 33–34, 248–250, passim. Reprinted by permission of Routledge Ltd.

Source 92: Alfred J. Andrea, ed. and trans., *The Capture of Constantinople: The* Hystoria Constantinopolitana *of Gunther of Pairis,* University of Pennsylvania Press, 1997, pp. 90–91, 105–106. Copyright University of Pennsylvania Press. Reprinted by permission of the publisher.

Chapter 11

Source 93: G. S. P. Freeman-Grenville, ed. and trans., *The East African Coast: Select Documents* (Oxford: Clarendon Press, 1962), pp. 14–17, passim. Reprinted by permission of Mr. Freeman-Grenville.

Source 94: J. F. P. Hopkins, trans., and N. Levtzion and J. F. P. Hopkins, eds., *Corpus of Early Arabic Sources for West African History* (Cambridge: Cambridge University Press, 1981), pp. 79–83, passim. Copyright © University of Ghana, International Academic Union, Cambridge University Press, 1981. Reprinted with permission of Cambridge University Press.

Source 95: G. W. B. Huntingford, *The Glorious Victories of 'Amda Seyon, King of Ethiopia* (Oxford: Oxford University Press, 1965), pp. 53–65, passim. Copyright © 1965 Oxford University Press. Reprinted by permission of Oxford University Press.

Source 96: Phillips Stevens, *The Stone Images of Esie, Nigeria* (New York: Africana Publishing Co., a division of Holmes and Meier, 1978), p. 205, photo 383. Copyright © 1978 Ibadan University Press and the Nigerian Federal Department of Antiquities. Photo courtesy of the Library of Congress.

Source 97: Courtesy of The Metropolitan Museum of Art, Gift of Nathan Cummings, 1964 (64.228.63).

Source 98: Benjamin Keen, ed., *The Life of the Admiral Christopher Columbus by His Son Ferdinand* (pp. 153, 157–164). Copyright © 1959 by Rutgers, the State University. Reprinted by permission of Rutgers University Press.

Source 99: Adrian Recinos, trans., *Popol Vuh: The Sacred Book of the Ancient Quiché Maya* (Norman, OK: University of Oklahoma Press, 1950).

Source 100: Harriet de Onis, trans., and Victor W. Von Hagen, ed., *The Incas of Pedro de Cieza de Leon* (Norman, OK: University of Oklahoma Press, 1959), pp. 165–167, 169–174, 177–178, passim. Copyright © 1959 by the University of Oklahoma Press.

Part Four ▼ Travel, Encounter, and Exchange: 1000–1700

Chapter 12

Source 101: Francis Morgan Nichols, ed. and trans., *The Marvels of Rome* (London: Ellis and Elvey, 1889), pp. 17–18, 21–23, 29–30, 46.

Source 102: S. D. Goitein, ed. and trans., *Letters of Medieval Jewish Travelers* (pp. 221–225), Copyright © 1973 by Princeton University Press. Reprinted by permission of Princeton University Press.

Source 103: Christopher Dawson, ed., *The Mongol Mission* (New York: Sheed and Ward, 1955), pp. 93–98, 103–104, passim.

Source 104: W. Marsden, trans., *The Travels of Marco Polo* (1818); adapted into modern English by A. J. Andrea.

Source 105: Henry Yule, ed. and trans., *Cathay and the Way Thither,* 2nd ed. (rev. by H. Cordier), 4 vols. (London: Hakluyt Society, 1913–1916), pp. 45–51.

Source 106: Jeannette Mirsky, ed., *The Great Chinese Travelers* (New York: Pantheon Books, 1964), pp. 214–216, 222–224, 231–233, passim.

Source 107: Henry Yule, ed. and trans., *Cathay and the Way Thither,* 2nd ed (rev. by H. Cordier), 4 vols. (London: Hakluyt Society, 1913–1916), vol. 3, pp. 151–155.

Source 108: J. F. P. Hopkins, trans., and N. Levtzion and J. F. P. Hopkins, eds., *Corpus of Early Arabic Sources for West African History* (Cambridge: Cambridge University Press, 1981), pp. 284–286, 288–291, 296–297, passim. Copyright © University of Ghana, International Academic Union, Cambridge University Press, 1981. Reprinted with permission of Cambridge University Press.

Source 109: The "Cotton Manuscript" of the British Museum, printed 1625, ch. 20, 30; adapted into modern English by A. J. Andrea.

Source 110: Ma Huan, *The Overall Survey of the Ocean's Shores* (London: Hakluyt Society, 1970), pp. 108–109, 113–117, 120, 137–140, 165, 172. Copyright © 1970. Used by permission of the publisher.

Source 111: Gomes Eannes de Azurara, *The Chronicle of the Discovery and Conquest of Guinea,* trans. Charles Raymond Beazely and Edgar Prestage, 2 vols. (London: Hakluyt Society, 1896), vol. 1, pp. 27–29, 83–85.

Chapter 13

Source 112: James Lockhart, ed., *We People Here: Nahuatl Accounts of the Conquest of Mexico* (Berkeley: University of California Press, 1993), pp. 96, 98, 100, 106, 108, 110, 112, 132, 134, 136, 180, 182, 186, 188, 210, 216, 218, 238, 240, 242.

Source 113: Antonio Vasquez de Espinosa, *Compendium and Description of the West Indies* (Washington, DC: Smithsonian Institution, 1942), pp. 621–625, 629, 631–634.

Source 114: Extracts from Letters of King Afonso to King of Portugal, 1526. Translated and published in *The African Past,* by Basil Davidson. Reprinted by permission of Curtis Brown, Ltd. Copyright © 1964 by Basil Davidson.

Source 115: (1) Courtesy of the Museum of Mankind in London, a subsidiary of the British Museum. (2) Photograph by Franko Khoury. Courtesy of National Museum of African Art, Eliot Elisofon Photographic Archives, Smithsonian Institution.

Source 116: Awnsham Churchill and John Churchill, eds., *Collections of Voyages and Travels,* 3rd ed., 8 vols. (London: H. Lintor, 1744–1747), vol. 5, p. 459; modernized by A. J. Andrea.

Source 117: Louis J. Gallagher, S.J., trans., *China in the Sixteenth Century: The Journals of Matthew Ricci: 1583–1610* (New York: Random House, 1953).

Source 118: David John Lu, ed. and trans., *Sources of Japanese History* (New York: McGraw-Hill, 1974), vol. 1, pp. 207–209.

Source 119: Henry Beveridge, trans., *The Akbar Nama of Abu-l-Fazl,* 3 vols. (New Delhi: Ess Ess Publications, 1902–1939), vol. 1, pp. 37, 207, 322–323, 368–370, 410–411.

Source 120: Jean-Baptiste Tavernier, *Travels in India,* 2nd ed., ed. William Ball, trans. V. Ball (Oxford: Oxford University Press, 1925), pp. 7–11. Used by permission of the publisher.